Ana M. López

SUNY series in Latin American Cinema
———
Ignacio M. Sánchez Prado and Leslie L. Marsh, editors

Ana M. López
Essays

Edited and with an introduction by
Laura Podalsky and Dolores Tierney

Cover credit: Illustration of flying motion picture camera in front of the Earth, set among stellar clouds in the night sky; the Earth is rotated to show North and South America with labels for selected Latin American cities. Original artwork by Douglas Miller. Used with permission.

Published by State University of New York Press, Albany

© 2023 State University of New York

All rights reserved

Printed in the United States of America

No part of this book may be used or reproduced in any manner whatsoever without written permission. No part of this book may be stored in a retrieval system or transmitted in any form or by any means including electronic, electrostatic, magnetic tape, mechanical, photocopying, recording, or otherwise without the prior permission in writing of the publisher.

For information, contact State University of New York Press, Albany, NY
www.sunypress.edu

Library of Congress Cataloging-in-Publication Data

Names: López, Ana M., author. | Podalsky, Laura, 1964– editor. | Tierney, Dolores, editor.
Title: Ana M. López : essays / edited and with introductions by Laura Podalsky and Dolores Tierney.
Description: Albany : State University of New York Press, [2023] | Includes bibliographical references and index.
Identifiers: LCCN 2022013456 | ISBN 9781438491097 (hardcover : alk. paper) | ISBN 9781438491103 (ebook) | ISBN 9781438491080 (pbk. : alk. paper)
Subjects: LCSH: Motion pictures—Latin America—History. | Motion pictures—Social aspects—Latin America. | Mass media—Latin America—History. | Mass media—Social aspects—Latin America. | Latin Americans in motion pictures.
Classification: LCC PN1993.5.L3 L659 2022 | DDC 791.43098—dc23/eng/20220910
LC record available at https://lccn.loc.gov/2022013456

10 9 8 7 6 5 4 3 2 1

Contents

List of Illustrations	ix
Acknowledgments	xiii
Foreword *Ignacio M. Sánchez Prado*	xvii
Introduction: At the Interface and Beyond *Laura Podalsky and Dolores Tierney*	1

Part 1. Latin American Cinema/s:
The Transnational Turn

Editors' Introduction	13
1 A Cinema for the Continent (1994)	17
2 National History, Transnational History (1998)	29
3 Facing Up to Hollywood (2000)	37
4 Early Cinema and Modernity in Latin America (2000)	61
5 Film and Radio Intermedialities in Early Latin American Sound Cinema (2017)	91
6 From Hollywood and Back: Dolores Del Rio, a (Trans)national Star (1998)	109

7 The São Paulo Connection: The Companhia Cinematográfica
   Vera Cruz and *O Cangaceiro* (1998)   135

8 Crossing Nations and Genres: Traveling Filmmakers (2000)   163

Part 2. Of Modes and Genres

Editors' Introduction   183

9 Tears and Desire: Women and Melodrama in the "Old"
   Mexican Cinema (1994)   187

10 Our Welcomed Guests: Telenovelas in Latin America (1995)   203

11 Of Rhythms and Borders (1997)   221

12 Mexico (2012)   251

13 Before Exploitation: Three Men of the Cinema in Mexico
    (2009)   271

14 (Not) Looking for Origins: Postmodernism, Documentary,
    and *America* (1993)   295

15 Revolution and Dreams: The Cuban Documentary Today
    (1992)   309

16 *The Battle of Chile*: Documentary, Political Process, and
    Representation (1990)   323

17 At the Limits of Documentary: Hypertextual Transformation
    and the New Latin American Cinema (1990)   341

18 A Poetics of the Trace (2014)   367

Part 3. Intersections: Race, Ethnicity, and Gender

Editors' Introduction   389

19 Not Only a Question of Color: Afro-Latino/a Images in
    Latin American Cinema Today (1992)   393

20 African Roots: Images of Black People in Cuban Cinema
    (1988)   401

21 Sergio Giral on Filmmaking in Cuba (1986–1987)   411
    With Nicholas Peter Humy

22 Are All Latins from Manhattan? Hollywood, Ethnography,
    and Cultural Colonialism (1991)   419

23 Greater Cuba (1996)   437

24 I (Also) Love Ricky: The Oft-Forgotten Cuban-in-the-Text
    (2012)   455

Part 4. Final Thoughts, Metacritical Reflections

25 López on López: Liminal Words (2012)   469

"Siete Veces Ana": An Afterword   475
    Nilo Couret

Notes   479

Works Cited   517

Index   549

Illustrations

Figure 1.1	Cantina scene from *Allá en el Rancho Grande* (Fernando de Fuentes, 1936).	20
Figure 4.1	Alfonso Segreto shows off his equipment shortly after his return to Rio de Janeiro from Europe (1898).	70
Figure 4.2	The Alva Brothers—Salvador, Guillermo, and Eduardo—take a lunch break from filming (circa 1910–1912).	83
Figure 4.3	Emma Padilla imitated the Italian actress Pina Menichelli in Ezequiel Carrasco's *La luz* (The Light, 1917). Padilla was the first Mexican "actress" to become a "star."	87
Figure 4.4	Enrique Rosa's *El automóvil gris* (The Grey Automobile, 1919) was the most significant Mexican film of its era.	88
Figure 5.1	The electrical cord of the radio in the living room links to the microphone in the radio station in *Ídolos de la radio* (Radio Idols, Eduardo Morera, 1934).	102
Figure 5.2	Embodying the new social position of "listeners." *Madre querida* (Dear Mother, Juan Orol, 1934).	104
Figure 5.3	Sara García's radiophonic apotheosis from *Cuando los hijos se van* (When the Children Leave, Juan Bustillo Oro, 1941).	106

Figure 6.1	Dolores Del Rio in the silent era: a female Valentino.	114
Figure 6.2	The "new" art deco Dolores Del Rio in the 1930s Hollywood.	122
Figure 6.3	"Framed by braids" and enshrined in the Mexican landscape: Del Rio in *María Candelaria* (1943).	127
Figure 6.4	Dolores Del Rio on the altar of art as the "offering" of David Alfaro Siqueiros's *Imagen de Nuestro Tiempo* in Paris, 1952.	133
Figure 6.5	Amalia Mesa-Bains, *An Ofrenda for Dolores Del Rio*, 1984–1990.	133
Figure 7.1	Poster for *O Cangaceiro*.	138
Figure 7.2	Poster for *Tico-tico no fubá*.	146
Figure 7.3	Music for *O Cangaceiro*.	149
Figure 9.1	María Félix in *Doña Diabla* (Tito Davison, 1949).	197
Figure 11.1	Julia and her partner in *Danzón* (Maria Novaro, 1991).	244
Figure 13.1	Clenched fists in *La Llorona* (The Weeping Woman, Ramón Peón, 1934).	278
Figure 13.2	A transition from *La Llorona* (The Weeping Woman, Ramón Peón, 1934).	279
Figure 13.3	Ghostly effects in *La Llorona* (The Weeping Woman, Ramón Peón, 1934).	280
Figure 13.4	La Consolidada in Mexico City in *La sangre manda* (Blood Rules, José Bohr, 1934).	283
Figure 13.5	A mirror shot in *¿Quién mató a Eva?* (Who Killed Eva?, José Bohr, 1934).	285
Figure 13.6	Clenched-hand gesture in *Luponini (El terror de Chicago)* (Luponini, the Terror of Chicago, José Bohr, 1935).	290
Figure 13.7	Lupo in disguise in *Luponini (El terror de Chicago)* (Luponini, the Terror of Chicago, José Bohr, 1935).	291

Illustrations | xi

Figure 16.1 The pageantry of Popular Power in *La Batalla de Chile*, part 3. 337

Figure 16.2 The price of documentary witness: an Argentine cameraman records his own summary execution at the hands of mutinous Chilean troops in *La Batalla de Chile*. 338

Figure 16.3 The traitorous military under intimate scrutiny: *La Batalla de Chile*, part 2. 339

Figure 17.1 Playing himself in the film he coscripted, writer Edmundo Desnoes shares the dais with Argentine novelist David Viñas. *Memorias del subdesarrollo* (Tomás Gutiérrez Alea, 1968). 349

Figure 17.2 The still uncomprehending criminal cornered by the "long arm" of the press and the police. *El Chacal de Nahueltoro* (Miguel Littín, 1969). 352

Figure 17.3 In a paradox expressive of his extreme marginalization, José's only constructive socialization takes places behind bars. *El Chacal de Nahueltoro* (Miguel Littín, 1969). 354

Figure 17.4 Mario (Mario Balmaseda) and Yolanda (Yolanda Cuellar) seldom see eye to eye in *De cierta manera* (Sara Gómez, 1974–1977). 355

Figure 17.5 Unscripted contention: factory workers debate the ethics of Mario's actions in the conclusion of *De cierta manera* (Sara Gómez, 1974–1977). 357

Figure 18.1 The static, distant framing in *Santiago* (2007). 372

Figure 18.2 Santiago exercising his hands (*Santiago*, 2007). 373

Figure 18.3 Ad announcing a casting call for women who "have stories to tell" (*Jogo de Cena*, 2007). 376

Figure 18.4 Reenactment in *Jogo de Cena* (2007). 377

Figure 18.5 Nilza's surprising revelation in *Jogo de Cena* (2007). 379

Figure 18.6 Planning for unexpected events: framing in *Alamar* (2009). 383

Figure 18.7 Natán acknowledges the camera (*Alamar*, 2009). 384

Figure 19.1 Ganga Zumba tries to convince Zumbi in *Quilombo* (Carlos Diegues, 1984). 398

Figure 20.1 *De cierta manera* (*One Way or Another*, Sara Gómez, 1974–1977). 404

Figure 22.1 As "the world's greatest dancer," Dolores Del Rio was paired with Leo Carillo in Lloyd Bacon's *In Caliente* (1935), where she personifies the perfect cinematic example of the "colonial hybrid." 427

Figure 22.2 Echoes of Lupe Vélez's smoldering sexuality resonate in this publicity shot. 428

Figure 22.3 Attired in a hyper-version of the traditional *baianas* of Brazilian carnival, Carmen Miranda was the best known Latin American of the 1940s. 430

Figure 23.1 Final scene from León Ichaso and Manuel Arce's *Crossover Dreams*. 447

Figures 24.1 a–c. Desi Arnaz and the conga drums. 461

Figure 24.2 A scene from "Never Do Business with Friends" from the TV show *I Love Lucy*. 462

Figure 24.3 A recreation of a "real" episode of *I Love Lucy* in the film version of Oscar Hijuelos's novel *The Mambo Kings Play Songs of Love*. 464

Acknowledgments

The editors would like to express their gratitude to Wyatt Crider for his help in formatting the essays and to John Crider for sharpening our prose. We also appreciate Rebecca Colesworthy at State University of New York Press for her help (and patience!) and series editors Leslie Marsh and Ignacio Sánchez Prado for inviting us to edit this volume. We are equally appreciative of the copyeditors of this book, Dana Foote and Jenn Bennett-Genthner, for their precise and detailed work and thank Eileen Nizer for shepherding it through production. We also thank our colleagues with whom we corresponded in the process of compiling this collection of essays (Luisela Alvaray, Gilberto Blasini, Olivia Cosentino, Nilo Couret Tamara Falicov, Rielle Navitski, Ignacio Sánchez Prado, Laura Isabel Serna, and Cristina Venegas) and the broader SCMS (Society for Cinema and Media Studies) Latinx Caucus for crowd sourcing the practices and usage of certain key terms.

We would also like to express our gratitude to Ana for her very generous gifts: the wealth of her scholarship, mentorship, and friendship over the years. This manuscript comes wrapped in our thanks and love for you.

In assembling the essays for this volume, the editors reformatted all of the bibliographical references to conform to SUNY Press's style sheet, corrected minor textual errors, made small changes in terminology, and clarified citations and information, where necessary. In the case of essays that had been published in different versions, we generally selected the most extensive one. The full publication history for each essay and its variants is included in the endnotes. Translations of the essays published in this anthology were done by the editors.

Finally, we would like to thank our families. Nancy and Dulcie for helping out more with their little sister, Elsie, and loading the dishwasher, and our babysitter Susie Wisbey for the help she could give. And Lily

Alejandra for the backyard picnics. We finalized this manuscript in the middle of the COVID-19 pandemic and are grateful for their forbearance and making us laugh by joining our Zoom sessions now and again.

Essays in this collection originally appeared in the following publications and appear here with permission from the relevant publishers:

"A Cinema for the Continent." In *Mexican Cinema Project*, edited by Chon Noriega, 7–12. Los Angeles: UCLA Film Archives, 1994.

"National History, Transnational History." Originally published in Spanish as "Historia Nacional, Historia Transnacional" in *Horizontes del segundo siglo: Investigación y pedagogía del cine mexicano, latinoamericano y chicano*, edited by Patricia Torres San Martín, Julianne Burton, and Angel Miquel, 75–81. Guadalajara: Universidad de Guadalajara/IMCINE, 1998.

"Facing Up to Hollywood." In *Reinventing Film Studies*, edited by Christine Gledhill and Linda Williams, 419–37. London: Edward Arnold (UK), 2000.

"Early Cinema and Modernity in Latin America." *Cinema Journal* 40, no. 1 (Fall 2000): 48–78.

"Film and Radio Intermedialities in Early Latin American Sound Cinema." In *The Routledge Companion to Latin American Cinema*, edited by Marvin D'Lugo, Ana M. López, and Laura Podalsky, 316–28. New York: Routledge, 2017.

"From Hollywood and Back: Dolores Del Rio, (Trans) National Star." *Studies in Latin American Popular Culture* 17 (1998): 5–33. Copyright © 1998. Courtesy of the University of Texas Press. All rights reserved.

"The São Paulo Connection: The Companhia Cinematográfica Vera Cruz and *O Cangaceiro*." *Nuevo Texto Crítico* 11, no. 21/22 (1998): 127–54.

"Crossing Nations and Genres: Traveling Filmmakers in Latin America." In *Visible Nations*, edited by Chon Noriega, 33–50. Minneapolis: University of Minnesota Press, 2000. Copyright © 2000 by the Regents of the University of Minnesota.

"Tears and Desire: Women and Melodrama in the 'Old' Mexican Cinema." In *Multiple Voices in Feminist Film Criticism*, edited by Janice Welsch, Linda Dittmar, and Diane Carson, 254–70. Minneapolis: University of Minnesota Press, 1994. Copyright © 1994 by the Regents of the University of Minnesota.

"Our Welcomed Guests: *Telenovelas* in Latin America." In *To Be Continued . . . Soap Operas around the World*, edited by Robert Allen, 256–75. London: Routledge, 1995.

"Of Rhythms and Borders." In *Everynight Life*, edited by Jose Muñoz and Celeste Fraser Delgado, 310–44. Durham, NC: Duke University Press, 1997. All rights reserved. Republished by permission of the copyright holder. www.dukeupress.edu.

"Mexico." In *The International Film Musical*, edited by Corey Creekmoor and Linda Mokdad, 121–40. Edinburgh: University of Edinburgh Press, 2012.

"Before Exploitation: Three Men of the Cinema in Mexico." In *Latsploitation, Exploitation Cinemas, and Latin America*, edited by Victoria Ruétalo and Dolores Tierney, 13–33. London: Routledge, 2009.

"(Not) Looking for Origins: Postmodernism, Documentary and *America*." In *Theorizing Documentary*, edited by Michael Renov, 151–63. London: Routledge, 1993.

"Revolution and Dreams: The Cuban Documentary Today." *Studies in Latin American Popular Culture* 11 (1992): 45–57. Copyright © 1992. Courtesy of the University of Texas Press. All rights reserved.

"*The Battle of Chile*: Documentary, Political Process, and Representation." In *The Social Documentary in Latin American Cinema*, edited by Julianne Burton, 267–97. Pittsburgh: University of Pittsburgh Press, 1990. Copyright © 1990. Reprinted by permission of the University of Pittsburgh Press.

"At the Limits of Documentary: Hypertextual Transformation and the New Latin American Cinema." In *The Social Documentary in Latin American Cinema*, edited by Julianne Burton, 403–32. Pittsburgh: University of Pittsburgh Press, 1990. Copyright © 1990. Reprinted by permission of the University of Pittsburgh Press.

"A Poetics of the Trace." In *New Documentaries in Latin America*, edited by Vinicius Navarro and Juan Carlos Rodríguez, 25–43. London: Palgrave Macmillan, 2014.

"Not Only a Question of Color: Afro-Latino/a Images in Latin American Cinema." *Tonantzin* 9, no. 1 (1992): 20.

"African Roots: Images of Blacks in Cuban Cinema." *Black Film Review* 4, no. 3 (1988): 5–9.

"Sergio Giral on Filmmaking in Cuba" (coauthored with Nicholas Peter Humy). *Black Film Review* 3, no. 1 (1986–1987): 4–7.

"Are All Latins from Manhattan? Hollywood, Ethnography, and Cultural Colonialism." In *Unspeakable Images: Ethnicity and the American Cinema*, edited by Lester D. Friedman, 404–24. Urbana: University of Illinois Press, 1991.

"Greater Cuba." In *The Ethnic Eye: Latino Media Arts*, edited by Chon Noriega and Ana M. López, 38–58. Minneapolis: University of Minnesota Press, 1996. Copyright © 1996 by the Regents of the University of Minnesota.

"I (Also) Love Ricky: The Oft-Forgotten Cuban-in-the-Text." Originally published in Spanish as "Yo también amo a Ricky: el cubano que muchas veces se olvida" in *Hollywood, Nuestra América y los Latinos*, 254–63. Havana: Ediciones Unión, 2012.

"Liminal Words." Originally published in Spanish as "Palabras liminales" in *Hollywood, Nuestra América y los Latinos*, 5–10. Havana: Ediciones Unión, 2012.

Foreword

IGNACIO M. SÁNCHEZ PRADO

As a coeditor of the SUNY series in Latin American Cinema, contributing to the existence of this book is very meaningful. As a self-trained latecomer to Latin American film studies, I have always found Ana López's work to be a clear compass to the field, its debates, and its ideas. A generous mentor, a kind friend, and an exemplary scholar, Ana has created a body of work that is generative. Her essays often result in long-living lines of inquiry and even entire subfields. Some of my favorite pieces, like her paradigm-shaping essay on early cinema, demonstrate her uncanny ability to capture the spirit of a time or a mode of cultural production, distilling them with precision into critical and analytical arguments. In an academy where the book-length monograph has become excessively centered, Ana's writings are one of the prime examples of the value and rigor that the essay genre can be. Ana's work brims with precision, while covering a truly extensive cartography of theoretical, historiographic, and geographical material. This book, I hope, is not only a retrospective of a trajectory that remains very much alive, but also a tribute to a scholar whose future contributions will be equally fundamental for our field. Due to Ana's trajectory and her extensive legacies in the field as an author, a researcher, a mentor, an editor, and a leader, this collection will be an essential document in understanding the rise and consolidation of Latin American film studies in general, geographical subfields around Brazil and Cuba, and thematic subfields contending with the melodrama, the musical, and other areas. All of us working in Latin American film studies are indebted to Ana's career and dedication.

Introduction

At the Interface and Beyond

LAURA PODALSKY AND DOLORES TIERNEY

Ana López is one of the foremost Latin Americanist film and media scholars in the world. Her work has addressed filmmaking in every historical period, in numerous countries and in multiple modes—from early cinema (2000b) to the present; from Brazil (1998c, 1999), Cuba (1992b), and Mexico (1994b, 2012a) to diaspora, exile (1996), and Latinx cinemas in the United States; from documentary (1990a, 2014b) to fiction; from melodrama to politically militant film (1988b). Her contributions extend beyond cinema to analyze telenovelas (1985b, 1995b) and the intermedial relationship between film and radio (2014a, 2017). More notable than the scope of her endeavors is how her groundbreaking essays have fundamentally transformed the field of Latin American film studies, opening up new approaches, theoretical frameworks, and lines of investigation.

For three decades, she has worked at the interface between different academic fields and geocultural traditions—from US-based film studies to Latin American–based film studies to Latin American cultural studies. In bringing together these lines of thought, López has been able to challenge the interpretive frameworks of each. For example, in early essays (1986–1987, 1988a, 1992d), she countered overly broad discussions of "Black cinema" in the Anglo-American academy by delineating the differential histories of racialization and racialized representation in Latin American film. Her discussion of melodrama in "women's films" and telenovelas dialogued with the theoretical proposals of Christine Gledhill, E. Ann

Kaplan, Laura Mulvey, and others, but also drew on the rich conceptual frameworks of Jesús Martín-Barbero and Carlos Monsiváis who traced the success of the melodramatic mode in Latin American media to the urbanization process and incorporation of oral traditions.

Throughout her career, López has helped to bring US-, UK-, and Latin America–based film scholarship into more productive dialogue and to forge a place for Latin American film studies within the Anglo-American academy.[1] Beyond the aforementioned contributions, she has recognized and built off of Spanish- and Portuguese-language scholarship by Argentine, Brazilian, Colombian, Cuban, and Mexican researchers in her own analyses and propositions. She has provided fundamental support for initiatives such as *Cine cubano, la pupila insomne* and *Enciclopedia digital del audiovisual cubano*, Cuban critic Juan Antonio García Borrero's innovative blog and digital encyclopedia (or multisourced, cloud-based "film club without walls"). For English-language readers, she has composed synthetic overviews of Latin America–based film scholarship (1985a, 1988b) as well as English-language translations of important books such as *Le cinéma mexicain* (edited by Paulo Antonio Paranaguá, 1992; *Mexican Cinema*, 1995). In December 2015, she took over the editorship of *Studies in Spanish and Latin American Cinemas*, the first and only academic journal dedicated to those cinemas published in the United States. In addition to her many publications, translations, and editorial work, she has hosted Latin American filmmakers and scholars, curated traveling film series, and chaired panels with diverse colleagues at professional conferences. She has also organized international symposia to promote Latin American film within the US and create opportunities for networking and substantive exchanges between scholars and filmmakers from different geocultural traditions—often with the support of Tulane University's Roger Thayer Stone Center for Latin American Studies and the Cuban and Caribbean Studies Institute (which she has led since 2000). These events include the 1994 Nobody's Women film series (named for Adela Sequeyro's 1937 *La mujer de nadie*) featuring the work of Mexican women filmmakers and the participation of Mexican film scholar Patricia Torres San Martín and filmmaker Marcela Fernández Violante; the 1996 Popular Cinemas conference with Carlos Monsiváis as keynote speaker; the 1999 40 Years of ICAIC: Cuban Cinema Series and Symposium with lectures by Julio García Espinosa and Lola Calviño; the 2009 Geographical Imaginaries conference codirected with Tatjana Pavlovic; and numerous other conferences on Cuban and Caribbean culture.

Through these intellectual and institutional contributions, López has helped to forge a community of teachers, critics, and researchers. This has long been evident to the editors of this volume and to other former students (such as Gabriela Alemán, Misha MacLaird, and Victoria Ruétalo) from Tulane University, where she has taught since 1985. As younger (and then older!) scholars, we benefited immensely from her efforts to draw us into larger scholarly debates and exchanges through invitations to present on panels at SCMS, join externally funded projects with Cuban colleagues, participate in Latin American film events (such as the 1995 Mexican Film Project conference at UCLA), or publish a first article in volumes that she edited. Her contributions to the construction of a productive and supportive network of Latin American scholars go beyond her former students. Colleagues whom we contacted while compiling this volume all note Ana's impact on their intellectual growth. Luisela Alvaray, Gilberto Blasini, and Cristina Venegas remember meeting her and becoming familiar with her essays when they were graduate students in the mid-1990s while Ana was a visiting professor at USC in spring 1995, and/or during Latin American film conferences at UCLA in 1994 and 1995, and at UC Santa Cruz/Stanford in 1997 (organized by Chon Noriega and Julianne Burton/Jorge Ruffinelli, respectively). Alvaray remembers that López's writings always contained "some elegant subtlety, a reframing of an old topic, or a new set of associations that brought her work to the forefront of what we were thinking in our own graduate work. We would start anticipating Ana's next article, and craving it like candy, once it came out. What new, challenging ideas was it going to bring?" (2021). Other, younger scholars like Olivia Cosentino, Nilo Couret, and Rielle Navitski point to her generosity to junior colleagues through conversations at conferences, email exchanges, and invitations to collaborate. As neatly summarized by Tamara Falicov, "[López] is a brilliant scholar but is not living in her cloistered world of ideas. . . . [She leads] study abroad trips, edit[s] books and journal issues, convers[es] with colleagues at SCMS and other conferences, [participates in] international conferences [and] on listservs and provid[es] opportunities for up and coming graduate students and faculty (as well as oldies!)" (2021). For her part, Navitski summarizes the thoughts of many colleagues when she calls López a "treasured mentor for generations of scholars" (2021). Ana has been a particularly important role model for younger women and Latinx scholars. Alvaray comments that as a graduate student she could "relate to [Ana] in more than one way," given that she was a "Cuban American scholar who had already [trod] the path of working on uncharted territory—Latin American cinema—within a U.S. academy not used to this divergent view" (2021).

For all of these reasons, we have compiled *Ana M. López: Essays* as the first English-language book to feature a large selection of her scholarship in a single volume.[2] It includes foundational essays along with some lesser-known works and three translations that will appear in English for the first time.[3] The collection will serve as a resource for newcomers and seasoned scholars alike—whether they are from Latin American film and cultural studies or Anglo-American film studies—who up until now have had to search for her essays in numerous journals and edited volumes. Given López's own ongoing metacritical efforts to map the field of Latin American film studies (1985a, 1988b, 1991d, 1998b, 2006, 2010, 2011, 2012b), it is only fitting that we begin by tracing her intellectual trajectory from the 1980s until the present. As with any scholar, her ideas did not evolve in a linear fashion; thus, rather than suggesting a strict chronology, the "short history" traces some of her engagements with key scholarly debates during her career.

A Short History

López began taking film classes at Queens College in New York City, where she received a BA in accounting in 1978. A few years later, she started a graduate program in what was then the Department of Communication Studies at the University of Iowa, under the direction of Dudley Andrew. There she benefited from the mentorship of Andrew, Rick Altman, and numerous other visiting film scholars (Jacques Aumont, David Bordwell, Thomas Elsaesser, Kristin Thompson), and the guidance of Mexican historian Charles Hale and literary scholar Tom Lewis (Venegas 2017). Julianne Burton (then at University of California, Santa Cruz) was also a formative influence. As one of the first US academics to focus their scholarship on Latin American film, Burton modeled the importance of foregrounding the voices of Latin American filmmakers themselves and eschewing an "extractive" mentality of film scholarship (Venegas 2017).[4]

At Iowa, López was part of a transformational group of graduate students, many of whom (Robert Allen, Mary Ann Doane, Philip Rosen, David Rodowick, Patrice Petro, and Henry Jenkins) would also go on to distinguished careers.[5] It is perhaps notable that she and her colleagues were being trained at a time when the era of high theory (or *Screen*

Theory) was slowly giving way to what became characterized as the "historical turn" in US film studies—that is, from a focus on expansive questions about film, subjectivity, ideology, and gender norms (considered in transhistorical and universal terms) to an emphasis on situated practices in time and space, including conditions of production, contexts of reception, and transformations in technology (Baer 2018). The scholarship of the entire cohort would reflect the shift—albeit in varied ways. In the case of López, her interest in Latin American film led her to be attentive to the influence of local, national, and regional traditions on the production and reception of cinema. Rather than eschewing theoretical concerns, her work tackled "big questions" from a situated perspective. As noted by Blasini, López's essays showed subsequent Latin American film scholars "how to establish a fruitful dialogue between theory and history . . . during the high theory period that had been ushered in by poststructuralism and postmodernism (and that lasted way into the late 1990s)" (2021). Also notable is the way that her understanding of "theory" itself recognized, conversed with, and interrogated traditions of thought outside of or disruptive to Europe and the US—from dependency theory (Cardoso/Faletto) to postcolonial theory (Said, Bhabha) to theories about the coloniality of power (Quijano, Mignolo).

This dual interest in theory and history would be evident in her earliest work on the New Latin American Cinema (NLAC), the politically militant and aesthetically experimental cinema that emerged in many countries in the late 1950s. Her dissertation (1986) was one of the first to offer a comprehensive account of the NLAC as a pan-continental phenomenon in contrast to other contemporaneous studies that mainly focused on specific national cases.[6] Her doctoral thesis would be reworked into articles and book chapters such as "Unleashing the Margins: Argentine Cinema, 1955–1976" (1987) and "An 'Other' History: The New Latin American Cinema" (1988b). In these and other essays, she provided detailed historical accounts of the emergence of the NLAC from the national film movements and sociopolitical conditions that nurtured it. At the same time, her scholarship had larger conceptual goals—namely, to craft interpretive frameworks that identified common, cross-national aesthetic strategies, such as the recurrent mixing of fictional and documentary modes. For example, in "Parody, Underdevelopment, and the New Latin American Cinema" (1990c)—and the expanded version "At the Limits of Documentary: Hypertextual Transformation and the New Latin American Cinema" (1990a), she offered a provocative challenge to contemporaneous readings of NLAC films as "straight" (serious) political films. Drawing on the work of postmodern theorists like Linda Hutcheon, López argued that the fictional films of the NLAC that incorporated documentary conventions should be understood as parodies—that is, as hypertextual interventions that comment critically on the documentary form itself as well as on history, understood as intertext.

In this same period (mid-1980s to mid-1990s), even as López was offering nuanced analyses of the aesthetic contributions of the NLAC, she was tackling the cultural politics of telenovelas and critiquing the cultural dependency model that characterized television and film as imperialist tools. On one level, she was challenging Latin America–based scholars and artists—including some of the NLAC filmmakers who railed against cultural imperialism and rejected the continent's heavily melodramatic classical cinemas as imperfect imitations of Hollywood. In essays like the much-cited "Our Welcomed Guests," López drew on Martín-Barbero's notion of "mediations" to argue that domestic mass media was not imposing foreign models as much as allowing local audiences to reckon with rapid societal transformation and to acquire new cultural habits through media forms that drew on long-established oral traditions and ideological frameworks (1995b, 257). On another level, she was beginning her critique of US-based film and media scholars who would frame any commentary on Latin American media in terms of a base comparison to US or European cultural forms and industrial structures. In "The Melodrama in Latin America" (1985b), she noted the clear distinctions between telenovelas and US soap operas in terms of narrative scope, industrial dynamics, and reception or, more specifically, by commenting on differential star systems, scheduling practices, and target audiences. In "A Cinema for the Continent" (1994a) and again in "Facing Up to Hollywood" (2000c), she countered arguments about Hollywood as the singular external influence in the region by recognizing the Mexican industry's success in the 1930s–1950s in markets in Argentina, Colombia, and other Latin American countries.[7]

Well into the 1990s, US-based Latin American film scholarship still tended to utilize the New Latin American Cinema of the 1960s and 1970s as the yardstick by which to assess later works. In the wake of crises in state funding and the rise of new industrial dynamics, many scholars highlighted (quite rightly) how contemporary Latin American cinemas mobilized an NLAC sensibility to rework genre films and modes—from melodrama and musicals (King 2000 [1990]; Newman 1993; Tierney 1997;

D'Lugo 2003) to road films and even horror and westerns (Stock 1999). In other words, such studies highlighted how a new generation of filmmakers (along with some older directors like Fernando Solanas) was inserting political critique into formula films as a means to reach wider audiences.

Within this context, López turned her attention slightly elsewhere to study popular or mainstream cinema. She began to call for US-based Latin American film scholars to historicize how popular genres had functioned in the region's "studio era" (1930s–1950s) to understand the historical trajectory of melodrama from the past to more contemporary popular films (like María Novaro's *Danzón* 1993) (López 1997). In doing so, she drew on the feminist revisions of melodrama and the women's film taking place in Anglophone film studies. At the same time, she cogently argued for the importance of recognizing the differential function and meanings of given modes and genres within Latin America and the US. In a parallel fashion to her argument about melodrama, López insisted that "the musical" in Latin America didn't always function as theorized by US film scholars like Jane Feuer. In essays such as "Of Rhythms and Borders" (1997) and again later in "Mexico" (2012a), she would put forth an alternate conceptual model, underscoring how the recourse to music and dance in Latin American films allowed for border crossings—as audiences in many different countries shared an affinity for *bolero, son, danzón, salsa* and other sonic and performative traditions that themselves were the hybrid products of cultural flows across national borders. Sharing an affinity with the approach of British film scholar Richard Dyer to Hollywood (1981), López located the (political) utopian possibilities of "old" and "new" Latin American musicals in their music and dance sequences (1997, 335). In general, her essays on popular genres helped to broaden the notion of the "political" in Latin American cinema by acknowledging the contestatory potential of pleasurable forms. This was a notable departure from the characterization of genre films in the historical accounts written by Latin America–based scholars like Emilio García Riera, Aurelio de los Reyes, and Domingo Di Núbila, but it resonated with the approach of other Latin American–based scholars such as João Luiz Vieira and US collaborator Robert Stam and their work on the Brazilian *chanchada* (Vieira 1987; Vieira and Stam 1985).

In the 1990s, López also wrote essays on the representation of Latinx people in classic Hollywood film and also on the work of Latinx filmmakers. Engaging with the emerging field of postcolonial theory and the work of Edward Said, James Clifford, and Homi K. Bhabha, López addressed how Hollywood's representational strategies reproduced colonial imaginaries even while the performative tactics of Latinx stars subtly undermined Hollywood's authority and ability to fix identities. In "Are All Latins from Manhattan?" (1991a), she explored how the ethnographic imperatives of Hollywood in the 1940s shaped the representation of three "Latin" stars: Dolores Del Rio, Lupe Vélez, and Carmen Miranda. In other essays, her interest in the agency of Latinx subjects extended into analyses of Latinx directors. In "The 'Other' Island" (1993) and the revised version published as "Greater Cuba" (1996), López explored the video practices of post-1959 Cuban exiles and how the heterogeneity of their efforts to produce a national identity in exile produced an "other" island. López's work on diasporic, exilic, and Latinx image-making culminated in *The Ethnic Eye: Latino Media Arts* (Noriega and López 1996), a significant anthology in which López and coeditor Chon Noriega brought together a new generation of Latinx film scholars to address a heterogeneous body of Latinx film/video including *Born in East L.A.* (Cheech Marin, 1987) and *Carmelita Tropicana* (Ela Troyano, 1993).

At this time, López's work on Latin American cinemas, Latinx representation within Hollywood, and Latinx filmmakers' self-representation participated in the growing visibility of those fields within what was then known as the Society of Cinema Studies or SCS (that later became the Society for Cinema and Media Studies or SCMS). The establishment of the Latino Caucus in 1990 by Chon Noriega and Charles Ramírez Berg was absolutely key to this increased institutional presence.[8] The caucus was initially conceived as a means to support the efforts of Latinx scholars in the academy and diversify the society's membership, while also promoting the work of Latinx filmmakers (such as Lourdes Portillo, Paul Espinosa, and Isaac Artenstein) who were invited to participate. However, the caucus's mission quickly expanded to welcome and support all scholars researching Latino/a and Latin American media in recognition of the different constituencies attending its inaugural meeting that very year.[9] This tactical professional alliance permitted Latinx and Latin Americanist film scholars to intervene more forcefully in SCMS and in US-based film studies. There was also a recognition of shared concerns—particularly about the political and politicizing potential of film/media, the role of film/media in racialization processes, and the fruitfulness of intersectional approaches—as well as of parallels and lines of influence between the New Latin American Cinema and independent Chicano media-making in the 1970s–1980s. That said, these two subfields remained distinct, particularly as scholarship flourished in the 2000s at the hands of a new generation of academics. For her part, while López continues to present conference papers on Latinx topics (such as the television series *Devious Maids*, 2013–2016, Lifetime), the bulk of her work after this point has focused on Latin American media.

In the late 1990s and early 2000s, her previous work on the shared aesthetic tendencies of the NLAC (1990a) and the continental appeal of Mexican cinema (1994a) began to coalesce into a more pointed, overarching argument about the transnational tendencies of Latin American cinemas. Of course, López was not alone. Among Latin Americanist film scholars, there was a growing interest in the recent surge of coproductions and the emergence of new alignments between film industries in different countries that had resulted from the rise of neoliberal platforms and the crisis of state subsidies for domestic film industries in Latin America as well as the broader intensification of economic globalization and Hollywood's search for increased penetration of foreign markets. López's contribution was to recognize that the presence of transnational dynamics and networks between Latin American countries, the United States, and the Hispanic Atlantic actually predated the contemporary moment and could be traced back to the studio era and before (1998b, 2009).

This call for a "transnational turn" in Latin American film studies responded to the limitations of the nation-centric accounts of Argentina, Bolivia, Brazil, Mexico, Peru, among others, written by both US- and Latin America–based scholars focused on film and national identity. At the same time, her essays coincided with the questioning of the national by postcolonial scholars like Homi K. Bhabha as well as the very notion of national cinema that was taking place among British and US scholars. The latter, among other things, insisted on the need to reconsider the text-based criteria used to define aesthetic canons within given countries and to debate the very merits of a unitary and/or unifying notion of national cinema (Crofts 1993; Higson 1989, 2000).

No "short history" would be complete without mentioning López's influential "Early Cinema and Modernity in Latin America" (2000b)—an expansive view of cross-border flows and mediated sociocultural transformation between the 1890s and 1920s. That essay and her more recent "Film and Radio Intermedialities . . ." (2017) on the "radiophonic imaginary" in the 1930s–1940s continue to challenge many of the assumptions about those earlier historical periods. López eschews historicizing models that are teleological and that foreground linear lines of influence between technologies and cultural forms. For example, in the latter essay, she contests descriptions of early filmmaking that characterize it as simply the outgrowth of existing popular theatrical forms (such as the *teatro bufo* and *carpa*) and narrative modes like melodrama present in both radio programs and nineteenth-century theater. Here, again, she insists on the importance of acknowledging the differential historical development of media industries in Latin American countries versus the US and Europe. Rather than emerging in succession, the radio and film industries grew up alongside each other in countries like Argentina. The two essays cogently demonstrate the productivity of examining broader media horizons to reveal how film (and radio) participated in a "perceptual revolution" and reimagination of community in an era of rapid modernization. For its part, the 2017 essay joins in the proliferation of intermedial approaches to Latin American media and substantive discussions of media horizons in the early twenty-first century, through the work of younger scholars like Andrea Cuarterolo (2013) and Rielle Navitski (2017).

Over the last three decades, Ana López has acted as a media archeologist, locating, chronicling, and theorizing not only lesser-known texts but also underappreciated media dynamics. Her metacritical sensibility produces a delightfully perverse tendency to push against staid interpretative parameters. As noted by Couret in his afterword, López's work has always been "an invitation to historicize otherwise, to understand the messiness of the archive, the ambivalence of the apparatus, and the limitations of the national." She can certainly be considered a "Latin Americanist," but her contributions move beyond that region. Without overlooking the power of colonialist imaginaries and economies, López has helped to question Eurocentric notions of media influence that have long positioned the US and Europe as starting points for aesthetic change and technological innovation, whether through her efforts to break away from a model of media imperialism or to bring into relief transnational flows *within* Latin America. This volume provides a glimpse of López's innovative scholarship up to 2020; we look forward to her future contributions.

Part 1

Latin American Cinema/s

The Transnational Turn

Editors' Introduction

We begin this anthology with eight essays that highlight López's transnationally focused approach to Latin American film and media. In the wake of Higson's seminal work on national cinema (1989) plus his equally significant essay interrogating national cinema (2000), the concept of cinematic transnationalism has gained increasing currency among film scholars. This is evident in the proliferation of edited volumes on the topic (Ezra and Rowden 2006; Ďurovičová and Newman 2010; Higbee and Lim 2010; Lefere and Lie 2016; Lusnich, Aisemberg, and Cuarterolo 2017) as well as in the establishment in 2010 of *Transnational Cinemas*, an academic journal founded by Deborah Shaw and Armida de la Garza (both of whom have written on Latin American film), and Ruth Doughty, that was renamed *Transnational Screens* in 2019. Acting as a hold-all to describe a range of complex extra-national practices including "production and distribution [and] sources of funding and thematic concerns" (Hjort 2010, 12), cinematic transnationalism also offers scholars of contemporary and earlier modes of image-making a means of theorizing the movement and displacement of cinemas, directors, actors, and film personnel across national and regional borders. Feeding into this expanding body of research were the efforts of Latin Americanists who, in the 1990s, utilized transnationalism (even though it was not necessarily named as such at the time) as the paradigm through which to explore the intense contemporary neoliberal transitions taking place in the filmmaking economies of the region's different nations, including state backed coproductions with European cultural institutions (King 2000a [1990]; Stock 1997).[1]

As noted briefly in the introduction to this volume, during this same period, López took her cue from postcolonial theory, calling into question the totalizing and hegemonic nature of constructions of the nation, while also turning attention to filmmaking dynamics in earlier periods (Bhabha 1994, 297). "A Cinema for the Continent" (1994a) was the opening salvo in the marshalling of an approach that examined the multiple ways that Mexican classical cinema (1930s–1950s) operated regionally, nationally, and transnationally. Unlike previous accounts that foregrounded the role of domestic entrepreneurs, filmmakers and actors, state-industry relations, and the incorporation of local musical traditions, López contended that it was as much what was happening internationally that fostered the (regional) success of Mexico's cinema in this period. A few years later, in 1997, she presented "Historia nacional, historia transnacional" at a pre-LASA conference in Guadalajara (later published in *Horizontes del segundo siglo* in 1998) where she used the term "transnational" for the first time to describe the need to rethink the older national cinema model, sketching in broad strokes the impact and influence of "traveling filmmakers" moving between Latin America, the United States, and Europe. As noted by Laura Isabel Serna, in these and other essays, Lopez's work on transnationalism "functioned as a model for how to theorize space and media." Her innovative "methodology . . . prompted [scholars] to think about the meaning of cultural objects and formation across borders" (Serna 2021) and was influential for later studies, including Tierney's 2007 *Emilio Fernández: Pictures in the Margins*, Serna's own 2014 *Making Cinelandia: American Films and Mexican Film Culture before the Golden Age*, and Nicolas Poppe's *Alton's Paradox: Foreign Film Workers and the Emergence of Industrial Cinema in Latin America* (2021).[2]

In her studies on transnationalism, López has been particularly attentive to chronicling *intra*regional flows and exchanges within Latin America. She emphasized the contributions of Latin American–born/ trained filmmakers (like Argentine-born Carlos Hugo Christensen) on the film industries in other countries (like Venezuela). She traced the filmic constitution of certain national imaginaries (in Mexico and Venezuela) to the "othering" of other Latin American countries/cultures (Cuba) within given films, as well as to the sonic terrain (from linguistic commonalities and variations to musical traditions) that facilitated cross-border flows. This emphasis on intraregional exchanges rejected the previous tendency to see Latin American cinema as determined by one-way flows of technological, aesthetic, and industrial innovations from colonizing nations (France, the United States, Italy, Great Britain) to the "periphery."[3]

Finally, it's important to distinguish López's scholarship from recent volumes on "world cinema" that take an additive approach (Hollywood+

or Hollywood/European cinemas+) to mapping filmmaking around the globe. For example, Geoffrey Nowell-Smith's edited volume *The Oxford History of World Cinema* (1996)—published around the same time that López began her transnational turn—offers a historical account that is Hollywood-centric and categorizes filmmaking elsewhere mainly as unique "national cases" or, occasionally, as regional cases (e.g., cinemas of Latin America or sub-Saharan Africa) (for similar tendencies, see Gazetas 2000; Hill and Church Gibson 2000). In contrast, López helped to pave the way for more in-depth reconceptualizations of film industries and aesthetics as the product of networks and flows, exemplified in the volumes mentioned at the beginning of this introduction (e.g., Ďurovičová and Newman 2010; Higbee and Lim 2010) as well as in works that explicitly take on the notion of "world cinema" (Nagib, Perriam, and Dudrah 2012).

1

A Cinema for the Continent (1994)

This is López's first, pioneering essay on the transnational nature of Latin American film industries.¹ It was originally published in a catalog edited by Chon A. Noriega and Steven Ricci that was an outgrowth of the multiyear Mexican Film Project developed through the UCLA Film and Television Archive. Even as the essay's overall goal sought to foster awareness and appreciation of Mexican film culture among US (scholarly and popular) audiences, López's article complicated the notion of Mexican cinema as a hermetically sealed "national case" by tracing its continental reach. The essay identifies multiple economic, geopolitical, cultural, and aesthetic factors that helped to make Mexican films attractive to other markets in the region and in Spanish-language theaters in the US—placing particular emphasis on the 1930s–1950s. "A Cinema for the Continent" coincided with Andrew Higson (1989) and Stephen Crofts's (1993) interrogations of the notion of national cinema.

I

Mexico has always played a crucial role within Latin America, yet in the twentieth century it has also always been somewhat asynchronous to the other major countries of the continent. Caught in the wheels of a radical revolution that began in 1910, ended only a decade later, and eventually resulted in the formation of an official "revolutionary" political party that has ruled the country since then, Mexican history, from a Latin American perspective, always seems insular: exotically different yet familiar. Mexico's "revolution" was a twentieth-century "first" among Latin American countries. Mexican cinema, like the revolution, has been a "frozen" icon: often a hegemonic cultural force throughout the Americas while interestingly (between the 1960s and 1980s) dissociated from the principal cinematic trends of the continent. The Mexican cinema has been the only Latin American cinema to have successfully and consistently exceeded the limits of its national borders: since the 1930s and especially in the 1940s and '50s, almost all Latin Americans with access to the cinema watched and loved Mexican films. From Havana to Rio de Janeiro and Santiago de Chile, most Latin American cities had well-attended theaters that regularly scheduled Mexican films well into the 1960s. To this day and throughout the continent, one still speaks as often of Cantinflas as of Chaplin, of María Félix as of Marilyn Monroe, of Jorge Negrete as of Clark Gable.

Why did Mexican films—often resoundingly nationalistic and apparently insular—resonate so powerfully in Latin American popular culture and in the continental unconscious? How could the film of a nation that has so often been simultaneously on the vanguard of and "off course" from continental politics and social movements consistently penetrate deep into the heart of Latin America? How was the Mexican film industry able to negotiate the commercial barriers that made the Latin American continent a "natural" market only for Hollywood and that problematized intercontinental distribution? What is the international market for Mexican films today, when Latin American theatrical attendance has dropped to disastrously low levels that have crippled most national industries? What keeps alive the continental myths (and realities) of the "Mexican cinema" today?

Answering these questions requires weaving together several explanatory theses. First of all, the presence of Mexican films throughout Latin America must be understood in economic terms. For years, the Mexican film industry was the best capitalized and the most productive in the continent. At its height in the 1940s and '50s, the Mexican industry's dozen or so active studios invested as much as 144 million dollars to produce between 80 and 136 films per year.[2] Well protected by the state, intimately linked to US/Hollywood investors, and increasingly popular at home (thus able to recoup production costs domestically), the Mexican cinema could enter the continent with a confidence and an economic advantage that no other Latin American film-producing nation could afford.

A Cinema for the Continent | 19

But the links between the economic clout of the industry and its appeal to Latin American audiences are complex and exceed purely economic explanations. Most obviously, we must position the Mexican cinema as a Spanish-language cinema. This linguistic advantage allowed the Mexican cinema to create a market for itself in Latin America that Hollywood, with its subtitled and/or inappropriately dubbed films, could not easily tap. In the poorer sectors of large urban centers and in rural areas where illiteracy was the norm, the easy-to-understand Mexican cinema was, for decades, almost synonymous with cinema itself. Thus, the success of Mexican films in Latin America must be analyzed in relation to other Spanish-language film producers and their histories—Hollywood in the early 1930s, Argentina in the 1930s–1940s, Spain in the late 1950s–1960s—all in the context of Hollywood's constant presence in the Latin American market. After all, even at the peak of its popularity, the Mexican cinema never had more than 25 to 35 percent of any one Latin American market.

Although a good part of the appeal of Mexican cinema throughout Latin America is undoubtedly based on its immediate linguistic accessibility, we must also attempt to explain how a national cinema's concerns evolved so as to appeal to an entire continent. The Mexican cinema's obsessive reworking of national characteristics was profoundly appealing to other nations that were perhaps less archetypally defined, less powerful, and/or less visible internationally. Understanding this process requires an analysis of how a national cinema expands, absorbs other national differences, and produces a continental voice that is, nevertheless, deeply nationalistic.

II

The story of the Mexican cinema's success in Latin America begins with *Allá en el Rancho Grande* (Over on the Big Ranch, Fernando de Fuentes, 1936). Mexico had already produced a significant number of films in the silent period, and the early days of sound production had witnessed spectacular films,[3] but *Rancho Grande* (fig. 1.1) focused both the economic drives of the nascent industry as well as the attention of the continent. *Rancho Grande* is set in the present, but in a bucolic, mythical rural area where neither the Revolution nor the recent Agrarian Reform have left any traces and where conflict emerges only from love affairs, wounded male pride, and misunderstandings. Its narrative is melodramatic: *hacendado* (René Cardona) falls for the girlfriend (Esther Fernández) of his *caporal*

(Tito Guízar), with whom he had been friends since childhood. The former friends become enemies, but ultimately, despite misunderstandings, macho attitudes, and fights, the bonds of their friendship prevail and all are reconciled with the aid of much singing and dancing. Thus, the film posits the possibility of a perfectly harmonious relationship between the rich *hacendado* and his employee—exalting precisely that which the radical Lázaro Cárdenas government then in place was attempting to eliminate and promotes the maintenance of the sociopolitical status quo through an unbridled nostalgia for an imaginary past where such relationships could be conceived. Perhaps most significantly, however, *Rancho Grande* also cinematically reworks a series of popular and folkloric elements that would define the *comedia ranchera* genre: popular music in the form of *rancheras*, here sung by Tito Guízar and Lorenzo Barcelata; a loose and episodic narrative structure derived from variety theater, with songs often taking the place of dialogue; and the introduction of familiar yet picturesque character types (*charros*, innocent señoritas with long braided hair, and peppery old housekeepers) and situations (cockfights, *fiestas*, and *jarabes tapatíos*).

Despite a weak opening run in Mexico City, the film was eventually very popular, and was even more widely distributed after Gabriel Figueroa

Figure 1.1. Cantina scene from *Allá en el Rancho Grande* (Fernando de Fuentes, 1936). Fair use.

received the Mexican cinema's first international festival prize for its cinematography in Venice. Nationally, it spurred investment in the industry and production. The year *Rancho Grande* was released (1936), Mexico produced twenty-five films. By 1937 production grew to thirty-eight films, of which twenty exploited the *ranchera* model. In 1939 production again increased: out of fifty-seven films, twenty exploited *ranchera* formula and local color.

Rancho Grande was also seen throughout the Spanish-speaking Latin American market, and subtitled versions were even released in the United States (always the market most resistant to cinematic imports). But even this first moment of nationalist expansion was mediated by the participation of Hollywood. International distribution was coordinated by United Artists, which struck an advantageous agreement with the film's producer (40 to 60 percent split of gross revenues). Until United Artists got out of Latin American distribution in the 1950s, *Rancho Grande* was one of its highest grossing films, in 1939 surpassed only by *Modern Times* (Charlie Chaplin, 1931) and *The Garden of Allah* (Richard Boleslawski, 1936) (de Usabel 1982, 140-41). As would be the case throughout most of its history, Mexican cinema expanded with the cooperation of Hollywood, which favored it more than any other Latin American film producer. As Paulo Antonio Paranaguá has succinctly expressed it: "Poor Mexico, so far from God and so close Hollywood" (1992, 18).[4]

In any case, the release of *Rancho Grande* in Latin America could not have occurred at a more propitious moment. Other Spanish-language cinemas that had competed for the Latin American market were going through difficult times. Spain was involved in a bloody civil war that would temporarily cripple production. Argentine films—of much higher technical quality than the Mexican but also becoming very Europeanized—were waning in popularity and Argentine production, although increasing, had not matched the levels of the Mexican industry (Argentina produced fifteen films in 1936, twenty-eight in 1937, and forty-one in 1938). The *Rancho Grande* formula unearthed what Latin American audiences seemed to have been looking for in the Mexican cinema: the presentation of a "Mexican" vision of Mexico that coincided with their expectations of the nature of national local color. As Emilio García Riera has argued, after *Rancho Grande*, the Mexican cinema "enjoyed the prestige of authenticity granted by even the most adulterated folklore" (1969, 140). The *ranchera* vision of Mexico, albeit decidedly distinct from other Latin American national stereotypes, was still recognizable. It combined an appealing exoticism with a comforting familiarity that easily won over Latin American audiences looking for points of cinematic identification.

Furthermore, the nostalgia for an imaginary bucolic past where macho pride and true love always prevailed—as invoked by *Rancho Grande* and its successors—also echoed throughout other Latin American countries where, despite different political histories, the present was burdened by the legacies of colonization and the frustrations of independence.

Rancho Grande opened the doors, and the industry rushed to keep them open: the Mexican cinema consolidated its strength by copying, expanding, and improvising upon the formula of the *comedia ranchera*, introduced variations of other well-rehearsed generic formulas like the maternal melodramas and the picaresque comedy, and attempted to develop its own "star system" comparable to that of Hollywood.

At the end of the 1930s the popularity of *rancheras* seemed to be waning, Argentine production was increasing, and few Mexican films were truly successful at the box office. This temporary "crisis" ended due to an historical accident: World War II. Wartime pressures temporarily weakened Hollywood's hold on the Latin American market (Hollywood imports began to arrive sporadically) and exhibitors used Latin American productions to fill programming gaps in many of the 4,200 theaters in Latin America. With Mexican and Argentine films screened more regularly and even appearing in first-run theaters, Latin American audiences began to develop a consistent "taste" for Spanish-language films and began to favor them over the war-obsessed Hollywood productions.[5] Furthermore, because US retaliations against Argentina favored the Mexican film industry with extra film stock shipments (and crippled the Argentine industry), the future of the Mexican industry seemed "golden" at home and in the Latin American market. With increasing state and private investment (the establishment of the Banco Cinematográfico in 1942 and, in 1945, the opening of the Churubusco studios [50 percent financed by RKO], and the creation of PELMEX to handle foreign distribution), the industry was set to strengthen its position in the Latin American market.

Some of its most visible efforts to widen this market involved filming explicitly Latin American stories—for example, *Simon Bolívar* (Miguel Contreras Torres, 1941) and *Cristóbal Colón: La grandeza de América* (Christopher Columbus: The Greatness of America, José Díaz Morales, 1943)—and emulating Hollywood's Pan-American/Good Neighbor Policy films. These latter films refashioned the Hollywood "Good Neighbor" formula (exemplified in *Panamericana*, John H. Auer, 1965; *The Gang's All Here*, Busby Berkeley, 1943; and dozens of others) whereby entertainers from various Latin American nations perform almost continuously while the Anglo stars develop the principal narrative lines. In contrast, films like

Las cinco noches de Adán (The Five Nights of Adam, Agustín Martínez Solares, 1941), *La liga de las canciones* (The League of Songs, Chano Urueta, 1941), and *Cuando viajan las estrellas* (When the Stars Travel, Alberto Gout, 1942) featured the usual multinational cast of singers, dancers, and performers, but emphasized inter–Latin American unity at the expense of the Anglo characters and situations. In these films (and without the reticence of their Hollywood counterparts), the Mexican protagonist *always* gets the "girl," even when she is Anglo (as in *Cuando viajan las estrellas*). Others, like *Canto a las Américas* (Song to the Americas, Ramón Pereda, 1942) and *Hotel de verano* (Summer Hotel, René Cardona, 1943) deployed only Latin American talent, although the latter film features the first cinematic appearance of German Valdés "Tin Tan," a singer/dancer/performer whose *pachuco* style at the very least invokes the closeness and cultural influences of Mexico's Northern neighbor.

But by 1943 ("el Gran Año"), as García Riera argues, the Mexican cinema had "achieved a greater fit between the national cinema and the taste of the Latin American public" (1970, 111). The best and most popular films of that year—*María Candelaria* (Emilio Fernández), *Doña Bárbara* (Fernando de Fuentes), *Distinto amanecer* (A Different Dawn, Julio Bracho), and *Flor silvestre* (Wildflower, Emilio Fernández)—for the most part abandoned foreign exoticism and left behind "universalizing" or Pan–Latin Americanist tendencies to focus on markedly "Mexican" themes and problems.[6] These themes—*indigenismo*, the Revolution, the melodramatic angst (and humor) of urban life, and, of course, *rancheras*—would constitute the backbone of Mexican cinema's popularity in Latin America.

The industry's attention to the Latin American market was also evidenced by the growth of the tendency to import and harbor talent from other Latin American countries. Mexico had imported talent since the earliest days of the sound era,[7] but in the 1940s it "open[ed] its arms to the many foreigners that come to contribute to the growth of the industry" (García Riera 1970, 209) and welcomed a wide assortment of Latin American actors and performers. In the mid-1940s, for example, a number of very prominent Argentine actors—Libertad Lamarque, Nini Marshall, Hugo del Carril, Luis Sandrini, and others—sought refuge in Mexico from the Perón regime. Their subsequent appearance in the Mexican cinema served to further "Latin Americanize" its appeal. As a Cuban critic writing in Mexico argued in 1944, "The artistic exchange among us will always be a way of opening the doors of the market: in each country in which a [Mexican] film is shown featuring a national of that country, that film will be doubly well received, since everyone likes to see their own being well treated" (García Riera 1970, 209). Spanish talent was also welcomed, most notably in the case of Luis Buñuel, who went on to win more international critical acclaim for the Mexican cinema than any other director. But his is a different, and well-studied, other case.

In the late 1940s and '50s, once again facing competition from Hollywood and other Latin American producers, as well as spiraling production costs at home, Mexican producers looked abroad for production possibilities and began what would turn out to be a rather profitable practice within the Latin American (and Spanish-speaking) market: coproductions. Curiously, the most favored coproduction partner until the mid-1950s was Cuba, a nation without an established filmmaking industry. Several factors made Cuba a natural coproduction partner for Mexico. Since the 1930s, Cubans and Cuban rhythms had "livened up" Mexican films and brought along heavy doses of exoticism and sensuality. Imported Cuban stars like Ninón Sevilla and María Antonieta Pons, the two best-known *cabareteras*, were extraordinarily popular in Mexico and throughout the continent. Cuba could provide cheap labor and exotic landscapes. Besides, despite its small size, Cuba was proportionately one of the biggest markets for the Mexican cinema in all of Latin America.[8] For Cuban producers, Mexico was a desirable ally. With the clout of Mexican financing and technical expertise, the Cubans hoped to improve their skills and to open up the foreign market for their own subsequent productions.

The initiator of the coproduction trend was director Juan Orol, a Galician immigrant to Mexico with close ties to the island, who filmed *Embrujo antillano* (1945) and *El amor de mi bohío* (1946) as well as several other films in the 1950s. *María de la O* (1947), an adaptation of a *zarzuela* (Spanish musical comedy) set in Havana in the 1840s and written by the archetypal Cuban composer Ernesto Lecuona, that best identified the advantages of coproductions with Cuba. Working with a typical coproduction arrangement that would not become common international practice for quite some years, Fernández Bustamante found in Cuba—especially in its history, music, dance, and racial mixtures—an exoticism that was more easily circulated and better received than its Mexican equivalents. As García Riera writes in reference to *María de la O*:

> The cinematographic exchange between Cuba and Mexico consisted of the former giving the latter the opportunity to share its sorrow over the pain and fatality of its black people. The Mexican cinema could now consider as its own the difficulties

of racial mixing undertaken in a climate of sin, voluptuousness, superstition, discrimination, fortune telling, and *pasitos tan chéveres*. (1971, 230)

The most important years for coproduction with Cuba were 1953 and 1954 (respectively, six and eight films), although Mexican producers continued to coproduce with Cuba regularly. Most of these films—most notably *Mulata* (Gilberto Martínez Solares, 1953) and *Sandra, la mujer de fuego* (Sandra, the Woman of Fire, Juan Orol, 1952)—served to relativize the usual nationalist fervor of the Mexican cinema, setting it against films about far more exotic, often racially differentiated "others" in Cuba. These representations could be enjoyed without the ideological and political burden of the national "Indian" problem in Mexico (Podalsky 1994).

As further coproductions were quickly sought, the Cuban-Mexican partnership served as a model. The Spanish singer Sarita Montiel, for example, was redefined as a "Cuban" and starred in several coproductions of the 1950s. And a later series of coproductions with Spain featured and marketed the "national" exoticism of the flamenco dancer and singer Lola Flores. In general, the coproductions allowed the Mexican cinema to expand its national horizons without (apparently) contradicting or compromising its own national imperatives. By paying little attention to the specificities of other nations and/or subsuming them under romantic, folkloric, or exoticizing narrative schemas, the Mexican cinema could retain its currency.[9]

The importation of Latin American and other Spanish-speaking talent, Latin American themes, and coproductions transformed the definition of "Mexican" within the industry. In other words, from the centrality of its national concerns, the Mexican cinema expanded its own borders and produced, no matter how stereotypically, a vision of a Latin American/Spanish-speaking commonality. That vision was at once self-serving (in its efforts to sustain the Latin American market) and unique, for in this period, Latin Americans could not really find a common ground anywhere else in the cinema.

III

After such heights of Latin American interpenetration, in the 1960s the Mexican cinema began to fall out of synch with the principal cinematic trends sweeping through the continent. Industrial production became mired within the stultifying bureaucracy of the state: repetitive, self-indulgent, and far too accustomed to thinking of itself as in "crisis." Mexican films continued to be shown throughout Latin America, but fewer and fewer films were as successful as their predecessors in the 1940s and 1950s. Increasingly, Mexican films were relegated to second- and third-run houses in most Latin American urban centers.

In some parts of the continent, the three-decade-long cinematic presence of the Mexican cinema on Latin American screens began to be perceived as an extension of the cultural imperialism epitomized by Hollywood. For example, in the 1970s, Cuban critics Enrique Colina and Daniel Díaz Torres argued in the pages of *Cine Cubano* that the "old" Mexican and Argentine cinemas had functioned to sustain "the cultural underdevelopment of the people's consciousness." In their assessment, Latin American films of the 1930s, 1940s, and 1950s were poor imitations of Hollywood productions "which opened the floodgates to a manifold process of cultural colonization in Latin America" (1971, 15). A decade later, Mexican critic Jorge Ayala Blanco expressed a similar sentiment:

> The Mexican cinema functioned imperialistically in most Spanish-speaking countries of the continent without their own film industry. In other words, it proposed aesthetic tastes and values to the great semi-literate masses, it created and reversed social and individual myths, it opened and exploited markets at its own volition. (1986, 508)

Focusing on its pervasiveness and populist tendencies, Colina and Díaz Torres, Ayala Blanco, and other contemporary critics failed to take into account that this was the first indigenous cinema to dent the Hollywood industry's presence in Latin America; the first to consistently circulate Latin American images, voices, songs, and histories; and the first to capture and sustain the interest of multinational audiences throughout the continent for several decades.

However, in the 1960s, the Mexican cinema did seem increasingly distant from the exciting new cinematic movements and radical proposals emerging elsewhere in the continent. In Cuba, Brazil, Argentina, Bolivia, Chile, and elsewhere, a younger generation of filmmakers was attempting to produce a different kind of national/Pan–Latin American cinema predicated upon social change, a movement that would later be identified as the New Latin American Cinema. Although in Mexico there were also a number of young and amateur filmmakers struggling to redefine the cinema—especially the Nuevo Cine group—their efforts would not be circulated outside of Mexico City and had almost no impact upon the work of the dominant commercial producers. With few exceptions, until the late 1970s the Mexican cinema had become a continental dinosaur.

The Mexican film renaissance in the late 1980s and 1990s chronicled elsewhere in this catalog is thus doubly surprising within a Latin American context. Over the last two decades, Latin Americans' familiarity with the Mexican cinema has been based upon the constant recirculation of classics from the Golden Age and contemporary sex-drugs-and-violence exploitation movies on Spanish-language television. Controlled by Mexican interests, chains like Univisión and Galavision (which are available throughout Latin America as well as in the US) have sustained a certain retrograde vision of the Mexican cinema. It is a vision in which the Golden Age films are the frozen icons of a Latin American cinematic presence which is no longer viable for the Mexican cinema. In the US Latino community, in fact, the Golden Age cinema has become a source of chic kitsch,[10] while the contemporary commercial exploitation films are perceived as entertainment fodder for the *recién llegados* who still do not speak English.

The contemporary Latin American theatrical film market, reduced by political and economic exigencies, finds itself unable to compete with the ever growing dominance of both television and Hollywood. Thus, the commercial and critical success of recent films like *Cabeza de Vaca* (Nicolás Echeverría, 1991), *Danzón* (María Novaro, 1991), and *Como agua para chocolate* (Alfonso Arau, 1992) has taken place in an international context that is radically different from that of the Golden Age. When and if they are distributed in Latin America, these films are circulated as part of an international "art cinema" practice within which national specificities are almost of no consequence. In an international context, this "new" Mexican cinema speaks with a different voice and to a radically different audience. The international market it seeks is no longer defined by language or geography, but by a network of financers and distributors that direct it north (to the US) rather than south, and to elite rather than to mass audiences.

Perhaps it is impossible for the contemporary Mexican cinema to aspire to the kind of hold on the Latin American imaginary that it once had. But the history of the Latin American trajectory of the Mexican cinema is already embedded in contemporary Latin American and US Latino identity. We remember—and often see ourselves in—Cantinflas,

Jorge Negrete, and María Félix: *rancheras*, melodramas, and *cabareteras*. The symbolic linkages wrought by the history of over five thousand Mexican films shared continentally will not easily disappear from our collective imaginary, for, to some degree, the Mexican cinema has been our only version of Jose Martí's utopian "Nuestra America."

2

National History, Transnational History (1998)

This is the first essay in which López explicitly calls for a rethinking of Latin American cinema in terms of transnational dynamics. Rather than seeing film in the region as a group of "national cinemas," scholars should recognize the transnational flows of technologies, economics, and personnel between countries within the region (as well as with the US and Europe) that have helped to constitute film industries, practices, and textual/aesthetic forms from the 1890s to the present. To exemplify this argument, López focuses on the role of traveling filmmakers such as Carlos Hugo Christensen who worked in several different industries within the region during the "studio" era (1930s–1950s). Never published in English, this important essay sets out her larger rationale for a shift in the field of Latin American film studies; as such, it deserves wider circulation to English-language audiences.

Latin American film research has reached a crucial stage of its relatively short history. Today, in 1997 we can ascertain that the histories of Latin American national cinemas are now being thoroughly documented and that this process has grown exponentially since the 1960s, when there were few specialized books in circulation and the research taking place was still rather basic. Although the national cinemas of some countries have been documented more rigorously than others—highlighting, for example, the vast bibliography that now exists on Mexican cinema—almost all of the

---

Originally published in Spanish as "Historia nacional, historia transnacional" (1998), the essay is translated by Dolores Tierney and Ana M. López.

continent's national cinemas have been the focus of at least one or two books published in the 1980s or 1990s, sometimes published with the support of cinematheques, or sometimes through the individual efforts of researchers and university professors. Currently we have bibliographic information on national cinemas that until recently we didn't know existed (Costa Rican cinema, for example, through the work of Daniel Marranghello) and we have begun to develop different strategies for studying key eras with scarce resources, especially silent cinema (in recent publications in Argentina, Mexico, Chile, Peru, Colombia, and Cuba).

Even though this process of rescuing the history of national cinemas is of the utmost importance, the focus on the national has not allowed us to fully understand the transnationality of all Latin American cinema. In general, the New Latin American Cinema, especially in the 1960s, is the only movement to have been considered transnational, and the only one to have been studied from a continental perspective. We know that those filmmakers who began the "new" cinemas in their own countries started to meet each other at festivals both in Latin America and in Europe, where they exchanged ideas and aesthetic and sociopolitical projects and reimagined their movement as a continental project. Thus, under the banner of the new cinemas and the new national cinemas (especially Cuban cinema of the 1960s), these intercontinental collaborations have been hailed in multiple accounts as one of the central characteristics of the new pancontinental movement even though many of the accounts of this period continue to treat the new cinemas of each country as national projects above anything else, formed under the politics and society of each state and only coincidentally linked to social changes and movements across the continent. For example, although it is impossible to think of the Chilean cinema in exile without taking into consideration continental collaborations or to think of ICAIC's Cuban cinema or the Brazilian Cinema Novo without taking into account continental influences and relationships, these dimensions have yet to be researched and adequately accounted for.

Given this absence of a transnational perspective on the new cinemas, it should be of no surprise that the most insular cinemas, those of the classical era, and of the "golden age" of the 1930s, 1940s, and 1950s have been studied almost always as exclusively national phenomena. Despite the fact that historians have recognized and analyzed the susceptibility of national cinemas to economic and political changes taking place internationally (for example, the Spanish Civil War and the often-cited embargo of virgin film stock by the United States against Argentina during the

Second World War), as much as the effects on national production of the presence or absence of films imported from Hollywood or other countries in the exhibition circuit, most commonly national cinemas are studied in relation to state politics and national culture. Therefore, almost all the accounts of this period focus exclusively on sociopolitical determinants and the national figures that forged national cinemas.

What are the transnational forces that we have ignored in classical cinemas? Even though they are not circumscribed by a sociopolitical ideology linked to a specific movement like the New Cinemas, Latin America's classical cinemas were undoubtedly marked by important transnational shifts: in technology, obviously (as Paulo Antonio Paranaguá mentioned in *Cinema na América Latina* close to fifteen years ago, Latin American cinema began as an imported phenomenon that developed under the sign of radical otherness), in capital (as shown in the recent work of Seth Fein and other researchers), and of technical and creative personnel (like the travelers who moved around the continent uprooted by social and political events—the Spanish Civil War, Peronism—or looking for better economic opportunities for other reasons such as education or apprenticeship [Fein 1994; Paranaguá 1985, 11]).

Starting with the idea of Latin American cinema as a giant "contact zone" (Pratt 1991), my research project tackles the idea of transnationality through the figure of the traveler in classical cinema. In other words, instead of taking on the challenge of a comparative history with a generalizing perspective or an industrial focus, I want to begin with the specificity of a more local phenomenon—traveling auteurs—so that they might lead us to perceive a "continental" dimension that is both a historical fact as well as a complex textual production.

Although the influence and impact of traveling filmmakers is less obvious than, for example, the coproductions that were in fashion in the 1940s and 1950, they contributed a lot to the development of the classical cinemas in Latin America. Without a doubt, the journeys to the other side of the Rio Grande, for example, were very important in the early sound period: many of our pioneers learned to make sound cinema in Hollywood, especially during the period of the "Hispanic boom." Even though many like Emilio Fernández were just extras or took on secondary roles (assistants, etc.), they returned "home" bitten by the cinematic bug and determined to build their national industries: Emilio Fernández, Gabriel Soria, Miguel Zacarias, Alejandro Galindo, Alberto Gout, Chano Urueta, Raphael J. Sevilla, Fernando Méndez, Raúl de Anda, Gilberto Martínez

Solares, René Cardona, Tito Davison, and many others. As we already know, *Santa* (1931), the first success of Mexican sound cinema, was produced by a team trained in Hollywood: the director Antonio Moreno had been an actor, like the actress Lupita Tovar (the star of the Spanish version of *Dracula*) and the actor Donald Reed (Ernesto Guillén); born in Russia, the cinematographer Alex Phillips had worked on many Hollywood films and had worked as an assistant to the great cinematographer Gregg Toland. Like Phillips, others arrived in Mexico from the "other" side and became a part of the industry: David Kirkland, John H. Auer, Robert Curwood, Roberto O'Quigley, Jack Draper, Ross Fisher. Others like Paul Strand traveled to Mexico for short periods of time or to make specific projects like *Redes* (Fred Zinnemann and Emilio Gómez Muriel, 1934).

Journeys across the Atlantic were also very fruitful. Many of the most famous traveling filmmakers in Latin America arrived from Europe. Sergei Eisenstein's trip to Mexico left a profound mark on Mexican cinema and the impact of Luis Buñuel's lengthy "visit" in Mexico continues to be a fascinating subject to be explored further. Although less well known, the time that Alberto Cavalcanti spent in Brazil as the executive director of the Vera Cruz studio in São Paulo at the end of the 1950s was no less important. The case of Vera Cruz—the failure of its studio system of production—initiated important debates about national cinema in the 1950s that established the parameters for the subsequent Cinema Novo movement.

Even though these transnational journeys are fascinating, what interests me most is the history of the intracontinental journeys, in other words, the effects and influences of filmmakers, producers, and actors who traveled within Latin America and participated in collaborative projects in other countries. The idea of intracontinental influences is not just an interesting historical puzzle; it also questions the viability of the national as a central axis of histories of Latin America's classical cinemas and underlines the hybridity of all the national cinemas. Against the myth of cinematographic national insularity and stories of national achievements and failures, I insist on a continental perspective that includes but transcends the national. In this context, the figure of the traveler/traveling filmmaker as the axis for the mediation of the national could be the key that opens the door to transnational analyses of classical Latin American cinema.

Among the travelers that we could consider in this context is Carlos Hugo Christensen, who after a significant career in Argentina (where he led the so-called "Christensen era" at the Lumiton studios and was recognized for the eroticism of his films), worked for the first incarnation of Chile films in the mid-1940s and directed *La balandra Isabel llegó esta tarde* (The Isabel Arrived This Afternoon, 1949) and other films in Venezuela. *La balandra* is perhaps the best example of a supremely nationalist film, touted as the beginning of Venezuelan cinema, that is marked by transnationality. The almost documentary level of naturalism, the melodrama, and the erotic and exotic folkloricism of *La balandra* come together in the intersection of the national with transnational forces. These elements as well as the presence of an international cast (especially the then super famous Arturo de Córdova) and the film's generic hybridity codify the auteur's expression and his gaze as both national and necessarily multinational, both foundational and destabilizing. More than anything, *La balandra* exposes the paradoxical nature of the "national" in national cinemas and the impossibility of separating out the "foreign" gaze from any kind of vision of the nation.[1] Fleeing from Peronism in Argentina, Christensen continued his travels and moved permanently to Brazil, where he continued his work in film. Working in a commercial environment, on the edges of the beginnings of Cinema Novo, this period in his career continues to be marked by transnationality (he "imported" Arturo de Córdova for two films, transnationality is the implicit theme of *O Menino e o Vento* [The Boy and the Wind, 1967]) and is deserving of an in-depth study.

Other "travelers" were filmmakers that are generally marginalized by official accounts of national cinemas like José Bohr, who made great contributions to both Mexican and Chilean cinemas (after his sojourn in Hollywood and its Hispanic cinema) and Juan Orol, king of melodrama and a key figure in the wave of Mexican-Cuban coproductions of the 1940s and 1950s. One also has to include the traveling actors, authors of their own careers, whose star images and stardom were determined by multiple journeys and exiles, including among the most notable: Dolores Del Rio, Libertad Lamarque, Arturo de Córdova, and Pedro Armendáriz, as well as Ninón Sevilla, María Antonieta Pons, and many others. As continental icons, signifiers of particular genres and tropes, these travelers contributed very specifically to the transnationalism of the classical cinemas, especially classical Mexican cinema, that fed off their "foreign" qualities, their fame, and their rhythms. The travelers, the timely topical Latin American content and the coproductions transformed the definition of *lo mexicano* (Mexicanness) in the industry. In other words, from a position in which the national was central to Mexican cinema, the industry broadened its own horizons to produce a vision of a Latin American transnational community, albeit a stereotypical one. This broad vision was part of a deliberate industrial strategy given that continental distribution was the bedrock of the Mexican industry, but it also gave rise to the sense of a pancontinental culture: cinema joined with popular musical forms—another great traveler—to form a common cultural experience across the continent, which in a broad sense could be described as a cultural version of José Martí's "Our America."

And despite thinking that the analysis of classical cinema through these traveling filmmakers could be a very productive route to embark upon, I also think that approaching cinema from a transnational perspective might also help us to analyze contemporary cinema in the context of globalization and postmodernity of the 1980s. For example, the hierarchization of production—films made for inside and outside, for the domestic market and those (popular and international ones) made for the external markets, and all of these subjected to the effect of globalized cultural policies. On the one hand we have an "inside" that is also an "outside," in the shape of the Latino/a audience in the United States, who see *La risa en vacaciones 1-8* (René Cardona Jr., 1988–1996) on Spanish-language television or on video as eagerly and with as much viewing pleasure as popular Mexican audiences. On the other hand, we have a cinema with artistic pretensions of international distribution and exhibition at film festivals and in art cinema circuits. Alfonso Arau has gone to Hollywood and Robert Rodríguez is filming in Mexico. Reversing the trajectory of Dolores Del Rio, but still imbricated in a continental aura of Latinness, Salma Hayek has gone from the telenovela and Mexican cinema to Hollywood with *Fools Rush In* (Andy Tennant, 1997).

As a different and very particular example, it is interesting to think about what has happened in Cuba and in the studies of Cuban cinema through the matrix of transnationality. Ten years ago it was impossible to think about Latin American cinema without talking about Cuban cinema. Today Cuban films are as scarce as research on Cuban cinema. There's very little contemporary material on Cuban cinema—some articles, none of which are comprehensive; Michael Chanan's out-of-print *The Cuban Image* (1985);[2] the subgenre of recent homages to Tomás Gutiérrez Alea—and every day we realize that we don't even know what we thought we knew and that the studies have to start from the beginning. Our knowledge about Cuban cinema suffers from an excessively statist rather than national focus: the history of cinema made within the ICAIC—which should be thought of as such and not mistaken for national cinema—has to be reinvented. And the borders of Cuban cinema can also be opened through an approach that stresses the importance of traveling filmmakers, which have been a constant presence in the very transnational history of the entirety of Cuban cinema, from the French Gabriel Veyre who appeared in Havana in 1896 with the Lumière equipment and Mexican actualities, continuing on with Juan Orol and his *rumberas*, the specialists imported in the first years of ICAIC to nurture its inexperienced filmmakers (from Barbachano Ponce and Cesare Zavattini to Mikhail Kalatozov, Chris Marker, and Joris Ivens), and the refugees from the various military dictatorships welcomed in the 1970s (Miguel Littín, Patricio Guzmán, etc.). Of course, journeys were also made in the opposite direction and many fled abroad after the Revolution, bringing their Cubanness to the world (from Goar Mestre to Néstor Almendros). Today these journeys go the opposite way with Cuban filmmakers—and not just films—traveling the world. Before he died, Tomás Gutiérrez Alea became a Spanish citizen to facilitate international coproductions; other, less famous filmmakers go back and forth between Havana and the world; and still others continue to make "Cuban" cinema but do it from Miami or New York (Sergio Giral, for example). The history of Cuban cinema is the history of travelers and traveling that ruptures the insularity of the island and ICAIC to follow in the footsteps of those who arrived, and left, came back, and come and go.

With the millennium a few years away we begin to realize that globalization is not just a postmodern and post-NAFTA invention, but something that, in one way or another, has always been with us and has been a feature of our cinemas. The paradox of a national cinema—imagined, dreamed, and debated—has been and continues to be formed by a transnationality that exceeds and extends across all borders. The perversity of approaching the national through transnationalism might actually be a useful way of rethinking and reinventing the histories of our cinemas.

3

Facing Up to Hollywood (2000)

"Facing Up to Hollywood" further develops López's transnational perspective on a metacritical level. Written for the collection Reinventing Film Studies *(edited by Christine Gledhill and Linda Williams) and directed at a wider film studies scholarly community, the essay is an expansive overview of how film industries in Latin America have "faced up" to Hollywood's hegemonic status from the 1930s to the 1990s. López begins by identifying the economic, political, and ideological means by which Hollywood achieved its dominance of world markets as early as the 1910s, before turning to numerous case studies—from the efforts to establish a commercial industry in Mexico in the 1930s, to the rise of the short-lived Vera Cruz studio in the late 1940s in Brazil, to the pan-regional New Latin American Cinema in the 1960s, to the emergence of new crossover directors like Alfonso Arau, Guillermo del Toro, and Bruno Barreto in the 1990s. The essay showcases López's comprehensive understanding of the twentieth-century film industries in various Latin American countries and the complex international and national dynamics that shaped them. "Facing Up to Hollywood" further exemplifies how her transnational approach calls for a more complex understanding of the porous nature of Hollywood, insisting on the centrality of its engagements with non-US industries, markets, and talent in Latin America (as well as Europe) from the post-WWI period to the present. The essay enacts a relational model for film studies—anticipating the less binary, more networked models proposed by others (such as the authors included in Ďurovičová and Newman 2010; Higbee and Lim 2010).*

Although resolutely national, the US film industry—Hollywood—has always also been profoundly international. Hollywood's international presence has had acute effects not only on Hollywood itself—upon its production and textual practices—but on all other filmmaking nations. One way or another, all other nations aspiring to produce a "national" cinema have always had to deal with Hollywood's presence or, sometimes, its absence. For almost a century, Hollywood films have been a constant source of entertainment pleasure for international audiences and the Hollywood style of production the goal that national cinemas have striven to achieve. Perceived as the industrial "vanguard," Hollywood always seems to lead the way in technology, capital investments, and pleasure-producing innovations. Yet paradoxically, "Hollywood" and everything it stands for have also been the nemesis of national cinemas throughout the world: the seductive polish, production values, and constant presence of Hollywood films invariably precluded or prejudiced the industrial development of indigenous production.

Understanding the impact of Hollywood's international ubiquity and developing strategies to "face up" to it is a considerable challenge for producers in other cultural/national contexts. This essay begins by providing a summary of the context in which Hollywood acquired its hegemony over international markets and then traces the historical development of the strategies and theoretical rationales that have been deployed to deal with it. In the period between the coming of sound and the 1950s, national cinemas generally "faced up" to Hollywood by addressing specific market segments (art/high culture or language based, for example) and/ or by imitation. I will illustrate these strategies via two "case studies," the development of a film industry in Mexico in the 1930s and the attempt to create a "Brazilian Hollywood" by the Vera Cruz studio in the late 1940s/ early 1950s. In the 1960s, the theories of dependency that emerged from Latin America, coupled with post–World War II alternative models of film production and expression such as Italian neorealism and the French New Wave, altered this paradigm. Rather than an admired ideal, Hollywood's ubiquity became a predominant symbol of the strength of US cultural imperialism, and its practices and appeals were to be shunned in the interests of national cultural specificity. The most illustrative cinematic response to this conceptual and political shift was the New Latin American Cinema movement of the 1960s and 1970s. By the 1970s and 1980s, however, a recognition of new patterns of economic and cultural exchanges led to an important reconceptualization of the cultural imperialism approach. The concepts of globalization and postmodernity, acknowledging the growing speed and international interdependence of contemporary economics and culture, have opened a space for rethinking the strategies through which Hollywood needs to be "faced" and the histories of national cinemas.

How Hollywood Became an International Force: Economics, Politics, and Ideology

Even before the full establishment of the classical Hollywood studio system of production in the late 1910s, the cinema was already global, in the sense that it was recognized as an international business. The first attempt to monopolize the industry, Thomas Alva Edison's Motion Picture Patents Company ("the Trust"), strategically included significant non-American film concerns: its "continental wing" comprised alliances with two French companies, Pathé Frères—at the time the most powerful international company, already vertically integrated—and Georges Méliès's Star Films.

Nevertheless, despite the Trust's early efforts, the US film industry did not really acquire hegemony over world markets until World War I (Thompson 1985). Previously, the huge size of its domestic audience and its vertiginous growth had kept the industry more than profitable, since the domestic market fully amortized production expenses. In fact, several European companies (Pathé from France, Nordisk from Denmark) who depended upon export revenues to amortize production because of their small domestic markets had already a well-established competitive presence within the USA. But by the immediate prewar years, the industry had organized and consolidated its activities sufficiently to saturate the domestic market and expand into foreign markets by tailoring its pricing structures and establishing new distribution procedures. Since production costs could be recouped in the domestic market, international film sales could be priced differentially, according to what specific national/regional markets could bear and undercutting the local competition. This made Hollywood films very attractive to local exhibitors and distributors, who quickly saw that they could gain higher profits by showing Hollywood films rather than local productions. Furthermore, rather than relegate all international trade to agents in London, Hollywood producers began to open their own local offices in the major foreign markets. In Brazil, for example, the sudden appearance of well-funded branches of Hollywood studios who bought out local distributors essentially wiped out all domestic production (Johnson and Stam 1995).

In general industrial terms, World War I was a godsend for Hollywood because it allowed for the solidification of its international operations. First, while the war raged in Europe, filmmaking there was disrupted and production plummeted, while the US cinema prospered: Cook, citing Lewis Jacobs, estimates that while in 1914 the USA produced slightly over half the world's films, by 1918 it was making nearly all of them (1996, 47). Simultaneously, the US industry took advantage of its competitors' distractions by aggressively going after the export markets they had previously dominated, especially Australia, New Zealand, and Latin America. By eroding the European industry's international base of support, Hollywood permanently weakened the formerly strong European producing countries. Since 1919, overseas receipts have regularly been factored into Hollywood's budgets and, since the 1930s, foreign markets have provided between a third and a half of all industry revenues. World War I—and later World War II—placed the US industry in a position of indisputable economic and productive leadership that, with variations, it would never again relinquish.

ECONOMIC STRATEGIES AND POLITICAL ALLIANCES

To never again loosen its hold of the international film marketplace, the Hollywood industry developed complex strategies to sustain and augment its power. In economic terms, this has been described as the industry's flexible managerial structure and open and innovative financial systems (Acheson and Maule 1994). However, most important in the immediate post–World War I years was establishing the terms of Hollywood's relationship to Europe. A first step was to co-opt foreign producers. For example, Germany, which had emerged from the war with a relatively strong industry, was resisting the US takeover of its market and had innovated with protective legislation (quotas on imports since 1921). Therefore, when for complex reasons the powerful and very successful German producer UFA found itself in dire financial trouble in 1925, Paramount and Metro Goldwyn Mayer stepped in with a large loan in exchange for the right to release ten UFA films annually in the USA and the creation of a joint distribution company, Parufamet, to distribute Paramount/MGM films in Germany. Offering much-needed capital to financially strapped foreign producers who could conceivably have an edge in some important foreign market to establish binational production and distribution agreements would continue to be a favorite Hollywood strategy.

A second, ancillary strategy involved attempts to diversify the Hollywood talent pool. Consciousness of the international market led producers to seek out foreign actors, positioning Hollywood as the home base of a broad constellation of international stars. Thus, for example, a canny producer imported Dolores Del Rio from Mexico in the 1920s and made her a star who could fit the exotic foreigner role to perfection. European talent was always particularly attractive. In fact, immediately after the Parufamet agreement, many UFA artists and technicians migrated to Hollywood. Director Ernst Lubitsch and actress Pola Negri, in Hollywood since the early 1920s, were joined by several directors (among them, F. W. Murnau and Michael Curtiz); cinematographer Karl Freund; actors Emil Jannings, Conrad Veidt, and Greta Garbo; producer Erich Pommer; and set designer Carl Mayer. Others, from Germany and elsewhere in Europe, would join them throughout the late 1920s and through the 1940s, among them Jean Renoir from France, Alfred Hitchcock from England, and Fritz Lang, Robert Siodmak, Douglas Sirk, Billy Wilder, and Otto Preminger from Germany. The studios also eagerly sought talent from less well-established film producers who had nevertheless established a firm regional reputation: Mexican heartthrobs Pedro Armendáriz and Arturo de Córdova, for example, worked for Hollywood studios in the 1940s and 1950s.

Beyond purely financial and importation deals, however, the Hollywood studios also established a firm connection with the US State Department and other governmental agencies that allowed the industry to wield extraordinary diplomatic clout—always, of course, in the service of its own international position. In 1922, the US studios established a trade association, the Motion Picture Producers and Distributors of America (MPPDA) and hired the well-connected ex–Postmaster General Will Hays to direct it. Although primarily designed to clean up Hollywood's somewhat tarnished national image, the MPPDA was also empowered to represent the industry's trade interests abroad. In fact, the MPPDA and its offshoot since World War II, the Motion Picture Export Association of America (MPEAA), have acted as a legal cartel for foreign trade. Both the MPPDA and the MPEAA have successfully negotiated with foreign governments to fight quota legislations curtailing the presence of Hollywood films in particular countries. Representing the entire industry, they could not only threaten—and carry out—boycotts, but also negotiate enforceable agreements. Furthermore, the US government often fully backed their endeavors, either via the Motion Picture Division of the Department of Commerce (established in 1929) or directly via the State Department. Jack Valenti, head of the MPEAA since the 1940s, endearingly dubbed the agency "the little State Department" because of its close alliances with US policy and ideology (Guback 1969).

These alliances were more than strengthened during and after World War II, when the government saw Hollywood films as propaganda for democracy and "the American way of life" (Schatz 1988) and facilitated film exports through Commerce Department initiatives and diplomatic pressures. During the war, the Hollywood cinema was perceived as a crucial weapon, extraordinarily valuable to maintain not only national morale but also the political alliances of the USA's South American "neighbors." Not coincidentally, these South American neighbors were also one of the industry's few remaining foreign markets, since this war again paralyzed the market in continental Europe (which had previously provided the industry with 25 percent of its foreign revenues). Reviving the dormant "Good Neighbor Policy," the State Department created the Office of the Coordinator of Inter-American Affairs in 1940 to combat pro-Axis sentiment in Latin America, and its Motion Picture division worked with Hollywood producers to ensure the production of films to please this suddenly significant market: Latin American themes, locations, rhythms, and talent invaded Hollywood films during the war (Woll 1980 [1977]).

Similarly, the post–World War II dismantling of the film industries of the former Axis nations fully complemented Hollywood's economic plans with the USA's antifascist and anticommunist political agendas. The alliance between the MPEAA and the State Department continues to this day. For example, in 1970–1971, the MPEAA collaborated with the USA's efforts to undermine president Salvador Allende's Popular Unity government by participating in an "invisible blockade" against Chile. The majors stopped shipping prints and demanded advance payments on rentals, which effectively eliminated Hollywood films from Chilean screens, further discredited the regime, and increased popular dissatisfaction (Chanan 1976). In contrast, the US government collaborated explicitly with MPEAA efforts: in 1985 Congress and the US embassy demanded that South Korea allow Hollywood to establish its own distribution companies and shortly thereafter South Korea became Hollywood's second largest market in Asia (Bordwell and Thompson 1994).

BEYOND ECONOMICS

As a complement to the canny business and lobbying practices that transformed the USA into the world leader of cinema, Hollywood also had a stake in making its own nationality invisible. Since its earliest days, cinema had often been posited as a *universal* medium that could surmount linguistic differences, overcome distances, and be understood by all, and

Hollywood had a particular practical interest in promoting this position as it came to dominate world markets (Sklar 1993). That cinema was a universal medium was an especially handy counterargument against those wishing either to use film to represent national/local interests or to erect import barriers. And it also served to naturalize Hollywood's own nationality by equating Hollywood cinema's undeniable American "accent" with a universal language. Given Hollywood's worldwide prominence and the rhetoric of universality, the style and practice of filmmaking developed by Hollywood in the late 1910s and 1920s became international norms: studio-based production, expensive production values, rapid cutting, shot variety, continuity editing. However, to the same degree that people in all countries could see and understand the Hollywood cinema, when it represented those peoples and nations it did so, invariably, though its own very American eyes. As Sklar argues, the aspiration to global leadership was not accompanied by an effort to construct a global perspective on human lives and cultures. The Mexican government's reaction to Hollywood's hegemony on Mexican screens in the 1920s is especially telling in this respect. Whereas other nations demanded protective legislation (such as quotas) on economic terms, Mexico was the first country to protest against the USA on ideological grounds. Offended by the too-frequent stereotypical representation of Mexicans as "greasers," evil bandidos, and sexy señoritas, in 1922 the Mexican government banned the films of any company making films portraying Mexicans offensively, even when the films themselves were not distributed in Mexico (García Riera 1987a, 109–11, 125–26). Because the Mexican market was already lucrative enough to be of interest, US producers promised to comply. In fact, one of the earliest charges of the MPPDA, included in lists of "Don'ts and Be Carefuls" to producers, was to ensure that "foreigners" were not depicted offensively. In practice, the greasers and señoritas did not disappear, but the narratives in which they appeared were relocated from Mexico to imaginary tropical nations or to unidentified "Spanish" California locales.

The Effects of Hollywood's International Dominance: The Problems of National Cinemas

The range and depth of the Hollywood industry's historical control over international film markets have forced filmmakers aspiring or struggling to produce national cinemas always to have to establish a dialogue with Hollywood. If not a universal medium, the very presence of Hollywood films everywhere proved that cinema was at the very least international and, outside Hollywood, raised questions of national provenance with which Hollywood had not previously been concerned. What could be deemed "national" in film? National ownership of the means of production, distribution, and exhibition? The nationality of the creative personnel? Narrative content/style and their cultural specificity (Crofts 1993)?

In Europe, after World War I, the dominance of Hollywood films was seen "as a crisis not only of cinema, but of civilization" (Sklar 1993, 126). It gave rise to significant comparative debates over economic, aesthetic, and social issues. Was the dominance of Hollywood films a purely economic factor, linked to the industry's ability to gain distribution and exhibition outlets and cutting film rental prices below that of local producers? Or was it that Hollywood films were indeed better than national efforts; that is, that their polish and technological sophistication offered greater entertainment value and textual pleasure? Or was their popularity perhaps a sign of the disintegration of the national culture and its values, part of the process of commercialization into a homogeneous international mass culture driven by consumerism and technology in the service of capital? In this context, what responsibility does the state have to protect and/or foster a national cinema?

In one form or another, these debates have been echoed since then in all nations or regions aspiring to indigenous cinematic production since the end of World War I. After the coming of sound, Hollywood became more entrenched in international markets, although it had become, obviously, less universal when speaking English. Because the costs of the transition to sound were enormous—wiring theaters, acquiring new equipment—local investment throughout most of the world lagged behind that of Hollywood and allowed the industry to maintain its dominance. However, the difficulties of translation did open up a potential window of opportunity for local producers in non-English-speaking markets who suddenly had, on the surface, an easy answer to the question of "national" differences in cinema: language and music.

Hollywood's efforts to produce foreign-language versions (for example, the "Hispanic cinema") and multiple language versions of its films for export had been singularly unsuccessful. They were expensive to produce and, worst of all, usually box office failures because they failed to offer audiences any kind of cultural specificity or the lure of the appeal of established stars (Ďurovičová 1992). But resorting to subtitling automatically eliminated the segment of the popular audience that was either unable or unwilling to read at the movies, while dubbing produced a singular disruption of the spectatorial experience and the requisite suspension of disbelief. Furthermore, in some areas of the world linguistic commonalities seemed to offer natural well-differentiated markets for regional exploitation, creating a favorable climate for the development of industries, for example, in the larger Spanish-speaking nations such as Mexico, Argentina, and Spain. The history of the development of the Mexican sound cinema—its "Golden Age"—provides an especially illustrative example of the complex issues and negotiations involved in creating a national cinema in the face of Hollywood's international dominance.

THE CASE OF MEXICO: A "NATIONAL" CINEMA IN THE
SHADOW OF HOLLYWOOD

By the late 1920s (and despite earlier achievements), Mexican production had come to an almost complete standstill. The crisis was so dire that then minister of Public Education José Vasconcelos even argued that the cinema was "a typically US cultural product impossible to develop as a national form" (De la Vega 1995, 79). But after the success of the first sound films and the failure of the "Hispanic films," Mexico attempted to compete with Hollywood on its own terms. A group of exhibitors and journalists committed to the idea of a national cinema invested in optical sound-on-film production using a system patented by two Mexican engineers who had lived in Los Angeles, the brothers Joselito and Roberto Rodríguez. They produced an adaptation of *Santa* (Antonio Moreno, 1931), a canonical novel by Federico Gamboa (the Mexican Zola) about a sex worker with a heart of gold, that established a basis for the future development of the desired national film industry. *Santa* also included the romantic music of Agustín Lara and established an important connection between the cinema and the national radio and record industries which promoted the development of a regional mass culture industry.

The production of *Santa* coincided with a campaign led by a group of congresspeople to raise the consciousness of Mexicans to consume only national products (De la Vega 1995, 81). Although this campaign was short lived, it helped to establish protectionist trade barriers that facilitated the production of *Santa* and its subsequent success. In other words, the state was finally supporting, even if only indirectly, a Mexican film industry. *Santa* also coincided with the arrival of a famous and polemical visitor: Sergei Eisenstein, who had obtained funding from Upton Sinclair to shoot a paean to Mexican culture, *Que Viva Mexico*. Eisenstein was never able to complete his film but left an undeniable legacy to the Mexican cinema in his translation to film of some of the visual characteristics of the muralist, engraving, and photography movements that were cultivated in Mexico in the 1920s as part of the postrevolutionary "national culture" project (for example, the murals and paintings of Diego Rivera, José Clemente Orozco, and David Alfaro Siqueiros).

Thus, by 1932, the Mexican cinema already possessed some of the essential requirements for the development of industrial film production: a trustworthy sound system, an idea of a nationalist aesthetic, and the precedent of state support. Furthermore, Mexico was in the last stages of its postrevolutionary national reconstruction and, for the first time in decades, enjoying the benefits of political stability and capitalist development. What was needed to infiltrate the market, however, were distinctively local themes and genres. Given that Hollywood had not yet abandoned "Hispanic" films, even though they were in crisis, the incipient Mexican cinema bourgeoisie had sufficient time to experiment and to find a type of cinema to woo the Spanish-language foreign market; this was the only way to develop the national film industry.

The generic experimentation of the period 1933-1937 was broad based, aesthetically and commercially successful, and encompassed a variety of approaches to the medium. Some directors approached the cinema primarily as a business and were primarily concerned with box office receipts and offering entertainment value. Perhaps the most prototypical was the Spanish-Mexican Juan Orol, producer and director of lachrymose melodramas directly influenced by the popularity of serial radio dramas. Clearly a part of an incipient pan-Latin American mass culture industry, these films were among the first to prove successful in non-Mexican markets, especially in Central America and the Caribbean, and began to establish a distribution base for Mexican producers. At the opposite end of the spectrum, we find the avant-garde playwright Juan Bustillo Oro whose films followed a more traditional artistic model, influenced by literary trends and German expressionist styles. Between these two extremes, a third strand of films benefited from state support. Under the influence of the radical social policies of President Lázaro Cárdenas (1934-1940), the state funded the production of films with a marked social content, including *Redes* (Nets, Fred Zinnemann and Emilio Gómez Muriel, 1934), *¡Vámonos con Pancho Villa!* (Let's Go with Pancho Villa!, Fernando de Fuentes, 1935), and many documentaries and newsreels exalting the popular politics and economic progress of the Cárdenas regime. Yet a fourth tendency was exemplified by directors who managed to articulate commercial and aesthetic demands with extraordinary results, for example, Arcady Boytler in *La mujer del puerto* (The Woman of the Port, 1933), a brilliant brothel melodrama; Fernando de Fuentes in *El fantasma del convento* (The Convent Ghost, 1934), an innovative horror film; and José Bohr, whose delirious but well-made gangster-detective trilogy is often considered among the best work of the period: *¿Quien mató a Eva?* (Who Killed Eva?, 1934), *Luponini (El terror de Chicago)* (Luponini [The Chicago Terror]), and *Marihuana (El Monstruo Verde)* (Marijuana [The Green Monster]) shot, respectively, in 1935 and 1936.

Mexican cinematic nationalism took two distinct forms in this period. On the one hand, some films explicitly reflected the liberal nationalism of Lázaro Cárdenas's policies and were influenced by Eisenstein's visualization of Mexico and the prevalent musical nationalism of art music (composers such as Manuel Castro Pasilla, Silvestre Revueltas, Manuel M. Ponce, and Carlos Chávez). On the other hand were films that focused on the prerevolutionary agrarian world (ruled by the dictator Porfirio Díaz and called the Porfiriato), "putting aside the social changes brought about by the Revolution and defending the established order," which were influenced by popular theater and music rather than elite culture (de los Reyes 1987, 187). The international success of one of these, Fernando de Fuentes's *Allá en el Rancho Grande* (Over on the Big Ranch, 1936) determined the nature of the Mexican industry, which would develop commercially under the influence of popular cultural forms—popular music, comedy/vaudeville, melodrama—to the detriment of a state-sponsored cinema inspired by elite art forms.

To understand this shift, consider a brief analysis of the textual work of *Allá en el Rancho Grande*. *Rancho Grande* is set in the present, but in a bucolic mythical rural area where neither the Revolution nor the recent Agrarian Reform has left any traces and where conflicts emerge only from love affairs, wounded male pride, and misunderstandings. Its narrative is pure melodrama: a landowner falls for the girlfriend of his foreman, with whom he has been friends since childhood. The former friends become enemies, but ultimately, despite macho attitudes and fights, the bonds of their friendship prevail and all are reconciled with the aid of much singing and dancing. Beyond its nostalgia for an imaginary past in which such simple relationships could have been conceived, the film reworks a series of popular and folkloric elements that would define the *comedia ranchera* genre: popular music in the form of *ranchera* songs; a loose, episodic narrative structure derived from variety theater in which songs often take the place of dialogue; and familiar yet picturesque character types (charros, innocent señoritas with long braided hair, peppery old housekeepers) and situations (cockfights, fiestas, horse races, etc.).

The film was eventually very popular and was even more widely distributed after cinematographer Gabriel Figueroa received the Mexican cinema's first international festival prize for its cinematography in Venice. Nationally, it spurred investment in the industry and production. The year *Rancho Grande* was released (1936), Mexico produced twenty-five films. By 1937 production grew to thirty-eight films, of which twenty followed the *ranchera* model. In 1939 production again increased: out of fifty-seven films, twenty exploited the *ranchera* formula and "local color."

Rancho Grande was also seen throughout the Spanish-speaking Latin American market and subtitled versions were even released in the USA (always the market most resistant to cinematic imports). But this first moment of nationalist expansion was already mediated by Hollywood. International distribution was coordinated by United Artists, who struck a most advantageous agreement with the film's producer (60 to 40 percent split of gross revenues). Until United Artists got out of Latin American distribution in the 1950s, *Rancho Grande* was one of its highest grossing films, in 1939 surpassed only by *Modern Times* and *The Garden of Allah* (de Usabel 1992, 140–41). As would be the case throughout most of its history, Mexican cinema expanded with the cooperation of Hollywood, which favored it more than any other Latin American film producer. As Paulo Antonio Paranaguá has succinctly expressed it: "Poor Mexico, so far from God and so close to Hollywood" (1995a, 9).

In any case, the release of *Rancho Grande* in Latin America could not have occurred at a more propitious moment. Other Spanish-language cinemas that had competed for the Latin American market were going through difficult times. Spain was involved in a bloody civil war that would temporarily cripple production. Argentine films—of much higher technical quality than the Mexican but also becoming very Europeanized—were waning in popularity, and Argentine production, although increasing, had not matched the levels of the Mexican industry (Argentina produced fifteen films in 1936, twenty-eight in 1937, and forty-one in 1938). The *Rancho Grande* formula unearthed what Latin American audiences seemed to have been looking for in the Mexican cinema: the presentation of a "Mexican" vision of Mexico that coincided with their expectations of the nature of national "local color." As Emilio García Riera has argued, after *Rancho Grande*, the Mexican cinema "enjoyed the prestige of authenticity granted by even the most adulterated folklore" (1987a, 111). The *ranchera* vision of Mexico, albeit decidedly distinct from other Latin American national stereotypes, was simultaneously still recognizable. It combined an appealing exoticism with a comforting familiarity that easily won over Latin American audiences looking for points of cinematic identification. Furthermore, the nostalgia for an imaginary bucolic past where macho pride and true love always prevailed invoked by *Rancho Grande* and its successors also echoed throughout other Latin American countries where, despite different political histories, the present was burdened by the legacies of colonization and the frustrations of independence (López 1994a).

Rancho Grande opened the doors, the industry rushed to keep them open: the Mexican cinema consolidated its strength by copying, expanding, and improvising upon the formula of the *comedia ranchera*, introduced variations of other well-rehearsed generic formulas such as the maternal melodramas and the picaresque comedy, and attempted to develop a "star system" of its own comparable to that of Hollywood. Some fifty-seven features were produced in 1938, and the Mexican film industry was officially born. The industrial transformation of the Mexican cinema involved the defeat of the Hollywood "Hispanic" cinema and constant supremacy over the other Spanish-language producers. But the other US-produced cinema never lost its hegemony over Latin American or Mexican screens: of the 3,081 feature films premiered in the capital in the 1930s, 2,338 (76 percent) were from the USA, 544 (18 percent) were from other foreign nations, and only 199 (6 percent) were Mexican (Ayala Blanco and Amador 1980). In this sense, neither the Mexican cinema nor the cinemas of other underdeveloped nations have ever been a serious threat to Hollywood.

THE CASE OF VERA CRUZ: THE FAILURE OF STUDIO-BASED
BRAZILIAN PRODUCTION

The Companhia Cinematográfica Vera Cruz, in existence between 1949 and 1954, represents the most concerted effort to implement studio-based filmmaking in Brazil. In Rio de Janeiro, other companies such as Atlântida and Cinédia were also studio based, but unlike them Vera Cruz was modern, well equipped, and, since it was backed by the wealthy São Paulo bourgeoisie, well financed. For its founders, the great industrialists Francisco Matarazzo Sobrinho and Franco Zampari, Vera Cruz—like the

Museu de Arte Moderna and the Teatro Brasileiro de Comédia that they had also created—was a symbol not only of their own cultural aspirations but of the modernity and effervescence of the São Paulo bourgeoisie in general. If anyone could, they would be the ones finally to produce a Brazilian cinema of international "quality," the opposite of the much-detested *chanchadas* or carnivalesque comedies produced by the Rio de Janeiro companies. Their "internationalism" was inspired by Hollywood's universality (and the studio mode of production), but the technical know-how for the company was all European. Among the talent imported by Vera Cruz were British cinematographer Chick Fowle, Austrian editor Oswald Haffenrichter, Danish sound engineer Eric Rasmussen, and several Italian directors (Adolfo Celi, Luciano Salce, and Ruggero Jacobbi) associated with the Teatro Brasileiro de Comédia. Of course, the principal "import" was not really an importation, but the return of a prodigal son: Vera Cruz hired as its executive producer the Brazilian-born director-producer Alberto Cavalcanti, who had begun his career with the French avant-garde, worked at Joinville in multilingual productions, had participated in the establishment of the British documentary movement, and greatly contributed to the success of the Ealing studios. Under his tutelage, Vera Cruz established a complex system of studio production, fully staffed and with large facilities (Galvão 1981; Johnson and Stam 1995; Ramos 1987).

In its five years of intense activities, Vera Cruz produced some documentaries (including two shorts directed by Lima Barreto) and eighteen feature films, ranging from historical and contemporary melodramas to biographical films, historical epics, and comedies. Its greatest success was Lima Barreto's *O Cangaceiro* (1953), which won two awards at Cannes and was distributed worldwide. Vera Cruz's output, coupled with increasing filmmaking activity in São Paulo itself and in Rio, led to a general euphoria over the real possibilities of Brazilian filmmaking: national film production rose from ten films in 1947 to twenty in 1950. Above and beyond production numbers, it was also evident that the Vera Cruz studios had, almost overnight, improved the technical quality of Brazilian cinema, especially in relation to cinematography, sound, editing, and lab work. As Johnson and Stam argue, "Through their themes, genres, and production values they achieved the 'look' of First World Cinema" (1995, 28).

Nevertheless, critics complained about the lack of national specificity in this "international style." Vera Cruz films were accused of "foreignness" because of their foreign technical personnel as well as the perceived inauthenticity of its formal paradigms. And the markets were much more difficult to conquer than Vera Cruz had estimated. Inexplicably, Vera Cruz did not take into account the limitations of the domestic market and the difficulties of breaking into the international market. Returns on investment were simply too slow to sustain big studio production: its big-budget films (the average Vera Cruz film cost ten times more than a Rio *chanchada*), extraordinarily high overhead costs, and, eventually, its indebtedness to the Bank of Brazil and the Bank of the State of São Paulo bankrupted the company. Even the 1953 success of *O Cangaceiro*, the first Vera Cruz film to break into the international market, came too late. Strapped by debts, the company sold its international distribution rights to Columbia Pictures, which was the only one to profit from the film's groundbreaking success.

Although Vera Cruz's failure proved the economic unsuitability of Hollywood-modeled studio film production in Brazil, its achievements were very significant. Beyond its individual films, the company and its foreign technicians trained a cadre of professionals in the field who would later contribute greatly to Brazilian film and television production (López 1998c). Furthermore, the extraordinary impact of its failure led to a broad debate among critics and filmmakers and a search for new aesthetic and production models more appropriate to the social and economic conditions of the nations which would eventually evolve into the Cinema Novo movement of the 1960s.

Dependency Theory and Cultural Imperialism: Facing Up to Hollywood in the 1960s

The nations in the periphery of the international superpowers have always been cognizant of the uneven nature of cultural flows, especially of the cinema, and of the potentially negative effects of Hollywood's pleasure machine on national cultures. People all over the world and in every conceivable cultural and social context were exposed not only to narrative and spectacular pleasures, but also, as part of the "American way of life," to the wonders of US modern consumer technology (cars, furniture, fashions, etc.). That Hollywood films clearly created a desire for US-made consumer goods was not lost upon Hollywood exporters or national agencies, which regularly protested against specific market disruptions caused by films. In the mid-1930s, for example, a group of Argentine merchants protested to the US embassy about Clark Gable's lack of an undershirt in a crucial scene of *It Happened One Night* (1934) because it had created a surplus of undershirts in their warehouse (King 1990, 32).

However, beginning in the post–World War II period, and especially among poorer nations, this discourse took on different overtones. In an environment in which exported consumer goods and modernized markets were positioned as important contributors to modernizing developmental processes, social critics foregrounded the capitalist media as the principal vehicles for the commodification and political and economic exploitation of their societies. Development through commercialism meant dependence: slow economic growth, disenfranchised local cultures, emergent local ruling classes reliant on foreign capital and ideology (Mattelart 1979; Tomlinson 1991; Turnstall 1977).

Significant international political realignments in 1959–1960 added an additional facet. While in Africa the old European colonial empires crumbled and new nations were quickly emerging, in Latin America, cultural renewal and political debates acquired a new urgency and viability after the spectacular success of Fidel Castro's guerrilla forces against a dictator in Cuba (Castro took power on January 1, 1959). The nonaligned movement of the 1950s, which had sought a way out of the polarizations of the Cold War, soon became a "third" way and those nations collectively known as the "Third World."

Perhaps the most sustained attempt to translate dependency theory into practice in the realm of culture and cultural critique occurred in the debates and films of the New Latin American Cinema (NLAC) movement. A central focus of this movement, which emerged as the synthesis of a series of "new" national cinemas in Argentina (La Nueva Ola), Brazil (Cinema Novo), and Cuba, was the rejection of the mode of production, style, and ideology of the Hollywood cinema. Filmmakers and critics were influenced by the aesthetic innovations and new modes of production of European film movements, especially Italian neorealism and the French New Wave, which proved the viability of non-studio-based production. They were also, simultaneously, immersed in the maelstrom of political and social debates and revolutions that traversed the continent from Cuba to Patagonia and were eager to "liberate" the cinema; that is, to change its social function. The "new" cinemas would serve as forms of national expression but would also be active weapons in the transformation of the underdevelopment and political oppression that characterized Latin America (López 1990a). Manifestos such as Julio García Espinosa's "For an Imperfect Cinema" (Cuba) and the Grupo Cine Liberación's "Toward a Third Cinema" (Argentina) critiqued the "perfection" and ideological complicity of Hollywood films while arguing for the need for a new, imperfect, cinema of liberation for the continent. Filmmakers throughout the continent attempted to put theory into practice and produced some of the most innovative and far-reaching works of the decade, ranging from, in Cuba, Tomás Gutiérrez Alea's *Memories of Underdevelopment* (1968) and Humberto Solás's *Lucía* (1968); in Argentina, Fernando Solanas and Octavio Getino's *The Hour of the Furnaces* (1968); in Chile, Miguel Littín's *The Jackal of Nahueltoro* (1969) and Patricio Guzmán's *The Battle of Chile* (1975-1979); in Bolivia, Jorge Sanjinés's *Blood of the Condor* (1969); and, in Brazil, Glauber Rocha's *Terra em Transe* (1967) and *Antonio das Mortes* (1969), Nelson Pereira dos Santos's *Vidas Secas* (1963) and Joaquim Pedro de Andrade's *Macunaima* (1969).

The films of the NLAC were often revolutionary and explicitly political, taking on the medium as political instrument. In the fictional realm, they were films that took on the cinema as a medium for entertainment but attempted to transform and demystify its standard parameters, resorting either to "realism" or to "history" as privileged realms. They were not, however, industrial films. Above all, these were independent films, marginal cinemas on the fringes of existing industries or artisanal practices in nations without a national cinematic infrastructure such as Chile, Uruguay, and Bolivia. Cuba has been a case apart because of the stability (until recently) and extraordinary longevity of the Castro regime.

Unlike Cuba, almost all other Latin American nations underwent cataclysmic political changes in the 1970s and 1980s that undermined the viability of an alternative revolutionary cinematic movement such as the NLAC: repressive regimes, military coup d'états, failed socialist experiments, ballooning foreign debts, and deteriorating economic conditions. Furthermore, the NLAC was simultaneously challenged by another problem. Despite its challenges to dominant cinemas and its desire to subvert and demystify, the NLAC was also interested in fostering the national presence of the cinema and to encourage sustained production. These kinds of concerns cannot be addressed from the margins, but must be articulated in relation to mainstream national cinematic production, state protection of the national cinema, and the cinema's popular or commercial potential. Thus, in nations with developed or developing national industries, the NLAC, in its search for ways to become popular, gradually found itself incorporated into mainstream—albeit somewhat modified—commercial operations. When combined with political pressures, this trend toward industrial practices conclusively altered the NLAC project.

In Brazil, for example, the Cinema Novo disappeared under the hegemonic power of the state agency for the cinema Embrafilme. After democratization, Argentine filmmakers focused on redeveloping the industrial filmmaking sector. In Cuba, although still a case apart, the longevity of the state agency for the cinema (ICAIC) has also meant that the Cuban cinema is an official (rather than a marginal) cinema with different national imperatives.

Perhaps even more conclusive from a theoretical perspective, some of the basic premises underpinning the NLAC have also been put into question. For example, the articles and manifestos that denounced Hollywood's cinematic imperialism also rejected the "classical" cinemas produced in Latin America between the 1930s and 1950s as imitative of Hollywood, unrealistic, alienating, and ideologically complicit and servile to the interests of the dominant classes. The old cinema's principal sin was, as the Cuban critics Enrique Colina and Daniel Díaz Torres argued in 1971 in the pages of *Cine Cubano*, its melodramatic proclivities. Making the melodrama synonymous with the Hollywood cinema, they argued that these Latin American films were little else than a poor imitation "which opened the floodgates to a manifold process of cultural colonization" in Latin America (1971, 15). However, Colina and Díaz Torres did not take into account that this was the first indigenous cinema to dent the Hollywood industry's pervasive presence in Latin America; the first consistently to circulate Latin American images, voices, songs, and history; the first to capture and sustain the interest of multinational audiences throughout the continent for several decades (López 1991b).

The melodramatic was so easily identified with cultural colonization because of its popularity. Simplistically reproducing an elitist mistrust of mass communication and popular culture, critics influenced by theories of cultural imperialism were often unable to see in the popularity of the melodrama or other forms of popular culture anything but the alienation of a mass audience controlled by the dominant classes' capitalist interests. With little differentiation or attention to the processes of reception and identification, they rejected the melodrama as "false" communication. It is ironic, however, that the new cinema's efforts to establish so-called "real" communication—as important as they have been—have rarely attained the levels of popular acceptance of the old cinemas. And when that popular success has been achieved, as in *La historia oficial* (The Official Story,

Luis Carlos Puenzo, 1986, Argentina), for example, it has been precisely by recourse to the melodramatic.

This example points to some of the fatal flaws of the cultural imperialism thesis and dependency theory, in particular their inability to address the specificity of cinematic reception and identification, what Miller calls "the mediation of Hollywood's output by indigenous cultures" (1998a, 375). An additional flaw proved to be the unproblematized approach to "national" cultures, which assumed the existence of some authentic core of national issues/concerns that the cinema had to address and, furthermore, privileged all national producers irrespective of their mediations and relationships with international practices. However, the discussions mobilized by cultural imperialism and dependency theory did allow for the recognition of important cultural inequalities, and pointed the way for the reconceptualization of differences and cultural specificity that constitutes the core of the globalization approach.

TO BE OR NOT TO BE . . . GLOBAL

In the late 1990s, this can hardly be the question. Whether individuals or nations recognize it or not, we are "global." Since the 1970s the speed and range of economic and cultural exchanges have increased vertiginously, allowing companies to sell to customers all over the world. Technology transfers have also contributed to globalization, accelerating the flow of information across, and often without regard to, national borders. These days, financial decisions and events in one part of the world have immediate ripple effects throughout the rest (witness the collapse of the Asian financial markets and its reverberations on Mexico and the USA). Corporations are increasingly multinational and unfettered by national policies and legislation (or attempts to curb them). Whether Mercedes Benz constructs factories in the USA and Brazil or whether US fund managers invest millions in Thai stocks, the economies of individual nations are increasingly integrated by private, cross-border financial flows. In this sense, Hollywood is part of the USA perhaps only in theory, since the major production companies are owned by large international conglomerates, almost half of them not even US based (as with Sony, Rupert Murdoch). In general terms, industrial production—a practice firmly rooted in a location, the factory—has become both increasingly mobile (the maquiladoras in the US-Mexico border) and insignificant: the real profits are to be made trading and speculating on securities and selling services rather than products. Similarly, the production of films is no longer necessarily the main source of profits for conglomerates that sell everything from books and magazines to sneakers, toys, and breakfast cereals: for blockbusters, the ancillary products are often as profitable as box office revenues (Wasko 1994). International credit policies have meant the end of import-substitution industrialization for "developing" nations and the institution of export-based economies linked to an "open" world marketplace, limited perhaps only by regional trade agreements (North Atlantic Free Trade Agreement [NAFTA], General Agreement on Tariffs and Trade [GATT], etc.). Thus commodities are increasingly produced for specific international markets: Chile sells its extraordinary Pacific fish to the Japanese for sushi, Sean Connery remains a "star" because of his appeal to European audiences, and Kevin Costner's *Dances with Wolves* (1990) is sold to the French as a semi-documentary on Native Americans (Danan 1995). As Miller argues, in the era of globalization, the national has become paradigmatic: "New forms of rationalization standardize the acknowledgment of difference as part of capital's need for local marketability" (1998a, 377). The speed and frequency of cultural transfers have given consumers throughout the world "global" tastes, accelerating the demand for cultural imports of all kinds—from movies and music to fashion and food. And this has taken place, at a somewhat similar pace, throughout the world, irrespective of first, second, or third "barriers."

Some of the changes we have seen in the cinema include the growth and mutation of coproductions. Originally, the Hollywood studios used coproductions to defeat restrictions upon earnings imposed by foreign nations after World War II (reinvesting the frozen funds in "local" productions that would have the benefits of two nationalities for distribution quotas elsewhere). They were seen as a strategy that undermined the potential of the national cinema, yet another one of Hollywood's unfair competitive advantages. Yet, as the studios purchased facilities throughout the world to take advantage of lower labor costs, production increasingly shifted away from the locatedness of "Hollywood" and became ever more global. At the same time, coproductions have also become the lifesaver of struggling national cinemas. For example, since the 1970s Latin American filmmakers have eagerly sought coproduction arrangements—either with European and/or with Hollywood producers—as sometimes the only way to make any kind of national production possible. Such has been the extreme case of Cuba in the 1990s, when the financial crisis brought about by the collapse of the Soviet Union (known as the "special period") abruptly immersed the formerly isolated nation into the global arena and decimated the national cinema: the only films that can be made in Cuba today are ones with international financing. A less extreme example is that of Brazil, where the new cinema legislation enacted in the mid-1990s encouraging local investments in culture via tax breaks has proven useful primarily in conjunction with international coproduction deals.

In a global universe, "facing up to" Hollywood has become an increasingly amorphous project. The extreme globalization of film production has made the idea of national cinemas more problematic than ever before. Alongside the eternal desire to use the medium to address national history and cultural values, all producers of national cinemas are also aware that much greater profits and prestige are to be found in a reconfigured international film market now driven by "global" tastes. The US market has never been more open to exotic—and profitable for the US distributors representing them—imports. Thus the spectacular success of *Like Water for Chocolate* (Alfonso Arau, 1991)—the highest grossing foreign film in US history—must be understood as a function of the film's canny recycling of Mexicanisms in a global context: its reimagining of the iconography of 1940s Mexican revolutionary melodramas through the metaphor of its own international consumption.

At the same time, the growing traffic in cultural products inherent to globalization has also meant that filmmakers and creative personnel cross borders with increasing regularity. International success may also mean following the inevitable road to the Hollywood "Mecca." Like Alfonso Arau, for example, Mexican director Guillermo del Toro followed up the international success of his quirky *Cronos* (1993) produced with the support of IMCINE (the Mexican state agency for the cinema) by moving to Hollywood and making the big-budget horror *Mimic* (1997). Mexican star Salma Hayek, a new national icon, is currently attempting to fill (or create) a space for a Latina actress in Hollywood productions such as *Fools Rush In* (1996). But these kinds of exchanges are rarely unidirectional now. Brazilian director Bruno Barreto—who was responsible for some of the greatest box office successes of Brazilian cinema in the 1970s and 1980s such as *Dona Flor and Her Two Husbands* (1976)—has lived and worked in the US for a decade. But he also directed *O que é isso companheiro?* (1997) in Brazil, which was nominated for the foreign film Academy Award. Meanwhile, Carlos Marcovich, who has worked primarily in music videos and advertising in Mexico City, went to Cuba to direct *¿Quién diablos es Juliette?* (1996), to date the most incisive analysis of the intersection of globality and gendered identities in contemporary Cuba. Another, among many other transnational travelers, is the Brazilian José Araujo, who works as an independent sound editor in US independent productions (such as Lourdes Portillo's *El diablo nunca duerme* [The Devil Never Sleeps, 1995]) but directed his well-received *opera prima*, *O Sertão das Memorias* (1996), in his native state of Ceará exclusively with local funding. In yet another ironic contemporary transnational twist, the renowned Cuban director Tomás Gutiérrez Alea became a Spanish citizen to facilitate coproduction deals—and enable his last film, *Guantanamera* (1995)—a few years before his death in 1996.

These multiple and diverse "border crossings" point to the fact that film production, despite the continued financial hegemony of the Hollywood machine, has become as deterritorialized, diasporic, and transnational as the rest of our world. While Hollywood's own profitability has never been more dependent on foreign revenues, the industry has never been more open to the differences to be found elsewhere. And while we may sometimes worry about its absorption of different cultures, knowledges, and landscapes, it is also true that globalization has contributed to the spread of cinematic activity and to the recognition of filmmakers and filmmaking traditions that had never appeared on the US motion picture map. This may not constitute an assault on Hollywood's hegemony, but it is a visible and significant constant reminder of difference, perhaps globality's greatest contribution to our understanding of culture.

Our critical awareness of global forces and practices has had a significant impact upon the theorization of international cinematic relations, that is, on the practices and consequences of "facing up to" Hollywood. Earlier approaches such as purely economic analyses or the cultural imperialism/dependency thesis have given way under the pressure of the shifting cultural paradigms of globality to what we may call "transnational" film studies. Under the banner of transnationality, scholars have begun to question many central paradigms of the field through relational (rather than merely comparative) prisms that reposition the center/periphery and national/foreign dichotomies. Thus, for example, Ella Shohat and Bob Stam's *Unthinking Eurocentrism* (1994) brilliantly unpacks complex international textual and productive relationships through the lens of multiculturalism and postcolonialism. Without negating the uniqueness of the contemporary situation, what Toby Miller has dubbed the "New International Division of Cultural Labor" (1998b, 171), scholars have also begun to apply the lessons of the present to their historical research. One privileged object of study has been the Mexican Golden Age cinema (1930s–1950s), traditionally considered the most stalwartly nationalistic of all Latin American cinemas. Fein, O'Neil, and I have begun an important reconsideration of this period as already profoundly transnational: Fein (1998a, 1998b) has focused on the imbrication of Mexican and US interests in a series of productions during and after World War II, O'Neil (1998) has analyzed Hollywood's second attempt to make Spanish-language films in the late 1930s as illustrative of the Mexican cinema's own hybridity; and I (López 1998a) have chronicled the "reverse flow" of Dolores Del Rio, who left Hollywood and became the foremost icon of the Mexican cinema, and have explored the impact of intercontinental traveling auteurs such as José Bohr, Juan Orol, and others in the development of the industry (López 1998b). Similarly, Ann Marie Stock's anthology *Framing Latin American Cinema* (1997) gathers recent work which focuses on the transactions and interconnections in the history of Latin American cinema, while Chon Noriega's collection *Visible Nations*, returns to the question of the national in Latin American cinema with a difference, placing the nation itself under the lens of a transnational gaze.

Rather than a face-off between Hollywood and its others, what we now seek to understand is a broader zone of cultural debate and economic relationships in which we can trace the tensions and contradictions between national sites and transnational processes. It is in this zone, after all, that the cinema is and has been "lived" as a part of public culture (Appadurai and Breckenridge 1995).

4

Early Cinema and Modernity in Latin America (2000)

This immensely influential and widely anthologized essay provided the first comprehensive overview of early or "silent" cinema in Latin America, based in part on López's Guggenheim-funded fieldwork in various film archives in the region. As in her earlier work, she develops a critical framework that draws on both Anglo-American film studies and Latin American cultural studies. While utilizing Tom Gunning's notion of early cinema as a "cinema of attractions," López contends that the relationship between cinema and modernity was not one of "reflection and convergence" (as argued by US film historians). Instead, she argues that these early films allowed audiences in the region to negotiate modernity. In other words, audiences were at once voyeurs to technological wonders located elsewhere (via imported films) and, at the same time, in synch with the perceptual changes emerging out the new rhythms of modern life and, thus, able to assert the self (and one's nation) as modern. Arguing against teleological models of film history, "Early Cinema and Modernity in Latin America" would be immensely influential on younger scholars in and outside the US, including Maite Conde, Nilo Couret, Andrea Cuarterolo, Rielle Navitski, and Laura Isabel Serna. Translated into Spanish, "Early Cinema" appeared in the inaugural edition of Vivomatografías: Revista de estudios sobre precine y cine silente en

---

Research for this essay was made possible, in part, by grants from the Stone Center for Latin American Studies at Tulane University. My thanks to Hamilton Costa Pinto for his constant companionship, astute movie-watching, and patient fact-seeking over the years.

Latinoamérica *(2015)*, alongside a translation of Gunning's "Early Cinema as Global Cinema."

The early years of the silent cinema in Latin America, roughly 1896–1920, are the least discussed and most difficult to document in Latin American media history. This period was overshadowed by wars and other cataclysmic political and social events and, subsequently, its significance was eclipsed by the introduction and development of other media—the "Golden Ages" of sound cinema and radio in the 1940s and 1950s, television in the 1960s and 1970s. These developments seem to "fit" better with the narratives of Latin American modernity some scholars want to tell, be they tales of foreign technological and ideological domination and inadequate imitation (à la Armand Mattelart [1983] and Herbert Schiller [1976]) or contemporary chronicles of global mediations (à la Martín-Barbero [1987]). Nonetheless, in this early period, we find not only complex global interactions but also extensive evidence of the contradictory and ambivalent transformative processes that would mark the later reception and development of the sound cinema and other media. These early forms of mediated modernities already complexly refracted and inflected the production of self and other imagined communities and, I argue, lay bare the central characteristics of the processes through which subsequent media engaged with and contributed to the specificity of Latin American modernity.

The Arrival

According to Paulo Antonio Paranaguá, "The cinema appear[ed] in Latin America as another foreign import" (1985, 9).[1] This is perhaps the most salient characteristic of the experience of early Latin American cinema: rather than developed in proto-organic synchronicity with the changes, technological inventions, and "revolutions" that produced modernity in Western Europe and the US, the appearance and diffusion of the cinema in Latin America followed the patterns of neocolonial dependency typical of the region's position in the global capitalist system at the turn of the century. As Ella Shohat and Robert Stam point out, "The beginnings of cinema coincided with the giddy heights of the imperial project," and "the most prolific film-producing countries . . . also 'happened' to be among the leading imperialists" (1994, 100).

The cinematic apparatus—a manufactured product—appeared, fully formed, in Latin American soil a few months after its commercial introduction abroad. Subsequently, on the very same ships and railroads that carried raw materials and agricultural products to Europe and the US, Lumière and Edison cameramen returned with fascinating views of exotic lands, peoples, and their customs. Thus, in reference to Latin America, it is difficult to speak of the cinema and modernity as "points of reflection and convergence" (Charney and Schwartz 1995, 1), as is the presumption in US and European early cinema scholarship. Rather, the development of early cinema in Latin America was not directly linked to previous large-scale transformations of daily experience resulting from industrialization, rationality, and the technological transformation of modern life, because those processes were only just beginning to occur across the continent. In turn-of-the-century Latin America, modernity was, above all, still a fantasy and a profound desire.

In Latin America, modernization has been a decentered, fragmentary, and uneven process.[2] As José Joaquín Brunner (1993) has argued, modernity (and, simultaneously, postmodernity) in Latin America is characterized by cultural heterogeneity, by the multiple rationalities and impulses of private and public life. Unequal development led not only to "segmentation and segmented participation in the world market of messages and symbols" but also to "differential participation according to *local codes of reception*" that produced a decentering of "Western culture as it [was] represented by the manuals" (41). In other words, Latin American modernity has been a global, intertextual experience, addressing impulses and models from abroad, in which every nation and region created, and creates, its own ways of playing with and at modernity. These "spectacular experiments" (Appadurai 1995, 24)[3] constituted what Angel Rama called "the momentous second birth of modern Latin America," which took place as *la ciudad letrada* or the lettered city—the nexus of lettered culture, state power, and urban location that had facilitated the continent-wide colonizing process—entered the twentieth century (1996, 99). Albeit intensely engaging with European and, later, US culture, the intellectual sectors Rama dubbed the *letrados* were nevertheless able to define local modernities.

Another crucial sign of Latin American modernity is a kind of temporal warp in which the premodern coexists and interacts with the modern, a differential plotting of time and space, and, subsequently, of history and time. In Aníbal Quijano's words, "In Latin America, what is sequence in other countries is a simultaneity. It is also a sequence. But in the first place it is a simultaneity" (1993, 149). Rather than a devastating process that plows over the traditional bases of a social formation—all that is solid melting into air—Latin American modernity is produced via an ambiguous symbiosis of traditional experiences/practices and modernizing innovations, such as the technologies of visuality epitomized by the cinema. To quote Brunner again, "Not all solid things but rather all symbols melt into air" (1993, 53). This warp has profound consequences for any historical project: because of temporal ambiguity and asynchronicity, teleological narratives of evolution become mired in dead ends and failed efforts and do not do justice to the circuitous routes of Latin American modernity.

If we are to understand the "indigenization" of the cinema in Latin America, the "spectacular experiments" through which it was inserted into and contributed to the specificity of the experience of Latin American modernity, our conceptual framework must link the national and continental with global practices, tracing the complex and specific negotiations between local histories and globality through differential and overlapping chronologies. Any attempt to directly superimpose the developmental grid of US and European early film history (albeit with its own discontinuities and heterogeneity) on the Latin American experience is doomed to failure and frustration, for the early history of Latin American cinema already points to the complexly intertwined chronologies and multiple branchings that later characterized the development of subsequent media.

Likewise, it is not productive to seek replicas of the technological and narrative experiments associated with early cinema in the developed West, for the history of filmmaking in Latin America is too profoundly marked by differences in global position, forms of social infrastructure, economic stability, and technical infrastructure. Studying this period is made even more daunting by the paucity of available material; most of the films produced in Latin America between 1896 and 1930 have disappeared, victims of the inevitable ravages of time (and fires) and the official neglect of cultural preservation. Scholarship on this period is necessarily tenuous, limited to a few dozen extant films, and for the most part is based on secondary materials, especially press coverage. Nevertheless, this history in some countries, especially Argentina, Brazil, and Mexico, has been fairly well documented; conversely, few have attempted transnational comparative studies, since so much of the available material seems bound by "nationness."[4]

Early Cinema and Modernity in Latin America | 65

The first step befuddling any continental chronology is the cinema's uneven diffusion and development. The cinematic apparatus appeared in Latin America quickly, less than six months after its commercial introduction in Europe. There is journalistic evidence that British Brighton School films (using the Vivomatograph) were premiered in Buenos Aires as early as July 6, 1896 (not surprising, given the ongoing neocolonial relationship between Argentina and England during this period) (Caneto et al. 1996, 25–26). Confirmed screenings using the Lumière apparatus (the Cinématographe) took place shortly thereafter: in Rio de Janeiro (July 8, 1896), Montevideo and Buenos Aires (July 18), Mexico City (August 14), Santiago de Chile (August 25), Guatemala City (September 26), and Havana (January 24, 1897). Edison's Vitascope took only slightly longer to arrive. First was Buenos Aires (July 20, 1896), followed by Mexico City (October 22), Lima (January 2, 1897), and Rio de Janeiro (January 30) (Caneto et al. 1996, 27–28; Paranaguá 1987, 24; 1985, 10–11; Dávalos Orozco 1996, 12; de los Reyes 1972, 40; Hintz 1988, 11). These locations are not surprising, for they follow well-established routes of transatlantic commerce through the most advanced cities of the continent, which were already in the throes of modernization.

Arguably, Buenos Aires was ahead of the pack. Looking at some of the most salient indicators typically used to assess modernization, Buenos Aires was the center of national industrial activity (through its ports flowed the wool, beef, and leather that arrived on the British-sponsored railroad system linking the city to interior production centers; it housed six hundred thousand of the nation's four million inhabitants); it had an efficient electric streetcar system (since 1890), a reliable electrical infrastructure that serviced business interests, and two telephone companies (with more than ten thousand subscribers by 1900) (Romero and Romero 1983; Walter 1996, 480–83). Furthermore, its population was cosmopolitan; the government-encouraged waves of immigration from Europe, beginning in 1895, had changed the physiognomy of the city, producing a fluid constituency and sumptuous public works and private palaces that coexisted alongside *conventillos* (tenement housing) where laborers and poor immigrants resided (Sargent 1994). Also quite modern by continental standards, Rio had electric streetcars, telegraphs, telephones, and electricity, although the latter was unstable until completion of a hydroelectric plant in nearby Ribeirão das Lajes in 1905. Like Buenos Aires, Rio's population was cosmopolitan: Rio (and later São Paulo) was a magnet for migrants from the Northeast and immigrants from Europe (Adamo 1998; Moura

1987, 13–20). In contrast, a capital city like Lima was showing only the beginning signs of modernization. Despite urban renewal, funded by the rubber boom that would eventually modernize the city (especially significant was the redesign of the principal urban arteries of La Colmena and the Paseo Colón), Lima lacked a reliable source of electricity and was the center of a quasi-feudal state that historian Jorge Basadre calls the "República Aristocrática" (1968–1970). Peru was a nation in which only 5 percent of the population had the right to vote and in which that 5 percent governed and suppressed all peasant protests and urban popular movements. Further, its Europeanized elites, not the nation's majority indigenous population, controlled the country (Parker 1998, 153–78). Thus, it is not surprising that the "modernity" of early cinema echoed more resoundingly—and lastingly—in Buenos Aires and Rio than in Lima, since even the simple films shown at these first screenings already exemplified a particularly modern form of aesthetics responding to the specificity of modern urban life.

Porteños (Buenos Aires residents) took to the medium immediately; there is evidence that the first Argentine film—views of Buenos Aires—may have been produced as early as 1896. By the turn of the century, businessmen specializing in photography had mastered the new medium's technology and begun to produce a steady stream of actualities and proto-fictional shorts. Other impresarios included imported and national films in their popular public entertainment venues (theaters and, in the summer, open-air festivals) and, as early as 1901, had even built dedicated movie houses. *Cariocas* (Rio de Janeiro residents) also became early enthusiasts, but despite a series of "firsts" and the efforts of pioneers, the medium did not become established until reliable electricity was available in 1905. In contrast, the cinema acquired a foothold in Lima much more slowly. Although there is evidence that a national short may have been produced in 1899, the first confirmed filming did not take place in Peru until 1904, newsreel or actuality production was not consistent until 1909–1915, dedicated movie theaters did not appear until 1909, the first fiction film was not produced until 1915, and the cinema did not develop beyond its first documentary impulses until the 1920s (Bedoya 1992; Carbone 1992).

The diffusion of the cinema throughout the interior of Latin American countries followed a pattern determined by, among other things, the level of development of railroads and other modern infrastructures. In Mexico, for example, where a national railroad system was already well established by the turn of the century,[5] the Edison equipment enchanted Guadalajara, the nation's second-largest city, in 1896, and by 1898 the Lumière apparatus had already appeared in Mérida, San Juan Bautista, Puebla, and San Luis Potosí (de los Reyes 1972, 91). Conversely, more inaccessible regions—that is, regions marginal to international trade—were not exposed to the new invention until significantly later. For example, residents of the remote community of Los Mulos in Cuba's Oriente province did not see movies "for the first time" until the mid-1960s, made possible through the auspices of the Cuban film institute's (ICAIC) *cine-móvil* program. The experience is documented in Octavio Cortázar's short film *Por primera vez* (For the First Time, 1967).

More significant than the speed of diffusion of the technological apparatus is how it was used at various sites and locales—the process of adaptation, contestation, and innovation in the context of the international cinematic marketplace. The cinema experienced by Latin Americans was—and still is—predominantly foreign. This is a factor of tremendous significance in the complex development of indigenous forms, always caught in a hybrid dialectics of invention and imitation, as well as in the development of the form of experience—mass spectatorship—necessary to sustain the medium.

Peripheral Attractions

The early films that arrived in Latin America alongside the new technology were part of what Tom Gunning and other film scholars have characterized as the "cinema of attractions" (1990, 56–62). Instead of the narrative forms that would later become hegemonic, the cinema of attractions (predominant in the US until 1903–1904) was based on an aesthetics of astonishment; it appealed to viewers' curiosity about the new technology and fulfilled it with brief moments of images in movement. It was, above all, a cinema of thrills and surprises, assaulting viewers with stimulating sights; in Miriam Hansen's terms, it was "presentational rather than representational" (137).

In Latin America, this aesthetics of astonishment was complicated by the ontological and epistemological status of the apparatus. In fact, the Latin American context, in which, despite all attempts to produce films locally, imported films tended to dominate the market and have usually been the most popular, leads us to pose the question "indeed attracted, but to what?" The cinematic attraction is "attractive" in and of itself *and* as an import. However, beyond any purported fit with the experience of modernity in local urban life, its appeal is—and perhaps first of all—the appeal of the other, the shock of difference. With its vistas of sophisticated modern cities and customs (ranging from the Lumières' rather sophisticated workers leaving the factory and magnificent locomotives to Edison's scandalous kiss), the imported views could produce the experience of an *accessible* globality among the urban citizens of Latin America, many of them less than a generation away from the "old world." Fashion, consumer products, other new technologies, and different ways of experiencing modern life and its emotions and challenges[6] were suddenly available with tremendous immediacy: "In its earliest days . . . the cinema was an opening to the world" (Caneto et al. 1996, 31). But to the degree that that experience was desired and delightful, it also created profound ambivalence and was a source of anxiety.

The cinema's complex images of distance and otherness problematized the meaning of locality and self. Where were they to be found—these spectators of the "new world"—in this brave new "other" world of specular and spectacular thrills? On the one hand, the cinema fed the national self-confidence that its own modernity was "in progress" by enabling viewers to share and participate in the experience of modernity as developed elsewhere, to respond to the thrill. On the other hand, to do so, the national subject was also caught up in a dialectics of seeing: viewers had to assume the position of spectators and become voyeurs of, rather than participants in, modernity. To the degree that the cinema of attractions depended on a highly conscious awareness of the film image *as* image and of the act of looking itself, it also produced a tremendously self-conscious form of spectatorship in that Latin America was almost immediately translated as the need to assert the self as modern but also and, more lastingly, as different, ultimately as a national subject. Thus, the earliest Latin American films recirculated the parameters of modernity as cinematically experienced elsewhere, while simultaneously enabling viewers to participate in and promote whatever forms of that modernity were available locally.

In its form and content, early Latin American cinema clearly resonates with the technological changes and innovations generally associated with modernization, echoing how the intersection of cinema and modernity was evidenced in Western Europe and the US while demonstrating the desire to identify "attractions" locally in order to exploit the incipient modernity of each site. For example, in response to the great impact of the Lumières' *Arrival of a Train at the Station* (1895), one of the films included in most "first" Latin American screenings, local filmmakers sought in the developed and/or developing national railroad and transportation systems an equivalent symbol and the duplication of the amazement produced by the French film. One of the first national "views" filmed in Buenos Aires, screened in November 1896, was precisely of the arrival of a train at a local station, described pointedly in the press as "the arrivals of *our* trains" (Caneto et al. 1996, 34, emphasis added). Slightly later, in 1901, Eugenio Py chronicled the *Llegada de un tramway* (Arrival of a Streetcar), undoubtedly seeking a similar effect. In Brazil, Vittorio de Maio filmed *Chegada de um tren a Petrópolis* (Arrival of a Train in Petrópolis) and *Ponto Terminal da Linha dos Bondes* (Streetcar Line Terminal) in 1897; their exhibition at the Teatro Casino Fluminense in Petrópolis (a mountain resort city near Rio) in May 1897 was widely advertised (Monteiro 1996, 13).

As in the rest of the world, all modern modes of transport were quickly imbricated with the emerging medium, not only as subject but also by reproducing the perceptual changes they embodied. Railroad travel, in particular, profoundly altered the human sensorium and produced a specifically modern perceptual paradigm marked by what Wolfgang Schivelbusch calls "panoramic perception"—the experience of passengers looking out of a moving train window—as well as a changed temporal consciousness, an orientation to synchronicity and simultaneity (Schivelbusch 1971, 57–72; Kirby 1997). The cinema in Latin America developed a similar natural affinity with this panoramic mode of perception within its first decade; the railroad "view" became the logical predecessor and producer of early traveling shots. For *Los festejos de la Caridad* (The Festivities of St. Charity, 1909), for example, Cuban film pioneer Enrique Díaz Quesada put his camera on a streetcar to produce a traveling shot of festivities in Camagüey province. Alfonso Segreto produced a similar, albeit slower, effect with his Brazilian "views" from his ship pulling into the Bay of Guanabara in Rio de Janeiro in June 1898 upon his return from a trip to Europe (where he had purchased equipment from the Lumières) (fig. 4.1).

Mexican filmmakers assiduously followed President Porfirio Díaz's many train trips, beginning with a sojourn to Puebla in 1900; during a later trip to Tehuantepec (to inaugurate a rail line linking the Gulf of Mexico with the Pacific), actualities captured "fugitive" images of the pyramids at San Juan Teotihuacán. In Chile, Arturo Larraín filmed the funeral of President Pedro Montt in 1910 and included an extended sequence shot

Figure 4.1. Alfonso Segreto shows off his equipment shortly after his return to Rio de Janeiro from Europe (1898). Public domain.

from the last wagon of the train that carried his remains to the capital from the port in Valparaíso (Montt died in Germany). In *Missão militar e diplomática Alemã* (German Military and Diplomatic Mission), an actuality about the 1913 visit of a German diplomatic mission to Rio de Janeiro, shot by Alfredo Musson, what is of greatest interest is not the visiting dignitaries but the extraordinary, elegantly functioning transportation infrastructure, including the electric streetcar shown climbing the steep Corcovado mountain and the monorail to Pão de Açúcar (Sugarloaf Mountain). The vistas shot from inside both vehicles are magnificent.

Sometimes the "train effect" was pushed to its limits to produce the phenomenological experience of railroad travel (akin to the Hale's Tours popular in the US from 1906 to 1910); according to the Curitiba (Brazil) newspaper *A República*, to watch the 1910 film *Viagem à serra do mar* (Trip from the Mountains to the Sea), spectators "enter a simulacrum of a fully outfitted railroad car, including a machine on top providing the noise and vibrations of a moving railroad. Spectators receive a total illusion of a railroad trip, topped by the projection in the front end of the car of the amazing landscapes (visible from) our railroads, especially our marvelous mountains" (Noronha 1997).

Mobility in general was a great attraction. In the Brazilian films *Carnaval em Curitiba* (Carnival in Curitiba, 1910) and *Desfile militar* (Military Parade, 1910), for example, the camera's focus on the various means of transport overwhelms the alleged subject of the shorts (carnival festivities in Curitiba and a military parade in Rio). In both films, we witness a veritable melee of mobility as cars, electric streetcars, and horse-drawn carriages parade in front of the cameras. Here and elsewhere, the earliest Latin American films produce an extraordinary catalog of mobility; early films privilege travel, races of all kinds of vehicles (from bicycles to airplanes), mechanized journeys, and international visitors and tourists. As epistemologically unstable as the new medium's predominant characteristic, the illusion of movement, these new "visions" offered fleeting (one-to-three-minute-long) fragments of the experience of mobility in and around a modern metropolis.

In Latin America, as elsewhere, the early cinema capitalized on the panoply of modern technologies, including urban developments, media, and new amusements. In *Melhoramentos do Rio de Janeiro* (Improvements in Rio de Janeiro, 1908), for example, Brazilian Antonio Leal documented the 1905 opening of the urban artery the Avenida Central (today's Rio Branco), which changed the physiognomy of the city, and other urban improvements. Sophisticated firefighting organizations were the focus of early films in both Chile and Cuba. In Chile, *Ejército general de bombas* (Firefighters' Corps, 1902) was a three-minute view of the city's firefighters on parade and the first national "view" on record. The first film recorded on Cuban soil, *Simulacro de un incendio* (Simulacrum of a Fire, 1897), was shot by Lumière cameraman Gabriel Veyre; it documented a staged firefighting incident and featured a well-known Spanish stage actress (Rodríguez 1993, 33).[7] In the area of communication, the telephone was at the center of the proto-narrative of Argentinian Eugenio Py's *Noticia telefónica angustiosa* (Sorrowful Telephone News, 1906), while the popularity of the phonograph suggested a series of experiments in which music and sound were added to films, in particular, Py's thirty-two very popular "sonorized films" for the Casa Lepage (1907–1911) (Caneto et al. 1996, 85).[8]

Meanwhile, the still-in-development fields of public relations and advertising were exploited early in Cuba, following US trends. In José E. Casasús's *El brujo desaparecido* (The Disappearing Witch-Doctor, 1898), a trick film in the style of Georges Méliès, a magician "disappeared" to drink a beer. Somewhat later, Enrique Díaz Quesada's *El parque de*

Palatino (Palatino Park, 1906) chronicled and reproduced the thrills of the rides at the newly opened Palatino amusement park, a mini–Coney Island that included a movie theater (Rodríguez 1993; Douglas 1996). Influenced by the popularity and foreign novelty of the *bel canto* series at the newly inaugurated Teatro Municipal and other theatrical revues in Rio, Brazilian producers created what is perhaps the "first" Brazilian film genre: the *falados e cantantes* (spoken-and-sung) films. With actors speaking and singing behind a screen, these films were wildly successful between 1908 and 1912. They began as simple illustrated songs but quickly introduced complicated stagings of operas, zarzuelas, and operettas; eventually, producers developed their own "scripts," using well-known and new songs, as in Alberto Botelho's *Paz e Amor* (Peace and Love, 1910), a thinly disguised parody of the newly inaugurated president Nilo Peçanha.[9] In short, the cinema very quickly became emblematic of modernity, while the specularity and spectacularity of its fragmentary processes came to epitomize local forms of a modern sensibility.[10]

The Novelty of Objectivity

The cinema's impulse toward display and spectacle was ambivalently linked with the technology's purported affinity with science, much lauded in Latin America[11] and aligned with then hegemonic positivist ideologies of progress. Positivism and modernity were themselves inextricably linked; the former was perceived as the theoretical matrix that would permit the achievement of the latter. The idea that "scientific" rational knowledge could control the chaos of natural forces and social life was the intellectual rationale for the ideology of "Order and Progress," the motto of more than one nation and a sublation that condensed the contradictory impulses of the evolving "modern" rationalities of economics and politics in still overwhelmingly traditional societies. In fact, only a few early films documented "scientific" projects. In Argentina, surgical pioneer Alejandro Posadas recorded two of his surgeries—a hernia operation and the removal of a pulmonary cyst—in Buenos Aires in 1900 (both films are extant). In Brazil, the preventive work of Oswaldo Cruz was the subject of *Erradicação da Febre Amarela no Rio de Janeiro* (Eradication of Yellow Fever in Rio, 1909), while a somewhat precarious dental extraction in Venezuela was the subject of what may be the earliest views shot in Latin America. The film, *Un célebre especialista sacando muelas en el Gran Hotel Europa* (A

Famous Specialist Pulling Teeth in the Gran Hotel Europa), was made by Guillermo and Manuel Trujillo Durán and shown for the first time in January 1897. The cinema's veneer of scientific objectivity—its ability to display the physical world—perfectly rationalized its more thrilling appeals.

Also linked to the ideology of scientific rationality and progress was the insistence of local inventors on improving and expanding the medium. In 1898 Mexico, for example, someone "invented" the "ciclofotógrafo," a camera attached to a bicycle for traveling shots, and Luis Adrián Lavie announced his "aristógrafo," which allowed spectators to see motion pictures in 3-D (de los Reyes 1972, 174–78). In Argentina, three inventors patented a series of machines, among them the "estereobioscopio," which produced moving images with depth (Caneto et al. 1996, 47–48). The cinema was welcomed first and foremost as a sign of and tool for expressing the rationalist impetus of the modern. It was thoroughly aligned with the civilizing desires of the urban modernizing elites and disassociated from the "barbarism" of national "others."

In Mexico, it was, above all, the cinema's purported objectivity that first endeared it to the highly positivist intelligentsia of the Porfiriato, who were fully committed to its leader's "Order and Progress" motto. Linking the cinema with the also new and booming illustrated press and arguing that it was against the medium's nature to lie, early commentators railed stridently against the film *Duelo a pistola en el bosque de Chapultepec* (Pistol Duel in Chapultepec Forest, 1896), a reconstruction shot by Lumière cameramen Bertrand von Bernard and Gabriel Veyre of a duel between two deputies, as "the most serious of deceits, because audiences, perhaps the uninformed or foreigners . . . will not be able to tell whether it is a simulacrum of a duel or a real honorific dispute" (de los Reyes 1972, 104). The concern over Mexico's image abroad is explicit; after all, the film was shot by Lumière cameramen charged with collecting foreign views for international distribution, at a time when the government was already beginning to organize its pavilion for the 1900 Paris Universal Exhibition. But the paternalism explicit in this commentary—the "uninformed" (i.e., the national illiterate masses)—indicates the unstable relationship between the regime's much-touted "progress" and those it had bypassed. For the majority of Mexico City inhabitants, "progress" was experienced as entertainment, not science; they had already gathered in the streets to watch the installation of electrical power posts and a parade of new bicycles they still could not afford. The cinema was next in line, and, to the degree that it was adopted by the masses and developed its "attractions," it was repudiated by the elites. Thus, the cinema functioned as a modernizing force, not according to positivist scientific parameters but by consolidating the formation of a modern urban audience. Nonetheless, although abandoned by the *científicos*[12] and eventually given over to the masses as spectacle, the Mexican cinema remained bound to the myth of objectivity, to its value as "truth."

If at first the illusion of movement necessarily involved the disavowal of the frailty of our knowledge of the physical world, that thrilling anxiety was quickly sublimated into the still-shocking experience of seeing "history"—near and far—as it happened. Stimulated by the surprise of being able to see imported images, whether real or reconstructed, of the Spanish-American War,[13] local filmmakers throughout the continent exploited the ostensible objectivity of the medium to record current events. The attraction of history-in-the-making allowed the still economically unstable medium to continue to attract audiences and develop commercially; as the novelty of the first shocks of movement wore off, the focus shifted to monumental current events. In fact, it has been argued that locally financed and local-interest actuality newsreels constitute the only consistent and unbroken cinematic tradition of early Latin American cinema. Beginning with the chronicling of the visit to Buenos Aires by the Brazilian president—*Viaje del Doctor Campos Salles a Buenos Aires* (Trip of Dr. Campos Salles to Buenos Aires, 1900)—and, the next year, naval operations—*Maniobras navales de Bahía Blanca* (Naval Operations in Bahia Blanca, 1901)—the company of Argentine pioneer Max Glucksmann, Casa Lepage, which specialized in actualities, produced an outstanding record of the Argentine public sphere throughout the silent and sound periods. Joining in this endeavor were other entrepreneurs, among them Julio Irigoyen (*Noticiero Buenos Aires*) and Federico Valle. Valle entered the field shortly after his 1911 arrival in Argentina (after working with Méliès in France) and produced, among other films, the *Film Revista Valle* weekly newsreel from 1920 to 1930.

Actualities were also the mainstay of the early film business in Brazil. Antonio Leal in Rio and regional producers (especially in Curitiba) were soon joined by Marc Ferrez and his son Julio, Francisco Serrador, the Botelho brothers, and others in the provinces. In Brazil, however, the novelty of news also took on a spectacular character as sensational crimes, already popularized by the illustrated press, were meticulously restaged and shot on location. Films like *Os Estranguladores* (The Stranglers, Francisco Marzullo or Antonio Leal, 1908) and the two versions of *O crime da mala* (The Suitcase Crime, Francisco Serrador and Marc Ferrez and son, respectively, both 1908) were wildly successful: the audience's familiarity with the crimes enabled the filmmakers to tell their "stories" efficiently without intertitles or internal continuity.

Another restaging of a news story, Antonio Leal's *O Comprador de Ratos* (The Rat Buyer, 1908) is of particular interest, as it unwittingly captures the idiosyncrasies of modernity in the midst of underdevelopment, thus serving as a particularly vivid example of the contradictions produced by "misplaced ideas."[14] During the Oswaldo Cruz–led campaign to eradicate yellow fever in Rio, the government announced that it would buy dead rats by the pound. The inhabitants of Rio's poor neighborhoods found themselves in the midst of a thriving industry, breeding and fattening rats to sell to the government. In a brilliant allegory of modernity in Latin America, *O Comprador* tells the story of a Niterói native who attempted to sell thousands of rodents until the scam was discovered (Araújo 1976, 229–79; Galvão 1987, 51–64).

Following the Lumière model, Mexican pioneers also took to current events, perhaps with the greatest enthusiasm after Salvador Toscano exhibited the actualities *Guanajuato destruido por las inundaciones* (Guanajuato Destroyed by Floods, 1905) and *Incendio del cajón de la Valenciana* (Fire at the Valenciana Warehouse, 1905). In 1906, both Toscano and his principal competitor, Enrique Rosas, rushed to chronicle an official trip to Yucatán by President Díaz, whose image was still of great interest to audiences; their films exhibited a preoccupation with formal structure that pushed them beyond the simplicity of the typical actuality. Following an excruciatingly linear logic dependent on editing, Toscano's film narrated the presidential trip from beginning (Díaz's departure by train from Mexico City) to end (his farewells to Yucatán), thus substituting a chronology that was absolutely faithful to the profilmic event for narrative development.

Similarly, the Alva brothers' *Entrevista Díaz-Taft* (Díaz-Taft Interview, 1909), a report of the Díaz–William Howard Taft meetings in Ciudad Juárez and El Paso, employs the chronological "record of a trip" structure, but it is mediated by two additional concerns: a visible effort to record both sides of the event (some of President Taft's trip as well as Díaz's) and a willingness to fiddle with the chronology of the profilmic event to augment the narrative impact. As Aurelio de los Reyes demonstrates, the filmmakers altered the sequence of events toward the end of the film in order to have the film end on an apotheosis, with the image of both presidents on the steps of the Customs Building in Juárez (1983,

95–98). This image is the visual equivalent of their interview, but it is also strongly marked by an accidental profilmic action: as the presidents descend the steps, an observer waves a flag in front of the camera and, for an instant, the screen is filled by the flag and its large slogan, "Viva la República," visually affirming the national despite the alleged impartiality of its treatment. In fact, the cinema's "truth value" was selectively applied: the Porfirian cinema was basically escapist and did not record the more disagreeable aspects of national life, such as the bloody strikes in Cananea (1906) and Río Blanco (1907), the violence and poverty of urban ghettos, or the injustices of rural life.

Attraction of Nationness

Beyond the drive to identify "local" modern thrills—almost, but not quite, the same as those of the imported views—or to record current events, the new technology was used for the benefit of the imagined national community, to negotiate precisely the conflicts generated by the dilemmas of a modernity that was precariously balanced between indigenous traditions and foreign influences, between nationalist aspirations and internationalist desires. Thus, the fascination with the epiphenomenal manifestations of modernity and their perceptual thrills was inflected with explicit exaltations of nationness—these are not just "our" railroads but symbols of our national *belongingness*, in a sense as "modern" as the new technological forms themselves—linked in many instances to current events.

Following the nonchronological plotting of time and history suggested earlier, this process occurred both sequentially and simultaneously with the fascination with modern technology and current events described earlier. In late 1897, for example, a notice in the Buenos Aires newspaper *El Diario* announced not only a filming of local events but the time and location: "The views will be photographed in the morning. The first will be of bicyclists in Palermo park at 7:30 a.m. Those who would like to see their figures circulating on the screen of this theater should take notice" (Caneto et al. 1996, 35). Similarly, a few months later, *La Nación* remarked in its column "Vida Social":

> The views shot in Palermo, which will be projected by the marvelous machine next Monday on the stage of the Casino theater, will perhaps be of greater interest than the landscapes and exotic scenes reproduced by the "American Biograph." We

are assured that these views are as sharp as the European and that we shall clearly recognize many of our socially prominent citizens. (Caneto et al. 1996, 35)[15]

Clearly invoking another kind of desire or "attraction," these notices posited a spectatorial position predicated on identification and self-recognition, which was but an embryonic form of cinematic nationness. It was also a process markedly aligned with the existing power structure: the appeal was not just that one would see ordinary Buenos Aires citizens but socially prominent ones—metaphorical stand-ins for the nation itself.

In Latin America as a whole, the cinema was, from its earliest moments, closely aligned with those in power, be they wealthy and socially prominent or simply in government, and this alignment was a first step toward nationalist projects. The first films photographed in Mexico, for example, were not landscapes or street scenes but carefully orchestrated views of Porfirio Díaz (recently reelected for a fourth presidential term), his family, and his official retinue shot by Lumière cameramen von Bernard and Veyre in 1898. The young Frenchmen recognized the need to secure the dictator's goodwill to proceed in their commercial enterprises and arranged a private screening of the new technology for Díaz and his family in Chapultepec. During the five months they remained in Mexico, they filmed the president, who quickly recognized the propagandistic value of the new medium, at all sorts of official and familiar events. As one historian has remarked, Porfirio Díaz was, by default, the first "star" (attraction?) of the Mexican cinema (Dávalos Orozco 1996, 14): his on-screen appearances were enthusiastically hailed with rousing "Vivas!" (de los Reyes 1972, 153; 1983, 54).

Akin to the Mexican example, the first two views filmed in Bolivia were explicit paeans to the power structure. Both *Retratos de personajes históricos y de actualidad* (Portraits of Historical and Contemporary Figures, 1904) and the very popular *La exhibición de todos los personajes ilustres de Bolivia* (The Exhibition of All the Illustrious Characters of Bolivia, 1909) were designed to align the new technology with those who effectively controlled and defined the nation *and* to display them for the enjoyment and recognition of the new audiences. In Mexico, however, the initial links between cinema and the urban power elites was short lived. Production/exhibition pioneers, motivated by the 1900 closing down of Mexico City's exhibition sites—primarily *carpas* or tents—because of city safety regulations designed to curb the "uncivilized" behavior of popular spectators and to diminish the risk of fires, became itinerant and left

Mexico City, taking the cinema with them (there were only a handful of film exhibitions in the capital between 1901 and 1905) (de los Reyes 1983, 32–34, 55). They traveled throughout the national territory showing the films in their repertories but also regularly producing local views to entice the various regional audiences. These views chronicled the activities of small cities and towns: the crowds leaving church after Sunday Mass, workers outside factories, and local celebrations and festivities. Rather than focusing on modern life and technology, this early cinema took a turn toward the people—positioned in their local landscapes and captured in their everyday activities. Its attraction was self-recognition: "On premiere nights the improvised actors would come to the shows en masse to see themselves on film; the enthusiasm of each and every one when they saw themselves or their friends and relatives on screen was great" (Sánchez García cited in de los Reyes 1983, 53–54). But through that self-recognition, these actors also began the process of producing an image of the nation based on its traditional sectors and ways of life—the peoples and customs of the interior rather than the modernity of the capital city—and a more broad-based audience for the cinema.

The linchpin of the cinema-nation symbiosis coincided with the various centennial celebrations around 1910. In Argentina and Mexico (Chile also celebrated its centennial in 1910), filmmakers competed fiercely to record the festivities, and their films were quickly exhibited to great public acclaim. Aurelio de los Reyes reproduces a telling photograph in his book *Filmografía del cine mudo mexicano, 1896–1920*: while President Díaz is placing the cornerstone of a monument to Louis Pasteur, three cameramen vie for the best angle (1986, 61). At least three filmmakers—the Alva brothers, Salvador Toscano, and Guillermo Becerril—competed to record the events that were the apotheosis and swan song of the Porfirian era. Actualities such as *El desfile histórico del Centenario* (The Historic Centennial Parade), *Gran desfile militar del 16 de septiembre* (Great Military Parade of September 16), and *Entrega del uniforme de Morelos* (Presentation of Morelo's Uniform) illustrated the magnificence of the events as well as the exuberance and optimism of the crowds. But the paroxysms of patriotism elicited by the centennials and their preparations also motivated filmmakers in a different direction, away from current events and toward the reconstruction of key patriotic moments, in an effort to further mobilize the new medium in the service of nationhood.

National Narratives

Undoubtedly, Latin American audiences were already quite familiar with the post-1904 productions imported from the US and Europe—dubbed "transitional narratives"[16] to highlight their status in between the cinema of attractions and full-fledged narrative cinema—and had begun to experience the appeal of a different kind of cinematic identification, one that filmmakers sought to exploit for national celebrations. Viewers were influenced less by the chase films and Westerns arriving from the US than by the theatrical adaptations filled with artistic aspirations produced by the Societé Film d'Art and other European producers. The theater was already an art form with an extensive history and of great elite and popular appeal throughout Latin America. As such, it was a natural source of inspiration for filmmakers seeking to narrativize the medium. This process is most evident in Argentina, where the appeal of actualities of current events waned in comparison to the enthusiasm generated by a new series of proto-narratives, beginning with Mario Gallo's *La Revolución de Mayo* (The May Revolution, 1909).

A perfect example of a transitional film, *La Revolución* has neither a self-sufficient nor an internally coherent narrative. To make sense of the film and understand the motivations linking the various tableaux, the spectator must have extensive knowledge of the historical event being represented, as the intertitles are identificatory rather than expository. Furthermore, the style is thoroughly presentational, ranging from direct address to mise-en-scène (theatrical acting and theatrical backdrops suggesting depth and perspective rather than reproducing it). Its one purely "cinematic" moment occurs in the last tableaux, in which a visual device effectively supplements the film's patriotic enthusiasm: while the patriot leader Saavedra speaks from a balcony to a throng, an image of General San Martín in uniform and wrapped in the Argentine flag appears unexpectedly over a painted backdrop of the Cabildo; the people and the army salute him and shout "Viva la República" (according to the titles). Other Gallo historical reconstructions further developed this patriotic theme and style (utilizing well-known popular stage actors), as seen, for example, in *La creación del himno* (The Creation of the National Anthem, 1909), an homage to the writing and first performance of the national anthem, and *El fusilamiento de Dorrego* (Dorrego's Execution), *Juan Moreira*, *Güemes y sus gauchos* (Güemes and His Gauchos), and *Camila O'Gorman* (all 1910).

Humberto Cairo's *Nobleza gaucha* (Gaucho Nobility, 1915) further developed Gallo's narrative-nationalist impetus. This film most clearly exemplifies the nationalist sentiments and contradictions of this period and was perhaps the first to develop the city-countryside dialectic central to Latin America's modernity debates. Although much closer to a classical style than *La Revolución*, *Nobleza* is still a transitional narrative. Rather than depend on the audience's prior historical knowledge, however, its intertext is cultural; the intertitles cite the great Argentine epic poem *Martín Fierro* to recount the story of a courageous gaucho who saves his beautiful girlfriend from the evil clutches of a ranch owner who abducted her to his palatial city mansion. The ranch owner falsely accuses the gaucho of theft but dies when he falls off a cliff while being chased by the hero on horseback. Skillfully filmed—with well-placed close-ups, elegant lighting, and diverse camera movements, including tracking shots from trains and streetcars—and acted naturalistically, the story line allowed Cairo to focus on the always appealing folklore of the countryside (songs, ranchos, gauchos, and barbecues), as well as the modernity of the city: shots of Constitución Avenue, Avenida de Mayo, Congress, the Armenonville station, and even nighttime urban illuminations. *Nobleza* simultaneously exalts the traditional values of rural life—indulging in what Rey Chow (1995) calls "primitive passions"[17]—while displaying in all its splendor the modern urbanity that would make it obsolete; the gaucho may have been the hero of the narrative, but he was already relegated to the status of a foundational myth like *Martín Fierro*. *Nobleza*'s exploration of the crisis in national identity generated by the conflict between traditional experiences and values and the internationalization endemic to modernity was extraordinarily well received: the film cost only twenty thousand pesos to produce but made more than six hundred thousand from its many national and international screenings (Di Núbila 1959a, 18–20).

Thus, transitional narrative styles, in all their diverse forms, were almost naturally linked to the project of modern nation-building. Once the cinema had exhausted its purely specular attractions and sought new storytelling possibilities, the task of generating narratives about the nation inevitably led to the problematization of modernization itself. The epidermal modernity of urban daily life—with its railroads, mobility, and technology—had been exalted earlier. Narratives now required the exploration of the contradictions of that process at a national level. With few exceptions, the earliest successful Latin American films identified as "narratives" were linked to patriotic themes. In Mexico, for example, Carlos

Mongrand invoked well-known historical figures in *Cuauhtémoc y Benito Juárez* and *Hernán Cortés, Hidalgo y Morelos* (both 1904); later Felipe de Jesús Haro and the American Amusement Co. (*sic*) produced the elaborate (seven tableaux) *Grito de Dolores* (The Shout of Dolores, 1907), which was usually screened with live actors declaiming the dialogue behind the screen (de los Reyes 1986, 42–47). In Brazil, in addition to addressing historical events and figures (for example, Alberto Botelho's *A vida do Barão do Rio Branco* [The Life of the Rio Branco Baron, 1910]), similar to *Nobleza Gaucha*, narrative was aligned with comedy and contrasted with urban and rural lives. Julio Ferrez's *Nhô Anastacio chegou de viagem* (Mr. Anastacio Returned from a Trip, 1908), recognized as the first Brazilian fiction film, presents the misadventures of a country bumpkin newly arrived in Rio, including his encounters with urban modernity (railroads, monuments, etc.) within a mistaken-identity love plot. It engendered a series of similar comedies, focused on the conflicts between traditional rural ways and the modernity of cities filled with foreign immigrants and twentieth-century technologies. Throughout these comedies, which attempt to produce the discursive triumph of positivism, the traditional/rural is figured as nostalgically obsolete, a cultural remnant being willed into history, while the modernity of the metropolis is presented as inevitable, "natural," and national.

Although problematized by differential chronologies, similar efforts occurred in other parts of the continent. On the one hand, it is as if developments that took place in, say, Argentina or Brazil, in the early to mid-1910s began to unfold in nations like Chile, Bolivia, and Colombia in the 1920s. On the other hand, the films of the 1920s in Chile, Bolivia, and Colombia were very much produced in the context of 1920s global trends—familiar through always-abundant imported films—and had, to some degree, already abandoned the parameters of the 1910s. Thus, instead of rough transitional narratives, the first Chilean, Bolivian, and Colombian fiction films follow very closely the hegemonic representational parameters of the era—continuity editing, self-sufficient internal narration, and feature length—yet return to the nationalistic concerns of the earlier era elsewhere. In Bolivia, for example, the conflict between indigenous/rural existence and urban life was explored in José María Velasco Maidana's *La profecía del lago* (The Prophecy of the Lake, 1925) and Pedro Sambarino's *Corazón Aymara* (Aymara Heart, 1925). In Colombia, we find skillful adaptations of foundational fictions mediated through the conventions of European-inspired film melodrama: *María* (Alfredo del Diestro and Máximo Calvo,

1921–1922) and Di Doménico's *Aura o las violetas* (Dawn or the Violets, 1923). Chile's version of *Nobleza Gaucha, Alma chilena* (Chilean Soul, 1917), was directed by Arturo Mario, the star of the Argentine film, while Gabriella von Bussenius and Salvador Giambastiani's *La agonía del Arauco* (Arauco Agony, 1917) contrasted the Mapuche landscape and people with the melodramatic foibles of its urban protagonists, and Pedro Sienna's *El húsar de la muerte* (The Hussar of Death, 1925) chronicled the exploits of national hero Manuel Rodríguez.

The Chilean example highlights a curious characteristic of early Latin American cinema that perhaps explains, in part, its obsessive concern with nationness: throughout the continent, the overwhelming majority of early filmmakers were first-generation immigrants. The evidence to support this assertion is too vast to summarize efficiently, so a few names must suffice: in Brazil, the Segreto family came from Italy, Antonio Leal from Portugal, and Francisco Serrador from Spain. In Argentina, Enrique Lepage was Belgian, Federico Figner Czech, Max Glucksmann Austrian, Eugenio Py French, and Mario Gallo and Federico Valle Italian. In Chile, Salvador Giambastiani was Italian (and had worked in Argentina before arriving in Chile in 1915), and the Argentine actors Arturo Mario and María Padín became producers/directors in 1917. In Uruguay, the branch of Max Glucksmann's Argentine company was the principal producer of actualities between 1913 and 1931. Pedro Sambarino, an Italian, worked in Bolivia and Peru. Originally from Italy, the Di Doménico family was instrumental in establishing the cinema in Colombia and Central America. After immigrating to Panama, they acquired filmmaking equipment from Europe and traveled through the Antilles and Venezuela, arriving in Barranquilla in 1910 and settling in La Paz in 1911, where they established a regional distribution/production company of great significance until the arrival of sound (Nieto and Rojas 1992). Thus, the cinema was a medium not only of mobility but also of great appeal to the mobile, to immigrants seeking to make their fortunes in the new world through the apparatuses of modernity yet eager to assert their new national affiliations, and to those who restlessly traveled throughout the continent.

A Nation at War and Beyond

Mexico is a case apart, not only because its cinema pioneers were not foreign immigrants, with a few exceptions (Henri Moulinié and Carlos

Mongrand were French), but because its cataclysmic revolution determined a different, although no less nationalistic, path for the cinema between 1910 and 1918.[18] The films of the Mexican Revolution were the direct heirs of the passion for objectivity and reportage of the earlier actualities. Just as Díaz had been the "star" of early Mexican views, Francisco Madero, the other *caudillos*, and the armed struggle became the stars of the next decade. The success of the Alva brothers' *Insurrección de México* (Mexican Insurrection, 1911), one of the first films depicting revolutionary events, demonstrated that audiences were avid for news of the revolution, and most filmmakers followed the *caudillos* and fighting troops to capture images of the complicated events taking place (fig. 4.2). Alongside the increase in production, movie theaters mushroomed in the capital to accommodate new capacity crowds, many composed of newly arrived peasants escaping from the fighting and violence in the provinces.

Figure 4.2. The Alva Brothers—Salvador, Guillermo, and Eduardo—take a lunch break from filming (circa 1910-1912). Courtesy of IMCINE (Instituto Mexicano de Cinematografía).

In the first films of the Revolution, filmmakers continued to adapt narrative strategies to the documentation of events. *Asalto y toma de Ciudad Juárez* (Assault and Takeover of Ciudad Juarez, 1911), for example, the third part of the Alva brothers' *Insurrección en México*, was subdivided into four parts and consisted of thirty-six scenes, the last of which was the "apotheosis" or grand climax, in which the people acclaim the victory of the hero, Pascual Orozco. Similarly, the Alva brothers' *Las conferencias de paz y toma de Ciudad Juárez* (The Peace Conferences and Takeover of Ciudad Juarez, 1911) ended with the military's triumphant entry into Ciudad Juárez, and their *Viaje del señor Madero de Ciudad Juárez hasta Ciudad de México* (Mr. Madero's Trip from Ciudad Juarez to Mexico City, 1911) climaxed at the intersection of two parallel narrative lines (Venustiano Carranza and Madero's journeys, culminating in two apotheosis scenes). Finally, Guillermo Becerril Jr.'s *Los últimos sucesos de Puebla y la llegada de Madero a esa ciudad* (The Latest Events in Puebla and Madero's Arrival to This City, 1911) ended with the "apotheosis" image of President Madero and his wife posing for the camera. All these films respected the chronological sequence of the events and simultaneously adopted a clearly dramatic/narrative structure for their representation.

Potentially the most ambitious of all the revolutionary films was the Alva brothers' *Revolución orozquista* (Orozquista Revolution, 1912). It documented the battles between General Victoriano Huerta's and Orozco's troops and was shot under extremely dangerous circumstances. The filmmakers chose to present both sides of the battle with a great degree of objectivity and thus structured the film to tell two parallel stories without providing explanations or justifying the actions of either side: in the first part, we see the activities of the Orozquista camp, in the second the Huertistas. The third part features the battle between the two camps, but we are not shown the outcome—that is, who won is withheld from the report. Believing that the events were powerful enough to speak for themselves, the filmmakers attempted to assume the impartiality required of the positivist historian and thus produced a spectacular transitional form that engaged narrative protocols while remaining wedded to documentary objectivity and that aimed, above all, to inform. This form would be exploited and further developed by all the filmmakers active in this period, especially in the several films dealing with the events of the Decena Trágica in February 1913 (the ten days of violence in Mexico City following an armed uprising led by Félix Díaz, Porfirio's nephew, that culminated in Huerta's triumph over Madero).

It is important to note that each of the principal combatants had his "own" camera crews on hand to record his achievements. The Alva brothers followed Madero's activities; Jesús Abitia covered General Obregón—a former friend of his family—and also filmed Carranza; the Zapatistas were filmed by several cameramen; Pancho Villa and Carranza favored the US cinematographers, who rushed across the border to produce newsreels and documentaries. Villa, in particular, signed an exclusive contract with the Mutual Film Co. and was known to stage battles and events such as hangings in the daytime so that they could be filmed (de los Reyes 1985; de Orellana 1991). Huerta's takeover in 1913 had a great impact on the development of the revolutionary documentary; because the films often awakened violent reactions in their already partisan audiences, Huerta approved legislation requiring "moral and political" censorship prior to exhibition. Thereafter, filmmakers gave up striving for "objectivity" and assumed the point of view of those in power. *Sangre hermana* (Fraternal Blood, 1914), for example, is told from a marked federalist and propagandistic perspective. Other films focused on using previously shot materials to produce "reviews" of the Revolution that were then updated regularly and shown in their entirety: for example, Enrique Echániz Brust and Salvador Toscano's *Historia completa de la Revolución de 1910–1915* (Complete History of the Revolution, 1910–1915, 1915) and Enrique Rosas's *Documentación histórica nacional, 1915–1916* (National Historical Documentation, 1915–1916, 1916). Eventually, the Revolution disappeared from Mexican screens and was replaced by a new fiction cinema:

> Before, filmmakers were pragmatists who had learned their craft by documenting people and events in order to attract audiences. . . . National producers had never before dealt with narrative, a term that had been used exclusively to refer to foreign fiction films. . . . Now a different conception of cinema made its way. The "views" had lost their appeal and the desire was for *films d'art* based on foreign models. (de los Reyes 1995b, 72)

An important predecessor was the Alva brothers' *El aniversario del fallecimiento de la suegra de Enhart* (The Anniversary of the Death of Enhart's Mother-in-Law, 1912), a short comedy about the "daily life" of two very popular theatrical comedians (Alegría and Enhart) in the style of the French films of Max Linder. Although "fiction," the narrative focuses on the domestic as well as the professional lives of the two comedians. The Alvas apparently had not given up on their use of the medium to capture the real world, and the camera scrutinizes the very real Mexico City locations in which the fictional mise-en-scène takes place. The film is skillfully constructed, with editing that contributes to the narrative coherence by alternating between two parallel story lines, inserts (such as intertitles) that add to the suspense/humor, judicious use of special effects (like the old Méliès magic disappearing trick), and close-ups for comic/ performative emphasis. The Alvas were perfecting their technique, only now in the service of narrative entertainment rather than information.

Beginning in 1916, Mexican filmmaking turned to fictional narratives in the style of the French *film d'art* and ignored the revolution and the revolutionary documentary. This change can be attributed to a number of interrelated factors: the political restrictions imposed by the Carranza government, a desire to improve the image of the nation (which had been sullied by the Revolution itself but also by how Hollywood films represented it), the popularity of Italian melodramas, and a widespread desire to leave the Revolution behind (especially after the 1917 constitution and the 1919 assassination of Emiliano Zapata).

Two potentially contradictory tendencies were evident in the efforts to develop a Mexican industry: nationalism and the influence of Italian melodramas. The first tendency was exemplified by the work of Carlos Martínez de Arredondo and Manuel Cirerol Sansores, who founded the company Cirmar Films in Mérida. After making some fictional shorts with indigenous themes, such as *La voz de su raza* (The Voice of Your Race, 1914) and *Tiempos mayas* (Mayan Times, 1915–1916), they produced the first Mexican fictional feature film with a clear nationalist spirit: *1810 o los libertadores* (1810 or the Liberators, 1916). Meanwhile, the tremendous influence of Italian film melodramas was perhaps nowhere better illustrated than in Ezequiel Carrasco's *La luz* (The Light, 1917), the second Mexican feature-length fiction film. Clearly plagiarizing the popular Italian film *Il fuoco* (The Light, Piero Fosco, 1915), starring Pina Menichelli, *La luz* featured Emma Padilla, who not only resembled Menichelli but also copied her mannerisms and postures (fig. 4.3). In fact, Padilla was the first "actress" to become a "star," a position that had previously been occupied by real historical figures. The story (a tripartite tale of misguided passions following the trajectory of daily light—dawn, zenith, dusk) followed the melodramatic style of Italian films, although, as Aurelio de los Reyes has indicated, it was set in a very Mexican landscape, thus pointing to what

Early Cinema and Modernity in Latin America | 87

Figure 4.3. Emma Padilla imitated the Italian actress Pina Menichelli in Ezequiel Carrasco's *La luz* (The Light, 1917). Padilla was the first Mexican "actress" to become a "star." Courtesy of IMCINE (Instituto Mexicano de Cinematografía).

would become a characteristic of the Mexican cinema throughout the rest of the silent and early sound periods: transforming foreign narrative models by setting them in explicitly Mexican mise-en-scènes (de los Reyes 1995b, 73).

Approximately seventy-five feature-length fiction films were produced in the period 1917–1921, the most prolific in the history of the Mexican silent cinema. The most significant film of this period, Enrique Rosas's *El automóvil gris* (The Grey Automobile, 1919), evidences the complex negotiations between the almost-forgotten devotion to objectivity of the Revolutionary documentary and the more modern narrative film styles from abroad. Originally a twelve-part serial with explicit documentary ambitions, the film tells the real-life story of a band of thieves who pretended to be *carrancista* troops and robbed and kidnapped wealthy families throughout 1915 (fig. 4.4). The members of the band were eventually captured, tried, and sentenced to death. Their execution took place on December 24, 1915, and Rosas had filmed the event for his documentary

Documentación histórica nacional, 1915–1916. Because the band was linked to various military factions, the entire event was politically charged and Rosas's film version, combining historical facts and legends, vindicates and clears the image of the *carrancistas*. Like Toscano's *Viaje a Yucatán* and the Alva brothers' *Revolución orozquista*, however, the central structuring element of Rosas's film is the historical chronology of the events: the film presents the various robberies and the subsequent chase by the police in strict chronological order. Like *Aniversario del fallecimiento de la suegra de Enhart*, *El automóvil gris* was shot on location, where the robberies and chases took place (and includes footage of the execution of the gang members previously shot by Rosas). By comparing the two films, we can see how drastically Mexico City had changed in the intervening seven years: whereas in the earlier film we see people walking, interacting, and engaging in commerce in a clean and orderly city, in *El automóvil*, the city is in ruins, dirty, and almost completely empty.

El automóvil gris is the last Mexican silent film to have this kind of documentary feel—the last gasp of the previous documentary tradition—and, in its combination of documentary realism with touches of Italian melodrama, and sophisticated Hollywood-style cinematic syntax (i.e.,

Figure 4.4. Enrique Rosa's *El automóvil gris* (The Grey Automobile, 1919) was the most significant Mexican film of its era. Fair use.

irises, close-ups, the serial structure), it points to the future of Mexican sound cinema.

Peripheral Displacements

In complex negotiations between national events/traditions and foreign models and the demands of Westernization, Latin America produced a series of "spectacular experiments" that dialectically inscribed the cinema in national histories while simultaneously recognizing it as the embodiment of always differential dreams of modernity. Parochial yet also of the "world at large," the silent cinema was a key agent of both nationalism and globalization. With few if any proprietary claims to technology (the technology remained primarily an import), early cinema nevertheless contributed to the construction of strong nationalistic discourses of modernity. As evidenced by this comparative analysis, throughout the continent and despite certain regional differences, filmic visuality came to define the necessarily ambivalent position of those caught in the whirlpools of change, whether because of the shift from rural to urban life, displacements caused by immigration, or the cataclysms of civil war. A mechanism for accessible globality, the cinema captured and accompanied the vertiginous modernization of urban sectors, as well as the simultaneous inertia of other zones and territories: in the discursive struggle between the urban and the rural as icons of nationalisms, the cinema—the urban instrument par excellence—actively contributed to the postulation of the nonurban as a folkloric past or an anachronistic vestige.

Throughout the continent, national producers were faced with two significant changes in subsequent decades. The onset of World War I redefined the international cinematic marketplace; blocked from its usual markets and practices in Europe, US producers "discovered" the potential of the Latin American market and moved in aggressively. They consolidated their presence throughout the continent and, in most instances, effectively precluded national production from prospering commercially. This was quite marked in Brazil, for example, where the end of the *bela época* (circa 1912) coincided with the development of a strong distribution/exhibition sector geared to imports[19] and the subsequent arrival of subsidiaries of US firms.[20]

This shift was soon followed by a far more devastating change: the arrival of sound. Aggressively marketed, sound films from the US quickly took over the exhibition and distribution sectors, while national producers scrambled for capital, technology, and know-how. In some cases, the arrival of sound severed all cinematic activities: several nations—notably Bolivia, Venezuela, and Colombia—were not able to resume filmmaking until nearly a decade after the introduction of sound. Others—principally Mexico, Argentina, and Brazil—by hook or by crook, invented, adapted, and experimented, producing a different yet resonant version of early cinema. The sound cinema of the 1930s, 1940s, and 1950s would become the principal interlocutor of Latin American modernity—as Carlos Monsiváis (1997b) says, where Latin Americans went not to dream but to learn to be modern.

5

Film and Radio Intermedialities in Early Latin American Sound Cinema (2017)

This essay exemplifies the recent shift in López's scholarship to explore intermediality, or the relationship between different media—in this case between radio and film. Film scholars have portrayed the relationship between radio and early sound cinema in Latin America and elsewhere in terms of the "transfer" of recognizable stars, song forms, and narrative formulas from one well-established medium (radio) to another, newer one (film). However, in this essay, López argues that we must rethink this historiographical paradigm—noting that in Latin America the consolidation of radio as a mass medium occurred at the same time as the growth of film as a culture industry. The essay underscores the mutual relationship between these media and the way in which they both participated in a "perceptual revolution" and the reimagination of community in an era of rapid modernization. She demonstrates this through an analysis of three films from the 1930s–1940s: Ídolos de la radio *(Argentina, Eduardo Moreira, 1934),* Madre querida *(Mexico, Juan Orol, 1934), and* Cuando los hijos se van *(Mexico, Juan Bustillo Oro, 1941). Her intermedial approach to early sound cinema aligns with the work of younger scholars looking at the interface between photography and the cinema and the illustrated press and the cinema (Cuarterolo 2013; Navitski 2017, respectively). It also participates in a larger shift toward the investigation of media horizons and audiovisual landscapes as evident in the efforts of established academics like Paul Julian Smith (2017, 2018, 2019) and younger scholars such as Jacqueline Ávila and Olivia Cosentino.*

> Perhaps silencing the noise of the gaze we shall manage to listen, in
> new ways, to this long twentieth century and its contemporary legacies.
>
> —Ana María Ochoa Gautier,
> "El sonido y el largo siglo XX"

Radio Challenges to Latin American Film History

By the mid-1930s, radio and sound cinema had become commercially viable mass media in Latin America. Both were "new" media, and their parameters, powered by industrial and commercial imperatives, had yet to be fully refined. Radio and sound cinema would intersect, defining the overall mediascape of mid- to late 1930s Latin America. Therefore, this crucial decade needs to be seen as years of profound intermediality that reveal strategies of appropriation, accommodation, and, ultimately, layers of differentiation. As film scholars have noted, this was a moment of "crisis" for the cinema. But, rather than a period in which the new swept out the old, it was a period in which old and new media collided (Altman 2004, 13) and in which parallel intermedial processes served as the shifting base for the development of the "golden age" of Latin American national cinemas in the 1930s and 1940s. Focusing on the echoes of the radiophonic in early sound cinema, this chapter will explore the intersections, complements, and rivalries between sound cinema and radio in this period. Following Elsaesser (2004), it questions some of the standard historiographical assumptions through which this period has been understood. I want to interrogate a broader intermedial horizon in which we can trace the emergence of new audiovisual practices and social agents that set the stage for the regional appropriation and adaptation of sound cinema.

In standard histories of Latin American cinemas, this period of uncertainty and experimentation in between silent cinema and more industrial sound film production is typically presented as a necessary transition between almost artisanal silent cinema practices that continued through the 1930s, in some instances aligned with artistic avant-gardes (as with *Limite* in Brazil [Mário Peixoto 1931], *La mancha de sangre* in Mexico [The Bloodstain, Adolfo Best Maugard, 1937], and *Así nació el obelisco* in Argentina [Thus the Obelisk Was Born, Horacio Coppola, 1936]), and the institutionalization of the "Cinema" as an industrial or proto-industrial practice and an institutional mode of representation in the mid- to late 1930s and into the 1940s (King 1990, 23–36; Paranaguá 1996,

Film and Radio Intermedialities | 93

222–33). In most histories of national cinemas, the period is presented as one of "paralysis," representing the interruption of certain nation-based trajectories by the dislocating power of the new imported technologies and establishing a so-called need to "start from zero" (Machado 1987, 127; García Riera 1993a, 11–15; Maranghello 2005, 64). In fact, in a teleological historiographical move, the silent cinema is often subsequently refigured as the "prehistory" of what would become the national cinema "proper." As Argentine historian Domingo Di Núbila most eloquently expressed it, "The advent of sound established the frontier between the prehistory and the history of Argentine cinema" (Di Núbila 1998, 51).

In 1930–1931, filmmaking in Latin America certainly seemed on the brink of crisis. Hollywood sound feature films had spectacularly arrived in the preceding years and profoundly changed the cultural sphere: 1928 in Havana; 1929 in Buenos Aires, Mexico City, Rio de Janeiro, and Lima; and 1930 in Santiago de Chile (Godoy Quezada 1966, 35; Vieira 1987, 140; Bedoya 1992, 87; García Riera 1993a, 15; Douglas 1996, 53; España 1999, 25). In Peru, Chile, and Colombia, for example, silent film production continued haltingly through the 1930s. In Rio de Janeiro, however, film attendance declined precipitously by more than 40 percent (Vieira 1987, 135). There was little intracontinental expertise on sound film production. Only Mexico was in a somewhat better position because of its proximity to Hollywood and the constant North-South travel of film personnel. In Mexico and elsewhere, would-be sound filmmakers and creative and technical personnel traveled to Hollywood to learn about the new technology, and often to participate in the first wave of "Hispanic" films produced by the studios, which served as training for would-be national filmmakers and began to delimit the linguistic and sonic communities of a new cinematic submarket in Spanish (D'Lugo 2010; Jarvinen 2012). Despite the appeal of the new modern technology, the appearance of sound cinema in the region also led to intense public debates about the dangers of the "Yanqui plague," that is, having to listen to English in a movie theater (García Riera 1993a, 15; Morais da Costa 2008, 91–92) and the infiltration of "Yanqui" mores and ways of being in the world (Miquel 2005, 106–08). The sudden aural deluge, its potential unintelligibility, and foreign cultural mores were not the only perceived seismic changes introduced by sound cinema. As Otávio Gabus Mendes ironically argued in Brazil, "The cinema has become an auditory spectacle [in which] audiences must be rigorously silenced . . . silence the mouth, the feet, the seats" (Gabus Mendes 1929, 20).

The few films produced in 1930–1932 in Latin America either continued with silent cinema practices, sometimes rather spectacularly, and/or experimented with mostly homegrown sound-on-disc technologies (in fact, all the larger nations experimented with domestic sound-recording technologies): *Acabarem-se os Otários* (The End of the Simpletons, Luiz de Barros, 1929) and *Coisas Nossas* (Our Things, Wallace Downey, 1931) in Brazil; *Muñequitas porteñas* (Buenos Aires Dolls, José Agustín Ferreyra, 1931) in Argentina; and *Abismos* or *Náufragos de la vida* (Abysses or Castaways from Life, Salvador Pruneda, 1930), *Más fuerte que el deber* (Stronger than Duty, Raphael J. Sevilla, 1930), and *Santa* (Antonio Moreno, 1931) in Mexico. Many of these experimental sound-recording systems exploited existing disc-recording technologies and innovated mechanisms to synchronize sound with image and to project it, a bricolage deemed necessary given the inaccessibility and expense of the imported technological apparatuses. Thus, we need to move beyond what are at best "confused chronologies" to consider the interaction between the two mass media in order to better understand the impact of both popular media on the shaping of audiences.

New Intermedial Chronologies

That the emergence of locally produced sound films coincides with the consolidation of radio as a mass medium is of significance on at least two levels. First, it means that the chronology of the massification of the two media follows a more intermedial path than was the case elsewhere; second, the emergence of "national" styles/idioms occurs simultaneously in radio and in the cinema. In terms of the advent of mass audiences, in the US, for example, radio was already a mass medium by the late 1920s, as evidenced by the Radio Act of 1927 and the establishment of the Federal Radio Commission to regulate the airwaves.

By contrast, the diffusion of radio set ownership and the establishment of radio stations and national networks occurred later and more slowly in Latin America. Despite the fact that radio transmissions began in the region in the early 1920s (1920 in Buenos Aires, 1921 in Mexico City, 1922 in Rio de Janeiro and Montevideo), the diffusion of the medium was sluggish by comparison to the US, and radio ownership, radio stations, and networks only began to grow exponentially in the 1930s. In 1929, for example, Argentina indisputably led Latin America in radio set ownership, but with only 525,000 sets (22.86 per 1,000 inhabitants, or with a population of almost 12 million, a penetration rate of approximately 26 percent of families, estimating average family size of 6) and 22 stations. In the much larger Brazil, there were only 250,000 radio sets (6.43/1,000; penetration of 4.5 percent) and 15 stations, and in Mexico only 50,000 radio sets (3.49/1,000; penetration of 2 percent) and 19 operating radio stations (Batson 1929, 25). Other statistics suggest a somewhat higher level of penetration (Claxton 2007, 149), but the fact remains that the massiveness of radio was relative and uneven in the region. It is not until the mid- to late 1930s that Latin American radio would become a mass medium with national reach. According to an Argentine study from 1934, there were roughly 900,000 radio receivers in Latin America, two-thirds of them in Argentina (600,000), 150,000 in Brazil, and 100,000 in Montevideo (Matallana 2006, 36).

In the US, when sound fiction cinema became commercially viable circa 1929–1930, radio was already a well-established medium and had already created appropriate social subjects attuned to aurality: technologically shaped *listeners*. As noted by the *New York Times* in 1930, radio had already created a "sound receptive audience" for the talkies: "The spread of radio broadcasting had . . . familiarized the general public with dramatic dialogue and high-grade music to a far greater extent than ever before" (Crafton 2004, 150). In Latin America, on the other hand, radio and sound cinema became commercially viable only in the 1930s, synergistically feeding off each other's successes and strategies. Radio and incipient sound film practices were interdependent: they shared multiple economic interests throughout the continent, as well as important crossovers and interrelationships of creative personnel (stars, singers, and actors, but also writers, producers, announcers, and comedians). In 1930s Latin America, these new social subjects—the listeners, social agents who listen—and their new activity, "listening," were produced simultaneously by both sound cinema and radio.

Throughout Latin America, radio and sound cinema reconfigured the aurality of the public sphere and the sensorial competencies of audiences. Akin to what Susan J. Douglas has argued for the US, radio redefined a culture that had been "glutted with visual stimuli":

> With the introduction of the telephone, the phonograph, and then [more definitively] radio, there was a revolution in our aural environment that prompted a major perceptual and

cognitive shift in the country, with a new emphasis on hearing. Because sound is dynamic and fleeting, radio conveyed a powerful sense of "liveness." (Douglas 2004, 7)

Similarly, sound technologies also generated a renewed sense of aurality and reimagination of community that further challenged and reconfigured visual/literate culture. Douglas also emphasizes the need to recognize and identify different modes of "listening," arguing that *how* and *where* we listen and have historically listened to radio in America is crucial to understanding its impact in different eras, its particular ways of shaping individual and collective subjectivities (7-9). Although the literature on "listening" is relatively undeveloped in contrast to the literature on "spectatorship," it is clear that they constitute two different, albeit since the 1920s-1930s, complementary realms of the experience of media. In this context, then, the question is: How does the simultaneity of the perceptual revolution of radio and the redefinition of the cinema in Latin America as also an aural medium, speaking (and singing) in Spanish and Portuguese, impact the formation of "listeners" and the various modes through which Latin Americans learned and experimented with new ways of being as listeners? The construction of listening as a social practice was jointly undertaken by the two media, redefining leisure time. Radio trained listeners and created new social and social positions from which to listen: as a listening family, in the living room composed around the set; as sports fans, avidly following a game at home through the voice of the *locutor*; as a collective, in the auditorium shows in the studios where audiences could also see their favorite performers; as a housewife, while busy with tasks in the house but now with a new freedom: the acoustic time to listen (and to consume). Early sound cinema simultaneously reinforced and expanded these new social agents and positions, legitimizing them even while sometimes putting them into question.

Although not really discussed by Douglas (since being "modern" was not much of a concern in 1920s-1930s America), being a "listener" in Latin America also activated a significant cultural sense of modernity. As Jonathan Sterne (2003) has traced in *The Audible Past*, technology-mediated listening—and the skills necessary to decipher and decode what is heard—had been, at least since the eighteenth century, a signpost and constitutive of an evolving and ever-growing sense of modernity in the US and Western Europe, albeit not often necessarily acknowledged. Early silent cinema in Latin America allowed spectators to participate in a complex peripheral modernity centered on visuality, which resonated with the intellectual notion of a *ciudad letrada*/lettered city. Radio and sound cinema thus amplified and made accessible a new experience of modernity as "listener," appropriate for a different social and political context: new social subjects that assert their modernity and their locality and nationness, even as they assert their cosmopolitanism and incipient globality.

What makes these comparative chronologies of radio-film culture appear confused is that the establishment of sound cinema industries in Mexico, Argentina, and Brazil took place in the context of the insistent presence of Hollywood sound cinema. Without exception, sound cinema "arrived" in Latin America and did not have an "organic" evolution (although, of course, "sound" per se had always been available in movie theaters through live and recorded music, synchronization of live voices, and other "tricks"). Contemporary studies of the introduction of sound to cinema in the US have tended to downplay the transitional nature of this period, perhaps rightly so in the US context: "Sound cinema was not a radical alternative to silent filmmaking; sound as sound, as a material and as a set of technical procedures was inserted into the already-constituted system of the classical Hollywood style" (Bordwell et al. 1985, 301). Although synchronized sound did not "fundamentally change the textuality of Hollywood films, it did arguably make the system stronger and more normative" and shifted control from exhibitors to producers (Williams 1992, 128–29). In Latin America, however, even those countries that had sustained production through the 1920s were caught in a profound transitional mode and hard-pressed by the simultaneous technical and economic demands of sound cinema and the very precise and loudly proclaimed demands for nationness from critics, intellectuals, and audiences, who demanded linguistic authenticity and an imaginary national singularity from domestic producers.

Hollywood films were steadily exported to Latin America throughout this period and beyond, especially after the Hollywood studios invested in theaters in Latin America equipped with sound technology to help diffuse the "new" medium. As Gaizka S. de Usabel argues, in the early sound era Latin America was "the leading market for Hollywood films . . . and was ahead of Europe in the number of big capacity theaters" (de Usabel 1982, 80). The Hollywood studios invested heavily in updating the exhibition infrastructure of theaters in Latin American capitals, even in cities such as Buenos Aires, where some distributors, such as Max Glücksmann, who was also heavily invested in discography, were already beginning to self-finance the retrofitting of theaters (Maranghello 2005, 56). As early as 1930, 132 of the 830 movie theaters in Mexico had already been outfitted for sound (de los Reyes 1987, 118), and by 1937 there were close to 125,000 theater seats in houses outfitted for sound (Alfaro Salazar and Ochoa Vega 1997, 221–24). By 1932, 25 percent of film theaters in Latin America had been wired for sound and were ready to receive the ever-increasing output of Hollywood sound films and national productions (de Usabel 1982, 81).

This second layer of intermediality is of great importance, since subsequent "national" styles/idioms and cinematic strategies were therefore also inescapably linked to a panoply of Hollywood influences and practices. The intermedial matrix of this period is thus not only film and radio (and other sound reproduction technologies), but "film," "Hollywood film," and radio/sound reproduction. When we stop to consider that Hollywood sound films in English were initially unintelligible to most audiences unless subtitled and/or dubbed, the interrelationship among these interlocking technologies becomes even more complicated, since the standard Spanish-speaking spectator would have had to read, exercising the visual and literate, rather than fully engage in the new social and ostensibly very modern role of being a "listener" that the new technologies promised. As José Gatti suggests, an audience who must read subtitles will necessarily neither view nor hear carefully: the subtitles must be read first, and only if time permits can the eye focus on the image while the ear disconnects from foreign-language dialogue, and will at best only process music and noises (Gatti 2000, 94). How does this impact the experience and pleasure of being a modern listening subject of radio and sound cinema? Ultimately, it seems that in Latin America, being a fulfilled listening subject at the movies could only be realized through the imagined visual and sonic communities produced by national cinemas (in Spanish/Portuguese).

Finally in smaller Latin American countries such as Chile, Uruguay, Cuba, and Colombia, in which sound national cinemas appear much later (1934 in Chile with *Norte y sur* [North and South, Jorge Delano "Coke"], 1936 in Uruguay with *Dos destinos* [Two Destinies, Juan Etchebehere], 1937 in Cuba with *La serpiente roja* [The Red Serpent, Ernesto Caparrós], and 1938 in Colombia with *Al son de las guitarras* [To the Tune of the Guitars, Alberto Santana and Carlos Schroeder]), the chronology is different once again. In these countries, sound cinema emerges not only under the influence of radio and Hollywood films, but also under the often more significant influence of the films of the earlier Latin American innovators, especially the more widely exported Mexican and Argentine cinemas. It is therefore not surprising that intermedial relationships are quite complex in these other national sound cinemas, few of which would obtain "industrial" status (i.e., steady production) until much later, if at all.

Echoes of the Radiophonic

In general, intermedialities are textually evidenced in three areas that remain constant throughout the period: music and the performative; diegetic, formal, and stylistic cross-fertilizations; and melodramatic narrative platforms. Synergistically, the performative and the affective (sentimentalism, banality, and melodrama) were the principal registers of radiophonic intermedialities. There is also a historical progression: if, in the 1930s, music and performance are the primary sites of these intermedialities, by the end of the 1930s and into the early 1940s, films in the region exhibit more complex echoes of the radiophonic through narrative, especially through melodrama. Rather than present a catalog of filmic evidence from throughout the region to support this thesis, I will focus my analysis on key scenes from two films of the 1930s–1940s (alluding to a handful of others) that point to the textual complexities of this radio-film relationship and its evolution.

Musicality and the Performative

Early sound cinema and radio are linked by their dependence on music, more specifically by the development and consolidation of the nationness of music. Whether tango in Argentina, rancheras in Mexico, or sambas in Brazil, radio and sound cinema found in these national rhythms a way to assert their own singularity and national imaginaries and to create mass audiences. And for sound cinema, radio itself provided a framework through which to engage the new technology. Thus, popular rhythms are the engine that drove radio as well as early sound cinema in Latin America, establishing an exciting and complex synergy that defined the national as modern and incipient and their own singularity, national imaginaries, and mass audiences. In early sound cinema, the centrality of music is most evident not only because of its presence in the soundtrack, but because it is above all visibly performed and ostensibly experienced "live." It is not surprising therefore, that every national cinema explored and exploited the representation of musicality by seeking recourse to radio station settings and stories and performers who were becoming media stars through their exposure through radio and recorded music. Many of these films functioned to provide what the invisibility of radio precluded: the image of the singing body and the visual restaging of the moment of radio performance. As João Luiz Vieira has argued in regard to the two first Brazilian films with direct sound (*Alô, Alô Brasil* [Hello, Hello Brazil, 1935] and *Alô, Alô Carnaval* [Hello, Hello Carnaval, 1936], both directed by Wallace Downey), these films functioned as "a sort of visualized radio" that changed the position of the cinema spectator, supplementing the visual pleasure of the bodies of the singing radio stars. It was as if "had he closed his eyes, the spectator could have been sitting in front of a radio" (Vieira 2003, 48). Thus, it should not be a surprise that Latin American cinema through the 1940s and well into the 1950s privileged songs performed in their entirety rather than orchestral soundtracks. As a result, performance was always part of the diegesis, and the narrative actors were also coincidentally (and not always diegetically justified) musical performers: Libertad Lamarque in Argentina was always also a performer, even in the most lachrymose melodramas, but that Tito Guízar can sing like a radio star is never justified narratively in *Allá en el Rancho Grande* (Over on the Big Ranch, Fernando de Fuentes, 1936).

In Argentina, radio had been steadily popularizing singers, comedians, tango orchestras, and announcers (*locutores*) since the late 1920s and already had specialized publications dedicated to the medium and its stars: *Radiolandia* (1927), *Antena* (1930), and *Sintonía* (1933). *Ídolos de la radio* (Radio Idols, Eduardo Morera, 1934, Argentina) premiered at the Monumental Theater in Buenos Aires on October 24, 1934, and its huge popular success was almost guaranteed by its visual display of some of the most famous radio (and theater) stars of the time—Ada Falcón, Ignacio Corsini, Pablo Osvaldo Valle, Olinda Bozán, Tito Luisardo, and Ernesto Fama, among others. It was produced by the company Productora Cinematográfica Argentina Río de la Plata, an apparently hastily put together collaboration between tango composer/singer Francisco Canaro, radio magnate Jaime Yankelevich (owner of Radio Nacional, after 1935, Radio Belgrano), and lawyer and radio entrepreneur Juan Cossio, who aimed to maximize their radio enterprise through the new markets enabled by sound cinema. The artistic director of the production company and director of the film, Eduardo Morera (who had experience with sound film technology, having been in charge of the early Carlos Gardel shorts filmed in Buenos Aires), was in accord that their goal was to reach the same popular mass audience of Radio Nacional/Belgrano (Gómez Rial 1999, 250–60).

Certainly, *Ídolos de la radio* fulfilled this ambition. The inclusion of more than half a dozen complete musical numbers in one hundred minutes suggests that there was little time for narrative development. Although very much in the style of the musical revue films with which Hollywood had begun its incursions into sound but would soon abandon, in addition to all the musical performances, the film does have a well-developed dual-focus narrative: a love plot and a rags-to-stardom (in radio) plot. As if to highlight its intermedial origins, the credit sequence is superimposed atop silhouetted images of film and radio production scenarios—cameramen holding reels, silhouetted men speaking into microphones—and still photographs of its principal stars (reminiscent of similar photographs that would have already appeared in publicity magazines). Yet in its very first scene, the film already announces an alleged perceptual and/or experiential superiority over the radiophonic. Despite its economy of means, the film announces its status as "cinema" with an elegant track that shows decorations and stops at a hand annotating sheet music. At this point, a female voice in off seems to be reading a job ad from the newspaper. A pan left and a cut barely concealed by a wipe effect discloses the speaker, a young woman who comments on the difficulty of finding jobs. Another fake wipe brings us to a newspaper and the original voice is revealed, when the newspaper is dropped, as that of an older woman who continues reading job ads. After economically and very cinematically establishing a family unit of an Italian immigrant grandfather and two sisters looking for work (the younger played by the great tango singer Ada Falcón in a rare screen appearance), the scene shifts in tone when the doorbell rings to introduce a man (a German Jewish immigrant by his accent and attire) claiming to want to buy the family's radio. As they negotiate over the price of the radio, the Ada Falcón character asserts that one can hear all the stations very well and the older sister proceeds to adjust the dial, in an instructional close-up. The first station heard seems to be addressing the buyer directly: "Mister, don't let yourself be tricked, purchase cheaper!" She quickly retunes to another station airing a melodramatic *radionovela*. After alternating close-ups from the buyer and the sister to the radio apparatus as the third protagonist, a new shot focuses on the radio's electrical cord and, quickly panning left, uses the cord to establish an interesting sense of visual continuity with the cord of

Figure 5.1. The electrical cord of the radio in the living room links to the microphone in the radio station in *Ídolos de la radio* (Radio Idols, Eduardo Morera, 1934). Fair use.

a microphone in a radio studio, where the actors of the *radionovela* are performing (fig. 5.1). The scene in the studio discloses that the plaintive cry of a baby in the radio drama is produced by a fat mustachioed man straddling a chair before we cut back to the living room, where the sister and the radio buyer are visibly moved by the story. Cutting back to the studio, an announcer approaches the mic to announce that we have heard episode number 2,945 of the *radionovela* "The grief of a mother, or when pain hurts." Without a break, the announcer continues with a promotional spot: "If your shoes hurt, buy Double X shoes. They are the best."

Once again in the living room, we see the sister still raptly listening as the radio announcer continues and announces a contest to select the "Queen of Tango." This radio contest will serve as the narrative motor that will propel the rest of the plot, in which Ada will sing her grandfather's compositions to become a tango star and find true love in the arms of the already established star Ignacio Corsini.

Thus, although the film is clearly intended to build upon the success and penetration of radio with popular audiences, it also rather quickly asserts its own superiority as a medium that gives the cinematic audience vision as well as sound: its authority is legitimated by the fact that it can show the workings of radio, the lies and tricks that cannot be heard by the naïve radio listener. As well, radio gives it the tools through which to establish its own novel form of continuity: the radiophonic apparatus itself, the cord that visually links the receiver to the microphone through the otherwise invisible ether, narratively rationalizes the quick juxtaposition of vastly different spatial and sonic spaces through the radiophonic. Nevertheless, at the end of the sequence, the announcement of the tango queen contest is neither questioned nor doubted: the listeners in the living room "believe" and so must the narrative . . . and the audience.

Beyond Musicality and the "Broadcastings": The Radiophonic as Narrative and Stylistic Engine

To the degree that musicality and the performative were central to radiophonic filmic intermedialities, the establishment of a narrative platform centered on melodrama, sentimentalism, and banality was also a significant intermedial process. Melodrama was, of course, already an integral part of silent cinema throughout the region, often developing under the guise of nationalist themes and the influence of the very popular Italian diva films of the 1910s–1920s (especially in Mexico), melodramatic tango lyrics (the *arrabal* films of José Agustín Ferreyra in Argentina), and Hollywood films. Early radio throughout the region, although at first focused more on music and news, quickly began to experiment with narrative modes, developing novel ways of telling stories. It had to learn how to stimulate the imagination through aurality, extremely stylized voices, music, and noises to produce the necessary excess. The process began with radial adaptations of popular literature such as Alejandro Galindo and his brother Marcos Aurelio's 1932 adaptation of Dumas's *The Three Musketeers* for XEW, "The Voice of Latin America from Mexico," or popular/folkloric themes and *sainetes* exploited by traveling theatrical companies such as Andrés González Pulido's *Chispazos de tradición* (Sparks of Tradition, 1931) in Argentina. Listening to narratives on the radio became a popular pastime identified as *radionovelas* (and linked to commercial sponsorships not unlike that of US soap operas). *Radionovelas* emerged under the mantle of serial popular literature, the *folletín*, popular theatrical genres, and the Hollywood serial films that had already visualized these earlier forms.

In Latin America, we can trace a melodramatic radiophonic intermediality since the earliest days of sound cinema. For example, in *Madre querida* (Dear Mother, Juan Orol, 1934), an Ur-radiophonic melodrama, Juan Orol (who was affiliated with the XEB station, the oldest in Mexico, owned by the Compañía Cigarrera del Buen Tono) begins with a *locutor*-like preamble featuring Orol speaking directly to the spectators from behind a desk, like an embodied authoritative male radio announcer (the vast majority of *locutores* were male), dedicating the film to the *madrecitas* of the world who, as mothers, have inevitably suffered, and setting up the scene for the melodramatic excess to come. Later on, the film acknowledges and embodies the new social position of the listeners. In a crucial scene thick with longing, the boy without a mother and with a father who thinks he is widowed listen to a radio broadcast about Mother's Day in the living room (fig. 5.2). Intercut with shots of the *locutor* at the XEB

Figure 5.2. Embodying the new social position of "listeners." *Madre querida* (Dear Mother, Juan Orol, 1934). Fair use.

studios and other unidentified families also listening to the same broadcast exalting motherhood, the film acknowledges the listeners as an invisible community and reels them into the melodrama, a shared pathos, through the mediation of the radiophonic.

By 1941, almost a decade after the convergence of sound media had begun, the relationship between the cinema and radio had changed. Radio had consolidated its popularity and had become a ubiquitous mass medium, while nationally and internationally the Mexican national cinema had also begun to hit its stride since the success of *Allá en el Rancho Grande* in 1936 and found audience niches. In the realm of filmic melodrama, the national and international success of *Cuando los hijos se van* (When the Children Leave Home, 1941, Juan Bustillo Oro) was seen as an engine for the increasing prestige of the national cinema and for the consolidation of the genre of suffering mothers (Bustillo Oro 1984, 193–96). It is, as Ayala Blanco argued, "the archetype of the family melodrama genre" (Ayala Blanco 1979, 50–51).

Cuando los hijos se van begins with a radiophonic frame: the film exploits the certainty that audiences already knew how to be listeners, invokes them as listeners, and gifts them with the privilege to see. After the credits, the diegesis begins with a 2.5-minute voice-over sequence introducing the setting, a colonial home in Orizaba with multiple interior enclosures, and the date: "December 24th some years ago." The doors and porticos of the house open as the resonant male voice invites us to enter "with the same emotions we felt when crossing our own thresholds." The *locutor*-like voice describes the interior patio in detail, linking specific features—the rose bushes, the trees—to the labor and sacrifice of the father and mother and laying out explicit hooks for the audience to establish affective links with the empty and still sterile space. As the camera enters the living room, for example, the voice-over asks, in a very radiophonic aural invocation of the senses, "What aroma is that? It smells like distant and happy times . . . of pine . . . of nativity scenes!" The *locutor* we never see is Manuel Bernal, a beloved XEW *locutor* famous for arguing that "in radio the voice is the image," and therefore remaining a rather mysterious public figure throughout his career; his voice would have been instantly recognizable, believable, and trustworthy to a 1940s audience in Mexico (Mota Martínez and Nuñez Herrera 1998, 149–52). This was a voice the public knew how to listen and respond to. As Bernal's voice introduces the scenario and the camera penetrates the interior spaces, he remarks, "We are invisible witnesses. No one will hear our steps or even the accelerated beats of our hearts. No one will notice our presence. Invisible, just like the radio: imagine what my voice describes, nevertheless the film will show it to you." This voice-over introduces the narrative and will interrupt the plot three other times to move the story forward, to explain temporal changes, and to comment upon the passage of time. It is the structural thread that makes sense of the temporal elisions and it invokes something else: a desire for the guidance of that ethereal radio voice that gives shape and meaning to experience. Serving the same function that would be fulfilled by a *radionovela locutor*—extensively describing locales and linking them to affective states, establishing an initial enigma to be explored, guiding and manipulating the reading, and pointing to a certain moral order to be maintained—the voice-over uses the radiophonic as an affective shortcut to effectively begin the story, having already secured the desired listening and spectatorial state and interpellating the audience as part of an affective community.

Thus, enveloped by the aura and emotional appeal of the radiophonic, the story unfolds: the threat to the sanctity of the family and its dynamics when the children, seduced by circumstances and opportunities or unfairly banished, leave home for the city. The emotional climax of the narrative curiously occurs through the radiophonic not at the end, but about two-thirds of the way through the travails of the by then reduced family unit: father Pepe (Fernando Soler), mother Guadalupe (Sara García), and compadre Casimiro (Joaquín Pardavé), who lives across the street in a space we never see. It is May 10, Mother's Day, and Casimiro brings Guadalupe a radio set as a present and a newspaper clipping announcing that her beloved favorite son Raimundo (who had been unfairly banished from the family home) is going to sing on the radio in a special Mother's

Day program. However, saddled by debt she has incurred to help one of the least deserving of her children, the holder of her IOUs arrives to seize her furnishings, including the new radio, for repayment. The scene is then staged (for over ten minutes) in between staggering close-ups of Sara García weeping as she listens to her son singing and almost hugging the radio, and cutaways to Casimiro and to the men who had come to pick up her belongings (some of whom are visibly moved). Functioning as an umbilical cord that permits communication between mother and son, the radio set fulfills her oft-proclaimed desire to hear his voice again (fig. 5.3). To hear his voice, not just to see him. Once again, the film proclaims the importance of being a listener and wraps it up under the mantle of an affective miasma that sweeps all other concerns under the rug.

If the valence in earlier films was dismantling the veracity of radio, that is here disavowed. Radio is both a structuring principle for the narrative and the vehicle for its most affective denouement. The radiophonic and the filmic are one.

Figure 5.3. Sara García's radiophonic apotheosis from *Cuando los hijos se van* (When the Children Leave, Juan Bustillo Oro, 1941). Fair use.

Conclusions

By recognizing the multivalent intermedial relationships between radio and film in Latin America as both a comparative model with the US experience and as a contrastive study of uneven development within the region, we are able to formulate a series of questions that have usually been short-circuited by most Latin American film histories. Among these is the need to question the implications of the construction of mass audiences; we are speaking here of listeners and spectators who were also social subjects and whose social positioning was stabilized, if not formed, through the technological mediation of the practice of listening. Beyond questioning how the mediascape was constructed, in tandem, by technologies that learned and competed with each other to build mass audiences, we need to further interrogate the material practices of film and radio through which "listening" as a social position was stabilized. This is not simply a question of teasing out elements of class, ideology, or political manipulation in particular texts. The interrogation of the complementarity of intermedial practices leads, perhaps inevitably, to questions of cultural/ social identity formation in a period of rapid modernization.

To the degree that being modern in earlier decades meant being attuned to the spectacular visualities of the silent cinema, in the 1930s and early 1940s, that modernity had shifted and invoked listening in a new way as the crystallization of the attitudes required by the new media and their new commercial imperatives. An intermedial lens helps us to understand this period in greater depth and should also prove helpful to unravel the complexities of similar moments of "crisis" as transitions have occurred in the Latin American mediascape.

6

From Hollywood and Back

Dolores Del Rio, a Trans(national) Star (1998)

Published the same year as "National History, Transnational History," this essay exemplifies López's method of tracing transnational linkages between film industries through the analysis of the professional trajectories of "talent" (actors and directors). Here she explores the transnational stardom of Mexican actress Dolores Del Rio across her late silent/1930s Hollywood and classical Mexican cinema career. Arguing that earlier nation-focused star studies of Mexican and Latin American performers often obscure important transcontinental forces and exchanges in the classical period, López highlights how Del Rio's stardom is, like Latin American cinema itself in the classical era, a fundamentally transnational phenomenon. The essay provided a renovated model of star studies and served as a precursor to the proliferation of English-language scholarship on Latin American stars and Latina bodies in film and media in the 2000s (see Beltrán 2009, Hershfield 2000, Mendible 2007, Molina-Guzmán 2014, Peña Ovalle 2011).

Research for this essay was made possible, in part, by grants from the Royer Thayer Stone Center for Latin American Studies at Tulane University. My thanks to Rebecca Ellner for her diligent research of Dolores Del Rio's Hollywood career. Versions of this essay were presented at the National Film Theater (London) and the King Juan Carlos I of Spain Center (New York University).

Images of a Star

- Chicana artist Amalia Mesa-Bains produced a series of seven installation pieces or "altars" between 1983 and 1993 paying homage to Dolores Del Rio. Simultaneously of the home and of the public sphere, these altars reinscribe the figure of Dolores Del Rio into the museum and the Chicano imaginary.

- In David Avalos's *Ramona: Story of a Miscegenation* (1991), an experimental Chicano video, the figure of Del Rio—in *Ramona* but also in other films—is one of the narrative engines used to unpack a century's worth of stereotypes in the US representation of Latinos.

- A contemporary Los Angeles restaurant menu includes, as one of its salads, the "Dolores Del Rio," which is described as "a combination of tomatoes, red onions, zucchini, celery, carrots, cucumbers, and mushrooms, all on a bed of lettuce. Your choice of dressing." This is the only salad on the menu that offers such an option.

- In addition to copious press coverage, in 1930, even before she had made the transition to sound, Dolores had already been the subject of a book-length study, published simultaneously in Madrid, Barcelona, and Buenos Aires: *Dolores del Rio: La Triunfadora* by Rafael Martínez Gandía (1930).

- Many Mexican artists have used the figure of Dolores Del Rio in paintings, poetry, plays, and fiction, among them Adolfo Best Maugard, Diego Rivera, José Clemente Orozco, Salvador Novo, Carlos Pellicer, Alfonso Reyes, Jaime Torres Bodet, Paco Ignacio Taibo I with *Siempre Dolores* (1984) and Carlos Fuentes with *Orquídeas a la luz de la luna* (1982).

- A recent internet search disclosed not only several places in the world where her films were being shown, but also a bevy of sites in which her name appears, among them the site Romantically Linked, in which she is associated with a series of nine personalities, other than her husbands, including, of course, Orson Welles, but also Porfirio Rubirosa, Walt Disney, and Greta Garbo.

The central question that these facts and images suggest is, on the surface, straightforward: How to study a transnational star, an actress whose career overlapped with at least two national cinemas and who continues to have a presence in the US, Mexican, and Latin American imaginaries? First we must question the relationship between stardom and nationness. Hollywood stars and stardom have been copiously studied, but always through a hegemonic and often unconscious national prism that presumes that Hollywood stardom is stardom in and of itself. Even the most recent books and anthologies on stars and stardom barely acknowledge the troubling presence of other star systems, other bodies, and other nationalities.[1] Furthermore, Hollywood star studies rarely acknowledge stars' acting forays in other national cinemas or the repercussions of stardom—Hollywood or otherwise—in other cultural contexts. In other national cinemas, stardom as a phenomenon has barely begun to be theorized and most so-called star studies are little more than biography. There are a number of star biographies in Mexican film studies, for example, but the kind of transnational focus that I am calling for here goes against the grain of a scholarly project—the chronicle and defense of Mexican cinema—which is usually articulated in relationship to the national. Beyond a consideration of stars, the cinemas of Latin America, be they the New Latin American Cinema or the "Golden Age" cinemas of the 1930s and '40s, have generally been studied as discrete national phenomena, framed primarily by the sociopolitical vagaries of each state and only incidentally linked to continental or international social changes and movements.[2] This focus on nation and the corollary search for difference and uniqueness has obscured a series of important transcontinental forces and exchanges in the classical period because in the 1940s and '50s the cinema in Latin America was already—and perhaps had always been—a transnational phenomenon.

Thus the issue of transnational influences in the classical period that the case of Dolores Del Rio highlights is a fascinating historical puzzle that questions the viability of the "national" as the signpost of film histories by highlighting the hybridization potentially inherent to all national cinemas. Against the prevailing myth of national cinematic insularity and histories of national achievements and failures, I want to argue for the need to look at the history of Latin American cinema from a continental perspective that includes, but mediates, the national. The Mexican cinema, for example, was a national and nationalist cinema, but also profoundly transnational (Fein 1994). It is precisely its transnational contexts and alliances that allowed it to develop some of its most "nationalistic" characteristics, icons, and stars like Dolores Del Rio. I want to use Del Rio's unique career, which began in Hollywood in the silent period, continued and climaxed in Mexico in the 1940s, and also featured a few subsequent appearances in Hollywood, as a catalyst to enable a discussion of the transnationality of Hollywood and of postwar Mexican cinema and their mutual industrial and ideological linkages. Thus the figure of the traveling actor—Del Rio—as a site for tracing the mediation of nationness should function as a key for opening up a space for transnational analyses of the classic cinemas, be they Mexican or Hollywood.

Del Rio's transnational stardom suggests a series of overlapping questions: Why does Dolores Del Rio become a significant Hollywood star when so many others—especially Latin American women—failed? How and why does her return to Mexico shift her star persona and produce her as a national myth? What does it mean that she still fascinates us? How does she function as a symbol of Latinidad in the United States imaginary? In order to provisionally answer these questions, I shall attempt to weave a web of sociohistorical and cinematic evidence that addresses various levels of agency and determination, ranging from the individual herself—that is, from biography—to the social/national and the transnational.

How Hollywood Created a Star

"Lolita" was born Dolores Asúnsolo López Negrete on August 3, 1905, into an aristocratic Durango family that fled from Pancho Villa to Mexico City in 1910. After studying in a convent where she was educated in French and taking private lessons with a famous dancer, Lolita married her first husband, Jaime Martínez del Río, shortly after her sixteenth birthday. He was eighteen years her senior, a lawyer educated in Europe, and part of an old aristocratic Castilian family that had been in Mexico for decades and was socially prominent. After a long honeymoon in Europe, the couple settled into the elegant life of the Mexico City aristocracy: parties, dances, and teas.

Her entry into the cinema was accidental: Hollywood director Edwin Carewe, honeymooning in Mexico in the summer of 1925, was brought to her house (by painter and family friend Adolfo Best Maugard) for a "tea" and convinced her and her husband to go to Hollywood. The rationales for the move appear to have been multiple. First of all, like most young women of the period, Dolores adored the movies, read movie magazines, and collected star photographs. Simply meeting stars, much less becoming one, was an exciting prospect. Furthermore, there had already been several well-publicized Hollywood "star searches" in Mexico City that surely would have captured her interest (De la Vega Alfaro and Torres San Martín 1997). Perhaps most importantly, the move to Hollywood offered her and Jaime an opportunity to begin a new life, away from the conservative values of their respective families. For both the move represented affirming themselves against their families. In any case, within days of their arrival in Hollywood in late 1925, Dolores was in front of the cameras in a secondary role as a Spanish countess in *Joanna* (1925), the film Carewe was then directing.

Del Río's rise to stardom was as quick as the disintegration of her personal life. The cinema, rather than bring the couple closer, tore them apart. Jaime did not like being "Mr. Del Río" and his own career as a writer was going nowhere. After two trial separations Dolores filed for divorce in 1928,[3] while rumors about her relationship to Carewe were flying high. He was her manager and successfully got her roles in First National, Fox, Metro, Universal, and United Artists productions, several of which he directed himself.[4] While he directed her in *Ramona* in 1928 he also divorced his wife Mary Aiken, and he and Del Ríos traveled together to Mazatlán on his own yacht for some location shooting for their next film, *Revenge*. Dolores denied their relationship, but called her mother to live with her to suppress the gossip. As she said years later: "Everything happened to me. Things broke down around me. Terrible and tragic things" (Parrish 1978). In late 1928, Jaime del Río died suddenly of blood poisoning. Now Dolores was ostensibly free to concentrate upon her career in a different way.

In the silent period, Carewe was perhaps Del Río's best director; certainly they aided each other's careers. To begin with, Carewe's press agents were responsible for circulating constant releases about Dolores and gave her a "name" even before she had any starring roles. As Rafael Martínez Gandía, her first chronicler, astutely complained as early as 1930:

> What is most surprising in Dolores del Río's (*sic*) lightning fast climb to fame is that her triumph was not due to impeccable acting before the cameras. . . . Dolores del Río became a personality without proving her merits. Thanks to Carewe and to his publicity campaigns her name was known throughout the world much before her first films. (1930, 15, 16—17)[5]

This same press machinery is also the central topic of Paco Ignacio Taibo I's novel *Siempre Dolores*, in which the author's alter ego is none other than the young press agent/lover responsible for creating Dolores's Hollywood star image. In any case, critics did notice that in Carewe's films, Del Rio seemed at her best and he perfected her silent image as the "female Rudolf Valentino," a dark beauty with cupid lips who acted, above all, with her face, and, secondarily via hand and body movements (fig. 6.1). After the tremendous success of *Ramona* and *Revenge*, the couple arranged a lucrative five-million-dollar contract with United Artists. As their fortunes rose, however, their relationship cooled. Perhaps because of Jaime's death, Dolores withdrew from Carewe and, after they filmed *Evangeline* in 1929, Carewe sold her contract to United Artists.[6]

Carewe's role in the "creation" of Del Rio as a Hollywood star is important and linked to the already significant cinematic relations between

Figure 6.1. Dolores Del Rio in the silent era: a female Valentino. Courtesy of Centro de Estudios de Historia de México, Condumex.

Mexico and Hollywood. Carewe may have been on his honeymoon when he went to Mexico, but he must also have been thinking about his business. The previous two films that his small independent company had produced had been threatened with bans by the Mexican government for their depiction of Mexicans. And an independent producer with limited means like Carewe could not afford to lose the lucrative Mexican market, since his success was dependent upon quick returns on investment. The Mexican government's censorship policies were already well known and somewhat feared by Hollywood producers: rather than banning an individual film, the Mexican government had begun to ban all the films produced by companies distributing or producing offensive titles. Furthermore, they sought and began to obtain the solidarity of other Latin American nations who followed the Mexican example with similar legislation. Hollywood stood up and listened: First National, the first producer whose entire output was banned by Mexico, immediately published a statement that "the wishes of the government would be respected" (Woll 1978, 13; García Riera 1987a, 109–11, 125–26). In fact, however, rather than present "dignified" Mexicans, producers resorted to inventing imaginary countries and to "Hispanicizing" California without making it either Mexican or Spanish. Nevertheless, following the spirit of the period, Carewe was careful not to offend Mexican sensibilities and stated to the press during that first visit: "The production companies have been wrong to exploit Mexican characters of the 'with a gun in their belts' types as bandits and traitors when in Mexican society there are so many distinguished women and cultured men" (de los Reyes 1988, 320). These sentiments were echoed by Dolores shortly after her arrival in Hollywood:

> What [Hollywood] needs is a high-society Mexican woman, one who may have been exposed to foreign culture and customs through travel, but who maintains our customs and the traces of our Mexican land. And then the vulgar picturesque type, so damaging because it falsifies our image, will disappear naturally. . . . This is my goal in Hollywood: all my efforts are turned toward filling this gap in the cinema. . . . If I achieve this it will be the height of my artistic ambition and perhaps a small glory for Mexico. (de los Reyes 1988, 320)

Dolores became a Hollywood star, but she never achieved this dream.

What Price Glory? The First Hollywood Star Image

Dolores Del Rio's first successful starring role was her fifth film, *What Price Glory?* directed by Raoul Walsh and one of the *New York Times'* ten best films of 1926. As Charmaine, a French bar girl during World War I, she steals the hearts of two feuding American marines (Victor McLaglen and Edmund Lowe) who stoically face the horrors of war but would rather fight each other for her favors. In this film she solidified her image and there seems to be somewhat of a "fit" between her star image and her onscreen role. In other words, she fulfills the promise of stardom that the star's onscreen characters give audiences some kind of access to the personality itself. As in most of her other Hollywood films, especially in the silent period, she was a heavily sexualized and exotically beautiful foreigner, but here she also had a feisty humorous spirit that allowed for curiously independent actions. Charmaine is, above all, spontaneous, natural, innocently sexy—precisely the characteristics attributed to her great native/foreign beauty and a "fit" that Dolores herself underlined to the press: "I am not, by nature, melancholy, weepy, sorrowful, languishing, or sweet. I am the girl of *What Price Glory?* There, for a bit, I could show my real self. I am, by nature, tempestuous, fiery, stormy, eager" (Bodeen, 1967, 266–67).

Our first introduction to Charmaine crystallizes the naturalizing mechanics of her sexualization: rolling a heavy barrel on the floor of the barroom, her prominently displayed derriere is the compositional center of a rather unusual image in which the camera assumes the lecherous point of view of Captain Flagg (McLaglen) and Dolores is displayed for all to see what she herself cannot possibly appreciate. This introduction tellingly turns the table on the conventional marking of a star's entrance into the narrative via luminous close-ups that underline the star's presence. Rather than the face as the window onto the soul, her sexy derriere is what the audience first recognizes as characteristic of her persona.[7] However, as her appreciative once-over of Captain Flagg when she turns around demonstrates, seduction and seductive looks are something Charmaine can return as well as receive and her sexual freedom is the focus of the non-battle parts of the film: both marines fondle her outrageously and frequently and she sleeps with both of them (off screen). In fact, Charmaine is the only site of visual pleasure—with frequent close shots of buttocks, legs, and half-bared shoulders—in a film that is otherwise concerned with detailing the horrors of war. Curiously for a film of this period, she is not condemned for her explicit sexuality, what Kevin Brownlow has described as "the utterly unabashed sexual content of the love scenes" (Johnson 1982, 1210); on the contrary, it empowers her. When her father (Cognac Pete) attempts to force one of the men into a shotgun wedding for "ruining" her, the men acquiesce to the situation while she is the one that rebels, venting her fury on all the men around her with a virulence and freedom rather unthinkable for an "American" girl in an equivalent film situation. She is certainly neither a rebellious New Woman, an independent bachelorette, a fallen woman, nor a flapper.

At the end of the film, the men are at war and at war with each other, but Charmaine, in the act of choosing one over the other, is also able to reconcile them: Captain Flagg has her heart, but Sergeant Quirt her love. Positioned as a sexual object but also as a redeeming force—the power of love and a "pure" heart despite sexual freedom—her pathos at the men's departure to yet another battle ends the film and allows Del Rio one of her best acting moments in the film.

Although she went on to work with a variety of directors, Del Rio's image in the silent period remained fairly stable albeit with a complicated degree of interpenetration between her publicly available private life and her films. Despite being insistently identified as Mexican in the public sphere, she played sexy Russians (*Resurrection*, 1927, and *The Red Dance*, 1928), sexy Spanish dancers (*The Loves of Carmen*, 1927, and *The Bad One*, 1930), sexy half-breeds (Andean in *The Gateway of the Moon*, 1928, and North American in *Ramona*, 1929), sexy gypsies (*Revenge*, 1928), and even a fairly sexy Acadian (*Evangeline*, 1929). She was not identified with Latin American characters. Rather, hers was a vaguely upper-class exoticism articulated within a general category of "foreign/other" tragic sensuality. As a sensual "other"—an object of sexual fascination, transgression, fear, and capitulation—her on-screen image did not have a specific national or ethnic provenance, simply an aura of foreignness that accommodated the disruptive potential of her explicit sexuality. Her "otherness" was located and defined on a sexual register conflated over the foreign/exotic rather than the ethnic.

Within the industrial context of Hollywood, Dolores, who was still very young and a great beauty, fit in well into the late 1920s international constellation of talent. At a time of great expansion for the industry, the Hollywood studios had begun to attract—and recruit—a bevy of international stars and directors, not only to preclude competition from other national cinemas (such as the German) but also to increase its appeal to international audiences. Dolores Del Rio fit in perfectly with the new international crowd, which included, among others, Pola Negri, Greta Garbo, and Rudolf Valentino: with her elegant ways reminiscent of the "old Spanish tradition," the many stories circulated by the press about her exotic upper-class upbringing and travels, and her glamorous marriage (at least while it lasted) she complemented Hollywood's new self-conscious international image. Hollywood had needed a Mexican female star—few reviews or press releases failed to comment upon her nationality—and had finally produced it, yet this particular brand of Mexicanness—albeit based on the colonial legacy of the old Spanish tradition—which was so essential for her image was not specifically tapped on-screen. Rather, her ethnicity was submerged under the signpost of exoticism.

The Height and Fall

Her success in Hollywood in the silent period was spectacular, peaking after the release of *Ramona*, when United Artists also released a record that included Del Rio's rendering of the "Ramona" title song, which sold by the thousands. And she was also well liked by the Mexican public, even if some reviewers had mixed feelings. In 1926 she had been selected as one of the "WAMPAS Baby Stars," a yearly selection by the Western Association of Motion Picture Advertisers of thirteen young starlets headed for stardom. Among others, the 1926 roster included Mary Astor, Fay Wray, Joan Crawford, and Janet Gaynor (Parrish 1978, 16). She was picked the winner by the US public. A year later, trying to determine which of its previous roster of thirteen had in fact been most successful, WAMPAS had another contest open to voters from all nations. Dolores solicited the help of her compatriots via ads in the *Los Angeles Times* and the *Universal* in Mexico City and she received hundreds of thousands of votes, winning the contest by more than two hundred thousand.

But the arrival of sound complicated her career. Del Rio had put off the transition to sound for as long as she could. As late as 1928 she dismissed the new talkies as "a passing fancy" and tried to argue that sound would destroy the kinds of movies that were "Hollywood's greatest works" (Woll 1978, 40). It was already well known that the US public rejected foreign actors with accents and she was rightly worried about hers. As is evident in the "Ramona" recording, as of 1929 her accent was thick and her English almost unintelligible. Thus, to rationalize her accent, in *The Bad*

From Hollywood and Back | 119

One, her first sound film of 1930, she played a Spanish singer and began to fall into the trap of having to portray some kind of Latin American character. And this trap—added to a series of personal problems such as a protracted illness (or nervous breakdown) and a scandal surrounding her attorney, Gunther Lessing, who sued her "for ruining his marriage" and disclosed to the press a series of unsavory allegations—would sully her image significantly. Perhaps in an effort to reconstruct a version of her previous dignified, aristocratic, and "happily married" image, in 1931—the only year since her arrival in Hollywood in which she did not appear in a single film—she married the well-known MGM set designer Cedric Gibbons, the arbiter of style for the Hollywood jet set. Rather tellingly, in a *Photoplay* interview, she explained her marital choice in transnational terms, mentioning but eliding her nationality as well as Cedric's:[8]

"Cedric is perfect," she asserted, and her eyes lighted up like burning candles. "First, he is American, with that dash most American men seem to possess. And he is understanding and sympathetic. He has never been to Mexico and does not know my people—but he is an artist, and in his artist's appreciation he has been endowed with the sensitivity of the Latin. A perfect husband, no?" (Woll 1978, 42)

But sensitive to Latins was exactly what her second sound film, *Girl of the Rio*, was not. This film was a remake of *The Dove*, a 1927 Norma Talmadge vehicle that had been banned in Mexico and other Latin American countries, primarily because of its central character, Don José María López y Tostado (Leo Carrillo), a stereotypical bandit villain. In *Girl of the Rio*, Del Rio is a singer in the Purple Pigeon Night Club, just over the border. Outfitted in a Spanish-dancer white lace dress, huge hair combs, and a white *mantilla*, she entertains the bar patrons and falls in love with a goodhearted American, Johnny Powell (Norman Foster). Don Tostado decides he wants Dolores and arranges several mishaps for Johnny, including shooting him, but in the end relents and allows Dolores to go off with her American. Although *Girl of the Rio* was not banned by the Mexican censors, when it was exhibited as *La Paloma* it generated much ill will toward Del Rio in Mexico. According to one historian, "The theater which showed the film in Mexico City received continual threats of violence and a special delegation visited Mexican President Ortiz Rubio to request immediate suspension of the film" (Woll 1978, 42). And Luz

Alba, film critic for the Mexican newspaper *Ilustrado*, wrote a scathing critique of her acting abilities: "Dolores Del Rio is always the same. Endlessly she inflates her nostrils and manipulates her eyes with an excessive desire to make them seen incendiary. Her mannerisms are as bothersome as a speck of dust in the eye" (García Riera 1987a, 161).

Although she remained a visible presence in the Hollywood jet set until her departure in 1942, Del Rio never regained her former fame. She moved among the Hollywood elite, but over the next decade her roles became less and less significant and she became much more identified with Latin American and/or Mexican characters. Furthermore, her decline was also linked to the shifting imperatives of the industry throughout the 1930s and early '40s.

Most significantly, sound had opened the floodgates to music and by the mid-1930s it was almost impossible to conceive of "Latinness" in Hollywood without music. Although Del Rio starred in four musical vehicles in the early '30s and ostensibly had musical talent, especially dancing, she did not "take" as either a singer or a dancer. For example, although she was the top-billed actress of *Flying Down to Rio* (Thornton Freeland, 1933), she lost the film to the introduction of Fred Astaire and Ginger Rogers as a dancing couple. In *Wonder Bar* (Lloyd Bacon, 1934) she is only a featured player and got lost in the shuffle of a cast that included Al Jolson, Kay Francis, Dick Powell, Ricardo Cortez, and Busby Berkeley choreographies. To add insult to injury, another one of her musicals, *In Caliente* (Lloyd Bacon, 1935), had a border setting and was banned by Mexican censors because of its undignified depiction of Mexicans, which included songs with lyrics such as, "In the language of the gringo I'm so hotcha, muchacha, I'll watchya . . . just like a cat would watch a little cucaracha."

In addition to sound and the emphasis on musicality, other forces were also shifting Hollywood's interests. First of all, the July 1934 enforcement of the Production Code—the industry's self-censoring mechanism designed to forestall federal intervention—radically changed the level and intensity of sexuality that could be portrayed on-screen. That which had been Dolores's forte—her body, unabashed sensuality, and extraordinarily explicit sexuality—could no longer be represented. In fact, her first film to be submitted for Production Code approval, *Madame Du Barry* (William Dieterle, 1935), was a major cause of dispute between the studio and the Hays office, primarily because it presented the court of Louis XV as a sex farce centered around Del Rio.

Secondly, shortly thereafter the beginning of World War II shifted Hollywood's priorities. Prior to the war the industry had derived a large percentage of its gross revenues from foreign markets, and upon the closing of the European and Japanese markets, it set out, in Bosley Crowther's words, on "a campaign to woo Latin America" with films of "Pan-American" interest (Crowther 1949, 21). Pan-Americanism led to the creation in 1940 of the State Department Office of the Coordinator of Inter-American Affairs (OCIAA) headed by Nelson Rockefeller and to the resurrection of the Good Neighbor Policy. In addition to sponsoring the production of documentaries, newsreels, and shorts "to carry the message of democracy below the Rio Grande," the OCIAA worked with the Production Code Administration's newly appointed Latin American expert to pressure the studios to become more sensitive to Latin issues and portrayals (Woll 1977/1980; de Usabel 1982).

Thus the Good Neighbor Policy, among other things, further reinforced the musical tendency that was perceived as politically harmless and also redefined the terms of Hollywood's Latin/Latino representation. Dolores Del Rio's kind of ethnically undifferentiated sexual persona was no longer either adequate or desirable. For example, whereas in a precursor of the Production Code and the Good Neighbor films like *Flying Down to Rio*, the explicit and irresistible sensuality of her aristocratic Carioca character (all she has to do is look at a man across a crowded nightclub and he is smitten forever) could be articulated because in the end it would be tamed by marriage to the North American hero, in the films of the Good Neighbor period, that resolution/partial appeasement of the ethnic/ sexual threat of "otherness" she unleashed was no longer available. A kind of embryonic identity politics was beginning to emerge—symbolized by demands for authenticity in representation—which called for a sanitizing of sexuality: instead of Del Rio's sultriness, Hollywood produced Carmen Miranda in a tutti-frutti hat and tropicalization became the dominant trope for Hollywood Latins.

In order to recognize this shift, it is useful to analyze Del Rio's image in the pre–Production Code and pre–Good Neighbor Policy period as an elegant and sensual aristocrat in *Flying Down to Rio* and as the no less sensual, albeit less elegant, South Seas princess Luana in *Bird of Paradise* (King Vidor, 1932). Both films are significant within her filmography and demonstrate not only her new "look" but also her search for a different star image. In both, but especially in *Flying Down to Rio*, Del Rio appears sporting an absolutely "modern" look. Possibly influenced by the makeup revolution introduced by Joan Crawford and Marlene Dietrich or by her husband's (Gibbons) well-known fascination with art deco set design, almost overnight Del Rio's physical appearance changed (fig. 6.2): short soft hair rather than a severe center-parted chignon; a wider softer mouth rather than small heart-shaped lips; makeup that emphasized her high cheekbones and called even more attention to her luminous and well-made-up eyes; and, in *Flying Down to Rio*, elegant white or black svelte clothing that highlighted her famous *esquelético rumbero*.

Playing Carioca aristocrat Belinha Rezende in *Flying Down to Rio*, she is still extraordinarily sensual, but now suffused with elegance, sophistication, and glamour. As Aurelio de los Reyes has commented, this is the first time that her on-screen image fully coalesced with her off-screen persona, the elegant socialite Mrs. Cedric Gibbons who hobnobbed with the elite and had weekends at San Simeon with the Hearsts (1996, 80). However, already we can see traces of the changes about to come that would radically alter Hollywood's representation of Latinos and the place and function of Latinos in the industry. In the crucial scene early in the

Figure 6.2. The "new" art deco Dolores Del Rio in the 1930s Hollywood. Courtesy of Centro de Estudios de Historia de México, Condumex.

film when Belinha easily seduces Roger, the gringo bandleader, simply by setting her smoldering eyes upon him (emphasized in a close-up in which the rest of her face is framed by an evening hat low on her brow, the billowing sleeves of her white gown, and an evening purse mirror that she uses like a flirtatious mask), there is a clear hint of an important displacement. After Belinha and Roger begin to dance, one of the four blonde American women left behind at the table remarks to her companions: "What do these South Americans have below the equator that we haven't?" Ostensibly an innocent remark, her comment is nevertheless extraordinarily telling of how the film maps Del Rio's sexuality on a geopolitical axis. First, it is obviously a statement that textually produces the effect of difference ("What do *they* have that *we* don't have"), an "us" and a "them" with well-defined essentialized boundaries, but it can also be read as referring explicitly to Del Rio's sexuality ("What do these South Americans have below . . . the *waist?*") and how it can stand in as a characteristic of South Americans, especially women, in general: no matter how elegant, aristocratic, and/or glamorous, Latin American women are above all erotic, passionate, and mesmerizing. In the conjunction of region/nation ("South Americans") with implicit sexuality (below the waist), the statement also figuratively displaces that sexuality onto the map, and, by suggesting its tropicalization ("below the equator"), somewhat diffuses its implied threat (Ellner 1997). This tropicalization, albeit subtle, is pervasive: Belinha is, like her theme song in the movie, like an exquisite orchid, an exotic flower from a lush hot house like Del Rio herself, who was described by at least one critic as "orquidaceous" (Shipman 1970, 154). Similarly, within the diegesis, the "native" rhythm the "carioca" is easily learned and "transformed" by dancing stars Astaire and Rogers despite their original dismay at its verve, complexity, and entertainment value.

   Flying Down to Rio was one of Del Rio's last pre–Production Code screen appearances, but the film already seems to embody a consciousness of the repression of sexuality about to come.[9] When Belinha and Roger— who also happens to be a pilot—find themselves having to spend the night alone on a desert island (it is actually Haiti, and the bandleader has tricked her), they begin to fall in love as they sing "Orchids in the Moonlight." But what is most fascinating about this scene is not only the commonplace that a Latin American woman and an American are falling in love, but how the scene's potentially explicit sexuality is displaced. Rather than show their interaction, the characters' encounter is displaced onto "others," ghostly apparitions of themselves (alternatively their conscience or ids), who are then empowered to act out the forbidden (their kiss and passion) and are only subsequently—after the "fact"—incorporated into the "self."

Birds of Paradise, although produced a year earlier, is significant for pointing in a different direction—one which Del Rio would not follow—toward the explicit tropicalization that would eventually produce Carmen Miranda as an exuberant tropical rather than only a sexualized fetish. As the South Sea princess Luana, she is exquisitely sensual and given great freedom to display herself erotically and barely clothed in leis and sarongs (the Cecil Beaton photographs of her in costume are among her most revealing and exquisitely display her great beauty).[10] She is the object of the hero's (Joel McCrea) desire and reciprocates freely, unfettered by social taboos other than those of her own tribe. But here, as a racialized other, her sexuality, although available in terms of an interracial romance and played out on-screen explicitly—especially in the nude underwater sequence in which she lures McCrea off his friends' yacht like a mermaid, as *Variety* commented, "an eyeful of undraped symmetry" ("Bird of Paradise" 1983)—cannot be assimilated. This white American hero is one she cannot marry: "East is East and West is West and never the twain shall meet," as one character says at the end of the film right before Luana gives up Johnny and walks into a roaring volcano off screen.

Both films are significant because of the explicit sexuality of the characters Dolores plays, but in both we can also see why Del Rio could not establish herself as a musical star: in contrast, say, to her swimming or when she is being seductive, her dancing is stiff and tense. She already appears aware of herself as performer; the great star condescending to dance rather than a dancer. In contrast to the native extras' far more rhythmic moves in *Bird of Paradise*, for example, her tribal dancing sequences are stiff and self-consciously performed for the camera and/or white voyeur. Similarly, while dancing to "Orchids in the Moonlight" in *Flying Down to Rio* she manages to look utterly uncomfortable in Fred Astaire's arms, posing for the camera/diegetic nightclub audience rather than dancing with her partner.

In her 1930s/early 1940s films, Del Rio demonstrated her already sculptural great beauty—what Mexican poet/playwright Salvador Novo described as "only the material form of talent" (Monsiváis 1997a, 79)—but not her acting skills or popularity. As Aurelio de los Reyes remarks, "It seems that Dolores got her roles more because of her social relations than her box-office success" (1996, 83). Her life in the Hollywood jet set was, simultaneously, her highest achievement and part of her downfall. On the one hand, it secured her status—star-studded Sunday lunches, couture fashions, the best social connections—and international recognition: as one of the "Universal Mexicans" she was an official guest at the 1934 inauguration of the Palacio de Bellas Artes in Mexico City. On the other, it brought her to Orson Welles: their 1938-1940 secret affair caused a great scandal and led to her repudiation by the Hearsts and their crowd (because of *Citizen Kane*) and to her divorce from Cedric Gibbons in 1941. Welles cast her in his new film *Journey into Fear* (1943), but unfortunately, he lost the film—it was finished by Norman Foster—and Del Rio lost Welles, who left her for Rita Hayworth and the filming of *Lady of Shanghai*.

In *Journey into Fear*, Del Rio is a travesty of her former star persona. She is still exotic, but now she is a secondary character, a nightclub entertainer dressed in a catsuit, whom Joseph Cotten, the protagonist of the film, constantly refers to as "the girl that meant nothing to me" in his voice-over narration. Above all, here we recognize that, as Novo had intuited, her beauty *was* her talent. In *Journey into Fear* she remains magnificently beautiful, but static, immobile, a frozen effigy in the midst of a paradoxically fast-moving and convoluted espionage plot (based on the Eric Ambler novel). It was obviously time to leave: she sold her Hollywood home and fled back to Mexico, where, after all the film business was looking good.

The Myth Is Reborn

But in Mexico, although recognized as an "achiever," Dolores was not necessarily well liked by the public. As she remarked in the 1970s to Elena Poniatowska:

If my going to Hollywood was criticized by all Mexican society, my return was much worse. You can't imagine the rumors when I said that I wanted to make films in Mexico. They began to say: "With whom are you going to make films here?" I wanted to help to make Mexico known throughout the world. (1993, 25)

Nevertheless, astoundingly quickly, in Mexico Dolores Del Rio was reborn as a, if not *the*, great star of the newly thriving national industry. She was a founding member of the most famous filmmaking team of the industry, joining forces with director Emilio Fernández (the "Pygmalion" of her Mexican career), cinematographer Gabriel Figueroa, screenwriter Mauricio Magdaleno, and the actor Pedro Armendáriz, her most frequent on-screen partner (of her seventeen Mexican films between 1943 and 1966, she costarred with Armendáriz in ten). With this team, she starred in two of the most significant films of *el gran año* (the great year) of the Mexican Golden Age, 1943: *Flor silvestre* and *María Candelaria*, the most significant of the two because of its subsequent success at the first postwar Cannes Film Festival.

Now ensconced in an industry with an ostensible nationalist agenda, Del Rio's persona underwent a radical transformation. Her previous sophisticated exoticism disappeared under the weight of a new image premised on a then fashionable indigenismo. Advised by Diego Rivera and other intellectuals and artists, she jumped at the opportunity to be "Mexican" and took on Fernández's nationalist project:

> If to your beauty and fame we add the tragic spirit of the Mexican people, Lolita you can be sure to conquer Europe. You must win the hearts of the Mexican people, who have been resentful of your contemptuous attitude. . . . You must communicate that you are Mexican and proud of it and, moreover, that you identify with the oppressed classes. (Emilio Fernández cited in Fernández 1986, 190–91).

Stripped of her high-fashion gowns and Hollywood glamour, Dolores assumed the on-screen image of a prototypical meek, ignorant, and barefoot indigenous girl. She was finally portraying a Mexican woman, but not the sophisticated, cultured one that she had dreamt of introducing to Hollywood in 1925. With some exceptions, from *Flor Silvestre* in 1943 on, Del Rio played essentially the same character: a humble and/or quietly dignified indigenous and/or rural woman who suffers and must subordinate herself and her desires to a man and/or the nation. Confined to the melodramatic genre, her characters—although physically perfect, especially when photographed by Gabriel Figueroa or Alex Phillips—were always controlled or driven by others or external forces. The immobility already evident in her later Hollywood films was exacerbated, the phenomenon Monsiváis has dubbed a "facial ideology": "In order to excuse the unrepeatable beauty of a native, local racism makes her hieratic—the negation of happiness, a reservoir of suffering and dignity" (1997a, 81;

1983). In the 1940s, Del Rio became a larger than life archetype, a crucial emblem of Mexicanness, one of the great "myths" of the Mexican cinema. As Emilio García Riera argues: "The *new* tragic Dolores Del Rio who has had to return to her country in order to no longer be the impassive exotic beauty that Hollywood created, in the future will never stop playing this role, being faithful to her image rather than to her characters" (García Riera 1970, 121).

It is rather curious, however, that, internationally, this second "impassive" version of "Dolores Del Rio," star, crystallized in *Flor Silvestre* and especially *María Candelaria*, was perceived as real, as the "authentic" version (fig. 6.3). For example, Georges Sadoul, after watching *María Candelaria* at Cannes (where the film was well received and awarded), wrote the following in *Les Lettres Françaises* in 1946:

> We thought we knew her . . . but all we had seen was the Hollywood mask. . . . Without artifice, her pure face framed by long braids, and dressed with the simple clothes of a Mex-

Figure 6.3. "Framed by braids" and enshrined in the Mexican landscape: Del Rio in *María Candelaria* (1943). Fair use.

ican peasant, Dolores Del Rio appeared completely new and speaking her native tongue. Like her face, her acting lacked artifice. We did not face an actress, but rather, a woman. (García Riera 1970, 169)

Sadoul's comment about Del Rio's acting is rather perceptive, not because in *María Candelaria* she lacked artifice, but because after *María Candelaria* and once again winning an international reputation, cinematically Dolores Del Rio's star image functioned very differently in the Mexican cinema than it had in Hollywood. Despite her Hollywood "defeat," despite the Mexican public's initial resistance, she returned to Mexico a star and all her Mexican films, especially after *María Candelaria*, are overpowered by her presence as a star. The performative self-awareness that was already evident in her Hollywood dancing sequences in the 1930s was adopted as an acting style. In other words, the process of manufacturing the star image became an integral part of her acting. It is as if the distinction invoked by Jean-Louis Comolli (1978) between the "body acting" (the actor) and the "body acted" (the character) to explain the disjunction that occurs in historical films because the characters have real historical referents had become naturalized: the real historical referent here is always Dolores Del Rio, the star. She doesn't act anymore; she simply is Dolores Del Rio, the grande dame, the great face that after *Bugambilia* (Emilio Fernández, 1944) will be endowed with even more expressive eyes and extraordinarily mobile eyebrows.[11]

The visible split between her star and on-screen images in this period—society lady/all-powerful star versus endless humility, suffering, and abnegation—is disconcerting, producing fascinating tensions (for example, as María Candelaria she constantly walks around holding a pig, "la marranita" that will allow her to buy a wedding gown, but all we notice is her impeccable designer indigenous dress and the perfection of her features, which are, paradoxically, most evident in the films in which she does not play indigenous, rural, or historical characters. In *La otra*, a 1945 urban melodrama directed by Roberto Gavaldón, for example, she plays a double role as physically identical but vastly different twin sisters (María, a manicurist, and Magdalena, a millionaire), one of whom kills the other and takes her place. The narrative of the film is about otherness and María's struggles to pass herself off as Magdalena, but, as Emilio García Riera perceptively noted in a capsule review of the film: "a film which could have been about otherness—after all it is called The Other—ended up being about the film star being herself" (1971, 50). Nevertheless, *La otra* is perhaps her best Mexican film—rivaled only by *Doña Perfecta* (Alejandro Galindo, 1950)—and its double roles and byzantine plot (written by José Revueltas) allow Del Rio to turn the tables on her traditional melodramatic submissiveness to be simultaneously arrogant and aggressive. The diegetic emphasis on identity and the film's many scenes in which a silent María/Magdalena struggles with her fears, guilt, and the practical difficulties of pretending to be someone else are a perfect frame for Del Rio's kind of acting. For example, shortly after burying her sister, when she struggles with how to falsify her signature convincingly, we watch as frustration, fear, and ingenuity crisscross her face in complete silence, culminating in her decision to maim her right hand with a fire-iron in order to be able to justify signing with her left. The camera closes in on her face, marked by the shadows of the flickering fire, and the marked arching of her right eyebrow—inordinately sustained—communicate her decision to maim herself. An even tighter close-up documents the burn as her face becomes a mask of pain, relieved only by satisfaction when she realizes she has accomplished her objective and can now have a new signature.

If, as Christine Gledhill (1991) has argued, the first promise of the star is access to the personality, in this film the visibility of the star system itself discloses that possibility as an illusion. Here there is an excess of stardom produced by the emphasis on identity that the narrative can never fully recuperate. What is obvious in *La otra*, a film which includes a tremendous number of scenes without dialogue, is that Dolores Del Rio always remained a silent cinema actress even though it was the Mexican sound cinema that produced her as myth.

Transnationality and Returns

Del Rio's triumphant return to a thriving industry and transformation into a national myth and an international icon of Mexicanness must also be understood in the context of transnational relations. First of all, the OCIAA wartime programs instituted in Mexico had led to the modernization and expansion of Mexican film production in the style of Hollywood, providing raw film stock, equipment, and personnel. As Seth Fein (1998a) has argued, working through Hollywood, the OCIAA sought to develop the Mexican cinema sector as a publicly autonomous and culturally authentic source of mass entertainment propaganda for

Latin America. To a large degree, it was these economic arrangements that enabled the Golden Age of Mexican cinema. After the war, this integration and collaboration climaxed in the partnership between RKO and the group headed by Mexican media magnate Emilio Azcárraga to build Estudios Churubusco. Earlier, RKO had already been the studio that had collaborated the most with the US government's cultural/ideological agenda. Now, by providing a transnational mode of producing Mexican mass culture, RKO's investment in Estudios Churubusco was central to postwar US propaganda production in Mexico.

Coincidentally, these transnational arrangements were crystallized in a film that was also Del Rio's first return to a "Hollywood" now located in Mexico City: John Ford's *The Fugitive* (1947). Produced by Argosy, Ford's independent company, filmed at the Churubusco studios and distributed by RKO, *The Fugitive* shrewdly featured the Mexican cinema's best-known screen couple—Del Rio and Pedro Armendáriz, with well-known US star Henry Fonda—and reproduced the Golden Age visual style through Gabriel Figueroa's cinematography and Emilio Fernández's (uncredited) collaboration as assistant director.

Although an adaptation of Graham Greene's *The Power and the Glory*, a novel indicting Mexican anticlerical policies in the 1930s, the film takes place in an anonymous Latin American nation controlled by a corrupt authoritarian state that invokes pseudo-communist rhetoric and oppresses Catholic peasants and the clergy in the name of social equality and modernization.[12] The film not only fit the US's cold war ideological international imperatives but also coincided with the Mexican state's domestic policies: as its previous (1930s) commitment to social justice and agrarian reform waned, the regime needed to justify social status quo as consistent with the nation and to equate radicalism with subversion, while simultaneously clarifying the state's ideological stance during the cold war. In *The Fugitive* we have not only an example of transnationality that reveals the profound economic and ideological connections between the US and Mexico in this period, but also Dolores Del Rio's first reassociation with Hollywood. No longer the elegant exotic, she was now its antithesis although just as narrowly defined. Her character in the film, María Dolores, is an indigenous woman who, of course, suffers with great dignity. Seduced and abandoned by the Armendáriz character, a despotic police chief, she bears his child, works as a cantina girl, but risks all for her faith and its pursued representative, the intense priest played by Henry Fonda. She is appropriately introduced in the shadowy interior of a church, wrapped in a modest rebozo, holding a sleeping infant in her arms, and illuminated only by the sun streaming through a church window. She is silent, almost immobile, and the mise-en-scène compounds the tension by postponing the full revelation of her beauty. She is more sexualized here than in *María Candelaria*—the prototype for her character—since this is after all a Hollywood film, but she is on display as an object of desire only once, when she dances on top of a cantina table to distract the policemen from searching for the priest she has hidden in the back room. But even here, the moment is narratively contextualized and the camera treats her figure with devotion. When the exhausted priest arrives at the cantina, she offers to run away with him to "save" him by pretending to be his wife and child. But, immediately, she realizes that this suggestion of a forbidden sexuality is perhaps offensive and apologizes even though the priest has fainted and cannot hear her. Thus, narratively, her sexual potential is relegated to an other secular and inaccessible realm. Similarly, when she flirts with the police sergeant and offers to dance, it is clearly done in the spirit of a great sacrifice rather than of pleasure. Visually, her sexuality is dissected—her sexualized, beautiful legs and feet are self-consciously separate from her face/soul. Thus when she emerges from the back room in a flirtatious dress, an unexpected fast track follows her in a blur of movement from the doorway to the top of the cantina bar and ends in a level close shot of her bare feet and legs marking the beginning steps of a dance. A low-angle canted close-up then shows us her face, animated and fairly seductive, alternatively masked by the fan she rhythmically waves, but also in a very distinct visual space. It is only the third shot of the sequence that "joins" the sexualized body and the face: beginning with a medium shot of her bared legs and a policeman trying to peer up her skirt, the camera tilts up slowly on her body until it reaches her oddly animated face, which can now be read as utterly artificial. When several shots later the dancing is interrupted by the arrival of Rafael (Pedro Armendáriz), a visual echo corroborates her "purity" and, simultaneously, the high price and perhaps even the inadmissibility of sexuality as his entrance is marked by a close-up of his shiny black boots entering the doorway. In *The Fugitive* Del Rio's stardom is sanctified: she is a Madonna, the Virgin of Guadalupe, the ultimate figure of devotion. By 1947 Del Rio was already a national and Latin American icon with an immutable image and *The Fugitive* was the vehicle that reinscribed this new persona permanently within the Hollywood imaginary.

In all her subsequent Hollywood work, it is this quintessential Del Rio—framed by braids, as Sadoul says, but obviously no less a construct than her first star persona—that prevailed internationally. In other Hollywood forays she would always play strong yet suffering indigenous women: the "Spanish Woman" in John Ford's *Cheyenne Autumn* (1964), Elvis Presley's Kiowa mother in *Flaming Star*, and the grandmother in Hall Bartlett's *The Children of Sanchez* (1978), her last screen appearance.

Memory and Re-iconicity

In the US imaginary, once the distinction between the star as person and the star as performer had collapsed, Dolores Del Rio was wedded to her Mexicanness, this time not as an exotic other, but explicitly as an indigenous and/or ethnic other. Rather than across the axis of nationality, her star persona is now plotted upon a class-based register: as a too-youthful-looking grande dame she condescends to play "others" *because* she is a great actress and, *as* a great actress, literally condescending. Above all, we remember Del Rio as an image rather than as an actress, silent and unsmiling, a visual icon in stasis rather than in movement. In 1952, for example, the Parisian entertainment magazine *Cinemonde* featured her in an "exclusive" article in which she ostensibly "presents" an exhibit of Mexican art at the Louvre, but which really functions to position her on the same artistic altar—distanced, appreciative, priceless—as the works (fig. 6.4): the large earrings of a rare pre-Columbian figurine are just like her own gold hoops; the statue of Chacmol is significant because she appeared in a film with it; strategically positioned in front of David Alfaro Siqueiros's *Imagen de nuestro tiempo*, she is the object offered to the world by the painting's outstretched hands (Beaume 1952, 9–11).

Thus perhaps the Amalia Mesa-Bains altar installations cited earlier provide us with the most prescient—and most problematic—representation of her transnational stardom.[13] First of all, Dolores was herself a fan of "altars" and displayed objects: "When I was a little girl I collected all kinds of things: I had small boxes filled with rings, bracelets, earrings, beads . . . and boxes full of ribbons that I classified by color and width" (de los Reyes 1996, 192). When she went to Hollywood she took along many family heirlooms, which she exhibited in her homes and in many publicity stills as if to invoke her own personal and cultural identity. Secondly, she self-consciously positioned herself on altars—of stardom, high art, elegance, and sophistication—and was therefore enshrined as

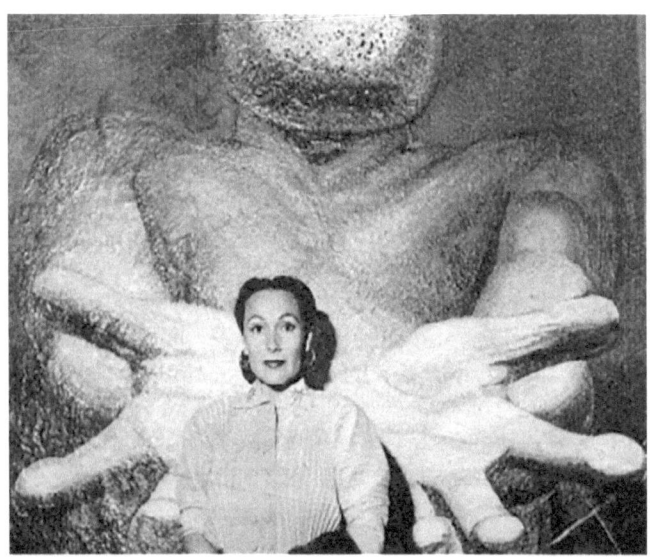

Figure 6.4. Dolores Del Rio on the altar of art as the "offering" of David Alfaro Siqueiros's *Imagen de Nuestro Tiempo* in Paris, 1952. Courtesy of the Cineteca Nacional de México.

Figure 6.5. Amalia Mesa-Bains, *An Ofrenda for Dolores Del Rio*, 1984–1990. Courtesy of Amalia Mesa-Bains.

a sculptural icon. The Mesa-Bains altars, filled with myriad personal objects that could have been hers and publicity stills, echo her own self-representations. They capture her as image, and, while providing a personal or human context through objects of everyday life, simultaneously transform her star glamour into a kind of divinity (the photos, lace, and glitter linked to the candles and religious icons): her Mexicanness, synonymous with her beauty, is reinscribed as sacred.[14] The altars contextualize her image domestically, but as a cinematic icon she is, by definition, not of the world of domesticity. In fact, the altars return her to the museum, the one site that most productively condenses her image and secular sainthood. But the altars also reinscribe her nationality: she is Mexican but of two "nations," of the world of Hollywood and a Mexico now also located in the US. Ironically, in the heterotopic space produced by these altar installations—her greatest transformation—the elite socialite Del Rio becomes a Chicana cultural heroine, rescued from Hollywood and Mexico for the transnation.

7

The São Paulo Connection

The Companhia Cinematográfica Vera Cruz and *O Cangaceiro* (1998)

This essay analyzes the national as well as international dimensions of the Vera Cruz studio, a unique, short-lived effort at an industrial mode of production underwritten by a group of entrepreneurs in São Paulo beginning in the late 1940s. López challenges existing characterizations of Vera Cruz as a mere prelude to the more radical, nationalist Cinema Novo film movement—characterizations that are based on the influence of foreign-trained filmmakers and Vera Cruz's "internationalism." To do this, she brings to light the studio's own efforts to frame its films as national(ist) and argues for Vera Cruz's long-lasting impact on "Brazilian film" through its function as a training ground for media professionals who had a profound impact on Brazilian audiovisual production (in film and TV) in later decades.

The experience of the Vera Cruz studios in São Paulo is a typically "fifties" moment in the history of Latin American filmmaking; a moment of change, debate, euphoria, increasing internationalism (of personnel, distribution, influences), and, of course, failure.

The Companhia Cinematográfica Vera Cruz, in existence between 1949 and 1954, represents the most concerted effort to implement studio-based filmmaking in Brazil. In Rio, other companies like Atlântida and Cinédia were also studio based, but unlike them, Vera Cruz was modern, well equipped, and, since it was backed by the wealthy São Paulo bourgeoisie, well financed. For its founders, the great industrialists Francisco

Matarazzo Sobrinho and Franco Zampari, Vera Cruz—like the Museu de Arte Moderna and the Teatro Brasileiro de Comédia that they had also created—was a symbol not only of their own cultural aspirations but of the modernity and effervescence of the *paulista* bourgeoisie in general. If anyone could, they would be the ones to finally produce a Brazilian cinema of international "quality," the opposite of the much-detested carioca *chanchada*. Their "internationalism" was certainly inspired by Hollywood's universality (and the studio mode of production), but the technical know-how for the company was all European. Among the talent imported by Vera Cruz were important figures such as the British cinematographer Chick Fowle, the Austrian editor Oswald Haffenrichter, the Danish sound engineer Eric Rasmussen, and a number of Italian directors (Adolfo Celi, Luciano Salce, and Ruggero Jacobbi) associated with the Teatro Brasileiro de Comédia. Of course, the principal "import" was not really an importation, but the return of a prodigal son: Vera Cruz hired as its executive producer the Brazilian-born director-producer Alberto Cavalcanti, who had begun his career with the French avant-garde, worked at Joinville in multilingual productions, participated in the establishment of the British documentary movement, and greatly contributed to the success of the Ealing studios. Cavalcanti's reign as director was short lived: by all accounts, he had a difficult personality and his high standards, cosmopolitanism, and sexual preferences quickly came into conflict with the company. Cavalcanti left Vera Cruz in 1951. Before returning to Europe, he directed three films (*Simão, o Caolho*, 1952, a political *chanchada* featuring the great comedian Mesquitinha; *Mulher de verdade*, 1954, another comedy; and *O canto do mar*, 1954, a restaging of his French port city film *En rade*, 1927, in Pernambuco) for Kino and Maristela, studios that had emerged in the shadows of Vera Cruz (Paranaguá 1996).

In its five years of activities, Vera Cruz produced a few documentaries (including two shorts directed by Lima Barreto) and eighteen feature films, ranging from historical and contemporary melodramas to "biopic" films, historical epics, and comedies. Its output, when coupled with increasing filmmaking activity in São Paulo itself and in Rio and with a general euphoria over the possibilities of Brazilian filmmaking, led critic Salvyano Cavalcanti de Paiva to predict in a 1952 cover article in the weekly news magazine *Manchete* (then in its first year of publication), based on the fact that national film production had doubled (from ten films in 1947 to twenty in 1950), that production would reach forty films per year in the near future. And echoing the famous nationalist cliché, he exhorted:

"Our three and a half million weekly spectators, eager and willing to pay to see films spoken in their own language with local actors and national themes, are waiting for a historical change. After all, is this or is it not the "Country of the Future"? (Cavalcanti de Paiva 1952, 14).[1]

As we know, in the short term it wasn't, and Vera Cruz was not the company of the future either. Vera Cruz had not taken into account the limitations of the domestic market and the difficulties of breaking into the international market: its big-budget productions (the average Vera Cruz film cost ten times more than a Rio *chanchada*), extraordinarily high overhead costs, and, eventually, its indebtedness to the Bank of Brazil and the Bank of the State of São Paulo, bankrupted the company.

These are the dry facts that are available in any history of Brazilian cinema. But there is also an accompanying standard reading or interpretation of Vera Cruz that has become a historical cliché: Vera Cruz's failure proved the economic unsuitability of studio-based film production in Brazil and, although the company's achievements are grudgingly acknowledged (with statements like "they achieved the 'look' of First World dominant cinema," Johnson and Stam 1995 [1982], 28), Vera Cruz is understood to have been merely a kind of necessary prelude, a historical footnote to, or maybe even a misguided digression from, the soon to emerge Cinema Novo movement. This standard critical and historical understanding of Vera Cruz—in part emerging from Maria Rita Galvão's (1981) brilliant sociohistorical analysis of the company and her oral histories, in part from Glauber Rocha's scathing critiques in *Revisão crítica do cinema brasileiro* (1963), but also indebted to our former fascination with the new cinemas of the 1960s—has allowed us essentially to dismiss, or at least invariably to always qualify the company's achievements and influence. Discussions of Vera Cruz focus on the sociological dimensions that the company's formation, staffing, and demise signal, while the films—accused of elitism, of being too technically perfect, of being too European—are handily dismissed under similar sociologically driven criteria.

Consistent with the spirit of historical revisionism with which we are tackling the analysis of 1950s Latin American film, and without dismissing what we have already learned about the sources and ideology of Vera Cruz and its practices, I want to argue that the time has come for us to revisit Vera Cruz from different perspectives. In fact, somewhat perversely, I would like to suggest that it is perhaps Vera Cruz and its films—rather than the Cinema Novo—that have left the most lasting legacy upon Brazilian media production. My analysis will focus on two aspects of the Vera Cruz period: first and more briefly, the company's much maligned "internationalism," and, second, its also much maligned films, especially Lima Barreto's *O Cangaceiro* (1953), the company's most notable box office success (fig. 7.1).

Figure 7.1. Poster for *O Cangaceiro*. Public domain.

The Foreigners

We are accustomed to thinking of Vera Cruz's massive importation of foreign technicians as a historical aberration, almost as if it were a unique event in the history of the cinema, without considering that even Hollywood—especially at the height of its internationalizing moment in the 1920s but also during and after World War II—depended heavily upon "foreigners" for crucial technical and creative support. If we stop to think about the thirties, that other crucial and misunderstood period in which the classic Latin American cinemas were established, what do we see? Foreigners, and foreign-trained talent and technicians everywhere. In Mexico, all we need to remember is the Hollywood-based cast and crew of *Santa* (Antonio Moreno, 1931), the work of Russian émigré Arcady Boytler (*La mujer del puerto*, 1933), and, of course, Eisenstein, Eduard Tissé, Alex Phillips, Juan Orol, José "Che" Bohr, and later, Luis Buñuel, Dolores Del Rio, Libertad Lamarque, Ninón Sevilla. The list is endless, for the Mexican cinema, that great nationalist cinema, was above all also an international melting pot.

The situation was not that different in other countries. *La balandra Isabel llegó esta tarde* (1949), directed by Argentine Carlos Hugo Christensen with the goal of jump-starting Venezuelan national cinema, featured a Mexican actor (Arturo de Córdova), an Argentine actress (Virginia Luque), and an almost all-Argentine crew, alongside the Spanish-born cinematographer José María Beltrán and a Venezuelan folklore specialist. The first version of Chile Films in the 1940s, admittedly a failure, imported its talent from Argentina. Cuba entered into a fairly extensive series of coproductions with Mexico in the late 1940s and '50s and imported directors as often as it could in order to stimulate its own technical development and the idea of a national cinema (Podalsky 1994, 59–70). Of course, there were émigrés from the Spanish Civil War everywhere. Finally, in a different period altogether, we must also remember that when faced with the so-called challenge of starting from scratch, Cuba's ICAIC also resorted to importing foreigners; the roster of visitors during its first few years reads like a who's who of the politically correct of the era.

Curiously, however, the case of Vera Cruz has always been read differently, as eccentric and unassimilable. In the *depoimentos* gathered by Maria Rita Galvão and in the contemporary Brazilian press we read, over and over again, how the foreigners did not understand "our Brazilian ways"—they insisted on having high tea and refused us our *cafezinhos*, they wanted perfection when we were used to *quebrar um galho* and *dar um jeito*, they expected regimentation and were elitist, while we were disorganized and less concerned with class differences.[2] Benedito J. Duarte in 1954 argued that both *O Cangaceiro* and *Sinhá Moça* (Tom Payne, 1953) were excellently photographed, but that their photographers (Chick Fowle and Ray Sturgess, respectively), "although competent technicians, have not yet assimilated the light and features of the land" (Galvão and Bernardet, 1983, 109). Even Cavalcanti, who was not a foreigner but had the misfortune of living abroad most of his life, is described as *estrangerizante*. Alex Viany, possibly Cavalcanti's harshest critic, considered him an *entreguista* and even in his later *Introdução ao cinema brasileiro* (1987), where he attempts a more balanced analysis, argued that Cavalcanti just couldn't understand the Brazilian *jeitão* (Viany cited in Galvão 1981, 204; Viany 1987, 113). Cavalcanti's own explanations about the imported technicians are also telling:

> I reject the allegation that by importing technicians from different countries I was attempting to facilitate the creation of a unique national film style that would therefore be free of any one national influence. . . . Even today I continue to think that only with the arrival of more foreigners will we be able to efficiently train Brazilian technicians, and without a doubt, this should be our primary concern. (1952, 39)

Vera Cruz itself was quite defensive about its nationness, insisting in its press releases and publicity materials that the company was 100 percent Brazilian, that its goal was to produce a "Brazilian" cinema of international quality, and that the "cosmopolitanism" of its films was ultimately a result of Brazil's own reality. In publicity materials for *Esquina da ilusão* (1953), for example, we read that the film is "polyglot, a heterogeneous gallery of characters from different nations and speaking different languages because Bras [the São Paulo neighborhood in which the film is set] is itself international and cosmopolitan, peopled by Brazilians, Japanese, Syrians, Spaniards, Germans, etc." (cited in Galvão and Bernardet 1983, 113–14). The company explained its foreign personnel, echoing the ideology of Brazilian *mestiçagem*, as follows:

> They came to renew the national cinema, giving it an international character . . . akin to our national capacity for assimilation.

[Without this] we would not have reached the stage in which we now find ourselves; just as the Brazilian people are a mixture of the most diverse races, our cinema, as the ultimate form of cultural expression, is also a synthesis of the most diverse filmmaking schools. (Cited in Galvão and Bernardet 1983, 114).

Rather typically, at the time of the Second National Congress (1953) Lima Barreto was one of the most outspoken critics of Vera Cruz's international staff: "Vera Cruz has become the monopoly of alien adventurers who know nothing about Brazil. Let's put an end to this discussion once and for all: a Brazilian cinema can only be made by Brazilians" (cited in Galvão and Bernardet 1983, 116). Of course, as Randal Johnson has chronicled, this was a period of intense nationalism and of complex debates over the constitution of "Brazilianness" in all facets of culture, and it should not surprise us that the presence and effect of foreigners in national culture should be questioned at the time (especially given the intense debates and nationalist thesis proposed by the Instituto Superior de Estudos Brasileiros [ISEB] shortly thereafter) (Johnson 1987). But that foreignness has continued at the forefront of discussions of Vera Cruz *is* surprising, especially given the critical turn toward hybridity and multiculturalism, and the reevaluation of difference and otherness within nationness. Even Paulo Emilio Salles Gomes, who spearheaded the critical reassessment of Brazilian popular cinema by recuperating the *chanchada*, arguing in his 1973 essay "A Trajectory within Underdevelopment," that lacking an original culture, nothing is foreign to us because everything is, was unable to place Vera Cruz within his famous "Brazilian incapacity for copying" paradigm. The foreign presence, in this instance, does seem to have mattered: "Dismissing the popular virtues of carioca cinema, the *paulistas*—encouraged by recently arrived European technician and artists—decided to point Brazilian cinema in a totally different direction" (Salles Gomes 1995, 249).

Can we begin to rethink the position of these foreigners, expert technicians in an alien nation, often working for months on location in the interior of São Paulo, barely understanding the language, the culture, the food, or the weather? Are there other ways of understanding their undeniable contribution to the Brazilian cinema? As even the most recalcitrant critics have acknowledged, almost overnight they improved the technical quality of Brazilian cinema 100 percent. Alex Viany reluctantly admitted that "technically, *Caiçara*, the first Vera Cruz film, in a flash recuperated a twenty-year lag in the field of Brazilian cinematography" (cited in Galvão and Bernardet 1983, 195). This was in the fifties, when Viany could also say that "a correção do técnica não e de espantar" (technical improvement shouldn't be surprising) (Viany cited by Galvão 1981, 228; this and the following translation are by the editors), and Vera Cruz's foreigners enabled the national cinema to achieve what later Glauber Rocha would discuss as a "a camera alfabetizada" (a literate camera). Without this literacy, the rebellion of Cinema Novo in the next decade seems hard to imagine. But this reading leaves us still in the realm of positing the achievement of technical competence—driven by foreigners—as a prelude to the subsequent development of a "real" Brazilian cinema.

In fact, the foreigners' most crucial contribution to Brazilian cinema was perhaps not so much the technical competence of their films, but that they, as Cavalcanti argued in an earlier quote, trained an entire generation of Brazilian technicians conscious of a certain *padrão de qualidade*. The cinematographers, editors, sound engineers, set designers, etc., who learned their crafts at Vera Cruz, working with the foreigners, would form the backbone for the next wave of *paulista* cinema in the 1960s and '70s, as the *depoimentos* in Maria Rita Galvão's *30 anos de cinema paulistano* (1980) prove. Furthermore, after the closing of the company, and given that jobs in production were generally scarce, many of those who stayed in Brazil ended up of course not directly affiliated with Cinema Novo, but with the emerging new medium, television, the real heir of Vera Cruz. For example, Jacques Deheinzelin, who went to Vera Cruz as a cameraman after studying at IDHEC (Paris), ended up in TV advertising and with his own pioneering company (founded in 1954), produced jingles and spots, and gave jobs and training to many of the new *paulista* film and video-makers of the 1970s and '80s. The significance of independent television professionals for Brazilian audiovisual production cannot be overestimated. As Roberto Santos argued in an interview with Maria Rita Galvão, the growth of these companies aligned with television created a truly professional production environment, including the constant renovation of equipment and studio facilities, which created another kind of "revolution" in the language of cinema (Galvão 1981, 209–20).

We must also note that although Vera Cruz officially went bankrupt in 1954, production continued in its São Bernardo do Campo studios under the name "Brasil Films" and the directorship of Abilio Pereira de Almeida (named director by the Bank of the State of São Paulo).[3] Pereira de Almeida had already appeared in and directed several Vera Cruz films, including *Sai da frente* (1952), *Nadando em dinheiro* (1952), and *Candinho*

(1953), which introduced the popular radio and TV comedian Amácio Mazzaropi to the cinema. He created Brasil Films in order to escape from Vera Cruz's distribution agreement with Columbia Pictures and produced at least seven films between 1956 and 1959. Shifting Vera Cruz's priorities, he provided opportunities to emerging *paulista* directors, among them Walter George Durst (*O Sobrado*, 1956), who had previously been one of the harshest critics of Vera Cruz; Walter Hugo Khouri (*Estranho encontro*, 1958); the brothers Geraldo and Renato Santos Pereira; Cesar Memolo Jr.; Carlo Alberto de Souza Barros; and Rubem Biáfora. Brasil Films provided not only cinematographic continuity in São Paulo but, perhaps following Pereira de Almeida's lead,[4] it was also the first film production company to recognize the significance of and profit from the popularity of television; the cast of Walter Durst's *O Sobrado* consisted of actors who had become famous via the *paulista* station TV-Tupi founded by Assis Chateaubriand in 1950 and, at the time, the industry and audience leader.[5] As a kind of coproduction between film and television, *O Sobrado* pointed the way to a collaborative road that, unfortunately for Brazilian cinema, was not taken until decades later.

The cosmopolitanism, classicism, and high production values that were so dear to Vera Cruz and its foreigners would be thoroughly Brazilianized in the following decades and transformed into the great TV-Globo *padrão de qualidade* that since then has been central to all discussion of audiovisual production in Brazil. Although Globo itself always resisted any affiliation with the cinema and developed its own artistic and technological base, the impact of the *padrão Globo de qualidade* (not only production values, but a specific dramatic and representational style that consolidated a series of prestigious actors) and the televisual itself has come back to haunt Embrafilme (with its quest to achieve a standard of quality for international distribution) and contemporary post-Embrafilme Brazilian cinema.

The reinscription of the Vera Cruz experience not as an anomaly but as an important stage in the history of Brazilian audiovisual production was crystallized in 1997 in the Projeto Nova Vera Cruz sponsored by TVCultura/ Fundação Padre Anchieta and the government of the State of São Paulo. Extraordinarily ambitious, although not without internal contradictions, the project combines a TVCultura/State of São Paulo initiative to fund at least twelve films per year (to be aired on TV and released theatrically) with the renovation of the Vera Cruz studio facilities in São Bernardo do Campo. Budgeted at R$15 million (one-third guaranteed by the state government), the renovation will include the refurbishing of the two original Vera Cruz studios, a postproduction facility, public areas (such as a theater and gallery spaces), and the Centro Experimental Alberto Cavalcanti, a school that will provide technical training and hands-on experience.[6] Behind the project is an explicit desire to recuperate the memory of Vera Cruz (archival preservation, promoting research, production of a CD-ROM), but also the desire to retake its original proposal: to make films on an industrial scale (Neto 1997). In March 1997, Guillerme de Almeida Prado reinaugurated the Vera Cruz facility when he began filming *A hora mágica*, based on a Cortázar short story ("Cambio de luces"), a story about the transformation of a radio station into a TV station in the 1950s.[7]

For better or for worse, since 1954, all Brazilian cinema activity has had as a reference point the success and failure of the Companhia Cinematográfica Vera Cruz. Although Paulo Emilio Salles Gomes argued that the Vera Cruz experience primarily prepared the ground for the great renovations of the 1960s, he also rallied against harsher critics with appropriate words: "Timid spirits insist on speaking of errors because they have not yet understood that the only fatal error is not to exist. If only we all had the errors and stimulating consequences of Franco Zampari's audacity!" (1982, 306).

THE "FOREIGN-LOOKING" FILMS

Of all the activities of Vera Cruz, its films have, paradoxically, been the least studied aspect. All too often they are dismissed en masse as too technically perfect, too European, too alienated from "the realities of Brazilian life," with perhaps only *O Cangaceiro*'s success, cited as an ironic anomaly. Although it is undoubtedly true that Vera Cruz's search for an international style for an international market—of which we find evidence in other Latin American national cinemas of the period, especially the Argentine—lent its films an almost excessive formal classicism that sometimes collided with their conscious effort to focus upon national content, the diversity of the films they produced by now should have precluded any categorical assessments or dismissals. The time has come to return to the films themselves and to reread them, not searching for their foreignness and certainly not looking for traces of Cinema Novo, but seeking to identify what Maria Rita Galvão, in *Le cinéma brésilien* describes, in a curious phrase, as their elusive "impregnation" with Brazilian reality (1987, 81). Such an analysis must begin with a consideration of how Vera Cruz adapted and transformed the standard genres of melodrama and comedy.

Melodrama was the basic staple of Vera Cruz. The company produced historical melodramas (*Sinhá Moça*, Tom Payne, 1953), a musical melodrama cum biography (*Tico-tico no fubá*, Adolfo Celi, 1952), contemporary urban melodramas (*Apassionata*, Fernando de Barros and Adolfo Celi, 1952; *Floradas na serra*, Luciano Salce, 1954), rural/provincial melodramas (*Caiçara*, Adolfo Celi, 1950; *Terra é sempre terra*, Tom Payne, 1951), and even a film-noirish looking melodrama (*Na senda do crime*, Flaminio Bollini Cerri, 1954). In all cases, the films closely followed classical structures and previously established generic universals, but almost in each instance with interesting differences. Thus, for example, *Sinhá Moça* is much more than an abolitionist drama à la *Gone with the Wind* with a Zorro-like male protagonist; it also offers significant and hitherto cinematically invisible images not only of the horrendous violence inflicted upon enslaved people[8] but of Black resistance to slavery. Despite its staginess and obsessive fidelity to the model of the Hollywood biopic, *Tico-tico no fubá*, the musical biography of composer Zequinha de Abreu, ironically presents not only a paean to the vivacity and seductiveness of nonmediated popular culture represented by the circus and its performers, but also a subtle critique of the culture industry that rejects and displaces Abreu until after his death (fig. 7.2). The most interesting moment of the film is, perhaps, the final montage coda in which that very culture industry—of which the film itself is part—is shown transforming Zequinha's famous song into a universal musical idiom: from the samba version of Rio's carnival celebrations into Egyptian, Japanese, French cancan, American bebop, and Cuban conga rhythms.

Although at first disdained because of its potential association with (or contamination by) the carioca *chanchada*, Vera Cruz also produced important innovations in comedy, diversifying the then-dominant model of grotesque parody and musical carnivalization. *Uma pulga na balança* (Luciano Salce, 1953), for example, was a sophisticated urban comedy about a thief who mounts an elaborate con system from inside prison. Most importantly, Vera Cruz also introduced the great popular comedian Amácio Mazzaropi as the prototypical *caipira* (hillbilly) attempting to deal with and adjust to life in the big city, giving cinematic life to what would become one of Brazil's most emblematic characters.

In the very popular *Sai da frente* and its sequel, *Nadando em dinheiro*, Mazzaropi played a humble truck driver living in São Paulo who must deal with the problems of everyday life and work in the suburbs of the big city. The latter is particularly interesting, because the plot (Mazzaropi dreams that he has inherited a fortune and everything that is good in his life disappears because of his new lifestyle) satirizes the attitudes and beliefs of the upper and upper-middle classes. In *Candinho*, Mazzaropi's last film

Figure 7.2. Poster for *Tico-tico no fubá*. Public domain.

for Vera Cruz, he plays a simple man who is expelled from the farm where he was raised. He goes off to the big city in search of his mother, ends up involved in many adventures, and finally marries his true love, a girl he saves from prostitution. All three films reenact the rite of passage from the interior into the city, from an innocent rural world into a complicated modern metropolis in which nothing is as it seems. Through comedy, they mediate a different kind of Brazilianness (and of foreignness) than the Vera Cruz melodramas: the contemporary estrangement and alienation incumbent upon rapid modernization and internal and external migrations. Thus in *Candinho*, when Mazzaropi's illiterate *caipira* is thrown in jail after a fight and cannot prove his identity, the sheriff calls upon other legitimate Brazilians who can do so—a German, a Japanese, and another "foreigner" who can produce proof of their nationality—and Candinho resolves that since he has no documents he must be a "Turk," the *caipira* generic category for foreigners. Above all and despite all difficulties, the *caipira* always prevails and, ultimately, finds happiness and accommodation in modernity without really having to change his ways. As critic Nuno César Abreu has argued, Mazzaropi's *caipiras* represented "the negation of underdevelopment" and an inside-out form of identification for mass audiences (cited in Mendes Catani 1987, 292).

After the collapse of Vera Cruz, Mazzaropi made five films for other producers before establishing his own production company in 1958 and refining his *caipira* persona into *Jeca Tatu* (Milton Amaral, 1959), an adaptation of the stereotypical character invented by writer Monteiro Lobato for a pharmaceutical company in 1919. Playing variations of Jeca Tatu, Mazzaropi made another two dozen films, all popular at the box office, at the rate of one or two per year until his death in the early 1980s. In the annals of Vera Cruz's achievements, the discovery and introduction of Mazzaropi was matched only by the success of *O Cangaceiro*, its most notorious film and greatest economic success.

O Cangaceiro

O Cangaceiro was Vera Cruz's ninth completed feature film. Set in the 1930s, the film is loosely based on the real-life exploits of Virgulino Ferreira "Lampião," the most famous of the *cangaceiros*, bandits who roamed—and to some degree ruled—the Northeast. The story revolves around a band of *cangaceiros* led by Capitão Galdino (Milton Ribeiro).

Following an elegiac shot of a band of men on horseback riding right to left across a landscape of brush and puffy clouds to the accompaniment of the song "Mulher rendeira," the *cangaceiros* run into and disband a team of government surveyors, then gallop off toward a village, which they violently attack and plunder. They capture the beautiful village school mistress Olivia (Marisa Prado) and hold her for ransom, which motivates the organization by official proclamation of a local posse to pursue them. Back in their camp, María Clodia—Galdino's woman (Vanja Orica)—makes advances to Teodoro (Alberto Ruschel), the most sympathetic, kind, and peace-loving of the bandits, but he is smitten by Olivia and rejects her. Galdino attempts to convince him to dedicate himself fully to the *cangaceiros*, but Teodoro manages to free Olivia and to escape with her into the *sertão* in the middle of the night. Galdino and the band pursue them relentlessly, violently punishing those who appear to have aided them. Meanwhile, Teodoro and Olivia get to know each other and fall in love. When the *cangaceiros* catch up to the couple, Teodoro makes Olivia escape to safety while he holds out against the twenty-three men and even wounds Galdino in the shoulder. Low in ammunition, he surrenders in the morning to Galdino, who asks him to choose how he will die. Teodoro's wish for a knife duel is not granted: instead he will walk a distance and, after passing under a tree, each *cangaceiro* will shoot once; if alive at the end he will be free to walk away. Spurred on by María Clodia, the wounded Galdino announces that he will be the last to shoot. Teodoro is hit three or four times and dies, disappearing into the ground, while Galdino also dies from his wounds, violently scratching the earth with his ring-covered fingers.[9] Following a fade and a sound bridge to "Mulher rendeira," a long shot shows a now retreating band of *cangaceiros* on horseback, this time riding across the landscape from left to right.

Released in early 1953, *O Cangaceiro* was a spectacular box office success nationally and abroad, winning a special prize for best adventure film and another for music at the Cannes Film Festival that year.[10] The film was widely distributed in Brazil and internationally (twenty-two countries) by Columbia Pictures, always eager to seize upon a profitable product from down South (they also distributed Cantinflas's films). In Brazil the film refocused national attention on the *cangaço*. The exploits of the *cangaceiros* had always been a fertile topic for northeastern popular culture—especially for *literatura de cordel* and itinerant musicians known as *violeiros*—and had entered erudite culture via literature in the 1930s (Graciliano Ramos, Rachel de Queiroz, and especially José Lins do Rego's *Os Cangaceiros*), but the film powerfully reinscribed the myth into the national cultural imaginary, ranging from stimulating academic historical and sociological research on the *cangaço* to inspiring painters (especially Aldemir Martins's important series) and playwrights to influencing fashion (the leather hats, sandals, and short skirts worn by Vanja Orica became the rage). Perhaps most influential was its music, which included northeastern folk songs and compositions by Zé do Norte, and which engendered several curious international cross-fertilizations (fig. 7.3).

Figure 7.3. Music for *O Cangaceiro*. Personal collection of Ana M. López.

In France, sheet music of the theme song "Mulher rendeira," circulated during the mid-1950s, rewrites the banditry thematic of the film into what was originally a rather simple folk love song. In the US, the release of the film generated a hit parade single, "The Bandit," sung by Eddie Barclay, subsequently rerecorded by a panoply of musicians ranging from Percy Faith to Joan Baez. International versions of "Mulher rendeira" continue to be recorded to this day: the French version catapulted Vietnamese singer Elvis Phuong to fame in the early 1960s, while most recently the Italian rock group Litfiba recorded an Italian version.[11] In Brazil "Mulher rendeira" itself inspired a broad range of subsequent works, including not only Gilberto Gil's classic "Renascer," but Chico Cesar's *Mangue Beat* hit "Folia de principe" in the CD *Cuscuz clã* (1996).

The film itself was well received by European, US, and Latin American critics. For example, in his review of the Cannes festival for *Les Lettres Françaises*, Jean Thévenot criticized the film's editing but praised its acting, photography, and music, describing it as strong, harsh, brutal, and strange work, the real surprise of the festival (Thévenot 1953, 10). For Georges Sadoul, *O Cangaceiro* was "seductive because of its picturesque exoticism" and "the first worthwhile film produced in Brazil by a young filmmaker" (1953, 5). In the US, Mosk in *Variety* relegated the film to "language spots and special situations" because of its violence, while praising the "authentic" feeling for countryside and ritual; the "fine" camera, editing, and compositional work; and the theme music, which "should make fine material for a pop song" (1953). Bosley Crowther compared the film's explicit representation of violent acts to Eisenstein's *Que Viva Mexico* and Elia Kazan's *Viva Zapata*, but argued that "the Latin director has found moments of beauty and poetry in some of the small things in this picture. . . . He is a poet with the camera, a master of an almost forgotten virtuosity." Finally, he concludes, "This *cangaceiro* is a picture that will cause Western fans to rub their eyes" (1954, 21).

In Latin America, the film was positioned in relation to the international film scene rather than to traditional Hollywood genres. Gabriel García Márquez, in Bogotá at the time writing film reviews and chronicles, adored the film. "What is wonderful about this story is how Lima Barreto tells it, with the prodigious technical assurance of the masters of the silent cinema and the inspiration, candor and pace of an ancient poet" (1982, 227). Perhaps already thinking about magical realism, the future novelist found that Lima Barreto, like Jean Renoir and Emilio Fernández, "had the magical ability to transform narrative raw materials into a pure lyrical substance. . . . This is a drama of bandits told in the language and style of a fairy tale" (García Márquez 1982, 238). In his year-end review of the Latin American film scene, Gabo noted the progressive decadence of Mexican cinema and argued that Argentina was "sterilized by contradictory influences, economic difficulties, and political problems," while "the presentation of *O Cangaceiro* in Bogotá was one of the stellar moments of the cinema this year. The feeling that the future lies in Brazil has not yet left those who had the privilege to see Lima Barreto's magisterial film" (García Márquez 1982, 435).

In Cuba the film was awarded the national critics' prize (ARTYC) and included among the best films of the year (1954) by the magazine *Carteles*, the cultural association Nuestro Tiempo (which that same year had also programmed a series of neorealist films), and the CCOC (Paranaguá 1990, 31). Leading critic and professor José Manuel Valdés Rodríguez, in his program notes for a screening of the film, after praising the authenticity of the acting and music, highlighted the film's "clean documentary feel." According to Valdés Rodríguez the film was comparable to the best neorealist films: "*O Cangaceiro* can occupy an eminent position alongside the fictional dramatic films admired for this noble trait, such as the best examples of Italian neorealism" (1966, 8).

In Brazil, the film's critical history has been as perverse as that of the Vera Cruz company. To put it bluntly, contemporary critics received the film according to their political allegiances: the Catholic conservatives praised it, while the left rejected it outright. In between these two extremes, some critics praised the film for putting the nation on screen. Braúlio Pedrosa, for example, argued that "there isn't an international formula for success, there aren't international characters that work as well here as in Afghanistan. The success of *O Cangaceiro* is due precisely to the fact that it reacted against such an internationalist leveling. . . . *O Cangaceiro* had the great merit of revealing its real nationality to the Brazilian cinema" (cited in Viany 1987, 116).

Most criticized the film's most obvious flaws: attempting to pass off the *gaucho* and *mineiro* accents of the romantic protagonists and the vastly different vegetation and topography of the *paulista* altiplano for the *sertão*. In *Introdução ao cinema brasileiro*, Alex Viany argued that Lima Barreto had shied away from the sociological and historical questions of the *cangaço*, but asserted that the film was an adventure film with a unique *rhythm* and timing already identified by Salvyano Cavalcanti de Paiva at the time of the film's release:

The so-called slowness or rhythmic flaws that some individuals have identified in the film are only the treachery of an unconscious accustomed to the dynamism of the US gangster and cowboy genres, a dynamism which would have been inadequate for a work that attempts to sincerely explore . . . the drama of the *bandoleiro de cabeça chata*, a phenomenon that is profoundly national and Brazilian. The more flagrant error of *O Cangaceiro* is the unhappy attempt to pass off the *paulista* altiplano landscape—radically different in vegetation and topography—for the landscape of the northeastern *sertão*, because even in a work without sociological intentions, with a topic like this, it will always be taken as a kind of veridical documentation. (Viany 1987, 116–17)

Subsequent critics would be much harsher, especially and most famously Glauber Rocha, who in *Revisão crítica do cinema brasileiro* lambasted Lima Barreto and the film as fascistic:

Without understanding *cangaço* fiction and without rendering the meaning of popular fiction from the Northeast, Lima Barreto created a conventional and psychologically basic adventure drama illustrated by mystical figures with leather hats, silver stars, and comic cruelty. The *cangaço*, as a phenomenon of mystic-anarchic rebellion emerging from the northeastern *latifundio* system and worsened by drought, was not represented. A story about the time of *cangaceiros*, a romantic fable exalting the land. (Rocha 1963, 69)

Almost all critics have commented on the visible mixture of styles and genres in the film, a combination of western-inspired mise-en-scène, Eisensteinian montage, and cinematography reminiscent of Emilio Fernández and Gabriel Figueroa. Partaking of the desire to identify national cinematic originality/uniqueness and a profound fear of influence, critics were anxious to denounce the film's eclecticism as imitative. For Glauber Rocha, for example,

Lima Barreto did nothing but repeat one of those Mexican epics on the *paulista planalto* costumed as the Northeast: he preserved the melodramatic spirit, the facile pictorialism, the

blackmail of great shots dynamically edited that mimic the
effects of the old Soviet cinema and more recent ones from
Hollywood. A western without great humanity or the purity
of John Ford's *My Darling Clementine*; an epic without the
mystical movement of Ford's *Stagecoach*; a nationalist drama
without the conviction of Eisenstein's *Alexander Nevsky*, a love
song to the land which, although romantic, lacks the authenticity of some of Emilio Fernández's scenes. A film bound by
ropes. (1963, 70)

Echoing Glauber decades later, Norberto Leal would argue in his *O Nordeste no cinema* (1982) that *O Cangaceiro* was an "artificial, lying, falsifying" work that "negated, lied about, and covered up" the men and culture of the Northeast and lacked vigor:

Not even its techniques have any validity today . . . , the film
is shocking because of its lies, for its Mexican visuals, and
Gabriel Migliori's musical *choradeira*. The dialogues have no
flavor. . . . And in the sequence show at the bandit's hideout,
the mystification, falsity . . . and low-quality copying of the
conventions of North American film reach their peak. (1982, 99)

Attempting to go beyond the labeling of foreign influences in *O Cangaceiro*, instead of imitative, I want to argue that the film's visual and thematic hybridity is transformative, as much so as the great parodic *chanchadas* of the period like *Carnaval Atlântida* (José Carlos Burle, 1952).[12] Like one of Roberto Schwarz's "misplaced ideas" (1992), *O Cangaceiro* transplanted a series of thematic and stylistic elements into an "other" audiovisual and historical context in which their function and effects were reinscribed. Unlike the *chanchadas*, *O Cangaceiro* is not parodic, but its self-conscious mixing of styles works just as efficiently as parody to denaturalize and relocate the text within a unique new space for cinematic representation. This space is, of course, the *sertão*, a Northeast that had not really been put on screen before (with the exception of an early documentary film shot by Benjamin Abrahão before Lampião's death in 1938)[13] and that is produced here as an explicitly cinematic space. Furthermore, *O Cangaceiro*'s stylistic hybridity and its articulation of a crucial mytheme for national representation coincides with an emerging affirmation of cinematic authorship in the figure of Lima Barreto, an auteur *avant la lettre*.

Hybrid Style: A National Space

O Cangaceiro's hybridity is systematic and unrelenting, mixing and matching, as most commentators noted, elements from diverse and potentially contradictory cinematic modes. However, rather than disjointed foreign borrowings, the deployment of these elements produces a coherent narrative and representational space. As Ismail Xavier argues in his analysis in *Sertão/Mar*, the film inherits a particular historical stance from its adhesion to some elements of the Hollywood western genre (1983, 123–35). Akin to the western's nostalgia for a now-extinct world—the already closed western frontier—*O Cangaceiro* positions its story as taking place in a past from which the film itself is distanced: as the opening epilogue proclaims, "Epoca: imprecisa, quando ainda havia cangaceiros" [Epoch: unspecified, when there were still *cangaceiros*]. This is not a film about a precise historical moment or a historical reconstruction (in fact, the preceding lines are followed by an odd disclaimer that "all similarities to real facts and persons are coincidental and unintentional"), but an evocation and cinematic reconstruction of history as national myth. Like the heroes and Indigenous Americans of the Hollywood western, the *cangaceiro* is available to the national cinematic imaginary precisely at the moment when "civilization" has made his position—indeed his very life—impossible.[14]

The film's position vis-à-vis its subject is reflected within the narrative itself. When Galdino and his band attack the village early in the film, they force an itinerant photographer to take their photograph, a moment that displays the process of production not only of the photograph but of the film itself. The photographer is, not coincidentally, a foreigner from Germany who barely speaks Portuguese ("Por que não fala cristão, gringo da peste? [Why don't you speak Christian, you stinky gringo?], Galdino asks him) who poses the group according to certain aesthetic parameters intrinsic to his medium to which only he seems privy. The *cangaceiros* gather in a semi-circle and, after a series of further adjustments (especially changing the direction of one of the *cangaceiro*'s rifles so as to not point directly at the camera), the photograph that fixes the *cangaceiros*' activities as myth is produced: the camera doubles the perspective of the immobile photographic apparatus, the lens is covered by a black cloth, the still image melds with the cinematic. Like the photograph, the film, not coincidentally also lensed and structured by "foreigners," follows its own aesthetic parameters and representational schema: it fixes the image and history of the *cangaceiro* as much as the still image does. It is only after this process has been identified and represented—and after the *cangaceiros* have been positioned within the realm of myth—that the film begins to develop characters in depth and to unravel the crucial romantic subplot.

The centrality of the romantic subplot is perhaps the film's most evident sign of hybridity and a dislocation of the previously established distanced historical stance. Although the film's mise-en-scène continues to bear a superficial similarity to the western—men on horseback wearing big hats, etc.—narratively *O Cangaceiro* markedly displaces the civilization versus wilderness opposition central to the western's epic project: in *O Cangaceiro* civilization is an unjust cadre of oppressors or an unfair police force rather than progress and industry, while the wilderness, despite the presence of an indigenous man with a magical leopard tooth necklace, is also threatening and harsh. Instead of the individualistic western hero of the wilderness, a man on horseback who uses his gun to uphold his personal code of honor, in *O Cangaceiro* the hero or *mocinho* is an outsider, pushed into the *cangaço* by an unjust police persecution.

While fleeing from Galdino, Teodoro explains to Olivia how he ended up in the *cangaço*: he had been unfairly accused of a crime and had no other option. As a "circumstantial *cangaceiro*" (Leal 1982, 92), Teodoro speaks the language of the civilized and does not seek revenge; he wants to find a place where he and Olivia can fulfill their romantic promise and the dream of family life. The "real" *cangaceiro* is Galdino. They share certain attributes—both are literate, astute, and intuitive—but Galdino, about whose past we know nothing, is the *cangaço* personified: violent, harsh, mystical, and driven by a magnificent spirit of survival. The effects of this dislocation are ideologically significant. Instead of nostalgically needing to be "saved from the blessing of civilization" (cf. Ringo Kid and Dallas at the end of John Ford's *Stagecoach*), Teodoro and Olivia need to escape from the wilderness/*sertão* and its evils and miseries, even though Teodoro claims not to be able to leave his land. The narrative conflict is traced along a moral spectrum in which the civilized and altruistic Teodoro is the "good" struggling against the organic selfish evilness of Galdino. Romance rather than absolute moral worth is crucially important in this equation, however, for what "civilizes" Teodoro—and in terms of the narrative develops his character in contrast to the other *cangaceiros*—is his love for Olivia. Thus as a redeeming civilizing force, the film posits romantic love as the ultimate value to be preserved, but at a price: rupturing the unity—and epic sweep—of the *cangaceiro* community.

That the *cangaceiros* are a community and not just a band of individuals is extraordinarily important, not only because it underlines Galdino's power as group leader (and a certain submissive spirit among the rest), but because of how the film produces this besieged spirit of community. *O Cangaceiro* narrativizes the community through music. It is not coincidental that the scenes in which characters and the romantic subplot begin to be developed take place in the *cangaceiro* camp, the ramshackle but communal everyday space in which their daily lives unfold. In a move functionally equivalent to how the Mexican genre of *comedias rancheras* (for example, *Allá en el Rancho Grande*, Fernando de Fuentes, 1936) creates a national communal space through music, *O Cangaceiro* plays out the tensions and pleasures of communal life through an obsessive musicality and performativity. In fact, other than a handful of short dialogue scenes, the camp sequence consists almost entirely of musical moments.

The equation of camp/community with musicality is first established nondiegetically. A folkloric tune accompanies our first views of the camp and a series of shots of everyday camp life: an old woman doing laundry while her lazy *cangaceiro* son lies on a hammock asking her for a glass of water, a sexy young woman flirting with various groups of men (and motivating the camera to move freely through the camp). Subsequently it is literalized by the presence in the camp of a gramophone—stolen from the ravaged village—that two *cangaceiros* attempt to operate unsuccessfully until the young woman adjusts the speed: it plays a jaunty carnival march (the "schottish" "Sempre Teu" recorded by the Rio de Janeiro Firemen's Band), music curiously foreign to this particular group that is never heard again. Finally, music is located within the community itself a few minutes later, when shots of María Clodia washing her hair are accompanied by a folkloric tune about the value of a woman's word sung by a woman working on a sewing machine. Later, at night, the *cangaceiros* amuse themselves around the campfire by singing, and their rendition of "Lua Bonita" is the background against which we see a woman who was kidnapped from the village and cruelly branded on the face wandering into Olivia's hut and wondering at her facial perfection. The *cangaceiro* group then begins to prepare for a *roda*, "Zequinho Olé," but their performance is interrupted by an unexpected remanifestation of their past violence: the branded woman sees a *cangaceiro* lighting a cigarette with his brand and screams hysterically. After she is silenced, the group performs and dances another *roda*, "Meu Pinhão" (led by Zé do Norte on accordion as one of the *cangaceiros*), which serves as background for the conversation in which Teodoro rejects María Clodia's love. Minutes later, the scorned María accompanied by a guitarist sings "Saudade, meu bem, Saudade" while the entire community, including a suspicious Galdino, listens. Almost without exception, all the songs performed in the camp are not only folkloric, but have lyrics that deal with romantic love. However, unlike the use of music and performance in the Hollywood musical—through which the romantic protagonists resolve their differences and ultimately rejoice in the joy of love—the protagonists of *O Cangaceiro*'s romance do not ever sing or dance. The community's paeans to love speak either of failed romances and promises or unfulfilled desires. Rather than a celebration of love, this is a discourse of dissatisfaction that sublimates their social condition.

To this immersion in musicality as the metaphorical equivalent of a community spirit linked to male-female love relationships, we must add that what at first seemed to be a nondiegetic association of the *cangaceiros* with the song "Mulher rendeira" as it accompanies their ride across the landscape in the beginning of the film is subsequently transformed into performance. After torturing to death a *cangaceiro* who had helped Teodoro and Olivia escape, the band of *cangaceiros* led by Galdino marches off in pursuit. Framed by medium shots rather than the extreme long shot of the opening scene, we can now clearly see that this group of *cangaceiros* sets off in search of revenge while playing guitars, tambourines, and an accordion and singing the romantic verses of "Mulher rendeira."[15] Without the film's previous development of musicality as that which cements the group, these images of revenge-seeking men on horseback singing a ballad would have seemed incongruous. But by this point, the film has thoroughly established that the *cangaceiros* are above all a group bound by music: their performativity is a central unifying force, what keeps them together, identifies them as other and simultaneously as a group. Music—and violence—are their means of expression and, simultaneously, their link to the landscape/region and, by extension, nation.[16]

As the flip side of their musicality, the *cangaceiros*' violence is brutally excessive and peaks in two moments of the film—the branding of the woman captured in the village and the torture to death of an alleged traitor by dragging him through the bush—that are explicitly linked to the group's musicality. In the first instance, the branding itself is one of a series of brutal acts committed during the attack on the village, but the branded woman's reentry into the narrative is framed by music: her hysterical insertion of the memory of violence into the *cangaceiro* camp interrupts the group's performance of "Zequinho Olé" and, after her screams subside, is followed by the performance of a different group *roda*. Similarly, the violence committed against Teodoro's ally is followed by the group's performance of "Mulher rendeira." Thus, following the pattern whereby the romantic plot mediates the previously established epic mode, individual and group violence is mediated by musicality.

Finally, music and violence intersect crucially with the cinematic evocation of a particular landscape as emblematic of the nation. *O Cangaceiro* produces a special way of placing the human figure in the landscape because the *sertão* is invoked cinematographically rather than through location. Framed by epic puffy clouds, thorny bushes, and dusty roads, the *cangaceiros* traverse and live in a landscape that is produced visually and cinematically for the first time. With their leather hats encrusted with silvery stars and symbols, bullet belts, scarves, and other finery, the *cangaceiros* (as recreated by set designer Carybé)[17] themselves are integral to and the most vibrant part of this harsh landscape. The inscription of this arid hostile space as a peopled visual archetype of the nation would be the film's great legacy: the creation of a new cinematic space.

Lima Barreto: A Pre-auteur

Originally a journalist and radio commentator (for Radio Tupi in São Paulo in the 1940s) and the author of many unpublished fictional works, Lima Barreto declared that he began in the cinema "carrying tripods for old man Del Picchia [a *paulista* silent cinema pioneer]. Later I borrowed a Kinamo camera and dug up 25 meters of film . . . and discovered my world always full of beauty, even when bread is lacking and love is scarce" (Barreto 1984, 19). He worked in the São Paulo industry making commercial films and documentaries. Brought in to work at Vera Cruz by Alberto Cavalcanti, he began as an actor, appearing in *Terra é sempre terra* and *Tico-tico no fubá*. Shortly thereafter he was second unit director for *Angela* and then directed two generally well-received documentary art shorts—*Painel* (1950), about Portinari's famous Inconfidência panels, and *Santuário* (1951) about Aleijadinho's masterpiece *Os doze profetas* (The Twelve Prophets). Barreto was irascible and bombastic, but he was well regarded by Cavalcanti and one of only two Brazilians at Vera Cruz in its early years.

Already in 1960–1961, Paulo Emilio Salles Gomes astutely recognized the uniqueness of Lima Barreto's position within Brazilian cinema. He argued that Lima Barreto, like Humberto Mauro and Mario Peixoto, the "three most celebrated filmmakers in Brazilian cinema," suffered from a kind of megalomania—an acute knack for self-promotion—but that his and the others' *mania de grandeza* was not a negative personality trait but "a weapon to fight the frustration that all artists and artisans of the Brazilian cinema face. In fact, their megalomania is a protest cry" (1986, 366). And Glauber Rocha, despite his critique of Barreto's politics, never questioned his commitment to the cinema. Barreto wrote the script and fought with Vera Cruz's management for years to get it produced. Apparently, he only managed to do so because he convinced one of the owners, Caio Guimarães Pinto, to talk Zampari into the project.

Vera Cruz had never made a film with this kind of epic sweep and the production was difficult, cumbersome, and problematic. The entire crew camped in the interior of São Paulo for months. Tons of materials—including horses and a leopard—had to be transported. For the attack on the village scene they had to enlist the help of the village's entire population while coordinating the actions of over eighty armed *cangaceiros* on horseback. Barreto was always difficult, but he was even worse during production and postproduction, arguing against Chick Fowle and Oswald Haffenrichter's judgments. In previous Vera Cruz productions Fowle and Haffenrichter had easily imposed their own style, knowledge, and experience on their films; directors like Adolfo Celi and Tom Payne had little or no cinema experience and simply followed their suggestions. Haffenrichter in particular was able to dramatically change the structure and final look of films in the editing room and to demand extensive reshooting (for example, *Tico-tico no fubá*) (Galvão 1981, 131–38). By continuing to be "difficult" and to challenge all decisions that interfered with his vision of the final product, Barreto was able to sustain a different style in *O Cangaceiro* (Galvão 1981, 140–41). It is no coincidence that *O Cangaceiro* does not look or feel like other Vera Cruz films and that Fowle's and Haffenrichter's work was in general quite different. Barreto may have been able to occupy the impossible position of an auteur in a system ostensibly centered on the hierarchical studio mode of production only, as Salles Gomes points out, because of his *mania de grandeza*. Maybe, as Glauber Rocha claims, he was even a closet fascist. But he was also the *inventor* of such a position in professional Brazilian film circles (Humberto Mauro being his counterpart in alternative filmmaking). Possibly a victim of his own audacity, Barreto never matched the success of *O Cangaceiro*. His only other fiction film, *A Primera Missa* (1960), was a commercial and critical failure and, although others filmed his scripts (*Quelé do Pajeú*, Anselmo Duarte, 1969, and *Inocência*, Walter Lima Jr., 1982), he never directed another film.

Conclusion: The Legacy

The fifties in Brazil were a fertile period of debate, invention, and reinvention that should not be dismissed as simply the era that preceded the turbulent 1960s. Vera Cruz left the universe of Brazilian technical production a most significant legacy of audiovisual quality and, with *O Cangaceiro*, a hybrid production that articulated an important new representational space for the nation: a cinematic *sertão* tapped by the commercial *cangaceiro* genre of the 1960s that emerged alongside the Cinema Novo revolutions. With films like *A Morte Comanda o Cangaço* (Carlos Coimbra, 1960), *Lampião Rei do Cangaço* (Carlos Coimbra, 1962), and *Três cobras de Lampião* (Aurélio Teixeira, 1962), the *cangaceiro* film developed as an adventure genre, with large doses of explicit violence (precursor of the spaghetti western) and romanticism, but also with a good deal of elasticity, embracing even a Mazzaropi comedy (*Lamparina*, Glauco Mirco Laurelli, 1963).[18] Dubbed the *nordestern* by the filmmakers/film critics of Cinema Novo, the *cangaceiro* genre was well received at the box office, and, unlike *O Cangaceiro* itself, generally liked by critics. Even Glauber Rocha stated that he was "one of the biggest defenders of the *nordesterns*" (Rocha 1963, 72). Curiously, the *nordestern* genre developed in dialogue with Cinema Novo's own dramatically different reappropriation of the thematic and landscape of the *sertão*, especially Glauber's "verticalization" (Senna 1997, 29) of the typical cause and effect relations of the genre in *Deus e o Diabo na Terra do Sol* (*Black God, White Devil*, 1963) and later in *O Dragão da Maldade contra o Santo Guerreiro* (Antonio das Mortes, 1969). Yet relations between the Cinema Novo filmmakers and the slightly older generation responsible for the *nordestern* genre were surprisingly cordial and respectful. In fact, although they followed different paths, both groups shared the same ambition for a Brazilian cinema that was beginning to attract consistent—rather than sporadic—international attention with the first films of Glauber Rocha, Carlos Diegues, Joaquim Pedro de Andrade, Nelson Pereira dos Santos, and Anselmo Duarte (*O Pagador de promessas*, 1962, winner of the Cannes Palme D'Or): to establish some kind of emblematic Brazilian type or landscape that would be fixed in the international cinematic imaginary. As Glauber said, "What we need is a filmmaker who will revise the patterns established by *O Cangaceiro*" (1963, 73).

The political debacle of the late 1960s that thwarted the development of Cinema Novo also essentially ended the *nordestern* genre; the military government was suspicious of the genre's espousal of banditry and its potential links to subversive activities in general. The last *nordestern* seems to have been Oswaldo Teixeira's *Cangaceiro sanguinário* in 1969. There were no *cangaço*-themed films at all in the 1970s. But, in the post-Embrafilme, late 1990s cinematic boom,[19] with filmmakers searching for national and international audiences and production funds, the *cangaço* has reemerged with a vengeance (coinciding with the Lampião centennial, July 7, 1997): Rosenberg Cariry's *Corisco e Dadá* (1996), Lirio Ferreira and Paulo Caldas's *Baile Perfumado* (1996), and a remake of *O Cangaceiro* by Aníbal Massaini (1997). To these films we must also add *Mandacaru*, a telenovela directed by Walter Avancini set in the *sertão* with *cangaceiros*, which began airing on the Manchete network in summer 1997.

As in the 1950s, the search for a relatively easy way to identify Brazilian iconicity has led filmmakers back to the *cangaceiro* and the *sertão* with varying degrees of success. More of a love story than a historical reconstruction, *Corisco e Dadá* recounts the relationship and exploits of this famous *cangaceiro* couple—the "Diabo Louro" (Blond Devil) and the twelve-year-old girl whom he abducted and seduced—who were the last to be defeated. *Baile Perfumado* is, ostensibly, the most ingenious, approaching Lampião from the point of view of photographer-cinematographer Benjamin Abrahão who filmed him in 1936, and incorporating some of the original footage. Rather than a fierce guerilla, this is the Lampião who was fascinated by the accoutrements of modernity: coffee makers, scotch whiskey, cameras, and French perfume. Of the three, the remake of *O Cangaceiro*—despite an obvious attempt to recreate the spirit of the original with set designs by Carybé, a story line that follows Lima Barreto's original script (which included a framing story not part of the original film), and makeup by Victor Mirinow[20] (who also did makeup for the 1953 version and appeared in it as the German photographer)—is the most disappointing. Pitched as a super-production, it attempts to outdo the original in every respect: it is extravagantly colorful, filled with gratuitous and explicit violence, as explicitly sexual and filled with nudity as a *pornochanchada*, and even more saturated with music.

Nevertheless, despite the relative faults and merits of these productions, the contemporary return to the *cangaço* reminds us of the viability and foibles of the Vera Cruz legacy—the aspiration for a Brazilian cinema of "international quality," the search for a uniquely Brazilian cinematic idiom—which continue to this day.

8

Crossing Nations and Genres

TRAVELING FILMMAKERS (2000)

This is another foundational essay that directly challenges nation-based accounts of cinemas in Latin America during the "studio era" (1930s–1950s). In this case, López analyzes the case of Argentine-born filmmaker Carlos Hugo Christensen (first mentioned in "National History . . ."1998b) who worked in Chile, Venezuela, and Brazil, as well as in his country of origin. While tracing his professional trajectory as a traveling filmmaker in diverse film industries and national spaces, "Crossing Nations and Genres" places particular attention on the role of the foreign and the "traveler's gaze" in La balandra Isabel llegó esta tarde *(The Isabel Arrived This Afternoon, 1949), the film that he made for Venezuela's Bolivar Films. This forceful, clearly delineated argument underscores the importance of examining transnational dynamics as constitutive of Latin American cinemas and of recognizing that those dynamics do not begin with the New Latin American Cinema, but rather were already in place in earlier periods.*

Within the general trajectory of Latin American filmmaking, the big moment of pancontinental travel and collaboration is generally said to have happened with the New Latin American Cinema in the 1960s. As this accepted historical narrative would have it, filmmakers who had been

---

Research for this essay was made possible, in part, by grants from the Roger Thayer Stone Center for Latin American Studies at Tulane University.

working independently to produce "new" cinemas in their respective countries began to meet on foreign and Latin American soil, to share ideas, and to think of themselves as a united—if not necessarily unified—movement. Thus under the banner of the new cinema movements and the new national cinemas of the 1960s (especially Cuba's), intercontinental cinematic collaborations were heralded as one of the central strategies of the new pan–Latin American movement. Even in this period, however, although there was indeed much cinematic collaboration among the various Latin American nations, the tendency of most film histories has been to treat the cinemas of each nation as discrete phenomena, framed primarily by the sociopolitical vagaries of each state and only incidentally linked to continental social changes and movements.[1]

Thus it is hardly surprising that the ostensibly far more insular "classical" or "Golden Age" cinemas of Latin America produced in the 1930s, 1940s, and 1950s have also been understood primarily as discrete national phenomena. Although historians have recognized and analyzed these cinemas' susceptibility to shifts in international policies and economics (for example, the oft-cited US embargo of raw film stock shipments to Argentina during World War II and the Spanish Civil War) and the effect of the presence of Hollywood and other imports upon local markets and production, the classical cinemas have nevertheless been analyzed as circumscribed primarily by state cinema policies and national cultural characteristics. Thus most histories and analyses (in English, Spanish, and/or Portuguese) of this period of Latin American filmmaking have dealt almost exclusively with the national forces and players that shaped the "national" cinema.[2]

This focus on nation has unfortunately obscured important intercontinental forces in the classical period. Although not defined by the unified ideology of a pancontinental social movement like the New Latin American Cinema, the classic cinemas were also marked by often intense and significant agenda and standard-setting transnational cross-fertilizations. The most obvious evidence of these cross-fertilizations are the coproductions among Latin American producers that became de rigueur in the 1950s but existed as early as the 1940s. Most often engineered through the Mexican or Argentine industries, these films have a curious status: in Mexican and Argentine film histories they tend to be included, although designated as inferior works, whereas in "other" contemporary national histories (for example, accounts of pre-Revolutionary Cuban film) they are, with few exceptions, highlighted as indigenous achievements and as evidence of the energy and potential of the nascent local cinema industry.

Although less evident than the recognized coproductions, traveling film personnel also provided for rich transnational exchanges. Of course, it goes without saying that Latin American filmmaking was profoundly influenced by travel across the Rio Grande. For example, many of the sound cinema pioneers of Latin America—especially from Mexico—learned the craft in the United States, especially in the days of the "Hispanic" cinema boom in the late 1920s and early 1930s. Although many only appeared as extras in "Hispanic" films or worked within the industry in secondary roles (assistants, makeup artists, translators, etc.), they later returned home bitten by the cinematographic bug and went on to produce the "national" cinema: Emilio Fernández, Gabriel Soria, Miguel Zacarías, Alejandro Galindo, Alberto Gout, Chano Urueta, Raphael Sevilla, Fernando Méndez, Raúl de Anda, Gilberto Martínez Solares, René Cardona, Tito Davison, and others.[3] In Mexico, *Santa* (1931), the first successful national sound film, was produced by a compendium of Hollywood-trained talent: director Antonio Moreno had worked in a number of silent films and early talkies, actress Lupita Tovar had also worked in silent films and starred in the Spanish-language version of *Dracula*, Donald Reed (aka Ernesto Guillén) was a silent film actor, the Russian-born cinematographer Alex Phillips had already worked on many Hollywood silent features and had been Greg Toland's assistant. In fact, Alex Phillips, like many other expatriates, arrived in Mexico in this period to stay and became one the most celebrated cinematographers of the Mexican cinema, with hundreds of films to his credit. Like Phillips, other US expatriates joined the nascent industry, crossing the Rio Grande in the "wrong" direction: David Kirkland, John H. Auer, Robert Curwood, Robert O'Quigley, Jack Lauron Draper, Ross Fisher. Others like Paul Strand traveled to Mexico for short periods or for specific projects such as Strand's work for *Redes* (Nets, 1934).

But travel across the Atlantic was also fruitful: some of the most celebrated cinematographic travelers to Latin America came from Europe. Sergei Eisenstein's trip to Mexico in 1930 left a significant imprint upon the nascent Mexican cinema, and Luis Buñuel's extended and productive stay continues to be the source of much debate. Alberto Cavalcanti's sojourn in Brazil as director of the Vera Cruz studios in São Paulo in the late 1940s and 1950s, although less discussed, was no less significant. The Vera Cruz experience—the failure of high-budget, studio-based filmmaking in Brazil—gave rise to important debates about the national cinema in the mid- to late 1950s that set the stage for the emergence of the Cinema Novo movement.

Despite the fascination of these already fairly well-tracked international trails, what interests me most is the history of *intra*continental travel and cinematic exchanges in this period: that is, the effect and influences of filmmakers and actors who traveled within Latin America and participated in collaborative film projects with nations other than the one with which they were professionally affiliated. The issue of intracontinental influences in the classical period is not only a fascinating historical puzzle but also one that questions the viability of the "national" as the signpost of classical Latin American film histories by highlighting the hybridization inherent to all national cinemas. Against the prevailing myth of national cinematic insularity and histories of national achievements and failures, I want to argue for the need to look at the history of Latin American cinema from a continental perspective that includes, but mediates, the national. This will require an analysis of official international agreements and collaborations but more important, much research into the networks of intellectual and cinematic exchanges established unofficially through interpersonal relationships and work-related travel. Thus, in this context, the figure of the traveling filmmaker—and the foreigner's gaze—as a site for tracing the mediation of nation is potentially a key for opening up a space for transnational analyses of the classic Latin American cinema.

Of the intracontinental travelers I have been able to track down, Carlos Hugo Christensen stands out because of the persistence of his pan-national efforts. He began his filmmaking career as a very young man in Argentina in the 1940s, worked in Chile and Venezuela, and ended up settling in Brazil in the mid-1950s, where he thrived despite his relative marginalization from the emergent (and later institutionally powerful) Cinema Novo crowd.

Christensen began his film career at a time of great growth for Latin American cinema. Both the Argentine and Mexican cinemas were thriving, having totally eclipsed the Spanish cinema (in crisis because of the civil war) in the internationally strong Spanish-language market: in 1940 there were 5,160 movie theaters in Latin America—Brazil had 1,450, Argentina 1,021, Mexico 823, and Cuba 375. Of the 17,829 theaters in the United States, 360 regularly played Spanish-language films (Oroz 1991, 121, 137). In Brazil the sound industry had found a firm commercial footing with carnival-inspired films and comedies. Simultaneously and inspired especially by the Mexican and Argentine examples, other nations had begun their efforts to produce national cinemas in the late 1930s and continued to do so—with various degrees of success—throughout the early 1940s (Peru, Uruguay, Cuba, Chile, Venezuela).

In Argentina, although there were approximately thirty functioning production companies (in 1942), most filmmaking revolved around two studios: Argentina Sono Films, the oldest, and Lumiton, founded in 1932 by three radio pioneers.[4] In the early 1930s, both studios produced an essentially "popular" cinema, with great emphasis on tangos and popular singers, melodramas set in the *arrabales* (popular neighborhoods), and populist comedy. Lumiton became well known for its tightly knit technical and artistic teams, quick production schedules, and efficient—if not minimal—budgets.[5] In this period, its principal director was Manuel Romero. Firmly convinced of the commercial potential of the new industry and attempting to attract middle-class and upper-class audiences, which disdained the national cinema, in the late 1930s Lumiton began to focus on more sophisticated subject matter and settings, producing a more romantic "bourgeois" cinema and highlighting the work of director Francisco Mugica (Di Núbila 1959b, 591). When Christensen directed his first film for Lumiton in 1940, the studio was again searching for new models and subject matter, still with an eye on the more elite sectors of the audience but also looking to make further inroads internationally via "universal" stories and styles.

In the mid-1940s, Christensen presented Lumiton with a viable option: explicit sexuality in either comedic or melodramatic scenarios. His 1943 film *Safo: Historia de una pasión* (Safo: The Story of a Passion) is credited for introducing "the erotic" into the Argentine cinema. It was an immediate success, transforming Roberto Escalada, the male lead, into an overnight star and consolidating the career of Mecha Ortiz, who played the sex worker. The film played for more than a year in Buenos Aires and was widely seen throughout the continent. In 1944, Christensen's *La pequeña señora de Pérez* (Little Mrs. Perez, 1944) duplicated the success of *Safo* in the realm of comedy. Thus began what Argentine historian Domingo Di Núbila has handily dubbed the "Christensen era" at Lumiton.

However, alongside Christensen's successes, the Argentine industry was beginning to feel the effects of the war and the US embargo on raw film stock imports. Although the studios set up a film black market (through third countries, especially Chile and Uruguay), the high costs of these transactions led to production cutbacks: from a high of fifty films in 1940, production dropped to a low of twenty-three in 1945. Despite stentorian efforts to control production costs (via even tighter production budgets and frenetic schedules), Lumiton had to cut back severely. Meanwhile, the Mexican industry had quickly filled in the gap in the international market created by the decrease in Argentine production. After the war, the Argentine industry was also affected by Juan Perón's rise to the presidency in 1946 and the subsequent political polarization of the nation. The cinema was placed under the jurisdiction of the Subsecretaría de Informaciones y Prensa de la Presidencia de la Nación (a sort of ministry of propaganda) and its director, Raúl Alejandro Apold, who subsequently became known as the "cinema czar." As a result of Apold's tight control over scripts and all facets of production and of modifications of the state protection laws between 1947 and 1950, the industry changed greatly in character, several studios closed (Lumiton stopped producing in 1952), and many actors and directors left to pursue their careers elsewhere (most notably, Libertad Lamarque, whose hostile relationship with Eva Perón led to her departure for Mexico in 1946).

While Mexico still had the strongest and most far-reaching cinema after the war, the overall market for Latin American films had begun to contract. Hollywood had very quickly reestablished its absolute dominance over all international markets, including the Spanish-language one, and all Latin American producers faced stiffer competition. Nevertheless, other Latin American nations—still awed by the accomplishments of the Mexican and Argentine industries in the 1930s and early 1940s—remained eager to tap into what was still perceived as a potentially lucrative and prestigious "national" enterprise. In these instances, state support for industrial development was often made available. Thus in 1946, Christensen was invited to direct in Chile by the recently established state-funded national producer Chile Films, initiating his continental filmmaking with *La dama de la muerte* (The Lady of Death, 1946). Accustomed to the industrial limitations of working for Lumiton, Christensen recalls that he was shocked by how Chile Films did business:

> The Chile Films studios were more modern than the Argentine and were excellently equipped. The personnel was also very professional. But they spent too much money: the manager used to come to work in the morning in a nineteenth-century horse-drawn carriage. (Oroz 1991, 139)[6]

Christensen's assessment of the inefficiency of the Chile Films setup is shared by Chilean film historian Alicia de la Vega, who dismisses this period of "importing talent" to build a national industry—of the nine films produced, only two were directed by Chileans while Argentines directed the remaining seven—as a "complete failure" because of poor scripts, the imported talent (which did not include big-name recognizable stars), the attempt to "internationalize" the content, and excessive production budgets (1979, 32–33, 379–80). It is interesting to note that Chile Films had contracted with Argentina Sono Films for "commercial, administrative, and technical" advice and that its model of studio organization, already causing difficulties nationally, was hardly appropriate for the Chilean scenario (Schnitman 1984). Although *La dama de la muerte* was among the best received of the studio's films, contemporary critics in the weeklies *Ecran* and *Ercilla* regularly lambasted all the Chile Films productions for the lack of "Chileanness resulting from their pancontinental creative and technical crews" (López Navarro 1994). In this instance, then, the national context ostensibly precluded the "traveler's gaze" from even being heralded as a contribution to the formation of a national cinema, although the period decidedly merits further research on just this account.

Shortly thereafter, following the extraordinary success of *El ángel desnudo* (The Naked Angel, 1946), which featured the first female nude of the Argentine cinema and transformed Olga Zubarry into its first "sexy" star, Christensen was once again invited to travel and encountered a vastly different scenario. His description of this experience provides interesting insights about the paradoxes of the formation of a national film industry:

> Some Venezuelans came to Lumiton and invited me to work at new studios that would be inaugurated with my film. They said that they wanted to develop a *Venezuelan* cinema and were willing to go to great lengths to achieve their objective. According to them, they had everything there. So, I went. Although the studios existed, there was nothing in them. I remember that I said to them, "But you said you had everything!" And they responded, "If we had told you the truth, you would not have come." Then, the owner of the studio, Villegas Blanco, told me to make a list of what they needed to import. Lights, cameras, everything necessary to make a feature-length film was brought in *by air*! Since there was no technical infrastructure, I brought technicians in from *Argentina*. (Oroz 1991, 164; emphasis by López)

The studio that brought Christensen to Venezuela was Bolivar Films. Owner Villegas Blanco had purchased the equipment and studios of

Condor Films (a firm started in 1940 by Rafael María Zambrano that had produced only two films before disappearing in 1942), then had contracted with the state to produce documentary, publicity, and newsreel shorts. Gradually, the company forged important alliances with other smaller producers and distributors until, in 1948–1950, it came to be perceived as the preeminent national producer and received funding from the state to finance feature-length fictional projects.

Why was the Venezuelan state interested in fostering a national cinema at this particular conjuncture? For one thing, after the 1945 coup, there had been a concerted movement to define a singular national identity. Echoing the foundational work of the characters of Rómulo Gallegos's novel *Doña Bárbara* (1929), who embody and act out the struggle between a primitive and violent past (Doña Bárbara) and the modernizing force of civilization (Santos Luzardo), the national culture was identified with the attributes of a subsector of the nation: the culture of the *llano*, or plains, with its mythic *llanero*—cowboys wearing spats and boots, and peasants shod in espadrilles. Within this paradigm, a national cinema was perceived as a modernizing force, but one that could still highlight the cultural element being promulgated in other cultural realms as the marks of national identity (González Ordosgoicci 1991, 69–75). In the period 1948–1958, the decade of the dictatorship (and especially after dictator Pérez Jiménez took over in 1950), this tendency was exacerbated: the officially promulgated *nuevo ideal nacional* included as one of its central dimensions an explicit celebration of folkloricism—especially the image of the *llanero* as the essence of national culture.

Christensen's second project for Bolivar films, the feature *La balandra Isabel llegó esta tarde* (The Isabel Arrived This Afternoon, 1949) was, in many ways, a perfect synthesis of the Venezuelan state's cultural and national agenda. As an adaptation of Venezuelan writer Guillermo de Meneses's 1934 short story of the same title, it was by default positioned as a celebration of national culture. Although Meneses would fall from grace during the decade of the dictatorship, in the late 1940s he was recognized as one of the principal voices of the national literature. His work in this period, including "La balandra Isabel," followed the realist tradition of Gallegos but with a difference. While Gallegos's positivist foundational fictions used the "local" referent—that is, regional settings and characters—as a source of national stability and an access to universal values, Meneses's work reconfigured similarly folkloric referents within radically unstable fictional universes. His focus on the power of sexuality to determine and drive human action and, even more significantly, his fascination with Afro-Venezuelan culture (rather than rural *llanero* culture), simultaneously marked his work with a "new" vanguard spirit while celebrating—and exoticizing—some of the most traditional, yet mysterious, aspects of the national imaginary. Much more indebted to Freud and Bergson than to nineteenth-century positivism, Meneses's fictions are peopled with characters who are adrift in, rather than grounded by, their regionality. Thus refigured as liminality, the regional/folkloric gives rise to doubts and uncertainties that threaten the social and psychic integrity of the individual. Having already been adapted for the stage in 1943 by Meneses himself, "La balandra Isabel" was thus positioned as a perfect symbol of a new Venezuelan national cultural identity.

Adapted to the screen by another Venezuelan writer, Aquiles Nazoa, and Christensen himself, the film version of *La balandra Isabel* pulled together a literary work of recognized national importance whose subject matter also addressed those folkloric elements in the forefront of official definitions of the nation, and with the same exoticizing impulse. *La balandra Isabel* was the most talked-about and awarded film of the period. Billed as the first Venezuelan "super-production," the film and its production were widely publicized. That its budget of nine hundred thousand bolivares (approximately US$270,000) was "suicidal" and almost double that of any other previous Venezuelan production was in itself a guarantee of prestige seconded only by the fame of the Mexican actor Arturo de Córdova, who received the then unheard of salary of $10,000 per week (Ricardo Tirado, cited in Solar 1991, 11). *La balandra Isabel* was widely heralded as the beginning of the national film industry. For example, Miguel Otero Silva in the newspaper *El Nacional* claimed that the film was "a revelation for natives and foreigners of all the grandeur and potential that the Venezuelan cinema can achieve." He went on to say: "Can a cinematography like this be ignored or stagnate? A nation that produces a film like *La balandra Isabel* will not remain on the margins and has the duty to continue offering us such works of art" (Silva cited in Solar 1991, 11). The film's pan-national case—not only Arturo de Córdova but also the Argentine actress Virginia Luque and a host of other secondary characters—and genesis disappeared under the pressure to highlight its foundational characteristics, especially after the film won the best cinematography award at the Cannes Film Festival for the work of its Spanish-born cinematographer José María Beltrán.

Of course, exoticizing the nation via folklore as a strategy for foundational national cinemas had already proven to be a viable strategy in Latin America, as the success of the Mexican *ranchera* genre had proven in the late 1930s. Here, however, more than a decade later, joined to the focus on sexuality in Meneses's story and to Christensen's already-established reputation as a "sexy" director, the folkloric nation is reinscribed as a locus for desire and a melodramatic engine. Rather than focus upon couple formation—the family romance—within a folkloric allegory of the nation, *La balandra Isabel* invokes the folkloric as an explicitly erotic subtext tinged with foreignness and with the potential to destabilize the family and the nation.

In the best Latin American melodramatic tradition, *La balandra Isabel* tells the story of Segundo, a captain from Isla Margarita who owns the ship *La Isabel*. Happily married and with a preadolescent son who is eager to follow in his seafaring footsteps, Segundo is introduced as a stable patriarchal figure with great authority. But when he goes off to sea, we discover that he is in fact unstable and obsessed by a powerful sexy woman, Esperanza, with whom he spends time in the port town of La Guaira. Esperanza wants Segundo to herself, and when her own sexual wiles seem insufficient to the task, she engages the help of Bocú, an Afro-Cuban/Venezuelan *santero* who puts a spell on Segundo to force him to return. The spell works. Segundo, even though accompanied by his son on this particular trip, is drawn inexorably to Esperanza, until he discovers that she is betraying him with Bocú. After he fights with Bocú, the power of the spell and of Esperanza's sexuality are dispelled and he is able to return to his son and his ship and to head home to Isla Margarita, his wife, and a "normal" social order.

To read *La balandra Isabel* simultaneously as foundational for the national cinema and through the lens of a traveling filmmaker is thus especially apropos, because the film is itself, in part, about traveling. Furthermore, both impulses, although ostensibly contradictory, find cinematic expression in a similar kind of formal gesture: a double-voicedness or dual focus that mediates the melodramatic through an appeal to the documentary power of the image and its potential ethnographic truth.

The film begins with a documentary-like move. The credits are superimposed upon a freeze-frame of waves violently crashing on a jagged rock and accompanied by dramatic orchestral scoring that approximates the sound of the ocean. Following the director's name, the frozen image is animated and dissolves into a sailboat upon which a rather crudely drawn map of northern Venezuela is superimposed. On the upper half of the map is Isla Margarita, and while the camera slowly reframes to center the small island, an obtrusive authoritarian male voice-over (with a marked

Venezuelan accent) identifies and describes the locale where the story will be set: "Land of sailors, at other times a mecca for greedy adventurers attracted by the fame of its pearls, Margarita dazzles like an invocation to the world of fauna." As the narrator finishes his poetic description, a series of dissolves shows the "land of sailors" and the cycles of the "world of fauna": nets drying on the beach; a large group of men, women, and children pushing a boat out to sea; the women and children standing on the beach as the boat sets off; pulling a net in (shot from three different directions); pulling the boat out of the water; the men using baskets to transfer tiny little fish to buckets; a closer shot of the leaping fish in the basket. Thus the film interrupts the trajectory of its very melodramatic credit sequence to begin with a minidocumentary treatise—in almost perfect travelogue style—that succinctly introduces and describes the life cycle of the island with images that scream out their "authenticity." The people here are obviously non-actors and the action is clearly unstaged. Furthermore, we can briefly see the bemused glances of several of the participants who occasionally look at the camera and smile shyly amid all their activity. Formally embracing this "other" island into the nation but through the eye of the foreign traveler, this documentary introduction simultaneously exalts and exoticizes Isla Margarita and the humble "natives" who work the sea by inserting them into diegesis as little else but the "world of the fauna" of the island.

Echoing this gesture, the first dramatic scene of the film is also marked by a traveler's gaze. Following a fade to black after the close-up of the tiny fish leaping in a basket, a high-angle shot shows a bunch of kids paddling in the water yelling, "El último, mister, el último!" ("The last one, mister, the last one!"]. A man visually coded as a foreigner—sweating profusely and wearing a white linen suit and hat, a loud flowered shirt, camera around his neck, and smoking a cigar—stands on the pier and pitches coins into the sea for local kids to dive for. Identified as "Monsieur" (one of the kids even yells out to him, "¡Monsieur-cito!"), this character is a typical "foreigner," like many others in Latin American films of the period and his actions those of a typical visitor to a colonial outpost. After one last big pitch, one of the kids gets a cramp, and a handsome man, observing the foreigner disapprovingly, dives in to pull him out. The man is the boy's father, Segundo, played by the easily recognized (especially after a strikingly beautiful close-up) Arturo de Córdova. When he comes out of the water, Segundo squares off with the foreigner, pushes him off the pier, and walks off with his son.

Narratively, this sequence serves to introduce two of our principal characters—Segundo and his son—and to characterize the father-son relationship and patriarchal lines of descent as central and linked to the sea and seafaring. But beyond its service to the plot, it also begins the film with a curious, determining, and very telling gesture. What can we make of the figure of the foreigner here? He is of no further narrative significance and never reappears, but his presence—like that of the map—is an index of the film's necessarily ambivalent position vis-à-vis its problematic, if not impossible, national commitments. By focusing on the diegetic foreignness of "Monsieur," the film can relativize the extra-diegetic otherness of Arturo de Córdova as a Venezuelan ship captain into a cinematic imaginary structured by the melodramatic. Recognized and displaced, foreignness itself becomes the principal source of melodramatic excess. Thus the film sets the terms for Segundo's redemption—he must reject the foreign, the other, his own foreignness—wherein the national becomes a question of taming the excess of foreignness rather than only a battle over emotions, passion, and desire.

This initial insistence on highlighting "otherness" is echoed, narratively and visually, throughout the rest of the film. For example, early in the film, after we have been introduced to his idyllic and quite bourgeois home life with wife and son, Segundo leaves Isla Margarita for La Guaira, a port town where he himself is a stranger and a traveler, an outsider.[7] His earlier locatedness and integrity—sources of his authority—begin to wane while still at sea. He is haunted by a song—identified by his noticeably Argentine first mate, Martinote, as "Esperanza's song"—and stares at the sea longingly while his sailors joke about the women waiting for them in La Guaira (in Venezuelan slang). When they arrive at La Guaira (a crowded prototypical port town in which nationalities, races, classes, and genders seem to coexist easily), Segundo dons a dapper white linen suit and straw hat and goes ashore, where he is greeted warmly by a series of women asking after his sailors. Reenacting "Monsieur's" stance and clothing, he is jovial and self-assured with all of them, a man completely in control of himself and his element, *un capitán*. Before entering El Cuerno de la Fortuna (The Horn of Plenty), the bar where Esperanza sings, he runs into a crazed old woman, María, who prepares him for what he is about to find: Esperanza is with another man. Inside the bar, Esperanza is next to an older man in a card game and singing with her back to the door; she does not see Segundo enter. Our first close-up of her discloses a beautifully excessive face, markedly sensual, already glistening with desire (the complete opposite of his wife's proper beauty). Segundo waits until the end of her song and then moves in to take her away. When challenged by the old man, they first duel at cards (Segundo wins), and finally they fistfight. At the end, the old man is beaten to a bloody pulp and gives up, while Segundo is barely mussed (only a little strand of curly hair has fallen onto his forehead). When he comes to Esperanza, they kiss passionately and leave the bar after Segundo throws the bartender a golden coin. Literally repeating "Monsieur's" actions in the first sequence, Segundo's aggressiveness and conquering spirit are not that different from those of the prototypical foreigner. Like Monsieur, he watches the natives bemusedly and has no respect for the life of this "other" world. He has money and, as he tells Esperanza, no man there is "man" enough to take her away from him. Subsequently, Esperanza begs him to stay with her, and in the throes of passion, he promises to stay with her forever. But after spending three days in her messy, crowded, and noisy apartment—surrounded by flypaper, bottles of liquor, and squabbles among neighboring women—he is utterly disgusted by the exotic, yet squalid, banality and vulgarity of her life.[8] When subsequently confronted by his first mate's song—a folk ballad with the refrain "la mujer margariteña siempre tiene su nobleza" (the woman from Margarita is always noble)—he orders his men to set sail.

A similar layering of otherness occurs when on the way back home, after Bocú's spell begins to affect Segundo, a storm forces the ship to stop at Carenero, another island port. In this even more exotic locale—an other to the other of La Guaira—the primarily Afro-Venezuelan natives are celebrating the feast of San Juan with *santería* drumming, singing, and dancing. Here there is no "normalcy"; it is night and the otherness is explicit and all-encompassing. And Segundo is no longer in control: he is driven to drink and into a mad frenzy—beautifully photographed in canted medium and close-up shots—by Bocú's spell and by the powerful ritualistic festivities. The otherness here is utterly foreign, excessive, dangerous, unmediated, intolerable.

Later, when Segundo seems to have moved permanently to La Guaira, where Bocú's spell keeps him enslaved to Esperanza's sexuality, he becomes a complete moral weakling and physical bully. The formerly dapper *capitán* becomes a besotted drunk; all he can do is hang around Esperanza, listen to her singing, and bully the bar patrons to be as entranced by her as he is. Here, Segundo has been completely depersonalized. His passion has denuded him and transformed him into a caricature of his former powerful self. Driven only by a mad desire and sweating rather unbecomingly (again, like Monsieur in the first sequence), he ignores his work, his sailors, certainly the memory of his wife waiting for him back home, but, most significantly, even his own son. He has become an other to himself.

Finally, a further layering effect is produced by the film's curious international mix of professional and nonprofessional actors and of extraordinarily popular stars and relative unknowns. Alongside Arturo de Córdova, arguably the most recognizable male star of the period,[9] is a series of lesser-known actors and a large number of non-actors who, with few speaking parts, provide a significant "authentic" backdrop for the unfolding melodrama. In his first screen appearance, Nestor Zavarce, the child who plays the son, mediates between the professional actors and the non-actors to provide local color: his more awkwardly delivered lines are touchingly sincere, appropriate to a child, and help diminish the difference between the two groups.

The international provenance of the actors and the curious mix of their various accents are similarly elided, but through an additional displacement that further complicates the work of nationality in the film. First of all, the location for most of the action—La Guaira—is established as remote and distant, far from the national stability and belongingness of Isla Margarita. Although cartographically La Guaira is on the mainland and centrally located (and the port for the capital city of Caracas), in the melodramatic geography of the film La Guaira is other: it does not appear on the map and is figured as an uncharted national territory, a Caribbean contact zone. Although races and nationalities seem to mix with impunity (one of the La Guaira women we see early in the film is called Olga and speaks with a European accent), the dominant thread of La Guaira is carried by a specific foreign influence: African religious rituals. Handily ignoring all demographic evidence to the contrary (Pollak-Eltz 1972), the film carefully confines *santería* to the cinematic outposts (La Guaira and, later, Carenero). In Isla Margarita, the furthest region of the cartographical nation of the introduction, Segundo's wife, Isabel, is a proper Catholic who has pictures of saints on her walls, makes son and husband say grace and cross themselves before dinner ("¡Santíguense, herejes!" [Cross yourselves, heretics!] she tells them), and attends Sunday mass dutifully. She even gives Segundo a small medal of the Virgin of the Valley on a chain for "protection." Despite its cartographical distance—or perhaps precisely because of it—Isla Margarita is the haven for the pure national values that will win the day: home, church, and patriarchy. The source of

La Guaira's otherness is clearly identified: Bocú is described as the son of a powerful and well-known Cuban *santero*, who sired him as well as the madwoman María. By displacing the source of the supernatural force that threatens the stability of man, patriarchy, and family onto a Cuban Black man and onto Afro-Cuban—rather than Afro-Venezuelan—rituals, the film is able to simultaneously present pan-national movement as a given while reinforcing the desire and need for a national stability centered on its rejection. *Mestizaje* may be an unavoidable given, but the terms of its incorporation into nationness will be closely regulated.

The scenes of the film that focus on *santería* activities are effective in yet another register, for they echo all too well the substance of authentic *santería* practices as well as their performative power and visual excess. Ranging from the detailed (and dramatically filmed) presentation of Bocú's house and altar when he puts the spell on Segundo in the cigar smoke ceremony—using the religious medal that Isabel had given Segundo for protection—to the festivities of San Juan in Carenero, the "folkloric" scenes were orchestrated by Juan Liscano, a well-known Venezuelan folklore expert whose name features prominently in the credits and whose collaboration grants these aspects of the film an even greater legitimacy. Presenting Afro-Venezuelans who, with the exception of Bocú, are obviously non-actors, these sequences are explicitly linked to the film's initial documentary and distancing gesture as yet additional evidence of the authenticity of its national representation. But they also further the film's peculiarly ambivalent position vis-à-vis the nation's internal otherness: despite the film's emphasis on "folkloricism," the nationness it promotes is not itself folkloric. How else can we read the existence of a folklore "expert"? Why would a folkloric national imaginary shared by all citizens require that an expert's testimonial evidence be explicitly acknowledged? Unlike the Mexican *comedia ranchera*'s effortless production of a folkloric world as national allegory—in which the autoreferentiality of an expert would be absurd—*La balandra Isabel* needs this mediating presence in order to constitute a specific paradigm of nationness vis-à-vis multiple and multicultural referents.

But what is at stake in *La balandra Isabel* is not simply positioning certain cultural elements as "foreign" within the national space of the narrative (this is obviously worked out diegetically) but a slippage of foreignness itself as a category. The crux of nationness here is not really the issue of foreign versus native but rather a question of two kinds of foreignness: primitive (erotic, uncontrollable, dangerous) and bourgeois

(Catholic, patriarchal, stable). In this way, the nation sees itself as exotic-erotic from a "foreigner's" perspective.

In the short story upon which the film is based, Meneses focused exclusively on painting a rich portrait of the Afro-Venezuelan life of his characters in the spirit of primitivism. The story lacks the film's crucial second tier of foreignness: we learn that Segundo is married and has children but we never meet them, and furthermore Segundo is called a "negro verde," a ladies' man with women in every port. Similarly, all of the characters are explicitly Black (and address each other as "negrito" and "negrita") and working-class poor, so there is no class or racial difference implicated in the drama. Most tellingly, in the story the spell upon Segundo doesn't work: he does not return to La Guaira, and Esperanza is left waiting for him at the docks. Although it does function as a sketch of a familiar yet implicitly distant other, the story's power is derived from its treatment of eroticism and sexuality. Frankly depicted and described, the erotic is what the story's location in otherness enables. In the film, however, which is aided by an internationally recognized melodramatic mode and star system, Segundo/Arturo de Córdova can overcome the primitive, for the film ultimately subordinates it to the ideals of a transnational bourgeois culture premised upon patriarchy and Catholicism.

Quasi-documentary naturalism, melodrama, and exoticized/eroticized folklore come together in *La balandra Isabel* at the intersection of the nation with pan-national forces, coding an auteurist impulse, star presence, and hybrid generic allusions as national and necessarily pan-national, foundational, and destabilizing. Straddling the difficult crossover of national and international aspirations, influences, and effects, *La balandra Isabel* highlights, above all, the paradoxical work of nationness in "national" cinemas and the impossibility of separating the "foreigner's" gaze from the nation's own best-intentioned introspections. That this perverse configuration was ostensibly designed to allow for the formation of a national cinema leads us to question to what degree other Latin American cinemas, and perhaps national cinemas in general, have been enabled by a figural or literal foreigner's gaze.

Despite all its complex slippages and national paradoxes, *La balandra Isabel* did not magically engender a national film industry in Venezuela. That dream was postponed—after a detour through the New Latin American Cinema of the 1960s—until the oil boom of the 1970s and 1980s. But it did generate a significant series of further pan–Latin American cinematic collaborations and imbrications. Cinematographer José María

Beltrán remained in Venezuela, while Arturo de Córdova continued his prolific traveling career. Christensen returned to Argentina, where he directed, among other films, *Si muero antes de despertar* (If I Die before Awakening, 1952), an adaptation of a short story by the US detective/thriller writer William Irish. A critically well-received and successful film, it was, according to Domingo Di Núbila, not only one of the best films of the year but also the indirect cause of Christensen's subsequent exile to Brazil: given the Peronist climate, "it was [politically] dangerous to make great films" (1959b, 1570). Christensen's career in Brazil, an indirect extension of *La balandra Isabel*, will constitute another chapter in the saga of Latin American traveling filmmakers and the persistence of the foreigner's gaze in national cinemas.

Part 2

Of Modes and Genres

Editors' Introduction

We continue this anthology with a part containing ten essays that embody López's transformative interventions in the study of Latin American modes and genres across the musical, the melodrama, exploitation cinema, and the documentary. While melodrama and music are discussed in essays included in other parts (such as "Film and Radio Intermedialities . . ." [2017] and "Are All Latins from Manhattan?" [1991]), genre issues are the primary focus of the essays in this part, all of which pay particular attention to how the melodrama, the musical, the documentary, and/or exploitation genres emerge, develop, and function differently in Latin America. That so many of the essays in this part straddle the multiple categories we have established to structure this anthology attests to the coherency of López's work and how it constitutes an "oeuvre."

Historically in Latin American film studies, certain discipline-related imperatives have encouraged scholars to undervalue mainstream genres and modes like the melodrama, the telenovela, and the musical. The Adornoian and anticolonialist-informed theoretical perspectives of the 1960s and 1970s, which shaped the new cinemas of that period, rejected genres as culturally derivative of the Hollywood industry, complicit with its bourgeois (patriarchal) ideologies (Colina and Díaz Torres 1971, 16), and consequently incompatible with the notion of Latin American cultural autonomy. Equally, in the Anglophone academy, melodrama was initially dismissed as less critically appealing by film theorists for its (female) excessiveness and its highly emotional context in favor of the (more manly) gangster movies and westerns. But subsequent (often feminist) reevaluations of melodrama rehabilitated the genre to make it a central concern of film studies and of the emerging discipline of cultural studies with its focus on mass and popular culture. In Anglophone scholarship of the 1970s and 1980s, Thomas Elsaesser, Geoffrey Nowell-Smith, Marcia Landy, Christine Gledhill, and others highlighted melodrama's potential to question (rather than uphold) the norms of patriarchal bourgeois society (Landy 1991, 14, 20) precisely because of its female centeredness. At the same time, in Latin Americanist cultural studies, a changed perspective toward mass culture led theorists to recognize melodrama in its different media forms (radionovela, classical cinema, telenovela, and the nineteenth-century *folletín* [serial literature]) as the privileged genre of Latin American identity that "personalizes the political" and "unifies" Latin America (Martín-Barbero 1987, 181; Monsiváis 1994).

López's foundational essays on melodrama "Our Welcomed Guests" and "Tears and Desire" (1995b, 1994b) emerged out of this broader disciplinary context of reevaluating melodrama and genre but did so with a geocultural specificity located in Latin America. First published as "The Melodrama in Latin America" in *Wide Angle* in 1985 (1985b) and then republished in expanded form, "Our Welcomed Guests" (1995b) argued for the distinctiveness of Latin American telenovelas from American soap operas and from each other, noting differences between the nationally produced telenovelas *and* also their transnational functioning across the region. First published in 1991 in the feminist film journal *Iris* as "Celluloid Tears" (1991b), "Tears and Desire" similarly argued for the discarding of melodrama's identification with cultural colonization and for the drawing out of the resistive possibilities and "multiple desires" of performative moments found in the melodramatic musical hybrid of the "old" Mexican cinema. Successive iterations of "Tears and Desire" and the sites of their publication in *Multiple Voices in Feminist Film Criticism* (Carson, Dittmar, and Welsch 1994) and *Mediating Two Worlds: Cinematic Encounters in the Americas* (King, López, and Alvarado 1993) further evidenced the strategic importance of, and the primacy of López's scholarship, to the kind of postcolonial film analysis she was championing: drawing attention to the importance of melodrama (the "old" Mexican cinema) as "an integral part of the Latin American and Mexican social formation" (1993b, 149) and, in turn, teaching younger scholars how "resistance may appear in the most unexpected texts" (Alvaray 2021).

Expanding this approach to other genres beyond melodrama, López's postcolonial scholarship similarly demonstrated how in hybrid cultures like those of Latin America, embracing colonialist forms such as the musical didn't necessarily imply a straightforward model of reproduction. Hence in two key essays that focus on Latin America's musical films, "Of

Rhythms and Borders" (1997) and "Mexico" (2012a), López noted how the specific Mexican genre of the *cabaretera* (urban nightclub/brothel film) defied genre definition "according to Hollywood formulas" mixing the melodrama and aspects of the musical so that music became less a way of communicating the heavenly feeling of heterosexual coupledom as in the Hollywood musical than a "central register for [melodramatic] excess" (López 2012a, 121; 1997, 322).

As with her work on melodramas and musicals, López's documentary pieces similarly emphasized the specific differences and historical formations of Latin American documentaries. For instance, "At the Limits of Documentary" (1990b) and *"The Battle of Chile"* (1990c) both argued that the key documentaries of the New Latin American Cinema (*Memories of Underdevelopment*, Tomás Gutiérrez Alea, 1968; *The Jackal of Nahueltoro*, Miguel Littín, 1969; *One Way or Another*, Sara Gómez, 1974–1977; *Yawar Mallku*, Jorge Sanjinés and Grupo Ukamau, 1969; and the three-part *The Battle of Chile* [Patricio Guzmán 1975–1979]) bring together documentary and fictional modes to deliberately "eschew . . . traditional distinctions between [them] in [the filmmakers']" search to produce a new "cinema with a renewed social function" (López 1991a, 404). Whereas, "(Not) Looking for Origins" (1992c) similarly pointed out how the five-part documentary series *America* (João Moreiras Salles, 1989) rejected documentary modes and categorizations such as verité, authenticity, among others.

This troubling of genre boundaries and definitions that runs through López's work on Latin American musicals, melodramas, and documentaries was equally the thrust of her essay on the anticipatory exploitation of some 1930s films from Mexico (2009). Positioning *La Llorona* (Ramón Peón, 1934), *La sangre manda* (José Bohr, 1934), and *Madre querida* (Juan Orol, 1934) as precursors to Mexico's exploitation cinemas of the 1950s–1970s, the essay was similarly focused on pinning down the regional specificity (such as mask-wearing villains) and genre hybridity (plots infused with melodramatic elements) in these films. In her close analyses of the films themselves, López took into consideration the presence of "generic strands popularized by Hollywood," noting how these are combined with "national themes and folklore" as well as "new formal strategies for storytelling" (2009, 14). More broadly, "Before Exploitation" examined the industrial differences between US and Latin American media industries that meant exploitation proper developed much later in the region.

By drawing attention to the importance, distinctiveness, and complexity of the popular genres and modes of Latin America's cinemas and saving them from critical dismissal, López paved the way for further work on modes and genres. This is evident in recent studies on Latin American melodrama from queer, feminist, and postcolonial perspectives (Dever 2003; de la Mora 2006; Tierney 2007; Sadlier 2009) and on the rehabilitation of other previously dismissed genres—from comedies in the classical era (Couret 2018), to the romantic comedy in the post-political-transition Mexico of the 2000s (MacLaird 2013, 10; Sánchez Prado 2014, 69), to exploitation and horror cinemas in various historical periods (Ruétalo and Tierney 2009; Tierney 2003; Syder and Tierney 2005).

9

Tears and Desire

Women and Melodrama in the "Old" Mexican Cinema (1994)

This canonical piece is one of López's most widely reprinted essays (along with "Early Cinema and Modernity" and "Are All Latins from Manhattan?"). Of particular interest to feminist film scholars, "Tears and Desire" took as its point of departure the theoretical rethinking of melodrama that took place in Anglo-American film studies in the 1980s through the work of Modleski (1982) and Gledhill (1987), among others. However, the essay questioned the way in which that initial scholarship had discussed melodrama without paying sufficient attention to cultural specificities or the variability of historical contexts and countered this tendency by examining the case of

---

Research for this essay was made possible, in part, by grants from the Mellon Foundation and the Roger Thayer Stone Center for Latin American Studies at Tulane University. Parts of this essay have appeared in "Celluloid Tears: Melodrama in the Classic Mexican Cinema," *Iris* 13 (Summer 1991), and in *Mediating Two Worlds*, ed. John King, Ana López, and Manuel Alvarado (London: British Film Institute, 1993).

Editors' note: The earliest version appeared in *Iris* as "Celluloid Tears: Melodrama in the Classic Mexican Cinema" (1991). Subsequent versions were (re)published under the current title in *Mediating Two Worlds* (1993, coedited by King, López, and Alvarado); *Multiple Voices in Feminist Film Criticism* (1994); *Feminism and Film* (2001); and *The Latin American Cultural Studies Reader* (2004). We selected the one published in *Multiple Voices . . .* (1994) because it places the study of melodrama much more firmly within the feminist mode and the history of feminist film scholarship.

187

188 | Ana M. López

Mexican melodrama in the 1930s–1940s. Rather than seeing melodrama as an alternative mode to the dominance of realism (as many Anglo-American researchers working on Hollywood cinema had argued), López utilized the work of Latinx and Mexican cultural studies scholars (Moraga, Monsiváis) to argue that melodrama has long been a dominant mode in Latin America and to trace the differential ways it emerged and developed.

The melodrama has been a crucial site for the interrogation of many of the categories utilized for the contemporary study of the cinema and for debates over questions of genre, narration, ideology, subjectivity, and representation (Gledhill 1987; Lang 1989; Altman 1989). Above all, however, film melodrama has been one of the most important areas for the development of feminist film criticism. Long considered a "feminine" mode because of its insistent attention to the domestic sphere and related emotional issues, the melodrama—especially that subset of the genre known as the "woman's film" and ostensibly addressed to female audiences—has proven to be a productive area for the investigation of the representation of women, female subjectivity, and desire, gendered critical categories, and the role of women as cultural producers and consumers (Gledhill 1987; Doane 1987). Emerging in the context of the 1960s–1970s rediscovery and reassessment of the classical Hollywood cinema and the 1970s–1980s boom in feminist scholarship, this investigation of the melodramatic mode was limited, until very recently, to the study of the Hollywood melodrama and its relationship to US society, ideology, and patriarchy. However, recent studies exploring the historical and international inscription of women and melodramatic representation (in cinemas as diverse as German Weimar films [Petro 1989], French films of the 1920s and '30s [Turim 1987; Vincendeau 1989], the *bourekas* films of 1970s Israeli cinema [Shohat 1989], and the commercial 1950s Hindi cinema [Vasudevan 1989]) have begun to delineate the complex lines of historical and cultural affiliations that link and differentiate the social functions of the melodramatic in specific moments of Western and non-Western societies. Above all, the investigation of the gendering of subjects in melodramatic representation in non-US societies has forced scholars to confront conflicting, historically specific claims of national, ethnic, and gender identity.

Within this context, I want to explore the placement of women in Mexican film melodramas of the 1940s and 1950s and its relationship to Mexican society. Rather than present a content-based description of the "types" of women represented (virgins/mothers versus whores, for example) or summarize clichéd plot resolutions (Mora 1985), I am concerned with the interrelations among patriarchal Mexican society, women's place in Mexican culture and national identity, and film production and consumption. Emphasizing the different articulations of gender and subjectivity in a society formed by colonization and marked by a history of violence and discontinuity, I attempt to link the history of the classical Mexican cinema melodrama with Mexican society, to trace the inscription of the melodramatic alongside the social positioning of women, and to highlight moments when conflicting voices and needs visibly erupt into the cinematic and social spheres.

The Melodrama and the Latin American Cinema

As has been extensively detailed elsewhere, the melodrama, along with music and comedy, became synonymous with the cinema in Latin America after the introduction of sound.[1] Taking advantage of Hollywood's temporary inability to satisfy the linguistic needs of the Latin American market, local producers used the new technology to exploit national characteristics. Argentina took on the tango and its melodramatic lyrics and developed the tango melodrama genre in the early 1930s. Similarly, Mexico made the melodrama a central genre of the sound cinema after the success of *Santa* (1931, Antonio Moreno), an adaptation of a well-known melodramatic novel by Federico Gamboa about an innocent provincial girl forced into urban prostitution and redeemed only in death.[2]

Furthermore, the rapid establishment of a specific Latin American star system heavily dependent on radio and popular musical entertainers gave rise to melodramas with at least one or two musical performances to heighten a film's "entertainment value." Starring singers-turned-actors, narratives about entertainers sprinkled with performances became de rigueur. Thus Libertad Lamarque's suffering mothers always also sang, Pedro Infante could weep over his little Black child with the popular song "Angelitos Negros" (Little Black Angels) in the film of the same title, and Ninón Sevilla could vent her sexual anger and frustration dancing wild rumbas in the *cabaretera* (brothel) films of the 1950s. In these and other films, the narrative stoppage usually generated by performances was reinvested with emotion, so that melodramatic pathos emerged in the moment of performance itself (through gesture, sentiment, interactions with the audience within the film, or simply music choice). And in a film such as *Amor en las Sombras* (Love in the Shadows, 1959, Tito Davison), which featured ten complete performances in less than two hours' screen time, music and song rather than dramatic action propel the narrative.

Despite this diversity, however, two basic melodramatic tendencies developed between 1930 and 1960: family melodramas that focused on the problems of love, sexuality, and parenting, and epic melodramas that reworked national history, especially the events of the Mexican Revolution. Although the two categories are somewhat fluid, with some family melodramas taking place in the context of the Revolution and its aftermath, I shall be concerned primarily with the operations of the former. The revolutionary melodramas are perhaps as significant for the development of a gendered "Mexican" consciousness as the family ones, but I am interested in analyzing the cinematic positioning of women within the Mexican domestic sphere, and the ideological operations of the family melodramas provide us with privileged access to that realm. Set in quintessential domestic spaces (homes or similar places) that, as Laura Mulvey says, "can hold a drama in claustrophobic intensity and represent . . . the passions and antagonisms that lie behind it" (1986, 95), the family melodramas map the repressions and contradictions of interiority and interior spaces—the home and unconscious—with more urgency than is possible within the cathartic large-scale action of revolutionary dramas.

The Melodrama, Women, and Mexico

The melodramatic is deeply embedded in Mexican and Hispanic culture and intersects with the three master narratives of Mexican society: religion, nationalism, and modernization. First of all, Hispanic culture carries the burden of its Christianity, which, as Susan Sontag argues in *Against Interpretation*, is already melodramatic—rather than tragic—in structure and intention. In Christianity, as Sontag says, "every crucifixion must be topped by a resurrection," an optimism inimical to the pessimism of tragedy (1966, 132–39). Furthermore, the staples of the family melodrama—sin and suffering abnegation—are essential components of the Christian tradition: sin allows for passion and, although it must always be punished, passion, after all, justifies life.

Perhaps most significantly, the melodrama always addresses questions of individual (gendered) identity within patriarchal culture and the heart of Mexico's definition as a nation. In Mexico, questions of individual identity are complicated by a colonial heritage that defines woman—and her alleged instability and unreliability—as the origin of *national* identity. The Mexican nation is defined, on the one hand, by Catholicism and the Virgin Guadalupe, the Virgin Mother and patron saint, and, on the other, by the *Chingada*, the national betrayal of Doña Marina—also known as La Malinche or Malintzin Tenepal—the Aztec princess who submitted to Cortéz and handed her people over to the conquistadores.[3] As Cherríe Moraga succinctly puts it: "Malinche fucked the white man who conquered the indigenous peoples of Mexico and destroyed their culture. Ever since, brown men have been accusing her of betraying her race, and over the centuries continue to blame her entire sex for this 'transgression'" (1986, 174–75). Raped, defiled, and abused, Malintzin/Malinche is the violated mother of modern Mexico, *la chingada*—the fucked one—or *la vendida*—the sellout. As Octavio Paz explains in *The Labyrinth of Solitude*, Malinche's "sons" (sic), the Mexican people, are "the sons of La Chingada, the fruits of a rape, a farce" (1961, 85). Thus the origins of the nation are located at a site—the violated mother—that is simultaneously an altar of veneration and the place of an original shame. The victim of a rape, Malinche/La Chingada, mother of the nation, carries the guilt of her victimization. Deeply marked by this "otherness," Mexican national identity rejects and celebrates its feminine origins while gender identity, in general, is problematized even further. To be Malinche—a woman—is to be a traitor, the great whore-mother of a bastard race. The melodramatic became the privileged place for the symbolic reenactment of this drama of identification and the only place where female desire—and the utopian dream of its realization—could be glimpsed. Mexico's colonial heritage—first Spanish and most recently North American—also affects the social functions of the melodrama. Colonialism always implies a crisis of identity for the colonial subject, caught between the impulse to imitate the colonizer and the desire for an always displaced autonomy. Like Caliban in Shakespeare's *Tempest*, the colonized must use the colonizer's "words"—the imported cinematic apparatus—and learn the colonizer's language before he or she can even think of articulating his or her own speech: "You taught me language and my profit on't is I know how to curse." Just as in Brazil the parodic *chanchada* genre can be seen as a response to the impossibility of thinking of a national cinema without considering the Hollywood cinema as well as Brazil's own underdevelopment, in Mexico, melodrama's excess explicitly defies the Hollywood dominant: "Since there can be no nostalgic return to pre-colonial purity, no unproblematic recovery of national origins undefiled by alien influences, the artist in the dominated culture cannot ignore the foreign presence but must rather swallow it and recycle it to national ends" (Vieira and Stam 1990 [1985], 96). As Carlos Monsiváis has said, "If competition with North America is impossible artistically or technically, the only defense is excess, the absence of limits of the melodrama" (1982b, 70). Thus the melodrama's exaggerated signification and hyperbole—its emphasis on anaphoric events pointing to other implied, absent meanings or origins—become, in the Mexican case, a way of cinematically working through the problematic of an underdeveloped national cinema.

The melodrama is also formally and practically linked with the specific trajectory of Mexican national identity and the significance of the Revolution for the nation-building project. If we agree with Peter Brooks that the melodrama is "a fictional system for making sense of experience as a semantic field of force" that "comes into being in a world where the traditional imperatives of truth and ethics have been violently thrown into question" (1976, xiii, 14–15), then we should not be surprised by the cultural currency of the melodrama in postrevolutionary Mexico. In the midst of the great social upheavals of this period, the country seemed ungovernable and the city an unruly mecca: the Revolution changed the nature of public life, mobilized the masses, shook up the structures of the family without changing its roots and, as Monsiváis says, "served as the inevitable mirror where the country recognized its physiognomy." The revolution may not have "invented" the Mexican nation, but "its vigor, for the first time, lent legendary characteristics to the masses that sustained it" (1982b, 27). In other words, the Revolution created a new class—the new urban poor soon to be a working class—whose willpower, roughness, and illiteracy became insistently visible in the formerly feudal national landscape.

The Revolution also further problematized the position of women in Mexico. Women had fought alongside the men and had followed the troops cooking, healing, and providing emotional and physical solace, either as legitimate wives, lovers, or paid companions. Known generally as *soldaderas*, these women formed the backbone of an incipient feminist movement that emerged after the Revolution. Yet as Jean Franco argues in *Plotting Women*: "The Revolution with its promise of social transformation encouraged a Messianic spirit that transformed mere human beings into supermen and constituted a discourse that associated virility with social transformation in a way that marginalized women at the very moment when they were, supposedly, liberated" (1989, 102). Precisely when the nation created itself anew under the aegis of revolutionary mythology and its male superhero redeemers, women were, once again, relegated to the background, and in cultural production—especially in national epic allegories—represented as a terrain to be traversed in the quest for male identity. Simultaneously, while the new secular state ostensibly promoted women's emancipation to combat Catholicism and its alleged counterrevolutionary ideology,[4] Mexico found itself caught in the wheels of capitalist modernization.

The new class created by the Revolution—an increasingly mobile, urban, migratory class of male and female workers—was entertained by the popular theater (*teatro frívolo* or *género chico*) before it found the cinema, but after the coming of sound, Spanish-language movies became the principal discursive tool for social mapping. While the *género chico* and its carnivalesque ribaldry[5] attracted a socially but not sexually mixed audience, the cinema was family entertainment and, by design and by commercial imperatives, broader based. By the late 1930s and through the 1940s and 1950s, the national cinema granted access not only to entertainment but also to vital behaviors and attitudes: "One didn't go to the cinema to dream, but to learn" (Monsiváis 1976, 446). There was not much room here for the carnivalesque celebration that continued to take place in the *teatro frívolo*: the cinema helped transmit new habits and reiterated codes of behavior, providing the new nation with the common bases and collective ties necessary for national unity. In fact, the cinema helped make a new postrevolutionary middle class viable.

If it is indeed true, as Monsiváis says, that film melodramas served this kind of socializing function, what exactly were the lessons they taught women? How did the melodrama mediate the postrevolutionary crisis of national and gendered identity and its subsequent institutionalization? Rather than blindly enforce or teach unambiguous high moral values, stable codes of behavior, or obedience to the patriarchal order, the family melodramas staged specific dramas of identity that often complicated straightforward ideological identification for men *and* women without precluding accommodation. However, the melodrama's contradictory play of identifications constituted neither false communication nor a simple lesson imposed upon the people from above. Rather, these films addressed pressing contradictions and desires within Mexican society. And even when their narrative work suggests utter complicity with the work of the Law, the emotional excesses set loose and the multiple desires detonated are not easily recuperated.

The narratives of the Mexican family melodrama deal with three principal conflicts: the clash between old (feudal, Porfirian) values and modern (industrialized, urban) life, the crisis of male identity that emerges as a result of this clash, and the instability of female identity that at once guarantees and threatens the passage from the old to the new. These conflicts are played out in two distinct physical and psychic spaces—the home, a private sphere valorized and sanctified by the Law, and the nightclub, a barely tolerated social space as liminal as the home is central. Only marginally acceptable, the nightclub is nevertheless the part of the patriarchal public sphere where the personal—and issues of female subjectivity, emotion, identity, and desire—finds its most complex articulation in the Mexican melodrama.

The Home: Mothers, Families, and Their Others

Although Mexican patriarchal values insist on the sanctity of the traditional home (as an extension of the "fatherland" blessed by God), the extended families in them are rarely well adjusted precisely because of the rigidity of the fathers' law and in spite of the saintliness of the mothers. In Mexico, the family as an institution has a contradictory symbolic status as a site for the crystallization of tensions between traditional patriarchal values (especially the cult of machismo) and modernizing tendencies and as a source of maternal support and nurturing the secular state could not replace (Franco 1986). This ambivalence is clearly evidenced in the deployment of the Mexican cinema's so-called mother obsession. Although it is undoubtedly true that the Mexican melodrama's fascination with saintly mother figures can be traced to the deeply conservative social impulses of the postrevolutionary middle classes, who countered their insecurity over the legitimacy of their status with aggressive nationalism and an obsessive attachment to traditional values, how this mother obsession is worked out in the melodrama complicates any assessment of the politics and social mapping of such representations.

Director Juan Orol and the actress Sara García created the archetypal mother of the Mexican melodrama in *Madre querida* (Dear Mother, 1934), the heart-wrenching story of a young boy who goes to a reformatory for arson and whose mother dies of grief precisely on the tenth of May (Mother's Day in Mexico). Over the next decades, García played suffering, self-sacrificing mothers in countless films such as *No basta ser madre* (It's Not Enough to Be a Mother, 1937), *Mi madrecita* (My Little Mother, 1940), and *Mi madre adorada* (Beloved Mother, 1948). However, despite their self-acknowledged narrative focus on mothers and their positioning of the mother as the central ideological tool for social and moral cohesion, these and other films ostensibly glorifying mothers as repositories of conservative family values were clearly maternal melodramas rather than women's films. This distinction, invoked by E. Ann Kaplan in her discussion of Hollywood 1920s and '30s melodramas (1987), is significant for Mexican cinema, because it helps to distinguish between films that focus on male oedipal dramas and films that more self-consciously address female spectators. Indeed, one could argue that despite their focus on mothers, these family melodramas are patriarchal rather than maternal because they attempt to preserve patriarchal values over the sanctity of the mother. In attempting to reinforce the patriarchy their narrative logic breaks down: the moral crisis created in these films revolves around the fathers' identity and not the mothers', whose position is never put into question.

In *Cuando los hijos se van* (When the Children Go Away, 1941, Juan Bustillo Oro), for example, a rigid provincial family is torn asunder by the father's (Fernando Soler) inability to see the true characters of his sons or to recognize their mother's (Sara García) more sensitive assessment of their characters. Influenced by the "bad" son, the father banishes the "good" son to the city, while the mother, with her unerring maternal instinct, never doubts his integrity and is ultimately proven right by the narrative: the banished son returns a popular radio star and saves the family from a bankruptcy engineered by his sibling. Despite the narrative's obvious privileging of the mother's sight, the film attempts to shore up a patriarchal family structure threatened not only by the patriarch's inability to see, but by the other world lying outside the patriarch's control: Mexico City, emblem of modernization and progress, and the modern and highly pleasurable world outside the family. The film attempts to idealize the family as a unit whose preservation is worth all sacrifices, even death, but its suggestion that the familial crisis is caused by the father's blindness and irrational rigidity, especially when compared to the mother's unerring instinct, puts in question the very patriarchal principle it seeks to assert. Mothers may have a guaranteed place in the home as pillars of strength, tolerance, and self-abnegation—in other words, as oedipal illusions—but outside the home they are prey to the male desires that the Mexican home and family disavow. As a foil to the mother's righteous suffering and masochistic respect for the Law, men, especially father figures, are self-indulgent and unable to obey the moral order. It is their desire—unleashed because of maternal asexuality—that most threatens and disturbs the stability of the family and its women. While denying desire within the family, outside it is a compelling and at times controlling force. Thus a variant of the family melodrama focuses on the impossible attraction of "other" women: the "bad" mothers (*las malas*), the vamps, the mistresses.

While Sara García portrayed the archetypal good mother, María Félix depicted her opposite, the *mala mujer* (bad woman): the haughty, independent woman, as passionate and devilish as the mothers are asexual and saintly. The titles of Félix's films clearly reveal her star persona: *Doña Bárbara* (Fernando de Fuentes, 1943), *La mujer de todos* (Everyone's Woman, Julio Bracho, 1946), *La Devoradora* (The Devourer, Fernando de Fuentes, 1946), *Doña Diabla* (Tito Davison, 1949). *Doña Bárbara*, her third film, most clearly defined this persona.[6] After being brutally raped as a young girl, Bárbara becomes a rich independent landowner—la Doña—who enjoys despoiling and humiliating others, especially men. She exults in her power and discards lovers and even her own daughter easily, exhibiting neither pity nor shame and relishing her hatred. Despite her power, Bárbara, like most of Félix's characters, is simply the vampiresque flip side of the saintly mothers of the family melodramas. Easily classified as antifamily melodramas insofar as they reject the surface accoutrements of the patriarchal family, ultimately her films forcefully reinscribe the need for the standard family. Despite titles focusing on the female character, Félix's films are male-centered narratives, where the specular pleasure lies with the woman (and her masquerades of masculinity), but the narrative remains with a male protagonist. Even in *Doña Bárbara*, the principal narrative agent is Santos Luzardo, a young man (Julián Soler) who challenges la Doña's power when he refuses her seduction. The film is more concerned with how he defeats Bárbara than with Bárbara's point of view or her downfall. Bárbara remains unknowable, an enigma given a sociological raison d'être—the rape—and the face of a goddess, but whose subjectivity and desires remain unknown. As a star, Félix could not embody female desire, for she was an ambivalent icon, as unknowable, cold, and pitiless as the mother figure was full of abnegation and tears (Monsiváis 1981, 161–68). Her presence is simply an echo of the dangers of desire for men rather than its realization for women.

Figure 9.1. María Félix in *Doña Diabla* (Tito Davison, 1949). Public domain.

Woman's Desire on the Margins of the Home

In general, only two kinds of Mexican melodramas were structured around woman's identity and presented from a female point of view: the fallen-but-redeemed-by-motherhood women's films and the *cabaretera* subgenre. Each type also had its prototypical female star: whereas the former films most often starred Dolores Del Rio or, somewhat later, Libertad Lamarque, two stars whose characters suffered copiously for their meager sins and relished child obsessions without equal, the latter were epitomized by the sexy *rumberas* portrayed by Cuban actress Ninón Sevilla. Since neither Lamarque nor Sevilla are Mexican, the relative independence achieved by Lamarque's characters and the sexual wantonness of Sevilla's could be distanced as foreign otherness even when the actresses portrayed Mexican women. However, Mexican-born Del Rio began her career in Hollywood, and, unlike the other two, was always considered a great actress, the grande dame of the Mexican cinema, whose face would acquire mythical status as *the* archetype of the moral and physical perfection of the indigenous woman.

Lamarque, singer and Argentine stage and movie star, acquired a tango-inspired star persona after successfully competing for screen time with singing idol Jorge Negrete in Luis Buñuel's *Gran Casino* (1946). Neither matriarchal mother, vampish other, nor a symbol of indigenous purity, Lamarque was most often a prototypically innocent fallen woman who also sang professionally. In *Soledad* (Solitude, Tito Davison, 1948), for example, Lamarque plays a young orphaned servant (Argentine!) tricked into a false marriage by the family heir, made pregnant, and abandoned but finally successful as an entertainer.

Despite their innocence, however, Lamarque's characters fall uneasily into the prevailing stereotypes of the Mexican cinema. In her best films, where she portrays entertainers with tragic pasts or fates, the need to position her simultaneously in relation to family life and to public life as a performer complicates the affirmation of standard social structures and woman's position vis-à-vis the private and public spheres. Her status as a respectable performer—and the incumbent independence of a salary, relationships outside the domestic sphere, and the adoring gaze of diegetic audiences—destabilizes her identity as a hopeless mother. Thus *Soledad* is unable to sustain the figurative melodramatic signification of its initial scenes (for example, prefiguring the falsity of the wedding ceremony via ominous mise-en-scènes and the *coup de théâtre* of a candle blown out by violent wind when the couple first embrace) and depends increasingly on Soledad's voice rather than her silence to unravel its melodrama. Told from her point of view and, by film's end, literally dependent on her voice, the melodrama of Soledad ends appropriately with her long-lost daughter's anguished cry of recognition: "Mother!" But by now Soledad is far more than "just a mother" and remains an outstanding model of self-sufficiency.

The Cabaret: *Rumberas* and Female Desire

Whereas Lamarque's characters are usually tricked or forced by circumstances into successful careers as singers while all they really want to be is wives and mothers, Ninón Sevilla and other *cabareteras* (María Antonieta Pons, Leticia Palma, and Meche Barba) present a different problematic. Much more sordid, their fates and entertainment activities project a virulent form of desire onto the screen. Nowhere else have screen women been so sexual, so willful, so excessive, so able to express their anger at their fate through vengeance. As François Truffaut (under the pseudonym Robert Lacheney) wrote in *Cahiers du cinéma* in 1954:

> From now on we must take note of Ninón Sevilla, no matter how little we may be concerned with feminine gestures on the screen or elsewhere. From her inflamed look to her fiery mouth, everything is heightened in Ninón (her forehead, her lashes, her nose, her upper lip, her throat, her voice). Like so many missed arrows, [she is an] oblique challenge to bourgeois, Catholic, and all other moralities. (Cited in García Riera 1971, 132–34, and Ayala Blanco 1968, 144–45)

Albeit uneasily, Lamarque's sophisticated performances could be narratively recuperated within an expanded domestic sphere, but Sevilla's excessively gendered gestures engaged melodramatic tropes beyond the point of hyperbole. Thus with Sevilla, the performative excess of the "musical/performance melodrama" reaches its zenith and the boundary between performance and melodrama disappears entirely.

The most virulent of Sevilla's *cabaretera* films was Alberto Gout's 1950 *Aventurera* (Adventuress). The plot is extraordinarily complicated and evidence of the excess associated with such films. Elena (Ninón Sevilla), a happy bourgeois girl, is left destitute when her mother runs away with a lover and her father commits suicide. Unable to find a job, she is tricked into a Juarez brothel, drugged, and gang-raped. Eventually, Elena becomes the star of and a sex worker at the nightclub, but she is so unruly that the madam (Andrea Palma) hires a thug to scar her in punishment. She runs away, becomes a nightclub star again, and meets and seduces Mario (Ruben Rojo), only to discover that his high-society mother is the madam of the Juarez brothel. After many other melodramatic twists and murders, the film finally ends with Mario and Elena supposedly free of their family traumas and about to enjoy a normal family life. The film's resolution imposes an end to the story, but it cannot contain the excess of signification circulated by the film: the malevolence of Andrea Palma's icy glance as she watches Elena's first tastes of champagne through an ominously barred lookout, Sevilla's haughty cigarette-swinging walk around the cabaret, her lascivious drunken revelry during her own wedding party, the sevenfold multiplication of her image while she sings "Arrímate cariñito" (Come Closer Little Love) in a Juarez nightclub. This excess is narrative and visual, for the plot is only as excessive as Elena's own physical presence, the sum of Sevilla's exaggeratedly sexual glance, overabundant figure, extraordinarily tight dresses, rolling hips, intemperate laughter, and menacing smoking. This excessive performance functions not so much as a parody of a mimetic performative ideal, but as an oblique affirmation of the gender identity that a mimetic repetition elides. Unlike the asexual mother figures of García, the suffering mothers of Lamarque, or the frozen sculptural beauty of María Félix's temptresses, Sevilla is made of flesh and blood, a bundle of unrepressed instinctive desires. If, as Judith Butler argues, the performative gesture "as a certain frozen stylization of the body" is the constitutive moment of feminine gender identity (1990b, 6), Sevilla—like a drag queen—melts the style. Her moral provocation is much greater than the admonitions provided by the narrative.

This provocation is not, however, as straightforward as it might seem. In Mexico, the "prostitute"[7] as emblem of desire, necessary evil, and mother of the nation (Malinche/Malintzin) has a prominent place in national cultural history. Prostitution might indeed be the oldest profession everywhere, but rarely have prostitutes been the preferred subject of so many popular culture texts as in Mexico. What we see in the *cabaretera* films of the late 1940s and 1950s is the culmination of a complex process in which the figure of the prostitute—albeit cloaked with the shameful aura of Malinche—became the site of a serious challenge to the Porfirian moral order and an emblem of modernity.

Officially regulated and socially shunned, the postrevolutionary prostitute and her spaces—the brothel, assignation house, and cabaret—had a distinct social function: they offered men a place to escape from the burdens of home and saintly wives and to engage in uninhibited conversations and the ambivalent pleasures of the flesh. Mexican culture always celebrated the myth of the prostitute, but in the 1920s the prostitute also assumed a different iconic status in the wildly popular romantic visions of singer-composer Agustín Lara. Idealized and simultaneously romantic and perverse, the prostitute of Lara's songs was not pitied for falling from grace. Lara's popular songs embodied a fatalistic worship of the "fallen woman" as the only possible source of pleasure for modern man.[8] Though at first considered scandalous (and prohibited in schools by the Mexican Ministry of Public Education), Lara's audacious songs were quickly absorbed as a new popular culture idiom, the exaltation of the Lost Woman.[9] By the late 1940s,[10] the cinema had completely assumed Lara's vision of the prostitute as an object of self-serving worship and his songs were the central dramatic impulse propelling the action of many *cabaretera* films. Thus, for example, *Aventurera* is clearly inspired by a song of the same title (sung by Pedro Vargas in the film):[11]

> Sell your love expensively, adventuress.
> Put the price of grief on your past.
> And he who wants the honey from your mouth
> Must pay with diamonds for your sin
> Since the infamy of your destiny
> Withered your admirable spring.
> Make your road less difficult,
> Sell your love dearly, adventuress.

Lara's songs idealized woman as a purchasable receptacle for man's physical needs—the ultimate commodity for modern Mexican society—but also invested her with the power of her sexuality: to sell at will, to name her price, to choose her victim. Nevertheless, as Monsiváis says, his songs also made the object of pleasure, once used, abstract: "The deified prostitute protects the familiar one, exalts the patriarchy, and even moves the real prostitute herself to tears, granting a homey warmth to its evocation of exploited lives" (1977, 60). In literature, in the songs of Agustín Lara and others, and finally in the cinema, the prostitute and the nightlife of which she is an emblem became an antiutopian paradigm for modern life. The exaltation of female desire and sin and of the nightlife of clubs and cabarets clearly symbolized Mexico's new (post–World War II) cosmopolitanism and the first waves of developmentalism. The *cabaretera* films were the first decisive cinematic break with Porfirian morality. Idealized, independent, and extravagantly sexual, the exotic *rumbera* was a social fantasy, but one through which *other* subjectivities could be envisioned, other psychosexual/social identities forged.

But the *rumbera* is not a simple model of resistance. When analyzed as part of a specific process of neurotic determinations (Hill 1986) and in the context of the suffering mother, the emerging image of female subjectivity is deeply contradictory and without an easy resolution. In fact, it is a fantasy. As Ninón Sevilla with much self-awareness explains to her lover in the *cabaretera* film *Mulata* (Gilberto Martínez Solares, 1953), the impossible challenge of female identity is the insecurity of "never knowing whether a man has loved me or desired me." Not that one is necessarily preferable to the other—she can be either the wife *or* the sexual object—but that Mexican society insists that they are mutually exclusive.

10

Our Welcomed Guests

Telenovelas in Latin America (1995)

In this essay, inspired by new paradigms for understanding Latin American mass media, López charts the shift from the cultural dependency model (focused on North American media imperialism) to a mediated model of mass media as a "welcome guest" addressing everyday concerns and specific cultural habits still within socially hegemonic discourses (Jesús Martín-Barbero). In this model, López reads the specific form of Latin American telenovela as an agent of modernization, nation-building, and increasing transnationalization. This essay outlines the principal characteristics of the genre, traces the cultural matrices within which it functions in Latin America and in the United States, and explores how it orchestrates complex mediations among the national, pan-national, and the melodramatic.

An article in *Variety* describing the growth of the Venezuelan TV network Radio Caracas was boldly titled "A Novel Rise to the Top," the "novel" referring not to the novelty of the event but to the fact that Radio Caracas is a network built, literally, by its successful telenovelas (among others,

---

Editors' note: The earliest version of this essay appeared in *Wide Angle* as "The Melodrama in Latin America: Telenovelas, Film, and the Currency of a Popular Form" (1985). The article was (re)published under the original title in *Imitations of Life: A Reader on Film and Television Melodrama* (1992) and in a revised and extended version under the new title "Our Welcomed Guests" in *To Be Continued . . . Soap Operas around the World* (1995b). We have selected to republish the expanded version here.

203

the wildly popular and much exported *Topacio and Cristal*) (Besas 1993, 1818). Radio Caracas is hardly an isolated example. Throughout the continent, networks and TV-based conglomerates have been consolidated upon the popularity of telenovelas and continue to depend upon their commercial potential. In fact, the persistence and frequency of the telenovela genre is the most marked characteristic of Latin American and Spanish-language television as a whole. Whether nationally produced or imported from other Latin American countries, telenovelas are the basic staple of all Latin American TV programming (day- and prime time), of Spanish-language programming in the US, and, to a lesser degree, of TV programming in Spain.

However, early studies of telenovelas in the 1970s, under the influence of the then dominant theories of cultural dependence and media imperialism, focused almost exclusively upon telenovelas' presumed alienation effect. The "alienating guest" of a study by Venezuelan scholars (Colomina de Rivera, 1968), telenovelas were posited as a harmful influence upon popular culture and consciousness and as agents for the creation of a capitalist and consumerist international global village engineered by the US and US-allied interests. In these studies, telenovelas were simply another example of the mind-numbing programming of the mass media as a whole. In fact, most of the myriad empirical studies and debates of the 1960s and 1970s over north-south flows of information and the deleterious presence of imported programming—albeit their political significance—failed to notice the sleeping, slumbering giants of telenovelas and the antidote they offered to the pessimism of media imperialism studies (Nordenstreng and Varis 1974).

Nevertheless, a "corrective" trend in 1980s research perhaps went too far in the opposite direction. Claiming a "reverse media imperialism" based on the extensive telenovela export activities of TV-Globo (Brazil) and Televisa (Mexico), scholars like Rogers, Schement, and others argued that the success of the telenovela allowed TV-Globo and Televisa to refute the "American hegemony paradigm" by substituting imported for domestic programming and by opening up international export markets (Schement and Rogers, 1984; Antola and Rogers 1984; Straubhaar 1984; Rogers and Antola 1985). The "alienating guest" was suddenly transformed into *O Salvador da Patria* (the savior of the nation, also the title of a popular 1989 TV-Globo telenovela), and the success of the telenovela equated with development, modernization, and the growing national/international clout of Latin American TV networks. As John Sinclair has argued, this second wave of research assumed that TV was "imposed upon helpless . . . nations as the ideological instrument of omnipotent international forces" without taking into consideration the active efforts of the national ruling classes to forge advantageous international connections. Furthermore, this research did not recognize that "the most consequential factor in the establishment of television in Latin America was not reliance on foreign programs but the institutionalization of the commercial model of [a] broadcasting structure which geared this medium into the more fundamental process of the transnationalization of their economies as a whole" (Sinclair 1990, 40–41).

To Sinclair's critique, still couched within the economistic terms of the media imperialism/cultural dependency debates, telenovela scholars in Latin America and elsewhere (for example, Jesús Martín-Barbero 1987; Martín-Barbero and Muñoz 1992; Mattelart and Mattelart 1990; Cano and Montoya Ferrer, 1989; Alfaro Moreno n.d.; Quiroz Velasco 1987; Vink 1988) have begun to add a different set of theoretical questions that address the insertion of telenovelas into daily life, the function of the telenovela vis-à-vis the "modernization" of Latin American societies, and the complicated relationship between production (and economic issues) and reception. Thus Jesús Martín-Barbero has argued that the telenovela is a site of "mediations," a place where the interaction between the forces of production and reception are crystallized. That is to say, the telenovela bears the marks of TV's commercial imperatives and responds to the demands of cultural habits and specific ways of seeing that are also in a constant state of transformation and adaptation. As Martín-Barbero, among others, has said, television only works in so far as it assumes—and therefore legitimizes—the demands and needs of spectators; but it does not legitimate these demands without redefining them according to what is acceptable within socially hegemonic discourses.

Thus refigured as a "welcomed guest" rather than an alienating poacher or national savior, the telenovela can be understood as an agent for and participant in the complex processes of Latin American modernization, nation-building, and increasing transnationalization. Although the magnitude of the telenovela phenomenon makes a synthetic analysis almost impossible, I shall attempt to briefly outline the principal characteristics of the genre in order to trace some of the complex economic and cultural matrices within which it functions in Latin America and in the Hispanic US, particularly in so far as it orchestrates complex mediations among the national, the pan-national, and the melodramatic.

What Is a Telenovela?

As a type of televisual serial narrative, the Latin American telenovela participates in the shared history that gave rise to other serial narrative models such as the US soap opera. It is an essentially melodramatic narrative mode, with roots that can be traced back to prior (Latin American and international) melodramatic forms (in the theater, serial literature, etc.) and their reinscription and recirculation by mass media in the cinema and radio. But even *Variety* has recognized the specificity of the genre: "The telenovela is a Latin American popular art form as distinctive and as filled with conventions as the norteamericanos' Western. . . . The telenovela is not a soap opera, although clearly the genres are close blood relations" (Anon. 1986, 142).

Certainly, the origins of the telenovela parallel those of the US soap: in the 1950s, soap companies (like Colgate and Lever Brothers) that had already sponsored radionovelas expanded into the new medium by sponsoring similar TV serials in a number of Latin American countries (Cuba, Venezuela, Mexico, Brazil).[1] However, from the start, the Latin American telenovelas were imagined differently from the US soaps.[2] Most significantly, telenovelas have always had clear-cut stories with definite endings that permit narrative closure. The historical development of the form and its singular place in Latin American television have also resulted in other important differences. Many US soaps continue to be sponsored by soap companies, are generally produced as daytime entertainment aimed at a female audience, are primarily destined for the national market, and are still considered a form of "slumming" by its workers (work on a soap being second best to film or theatrical work). On the other hand, telenovelas are prime-time entertainment for all audiences, financed directly by TV networks (or, most recently, by independent producers who subsequently sell advertising slots), widely exported, and definitive of the Latin American star system. Unlike the case in the US, where "stardom"—either of actors or writers and directors—is still defined by Hollywood, to work in a telenovela today is often to have reached the apex of one's professional career. In nations that are continuously struggling to sustain cinematic production (and often fail to do so), telenovelas produce indigenous star systems of great cultural (and economic) significance, for the great mass media icons are not movie stars but telenovela stars.[3] Furthermore, the star system reflects back upon the specificity of the telenovela format itself: the need to establish closure often means that the community of the text is narratively subordinate to a stellar couple with whom the audience is clearly meant to identify. Whereas the US soap's lack of closure implies a spectator that is knowledgeable of the history of the fictional community, the telenovela spectator recognizes actors and stars and awaits their appearance and fictional reincarnation in each new telenovela (Pumarejo 1987, 119). That telenovelas have had great economic impact hardly needs to be restated. As has been well chronicled in studies of the development of powerful TV-based conglomerates in Mexico and Brazil, for example, the popularity of telenovelas played a crucial role in their history and continues to be central to their revenues and power (Ortiz, Simoes, and Ortiz Ramos 1989; Caparelli 1982; Paterson 1982; Trejo Delarbre 1985; Besañez 1981). At least since the 1970s, the telenovela ceased to be cheaply produced filler material for daytime programming with content directly determined by advertisers and sponsors and began to successfully compete against the great US serials (like *Dallas*) for prime-time audiences. The telenovela (alongside the *show de auditorium*[4]) proved that national productions were attractive to audiences and could replace prime-time canned US programs. At least since the 1980s, both Globo and Televisa have imported only a small percentage of their programming from the US (in both cases, primarily feature-length films).

Furthermore, in the late 1970s–1980s, the telenovela also became prime export material. Within Latin America, the trade in telenovelas has been controlled by Mexican, Argentine, and Venezuelan producers: the airwaves of every Latin American nation have featured telenovelas from these countries in the last decade, even (as in Brazil) when airing dubbed versions. The norm for most Latin American television stations since the 1980s has been to program a steady stream of national and imported telenovelas, as many as six or seven in a programming day. In Lima in 1986, for example, an average of seven telenovelas were broadcast at one time, of which only two were nationally produced (Tello 1986, 141–42). In Brazil, where TV-Globo airs only its own telenovelas—since 1987, three first-run and one rerun daily—a rival network, SBT, began to successfully import Mexican productions in the early 1980s.[5] Although historically it has been less visible in Latin America than Telemundo or Venevisión, TV-Globo was the first to establish an expansive international distribution network.[6] In the 1990s, however, Telemundo, Venevisión, and other Latin American producers have begun to catch up. Thus, in the 1990s, it is not unusual to find Latin American telenovelas from nations (and television systems) as disparate as Brazil and Venezuela in the US (on the Spanish-language networks Univisión and Telemundo), Europe (especially in Spain, but also in Italy, France, Great Britain, and eastern European countries), Asia (including China), and Africa.

Because the costs of telenovela production are usually recouped with domestic advertising revenues, export revenues are extraordinarily attractive and valuable to producers.[7] Thus competition for the export market has generated a marked increase in average production costs. Whereas in 1985, the average cost of an hour-long Globo telenovela episode was US$20,000 to $30,000, in 1992, Globo executives declared that an "ambitious" novela could cost as much as US$120,000 per episode (Besas 1992, 82). Even less well-heeled producers, like Venezuela's Radio Caracas, are currently budgeting for increasingly more expensive productions, ranging between US$50,000 and $80,000 per segment (Besas 1993, 181–82). With revenues as high as US$15,000–$25,000 per episode for each foreign sale in a pool of more than thirty potential markets, however, the additional investments seem well worth the risk.

This constant production and the increasing sophistication of telenovelas have generated a solid capital base as well as a sophisticated professional and technical television infrastructure in the larger nations. Thus, primarily based upon the success of the telenovela, national networks and producers have been able to expand prodigiously in spite of their proximity to the US programming giant and without direct state intervention.[8] Whereas film production in Latin America has rarely been able to sustain itself industrially because of the competition from Hollywood and generally requires direct state investment and protection, television has gone through a markedly different development since the telenovela secured the national market and made exports possible. It is, therefore, perhaps not coincidental that the most commercially successful Latin American filmmaking efforts (in Mexico and Argentina in the 1930s, 1940s, and 1950s) were premised, like the telenovela, upon a melodramatic mode of expression.

Telenovelas and Melodrama

Beyond its sheer economic value, then, the telenovela's popularity and huge audiences also imply that each day a greater number of people throughout the Spanish-speaking world live with and recognize themselves in the world through telenovela melodramas. Although the melodramatic has always been central to the constitution of mass popular audiences in Latin America (in reverse historical order, through film, radio, serial literature, and popular entertainment/shows), its impact has never been as great or as focused as with the telenovela.

The trajectory of melodrama in Latin American culture differs from the European and US experiences. In the latter, as Christine Gledhill (1992) has recently argued, the melodramatic was devalued in favor of realism in the twentieth century through a gendering process: its emotionality and the centrality of socially mandated female concerns made it appealing to women and, thus feminized, the genre became a "women's" form. In Latin America, however, the devaluation of melodrama is explicitly class based rather than primarily gendered.[9] The telenovela's melodramatic antecedents were all, in their time, scorned by intellectuals and elites as *popular* forms, as entertainment with no cultural or redeeming value for the increasingly visible, primarily urban, masses.[10] Thus the telenovela is not associated explicitly with female consumption—as are "soap" operas—and its very name actively seeks prestige by citing an elite genre—novela—and a new technological medium associated with a much-desired modernization.[11] Furthermore, throughout Latin America, telenovela writers, not directors, are as respected, well known, and well paid as telenovela stars and often better known than their literary counterparts. Undoubtedly, the telenovela has also left its mark in Latin American literary production. Even Gabriel García Márquez argued in a recent TV interview that "the telenovela was a magnetic pole from which he could not escape."

In general, the telenovela melodrama is a specific appropriation of what Gledhill, following Peter Brooks, calls the "melodramatic project": the organizing mode of a world conceived "on the principle of terminal conflict between polarized moral forces that run through the social fabric and are expressed in personal and familial terms extending beyond the biological family into all areas of social life" (Gledhill 1992, 107). Like the US soap opera, the telenovela often displaces the flamboyant use of mise-en-scène typical of theatrical melodrama with an emphasis on dialogue and talk (because of its popular, oral tradition legacy, not because of an affiliation with women's fiction), but its narrative closure and extraordinarily persistent use of standard melodramatic devices (returns from the past, reversals of fortune, painful confrontations, etc.) square it firmly within a rather "purer" melodramatic tradition.

The telenovela exploits personalization—the individualization of the social world—as an epistemology. It ceaselessly offers its audience dramas of recognition and re-cognition by locating social and political issues in personal and familial terms and thus making sense of an increasingly complex world (Martín-Barbero 1992, 26–28). Thus it should not be surprising that the genre changes form historically and in different national contexts. If, in general, today's telenovelas often bear little resemblance to the products of the early 1970s, it is because, within the melodramatic paradigm, national characteristics have been accentuated even while international distribution and exposure have contributed to a complex web of pan–Latin American influences. What is most intriguing about the telenovela genre today is precisely how the melodramatic works with, on the one hand, the nation and its cultural characteristics and, on the other, a self-consciousness about other markets and other Latin American cultures.

Telenovelas and the National

The differences are so marked that almost anyone familiar with telenovelas can provide a general ahistorical sketch of the characteristics of the various national manifestations of the genre. Mexican telenovelas are notorious for their weepiness, extraordinarily Manichean vision of the world, and lack of specific historical referents. At the opposite end of the spectrum, the Brazilian telenovelas are luxurious, exploit cinematic production values, and are considered more "realistic" for their depiction of ambiguous and divided characters in contemporary (or specific historical) Brazilian contexts. The Venezuelan and Colombian telenovelas lie between these two extremes, assuming certain characteristics and establishing their own differences. The Venezuelan telenovelas are like the Mexican in so far as they tend to privilege primal emotions over sociohistorical context, but they substitute dialogue and utterly spartan sets for the signifying baroqueness of the Mexicans' mise-en-scène. The Colombians, on the other hand, have followed the Brazilian model, making specific and pointed reference to the history and culture of the nation, although not by recourse to "realism" but through the use of an ironic/parodic mode that combines the melodramatic with comedy.

Despite their visibility (and potential market value), these national characteristics—deeply ingrained in the specific history of each nation's appropriation of the genre—have begun to blur in the late 1980s and 1990s. The trajectory of the telenovela genre in most nations seems to have followed a not necessarily chronological pattern that oscillates between national, pancontinental, and international concerns.

Our Welcomed Guests | 211

MAKING NATION

First, and most obviously, the telenovela has served to create a televisual "national" in which the imagined community (Anderson 1991) rallies around specific images of itself. Following in the footsteps of radio and cinema, television increasingly makes "living" the nation a tangible and daily possibility. In other words, the otherwise invisible unity of the (political) idea of the nation becomes a part of everyday daily life. In this mode, the telenovela has become a privileged site for the translation of cultural, geographical, economic, and even political differences into the discourse of nationness.

For example, the Brazilian telenovela began to acquire its present format and popularity in 1969, when TV-Tupi (a now defunct network that was, at the time, TV-Globo's principal competitor) challenged the Globo style of telenovelas (usually historical, set in exotic locales, and resolutely non-Brazilian) with the wildly successful *Beto Rockefeller*, a novela that took place entirely in Brazil, was peopled with easily identifiable non-Manichean national characters like the *carioca malandro* (Rio de Janeiro scoundrel) protagonist Beto and representatives of other social classes, featured colloquial Portuguese and healthy doses of humor, and accompanied daily life by incorporating holidays into the narrative itself. As the first novela to use videotape, *Beto* was also more agile and relaxed, exploited different framing strategies, and featured some outdoor locations. Globo responded rapidly to this challenge by firing most of its novela personnel, building a new team of writers (many drawn from the theater), and developing its videotape technology and the skills of its personnel. From then on, the Globo novelas (and those of its competitors) have been based upon specifically Brazilian themes, characters, and landscapes, and have featured the topography, culture, and characters of the entire nation. Once featured on TV-Globo, all differences can be subsumed under the great banner of the nation. That this process took place at a time when Brazil was governed by a strict military regime whose need to rally a "new" nation coincided with Globo's desire to interpellate the nation through the airwaves of its network (and as potential consumers) is, obviously, not coincidental.

A similar process occurred in Colombia, as Martín-Barbero recounts, when the "traditional" model was transformed in the 1980s with telenovelas that brought in *costumbrismo*, a general parodic spirit (already evident in Colombian literature, which also often provides the source material) that undermines the typical melodramatic Manicheism with humor, with explicit attention to the details of Colombian social life, and even with touches of magical realism (Martín-Barbero 1992, 61–106). Circulating a wide spectrum of regional differences and styles and often using national "literature" as the context for the creation of new mass media narratives, the 1980s telenovela has provided the beleaguered nation with a self-image that differs markedly from the violent narco-trafficking for which it is known throughout the rest of the world.

An even more visible example of fashioning *and* interpellating the nation through the telenovela took place in Chile in the late 1980s, when Channel 13—the Catholic Church–owned-and-operated national television station—"adapted" the script of the rather racy Brazilian novela *Angel Malo* (Bad Angel) to suit not only the specificity of the Chilean "national characters" but the station's commitment to the Catholic Church's values and standards of decency. As Gertrude Yaeger argues in her study of the adaptation process, *Angel Malo*'s success "rested on its examination of the Chilean class system and the tensions or conflict between good and evil within every individual" (1990, 250). The Chilean version diminished the social and economic distance between rich and poor families represented in the Brazilian novela, eliminated racial elements in the plot, and highlighted Chilean views about sex and the family (for example, once pregnant, the protagonist never considers an abortion). Inspired by traditional Chilean literature—of the foundational kind[12]—the telenovela depicted a simple world populated by a rich and powerful aristocracy and poor, but ambitious, lower classes. The two classes come into contact only through domestic service and (often illicit) sex because in this universe, social mobility occurs not through hard work and effort but through marriage.

Angel Malo's "Chileanization" stratagem was successful: the telenovela averaged over a 60 percent share of the national audience and some episodes earned nearly a 90 percent share. In a country where most popular culture is imported from the US or Argentina, *Angel Malo* offered a clearly "national" alternative at a time when, nearing the end of a decade-long military dictatorship, the nation desperately needed to redefine itself and to seek solace and inspiration in its traditional foundational myths.

However, adaptation is not always necessary. As the case of Cuba demonstrates, imported telenovelas can also be used for nation-building projects. Throughout the 1960s and 1970s, Cuban television was a national laughing stock, for, to the same degree that the Cuban cinema developed prodigiously since the 1959 revolution, Cuban television had regressed from its prerevolutionary glory. Cuban television had been one of the principal legacies of US capitalism: in 1954, only four years after the medium's official introduction in Latin America, Cuba was the fourth TV nation in the world as well as an active exporter and programming innovator (Turnstall 1977, 293). But the elimination of all commercial broadcasting, the centralization and bureaucratization of production and transmission, equipment and financing difficulties, and the highly political and didactic imperatives forced upon the medium transformed Cuban TV into a national liability. Cubans watched TV because it was there, but without loyalty and with vociferous critiques. Telenovelas, once a national staple, had almost disappeared and national serial narratives had lost their popular appeal. Shot under extreme duress—with each thirty-minute show shot in one day to be broadcast a month later—serials had a rough, improvisational quality that demanded a very active audience and precluded easy identification. Furthermore, the official critique of melodrama—which equated the emotional excesses of the genre with capitalist consumerist alienation—required the development of other narrative strategies that proved anathema to the genre (or, at least, to audience desires).[13]

However, in the 1980s, when faced with the threat of Radio (and TV) Martí, the Instituto Cubano de Radio y Televisión (ICRT) reconsidered its programming practices and, in addition to livening up its own productions,[14] began to import telenovelas from other Latin American nations. The first highly popular import was TV-Globo's *La Escrava Isaura*. For the first time in decades, the nation rallied through fictional serial television: the country literally stood still during each evening's broadcast of the popular Brazilian novela and the ICRT had to arrange a morning rebroadcast to accommodate the demands of night-shift workers. Easily identifying with the historical theme of the novela (the story of Isaura, an enslaved woman[15] who can pass for white and suffers prodigiously), the Cuban audience rediscovered the pleasures of melodramatic identification and easily worked through the "foreignness" of the text—awkwardly dubbed into Spanish and filled with Brazilianisms—and the different narrative conventions of commercial Brazilian TV.

But the popularity of *Isaura* and the many other Brazilian telenovelas that have since aired in Cuba is not an index of nostalgia or of the longevity of presocialist ways of being. Through the Brazilian telenovela, Cuban audiences have worked through some of the anxieties of the country's isolation, reaffirming the national in a much-desired popular encounter with cultural differences. In fact, for close to a decade, the Brazilian telenovela has functioned as a funky Caribbean glasnost—as a symbolic (and practical)[16] "opening up" of the nation toward the popular mass culture of the Latin American continent. Even under the difficult conditions imposed by the current "special period" of crisis in Cuba, Brazilian novelas are still successfully aired and continue to contribute to "national" life. Thus, for example, *Vale Tudo* (*Anything Goes*), aired in 1993, recently provided the slang name *paladares* (the tasties) for the domestic dollar-only speakeasy-like restaurants mushrooming throughout Havana in the wake of the legalization of the dollar within the Cuban economy.

SELLING NATION

Almost to the same degree that the telenovela has been activated in the service of nation-building projects, it has also been used to sell "nation" and specific images of the nation to others. But exporting the nation is a complicated enterprise: what is popular and/or welcomed within the nation is not always what will be understood or appreciated outside of it. For example, historical novelas, always programmed by Globo in the least popular 6:00 p.m. time slot, have proven to be its most successful exports, perhaps because, like *La Escrava Isaura*, they focus upon historical processes common to or recognizable by many nations. Its domestically successful contemporary novelas have proven to be too "Brazilian" or too insular for most other markets.

Once export potential is taken into consideration when making production decisions, telenovelas can no longer address the nation too specifically and cannot afford to be insular, but they must still retain some national specificity in order to attract audiences. One solution, exploited by TV-Globo, has been to transform internationally known national novels—like the works of Jorge Amado—into telenovelas. Another solution, favored by Televisa in telenovelas like *Topacio* and *Simplemente María*, for example, has been to create non-nation-specific locales that exploit the urban/rural differences common to the continent as a whole. Yet another solution presented in the late 1980s was the development of telenovela stories set in multinational contexts and featuring, most often, Miami resort sites, and the experiences of world travelers whose home base is always the national capital. Exploiting the increasing international mobility afforded to the middle and upper classes by accessible air travel (it is often less expensive to fly to Miami than to fly to the interior or to go to another Latin American country), *Amándote*, an Argentine telenovela of the mid-1980s, featured a protagonist who was a pilot on the Miami–Buenos Aires route and who oscillated between the love of a young

Venezuelan girl he seduced during a Miami layover and his aristocratic fiancée back in Buenos Aires.

MEDIATING NATION

Thus the contemporary national spectrum of telenovela production is complicated by the contradictory pull of the desire for national identification/representation/mediation and exporting (marketing) strategies that demand at the very least a more pan-Latin American focus/acceptability. This is not to say that national imperatives have disappeared. In fact, in the early 1990s, the interplay of nation with telenovela melodrama resonates more strongly than ever.

In Venezuela, for example, the story of Radio Caracas's nationally very popular 1993 novela, *Por estas calles* (In These Streets), was directly inspired by the antics of national politicians gearing up for the presidential election (in December 1993) and so "realistic" that episodes were often reedited only hours before airing time so as to coincide more directly with each day's political developments (Besas 1993, 181).

Brazil recently offered an even more extreme example of the complicated relationships among national politics, national life, and telenovela melodrama. At the same time that President Fernando Collor was being impeached by Congress for corruption, Daniella Perez, an actress of the novela *De Corpo e Alma* (Body and Soul) was found brutally murdered and Guilherme de Pádua, the actor who played her abusive boyfriend in the novela, confessed to her murder. Shortly thereafter, de Pádua's real-life pregnant wife was also charged with murder and arrested. The "real" melodrama of the telenovela characters took over the national imagination and easily eclipsed the "other" drama taking place in the public sphere: the front page of the daily newspaper *O Jornal do Brasil* on December 30, 1992, featured headlines announcing the senate's vote impeaching Collor, but the picture of the murdered actress and the news of de Pádua's confession were far more prominent and of greater fascination. Although the presidential saga had also acquired its own telenovelistic characteristics, it was easily eclipsed by the real melodrama of the telenovela actors who were still appearing daily on the TV drama written by Gloria Pérez, the murdered actress's own mother (*De Corpo e Alma* ran for another two months after Daniella's murder and once all the scenes she had taped had been used up, the producers and the author continued to present her in flashbacks).[17]

Inventing "Nation"

An even more hybrid scenario of nation, melodrama, and the telenovela is being produced by the characteristics of the US Spanish-speaking market and its specific demands. Here the telenovela is making "nation" where there is no coincidence between nation and state.

The US Hispanic market, like the Hispanic vote, was long considered yet another "sleeping giant," a dream of great things to come maybe in the year 2000. Yet in the last decade or so, Spanish-language television and its telenovelas have undergone radical changes that are a direct reflection of the increasing visibility and importance of a market that is no longer perceived as either transitional or ephemeral. With purchasing power of over US$205 billion in 1992 and statistics demonstrating that 65 percent of the Hispanic population prefers to or can only speak Spanish, Spanish-language television has recognized its unique and powerful position within the US: its audience pool is not only the *recién llegados* who still don't speak English but also potentially the large group of "born-again Hispanics" who were born in the US but retain Spanish and a Hispanic or Latino cultural identity.

The two principal Spanish-language networks, Univisión and Telemundo, have been competing intensely not only for a bigger share of this market but also to increase and improve the quality of the market itself. As *Variety* summarized it in a recent headline, "Want a Bigger Slice? You Bake a Bigger Pie" (Levantal 1993, 62).

Univisión has a longer history and has historically dominated the market. Founded in 1961 by Emilio Azcárraga Vidaurreta (the Mexican media magnate, owner of Televisa until his death in 1972), his son Emilio Azcárraga Milmo (current owner of Televisa), and financier René Anselmo, Univisión was designed to function as a conduit for Mexican programming. Except for innovative news and current event programs and some variety shows in the 1970s and 1980s, Protele, Televisa's export subsidiary, provided the bulk of all programs, including its telenovelas. Hispanics in New York, Florida, California, and the Southwest watched *Simplemente María* together with Mexico City. When Hallmark Inc. and First Capital bought Univisión (then called SIN or Spanish International Network) in 1988 as a result of an FCC (Federal Communication Commission) decision against the network's foreign owners, the umbilical cord to Televisa, if not severed, was fractured. Argentine and Venezuelan telenovelas were programmed more frequently, surprising viewers with their marked regional characteristics and often more sophisticated narrative styles. In this context, telenovelas like the multinational *Amándote* and its world-traveling characters and constantly shifting locales began the process of winning over new generations of viewers.

But in the background of Univisión's changes, Telemundo had also begun to assiduously court that "born-again" viewer. In development since 1985, the Telemundo network was formed in 1987, and by 1988 covered 61.3 percent of the US's Hispanic households. Its calling card was, from the beginning, a focus on domestic production.[18] In 1988 Telemundo produced *Angélica, mi vida* (Angelica, My Love), the first telenovela produced in the US, which featured Puerto Rican, Mexican, and Cuban immigrants as central characters. Subsequently, *El Magnate* (1991) and *MaríElena* (1992) were also produced in the US; both telenovelas were set in Latino communities and featured, as principal characters, a hodgepodge of exiles and immigrants in various stages of assimilation. Written by Delia Fiallo, a veteran Cuban writer with a long career in Venezuela, *MaríElena* was especially successful because its protagonist, the Mexican actress Lucia Méndez, had long been a favorite of Televisa's novelas and, like Fiallo, was now Miami based (part of the community) and working for Telemundo. The impact of these telenovelas on the viewing public was remarkable: with fairly high production values, US Latinos recognized themselves through television melodrama and cherished their own, crossover, star system.

When Emilio Azcárraga Milmo reacquired Univisión in 1992 (in partnership with US businessman Jerrold Perenchio and the Venezuelan media magnates Gustavo and Ricardo Cisneros, owners of Venevisión),[19] Telemundo's successful telenovela programming strategies did not go unnoticed.[20] Although Univisión had increased its overall domestic production since 1988 (from 7 percent to 44 percent in 1992), it was essentially limited to news, talk shows, comedic programs, and *shows de auditorium* produced in its new extensive Miami facility. Meanwhile, Televisa's new competitor within the Mexican market, TV Azteca Channel 13, began to import Telemundo telenovelas: *MaríElena* was the runaway success of Mexican television in 1993, beating all Televisa programming and even forcing the network to reschedule its popular news show *24 Horas* to avoid competing directly with the serial. In mid-1993, the fact that change was taking place not only at Univisión but within Televisa itself became clearly visible with the airing of two telenovelas—*Valentina* and *Dos mujeres, un camino* (Two Women, a Road)—that represent and implicitly address and attempt to appeal to the US Latino community.[21]

Dos mujeres, un camino is the most obvious of the two. Erik Estrada, a New York–born actor of Puerto Rican descent who played Poncherello in the US TV series *Chips*, plays Johnny, an LA-based truck driver on a route that regularly takes him across the border. He is married to Ana María (veteran actress Laura León), but while on the road, meets and falls in love with the young aspiring singer Tania (singing starlet Bibi Gaytán). The complications that ensue are not particularly surprising, but Televisa's conscious effort to enlarge the fictional space of telenovela melodrama is. The explicit representation of the border-crossing scenario and the eventual blurring and disappearance of the border itself within the melodramatic work of the serial transforms it into another "lived" space consequent to those north and south of the border that unmasks the limits of official geography. That Erik Estrada—who claims to have done a Berlitz crash course in Spanish before accepting the role—speaks awkwardly and with a marked accent only adds to the serial's attractive gritty-realistic ambience produced by its frequent location shots throughout border states/cities and the Tex-Mex music of Grupo Bronco (in their first telenovela appearance).

Valentina is a more complicated example. Designed as a telenovela comeback vehicle (and first telenovela production effort) for Televisa veteran actress, singer, and, most recently, successful talk show hostess Verónica Castro, it was originally premised upon a complex international exchange meant to climax in the imaginary resort of Isla Escondida. The first two dozen episodes or so were visually spectacular, with complex narration, rapid editing, and much location shooting. The plot was less thrilling: his wife's botched attempt to murder him while on a cruise renders Fernando Alcántara (Juan Ferrera) amnesiac. He washes up at the resort, where he meets and falls in love with Valentina (Verónica Castro), the daughter of a once wealthy man who owned the resort, but where he is also seduced and confused by the evil Deborah Andrade (Blanca Guerra) who is the resort's present owner.

This typical melodramatic plot takes place on an island that, although ostensibly in Mexico (location shooting was done in Quintana Roo), is figured more as a mythical Caribbean locale. First of all, the island is linked more directly to Miami than to Mexico City: Fernando washes up there while on a cruise ship departing from Miami, it takes months for detectives from Mexico City to find him there. Second, it is a universe curiously bereft of marked class differences. Some characters are richer than others, there are employers, servants, employees, and even a homeless orphan boy whom Fernando befriends and unofficially adopts, but these differences are subsumed by the leveling isolation of the resort and the island itself. Owners and workers interact indiscriminately, even incestuously, and all ultimately end up on the beach. Most importantly, the central "native" character is "la negra Lucumé," an old *santera* played by the well-known Cuban salsa singer Celia Cruz (whose only other big- or small-screen appearance was in the film *The Mambo Kings*). Cruz's character, "imported" from the Caribbean and dropped into an inappropriate Mexican context, was obviously meant to be the serial's trump card for the US Hispanic market. Cruz's popularity and the audience's curiosity to see her acting rather than singing were activated before the telenovela's premiere and during its first few weeks on the air. Univisión featured Cruz in its talk shows, devoted a special one-hour homage to her "Cubanness" hosted by the also Cuban-born Cristina Saralegui and featured her almost as much as Verónica Castro in commercials and in the telenovela's precredit sequence.

Unfortunately, *Valentina*'s emphasis on place rather than characters did not sit well with audiences. Its ratings were so poor (in Mexico and in the US) that after two months it underwent a radical transformation (engineered by a new team of writers): after disclosing that Valentina's twin sister (also called Valentina and played by Castro) had been kidnapped at birth, the two central characters were promptly killed (as they stepped out of the church after their wedding), and the action relocated to the more familiar ambience of the poor and rich neighborhoods of Mexico City and focused upon the "other" Valentina, a typical lower-class girl with an atypical profession (she drives a taxi) who is deceived and abandoned by a man she thinks she loves but finds "true" love—and happiness, money, and her real father—across class differences.

Conclusion

Perhaps *Valentina* didn't work for audiences precisely because, in de Certeau's sense, its place was not a space (1984, 117). The imaginary stability and locatedness of Isla Escondida was not actualized or practiced: it was too fictionally arid, too composite, its hybridity too out of context. Unlike *Dos Caminos*, where a vibrant fictional space is created through the actions of characters that traverse through it, *Valentina*'s "place" figured primarily as a backdrop (and an excuse for breathtaking long shots of the landscape) and not as a practiced signifying context. Its willful abstraction and heterogeneity denied the spectator the possibility of identifying with a cultural territory that does not coincide with administrative and political demarcations.

Valentina's failure and *Dos Caminos*'s success clearly indicate that an awareness of the larger Spanish-speaking market has generated a different mediation between the national, the pan-national, and the melodramatic. It is not simply that there is now a telenovela subgenre that addresses a multinational audience, but that the telenovela genre itself (especially in Mexico and in the US) is undergoing a transformation where the national is melodramatically articulated in relationship to other, differentially constituted, imagined communities of viewers.

11

Of Rhythms and Borders (1997)

In this essay López explores the signifying of Latin American music and dance and their ability to cross and be crossed by borders. She specifically focuses on how music and dance have made such crossings in cinema, comparing the crossings of Latin American music and dance in the classic Hollywood cinema, in the classical Latin American cinema, in the New Latin American Cinema, and in contemporary Latin American and US Latinx cinemas.

Music has no borders.

—Amparo in *Break of Dawn*

We Got Rhythm?

Halfway through Isaac Artenstein's independently produced *Break of Dawn* (1990), the principal character, the Mexican singer and radio show host Pedro González, is at a fancy 1930s Los Angeles party in honor of a newly elected politician. He is introduced to an up-and-coming tango

---

Para Gervasio, que me enseñó a bailar.

My thanks to José Muñoz and Celeste Fraser Delgado, who encouraged me to write—and finish—this essay; and to Chon Noriega, for helpful critiques of earlier versions. The research for this article was, in part, funded by travel grants from the Mellon Foundation through the Roger Thayer Stone Center for Latin American Studies at Tulane University.

singer, a woman named Amparo, who sings a tango at his request. His newly instituted early-morning Spanish-language radio show (the first in the LA area) is a great success, and her performance is meant to serve as an informal audition. Afterwards, while sharing glasses of champagne in a quiet corner, he asks her, "How does a girl from Nogales end up singing tangos?" To which she responds flirtatiously, "Music has no borders."

Despite Amparo's remark, Latin American music and dance have been perfect markers of the instability of borders and have served as indices of the imaginary demarcations that constitute the process whereby Self/Nation defines itself (and is defined) in relationship to Others. If communities, as Benedict Anderson argues, "are to be distinguished not by their falsity/genuineness, but by the style in which they are imagined" (1991, 6), it is not surprising that the boundaries of the Latin American nation or Latino community have often been closely associated with music, dance, and their performance and representation as stylistic markers of (imagined) national essences: Argentine tangos; Brazilian sambas; Mexican mariachis and rancheras; the merengues of the Dominican Republic; the Cuban danzón, son, rhumba, mambo, and cha-cha-cha; the urban Latino salsa. In fact, we could argue that in addition to being "narrated"—a fictional or enunciated construct—the nation (and some more so than others) is also insistently sung and danced. Latin American nations have foundational literary romances (Sommer 1991), but they also have foundational rhythms that are fought over—and crossed—with as much regularity as their painfully real cartographical border. Rhythms have been an integral part of the complicated process of establishing and maintaining Latin American nations (creating the different "feeling" or style of the imaginary community), but Latin American music and dance have also been used by "others" to collapse such markers of national differences. Thus "Latin music" in the United States has often existed in a colonialist vacuum as a catchall category that collapses all the carefully nurtured (though often imagined) nationalistic origins of specific rhythms. By the same token, however, that colonial vacuum has also been the space where different notions of (an often gendered) *Latinidad* have emerged that realign the idea of "Latino" rhythms with a contestational pan–Latin American/Latino community and/or identity.

The position of music and dance as privileged signs of imagined Latin American nations/communities highlights what Homi K. Bhabha has so well characterized as the temporal split between the pedagogical and the performative in discourses of nationness (1990a, 291–322). According

Of Rhythms and Borders | 223

to Bhabha, such discourses must simultaneously sediment the nation's historical past—the pedagogical that signifies the people as an a priori historical presence—and provide the means for cultural identification in the present—the performative. This double inscription, as pedagogical objects and performative subjects, produces a double-time, a profound and ambivalent instability disavowed in historicist discourse. When music and dance are invoked as national discursive units of gestures and sounds, Bhabha's double-time becomes only too apparent. The rhythm must stand in as that which has always been part of the national imaginary, but it must also serve as that which can performatively interpellate social actors into a community in the present. Much more so than with narration, through music and dance "the nation reveals in its ambivalent and vacillating representation, the ethnography of its own historicity and opens up the possibility of other narratives of the people and their difference" (Bhabha 1990a, 300). Thus we cannot ignore the fact that Latin American national "rhythms" also have complicated histories marked by multiple attempts to erase/inscribe class, racial, and gendered differences in the service of the idea of nationness.[1] This is not the place to lay out this complicated history—the African roots of most Cuban rhythms, the French Creole roots of danzón, the African *and* working-class lunfardo genesis of the Argentine tango, the Afro-Brazilian-urban favela context for the development of samba. Nevertheless, one must stress that the idea of these specific rhythms as emblems of the nation already involves the process of appropriation and assimilation of differences that come into play when we talk about the circulation of such rhythms outside the nation-state in question. These are, indeed, ambivalent signs of nationness.

Yet music and dance also invoke another kind of troublesome splitting. Although by definition always evocative of the performative, music and dance can assume markedly different forms: they are vernacular forms of self-bodily expression as well as explicit performances for audiences that may acquire a representational half-life (or double life) through the mass media. First of all, then, beyond the national paradigm, music and dance operate in "other" spaces—domestic and semipublic spheres—where they serve as vehicles for different forms of transgressions and crossings linked to desire and other processes of identity formation and contestation. After all, Amparo's remark in *Break of Dawn* that "music has no borders" is meant not only to elide national boundaries but the domestic and social barriers that stand between her and the ostensibly happily married male protagonist who will become her lover that same evening. Preceding this scene of mutual seduction, Amparo's passionate public performance of the famous tango "Cuesta abajo" (the first lyrical lines of which already invoke the border-crossing scenario: "Si arrastre por este mundo la vergüenza de haber sido y el dolor de ya no ser")[2] is an act that may transgress national borders/identities, but which narratively initiates an ultimately very dangerous series of domestic and sexual transgressions that erupt onto the film's public sphere. Furthermore, just as in the film, I have not included an immediate translation of the lyrics of the tango "Downhill"; that they are untranslated in the film complicates processes of reception and the analyses of any such textual givens, for the bicultural spectator may identify with Amparo's transgression, while the monolingual Anglo audience may perhaps relegate her performance to the space of undecipherable and therefore safely meaningless local color of the gendered kind.

Second, as a bodily vernacular we can think of Latin American music and dance as forms of "signifying," as José Piedra argues in his suggestive essay about rumba, "Poetics for the Hip" (1991), and its companion piece about the Cuban son, "Through Blues" (1990). For Piedra, the rumba is a concentric form of signifying, "a questionably ethical and superficial means of compliance aimed at yielding a profound and aesthetic means of defiance" (1991, 634). But when this vernacular travels and crosses borders to become a musical fad or dance craze, it is also the means whereby others can sexily—yet safely—indulge in difference as a masquerade by performing the other and, as Jane Desmond (1997) argues, "inoculating" themselves against their potential danger. Even then the masquerade takes different forms: the colonizer slums by appropriating the subaltern's rhythms, but the subaltern also masquerades when she performs them for the other. As in all masquerade scenarios, the crucial point is not the masquerade itself, but what it conceals. Here it reveals not some genuine or authentic national or other essence but the means by which nationality, ethnicity, sexuality, and the contests over their authenticity are linked, reproduced, and marketed.

The third dimension of this problematic deals with the question of the representation and circulation of Latin American music and dance in the mass media, for this is the terrain where we can most clearly trace the processes whereby "performances" are inserted into the social imaginary to assume the emblematic power with which I began this essay.

In summary, then, my project involves a two-tiered, somewhat syncopated analysis. On the one hand, I am questioning the special "signifying" of Latin American music and dance and their ability to cross and be crossed by borders and, on the other, I am concerned with analyzing how music and dance have effected such troublesome crossings in one specific mass medium, the cinema. Of course, "the cinema" as such—in the abstract—is a film theorist's fantasy. My analysis derives its rhythm from a multiple historical focus that compares the crossings of Latin American music and dance in the classic Hollywood cinema, in the classic (or "golden") Latin American cinema, in the New Latin American Cinema, and in the contemporary Latin American and US Latino cinemas. Despite the linear history invoked in this chronological approach, I shall endeavor to demonstrate not a history of the overcoming of difference but the complex mediations effected by Latin American rhythms as markers of difference and identity, a process crystallized in the Mexican film *Danzón* (María Novaro, 1991), which I analyze in some detail in the last section of this essay.

The Movies Say We Got Rhythm?

Latin American rhythms and the cinema have had a long historical association. Certainly, even before the coming of sound, Hollywood films identified Latin Americans and Chicanos with rhythm, as witnessed by the early Edison kinetoscope *Carmencita, the Spanish Dancer*, featuring the vaguely "Spanish" turns of a dance that was all the rage at Koster and Bial's Music Hall in New York City in 1895 and 1896 (Ramsaye 1926, 117). Latin American rhythms were also already linked with an eroticized exoticism in the silent cinema. Even Rudolf Valentino's Latin lover, usually not associated with Latin Americanness, portrayed a stylized Argentine gaucho and danced a passionate and aggressive tango in *Four Horsemen of the Apocalypse* (Rex Ingram, 1921).[3] It is safe to assume, furthermore, that the many "fiesta" and "Latin"-inspired dance scenes common in Hollywood silent films were accompanied by appropriately "Latin"-inspired musical passages in theaters and nickelodeons (García Riera 1987a, 149–51). But sound unquestionably opened the floodgates in Hollywood, and Latin American rhythms poured in.

The affinity between the new technology and Latin rhythms was most consistently exploited in the western and musical genres (although "Latin" sounds often surfaced in any genre film that included cabaret or party scenes and often served to invoke excessive or forbidden sexuality[4] or to economically identify characters or settings as Latin).[5] In the western, Latin-inspired music and dance became an easy way to provide local color and to exploit the possibilities of sound. As early as 1928, the first "talkie" western, *In Old Arizona* (Raoul Walsh), featured Warren Baxter as the Cisco Kid singing a Mexican-inspired song entitled "My Toña." Throughout the 1930s and 1940s, the singing cowboys of the serials—Gene Autry, Roy Rogers, Tex Ritter, and others—would regularly be "inspired" by Mexican and/or Southwestern locales, inhabitants (especially the pretty señoritas), rhythms, and fiestas. Although the singing cowboys have been heralded as the principal agents for the subsequent popularity of Country (and Western) music (Hardy 1988, 193–95), they in turn also utilized and exploited Mexican themes and music: think only of the famous Gene Autry song "Down Mexico Way" in the 1940 film of the same title. But the "A" and almost "A" westerns also used Mexican- and Latin-inspired music and dances throughout the 1940s and 1950s. In *Stagecoach* (John Ford, 1939), for example, the Mexican singer Elvira Ríos (although portraying a Native American woman) sings a nostalgic ballad in Spanish linking a lost love with the distant nation and lamenting the loss of boundaries. However, here, as in most other instances of the Hollywood appropriation of Latin American music, the failure to translate the lyrics for the Anglo audience positions the song as a vague marker of a generalized Latin otherness, empty of specificity and indexing only the romanticized sexuality of the exotic.

The association of Latin American music and dance with female characters, usually but not necessarily of Mexican descent, is thus quite common in the classic Hollywood western. That Pearl Chavez in *Duel in the Sun* (King Vidor, 1946) is to be identified as Chicana is clear not because of her ancestors (upper-class, Spanish-speaking father and Native American mother is all the film tells us), but because her unbridled sexuality is rhythmically prefigured: when she is first introduced she is passionately dancing an unmistakably Latin number. In another western of the same year, *My Darling Clementine* (John Ford, 1946), Linda Darnell plays Chihuahua, a cantina girl who sings and dances in the Tombstone saloon where Wyatt Earp and Doc Holliday battle with the Clanton gang. Like other Mexican/Chicana women in Hollywood films, Chihuahua pays dearly for a sensuality that is graphically linked to her "profession" as a musical performer and to her ethnicity: pushed into the arms of a bad character by Doc Holliday's inattentions, she dies of a tragic gunshot wound. Pam Cook has argued that as the third term between the civilized schoolteacher Clementine and the uneasy taming of the Westerner Wyatt Earp, Chihuahua's "memory lurks in the shadows as a reminder of what civilization represses" (1988, 241). But that this "memory" is ethnically other is also no mere accident in a film suffused with the romanticism of paradises lost and regained.[6]

Despite its significant presence in westerns, Latin American rhythms would be most consistently exploited by the musical genre. Obviously based on a generic affinity, the Hollywood musical's attention to Latin America also paralleled the rise of the Latin music boom in the United States in the 1930s and 1940s. The cinematic musical genre and the popularity of Latin rhythms developed simultaneously, each feeding off the other to maximize their market potential. For example, as early as 1929 RKO made a most successful entry into the "all-talking, all-singing" genre with *Rio Rita* (Luther Reed), a musical western comedy set on the Texas-Mexico border. Based on a Ziegfeld show of 1927, *Rio Rita*'s combination of "colorful" characters (especially Bebe Daniels as a Mexican señorita fully equipped with mantillas, peinetas, and giant hoop earrings), sweeping action (the Texas Rangers riding horseback across the screen while singing in unison), and catchy and appropriately ethnified music set the stage for a decade's worth of Hollywood Latinisms in the musical.

Publicly enshrined at the same historical moment, the cinematic functions of the Latin American musical craze and the generic conventions of the Hollywood musical developed partly through each other's agency. Most early musicals followed the pattern of 1920s urban musical theater and motivated the genre's problematic combination of narrative and musical performances professionally, by featuring performers as characters and situating the action in theaters or nightclubs (Altman 1987, 119). But another solution was introduced as early as 1929 in Paramount's *Wolf Song* (Victor Fleming, with Lupe Vélez and Gary Cooper), where the awkward transitions between narrative action and singing were naturalized through the veil of ethnicity. As the *Variety* reviewer explained, it was "an old Spanish custom for the characters to sing at each other with guitar accompaniment at the slightest provocation" (cited in Richard 1992, 395; and García Riera 1987a, 155). Thus that "normal" people could break into song to express the joys of youthful coupling—when Lupe Vélez as Lola, the daughter of a California *hacendado*, sings "Mi amado" and "Yo le amo Means I Love You" to Gary Cooper, for example—was justified by claiming a mimetic realism based on the belief that musicality was an intrinsic Hispanic characteristic. The ethnic character—and apparently also those involved with her, since Gary Cooper carries a guitar throughout most of the film—is by necessity a *performative* subject that must enact and reenact his or her cultural identity. Shortly thereafter, once the musical's conventions were more formally established, the ethnic "cover" was hardly ever used; on the contrary, Latino/as and Latin Americans appeared most often as exotic performers rather than "regular" citizens driven by love to sing and dance their passions.[7] Such marks of citizenship would rarely be accorded to Hollywood's Latino/as and Latin Americans who were regularly called upon to perform their ethnicities.[8]

Besides lackluster efforts to invoke a (not necessarily appropriate) sense of Latin rhythms in films such as *The Kid from Spain* (Leo McCarey, 1932), Latin settings, music, and talent became de rigueur in at least one major musical film per year throughout the 1930s.[9] From *Cuban Love Song* (Willard S. Van Dyke, 1931) and *Flying Down to Rio* (Thornton Freeland, 1933) to *Under the Pampas Moon* (B. G. De Sylva, 1935), *Rose of the Rancho* (William Le Baron, 1935), and *Tropic Holiday* (Arthur Hornblow, 1938), the Hollywood musical traveled far and wide throughout Latin and Central America in search of "other" forms of musicality. The "South of the Border" musical peaked in the 1940s, when the combination of wartime interests, the popularity of Latin music (embodied in the figure of Xavier Cugat, the Catalan bandleader who epitomized the syrupy Latin big-band sound, and in Desi Arnaz, the conga king), the Good Neighbor Policy, and the box office success of "imported" performers (especially Carmen Miranda, the "Brazilian Bombshell") coalesced into a national obsession with things Latin American (López 1991a). Despite some efforts to deal with national specificities with sensitivity (Woll 1980 [1977]), overall these films participated in the general project of subsuming national rhythmic and other differences under the sign of Latinidad: all Latins and Latin Americans were from South of the Border and *that* border was the only one that mattered as far as Hollywood was concerned. Thus Carmen Miranda is incongruously "Brazilian" in a studio-produced Argentina (*Down Argentine Way*, Irving Cummings, 1940) and Cuban (*Weekend in Havana*, Walter Lang, 1941); Desi Arnaz an Argentine conga-playing student in a New Mexico college in *Too Many Girls* (George Abbott, 1940); Ricardo Montalbán a Mexican classical composer that dances Spanish flamenco in *Fiesta* (Jack Cummings, 1947); and Gene Kelly an Anglo sailor on leave who happens upon a stage version of Olvera Street in the Los Angeles of *Anchors Aweigh* (Stanley Donen, 1945) and dances a "Mexican Hat Dance" to the Argentine tango "La cumparsita." Although a self-declared top priority, national specificity was nearly impossible to represent by the terms of the Hollywood musical.

That Hollywood interest in all types of "Latin" musicality waned in the postwar period (*Nancy Goes to Rio* [1950] is considered the last "South of the Border" musical) has not, however, been convincingly explained by either musical or ethnic representation scholars. For example, Rick Altman argues that the fifties musical shift from South of the Border to Continental/Parisian settings and themes can be explained as part of the general evolution of "American utopian thought." During the war, "the characteristic Latin fiesta appeared to North Americans as a perpetual feast, a symbol of life in what seemed like an unhurried utopia," but postwar Paris seemed "to satisfy peace time pressures for a new utopia" (Altman 1987, 186, 193). The Mexican scholar Emilio García Riera (the most thorough chronicler of the Latin presence in the Hollywood cinema) presents a similar argument: Hollywood's excessive use of Latin sounds during the war years satiated the public. After the war, Latin America and Latin music were simply passé (García Riera 1987b, 104). As Betty Grable sings in the song "South America, Take It Away," featured in *Call Me Mister* (Lloyd Bacon, 1951): "Take back the rhumba, mambo and samba [because] my back is aching from all that shaking."

Nevertheless, it seems that Hollywood's fascination with music may also have cooled as a result of the increased *public* visibility of Latino/ as in US urban centers (growing waves of immigration in the late 1940s, 1950s, and 1960s, especially from Puerto Rico and Cuba) and in Hollywood (exemplified by the nonmusical "social consciousness" genre of the 1940s and 1950s) (Noriega 1993). Musically, the institutionalization of Latin rhythms as dance music (among others, the mambo in the 1950s) is also accompanied by a growing *mestizaje* between Latin and Anglo sounds. In Latin America, especially in the Caribbean, the influence of "foreign" musical signifiers would generate its own syncretic products such as the mambo, the cha-cha-cha, and the bossa nova.[10] In the United States, Latin musicians based in New York—like the Cubans Machito and Chano Pozo— would fuse rhythms to popularize dance music and "Latin jazz." In Los Angeles, the success of the Don Tosti Band's "Pachuco Boogie" (1948)—a mixture of *calo* lyrics, scat singing, and blues harmonies—and, somewhat later, the eclectic musical synthesizing of Ritchie Valens signaled yet a different kind of ethnic *mestizaje*. Even later, others would produce the syncretic mix called salsa, which has been associated almost exclusively with urban US Latinidad. Thus, the formerly exotic rhythms—syncretized, assimilated, transformed in and out of the United States—no longer invoke some pure exotic otherness, but rather the visible seams of US penetration abroad and ethnicity at home, where by 1951 Desi Arnaz already appeared every week as a conga-wielding Cuban bandleader married to the United States' favorite redhead in *I Love Lucy*.

Nevertheless, the reasons for Hollywood's original general interest in Latin American rhythms in the 1930s and 1940s as markers of otherness must be placed in a still broader context: besides the desire for "difference" with which to exploit the new technology in the 1930s and the stirrings of the Good Neighbor Policy in the 1940s, the Hollywood studios were quick to notice that "down South," dance and music had become important commercial markers for the nascent national cinemas that were beginning to successfully compete with Hollywood products for sectors of the Latin American market.[11] These early Latin American sound films exploited "national" talent (popularized through the also booming radio technology) in revue-type films; soon they would incorporate more narrative and assume specific national "forms" (while, alongside them, dance and musical performances would regularly appear in all genres, especially in the melodrama).

Argentina was the first Latin American nation to take advantage of the transition to sound by banking on the popularity of national rhythms. Argentine silent films had already used tango-inspired themes and iconography to good advantage,[12] but in addition, since 1924 in Buenos Aires, the exhibition of most films (national or imported) was usually accompanied by musical groups featuring the best tango musicians. At a time when the (developing) national radio industry denigrated the tango, the cinemas were the best and least expensive places to hear tangos and often the musicians were the principal attraction of the Calle Lavalle theaters in Buenos Aires. As Paulo Antonio Paranaguá has argued, sound came to the movies at the right time for Argentina, for by the late 1920s the tango was a mature and expanding form and the nation itself was ready to accept this quintessential porteño sound as the national rhythm (1985, 44).

It is therefore not surprising that the first Argentine experiment with optical sound, a series of ten shorts in 1929–1930, featured the popular tango singer Carlos Gardel. Gardel's growing national and international reputation, and the Latin American success of his films for Paramount at Joinville—especially *Luces de Buenos Aires* (Lights of Buenos Aires, Adelqui Millar, 1931) and *Melodía del arrabal* (Melody of the Arrabal, Louis Gasnier, 1932)—and later at the Astoria Studios in New York, stimulated the interest of national producers in the formerly denigrated musical form (Collier 1988). When Angel Mentasti established Argentina Sono Films, the company's first production was appropriately entitled *Tango!* (Luis Moglia Barth, 1933). Although little more than a revue-type film with a never-ending parade of singers and musicians, the success of the film consecrated the place of the tango in the Argentine sound cinema and its popularity engendered a number of sequels, some of them produced by a rival newcomer producer financed by Argentine radio entrepreneurs (Lumiton). But the affinity between the melodramatic nature of tango lyrics and musical narrative was most fully developed by silent cinema veteran José Agustín Ferreyra, who had already brought to national screens the urban iconography and popular stock characters of the tango and, with sound, would integrate them fully into a "new" national cinematic form: the "opera tanguera"[13] or tango melodrama. In *Ayúdame a vivir* (Help Me to Live, 1936), Ferreyra fully integrated tangos into the melodramatic diegesis using music for narrative development and punctuation and transforming tango singer Libertad Lamarque into an internationally known movie star. Beginning in the mid-1930s the Argentine cinema was nationally successful, exported widely throughout Latin America, and synonymous with the tango. As Jorge Miguel Couselo explains it, "The tango was the magic formula that opened all the doors" for the national industry.[14]

In Brazil, the "musical" genre would eventually become known as the *chanchada*, a carnivalesque combination of popular music—especially sambas—dance, and parodic comedy. The *chanchada* was preceded by "carnival films" that featured each year's most popular sambas, marches, and performers. Unlike the tango in Argentina, the samba was not yet considered a "national" rhythm and was socially and regionally segregated: as Paranaguá has argued, "samba era coisa de negro" (samba was associated with Black people) and of national interest primarily during carnival (1985, 42). At first simple reports of carnival festivities, the carnival films quickly evolved into narratives around which were interwoven the performances of the most popular radio and record personalities (often playing themselves). The success of *Alô, Alô, Brasil!* (Hello, Hello Brazil!, Wallace Downey, 1935) and *Alô, Alô, Carnaval!* (Hello, Hello, Carnaval!, Wallace Downey, 1936), released to coincide with the euphoria of carnival festivities and clearly alluding to their radiophonic allegiances, demonstrated that national music and dance, liberally combined with parodic comedy and performed by popular stars (like Carmen Miranda), were a popular draw for the nascent national sound cinema. The principal production companies of the era—Adhemar Gonzaga's Cinédia, Wallace

Downey's Downey Filmes and Sono-Filmes, and, in the 1940s, Moacyr Fenelon's Atlântida—devoted themselves quite successfully to the task of putting Brazilian music, dance, and its own stars on the national screens. Although often critically reviled, the Brazilian *chanchadas* perhaps represent the most sustained popular response to Hollywood's dominance of the Latin American film market: a popular, low-budget, and often quite biting national cinema for national consumption (linguistic and cultural barriers prevented Brazilian films from successfully exploiting the Latin American export market).

Although the Mexican sound cinema did not begin with musical revue-type films, music was always present and diegetically central in the films of the 1930s. The plot of the first sound feature—*Más fuerte que el deber* (Stronger than Duty, 1930)—for example, revolves around a young novice priest who prefers singing popular music to the church. And *Santa* (1931) prominently features a blind piano-playing singer and the music of Mexico's premier balladeer, Agustín Lara. Most early 1930s Mexican films invoke the musical, either as an explicit causal agent for the diegesis or as an essential part of the ambience. Nevertheless, the national cinema would not find its commercial footings until the 1936 release of *Allá en el Rancho Grande* (Over on the Big Ranch) and the establishment of the *comedia ranchera* genre—a peculiar combination of period/country nostalgia, comedy, and lots of *ranchera* music and dancing. As Carlos Monsiváis has argued, "After *Rancho*, the Mexican cinema could no longer do without one of its basic connotations—the songs. *Rancho grande* became our Paradise Lost, the image of a kind and idyllic Mexico destroyed by corrupt city life" (cited in García Riera 1969a, 132).

The *comedias rancheras*, like the Brazilian *chanchadas* and the Argentine tango melodramas, were not musicals in the style of Hollywood. Perhaps with the exception of José Agustín Ferreyra's films, Latin American films of this period do not weave music and dance into a dual-focus narrative focused on heterosexual romance and the joy of coupling. Instead, rhythms and performance are used as one signifying element in hybrid forms that defy generic definition according to Hollywood. In the *rancheras*, for example, music and performance often signal the genre's nostalgia for an idyllic past (in "old" Mexico everyone was happy, even when unhappy, thus they sang and danced), while in the more melodramatic films, music is used to mark moral opposites.[15] In melodramas, especially the *cabaretera* subgenre of the 1940s and 1950s, the Mexican cinema made great use of another great national musical icon: the bolero composer and singer

Agustín Lara. A former brothel pianist, Lara specialized in soulful songs exalting prostitutes[16] and fallen women that perfectly matched the needs of the melodramatic genre. Already world-famous by 1944—Walt Disney had used his song "Solamente una vez" (One Time Only) in *The Three Caballeros* (Norman Ferguson, 1944) and more than nineteen Mexican films had featured his music—by the late 1940s[17] the Mexican melodrama had completely assumed Lara's vision of the prostitute as an object of self-serving worship, and his songs became the central dramatic impulse propelling the action of many cabaretera films. *Aventurera* (*Adventuress*, Alberto Gout, 1950), for example, is clearly inspired by the song of the same name (sung by Pedro Vargas in the film).[18]

> Sell your love expensively, adventuress.
> Put the price of grief on your past.
> And he who wants the honey from your mouth
> Must pay with diamonds for your sin
> Since the infamy of your destiny
> Withered your admirable spring.
> Make your road less difficult,
> Sell your love dearly, adventuress.

Although difficult to conceive of as nationalistic icons, Lara's boleros and their cinematic renderings also participated in the complex process of Mexican nation-building. As I've argued elsewhere, musically and cinematically they served to inscribe the prostitute and the cabaret life with which she is associated as an antiutopian paradigm for a so-called modern Mexican life (1991b).

Overall there is very little singing and dancing in the classic Latin American cinema that is not diegetically motivated: characters are or have been performers or they go to places of performance. Nevertheless, rhythms are systematically invoked as markers of specific nationalities and as sites for national identification. The national rhythms are the rhythms of the "people" (rather than of individual characters) and simultaneously serve to unify the nation by providing an identity and to market the nation abroad. This is most apparent in those cinemas struggling to define themselves as "national" cinemas in relation to Hollywood and other imports. In the Cuban cinema of the 1930s, 1940s, and 1950s, for example, it is rare to find a film that does not feature the performance of a "typical" Cuban rhythm specifically advertised as such. As early as *El romance del Palmar* (Ramón

Peón, 1938), typical *guajiro* music and Rita Montaner's rendition of the popular song "El manisero" (The Peanut Vendor) are used to illustrate the nature and authenticity of the Cuban countryside. And even significantly later the melodramatic thriller *Siete muertes a plaza fijo* (Seven Deaths on the Installment Plan, Manolo Alonso, 1950) climaxes with a long musical performance of the history of Cuba through its rhythms, from the drums of enslaved people[19] to the urban comparsa and the contemporary mambo. However, despite various attempts to promote Cuba as a multiracial and multiethnic rhythmic landscape, prerevolutionary Cuban films consistently invoke musicality as a national trait—to be seductively performed—and an aberration resulting from the also performative process of syncretism. As Blanquita Amaro sings in *Bella, la salvaje* (Bella, the Savage, Raúl Medina, 1952), "Lo mismo yo bailo el mambo / Que el son guaracha o la rumba / Pues todas tienen sandunga / Igual que el ritmo africano."[20] With musical performance, the creation of a national space simultaneously invokes and elides the differences that constitute it, thus, also laying bare the traces of its production.

Although we can argue that Latin American national cinemas were literally empowered by the popular appeal and identifiability of "national" rhythms and performers, such rhythms regularly crossed cinematic and other borders throughout the 1930s, 1940s, and 1950s. Historically, Cuban musical performers and dancers had the greatest intercontinental cinematic mobility. The lack of sufficient local cinematic opportunities made Cuban performers a particularly attractive "export" item for other national cinemas. As early as 1933, for example, the Cuban singer Rita Montaner appeared in the Mexican film *La noche del pecado* (The Night of Sin, Miguel Contreras Torres) with her "Conjunto tropical." Even the often insular Brazilian cinema imported Cuban talent for the *chanchada* genre: *Carnaval Atlântida* (José Carlos Burle, 1952), a film considered a "practical manifesto for a realistic Brazilian cinematic practice" dealing with the (im)possibility of sustaining studio-type "quality" cinema in Brazil (João Luiz Vieira cited in Ramos 1987, 166) features the dancer María Antonieta Pons (aka "the Cuban Hurricane"), who intones the memorable line "El pueblo quer cantar, bailar, divertirse, tío!" (The people want to sing, dance, and have fun, uncle!).

However, the intercontinental traffic in rhythms was most often ordered by the shifting balance of power among the various national cinemas (and overseen by Hollywood, often with the first bidding rights on performers). While early on Argentina and even Cuba regularly imported talent, by the late 1940s the direction of rhythmic exchanges had been reversed and the now hegemonic Mexican cinema became the great musical equalizer, regularly featuring and absorbing popular Latin American rhythms and performers: Argentine tangos (via Libertad Lamarque), Cuban rumbas (Ninón Sevilla, María Antonieta Pons, Blanquita Amaro), sones (Rita Montaner), later mambos, cha-cha-chas, and even sambas. Thus, perhaps on a smaller scale but no less pervasively than in Hollywood, the Mexican cinema outside the *ranchera* genre posited Latin American music and dance as general markers of a "Latinness" increasingly dissociated from any national specificity and greatly invested with sexuality. Other national differences could be assimilated into a broadened, cosmopolitan vision of a "Mexico" that could absorb all the Latinidad of Latin America—and most often displace it onto the cabaret and its female denizens.

The comedy *Calabacitas tiernas* (Tender Pumpkins, Gilberto Martínez Solares, 1948)[21] starring the Pachuco-inspired comedian Tin Tan perfectly illustrates this homogenizing tendency. Tin Tan plays a frustrated and unemployed musician who assumes the identity of a cabaret impresario and orchestrates a show structured like a Pan-Americanist smorgasbord. Working for him are a beautiful Mexican maid (Rosita Quintana) who specializes in the latest rock and roll rhythms, a Cuban rumbera (Amalia Aguilar) and her entourage of *bongoceros* (bongo players), a refined Mexican bolero singer (Nelly Montiel), a Brazilian *samba-cantora* (samba singer) (Rosina Pagan) modeled on Carmen Miranda, and even an Argentine impresario (Jorge Reyes). With boundless energy (and some of the best comedic moments of his career), Tin Tan at will crosses all the borders that surround him: speaking and singing to the rumbera with a distinct Cuban accent and expressions, to the cantora in pidgin Portuguese, and in Spanglish to the maid. Above all, however, he dances smoothly and exuberantly to all the rhythms they embody and perform. Tin Tan energizes all the exchanges, arrivals, and departures and rehearses the performers to get their moves "right" (the rumbera is told to put more hip in her moves, the cantora instructed in how to use her hands more expressively). In his absence, the performers do not cohere as a group. But when rearticulated under his supranational rhythmic and spectacular tutelage, the show is a success, all the comedic mistaken identities are resolved, and the multicultural mosaic is dissolved into a new—and very Mexican—family unit: Tin Tan, the maid, and their five children. As in the Hollywood cinema, other national and exotic rhythmic differences are exploited and spectacularly figured by "others" (women, Afro-Cuban men) only to be subsumed by the greater force of *the* national paradigm of family life.

Aventurera is perhaps the most excessive example of the Mexican cinema's tendency to homogenize Latin rhythms and to identify them with the threat of excessive sexuality. In this cabaretera film, the Cuban rumbera Ninón Sevilla plays a Mexican girl who adapts with great relish to a life of prostitution and violence.[22] With more than ten musical production numbers, the film exalts the cosmopolitanism of Mexicanness by subsuming other national differences under the spell of Sevilla's virulent sexuality. The arrangements by Dámaso Pérez Prado, numbers by Pedro Vargas and the Trio los Panchos, and the suggestive and excessive performances of Ninón in every conceivable "South of the Border" cabaret landscape—including a Banana-land where she sings the sambas "Sigui-Sigui" and "Chiquita Banana" dressed à la Carmen Miranda—almost serve to dispel the myth of cosmopolitanism to reveal its inherently colonizing impulse.

Which Is My Rhythm?

By the 1950s the Mexican industry had thorough distribution networks in Latin America and a well-consolidated hold on the Latin American cinematic imaginary often exercised through rhythms. But growing state intervention and the producers' tendency to rely on formulas—especially melodramas and *rancheras* with lots of music and films capitalizing on dance fads—began to loosen that hold. Most importantly, the sociopolitical and cinematic climate of the continent was also radically changing. In the late 1950s and early 1960s, a significant nonindustrial cinematic current begins to emerge in Latin America: the cinema of the new Cuban Revolution, a Cine Joven in Argentina, a Cinema Novo in Brazil. Seeking different definitions of the nation and markers of national authenticity in other sectors, these new Latin American cinemas avoided the popular music canonized by the "old" cinemas. Such music was identified with the Hollywood (and, to some degree, Mexican) "tropicalizing" effect— with cultural colonization and alienation—and was, like the melodrama that often featured it, categorically rejected. However, in both Cuba and Brazil, films that are considered precursors of the "new" cinemas dealt specifically with the place of popular music and dance in national and individual life and explicitly used music to articulate a class analysis of the nation: Nelson Pereira dos Santos's *Rio, 40 Graus* (Rio, 40 Degrees, 1955)

Of Rhythms and Borders | 237

and *Rio, Zona Norte* (Rio, North Zone, 1957) and Julio García Espinosa's *Cuba baila* (Cuba Dances, 1960).

Rio, 40 Graus is a loving, albeit critical, homage to Rio de Janeiro, its people, and the spirit of samba. The film's first images are already indelibly identified with music: the magnificent aerial shots of the city—illustrating the beaches, the chic Zona Sul, and the tourist attractions as well as the Zona Norte and the *favelas* (shanty towns) on the hills—are accompanied by the popular samba "Voz do morro" (Voice of the Hill). But rather than serve as a nationalistic paradigm, music is invoked as a marker of class (and race) belongingness.

The narrative is structured around five young favela boys who sell peanuts around Rio's tourist attractions and, without explicit syntagmatic breaks, flows with the casual rhythm of a samba. *Rio, 40 Graus* presents a somewhat sentimentalist critique of the callousness of the Carioca bourgeoisie, but its analysis of the plight of the favelado is powerful precisely because the film is intoxicated with the image and sounds of the favela and represents them as a form of cultural capital. This fascination is most explicit in the last scenes of the film, shot on location in the rehearsal hall of the Unidos do Cabuçu samba school and featuring the special appearance of the samba school Portela. When the "samba-enredo" for that year's carnival—the one time of the year when the favelado takes over the city by right—is introduced, the plaintive voice of the *puxador* (singer) accompanying himself with a box of matches, the chorus joining in, and the dancing feet mark the end of the film with a joy that exceeds by leaps and bounds the doses of daily suffering it has recorded. As the music of the samba school wafts over the *morro* (hill), the camera soars also, in a long crane shot that discovers the mother of an accidentally dead peanut seller, still waiting by the window for his return, and, beyond her, the majestic beauty of Sugar Loaf and Guanabara Bay at night. Pereira dos Santos's accomplishment in *Rio, 40 Graus*, to produce a social critique based on the contrast between the *photogenie* and musicality of a popular class and the moral ugliness and inauthenticity of the bourgeoisie, would be an important precedent for the Cinema Novo, even though its practitioners would not return to the urban favela or to the samba for many years.[23]

Rio, zona norte (the second film of a never-completed trilogy about the city) also deals with samba, but in a more conventional, psychologically realist narrative mode. Structured by a series of flashbacks, the film tells the story of a samba composer of the northern suburbs of Rio, beginning with the accident that, at the end of the film, leads to his death. Once again intent upon contrasting popular and bourgeois universes and upon describing the exploitation and marginalization of one class by another, Pereira dos Santos uses samba as the narrative motor that drives the popular hero—Espírito da Luz Cardoso (played by Grande Otelo, a well-known and extremely popular Black *chanchada* actor)—against forces that alternately flatter him, cheat him of his chances, and ignore his pleas for help: the *malandro* (Jece Valadão) who steals his samba and refuses him credit and the concert violinist, Moacyr (Paulo Goulart), who admires his spontaneity, flatters him, offers help, and then systematically ignores him. Samba is simultaneously Espírito's gift and his problem—but it is above all a marker of his class and race and the only secure identity he has left.

Espírito's last encounter with Moacyr crystallizes the relationship of samba to the bourgeois nation. After convincing the famous singer Angela Maria (playing herself) to sing one of his sambas on the radio, Espírito needs to have his music transcribed. This opportunity is his last hope. He is well received by Moacyr and his intellectual friends, who politely listen to his samba and look upon Espírito as an exotic example of otherness. But soon their interest shifts and, ironically, they begin a heated aesthetic discussion about the place of popular culture and folklore in the theater. Ignored, Espírito sits by himself on the edge of a sofa, picks up the lyrics to his samba that a hand carelessly dropped on the center table, and gets up to leave. Too self-involved, the group fails to notice that a real representative of the *povo* is sitting in front of them. At the door, Moacyr thanks him for dropping by and casually says: "Oh, and about that music you wanted me to transcribe, why don't you come by next week sometime?" The question remains in the air as the dejected Espírito walks away, once again defeated.

With a somewhat heavy dose of self-flagellation, Pereira dos Santos here inaugurates a strategy that would be developed even further by the Cinema Novo: the bourgeoisie—the self, the audience—is severely criticized while simultaneously (and subsequently) allowed to feel exalted by its sentiment/compassion toward the *povo*. The political significance of the text resides precisely in the evocation of such sentiment and its association with popular music.

After his visit to Moacyr, Espírito heads toward the train station and home. On a crowded train he overhears two boys debating the merits of various sambas and he comes up with a fortuitous combination of words—"Samba meu / que e do Brasil também" (My samba / Which is also Brazil's)—and the rhythm for a new samba. No longer dejected, he changes trains among a milling throng and, barely on board and holding on to the open door for support, he begins to tap the rhythm on the edge of the door, humming, and then finally singing out loud. In his excitement and happy concentration he loosens his hold and falls. The film ends after his death in a hospital, where Moacyr, profoundly moved and ashamed, goes to Espírito's neighborhood to listen to and learn at least "two or three" of Espírito's sambas. "My samba / Which is also Brazil's" has obviously disappeared, yet another victim of class inequities. In Espírito's world, you may have your samba, but the nation—fractured, finally, rather than united by differential access to the circulation of rhythm—does not necessarily sing with you.

Although Cuban filmmaker Julio García Espinosa was also concerned with exposing the falsely established dichotomy between elite and popular rhythms and the private and public spaces in which they ambiguously (co)exist, his *Cuba baila* represents a much more complicated map of the interaction between class, rhythm, and pleasure. As the affirmation of the title indicates, the film does not question that the nation dances; what is at stake is rhythm itself and how the pleasure of the dance can be manipulated, if not corrupted, by dishonest political and social force.

The narrative of *Cuba baila* recounts the problems faced by the family of a minor functionary, Ramón, as they plan a big celebration for the daughter's *quince* (coming-out party celebrating a girl's fifteenth birthday). Flora (Raquel Revueltas), the mother, is determined to give her daughter Marcia a properly bourgeois party with the socially correct music—Viennese waltzes and North American music—even though the cost of such a band is well beyond the family's means. Ramón's efforts to ingratiate himself with his boss and local politicians to get a loan fail and, much to Flora's chagrin, the party can only take place in an open-air popular entertainment garden. What is most interesting about the film is not, however, this somewhat conventional plot, but the degree to which music defines the social spaces where it is played, heard, and danced to. The film begins with a popular dance at the same open-air garden where Marcia's party will eventually take place. In a seamless classical style, with measured tracking shots and few cuts, the camera captures both the pleasure of the crowd and the expertise and fluidity of individual couples focused upon for the pleasure of their performance. As the camera tracks among the swirling crowd, however, it also captures a curiously still figure on the margins: Flora, unmoved by the rhythm, looking disapprovingly at the gyrating bodies. Having identified itself with this popular act—this popular pleasure—the film also quickly sets up its opposite. The family attends the quince party of the daughter of Ramón's boss. Held at a swanky club and attended by the very North Americanized upper bourgeoisie, the music here is exactly what Flora wants for Marcia's party, but there is little pleasure among the stiff waltzing bodies, and the principal energy emanates not from the dance floor but from the political and financial connections being established among the guests. In this space, Marcia dances, but robotically and unsmiling. As Flora unwittingly discloses when she tries to compliment the hostess on the waltz with the statement "Su esposo y hija están como de película" (Your husband and daughter are like movie stars), the scene is patently artificial and its performance rehearsed rather than pleasurable.

However, the apparent simplicity of this crude opposition between popular and elite rhythms is quickly dispelled. Ramón attends a political rally to ingratiate himself to his boss and the film records how the pleasure of music and dance can be manipulated. When the politicians hire a band to pull in the crowd (since the turn of the century a common strategy in Cuban political rallies that was popularly called a *chambelona* or lollypop), the people seem unable to resist the rhythm and they abandon their errands and leave their homes to follow it. Like a mad pied piper, the band seduces the people with the pleasure of rhythm and deposits them at the feet of the politician. But when the band stops, the seduction is also abruptly cut short: the crowd does not forget its interests, boos the lies of the politician, and breaks out into a raucous fight.

Thus *Cuba baila* uses music and dance to articulate a keen critique of the prerevolutionary bourgeoisie and its conventions, but it also presents a subtle topography of how rhythm suffuses the nation by capitalizing on previously circulated stereotypes of Cuban musicality. As in the political rally scene, where rhythmic seduction is revealed as a potentially corruptible practice, that Cubans "dance" (or, as Benítez-Rojo would say, that they move "in a certain way") is taken for granted. What counts is how the pleasure is inserted into national life. In this prerevolutionary universe, "official" public spaces—the rally, the cabaret where Ramón goes to drown his sorrows—are sites for the corruption of popular pleasure by political greed, ideological manipulation, and Americanization. These are the spaces of the rumberas and bongoceros that peopled the Mexican cinema of the 1940s and 1950s and even the Cuban cinema itself. The domestic sphere is similarly infiltrated: Flora dreams of how her humble apartment could be transformed into a grand salon for the party (the answer: knocking down all the walls) and even holds rehearsals for the waltzing couples within its cramped quarters.

The rhythm of the popular only emerges in the interstices between these official public and domestic spaces where the distance between onlookers and participants literally disappears. The pleasure of rhythm is spontaneously expressed in places like the jukebox-equipped *cafetín* (bar, coffee shop) on the corner of Ramón's house, where a Black, female, and well-endowed patron languorously demonstrates the "poetics" of her hips to the admiring eyes of a friend (and the camera), positioned precisely at the crossroads of the inside of the bar and the street beyond it. And this curiously outdoor/indoor, private/public rhythm also reverberates within Marcia's bedroom. When Flora wakes her the morning of her birthday, Marcia is depressed by the uncertain status of the party. Flora tries to cheer her up by describing how the press will report on her party ("Do you realize the importance of a newspaper, daughter? Here on the same page, people will read 'Atomic Bomb Trials' and they will see your picture alongside it"), but Marcia stirs from her bed only when some music and singing, clearly Afro-Cuban and improvisational, rise up from the street. "Can you hear them? They are happy because today is your birthday," says Flora, as she uncharacteristically lets her body sway to the contagious rhythm. This unregulated and almost undefinable infiltration of rhythm effects a transformation of space—the private occurs in public (the pseudo-seduction in the *cafetín*), the public invades the private—into peculiar places at the crossroads of national life. These impossible narrative places demonstrate most clearly the ambiguity of rhythm as a national marker. Once again, rhythmic "Cubanness" is gendered and "colored"—the cinematic paradigm—but these scenes demonstrate how the stereotype is at once true and a stand-in for a much broader problematic.

García Espinosa's film, with its emphasis on a prerevolutionary world and popular music, was not exactly what the newly instituted Cuban film institute (ICAIC) was looking to celebrate in 1960. Although *Cuba baila* was in fact the first feature-length fiction film produced under the auspices of ICAIC (and in coproduction with the Mexican producer Barbachano Ponce), it was only released after Tomás Gutiérrez Alea's more properly celebratory *Historias de la revolución* (Stories of the Revolution).[24] Although rhythm (and the representation of musical and dance performance) would rarely be absent from subsequent ICAIC productions, the Cuban cinema would not focus on the place of popular rhythms in national life for more than two decades.

The new cinemas of the 1960s, in Cuba and elsewhere throughout the continent, looked for more "authentic," non-mass-mediated, purer "folk" musical forms. Glauber Rocha and others in Brazil found the harsh rhythms of the northeastern *sertão* a more authentic symbol than the urban samba, the ICAIC cinema in Cuba innovated with orchestral scoring and *la nueva trova* or new (protest) song movement rather than feature guarachas or rumbas. With few exceptions, the New Latin American Cinema simply did not address the nation through popular rhythms.[25]

In the late 1970s and early 1980s, however, several films took on the challenge of popular music and the musical film directly. For example, both *Quilombo* (Carlos Diegues, 1984, Brazil) and *Patakín* (Manuel Octavio Gómez, 1983, Cuba) use the form of the integrated Hollywood musical to reactivate the place of African myths/history in relation to specific social critiques. And Román Chalbaud's *Carmen, la que contaba 16 años* (Carmen, Who Was Sixteen, 1978, Venezuela) relocates the Bizet opera in the world of boleros and melodrama. But by the late 1980s and early 1990s, after decades of almost ignoring mass-market popular music and dance, Latin American filmmakers seem to have returned en masse to popular rhythms. Years after the first and last blushes of populist/socialist revolutions had long faded from the continent and in the context of contemporary international marketing practices and the ever more pressing need to secure international production and distribution deals, this is hardly surprising. As in the 1930s and 1940s, the need to secure local and Latin American—and preferably US and European—audiences is a top priority and often addressed through rhythm. Thus a number of recent Latin American and US Latino films, many of them coproductions among Latin American producers or between Latin American and European financiers, or both, have attempted to recapture the popularity of often archaic but deeply ingrained forms of music and dance as emblems of a national/ethnic unity and sensibility felt to be under siege.

In the United States, Latino filmmakers have regularly sought music and dance as emblems of their beleaguered specificity. The aforementioned *Break of Dawn*, but also *Zoot Suit* (Luis Valdez, 1981), *The Ballad of Gregorio Cortez* (Robert Young, 1982), *Crossover Dreams* (León Ichaso, 1985), and *La Bamba* (Luis Valdez, 1987) rework Hollywood's love affair with Latin American rhythms (most recently evidenced in *Salsa: The Motion Picture* [1989], *The Mambo Kings* [1992], and the lambada cycle). Whereas Hollywood's fascination with Latin American sounds continues to be superficial, the Latino films rework historically: they lay bare the contingent processes from which rhythms emerge and the uneven patterns of ethnic and class formations to which they, in tum, contribute.

In Latin America, perhaps the most famous example of this trend is the French-Argentine coproduction *Tangos: El exilio de Gardel* (Tangos: Gardel's Exile, Fernando Solanas, 1985), an invocation of the tango as the national essence par excellence, resistant even to the dirty war and exile.[26] But almost every nation with consistent cinematic production seems to have participated in this recent trend. Cuba, for example, produced *La bella del Alhambra* (The Beauty of the Alhambra, Enrique Pineda Barnet, 1989), a recreation of the rowdy spirit of a now-extinct Cuban burlesque tradition. The most remarkable, among the many Brazilian titles, are *A Opera do Malandro* (The Scoundrel's Opera, Ruy Guerra, 1986), a freewheeling French-Brazilian coproduction adapting *The Threepenny Opera* to the Carioca underworld, and *Stelinha* (Miguel Farias Jr., 1989), a nostalgic encounter between rock and radio-style balladry. The Chilean Valeria Sarmiento (*Amelia Lopes O'Neill*, 1990) and the Venezuelan Marilda Vera (*Señora Bolero*, 1990) explore the relationship between sentimentality, melodrama, and music. Finally, in Mexico, musical production has ranged from the extraordinarily experimental *Barroco* (Paul Leduc, 1988), a Spanish-Cuban-Mexican coproduction that eschews dialogue to present the history of musical exchanges between Spain, Mexico, and Cuba chronicled in Alejo Carpentier's *Concierto barroco*, to *Danzón* (María Novaro, 1991), a touching yet cinematically sophisticated homage to the empowering force of an old-fashioned dance.

In many of these films (especially the Latin American ones), the narrative focuses on a female protagonist who dances and/or sings and around whom national dramas are either explicitly or inadvertently played out. Thus music, dance, and gender once again intersect with the need to define and/or invoke the "nation" in terms that exceed the narrowly defined political. In crisis, the contemporary Latin American nation/community is once again (and with variations) represented primarily through the figure of woman as entertainer—dancer, singer, or both—whose nostalgic links with the past bridge the distance between once popular cultural forms and an uncertain present where their position is more problematic.

Danzón sets itself apart from these other films in various ways: directed by newcomer María Novaro (*Danzón* is her second feature film), its female protagonist is *not* a professional entertainer but a simple working-class woman whose passion for an old-fashioned dance empowers her to live, to make difficult choices, and, ultimately, to work out an independence rarely seen on Latin American screens. The music and her dancing pleasure are used neither for a large-scale invocation of the nation nor for gratuitous spectacle: deeply enmeshed with her identity as a contemporary Mexican woman, they curiously provide her with the backbone necessary to situate herself in a conflictual modern world.

Danzón is a film of deceptively simple pleasures. Julia (María Rojo), a quite capable thirty-something Mexico City telephone operator and single mother of a teenage daughter, indulges her passionate love of dancing, and especially of the measured elegance of the danzón, by frequenting a local dance hall with friends. There she always dances with the same man, the elegant Carmelo, whom she knows only through the dance (fig. 11.1). When he fails to show up several nights in a row, Julia realizes that perhaps she cares about him more than she had suspected and attempts to find him. She is unsuccessful, but upon hearing rumors that he has returned to his hometown to avoid a false burglary accusation, she travels to Veracruz to find him. Under the spell of the city's colonial and coastal charms, she befriends an odd assortment of characters who help her with

Figure 11.1. Julia and her partner in *Danzón* (Maria Novaro, 1991). Courtesy of the Cineteca Nacional de México.

her search—the hotel proprietress, a sex worker who lives in the hotel, two transgender performers,[27] and finally a very young and very handsome tugboat operator. She doesn't find Carmelo, but while looking for him she discovers much more than she had bargained for. Back in Mexico City, no longer anxious or depressed, Julia returns with her daughter and girlfriends to the usual dance hall. The band strikes up a danzón in her honor and, as she prepares to dance, Carmelo appears—as always enigmatically smiling—to resume a place, of sorts, in her life.

As this plot summary makes clear, *Danzón* is a melodrama that, faithful to the genre's development in the Mexican cinema, uses music and dance as a central register for excess. It depicts a resolutely feminine world shaped by romantic ideals and fantasies of the kind circulated by boleros, romantic ballads, and the cinema itself. All the women in this world—including the trans women—live their romantic fantasies through music and song. Nevertheless, *Danzón* also depicts a world of modern displacements in which the traditional anchors of Mexican society seem to have gone slightly awry: the city is the site for alienated labor and urban anomie; the "interior" (Veracruz), albeit still freeing, is no longer bucolic; the traditional family has all but disappeared; and, in the figures of the trans women, gendered identity is revealed as radically unstable. Thus the film invokes the spirit and iconography of the classic Mexican melodrama while turning its traditional referents inside out.

Similarly, the title's insistence on dance and the film's first image—a freeze-frame close-up of a woman's feet wearing dancing shoes—also ask us to consider the film's relationship to the Hollywood musical genre and its Latin American variants. This frozen image of a woman's shoes recalls the iconography of the Hollywood musical, especially the subgenre Rick Altman calls the fairy tale musical. But, whereas Fred Astaire's top hat and cane in *Top Hat* (Mark Sandrich, 1935) stand in for a world of sophistication and a universe of cinematic conventions, these shoes recall those conventions with a difference. First of all, we have a woman's shoes rather than a man's hat; the focus is on the feet, not on the head; and the image ultimately looks silly—or kitsch—rather than elegant and sophisticated. Not frozen icons, the feet "come alive" when the space of the image is invaded by the aggressive thrust of a man's shoes. Although the pleasure of the pose has been disrupted, the woman parries in response and the dance, a *danzón cerrado* (the traditional form [translation by the editors]), begins. As is always the case in danzón, the male dancer leads and the woman follows. The camera, possibly anticipating but miscalculating their next move, pans left and reveals other dancing feet, a community of dancing feet. This is not the rarefied world of the Hollywood fairy tale musical, but the world of working-class ballroom dancing; more precisely, the world where the myths of the Hollywood musical are simultaneously lived and displaced. The characters are neither professional performers who make a living by dancing nor members of a community that spontaneously break into song and dance to express emotions, but rather simple working-class people attempting to sweeten their lives and performing for the pleasure of the dance.

The title of the film and the music that accompanies the credit sequence also establish how the film will use the idiosyncrasies of rhythm as a marker of nationness to complicate questions of national and gendered identity. Danzón is a Cuban rhythm, often called the national dance of Cuba, that emerged—like most Cuban music—out of a complex process of transculturation at the turn of the century: Creole popular musicians who played in aristocratic salons transformed the French contradanza, brought to Cuba by French settlers escaping from Haiti in the mid-1800s, by adding elements of Spanish and African rhythmic modalities (Vásquez Millares 1970). Popularized in the 1910s and 1920s, the danzón and its successor, the even more popular danzonete, traveled quickly throughout Latin America and found a surprisingly receptive audience in Mexico, especially in Veracruz, a city that has, more than other parts of Mexico, a colonial legacy similar to Cuba's. To this day, the danzón endures in Veracruz as a viable form of popular entertainment, long after its popular appeal waned in Cuba (where it is now considered an almost folkloric dance), for this is a crucible city, where the colonial past visibly lives alongside the present. Thus as a marker of multiple processes of cultural repression, the danzón signals the always ambivalent relationship of rhythm to the task of imagining and sustaining communities and nationness.

And as a form of ballroom dancing—a performance that is simultaneously individual, couple, and group—danzón also signals to other processes of identity formation worked through the film in conjunction with the melodramatic. In *Danzón*, the swelling of surface signification typical of the melodrama affects the multiple registers of music, dance, mise-en-scène, and cinematography equally. The textual work of the credit sequence—where the image and sound-image relations are sites for complex intertextual and contextual referencing—continues throughout the film and is most consistently articulated in relation to questions of gender and identification.

Of Rhythms and Borders | 247

One of the clearest examples of the thoroughness of this melodramatic work occurs halfway through the film, when Julia, already somewhat doubtful that she will ever find Carmelo, first sees Rubén, the handsome tugboat operator. Immediately preceding this scene, Julia has undergone a makeover under the tutelage of her transgender friend, who claims that she is either afraid of "being taken for a whore" or of "looking good to men" and outfits her with a flirtatious red dress, full makeup, and a red flower behind her ear. Thus masquerading as the sexy woman of innumerable golden age films, she goes to the docks, looking for the Greek ship where Carmelo is said to have found work as a cook. Her walk is accompanied not only by the appreciative glances of the men she encounters but by a bolero with the telling refrain "amor es una angustia" (love is an anguish). During a series of point-of-view shots that narrate her search for the Greek ship (ironically called *Papanicolau*), the bolero ends with the lyrics "that to love is to become inconsequential," and turns into a danzón as the names of the ships are highlighted by canted close-ups: *L'Amour Fou* (Crazy Love), *Puras Ilusiones* (Pure Illusions), *Lágrimas Negras* (Black Tears), *Amor Perdido* (Lost Love), *Isla Verde* (Green Isle), *Mexican Azalea*, *Golden Empire*, and *African Azalea*. As if cued by this impossible list of names inspired by bolero titles and exoticism, Julia sees another ship passing by, a tugboat helmed by a handsome man. After an exchange of apparently flirtatious glances with the sailor, she sees the name on the boat: *Me Ves y Sufres* (See Me and Suffer). This exchange of glances is, however, complex, for she is the instigator of the look. Hers is the active, sexualized gaze, as evidenced by the closeness of the shot of her face, her expression of desire, her voyeurism, the emphasis on *his* physique, naked torso, and prowess. He looks back, but the exchange of glances is actually an illusion. Obviously, the tugboat is too far away for him to be smiling at her directly, or even for their eyes to meet. Thus suprafictionalized via this impossible series of shot-reverse shots, *Danzón* offers a beautiful example of the representation of a woman's desire. And a clear patriarchal warning on his boat: See me and suffer.

Julia's response to this warning is, not surprisingly, enacted on the margins of the dance floor, in a semiprivate space, and through the hip. On their first date, Julia and Rubén go to a popular open-air dance place, where all sorts of people, from little kids to old couples, dance effortlessly to the live music. On the dance floor, however, Rubén swings his hips like a salsero and is no match for Julia's danzón elegance. During a *descanso* (dance break built into the structure of danzón), Julia tries to explain the ethos and rules of danzón. We can't hear her words—the orchestra continues playing—but soon she herself gives up on them and uses her body, slowly twirling around Rubén's appreciative glance. Julia transforms what José Piedra calls a "meaningless" body part into a "signifying" bodily attitude: her hips become an icon of femininity activated in offense and defense. He can't dance, this is her dance. But her moves are not those of a *danzonera*, despite the fact that they are orchestrated to a danzón. These are rumba hips, exaggerated, marked, voyeuristic, exhibitionistic, deified; an acceptance of the bodily and a defiant desiring that, as we see in his visibly appreciative response, is clearly communicated.

Julia, an unlikely melodramatic heroine, does not suffer for appropriating desire, the gaze, the hip. She packs up and leaves Veracruz without even saying goodbye to her young lover. Denied pathos by a relentless, albeit subtle reflexivity, it is the spectator who suffers the most. But the film, like Julia and the female feet in the credit sequence, parries gracefully, for there is a "happy" ending.

Back in Mexico City, following the rhythm of her defiance and on the dance floor of their usual ballroom, Julia and Carmelo are reunited. But the victory is Pyrrhic for the spectator. Despite Julia's obsession, we know too little about Carmelo to really care about him as a character. Throughout the film he has simply served as an excuse to motivate Julia's development and her interpersonal encounters and he offers us none of the visual pleasure of Rubén's classic and fetishized beauty.

When Carmelo approaches Julia she is empowered by the very dance that would subjugate her and ready to dance a danzón number that has been publicly dedicated to her. Her dance would celebrate her return to the ordered and familiar world of the ballroom. But when the elegantly poised and silent Carmelo takes her in his arms and they begin the dance, things have obviously changed. Although Julia had demonstrated several times throughout the film the importance of the ritualized codes of the dance while attempting to teach others (her daughter, Suzy her trans woman friend), here she aggressively ignores them. She looks into Carmelo's eyes unwaveringly until, acknowledging defeat by a nod of the head, he breaks down, smiles, and returns her gaze. Thus the film ends with Julia and Carmelo, dancing and looking at each other, amid a community of dancing couples. Carmelo may still "lead" the dance, but Julia has discovered a way to assert her own position, her "certain way" of doing things.

Empowered by rhythm, through rhythm, and in rhythm, Julia has redesigned the stage of her performance and desire. Constituted through music and challenged through rhythm, her identity is reworked on the dance floor, where her performance produces a "different" space. Although physically the same, for Julia this ballroom is no longer the same place where the film began. Rather than a microcosm of the Mexican urban working class and its performative pleasures (a national public space) and patriarchal rigidity, the Salon Baile Colonial is now a place where her individual (gendered) identity is affirmed, contested, and reproduced. The danzón is a "cage," a social grid, but it is *her* grid and she can transform its pleasures and risk breaking its rules. As the Veracruz hotel proprietress tells her when she is getting ready to abandon her young lover to return to Mexico City, "Ya lo bailao nadie te lo quita" (No one can take away what you've already danced).

To Have a Rhythm

Unlike Julia in *Danzón*, Amparo in *Break of Dawn* cannot unsettle the codes of her life through border-crossing/rule-breaking rhythms. Her "transgression"—the appropriation of an "other" rhythm and of an "other's" husband—comes to naught. Pedro remains married to his decidedly nonmusical wife, although ultimately "rhythm" lies at the root of the false accusations that land him in jail for most of his life. Nevertheless, even in *Break of Dawn*, music and dance are figured as privileged spaces for the construction and contestation of ethnic/national *and* sexual/gendered identity.

As I hope my survey analysis of the history of cinematic uses of Latin American music and dance has begun to demonstrate, a multinational focus on music and dance opens up an unusual analytical space. Rhythm has been—and continues to be—used as a significant marker of national/ ethnic difference: the cinema locates and placates Latino/ as and Latin Americans rhythmically. But this placing has also served to provide a curiously unfettered space for ethnic and other nationals: a place for performance and a space of multiple identifications. Here we can perhaps begin to think about a different rhythmic cartography, not tied to borders to be crossed or transgressed, but where spaces become lived-in and dancing places in which the body—reclaimed from its subservience to work—can be a locus of resistance and desire and enjoyed on that basis. If at one level—that of supranational/colonialist appropriation—rhythm can be used to collapse the very differences it embodies, at another level—individual, subnational, contestational—rhythm has also served to posit spaces for rewriting and resisting the homogeneity of the generalizing force of nationness.

12

Mexico (2012)

In this essay, López explores the very different operation of the musical genre in Mexico during the classical era, arguing that, amid the multiplicity of genres in which music is deployed, narratives, songs, rhythms, and performances are usually invoked as markers of nationality and sites for national identification. López focuses in particular on two Mexican film genres (the comedia ranchera *and the* cabaretera*) and the representational spaces from which they emerged—the* hacienda *(country ranch) and the cabaret (urban nightclub). She notes the ways music is deployed as part of these films' melodramas of identity, nationhood, and male and female subjectivity.*

If, as Jane Feuer argues in *The Hollywood Musical*, "the musical is Hollywood writ large" (1993, xi), it is not surprising that the musical genre models introduced and subsequently developed by Hollywood underwent significant transformations and hybridizations as they crossed borders and oceans and landed in vastly different social, cultural, political, and economic contexts. In Latin America, a region always already associated with rhythm, the musical was not segregated as a separate cinematic genre. Instead of texts that weave music and dance into a dual-focus narrative focused on heterosexual romance and the joy of coupling (Altman 1987), music and performance are used as signifying elements in hybrid forms that defy generic definition according to Hollywood formulas.

Integral to the narratives, songs, rhythms, and performances are typically invoked as markers of nationality and as sites for national identification. In the Mexican "Golden Age" (1930–1960), cinema, music, and dance are constant across all "genres" but are always deployed within melodramatic narrative scenarios. At first, national rhythms are the rhythms of the "people" (rather than of individual characters) and simultaneously serve to unify the nation by providing an identity and to market the nation abroad (therefore articulating both the pedagogical and the performative aspects of discourses of nationhood) (López 1997). Subsequently, "national" rhythms regularly crossed cinematic and other borders. By the late 1940s the now hegemonic Mexican cinema became the great musical equalizer, regularly featuring and absorbing popular Latin American rhythms and performers: Argentine tangos (via Libertad Lamarque), Cuban rumbas (Ninón Sevilla, María Antonieta Pons, Blanquita Amaro), sones (Rita Montaner), and later mambos, cha-cha-chas, and even Brazilian sambas.

Musicality becomes a significant narrative and structural focus when inserted in two specific representational spaces: the *hacienda* or country ranch (that is, a rural universe) and the cabaret (that is, an urban nightlife universe).[1] This essay discusses the high points of the two Mexican film genres that emerged within these spaces, respectively: the *comedia ranchera* and the *cabaretera* film. Although "romance" is a constant across the two genres, rather than celebrating heterosexual romance, the films are melodramas of identity, nationhood, and male and female subjectivity. Often films end with one or more happy couples, but the work of getting there embodies differential visions of utopias. To the degree that, according to Caryl Flinn, the melodrama "defers or purloins its moment of utopia while musicals preserve it" (1992, 141), these films simultaneously engage in and disavow the possibility of utopia. In both instances driven by star power—of the music, the songs, and the performers—these two genres are difficult to classify as "musicals" according to Hollywood formulas, but they constitute the musical backbone of the classic or "Golden Age" Mexican cinema.

The Transition and Early Sound Cinema in Mexico: Context and Debates

The diffusion of the cinema throughout Latin America was defined by the technology's status as an import that embodied and was emblematic of modernity and by the technological infrastructure, political stability, industrialization, and economic activities at national and regional levels (López 2000b). By the late 1920s, nations like Mexico and Argentina had developed cinematic vernaculars and production infrastructures, and, above all, had captured national and regional audiences despite the constant competition from US and European imports. In Mexico, silent cinema inscribed the medium in the history of the nation (as chronicler of the Mexican Revolution) while it was also recognized as the embodiment of differential dreams of modernity; it was a *key* agent of both nationalism and globalization, and contributed to the construction of strong nationalistic discourses of modernity.

The introduction of sound brought this process to an abrupt halt. Once again dealing with an imported phenomenon, locals scrambled for capital, technology, and know-how as Hollywood aggressively marketed sound films and completed its takeover of the exhibition and distribution sectors. However, in Mexico, as in Hollywood, the introduction of sound also opened up the medium to generic experimentation (López 2009), including the exploitation of "national sonorities": spoken Spanish and music.

Even before the screening of the first sonorized film in April 1929 (Frank Capra's *Submarine*), the impact of sound on the medium and national culture was hotly debated in the press. Of concern were the impact of the talkies on the theater and, more heatedly, the impact of the "peaceful" linguistic invasion *by* the United States. As Luis Reyes de la Maza chronicles in *El cine sonoro en México*, the cultural intelligentsia presented a united front against the possibility that film would become an English-only medium, resisted Hollywood's inept efforts to produce Spanish-language films, clamored for a national cinema, and debated what it should embody (1973). By late 1930, Hollywood's Spanish-language productions had demonstrated most of their flaws, including problems with mixing accents and nationalities and the lack of convincing star power.

The late 1920s and early 1930s also witnessed the expansion of other forms of mass media—comics and serial books, the recording industry, and radio—that captured the public imagination and provided a synergistic context for the evolution of sound cinema. Primary among them was radio, marked by the launch of the two-hundred-kilowatt station XEW-AM in Mexico City in September 1930. Owned by Emilio Azcárraga Vidaurreta (also president of the Mexican Music Company, a record and sheet music distributor affiliated with RCA in the US), XEW launched as "la voz de América Latina desde México" (the voice of Latin America from Mexico). It was the first Latin American radio station powerful enough to reach a mass audience (exceeding the national borders and reaching into the US Southwest and the Caribbean basin). It was also armed with an extensive publicity machine and featured varied programming—popular music, dramas, news, children's programming, and sports—that easily captured audiences. Above all, however, music was the centerpiece of programming; since 1926, Mexican regulations required that all radio broadcasts be in Spanish only and, since 1932 to 1936, that at least 25 percent of the music aired consist of "typically Mexican" songs (Hayes 2000). This served to enshrine the already "official" repertoire of "typically Mexican" music.[2] The postrevolutionary government had promoted a version of national identity based on the concept of *mestizaje* located within rural expressive culture. As regional musical traditions became central elements in this official project of cultural nationalism, *mariachi* (a music and dance tradition from Mexico's western region) and *ranchera* songs (originating in the simple and direct melodies sung by *hacienda* workers) emerged as markers of national identity and symbols of *mexicanidad*. In the period 1920 to 1940, *mariachi* and *rancheras* were transformed from rural *mestizo* cultural expressions to international visual and sound symbols of national identity (Pérez Montfort 1994). Similarly, the *jarabe tapatío* (Mexican hat dance), a traditional courtship dance from central Mexico, and the figures of the *china poblana* (a young girl with long, thick plaits dressed in a long, full skirt with a white slip, embroidered blouse, and shawl), originally from western Mexico, and the *charro* (a cowboy dressed in the typical fancy style of the state of Jalisco, a three-piece suit composed of a waistcoat, jacket, and trousers bearing silver buttons down the seam) also became inscribed as prototypical symbols of *mexicanidad*.[3]

But the growth of radio and recording also created a tremendous demand for new songs and fueled the popularity of a very different genre: the Mexican *bolero*. Rooted in the Cuban *bolero*, which had earlier appeared in Veracruz, the *bolero* was reinvented by composer/singer Agustín Lara in a more metropolitan form, substituting a smaller ensemble of musicians for the solo guitar and placing emphasis on the singer's voice and the lyrics (Aura 1990):

> Through Lara's compositions, the bolero became an interlocutor between the provincial and the urbane, the foreign and the familiar. Lara combined an urban sophisticate's classical proclivities (signaled in Lara's use of piano, violin, and bel canto vocal techniques) and the popular styles favored by the masses. . . . It was both a liminal hybrid and something qualitatively new. (Pedelty 1999, 8)

Lara's lyrics, often set in the brothels and dance halls where he had begun his career, told tales of unrequited love—men hopelessly in love with prostitutes[4] and prostitutes seeking redemption. Idealized and simultaneously romantic and perverse, the prostitute of Lara's songs was not pitied for having fallen from grace, but the source of her admirer's poetic and spiritual empowerment. His songs embodied a fatalistic worship of the fallen woman not as a poor sinner whose only redemption was death, but as the only possible source of pleasure for modern man. Romantic to the extreme, almost to the point of corniness, the *bolero* celebrated a culture of sentimentality very similar in spirit to the narratives of radionovelas, which were second only to music in popularity on the radio. Drawing their talent from literature and theater—the very same pool that nourished the cinema[5]—radio dramas grew in popularity through the 1930s, becoming ubiquitous after 1940. (XEW aired as many as five different ones per day.) Above all, as in other parts of Latin America, radio dramas were notorious for their melodramatic and emotional excesses. The sentimental melodrama, punctuated by extreme pathos and enveloped in music, became, therefore, a sort of narrative lingua franca for the mass media in general. As poet Salvador Novo described it in the 1950s, it was "tequila espiritual a la garganta de todo mundo" (spiritual tequila in everybody's throat) (1951, 171).

Thus, throughout the 1930s, Mexican radio (led by XEW) codified, standardized, and institutionalized an "official" repertoire of what constituted "Mexican" popular music (*mariachis, rancheras,* and *boleros*) and popular melodrama, and created national musical "stars"—like Agustín Lara, but also Jorge Negrete, Pedro Infante, and many others—that would become very important for the cinema.

The *Comedia Ranchera*

The early 1930s were years of effervescent experimentation in which producers and filmmakers developed multiple alternative cinematic practices and attempted to define the national cinema and establish an autochthonous mass audience. In other words, they experimented with expressive styles and generic formulas to find the "magic bullet" for box office success and audience satisfaction (López 2009). The "bullet" was *Over on the Big Ranch (Allá en el Rancho Grande,* 1936) and the *comedia ranchera* genre.[6]

As Marina Díaz López notes in her detailed analysis of the genesis of *Rancho Grande*, this is an unusual instance in which one film single-handedly produced a genre that was taken up by the industry and national and international audiences alike and transformed the national industry (1996, 9). In fact, *Rancho Grande* adopted the already circulating semantic elements of *mexicanidad*—*charros, chinas poblanas, jarabes tapatíos, mariachis,* and *canciones rancheras*—and articulated them into a syntactic framework[7] based on simple melodramatic elements in the context of the structure of the *género chico* (musical variety theater akin to vaudeville).[8] In doing so it presented a new way of articulating the national through music and folklore as both performative and participatory.

After a brief introductory flashback to 1922, the narrative of *Rancho Grande* is set in the "present," but in a bucolic mythical rural area where neither the Revolution nor the recent Agrarian Reform has left any trace and where conflicts emerge only from love affairs, wounded male pride, and misunderstandings. Its narrative is based on a simple melodramatic triangle; Felipe, a *hacendado* (René Cardona), falls for Cruz (Esther Fernández), the girlfriend of José Francisco (popular singer Tito Guízar), his *caporal*. José Francisco and Felipe have been friends since childhood, when newly orphaned José Francisco and his sister Eulalia (Margarita Cortez) moved into the *rancho* community with their godmother Angela (Emma Roldán). With them came Cruz, another orphan who had been living with them. José Francisco is secretly in love with Cruz, who has always been considered slightly better than a servant by Angela, although Angela's permanently drunk "husband" Florentino (Carlos López "Chaflán") treats her like a daughter. This equilibrium is upset when Angela, desperate for a loan from the *patrón*, notices that Felipe also likes Cruz and offers to bring her to him at night. Although Felipe realizes that Cruz loves José Francisco after she faints in his arms and he behaves like a gentleman, she is seen leaving his house and therefore the entire community believes her to be "spoiled." When José Francisco dramatically (through the lyrics in a song) hears this gossip, the two men become enemies, but ultimately, despite misunderstandings and macho attitudes, the bonds of their friendship prevail, and all are reconciled.

The "musicality" of *Rancho Grande* evolves gradually. Diegetically motivated *ranchera* music only appears seventeen minutes into the film, when we first see the grown-up Cruz ironing. Florentino strums his guitar and naturalistically, Cruz begins to sing "Canción mixteca" (Song from Oaxaca), a *ranchera* song about longing for home. Here music reveals character—Cruz is not from Rancho Grande, but from Oaxaca—and is integrated into the rhythm and fabric of the quotidian as a natural form of expression in *hacienda* life. All of the *rancheras* of *Rancho Grande* are similarly naturalized and accompanied only by string instruments. Acoustically, there is little difference between the space of song and the space of dialogue/narrative. The next musical number—a tender serenade by Tito Guízar and a group of *mariachis* of "Las Mañanitas" and other songs—is sutured into the narrative, but the focus subtly shifts to the performative. With no camera movement (except for the beginning of the scene), the six-minute scene consists of static shots, alternating between medium close-ups and close-ups of Tito Guízar singing that force us to pay attention to Guízar's singing as performance. Indeed, this is also performance within the diegesis, since he is serenading Felipe's love object, not his own. But the camera's perspective is that of the nondiegetic audience, not that of the girl behind the shuttered window who is the object of the serenade.

The next musical number is diegetically integrated but assumes performativity and the variety theater presentational mode head-on. The entire *Rancho Grande* community is gathered for a cockfight with a neighboring rancher and is entertained before the actual fight by two musical "acts": two songs performed by dueling trios introduced as "los cancioneros del alma nacional" (the singers of the national soul) and a *jarabe tapatío*. The staging of these performances is traditional and essentially assumes the proscenium perspective of a diegetic spectator with a nod to the cinematic one; after introducing them via long shots, the camera moves in to frame them in medium close-ups and in artistically staged poses. Similarly, the presentation of the *jarabe tapatío*—with the exception of a close-up of the *charro*'s hat as the *china poblana* steps on its rim—first assumes the perspective of the diegetic audience. Here, however, the film cuts to show reaction shots of the (mostly male) audience; in medium close-ups we see the attentive appreciation of various men in the audience. Despite this thinly veiled voyeuristic move—are the men leering at the *china* or at the *charro*?—the performances of this sequence go beyond the naturalism and individuality of the earlier musical scenes and begin to produce a sense of the cohesiveness of a community linked explicitly to the national ethos, presenting just about all the traditional icons of *mexicanidad*: cockfights, *mariachi* trios, *charros*, a *china poblana*, and the *jarabe tapatío* define the pleasure, leisure, and tradition of this community, which stands in for the nation as a whole.

Finally, the musical apotheosis of the film occurs, appropriately, in another prototypical space: the town *cantina*. After a big win at a horse race, José Francisco returns to town and is feted at the *cantina* by his compatriots. When urged to sing, he breaks into a heroic rendition of the film's title song (which Guízar had already made famous on radio), "Allá en el Rancho Grande," accompanied by his own guitar. In one of the film's most beautifully shot sequences, José Francisco and every male of the community stage a superb act of communal bonding, singing loudly and energetically to proclaim their unity, manliness, cohesion, and happiness.

Unfortunately, this great communal feast is fractured during the subsequent musical/singing duel between José Francisco and his friend Martín (Lorenzo Barcalata), which serves as the musical and narrative climax of the film. In the heat of the singing "battle," Martín essentially sings the gossip that Cruz has been "ruined" by "el patrón." An integral part of the narrative denouement, this musical duel that reveals the "secret" is far more dramatic and of greater emotional and narrative impact than the subsequent revelation of the truth and the narrative reconciliation of José Francisco, Felipe, and Cruz (which is not accompanied by music). Music returns triumphantly, however, in the final scene of the film. As the community gathers outside the church, all the newly married couples exit to the accompaniment of a diegetic rendition of "Allá en el Rancho Grande" by *mariachis*, reestablishing the family unit at the core of utopian communality.

Rancho Grande posits the possibility of a perfectly harmonious relationship between the rich *hacendado* and his employees—exalting precisely that which the radical Lázaro Cárdenas government then in place was attempting to eliminate—and promotes the maintenance of the sociopolitical status quo and an unbridled nostalgia for an imaginary past where such relationships could be conceived. Rather than present an aspirational utopia, its appeal is that of nostalgia for an imagined Porfirian past. Or, to paraphrase Carlos Monsiváis, it inscribes for urban audiences an agrarian memory that never was: "lo urbano con memoria agraria" (1982a, 89).

After *Rancho Grande*

Despite a weak opening run in Mexico City, *Rancho Grande* eventually was extraordinarily popular and was even more widely distributed after cinematographer Gabriel Figueroa received the Mexican cinema's first international festival prize for its cinematography in Venice. Nationally, it spurred investment in the industry and production. The year *Rancho Grande* was released, Mexico produced twenty-five films. By 1937 production grew to thirty-eight films, of which twenty followed the *ranchera* model. In 1939 production again increased; out of fifty-seven films, twenty exploited the *ranchera* formula and "local color."[9]

These early *comedias rancheras* slavishly repeated the *Rancho Grande* scheme with only the slightest of variations, and a typically imaginary rural place (modeled most often on Jalisco) continued to be represented as a musical arcadia ruled by valiant machos where either a birthday, wedding, fair, or good horse race inevitably gave rise to the typical musical numbers. However, the genre was revived with the discovery of its first star in 1941: Jorge Negrete in *¡Ay Jalisco . . . no te rajes!* (Jalisco, Don't Backslide). A trained operatic singer, Negrete had become well known through radio and had already appeared onscreen as a *charro*, but in *Jalisco*, his masculinization and sexualization of the mild-mannered *charro* (as initially portrayed by Tito Guízar in *Rancho Grande*) transformed him into an international singing idol (Serna 1993).

Produced by the Rodríguez brothers (who were pioneers of the early sound cinema with *Santa* in 1931) and directed by one of them, José, *Jalisco* begins with a clear message that points to a change from the bucolic universe of *Rancho Grande*: "This film is inspired by events that could have taken place" in a time still close to the Mexican Revolution "in which, naturally, the excess of passions makes the exercise of law ineffectual." In this *ranchera* world, fists, guns, and macho posturing assume starring roles . . . alongside music and folkloric dancing. The violence in this world is quite explicit. The film begins in the countryside with the assassination of the parents of little Salvador ("Chavo"), who is left with his caretaker (the lazy and drunk Chaflán) and in the custody of his grandfather, Radilla (Antonio Bravo), a Spaniard who owns a *cantina*. Chavo swears that he will avenge his parents' death and Radilla, a determined misogynist, begins Chavo's education in *machismo* by teaching him to play cards, shoot guns, herd cattle, and distrust women. Pointing to a picture of a girl, he tells the young Chavo to look at her and to remember that women "are the most venomous animal in the world." A clever montage of the boy shuffling cards (with dissolves of cattle, horse riding, close-ups of women, and more card shuffling and dealing—the boy's education) brings us to the present, where he has grown into Jorge Negrete.[10]

As in *Rancho Grande*, in *Jalisco* music serves as a mechanism through which to express intimate emotions. Thus, a song cements Chavo's proclamation of love to the lovely Carmela (Gloria Marín, who would become Jorge Negrete's wife for twelve years); standing outside her window (but not in a serenading spirit), he asks her to join him in singing the verses he has composed because, after all, "todas las muchachas de Jalisco cantan" (all the girls of Jalisco sing). Despite this naturalization and elision of the professionalism of the performer, when he breaks into song the acoustical difference of the studio-recorded love song with full orchestral accompaniment is jarring, calling attention to the artifice of its production. Music and dance also function in large communal celebrations. During a trip diegetically motivated by Chavo's search for his parents' killers, he tours through fairs, cockfights, and celebrations where he watches a stirring performance of the film's title song by Lucha Reyes[11] and participates in a spectacular sing-along to the same tune in a large *cantina* in Guadalajara with dozens of *mariachis* (playing strings and trumpets), trios, and *chinas poblanas*. And in between all the singing and dancing, he also manages to kill nine men in cold blood, acquires the nickname "La Ametralladora" (the machine gun) for his shooting speed, and becomes the subject of a wanted poster pasted up in all *cantinas*. As in *Rancho Grande*, we also have the inevitable serenade with *mariachis*, but this time it turns into a musical duel and then into an actual fistfight between Chavo and Carmela's other suitor, the dandified aristocratic Felipe who is clearly no match for Chavo (he does not even sing and brings a surrogate singer to perform his serenade).

Despite the arrogant macho histrionics and violence, *Jalisco* remains what García Riera termed "an amiable comedy." Certain narrative elements contribute to this feeling of affability, among them the several charming small children that play significant roles, especially in relation to the romance between Chavo and Carmela (and despite his macho histrionics, Chavo is always kind and loving to the children, while Felipe is not) and a constant underlying stress on the goodness of families, for whom all sacrifices are feasible (García Riera 1993b, 205). To this I would add that music and performance also defamiliarize the violence and ultimately drive it away. In a world where music and dance bear such extraordinary emotional and narrative power, the violence and macho posturing lose their visceral edge and become only a necessary evil, to be discarded by the hero at the end of the film; rather than kill the last assassin, he hands him over to the law and goes off with Carmela (and Chaflán) to live happily ever after, reestablishing the utopian stability of nostalgia.

This kind of "naïve" *comedia ranchera* (Ayala Blanco 1985, 69–89) remained popular through the 1940s but eventually lost the innocence that had been its hallmark. By the 1950s *rancheras* featured characters who were irresponsible and even asocial, complicated plots, more and more songs, and an air of "festive insolence" (Ayala Blanco 1985, 83). The importance of the male hero also increased exponentially, so much so that films began routinely to offer two heroes (always played by big-name stars), not only to sustain the narrative but also, of course, to increase box office appeal.[12] The epitome of this buddy *comedia ranchera* is *Dos tipos de cuidado* (Ismael Rodríguez, 1952), which brought the singing stars Jorge Negrete and Pedro Infante together for the first and only time. (Pedro Infante had been introduced to the genre in another Ismael Rodríguez film, *The Three Garcias* [*Los Tres Garcia*, 1946]). With its two super-macho super-*charro* stars, *Dos tipos* is not interested in the social universe of the *hacienda*; it is nourished, as García Riera argues, by "the mythic weight" of the star figures of its heroes (1993f, 239) and fueled by the exhibitionism of Mexican masculinity.

The film begins with a prologue and with a somewhat self-reflexive gesture: a large group of young men and women are gathered for a group photograph of their country outing. As soon as the picture is taken, they disperse quickly and the focus shifts to Pedro Malo (Infante) and Jorge Bueno (Negrete) (dressed in identical outfits!); they both plan to ask their girls to marry them. After a quick dissolve we see Jorge with Rosario (Carmen González) in a pastoral setting while the soundtrack swells with the full orchestral introduction to "Olor de campo" (The Smell of the Earth), which he sings operatically as they stroll by a dramatic (back-projected) waterfall and, eventually, to a fishing spot. Jorge's strategy is to feign lack of interest in Rosario, and the artifice of the mise-en-scène and the grandiloquence of the music complement his arrogant stance. In another secluded spot (this time an unremarkable glade), Pedro, always honest and transparent, pleads with María (Jorge's sister, played by Yolanda Varela), to no avail; she reels off the names of the many girls he has been with, dismisses his ensuing pleas, and ends up clubbing him on the head after he dares to steal a kiss. Notably, Pedro does not sing to seduce.

This succinct precredit sequence effectively establishes the rural universe of the *ranchera* and plays off the star personas of the two men; Jorge is arrogant, affected, and egotistical, while Pedro is sincere, charming, and noble. As Monsiváis has argued, "Generosity, humbleness, contagious happiness and a lack of power are the predominant characteristics of Infante's persona. Infante never represented authority, while Negrete did" (1986, 6). But that this will also be a different type of *ranchera* world is evident in the first sequence after the credits, as Jorge pulls into a fancy petrol station and garage in a sparkling sedan. These may be modern times, but as the sign by a horse indicates ("we can lend you a horse while your car is being lubed"), old customs coexist within the modern. At the end, that is precisely the role the film itself plays in the universe of Mexican cinema, bringing together the "charm" of the *ranchera*—itself folkloric by 1952—with the modern star system of its thriving film and recording industry.

As we quickly learn, about a year has passed and Jorge is only now returning to the town. In the meantime, Pedro has married Rosario, Jorge's former sweetheart, and they have a brand-new baby girl, but he does not seem to have given up on his womanizing ways; to celebrate the baby's birth he brings a raucous bunch to the *cantina* to sing, drink, and dance. As Pedro explains during a lull in the dancing and singing, he has no luck with women; they don't want him because he is a womanizer and he is a womanizer because they don't want him. When Jorge runs into Pedro at the *cantina*, the tension escalates as Jorge accuses Pedro of betraying him and lays bare the gender politics of the film: "If a woman betrays us, we forgive her and are done with it because she is a woman. But when the betrayal comes from someone we believe to be our best friend, Chihuahua, how it hurts." In subsequent scenes, including a musical flashback where we learn that Jorge broke up with Rosario when she would not accept that he had taken another girl to a *kermes* (open-air bazaar) and a musical duel at a party, Jorge attempts to humiliate and provoke Pedro. Although he resists, Pedro is finally pulled into open confrontation. At the point that a duel with pistols seems inevitable, Pedro pulls Jorge into a back room for a private conversation. When they emerge fifteen minutes later, they seem reconciled, although the audience is not privy to their discussion. Only at the end of the film do we learn that Pedro married Rosario to "save" her because she was pregnant (the result of a rape when she traveled to Mexico City to forget Jorge after their breakup), thereby restoring Pedro to the position of a noble and loyal friend.

Without this knowledge, however, subsequent events in the film trouble the mores of Mexican masculinity *a la ranchera*,[13] especially when we see that Jorge is aggressively pursuing Rosario, thus putting Pedro in the position of a cuckold, and that Pedro is also pursuing Maria, thus being unfaithful to his wife and calling into question the sanctity of marriage and family. The contradiction is crystallized via simultaneous serenades—Jorge brings one to Pedro's wife, Pedro brings one to Jorge's

Mexico | 263

sister—presented via split screen. Calling attention to the men's narcissism and to the relationship between them at two moments they actually turn in the other's direction, as if redirecting their singing to each other—rather than the relationship between them and their female love objects, this sequence establishes the centrality of homosocial bonding for the narrative. Knowledge of the scandalous serenades quickly spreads through the town and Pedro is put in the unenviable position of being considered a cuckold, coward, womanizer, and irresponsible husband and father by both the townspeople and the spectators. In fact, as Sergio de la Mora argues in his acute queer reading of the film, Pedro is narratively and visually demeaned and feminized, as he is framed in front of the Virgin of Guadalupe and with a flower at crotch level while the General glowers at him for not addressing Jorge's aggressions, and later in front of mounted antlers, much to the amusement of the other partygoers (2006, 102–03). In fact, even after we learn that Pedro has not betrayed his friend and that he is neither cuckold nor coward, the final musical number (again, a folkloric *kermes* with *mariachis* galore), in which heterosexuality and families are firmly reestablished, visually pairs Pedro and Jorge together more frequently than with the women. As de la Mora says, "male friendship takes center stage" (115). And the women? Well, their place in this folkloric universe is on the outskirts of male life. Although they are finally empowered to sing along with the men in the final scene (for the first time in the film), the women are also identified with the *tamaleria* (food stand), ironically titled "La Malinche."[14]

The *Cabaretera*

To the degree that the *comedia ranchera* posited a musical rural utopia as the site for the exercise of multiple and contrasting forms of resolutely macho masculinities and its queer echoes, the *cabaretera* film produced a filmic musical space—the urban cabaret—for the interplay of differential female subjectivities.[15] With precedents in the long-standing tradition of prostitute films in the Mexican cinema—since the silent era but especially with the first sound film *Santa* (Antonio Moreno, 1931) and *The Woman of the Port* (*La mujer del puerto*, Arcady Boytler, 1933)—in which innocent girls, often from the provinces, are forced into prostitution in the big city and find redemption only in death, *cabaretera* films appear in the late 1940s, in a vastly different social context. Whereas the deeply conservative *comedia ranchera* emerged in spite of (or in response to) the progressive nature of Lázaro Cárdenas's government (which culminated with the expropriation of foreign oil companies in 1938),[16] a political turn to the right began with the Miguel Avila Camacho *sexenio* (1940 to 1946) and was institutionalized by Miguel Alemán (1946-1952) and successive presidents. Under *alemanismo*, the focus on nationalist economic policies and progressive social programs (focused on agrarian communities and organized labor) shifted to economic development, industrialization, and the rapid growth of the urban sphere. As scholars of the period have argued, Alemán fostered the symbiosis of political power and the national bourgeoisie under the slogan of "national unity" while simultaneously running a tremendously corrupt government and increasing Mexico's dependence on the US, especially after World War II (Medin 1990; Monsiváis 1990). The emergence of the *cabaretera* film can therefore be read as a response to the strains of sudden urbanization and the shift from proletarian moderation to urban conspicuous consumption in a city where the cabaret had become the quintessential space for entertainment: "Cabarets emerged throughout Mexico City and the fashionable rhythms vibrated with the roar that seemed to be that of prosperity on the march, although that prosperity would be illusory for the majority of the population" (García Riera 1993d, 108).

Whereas in the 1930s there were only a handful of cabarets in Mexico City by the late 1940s there were more than twenty, ranging from exclusive supper clubs like Ciro's in the Hotel Reforma (which featured Diego Rivera murals) to all-inclusive dance halls like El Pirata and Salón México (Berger 2006). As extolled by Salvador Novo in his *Nueva grandeza mexicana*, the cabaret represented the epitome of urban modernity and was a modernizing force; it was where the working class exchanged their sandals for shoes and their *pulque* (an alcoholic beverage associated with poor or rural areas) for beer (1946). But it was also a liminal space, "a moral hell and sensorial heaven where the forbidden was normalized" and where the powerless and disenfranchised land to dance a *danzón*, listen to a bolero . . . or find a way to make a living" (Monsiváis 1995, 118).

Unlike the Hollywood musical, which, as Dyer has argued, addresses "wants that (US) capitalism itself promises to meet" (1981, 84-85) and therefore typically excludes issues of class and race, these issues are at the crux of the *cabaretera* genre. In the already liminal and dystopic nature of its privileged space, the cabaret, music, and dance function not for national bonding or building community but as the vehicle for marginalized subjectivities.

The film that defined the *cabaretera* genre was Emilio Fernández's *Salón México* (1948). Noted for his earlier rural and *indigenista* films (that depicted the indigenous peoples of Mexico as simple and pure) such as *María Candelaria* (1943) and *Enamorada* (1946), Fernández and cinematographer Gabriel Figueroa transferred their skills to the new urbanscape of Mexico City: on the one hand, dark cabarets and tenements; on the other, schools, grand government edifices, and museums. Mercedes (Marga López) secretly works as a dance hall hostess (that is, sex worker) at the Salón México to pay for the private boarding school education of younger sister Beatriz. She also supports her pimp, Paco (Rodolfo Acosta), who refuses to part with the cash award they receive at a danzón contest that begins the film. Lupe (Miguel Inclán), a kindhearted policeman, is in love with Mercedes and tries to protect her, but she ends up in jail with Paco after a bank robbery. When freed, Mercedes agrees to the marriage between the handsome pilot Roberto and Beatriz, and later accepts Lupe's proposal. When Paco, who has escaped from jail, threatens to tell Beatriz the truth about Mercedes unless she escapes with him, Mercedes stabs him with a knife while Paco shoots her down. At the end, Beatriz finishes her studies and is lovingly embraced by Roberto, who now knows the truth.

Although many critics have read *Salón México*—and the *cabaretera* genre in general—within the terms of traditional bourgeois morality (the good woman versus the fallen woman) as ultimately serving to reinforce the patriarchal status quo, the visual, narrative, and musical dynamics of these films are, as Dolores Tierney has recently argued, much more complex (2007). Despite the conformity of the narrative and its privileging of "the Mexico that should be" (the bright and sunlit world of the school, the beautiful avenues and museums where Mercedes takes Beatriz on their weekly edifying outings, the heroism of the returned war veteran), even as it presents "the Mexico that should not be" (the dark and smoky cabaret and its edgy denizens) (García Riera 1993d, 264), *Salón México* produces an excess of signification regarding the latter that undermines the centrality of the former. As Tierney details, through camera work that lovingly—even "lustfully"—approaches the world of the cabaret and both its measured rhythms (the complex and precise footwork of the danzón contest with which the film begins) and its exuberant moments of tropicality (extraneous musical performances that interrupt the narrative proper), *Salón México* posits the interconnectedness of the two: "[the world] of moral orthodoxy in which Beatriz will marry the Pilot and gain ascendancy into Mexico's 'Revolutionary family' and . . . the underworld of the cabaret where pimping, prostitution and robbery happen daily and on which, ironically, this union depends" (2007, 136).

To the degree that *Salón México* sets out the parameters of the *cabaretera* genre, the creative trio of director Alberto Gout, screenwriter Alvaro Custodio, and the Cuban-born actress/dancer/singer Ninón Sevilla pushed the genre to its limits. Others—like Juan Orol—had pushed on the *Salón México* model, increasingly integrating Caribbean actresses/dancers and rhythms such as the rumba and the conga. Even Gout had already dabbled in the genre. He made *The Well-Paid One (La bien pagada,* 1947) with the Cuban dancer María Antonieta Pons but Ninón Sevilla would become his muse. No other screen woman in the classic Mexican cinema would be as sexual, willful, excessive, and able to express her anger at her fate through vengeance. As François Truffaut (under the pseudonym Robert Lacheney) wrote in *Cahiers du Cinéma* in 1954:

> From now on we must take note of Ninón Sevilla, no matter how little we may be concerned with feminine gestures on the screen or elsewhere. From her inflamed look to her fiery mouth, everything is heightened in Ninón (her forehead, her lashes, her nose, her upper lip, her throat her voice). . . . Like so many missed arrows, [she is an] oblique challenge to bourgeois, Catholic, and all other moralities. (Cited in Garcia Riera 1993d, 132–34, and Ayala Blanco 1985, 144–45)

What is striking in the Gout-Sevilla films, beginning with *Revenge (Revancha,* 1948), is the degree to which Sevilla asserts her own personality on-screen to create a remarkable self-reflexivity within the most conventional of narrative frameworks. As García Riera astutely commented with reference to her performance in *Revancha*:

> Thanks to Ninón Sevilla, the cabaret invented by the Mexican cinema was revealed as that which it really was: an invention. Film genres begin to exist when they accept their conventions. And the conventions lose their ability to conceal themselves when illustrated by a character as implacably real as Ninón Sevilla. (1993d, 213)

What García Riera defines as "real" is, in fact, Sevilla's excessively gendered presence that engages with melodramatic tropes beyond the point of hyperbole and pushes the genre to its zenith. Above all, the Gout-Sevilla films combine extraordinarily melodramatic plots with extensive (and excessive) musical performances (*Revancha* contains twelve musical numbers taking up approximately a third of the film's eighty-six minutes) in which Sevilla and others[17] engage with great glee. It is not coincidental that these incarnations of the cabaret began to be referred to as *rumbera* films, eliding the outright identification of the protagonist as a sex worker—though she typically is one—and aligning her with transnational rhythm instead. Favoring a combination of *boleros*—mostly by Agustín Lara—and Latin "rhythms" (rumbas, congas, mambos, and sambas), these later *cabareteras* transform the self-abnegating sex worker of *Salón México*. While Lara's *boleros* idealized woman as a purchasable receptacle for man's physical needs (the ultimate commodity for modern Mexican society) and also invested her with the power of her sexuality (as in the lyrics of "Aventurera,"[18] to sell at will, to name her price, to choose her victim), the Latin rhythms gave her the musical space to engage in what Piedra calls "the poetics for the hip" (1991). For Piedra, the rumba is a concentric form of signifying

> a questionably ethical and superficial means of compliance aimed at yielding a profound and aesthetic means of defiance.... The rumba hips, exaggerated, voyeuristic, exhibitionist, deified and prostituted as they appear to be, might also be a signifier of both acceptance of our bodies and defiance of foreign impositions, and even further: a substitute for the silent or muffled voice, and not just for women or through women. (1991, 636)

The *rumbera* and the nightlife of which she is an emblem became an antiutopian paradigm for modern Mexican urban life. Idealized, independent, and extravagantly sexual, the exotic *rumbera* was a social fantasy through which other subjectivities could be envisioned, and other psychosexual/social identities forged.

The most virulent of the Gout-Sevilla *cabaretera* films is *Aventurera* (1950). The plot is extraordinarily complicated and evidence of the excess associated with such films. Elena (Sevilla), a happy middle-class girl, is left destitute when her mother runs away with a lover and her father commits suicide. Unable to find a job, she is tricked into a Juárez brothel where she is drugged and gang-raped. She awakens bound to brothel employment.

Eventually, Elena becomes the star of/a sex worker at the nightclub, but she is unruly and given to such temper tantrums that the madam (Andrea Palma) hires a thug to scar her in punishment. She runs away to Mexico City, becomes a nightclub star again, and meets and seduces Marío (Rubén Rojo), only to discover that his high-society mother is the madam of the Juárez brothel. After many other melodramatic twists, seductions, and murders, the film finally ends with Marío and Elena supposedly free of their family traumas and about to enjoy a normal family life.

The film's resolution imposes an end to the story (which tellingly does not include the sex worker's death), but it cannot contain the excess of signification circulated by the film—the malevolence of Andrea Palma's icy glance as she watches Elena's first taste of champagne through an ominously barred lookout, Sevilla's haughty cigarette-swinging walk around the cabaret while Pedro Vargas sings the film's title song, her lascivious drunken revelry during her own wedding party, the sevenfold multiplication of her image while she sings "Arrímate cariñito" (Come Closer, Little Love) in a Juárez nightclub. This excess is narrative and visual, for the plot is only as excessive as Elena's own physical presence, the sum of Sevilla's exaggeratedly sexual glance, overabundant figure, extraordinarily tight dresses, rolling hips, excessive laughter, and menacing smoking. This excessive performance functions not so much as a parody of a mimetic performative ideal, but as an oblique affirmation of the gender identity that a mimetic repetition elides. Elena/Sevilla is more than a representation; she is a bundle of unrepressed instinctive desires. If, as Judith Butler argues, the performative gesture, "as a certain frozen stylization of the body is the constitutive moment of feminine gender identity," Sevilla, like a drama queen, melts the style (1990a, 140). This meltdown, her spectacular visual and musical provocation, is far greater than the moral admonitions provided by the narrative.

But the *rumbera* is not a simple model of resistance. In the context of Mexican musical genres like the conservative *ranchera* and maternal melodramas bursting with suffering mothers, the image of female subjectivity that emerges is deeply contradictory and without an easy resolution. In fact, it is a fantasy. As Sevilla, with much self-awareness, explains to her lover in *Mulata* (Gilberto Martínez Solares, 1953), another *cabaretera* film, the impossible challenge of female identity is summarized by the insecurity of "never knowing whether a man has loved me or desired me." It is not that one is necessarily preferable to the other—she can be either

Mexico | 269

the wife or the sexual object—but that Mexican society nevertheless still insists that they are mutually exclusive social categories.

In conclusion, in the "Golden Age" Mexican cinema, "the musical" did not function as a distinct entity comparable to the Hollywood genre. Instead, music and performance were incorporated into specific narrative spaces that served as utopian and/or dystopian allegories of nationhood. Whether in the *hacienda* or in the cabaret, musicality was the vehicle through which the melodramatic was exercised. In the early *comedia ranchera*, the impetus was for musicality to drive national bonding and community building but, by the late 1940s and 1950s, as we saw in *Dos tipos de cuidado*, even the *ranchera* had evolved and, as in the *cabaretera*, musicality became a vehicle for the articulation of marginalized subjectivities.

13

Before Exploitation

Three Men of the Cinema in Mexico (2009)

This essay explores the "proto-exploitation" practices of directors Juan Orol, José Bohr, and Ramón Peón in early 1930s Mexico, the period immediately following the introduction of sound and before the consolidation of the film industry in the 1940s when exploitation proper would emerge. López locates in these three filmmakers' works (including La Llorona *[Peón, 1934],* La sangre manda *[Bohr, 1934], and* Madre querida *[Orol, 1934]) a pronounced experimentation with narrative, themes, style, and genre that would lay the groundwork for both the future Mexican national industry and later exploitation cinemas throughout the region.*

> Yo tengo que vivir del público.
> I live from my audience.
>
> —Juan Orol in De La Vega Alfaro, *Juan Orol*

Eric Schaefer (1999) argues that exploitation film emerged as a discernible category in the United States around 1919–1920. Chronicling the public controversy over sex hygiene/anti-venereal disease films in this period, he argues that these films crystallized the possibility of an alternative film space at a moment when the mainstream industry had consolidated its industrial base in Hollywood, established a firm mode of production, and developed a stylistic system anchored in narrative and stylistic transparency. In Latin America, however, filmmaking developed at a different pace and under different kinds of contextual pressures. An exploitation cinema akin to that outlined by Schaefer could not even begin to emerge as an alternative filmic practice grounded in spectacle until the late 1940s–1950s, when the Mexican cinema had become established as *the* cinema for the continent (López 1994a). However, what emerged earlier, especially in the effervescent experimental period after the arrival of sound, were multiple alternative cinematic practices that, attempting to find the "magic" formulas for box office success and audience satisfaction, laid the groundwork for both the mainstream "national" cinema and future exploitation practices.

Focusing on Mexico in the period immediately after the coming of sound, this essay looks at the work of three filmmakers who arrived in Mexico and/or to the new medium in 1930–1931 and participated eagerly and with almost innocent glee in the rush to define a national cinema and establish an autochthonous mass audience: Juan Orol, José Bohr, and Ramón Peón. Originally from Spain, but in Mexico since youth, Orol had been a race car driver, boxer, actor, bullfighter, policeman, and artistic director for a radio station before taking up filmmaking with *Sagrario* (Sanctuary, 1933). Peón had been making films in his native Cuba (including the famous *La virgen de la Caridad* [Our Lady of Charity, 1930]) and had spent time in Hollywood before resettling in Mexico. He was assistant director for five films before directing his first Mexican feature, *La Llorona* (The Weeping Woman, 1934). Bohr had a long international career as a singer/composer and had worked on Spanish-language films in the United States; his first Mexican film was *La sangre manda* (Blood Rules, 1934). Eager for box office success and engaged in the collective exercise of establishing a "national" industry, all three directors (a few times in collaboration with each other) adopted a freewheeling syncretic style: they adapted and combined generic strands popularized by Hollywood with national themes and folklore and experimented with new formal strategies for storytelling. In the 1930s their work contributed significantly to the general experimentation and ebullience of a film industry attempting to find (and define) its audience.

The Context for Filmmaking in Mexico

As I have argued elsewhere (López 2000b), the diffusion of the cinema throughout the continent was defined by its status as an import emblematic of modernity and by the technological infrastructure, political stability, industrialization, and economic activities at national and regional levels. By the late 1920s the larger nations of Latin America had developed cinematic vernaculars and fairly solid production infrastructures, albeit with limited resources, and, above all, had captured national and regional audiences despite the constant competition from US and European imports. Latin American silent cinema inscribed the medium in national histories while simultaneously recognizing it as the embodiment of differential dreams of modernity.

In the late 1920s and early 1930s, however, the introduction of sound technology abruptly cut off this trajectory and, especially in Mexico, subtly shifted the terms of the cinema's main representational paradigms. Aggressively marketed, sound films from the United States quickly took over the exhibition and distribution sectors, while national producers scrambled for capital, technology, and know-how. In Mexico, the transition to sound took place at the end of the first decade of postrevolutionary state building, during which the nation engaged in complex negotiations to sustain governance over disparate and needy populations and to secure its place in the post–World War I international order. The end of the decade coincided with the end of Plutarco Elias Calles's official term as president (1928) and the end of the Cristero Rebellion (1926–1929). Unwilling to give up power after president-elect Alvaro Obregón was assassinated in 1927, Calles managed to secure his stronghold over national politics as the "Jefe Máximo" by appointing three interim puppet presidents over the next six years, a period known as the "Maximato" sexenio (1928–1934). This was also the period when Mexican artists and intellectuals, rallied by José Vasconcelos's exaltation of the mestizo as the future "cosmic race," the culmination of human evolution, and the embodiment of Mexican cultural identity (Vasconcelos 1925), were also deeply engaged in the project of building the cultural capital of the newly emerging nation. In the late 1920s and 1930s, cultural nationalism reigned supreme (Vaughan and Lewis 2006, 14).

It is important to note that the late 1920s to early 1930s also witnessed the blossoming of other mass media that quickly captured the public imagination. Primary among them was radio, marked by the launch of station XEW-AM in Mexico City in September 1930. Owned by Emilio Azcárraga Vidaurreta (also president of the Mexican Music Company, a record and sheet music distributor affiliated with RCA in the United States), XEW launched as "the voice of Latin America from Mexico." It was the first Latin American radio station powerful enough to reach a mass audience and featured an extensive publicity machine and varied programming that easily captured audiences.[1] Above all, music was the centerpiece of programming: in the 1930s, Mexican radio (led by XEW) codified, standardized, and institutionalized an "official" repertoire of "Mexican" popular music (*mariachis, boleros, rancheras*) and created national "stars" who became very important for the cinema. Second only to music, serial dramas, later known as radionovelas, also quickly grew in popularity. Drawing their talent from literature and theater—the very same pool that nourished the cinema[2]—radio dramas became popular in the 1930s and ubiquitous after 1940 (XEW aired as many as five different ones per day). Above all, as in other parts of Latin America, radio dramas were notorious for their melodramatic and emotional excesses. Sentimental melodramas punctuated by extreme pathos and enveloped in music became a narrative lingua franca for the mass media in general. As poet Salvador Novo described it in the 1950s, it was "spiritual tequila in everybody's throat" (1951, 171).

The arrival of sound to the cinema in this context of national high and popular cultural effervescence energized intellectuals and filmmakers. Even before the screening of the first sonorized film in April 1929 (Frank Capra's *Submarine*), the impact of sound on the medium and national culture was hotly debated in the press. As Luis Reyes de la Maza chronicles, the cultural intelligentsia presented a united front against the possibility that film would become an English-only medium, resisted Hollywood's inept efforts to produce Spanish-language films, clamored for a national cinema, and debated what it should embody (1973). By late 1930, Hollywood's Spanish-language productions had demonstrated their flaws, among them, problems with mixing accents and nationalities and the lack of convincing star power. Critics like Baltasar Fernández Cue argued in the pages of *El Ilustrado* that only Mexico was in a position to take over the Spanish-language market (de la Maza 1973, 246).

As if heeding the critics, President Pascual Ortiz Rubio included film in his 1931 Campaña Nacionalista (Nationalist Campaign): import duties were increased by almost 1,000 percent in July 1931 and, within three months, the exhibition sector was in crisis, since US distributors refused to pay the additional fees and stopped sending films (de los Reyes 1987, 118; de Usabel 1982, 93). This protectionist move was short lived: Rubio Ortiz rescinded the protectionist tariffs in late October 1931 since, as exhibitors rightly argued, there just weren't enough Mexican films to show in place of the imports.

Before Exploitation | 275

By this time, the Mexican exhibition sector was well established. In 1930 there were 830 movie theaters, 136 already outfitted for sound (de los Reyes 1987, 118). In Mexico City, between three and six major movie theaters were inaugurated yearly between 1930 and 1935. Whereas total capacity in Mexico City was only 32,888 seats in 1922, by 1937 the total number of seats had grown to almost 125,000 (Alfaro Salazar and Ochoa Vega 1997, 221-24). This growth paralleled the tremendous urbanization of Mexico City.[3] In the early 1920s the city's growth was concentrated in the old center, but in the 1930s its territory and population grew exponentially alongside the services and consumer options available to citizens. The larger and most elegant theaters remained in the *centro*, but after the implementation of the 1933 planning and rezoning law, the widening and lengthening of the city's main arteries led to the complete or partial demolition of many of the older theaters. Most were rebuilt throughout the 1930s and the exhibition sector developed a distinctly elegant and modern visage. The *colonias*, or planned neighborhoods, whether traditional or modern, also acquired their own theaters, often consonant with their own architectural vernaculars. Working-class *barrios* also had a cinematic infrastructure, though still much more precarious and associated with the *carpa* (tent theater) tradition (Pilcher 2001, 23-39). All that was needed to have an industry were Mexican films . . .

Foreigners, Adventurers, and Entrepreneurs

Mexico had always been a haven for foreign and foreign-trained film entrepreneurs and directors, even in the silent period (Ramírez Berg 1992; de Orellana 2004. But in the early 1930s it was a mecca. Eisenstein's famous 1930-1931 sojourn in Mexico set the stage, although it was sui generis: unlike others landing in Mexico in the early 1930s, Eisenstein had no desire to join and/or influence an industry and, as has been well chronicled elsewhere, his pursuits were instead intellectual and artistic (Nesbet 2003), although his visit left a lasting imprint on the cinema the future Mexican industry engendered (de los Reyes 1987, 96-116).

Many Mexicans had gone to Hollywood in the 1920s to become familiar with the US industry. Indeed, many had achieved success acting (Ramón Novarro, Lupita Tovar, Dolores Del Rio, Lupe Vélez, Gilbert Roland) while others worked as technicians or as extras or learned the trade as assistants (Miguel Contreras Torres, Raphael J. Sevilla, Miguel

Zacarías, Emilio Fernández, Chano Urueta). Many of the Europeans and North Americans that landed in Mexico after 1931 also came via Hollywood, for example, directors John Auer, David Kirkland, and Arcady Boytler (even Eisenstein himself) and cinematographers Alex Phillips and Ross Fisher. The three filmmakers considered here stand out from the rest insofar as they were native Spanish speakers and comfortable inhabitants of Spanish/Latin American culture. But what is most fascinating about this period is the incredible cross-fertilizations and collaborations that occurred across all job titles. Before the establishment of a tightly regimented "closed" union system in 1945, there were no limits to what anyone could do and/or contribute to the final product: every film was a collaborative experiment to see what would "take" and filmic authorship is even more problematic than usual to assert.

Orol-Bohr-Peón: First Films

Orol, Bohr, and Peón made their first films in Mexico in 1933, a year notable for a significant increase in national production: whereas only six films had been released in 1932, there were twenty-one in 1933. Bohr and Peón were recent arrivals to Mexico City; Orol had been in and out of the city for several years. All had spent time in Hollywood, learning about sound filmmaking and, in the case of Bohr, already an accomplished actor/singer, participating in Hollywood's Spanish-language productions. Witnessing its ebullience, they entered the Mexican film business in search of experience and financial success. Although none directed what were considered to be the "best" films of this period either by contemporary or later critics,[4] their films opened up new directions for the medium in Mexico and were often very well received by the public. In subsequent decades, the strands they wove in the 1930s led to the latsploitation cinema analyzed in Victoria Ruétalo and Dolores Tierney's edited volume on this topic (2009). Most importantly, there were deep interconnections among them and between them and others in the nascent film business. Particularly in this period (though the same would be true for the "classical" post-1943 period as well; see Tierney 2007), film production was a team effort and teams were fluid and collaborative in their endeavors to overcome production obstacles and achieve popular success.

Peón, with more filmmaking experience under his belt, was the first to direct and his *La Llorona* was the new industry's first attempt to establish a Mexican horror genre. A free adaptation of the popular myth of La Llorona—a woman who is rejected by her husband/lover and kills her children and then herself, either by stabbing or drowning—the film begins in the present as a well-off family celebrates the son's (Juanito) fourth birthday with an elaborate party. After the party, the grandfather warns the father, Ricardo, of a curse on the family that has caused the death of all their firstborn sons on their fourth birthday. The curse is explained via two long flashbacks. In the colonial period, an Indigenous princess was betrayed by a noble and killed herself and the son he wouldn't legitimize. When she falls to the ground, her spirit rises, spectacularly accompanied by a piercing wail that, literally, stops a sword fight cold. In the present, a masked intruder kills the grandfather and threatens Juanito. Through another flashback we learn that the curse goes back to the Conquest, when Cortéz took away Malinche's son. She went mad and in a fit of despair killed herself with a dagger. As her spirit also rises spectacularly with a long wail, her faithful servant vows to avenge her death for the rest of time. Returning to the present, the masked intruder drags Juanito to an Aztec temple's secret room and is ready to stab him when Ricardo and the police rush in, shoot the masked intruder, and eventually discover that she is the boy's caretaker: all the family's servants have been in their employ for generations and have carried out the legendary curse. Her spirit also rises with a long wail and the film ends with the nuclear family united and safe, but without dispelling the legend.

Peón's film is simultaneously heavily indebted to the silent cinema, especially in its pacing, as well as marvelously inventive in its mise-en-scène and editing. *La Llorona* begins by asserting its nationness by announcing that it is "a modern version of the popular Mexican legend." The rest of the credits unfold in front of dimly lit close-ups of Aztec-looking stone carvings, masks, and vessels that continue to assert Mexicanness as well as establish an apt mood for horror. The first scene (a prelude to the story proper) opens with a long shot of a city street at night. A well-dressed man walks toward the right and briefly stops to light a cigarette. Mid-frame, he gasps suddenly and falls to the ground. Cut to a close-up of his face; his eyes are open and the lit cigarette is still in his mouth, but he is clearly dead. Then the camera pans across his body to his hand as it clenches into a rigor mortis fist. A dissolve on the clenched fist leads to a different space, where a sheet is placed over the fist (fig. 13.1). As the camera pans left, and tilts up, we discover we are in a hospital or morgue, where a handsome doctor in scrubs proclaims to the medical

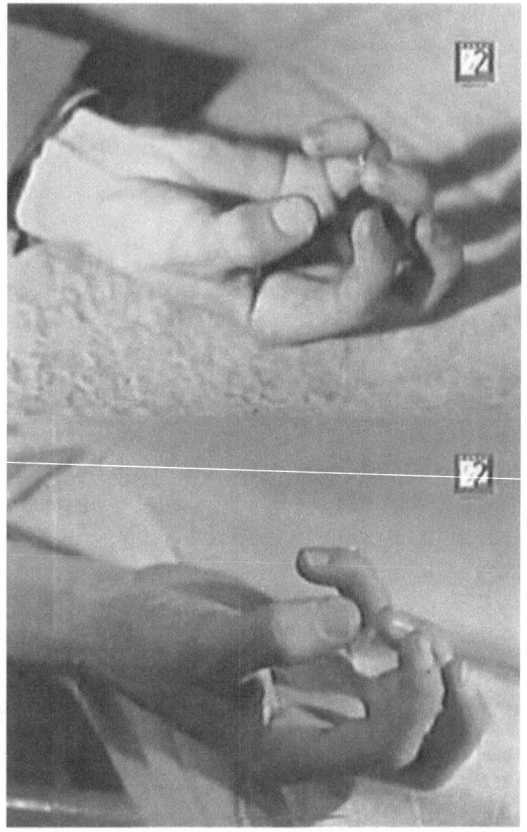

Figure 13.1. Clenched fists in *La Llorona* (The Weeping Woman, Ramón Peón, 1934). Fair use.

students surrounding him that the dead man is an example of a victim of a "typical" heart attack. This first scene economically establishes the horror scenario (mystery-death-ghosts), a contemporary setting ostensibly ruled by scientific rationality, and proclaims a unique style that Peón will sustain throughout the film: an attention to visual detail and a surprising emphasis on complex transitions that constantly call attention to themselves as artifice. Eschewing the parameters of invisible style editing, Peón's transitions catapult the spectator into a strange/estranging narrative universe and (perhaps unwittingly) greatly enhances the horror effect (which otherwise is fairly tame). As stated previously, very often the transitions between scenes occur on close-ups rather than the standard establishing shots and disorient and unsettle. When they do not, they are marked by spectacular diagonal wipes that call attention to themselves such as, for example, the transition between the hospital scene and Juanito's birthday party (fig. 13.2).

The birthday party scene also illustrates a unique—and disconcerting—attention to the mise-en-scène: the oddly shaped cloverleaf design on the floor, echoing the cloverleafs on the back of each chair to suggest a very modern setting and somewhat of an obsession with luck. Peón emphasizes these elements with a disturbingly long and measured 360-degree pan around the table focusing on each child at the party. Yet, we later see that the home is actually a traditional home that has been in the family for centuries (complete with secret underground passages). Visually, the scenes in the present (with the exception of the birthday party) are "realistic" in the gritty detective film style of Hollywood films of the 1930s, but each flashback adopts a different tone: the colonial flashback is visually lush in the style of a historical reconstruction and filled with ornamentation and

Figure 13.2. A transition from *La Llorona* (The Weeping Woman, Ramón Peón, 1934). Fair use.

dozens of extras, while the conquest one is minimalist—most of it filmed against a flat unadorned backdrop—and almost surreal with an almost exclusive focus on La Malinche and/or her servant.

Lastly, one must mention the ghostly special effects, which are spectacularly lurid (fig. 13.3) and, as García Riera puts it, "indescribable" (1993, 82). He is somewhat dismissive of the film ("not badly made and fairly amusing"), but I would argue that it represents an experimental milestone in the establishment of a full-fledged Mexican film industry and is also, to my knowledge, the first appearance of a masked menace in the Mexican cinema. Both the legend of La Llorona and masked characters played a significant role in Mexican exploitation cinema in subsequent decades. Peón also directed *Sagrario*, Juan Orol's first production. Orol had little filmmaking experience but liked the movies and invested capital from the sale of land in a production company, Aspa Films (De la Vega Alfaro 1987, 21–22). With a script by Quirico Michelena, he hired Peón to direct. Like *La Llorona*, *Sagrario* was generically innovative: it is the first film of the

Figure 13.3. Ghostly effects in *La Llorona* (The Weeping Woman, Ramón Peón, 1934). Fair use.

Before Exploitation | 281

Mexican sound cinema to feature *both* adultery and incestuous relations (it was produced and released before *La mujer del puerto* [The Woman of the Port, 1934]). Despite its soupçon of social aspirations (a working-class man who is wronged and jailed; a wife and daughter "helped" by a kindly "doctor" who makes the former his mistress and implicates the latter in symbolic incest), *Sagrario* was deeply marked by the melodramatic plot conventions of the by then booming radionovelas: illustrating the contradictions of the moralism of the times, female transgressions are splendidly—even luridly—aired but must be punished by either death or solitude. Unlike later *cabaretera* films in which performance and sexuality provided the women with agency (López 1994b), here they are pawns and victims to the end.

Stylistically, *Sagrario* is much more conventional than *La Llorona*, despite a few timely placed double exposures that display inner thoughts and mark flashbacks (reminiscent of the ghostly specters of Peón's film), a spectacular beginning that visually conveys the stifling routine of the factory where Juan works, and lovely scenes of the lovers in Chapultepec Park. Most interesting, however, is the nature of its melodramatic premises and its unprecedented success (ninety thousand pesos gross revenue in its first six months vs. thirty-two thousand production costs). The explicit representation of extreme female transgressions as the dramatic nexus (adultery, intended incest), despite the inevitable tragic end of those who transgress, heightens the melodramatic pitch and infuses a new kind of salacious energy into the genre, which presages one of the most persistent characteristics of later mainstream and exploitation efforts.

Some months after the release of *Sagrario*, José Bohr began production on his Mexican directorial debut, *La sangre manda*. Bohr had arrived in Mexico in 1932, still interested in pursuing a film career—"We need pictures filmed in our language" (Bohr, 1987, 207)—and was enchanted by opportunities in Mexico. Dissatisfied with the sound production facilities available (limited to the equipment used by the Rodríguez brothers for *Santa* two years earlier), Bohr went to Hollywood and bought a sound truck and cameras from a friend linked to a minor bankrupt studio (Tiffany Productions) (Bohr, 1987, 207–08). The filming of *La sangre manda* began in late 1933, with Bohr as producer/director, a script by Bohr and Eva "La Duquesa Olga" Limiñana (his longtime partner), and Alex Phillips as cinematographer.

La sangre manda stands out among its contemporaries. While it exhibits its very high production values, it is also the most indebted to the practices of Hollywood Spanish-language films (not surprising, given Bohr's lineage), evidenced first of all by its setting "in the world we live in, in contemporary times." The refusal to anchor the narrative in a real place, perhaps in an effort to achieve universal significance, undermines its impact, rendering its "message" abstract and, in the end, distant and ethereal.

José (Bohr) plays the playboy son of the owner of an ironworks. The film begins with a sophisticated credit sequence using a beautiful art deco font for the credits and a montage of busy office personnel as a backdrop. A close-up on a large clock of the Fundiciones Pedro Bolivar (Pedro Bolivar Ironworks) indicates it is 9:00 a.m. as owner Pedro Bolivar strolls in, noticing that his son's office is unoccupied. An hour later when he calls him, José is still in bed at home, drunk from the previous night's partying. This skillfully shot and edited opening sequence economically sets the dramatic stage for the film: the righteousness of work versus the irresponsible leisure of elites. That evening, the enraged Bolivar orders José to report to Chato López at the ironworks at 7:00 a.m. to work as a laborer. José's arrival at the factory the next morning is nothing short of spectacular: he drives up in an elegant convertible driven by a Black chauffeur, wearing tails and a top hat, and still visibly inebriated. This and other scenes shot on location at the foundry La Consolidada in Mexico City vividly capture the beauty of a steel plant and the harshness of working in one; simultaneously an ode to its symbolic modernity and an indictment of its effects (fig. 13.4).

As José befriends the workers and falls in love with Chato's adoptive sister Lupe, he advocates for workers' rights (minimum salaries and collective bargaining), and convinces his father to provide funding for a library, daycare center, and theater in the ironworks. Intending to marry Lupe, he withdraws from his family and former socialite girlfriend and moves in with her family. His relationship with Chato (who already calls him "hermano") is well developed, especially via two long exterior traveling shots that follow the pair as they walk to the factory after boxing lessons.

Fully transformed into a member of the working class, José inaugurates the library and theater and continues his romance with Lupe. The rehearsals for the theater's inaugural performances and the inauguration are the scenes that Bohr is most comfortable with, not only in terms of his acting but also in terms of the pacing and the actions of all the characters (Sara García makes her first appearance on film as a child performer's mother). However, in his own musical number, the specter of otherness

Figure 13.4. La Consolidada in Mexico City in *La sangre manda* (Blood Rules, José Bohr, 1934). Fair use.

that he had tried to suppress—his Chilean accent—bursts through in an all-too-jarring way as he sings cheek to cheek to Lupita.

That same evening, Chato's mother Amparo confesses on her deathbed that Pedro Bolivar is Chato's father and José's mother convinces Lupe to break up with José because of their social differences. When he loses his foothold in Chato's home and his loved one, José also seems to lose his class consciousness and in an argument with Chato at the factory, José angrily complains that the workers are usurping what his father amassed after years and that the workers have the same opportunity for growth as his father had. A worker listening wryly remarks, "There is no cure, boys, blood rules." José gets into a fight with El Pesao and is spectacularly wounded when he falls near a foundry.

When José is finally recovered, during a soiree in his honor, the workers Chato has organized to reclaim his patrimony threaten to attack the Bolivar home. Carrying blazing torches when the police arrive, El Pesao pulls a gun on José; Lupe, who had gone to the house to warn José, jumps in front of the bullet and is killed. The workers and Bolivar strike an accord, the brothers reconcile, and José picks up Lupe's body and walks off screen, uttering the apocryphal words: "He is my brother."

As is evident in this analysis, after an inventive and promising beginning, the universalizing impulse takes over the narrative once José is inscribed into factory life. His magical conversion into a proletariat is as facile as his reconversion into a callous aristocrat after being wounded. Visually, however, *La sangre manda* is rather extraordinary for its time and comparable only to *La mujer del puerto* in visual achievement. Phillip's cinematography—beautiful chiaroscuros in the cantina, long traveling shots, and luminous close-ups—is simply spectacular. Overall, the film is very evenhanded stylistically. For example, the juxtaposition of the luxurious life of the Bolivars with the clean simplicity of Chato's home and the poverty of another worker is vividly accomplished by the mise-en-scène but without jarring visual contrasts.

Although *La sangre manda* seemed an auspicious start, it was not especially successful and only lasted a week in a first-run theater. Not one to be easily dissuaded, Bohr immediately went into production for his second film, also cowritten with La Duquesa Olga—¿*Quien mató a Eva?* (Who Killed Eva?)—which premiered in August 1934.

With ¿*Quién mató a Eva?* Bohr found a more suitable genre for his talents, minus the social aspirations: the urban detective story. José (Bohr) is a young millionaire bored with his life. Returning from a gala in which he had just finished singing "I am so bored," José catches burglar Mario in his luxurious apartment and decides to join him in a burglary to inject some excitement into his life. Unfortunately, when they break into the house of famous actress Eva Orquiza, they find a squawking parrot and her dead body. José becomes the primary suspect after the police find his top hat at the scene and he goes "underground" with Mario (disguised as Luponini, a gangster from Chicago), committed to finding the real murderer using rationality and psychology. The ambiance of the "underground" provides

Bohr with a fabulous setting to people with extraordinary types, ranging from ingenues led astray and a scheming vamp to a marvelous quartet of police detectives who often break into song. Singing is a common denominator among all: in the rooming house where Mario and José hide out, the denizens entertain themselves in the dining room by frequently breaking into song (all of which are shown in their entirety). As with *La sangre manda*, Phillips's cinematography is astonishingly beautiful, with expressive close-ups and many chiaroscuro shots, including a striking mirror shot of José during one of his escapades (fig. 13.5). Without the narrative economy of a Howard Hawks in *The Big Sleep*, *¿Quién mató a Eva?* sustains a productive tension between José's search for Eva's killer, the mystery surrounding the characters of the underground, romance between José and one of the ingenues, and musical entertainment. The film was a worthy initiator of the detective/crime genre for the Mexican cinema.

Also in 1934, Orol partnered again with Peón to make *Mujeres sin alma* (Soulless Women). This time Orol played a much larger role in the creation of the film[5] and critics have argued that this film established the

Figure 13.5. A mirror shot in *¿Quién mató a Eva?* (Who Killed Eva?, José Bohr, 1934). Fair use.

"Orolian" universe. Orol plays Julián, an honest chauffeur at the Consolidada Ironworks who ends up in jail when he is framed for theft by his boss Carlos, who is also the lover of his frivolous wife Olga. Olga's infidelities and unsavory life continue and lead to another tragedy: another worker is framed by Carlos and imprisoned; his wife (played by Adela Sequeyro) dies from grief and their children are left orphaned. Julián eventually escapes from prison, uncovers the truth, and kills Olga and Carlos. He is chased by the police and wounded, and runs to his mother's house to die in her arms. Although the film begins with ambitions of realism (again, as in *La sangre manda*, beautiful imagery of the industrial milieu of La Consolidada shot by the ubiquitous Phillips), it quickly settles into the most torpid of male melodramas following the formula that Orol himself would exploit often later in his career: the loss of family values and female licentiousness cause the downfall of an honest man who, as a last recourse, must seek justice while never losing sight of his saintly mother.

Nineteen thirty-four was a significant year not only for the film industry (with total production increasing to twenty-three films that year) but for the nation. After a long campaign and despite the opposition of Calles, Lázaro Cárdenas was elected to the presidency and changed the shape of the nation, transforming the party of the revolution into a popular organization free from the control of Calles (Cárdenas forced Calles into exile in 1936). The political system established during his sexenio defined Mexican politics until the 1980s. During the Cárdenas sexenio, labor unions and *campesino* organizations were reorganized, urban and industrial workers gained unionization rights and wage increases, and the government finally fulfilled its revolutionary promises by expropriating and redistributing more than five hundred million acres to about eight hundred thousand *campesinos*. Under his leadership, the work of the Secretaría de Educación Pública and its socialist educational program, focused on the empowerment and enfranchisement of rural communities, also acquired renewed vigor (Knight 1994; Vaughn 1997). With a strong nationalist and populist agenda, Cárdenas had widespread popular support, which became almost unanimous when he masterminded the expropriation of foreign oil companies in 1938.

The new government also became interested in the burgeoning national cinema. Even before Cárdenas's inauguration, the Secretaría de Educación Pública financed the production of *Redes* (Nets) in 1934 (released in 1936). About a group of fishermen near Veracruz who rebel against their exploiters, *Redes* reflected what the artistic intelligentsia—among others, noted composer Carlos Chávez, prominent Marxist Narciso Bassols (who had been at the head of the Secretaría de Educación Pública), and the progressive US photographer Paul Strand—considered to be appropriate for the national cinema à la Eisenstein: *indigenismo* (faces, landscape, settings) and healthy—positive—doses of class struggle.[6] In January 1935, the Cárdenas administration promised via official decree to support the national industry and that same year provided railroad trains, a regiment, munitions, artillery, uniforms, and horses for Fernando de Fuentes's *¡Vámonos con Pancho Villa!* (Let's Go with Pancho Villa), produced by the recently opened modern studios of the Cinematográfica Latinoamericana, S.A. (CLASA). Despite this official propitious climate (and their artistic achievement and subsequent fame), these films did not capture the public imagination: the biggest box office hits of 1935 were directed by Orol and Bohr: respectively, *Madre querida* (Dear Mother) and *Luponini (El terror de Chicago)* (Luponini, the Terror of Chicago).

Possibly inspired by Bohr's 1934 *Tu hijo* (Your Son), which initiated the "cult of motherhood" films in the sound era but was not particularly successful with audiences or critics,[7] Orol adapted a sentimental story by Julián Cisneros Tamayo and hit the mother lode with *Madre querida*. Released on the tenth of May to coincide with Mother's Day in Mexico (a day that had acquired great significance since its "creation" in 1922),[8] the film was a resounding success, earning more than five hundred thousand pesos in the D.F. alone. In a sense, given its carefully arranged promotional angle, *Madre querida* could be considered the first Mexican film to be marketed with the panache and hucksterism later associated with exploitation cinema: in a later interview, Orol claimed that during the film's first theatrical run he handed out handkerchiefs as viewers bought their tickets, promising a complete refund if they were not used during the screening (De la Vega Alfaro 1987, 30).

Madre querida begins with a long introduction by Orol himself, dressed in suit and tie, in which he dedicates the film to the *madrecitas* of the world who, as mothers, have suffered. With a still-thick Castilian accent and speaking like a radio announcer, Orol emotionally exalts motherhood as that which "makes men more human" contrasted with images of various monuments to motherhood. Again inspired by radionovelas, the film proper begins in an elementary school during recess: a group of boys talk about what they are going to buy their mothers for Mother's Day. Juanito complains that he has no money to buy a present and Luisito, a younger boy, gives him fifty cents because he has lost his mother. Having already established its melodramatic premises, the film completes the background of each of the two boys. Luisito is a spirited prankster from a wealthy family; his mother died in childbirth. Manuel, his lonely father, confesses to his uncle the reason for his perennial sadness (via two elaborate flashbacks that include three musical numbers—his loved one was a singer—two of them in a sad Baja California cabaret): he once had a great love in Cuba, his family kept them apart, and when he returned to Cuba he could not find her. Juanito, on the other hand, is serious and hard-working (selling newspapers and pumping gas) to help his humble single mother, Adela, make ends meet. After Luisito accidentally sets a gas station on fire when playing with fireworks, Juanito is accused of arson and, rather than betray his friend, accepts the blame and goes to a reformatory. Brokenhearted, Juanito's mother becomes gravely ill. The remorseful Luisito finally confesses the truth to his father, who tries to help Juanito and his mother. Of course, the dying Adela is Manuel's long-lost love. She dies after telling Manuel that Juanito is his son. Meanwhile, Juanito has escaped from the reformatory to see his mother and, after learning of her death, takes to the streets. Finally, Manuel runs into Juanito at Adela's tomb, tells him he is his father, and takes him home, where he eventually recovers.

As this plot synopsis demonstrates, Orol managed to create the urtext of maternal exaltation and sentimentalism. Dripping in melodramatic excess, the film required few stylistic flourishes beyond its already excessive narrative, although Orol seemed much taken with superimpositions, using them extensively to illustrate the ferocity of the fire Luisito accidentally ignites and Juanito's delirious dreams in which his mother comes to his bedside as a ghostly apparition. Perhaps the key to understanding the film's success is to unravel its relationship to radio. *Madre querida* actually begins as an illustrated radio program and, building radio into the narrative itself, sustains a constant radiophonic vision and affect. Very early in the film, in the second flashback that explains the disappearance of Manuel's love in Cuba, he recounts that he learned that she had gone into radio to make a living and had later gone to Baja California. The flashback begins in the sleazy Baja nightclub, where Adela sings two numbers almost back-to-back in a decidedly radiophonic style: she stands frozen in front of a microphone, does not dance or emote, and barely acknowledges the audience. Later in the film, Luisito and his father sit by a large radio and listen to a radio announcer sending children a special Mother's Day message asking them to recognize the value of their mothers. Echoing Orol's sentiments and tone in the prologue, the presence

Before Exploitation | 289

of the radio positions the spectator into a similar heart-wrenching mode of spectatorship. Though cinematic, the experience translates into affective terms that would be instantly familiar and satisfying to audiences already well trained in—and in love with—the sentimentality of radionovelas.

The other big hit of 1935, *Luponini (El terror de Chicago)* took a very different approach to capturing the public's attention. Capitalizing on the popularity of Hollywood gangster films in the early 1930s and the fact that the post-1934 Production Code precluded the depiction of gangsters as tragic heroes, Bohr loosely adapted the story of notorious bank robber John Dillinger, who had been executed by the FBI in July 1934 as he was leaving a movie theater. In Bohr's version, Dillinger becomes Luponini (his character's alias in *¿Quién mató a Eva?*) who, in addition to having the physical agility that Dillinger had been famous for, is also a skilled singer and entertainer.

Once again exhibiting an excellent command of the medium, Bohr manages to take the more significant elements of the Dillinger story—his spectacular crimes and physical agility, the relentless taunting of the police, the daredevil escapes, the details of his death—and to embody them with a psychological motivation: Luponini, a somewhat frivolous bank teller with loose principles, wants to date the bank manager's daughter but is rebuffed because he doesn't have money. Later he marries another bank teller, Luisa, but after spending their first year of married life unemployed, she too rejects him to look for a man with money. At that crossroads, in a dramatic clenched-hand gesture that will become a leitmotif for the film (fig. 13.6), Lupo (as he is called by his friends) swears that he will get money, lots of money, and will throw it in her face. Elegantly matching the clenched fist, the next shot brings us to the pool hall, where Lupo's criminal life begins with his friend "El Chato."

Lupo's life of crime is quickly established and documented by the detailed presentation of their first successful bank heist—eerily featuring only ambient sounds, which renders it essentially silent—and a frenzied montage of newspaper headlines and radio announcers breaking the news of yet another bank robbery committed by the man the press had dubbed "el hombre mono" (the monkey man) because of his physical prowess. The crimes are, certainly by the standards of the Production Code-regimented Hollywood cinema, lurid: Lupo and his gang are indiscriminate shooters and have no qualms about killing anyone who stands in their way and/or shooting at innocent crowds. Then, in another long scene also with only ambient noises, Lupo robs the bank where he and Luisa worked.

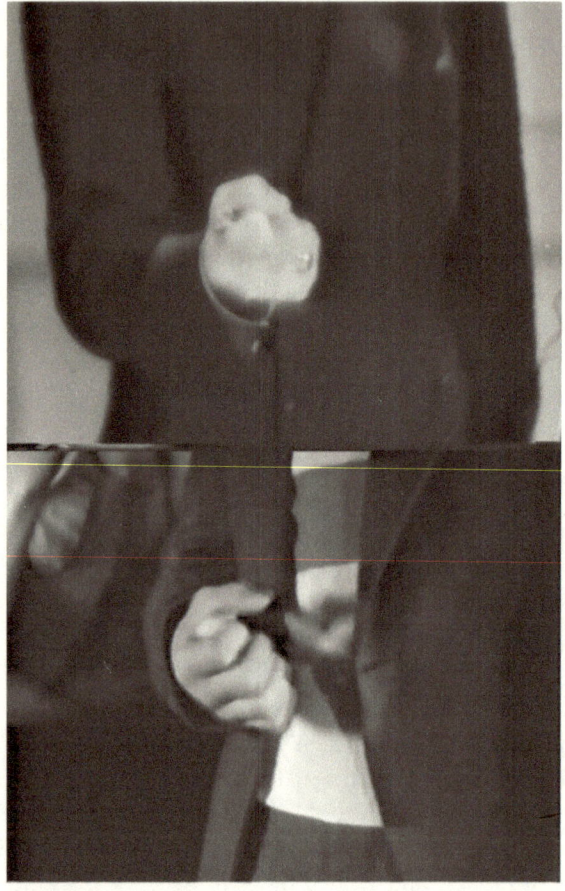

Figure 13.6. Clenched-hand gesture in *Luponini (El terror de Chicago)* (Luponini, the Terror of Chicago, José Bohr, 1935). Fair use.

This heist is complicated, but has been meticulously planned and timed, down to the arrival of a gang member dressed as a motorcycle courier who struts directly to the just-opened bank vault, empties it into his valise, and smoothly drives off with the loot. Another complication is that Luisa is still a teller in the bank; in fact, she is the first to come in and be tied up. As he gets ready to leave, Lupo grabs a fistful of money and, staring menacingly through a bandanna that covers most of his face, throws it at her. That stare will prove to be the beginning of his undoing: Luisa recognizes his eyes (fig. 13.7) and, without thinking, yells out: "Those eyes . . . It's him!"

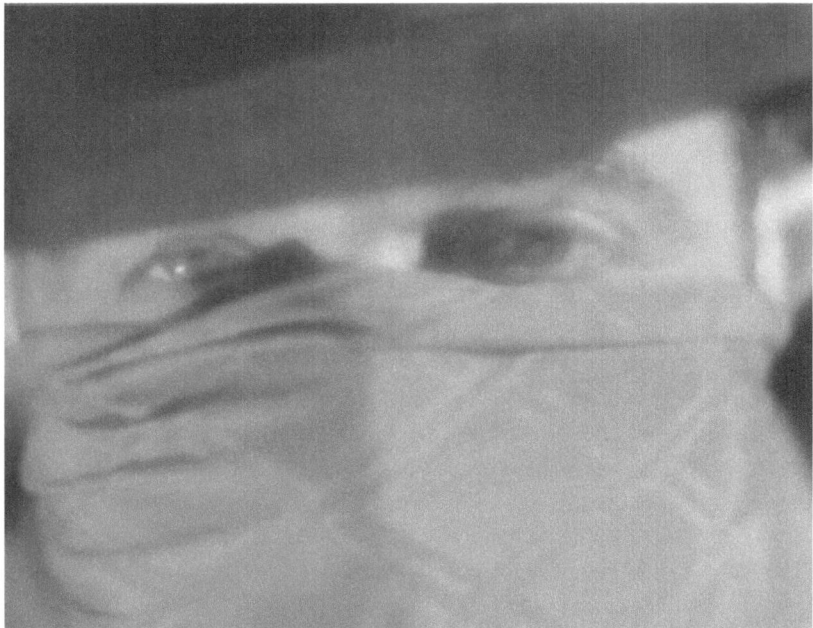

Figure 13.7. Lupo in disguise in *Luponini (El terror de Chicago)* (Luponini, the Terror of Chicago, José Bohr, 1935). Fair use.

Although she doesn't hand him over to the police, Luisa is suspected of helping "el hombre mono," loses her job, and goes to Lupo at his new place of employment: he has become an entertainer at a cinema and at El Chato's new oddly decorated restaurant/cabaret. The bulk of the rest of the film takes place in the milieu of this cabaret, where Lupo's new girlfriend, La Maravilla, is a singing/dancing attraction; another old friend Isabel is a hat-check girl; and Luisa becomes a tap dancer. The space of the cabaret, as in later *cabaretera* films, is luxuriously baroque—a mood generated via mise-en-scène and Bohr's exemplary use of mirror shots to create depth—and a microcosm of passions: the women are always at each other's throats. In between several performances and rehearsals, the police very effectively incite Luisa and La Maravilla's jealousy to break them down; through an informer they are convinced Lupo is "el hombre mono" despite a history of rheumatism (for which he ostentatiously puts a wool glove on his right hand) and childhood accidents that render him less than agile. Lupo and his gang are planning one last heist of the nightclub itself, but when it sours they barely make it out after killing and wounding many and a spectacular chase ensues, chronicled by a montage of police calls and radio announcers and punctuated by spectacular shots of cars and motorcycles careening around curves. Finally Lupo throws his car down an embankment and manages to crawl away and disappear . . . in order to find a plastic surgeon to change his face.

Sporting his Asian new look, Lupo locates Luisa and Isabel's hideout, reads about La Maravilla's success in a newspaper, and decides to go see her. Simultaneously hounded by the police, Luisa cannot control her jealousy and, after a long interrogation punctuated by a cop knocking on a wood table relentlessly, gives up his identity and location at the Cine Esperanza, where La Maravilla performs.

The cops set up a trap at the theater, but as Luisa approaches Lupo to lead him out, he breaks down, confesses his love, and asks her to remarry and go far away. In the lobby, with a big poster for *Delator* in the background (Spanish for John Ford's *The Informer*), Lupo swears his love. He is shot down spectacularly when he steps out of the theater and, after overhearing a report that Luisa has given up Lupo for fifty thousand pesos, kills her, bemoaning "money always money." The last shot of the film is a dramatic close-up of a mirror reflecting the word "Fin," which is gradually covered in blood.

Obviously very familiar with the Hollywood gangster film, Bohr adapted the genre to address his own creative strengths and attempted to localize it. Though the film is set in "any country in the world" (Bohr was worried about potential censorship), the ambience is unmistakably 100 percent urban Mexican. And, as inevitable in any Mexican film of the era, its copious musical numbers mark it as the product of generic hybridization not only of Hollywood musicals but of the musicality of radio. Here too, different than in *Madre querida*, radio leaves its mark: the instant communication provided by radio announcers with "breaking news" enables the police to close in on Luponini and the diegetic public to learn of his exploits.

After *Rancho Grande*

In 1936, the eventual unexpected success of Fernando de Fuentes's modest production *Allá en el Rancho Grande* (Over on the Big Ranch) radically changed the climate for filmmaking and introduced a new, uniquely Mexican genre, the *comedia ranchera* (the rural comedy) (López 1994a).

Before Exploitation | 293

Over the next two years, the febrile pace and experimentation of the early sound entrepreneurs dissipated as it became clear that one "formula" had risen above all others. Orol, Bohr, and Peón continued in the business, but their generic experiments lost their saliency. For example, Bohr produced another excellent crime film in 1936, *Marihuana, el monstruo verde* (Marijuana, the Green Monster),[9] but subsequently abandoned the genre, ostensibly looking for greater financial security, and jumped on the *comedia ranchera* bandwagon with *Por mis pistolas* (By My Guns, 1937) and *Canto a mi tierra* (Song to My Land, 1938), which introduced Pedro Vargas to the screen. In late 1939 he returned to Chile. Orol busily mined the suffering mother/wife genre with three films only to fall in with the *comedia ranchera* with *El derecho y el deber* (Right and Duty, 1937). By 1938 he was in financial trouble and decided to look for other opportunities in Cuba. He only returned to Mexico in 1943 and his subsequent work is part of a dramatically different industrial environment. Peón, always somewhat of a director-for-hire, worked ceaselessly across genres: historical dramas, suffering mothers and wives (*No basta ser madre* [Motherhood Isn't Enough, 1937] enshrined actress Sara García as "the mother of Mexico"), detective dramas, and the *comedia ranchera* (*La madrina del diablo* [*The* Godmother of the Devil, 1937] introducing Jorge Negrete). In 1938, excited about new possibilities after the creation of a new national producer, PECUSA, he also returned to Cuba (Agramonte and Castillo 2003, 99–106).

The legacies of Orol, Bohr, and Peón encompass many of the characteristics of the future exploitation cinema in Mexico. They made films quickly and inexpensively with often surprisingly good box office returns. Their films reflected both national concerns as well as their own transnationalities and were thus among the very first Mexican films to attract international audiences. They were generically hybrid, combining the most spectacular elements of the cinema and radio, whether extraordinary sentimentalism or crime and violence, with that one mainstay of the early Mexican sound cinema that would endure: music, dance, and performance. Some of the generic mixes they pioneered—maternal exaltation, salacious melodrama—would become central to Mexican cinema. Others—horror, gangsters, and crime—would disappear almost entirely from the post–*Allá en el Rancho Grande* "Golden Age," only to return, in the periphery, as that which we now call latsploitation cinema.

14

(Not) Looking for Origins

Postmodernism, Documentary, and *America* (1993)

This essay analyzes a five-part Brazilian documentary called America *that aired on Brazilian TV. López demonstrates how* America *does not easily fit into the categories of the documentary established by English-language scholarship (e.g., direct cinema, postmodern cinema). As in her other work, López helps to contextualize the series for English-language readers by tracing the film to Baudrillard's* America *(published in Brazil in 1986) and Brazilian author Mario Brissac Peixoto's book of essays,* Cenários em Ruínas. *She also situates the series within a larger media horizon as a Manchete production, an alternative from Globo-dominated Brazilian TV.*

> America is the original version of modernity. We are the dubbed or subtitled version.
>
> —Jean Baudrillard, *America*

I

The nation is a contested site. While many nations—in the Third World, in Eastern Europe—have, literally, only just begun the process of creating

---

Editors' note: An earlier version of this essay appeared as "Through Brazilian Eyes: *America*" in *Wide Angle* 13, no. 2 (1991): 20–30. We selected the more recent version published in Michael Renov, ed., *Theorizing Documentary* (Los Angeles: University of California Press, 1993), 151–63.

an "imagined community," the nation-state has simultaneously become impossible to sustain as a site for coherence or for unitary identification and representation. If, as theorists as diverse as Benedict Anderson, Tom Nairn, Eric Hobsbawm, and Homi K. Bhabha have argued, the national is by definition imagined, unstable, ambivalent, and Janus-faced, understanding a nation today demands a look that can see its narrations, ambivalences, and hybridity; that can see the international within the national. A privileged location for this look is the space of the margins, frontiers, and borders that simultaneously define and infiltrate the nation. The center—the nation—is always different when seen from its margins and finding the margin at the center's core involves the evocation of an even greater difference that challenges the transcendental status of the national while also revealing the very limits of modernity and its neocolonial justifications. As Bhabha argues in his introduction to *Nation and Narration*, the transnational dimensions of the nation-state can best be seen when "the margins of the nation displace the center [and] the peoples of the periphery return to rewrite the history and fiction of the metropolis (1990b, 6)."

Thus, modifying the title of Bhabha's book, which analyzes the narration of nations, we may ask: What does it mean to document a nation from the margin? In the case of the five-part Brazilian documentary series *America*, it means, literally, that its analysis of the United States must begin by challenging the national threshold: The series' first episode begins with an extensive precredit sequence in a small town, identified as "deep in the heart of Mexico," that sets the stage against which and through which a "look that shows that the known may be different" will be deployed.[1] In this 1989 TV documentary series, two Brazilians—the well-known writer Nelson Brissac Peixoto and filmmaker João Moreira Salles—"document" an America the likes of which we rarely see from this side of the equator. What is unusual in *America* is not only what the series explicitly attempts to show—an analysis of the North American imaginary focusing on its margins and frontiers—but also how the series positions itself as a documentary vis-à-vis the nation. In fact, *America* rejects all easy categorizations. Unlike cinema verité, for example, it is not interested in questioning the means of its own production or its representational work. Without any obvious material self-reflexivity, its structure has the complexity of postmodern fiction and its carefully composed and deftly juxtaposed images the plastic impact of contemporary representational art. Also unlike direct cinema (or the bastard form *verité*, identified by Brian

Winston as typical of contemporary TV documentaries on both sides of the Atlantic [1988, 518–19]) *America* makes no pretense at objectivity: its resonant poetic voice-over is clearly scripted and its images are composed with painterly care. Furthermore, the interviews with selected personalities (as diverse as Jean Baudrillard, Henry Kissinger, Laurie Anderson, David Rockefeller, and Octavio Paz) that grant authority to the text's various analyses are staged in dramatic mise-en-scène explicitly designed to highlight each individual's traits. Even the interviews with "real" people, albeit anonymous, are staged, insistently directed, and idiosyncratic. We also cannot compare *America* to historical or archival documentaries like the recent PBS *Civil War* series or even the more difficult to categorize *Atomic Cafe*. Although the series makes use of much archival footage and does, in its own way, establish a historical argument about the decay of North American society/culture, it is also singularly unconcerned with historical authenticity, facts, or statistics and demonstrates no desire to reconstruct or witness any specific historical moment other than its own present and the moment of its production and analysis.

After so many disclaimers, what, then, is *America* like? The series is divided into five independent but stylistically and thematically linked episodes identified via aphoristic titles: "Movement," "Mythology," "The Blues," "Speed," and "Screens." Composed of four or five sections also identified by brief suggestive phrases used as commercial break calls, each episode explores the full literal and metaphorical dimensions of its title. Thus, for example, the second episode dedicated to "Mythology," evokes Hollywood, the various American frontiers, steel men and new cowboys, supermarkets, and, in the section identified as "The History of a Return," Albany, William Kennedy's *Ironweed*, and the filming of the recent Héctor Babenco movie of the same title. Rather than follow a chronological or geographical logic, *America* sweeps over the American landscape and peoples, combining heterogeneous images and phenomena to produce a series of categories that define another kind of decentered totality. The associations between the images and phenomena featured are established by the voice-over narration. However, although authoritative, the voice-over refuses the logic of rhetorical persuasion and its reliance on poetic resonance and allusiveness suggests, instead, the openness and inconclusiveness of fiction.

Part of my argument is that *America* exhibits a hybrid documentary form combining self-consciousness, awareness, and fascination with the tenets of postmodernism with the seemingly contradictory desire to present a social critique. In fact, *America* is not "about" the United States, in the sense that a *National Geographic* documentary about an African tribe is *about* that tribe and ostensibly provides factual information about it. It is, instead, a documentary about multiple and varied representations of the United States that reworks those images and rhetorical *topoi*—whether clichéd or not—through a distinct filter of otherness. *America* explores the United States as an ambivalent and multifaceted cultural construct from a distinctly in-between position: in between cultures and nations, the political and the poetic, the past and the present, the documentary and the fictional. Thus, the portrait of a nation that emerges not only refuses standard ideas of a national totality, but also posits the possibility of a different documentary aesthetic.

Almost by definition, a Brazilian documentary about the United States has no access to the imperial authority of an ethnographic vision, nor can it easily exploit the exoticism of the tourist/native dichotomy. But *America* also rejects the transparency of straightforward ideological critique as well as the equation of self-reflexivity with critical acuity and distance. By dismissing questions of fact or "truth value," *America* highlights precisely the ambivalences of national-ideological constructions that most documentaries on foreign cultures or nations are forced to elide. It posits an aesthetics of displacement that pushes the documentary to assume a mapping function—linking places in space—as well as a narrative function that subjugates those links to nonchronological time. As such, the peculiar history of *America*'s production and the nature of its analysis of "America" helps to explain its unexpected appearance on Brazilian television and the significance of its particular vision of the United States for Brazil in 1989.[2]

II

The classification of *America* as a postmodern documentary is unlikely to be challenged by any of its spectators, especially in urban Brazil, where postmodernism is not simply a term bandied about by academics but an accepted concept regularly discussed by the media (and where Baudrillard and Lyotard are cult heroes whose visits to Brazil were given extensive front-page newspaper coverage). As is typical of "developing" countries, the Brazilian social formation combines, in an uneasy alliance, anachronistic, precapitalist elements with the most advanced capitalist (postcapitalist) forms, and in the last decade, postmodernism has found a secure cultural

(Not) Looking for Origins | 299

niche in the arts, media, and advertising in large urban centers (especially in São Paulo). In fact, we can trace the postmodernist sheen of *America* to two fairly well-circulated texts: Jean Baudrillard's *America*, published in Brazil almost immediately after its French release (in 1986, two years before the English-language edition), and Nelson Brissac Peixoto's *Cenários em Ruínas: A Realidade Imaginária Contemporanea* (Sets in Ruins: The Contemporary Imaginary Reality, 1987), a collection of stories by one of the coauthors of the documentary. Although the former clearly laid the theoretical groundwork for the documentary's analysis of the American condition, the latter already invoked many of the key images and stylistic devices subsequently used in *America*. More like a series of thematically linked meditations on contemporary fictional *topoi* derived from the cinema than a collection of short stories, *Cenários em Ruínas* couples contemporary subjecthood with internal exile: Always a foreigner in his own country, the unnamed "protagonist" of these essays is caught in a world of media-created pop imagery through which he searches via the plots of novels and films (and the narrativized creative sagas of contemporary film auteurs like Wim Wenders and Jim Jarmusch) for his own identity and place.

Despite the circulation of these literary texts, the appearance of what I am calling a postmodern documentary on prime-time Brazilian TV network programming is certainly not a common occurrence. In fact, the appearance of a documentary series of any kind on Brazilian television is already surprising given its constant concern with "entertainment" programming defined as lowest common denominator variety programs, telenovelas, and Hollywood serials and movies. Developed under the strict supervision of the military dictatorship that governed Brazil between 1964 and 1985, Brazilian television has been controlled by powerful private media monopolies that under the watchful eye of the military state transformed the medium into a powerful agent for the social and ideological unification of the nation. The Globo network, originally a partner of the Time-Life conglomerate, has been the single most powerful force in Brazilian television since the 1970s (its fifty affiliates attract approximately 70 percent of the national audience).[3] With access to the best technology, talent, and market research, Globo's telenovelas and other variety program formats have become definitive of Brazilian television.

However, the series *America* was not a Globo production. Independently produced by Videofilmes and financed by a number of private corporations,[4] *America* was aired by the Manchete network, a rival to

Globo formed in 1983 by the Bloch corporation (with interests primarily in publishing). Following a policy of purchasing some independent productions (instead of relying exclusively on in-house products as does Globo), the Manchete network began to make a small dent in Globo's hold of the national audience in 1989 with the popular period telenovela *Kananga do Japão*, the exploitative and sensationalistic current events series *Documento Especial* (Special Document), and several documentary series, most notably *African Pop* (a five-part, independently produced series about the worldwide influence and popularity of African music), and *America*. Although Manchete's biggest challenge to Globo's hegemony would be the telenovela *Pantanal*, aired in 1990, its innovative programming in 1989 set the stage for the massive channel turning to come the following year.[5]

III

How can *America* be considered a postmodern documentary? Certainly, the various definitions of postmodernism and arguments about its inevitability and/or effectivity are now quite familiar and hardly need lengthy reiteration. Suffice it, then, to cite, first, Charles Jencks, who talks about postmodernism as a "double coding" or pastiche that combines modernist and traditional techniques nonhierarchically, and Fredric Jameson, who provides, in "Postmodernism, or the Cultural Logic of Late Capitalism," the most complete catalog of the features of postmodernism: a "depthlessness" linked to the cult of the image or simulacrum; a weakening of historicity related to pastiche, historicism, and nostalgia; and the "waning of affect" replaced by *intensités* (Jencks 1986; Jameson 1984). Despite the specificity of these descriptions, the term "postmodernism" has become, as Dana Polan has argued, a "generative apparatus" or "machinal mechanism that encourages a recoding of previous forms and a proliferation of new ones" (1988, 49). Furthermore, the political effectivity of postmodernist culture and theory is a hotly contested terrain.[6] However, as Stanley Aronowitz and Henry Giroux argue, postmodernism has problematized popular culture by highlighting the conditions of knowledge embedded in new technologies, by positing the cultural as a field of domination *and* contestation, and by providing a theoretical framework for thinking of otherness as a source of "struggle, collective resistance and historical affirmation" (1991, 71). *America*'s postmodernism is, thus, a critical one that challenges the standards of the documentary by remapping its frontiers and simultaneously points

(Not) Looking for Origins | 301

to changing "configurations of power, knowledge, space, and time that characterize a world that is at once more global and more differentiated" to "effect a shift in power . . . to those . . . struggling to gain a measure of control over their lives" (Aronowitz and Giroux 1991, 151).

America is clearly a form of documentary pastiche that exhibits a fascination with and fetishization of the image. Each of its five episodes utilizes a variety of traditional and "modern" documentary strategies, combining them intensely but nonhierarchically. For example, each episode contains at least one sequence designed to function as an echo or reminder of its direct cinema predecessors, where the camera-documentarist enters a private space attempting to capture some kind of objective reality. The first episode, for example, includes a sequence in a California boxing academy, and the third, a "visit" to a blood bank close to the Mexican border. In both cases, the impetus for the images clearly seems to be direct cinema: invading a private space to record/find its truth. However, these sequences are neither given a special truth-value and epistemological significance, nor are they even stylistically pure. They are inserted, without any kind of special markers or commentary, as simply another kind of illustration of the basic theme of each segment. In the first case, what is highlighted is the idea of "movement" that the boxing academy sequence allegorizes in social terms ("making it" up and out of the ghetto) much like the strikingly composed images of highways, cars, and drive-ins that follow it do so physically (and in contrast to the "stillness" of the small Mexican town of the precredit sequence that precedes it). In the second example, the *topos* is the idea of the frontier, with the blood bank sequence (on the American side, but frequented only by destitute Mexicans) closely following a clip of the beginning of *Touch of Evil*. In both cases, the inherent social critique of each moment escapes, sliding away under pressure from its juxtaposition with the purely imagistic. The potentially direct here is contaminated even further by style and the series' fascination with the image. We may have sync sound and a nicely probing handheld camera in each of the sequences, but the spaces are carefully lit and the camera movements measured and graceful rather than obtrusively handheld. Furthermore, what may have been direct footage is, in both cases, edited briskly, denying the images any kind of spatiotemporal assertion of authenticity. The direct invoked here is, ultimately, simply another style to be used and aestheticized according to the logic of the image rather than a privileged mode of knowledge.

Similarly, the use of a poetic, authored voice-over that would seem to harken back to another, more traditional, style of socially relevant montagist documentary (one thinks of Pare Lorentz's *The River* as a model) is also contaminated by its own aesthetic excess and solipsism. The narration is so poetic, often so abstract, fragmentary, and self-consciously clever that it fails to connect with the images or to locate their place within an overarching argument.

Above all, *America* is a photographer's film. Its images are glossy, carefully composed to maximize their pictorial values, extraordinarily well lit, and rendered in brilliant colors. And it is the images themselves, as images, that capture our attention most. The words of the voice-over narration often seem to slip away, adding hardly more than a resonant complementary echo or aphoristic verbal image to accompany the visuals. The narration does not provide a model or guide for interpretation as much as it cognitively complements our specular pleasure. That photographs that served as an inspiration for the film *and* the texts of the interviews used by the narration were published as separate, glossy, and quite expensive coffee table books to coincide with the airing of the series is, therefore, not surprising (1989). *America* is a documentary of multiple surfaces that exploits imagistic intertextuality to further its own specularity: alongside its own images and staged (dramatically filmed) interviews, it uses a plethora of clips, ranging from archival footage of Martin Luther King and the first Americans on the moon to clips from *Que Viva México!*, *The Searchers*, *Easy Rider*, and *Ironweed*.

The intertextuality that is established is not only thematic, but also literally superficial—it is the very surfaces of the images rather than the specificity of their cultural meaning that is invoked. In other words, the collision of signs does not lead to a questioning of their status as representations (or even as clichés) but simply exalts them as such. Furthermore, bowing to the constraints of television and the necessity of commercial breaks, the series is also insistently reiterative, repeating images—original or "citations"—from episode to episode (even from section to section) to establish a sense of continuity and its own visual intratextuality. This fetishization of the image—whether visual or verbal—ultimately reduces the historical past invoked to a collection, the equivalent of a vast multimedia photo album with witty captions. And the affect produced is, as Jameson argues about *Diva*'s cult of the glossy image, curiously flat while simultaneously aesthetically sublime: "The silence of affect . . . is doubled with a new gratification in surfaces accompanied by a whole new ground tone in which the pathos of high modernism [i.e., Munch's

The Scream] has been inverted into a strange new exhilaration, the high, the *intensité*" (1990, 60-61). As a postmodern documentary, however, *America* also directly addresses the tension between epistemology and the aesthetic that troubles most theories of documentary. In "The Existence of Italy," Jameson argues that the postmodern or neodocumentary displaces the opposition between art and knowledge onto the image itself (1990, 155-229). The image's insistence on the "dual presence of the event," the act of its registration and the instant of history captured, becomes the substance of the documentary in films—like Eduardo Coutinho's *Cabra Marcado para Morrer* (*Twenty Years Later*, Brazil, 1984) and *Torre Bella* (Thomas Harlan, West Germany, 1977)—in which the process of production is itself violently inscribed into the texts as a visible historical presence that denies representation and asserts praxis. While these films do indeed "loathe" the fictive as Jameson argues, *America*, however, proposes a different answer to Jameson's question: "How to escape from the image by means of the image?" (1990, 162). In *America*, the documentary impulse is not a historical force through which the object is seen to be in perpetual change, but a position that allows the text to assert the geographical distance of its vision—a foreign look invested in the plasticity of the images and the poetics of the voice-over narration—with the freedom of a storyteller that, unlike Walter Benjamin's, is not threatened by information (1969). Perhaps because the fictional has always had a different, more problematic status for Brazilian culture, as Luiz Costa Lima argues in *Sociedade e Discurso Ficcional* (1986), rather than repudiate the fictive, *America* attempts to recapture it as a way to establish a difference that is historical and geographical. In *America*, "information" is neither a goal nor a challenge to the representational, but part of the telling function. Thus, not unlike those postcolonial novels analyzed by Timothy Brennan that combine the informational with the experiential "as voices from the Third World seeking to project themselves into a European setting" (1990, 56), *America* inverts the geographical violence of imperialism by proposing visual and aural images as records of experience, information, and fragments of stories that cannot be completed.

But perhaps what is most "postmodern" about *America* is precisely what a catalog of its postmodern characteristics, especially given that they are such self-consciously adopted ones, fails to elucidate. It is the very nature of the "America" analyzed by *America* that is most postmodern, that determines the necessity of the series' postmodernism, and that allows us to link the specificity of this documentary to the Brazilian context: *America*'s relationship to "America" is curiously replicated in *America*'s own relationship to Brazil.

IV

How is the postmodern voice of the text positioned vis-à-vis the "America" it purports to analyze? (I am using "voice" here as defined by Bill Nichols: "that which conveys to us a sense of the text's social point of view, of how it is speaking to us and how it is organizing the materials it is presenting to us . . . that intangible, moiré-like pattern formed by the unique interaction of all a film's codes" [1988, 50].) Claiming neither ethnographic authority nor empirical objectivity, *America*, nevertheless, establishes a necessary distance from its subject that is determined by its position as outsider and as other. Much as its analysis of the margins of America explains the center (the frontiers, immigrants, travelers, detectives, Mexican Americans, Jewish Americans, and African Americans that by their very outsiderness constitute the only possible center of America), the text also remains outside and by doing so acknowledges its inevitable relationship to the inside. As Jean Baudrillard says in his interview in the series, "America is our [everyone's] myth, our unconscious, our utopia." The America of *America* is everywhere, necessarily inside this text as well. Thus, the series' voice-over begins with a self-conscious assertion of location, describing its "look" as foreign and claiming that only that otherness can "reveal that the known may be different." Its analysis of the United States begins, paradoxically, with a look at a small town in the heart of Mexico. Claiming historicity, stillness, and respect for time and memory as Mexican characteristics that distinguish it from its neighbor, it poses Mexico as the closest "other" of the United States, in the words of Octavio Paz in his interview, "as different [from the US] as the wind is from the mountain."

However, *America*'s insistence on its own otherness and multiplicity also represses the position that seems most available to a Brazilian documentary about another nation: its own nationality as a place from which to speak and from which to define its alterity. The repression of the nation as a privileged site from which to look at the United States is already evident in the title of the series, *America*. Which America? North or South? All of it? Including Brazil? The "America" of the text is a stand-in, a simulacrum of an impossible continental totality to which Brazil belongs and from which it is simultaneously excluded.

That this is a Brazilian documentary made by Brazilians for Brazilian television is only acknowledged three times in *America*'s more than five hours. In the first episode, while analyzing the ahistorical and antihumanist nature of the American landscape and arguing that Las Vegas represents an inverted image of American values, the voice-over comments: "Americans do in Las Vegas what Brazilians do during carnival: invert daily experience." Obviously invoking Bakhtin-inspired theories of the function of carnival that have been widely circulated in Brazil,[7] the reference to carnival explicitly links a Brazilian phenomenon to the United States. But carnival as a point of reference for Brazil is problematic because what the comment refers to is precisely the contemporary transformation of the Brazilian carnival: its deterritorialization and institutionalization as a tourist industry (like Vegas, in fact) and the waning of the potentially subversive function its social inversions once may have had. As much as Vegas represents a perversion and commodification of the carnivalesque— the institutionalization of a carnivalesque inversion of the work ethic—the Brazilian carnival has also "perverted" its specificity and "Brazilianness" via commodification and tourist exploitation.

More markedly, however, the comment also invokes the important cultural significance of the carnivalesque for Brazil. Far more than just an annual festival of inversions, carnival is an emblem of national identity and, as Robert Stam argues in *Subversive Pleasures*, a master trope that invokes the necessary multiplicity and openness of cultures that are at once "national" and marginal in relation to the centers of power (1989, 122–56). Defined as cultural "anthropophagy" by the Brazilian modernists of the 1920s and as "tropicalism" by artists in the 1960s–1970s, the carnivalesque response to the liminality of Brazilian culture in the context of neocolonial cultural domination underscored the cannibalistic nature of processes of cultural assimilation via parody, irony, humor, and an aggressive and irreverent intertextuality. However, unlike the cinematic avant-garde of the 1960s–1970s that proclaimed an "aesthetics of garbage" (the sense of a marginal culture doomed to recycle the materials of the dominant one [Xavier 1982]) with films such as Rogerio Sganzerla's *Bandido da Luz Vermelha* (*Red Light Bandit*, 1968) and Artur Omar's *Triste Trópico* (1974), *America* assumes a different position vis-à-vis the nation and neocolonialism. Unlike the protagonist of *Triste Tropico* (a parodic anthropological fictive documentary) who reverses Levi-Strauss's journey of European self-discovery in Brazil and goes to Europe, like many Brazilian intellectuals, only to discover Brazil, in *America* the traveler has no recourse to an original purity or to a return home. The only points of reference are images that, like carnival, are simulacra of experiences that no longer have an original anywhere. The modernist recourse of devouring the foreign to affirm the national is no longer available, and the search for national identity becomes, therefore, a far more complicated enterprise.

The second reference to Brazil occurs in the second episode and, although explicit, its work is more subtle. While analyzing how US cities cultivate imaginary pasts, especially via images culled from the media (exemplified by a haunting image of San Francisco's Golden Gate Bridge used repeatedly in the credit sequences that is an explicit replica of a similar shot in Hitchcock's *Vertigo*), the text visits a number of small towns named after international metropolises (Paris, Lebanon, Moscow) and lingers in a small town called "Brazil" (in Indiana). The North American Brazil is, of course, a bucolic Midwestern community and the "Brazilian" senior citizen selected for an interview (photographed astride a riding lawn mower) could hardly be said to be representative of the Brazilian national character or identity. Although we do not hear the interviewer's questions, the citizen's comments are obviously responses to a query for difference: in December and January, it is very cold and snowy in Brazil; inflation is a phenomenon identified with big cities and not something the citizens of this Brazil are concerned about. The difference between this imaginary Brazil, a North American simulacrum, and the Brazil watching the documentary in November's sweltering 90-degree weather and with monthly inflation at a then all-time high of 50 percent is obvious. But what the documentary's insistence on the landscape and tangible existence of this other Brazil emphasizes is the inevitable coexistence of both. Is the Brazil that watches the documentary necessarily more "real" than the simulacrum? As the third reference to Brazil makes clear, hardly.

This final reference appears in the last episode of the series, where Brazil is once again alluded to by the voice-over, in a call for the next section preceding a commercial break: "In the next block, how to be in Paris without ever leaving Copacabana." The segment introduced by this title explores the ubiquity and deterritorialization of modern computer communication technology. In fact, the segment's analysis of the impact of technology on society could be applied to the documentary itself. How to be in America without leaving South America would perhaps be a more appropriate title because this is precisely the effect that the text aspires to produce: the effect of travel, a record of a journey that is simultaneously an assertion of presence (the camera, our foreign eye, was there), and a simulacrum of a necessarily impossible immediacy.

The last three episodes of *America* present a pointed analysis of America's decadence centered on the discussion of the impossibility of developing a historical consciousness because, for America, history—looking back—has meant acknowledging loss and discovering disenchantment (the contemporary impossibility of maintaining the national innocence that once allowed "America" to expand and conquer ubiquitously). Echoing the comments of Octavio Paz in one of the clips from his extensive interview, that "any nation with a history is doomed to decadence," the documentary convincingly argues that America—this America, but also, by extension, the greater America that includes Brazil and is elided from the surface of the text but remains an insistent intertext—necessarily exists in decadence, as a series of shifting and sliding screens (a metaphor of inviolability and transparency that serves as the title of the last episode) constituting an impossible totality that remains central, dominant, and present in its absence or impossibility.

Thus, in the documentary's analysis, the utopia of America—something that was lived as if realized—may now be impossible, not only for the United States, but also for the Brazil that insistently aspires to it. In 1989, a moment when Brazil seemed about to achieve its own utopian dream of democracy postponed by twenty-five years of military rule, *America* seems to warn that this dream, even before it happens, may be as impossible as any other "American" dream.

V

This brief analysis has hardly exhausted the complexity of *America*, the allusive richness of its metaphors, surfaces, and playfulness. But I hope to have suggested how this documentary series tackles postmodernity, as Fredric Jameson has said in another context, "homeopathically": "To work at dissolving the pastiche by using all the instruments of pastiche itself, to reconquer some genuine historical sense by using the instruments of what I have called substitutes for history. . . . The only way through a crisis of space is to invent a new space" (Stephanson 1987, 42). Appropriating the methods of postmodernism itself—pastiche, simulacra, images, gloss, and nostalgia—*America* charts a crisis of the American space and its imaginary that also potentially indicates the possibility of mapping a new space from the border and perhaps also *for* the border, the margin, the other everywhere. As Nelson Brissac Peixoto argues in *Cenários em Ruínas*, to survive the "void," "those who don't have names nor a place to go, may, nevertheless, begin all over, repossessing these images and banal stories, these fantasy sites now in ruins. The foreigners in their own countries can erect their own sets amid the ruins" (1987, 8).

Speaking from an in-between space to chart the transnational disruptions embedded in the national imaginary of the United States, *America* ends up elsewhere: neither in the Mexican border where it began, nor lost in the exorbitant images of decenteredness that it invokes, but finally addressing the necessary ambivalence of that "Brazilian" national identity it so steadfastly refuses to assume. Itself "Janus-faced," *America* thus addresses all of America, North and South and Brazil itself, with the paradoxical authority of its own neocolonialism. To Baudrillard's assertion that "America is the original version of modernity," *America* offers a postmodern minority discourse that renders inoperable the binarism of original/dubbed, inside/outside, national/foreign, center/periphery. Under erasure by pressure from the margin, the center can only be "documented" as an impossibility that may perhaps be used to renegotiate a different kind of space and time for the history of all forms of cultural difference.

15

Revolution and Dreams

The Cuban Documentary Today (1992)

*This essay examines Cuban documentary in the aftermath of the "heroic years" of the 1960s when there seemed to be no "contradiction between artistic production and political militancy." López addresses how Cuban government bureaucracies evolved during that later period and notes the "conservatism and dogmatism of other media, particularly the press and TV." After sketching this larger context, she points to the renewal of ICAIC (the state film institute) during the 1980s and the rise of new organizational structures (three working groups) that stimulated innovation. The essay incorporates a discussion of a series of short documentaries (*Kid Chocolate; Uno, dos, eso es; El viaje más largo;* and* Un día fui*) made in the late 1980s and early 1990s.*

Since the creation of the Instituto Cubano de Arte e Industria Cinematográficos (Cuban Film Institute, ICAIC) in 1959, the documentary has been an integral part of Cuban film and of Cuban life. Before the

---

In memory of Héctor Garcia Mesa (director, Cinemateca de Cuba, 1960–1989).

Neither this essay nor any research on Cuban film would be possible without the selfless devotion and conscientious work of the staff of the Cinemateca de Cuba in Havana. Many thanks to Mayuya (María Eulalia Douglas) and Teresita Toledo for their support and friendship. The author's research in Cuba was partly funded by grants from the Mellon Foundation and Tulane University's Roger Thayer Stone Center for Latin American Studies.

revolution, Cubans were already quite familiar with a kind of local newsreel production that, either sponsored by commercial interests or by wealthy individuals, claimed to "record" events of Cuban life. In fact, with few exceptions, these films simply promoted the interests and vanities of moneyed groups. However, these fledgling newsreels were the only consistent indigenous film production and they developed an important national familiarity with self-representation. Among the many newsreel producers of the 1940s and 1950s, mention must be made of the Mexican producer, Manuel Barbachano Ponce, whose *Cine revista* (film magazine), a nationally distributed ten-minute news magazine with ads, reportage, and humorous sketches, did attempt to explore the national landscape and served to train a number of future ICAIC personnel (among others, the director Tomás Gutiérrez Alea and cinematographers Jorge Herrera, José Tabío, and Iván Nápoles).

Capitalizing upon this long-standing familiarity with locally produced newsreel images and upon the support, advice, and solidarity of the best and most innovative documentary filmmakers of the 1950s and 1960s (Joris Ivens, Chris Marker, Agnès Varda, and Theodor Christensen, among others, spent time in ICAIC in the 1960s), ICAIC took on documentary filmmaking as one of its principal activities. Since 1959 it has produced some of its most accessible, immediate, politically effective, and innovative films within this genre: as of 1989, when ICAIC celebrated its thirtieth anniversary with a commemorative catalog entitled *Cine cubano: 30 años en revolución* (Cuban Cinema: 30 Years in Revolution), a staggering total of 1,064 documentary films had been produced (Espinoza and Llópiz 1989, 8).

Hardly more than an odd assortment of willing but barely experienced would-be filmmakers with little equipment and even fewer funds, ICAIC emphasized documentary production in the early 1960s for obvious practical reasons: documentaries were easier, faster, and less expensive to produce than feature fiction films. They also provided a relatively convenient training ground for the many filmmakers with little or no filmmaking experience who joined ICAIC in its early years. The documentary was also important, however, for theoretical and political reasons. Given the volatility of Cuban life in the early days of the revolution, the documentary provided ICAIC with immediate relevance and with a tool through which to begin to have an impact upon daily life. With documentaries, ICAIC recorded the many revolutionary changes taking place and provided a "catalog" of realistic images and sounds that belonged to the Cuban people. Furthermore, these images and sounds also began to encourage a different, more critical attitude, toward all image production, questioning "reality" as well as its cinematic reconstruction. Of course, this was not the exclusive domain of the documentary, since fiction and documentary filmmaking in ICAIC have always been deeply intertwined, sharing concerns, themes, and formal strategies. But the documentary was, for many years, in the vanguard of all Cuban image production. And, in fact, four of the most interesting fiction films of the early 1980s were fictionalizations of their directors' previous feature-length documentaries: Constante "Rapi" Diego's *El corazón sobre la tierra* (Heart above the Land, 1985), which was based on his 1982 documentary *Con el corazón en la tierra* (With the Heart on the Ground); Daniel Díaz Torres's *Jíbaro* (Wild Dog, 1985), which was based on his 1982 documentary of the same title; Luis Felipe Bernaza's *De tal Pedro tal astilla* (loosely, "Chip" Off the Old Block, 1985], which was based on his 1982 *Pedro cero por ciento* (Pedro Zero Percent); and Jesús Díaz's *Lejanía* (Parting of Ways, 1985), which was loosely inspired by his 1978 documentary *55 hermanos* (55 Brothers).

The history of the theoretical development of Cuban documentary practice, particularly the work of Cuba's most celebrated documentary filmmaker, Santiago Álvarez, has been well documented by Michael Chanan in his book *The Cuban Image* (the only book-length English-language study of the Cuban cinema).[1] The goal here is not to reiterate that history, but to analyze recent developments in the Cuban documentary, emphasizing how it has changed since the glorious days of the Santiago Álvarez–style experimentation highlighted in Chanan's text (and the drastic creative decline of the late 1970s *not* mentioned by Chanan). The aim is not to downplay Álvarez's and others' magnificent achievements in the genre, but rather to contextualize them, as well as the achievements of recent documentary work, with some recent social history. In Cuba, as in every other society, things change. And in the last thirty years, "things," including the ICAIC, have changed significantly. It is, therefore, hardly surprising that the documentary has also evolved, that filmmakers have not for many years exploited the montagist, high-modernist, agitprop style associated with Álvarez and with the Cuban documentary of the 1960s/early 1970s.

That form of experimentation was linked with the great political and social battles waged in Cuba then. It was a time of social, political, and economic upheavals and a time for artistic and political experimentation. As many have witnessed, it was a time when it was impossible to conceive of any contradiction between artistic production and political militancy. ICAIC and other Cuban cultural institutions worked through the established artistic canons, discussed the nature of revolutionary art, and attempted to define the role of the revolutionary artist.[2] It was also a time when Cuba and ICAIC turned toward the Latin American continent and established important social, political, and artistic alliances. For the cinema, the key moments were the Viña del Mar and Mérida festivals of 1967, 1968, and 1969, events at which the Cuban cinema was linked—practically, politically, and emotionally—to other Latin American film movements. It was, as Alfredo Guevara, the founder of ICAIC, argued at the 1987 Havana Film Festival in a talk celebrating the twentieth anniversary of the Viña del Mar festival, a time when the "double vocation" of ICAIC was clear: to sustain the links between revolution and poetry, to strive for aesthetic authenticity and cultural significance simultaneously (Guevara 1988, 7–8).

Since then, that "double vocation" has been challenged and threatened by the rigidity and orthodoxy of some of Cuba's socialist bureaucracies and by the conservatism and dogmatism of other media, particularly the press and TV. In the 1980s, the same period that was dreamt of as "the future" in the heyday of the revolution in the 1960s, the nature of the dreams that can be envisioned for the future has also changed. ICAIC continues to sustain its commitment to artistic risk-taking and a will to self-renewal. This was most recently evidenced by the reorganization of ICAIC into three independent production units where creative and budgetary control has once again been placed directly in the hands of the filmmakers themselves under the leadership of three senior filmmakers with clearly marked cinematic personalities: the dialectical Tomás Gutiérrez Alea, the operatic Humberto Solás, and the more commercial Manuel Pérez.

However, the changes that have taken place within documentary production in the 1980s are closely linked to ideological changes of Cuban society related to ever greater economic problems, the persistence of "tightening of the belts" initiatives, an aborted free market experiment for food products, and the growing awareness of the existence of high-level governmental corruption and incompetence.[3] The Cuban collective unconscious is now less focused on the "future," that magical moment of perfect socialist achievement once dreamt of as the inevitable outcome of the revolution, and which has been forever postponed. It has, instead, turned inward, toward a reassessment and reappreciation of facets of the past, and toward astute critical assessments of the present.

It is interesting to compare, for example, the differences between three boxing documentaries: one from the 1960s, Oscar Valdez's *El ring* (The Ring, 1966); and two from the late 1980s, Gerardo Chijona's *Kid*

Chocolate (1987) and Miriam Talavera's *Uno, dos, eso es* (One, Two, That's It, 1986). The 1966 film explores, via the juxtaposition of interviews with contemporary trainers and a retired fighter from the 1930s (the "Kid Chocolate" of the later film), the changes that had taken place in the sport since the revolution and highlights that, to the benefit of the sport, the revolution had eliminated the commercialism and exploitation of fighters that previously characterized Cuban boxing. The 1980s films, however, are concerned with markedly different issues.

Kid Chocolate focuses precisely on the most successful of the prerevolutionary and commercially exploited boxers, affectionately nicknamed Kid Chocolate ("el bonbón de Cuba" [the Cuban bonbon]). The film is based on a long interview with Kid Chocolate in his own humble house. Now an old man, he sits on a rocking chair (apparently somewhat under the influence of good Cuban rum) surrounded by the photos and trophies of his past and explains his life: "Recordar es volver a vivir, y yo vivo de mis recuerdos" (To remember is to live again, and I live on my memories). The interview is cross-cut with sequences of newsreel footage, newspaper headlines, and still photographs of the achievements Kid Chocolate recounts as well as by montage sequences of materials from the era that comment metacritically not upon the achievements of the man but upon the era itself. Creating an intertext within the film, these sequences, often embellished with extravagant wipes that also evoke the newsreels of the era, and a series of intertitles, discretely superimposed as period newspaper headlines, mark the different stages of the Kid's boxing history and position the interview historically, without denigrating either the man or his achievements, but immersing both in a critical "voice"[4] that resonates beyond the text of the interview itself. The film's mode of address is, therefore, far more complex than that of *El ring*'s, where the emphasis was on a straightforward celebration/reportage of contemporary achievements in boxing and the differences the revolution had brought about in the sport.

At the end, the film abandons the interview and the montage sequences. We see instead a medium traveling shot of an old man with shuffling feet, tentatively walking around the perimeter of a boxing ring by holding on to the ropes. We never see the man's body or his face, and, though it seems clear that it is *not* the Kid, a diegetic effect leads us to extrapolate the "fictional" image onto the documentary person/character. Accompanied by the sound of a plaintive, nostalgic horn, the last shot is a long shot of an empty auditorium, with a brightly lit and also empty ring in the center. Evoking an irresistible nostalgia, this metadocumentary ending adds an important dimension to the film, neither biographical celebration nor scathing analysis, but a loving *rescate* (rescue) and repositioning of a personal history that contributed much to Cuban life. Retrospectively and in the context of 1980s Cuban politics, what is also most interesting is that neither within the interview nor within the montage sequences is there any mention of what the Kid's life was like after his retirement and return to Cuba from New York, nor how it might have changed since the revolution.

Uno, dos, eso es is totally different. Ostensibly a documentary about boxing, it focuses, exclusively, on the always-ignored trainers. The film lacks interviews, voice-over commentary, or identifying titles, but has an extremely agile camera and excellent editing (the film's director, Miriam Talavera, has been an important ICAIC editor for many years). This short film challenges all our expectations about what a boxing film should be like. During the requisite fight sequence, for example, the camera focuses on both sets of trainers and shows us the fighters only after the bell rings, when they interact directly with their trainers. This film refuses to posit a hero, acknowledging neither individual nor revolutionary achievement: neither the boxers, who win and/or lose, nor any one trainer is favored. It's the training itself, the emotion and strain of the human activity, that is its focus.

In addition to these two films, there are a number of other recent documentaries that seem to exemplify the title of Alfredo Guevara's 1987 talk, "Reflexión nostálgica sobre el futuro" (Nostalgic Reflection about the Future) (1988). Especially noteworthy are two films from 1987, Rigoberto López's *El viaje más largo* (The Longest Trip) and Guillermo Centeno's *Un día fui* (One Day I Went). Both films are part of what might be called a contemporary *rescate cultural* (cultural rescue) genre that, with some crucial differences, can be traced back to the late Sara Gómez's documentary films of the late 1960s and early 1970s.[5] In the context of ICAIC's documentary-production history, these films are unique because they no longer look at the prerevolutionary past as something that must be criticized, soundly denounced, and abolished in order to represent contemporary improvements and the dream of an even better future. Rather, they analyze and critique the past—and the remnants of the past that survive in the present—because of its significance for contemporary Cuban cultural identity. The raw material of cultural sedimentation—past and present—is formally distanced and mediated via the filter of an explicit cinematic consciousness. Unlike many of the films of the 1960s, which used formal experimentation to aggressively question "other" systems of image production but rarely their own, these films of the 1980s rework their subject matter. They do not attempt to present objective representations of any one thing, person, or ideological position but recognize the unstable epistemological status of any cinematic representation and assert the filmmakers'—and the cinema's—own unstable place within the project of signifying a national cultural identity. In other words, they explore the dialectic between the social and discursive constitutions of the self, knowledge, and its mediators.

Rigoberto López's *El viaje más largo* is, on the surface, the most conventional of the two films, but its mixed modes radically challenge established preconceptions about documentary work. An exploration of Chinese immigration to Cuba, this short film exceeds the limits of the documentary by embedding a documentary about the lives and experiences of the now quite aged survivors of the early waves of Chinese immigration within a fictional, poetic, *and* autobiographical evocation of the phenomenological experience of that immigration. Working within the registers of memory and fiction, the film poetically evokes the immigrants' past—or what it might have felt like—in order to make these elderly Chinese figures, strolling through the streets of their old neighborhood in Havana, real characters of contemporary Cuban history.

The film begins with a precredits sequence: in complete silence, the viewer is presented with a Chinese proverb, source of the film's title: "El viaje más largo se inicia con el primer paso" (The longest trip begins with the first step), followed by a series of close-ups showing a man's hands clacking, dropping, and shaking a number of wooden objects. Although a high-angle shot discloses that some kind of ritual ceremony is taking place, the participants' identity and/or diegetic status are never clarified. Abruptly interrupted by a series of still, black-and-white close-up photographs of elderly Chinese men, this sequence is followed by the credits superimposed upon the photographs (which tellingly include credits for screenwriting). Immediately after the credits, another disorienting sequence: at dawn/dusk, in half-light, a tall ship battles the waves on the high ocean. No individuals are visible. Then a male, voice-of-God narrator interrupts: "Todo empezó esa noche . . ." (It all began that night . . .).

At first it seems as if the voice-of-God narration would serve to dispel the mystery of the images since it provides the viewer with factual data such as the date and length of the first Chinese sea voyage to

Cuba and the number of survivors. However, the voice's poetic tone and the rhythmic construction of the narration contribute to the increasing indeterminacy of the images: as the narrator describes the conditions that the Chinese found upon their arrival in Havana, burning torches in the dark illuminate catacomb-like spaces and a roaming camera shows close-up glimpses of men in the dark, massed together in some sort of sleeping barracks. Denied the totalizing vision of an establishing shot or three-point lighting, these images, regardless of the "data" provided by the narration, displace the spectator from the safety of the epistemological certainty of realistic representation onto the realm of evocative rather than official history.

As the film progresses, the voice-of-God narrator becomes less and less authoritative and more an element of indeterminacy, equal to the image track. In fact, rather than fix the polysemy of meaning of the image track, the narration works dialectically with and against the images, sometimes investing them with meaning and other times letting them roam free. For example, in a sequence exploring the central streets of the old Chinese ghetto in Havana (the streets Manrique and Dragones), the narrator introduces the streets, but remains curiously silent while a series of images systematically present different aspects of life in these streets today. The images themselves and their juxtaposition lead to the production of meanings not at all remarked upon by the narrator: the fact that those streets today are no longer Chinese-only ghettos. Within the short montage exploration of each street is included a shot of a member of another race (in both cases, Black women), happily coexisting with and looking out onto the Chinese life on the street. Finally, toward the end of the film the source of the narration's indeterminacy is disclosed when, unexpectedly, it begins to utilize the first-person singular: "Me gusta verlos asi, meditando sin culpa, caminando tranquilamente por las calles de su barrio" (I like to see them like this, meditating without guilt, walking calmly through the streets of their neighborhood). Shortly thereafter the status of the narration becomes clear: "Para mí, mi padre Lan Yan es un gran misterio. El romance entre un chino de Cantón y una mulata Cubana, mi madre" (To me, my father, Lan Yan is a great mystery. The romance between a Chinese from Canton and a Cuban mulatta, my mother). Repositioned as memory, as autobiographical evocation and homage to a family tradition/heritage that remains unknowable even though representable, the narration then is also inscribed within the fictional/documentary dichotomy of the film's images.

Whereas López's *El viaje más largo* produces its own textual voice by combining poetic, autobiographical, fictional, and documentary modes, Gerardo Chijona's *Un día fui* is more indebted to contemporary ethnographic practices. In fact, *Un día fui* could be considered a modern ethnographic portrait of the contradictions in the life and history of Baracoa, a small municipality in the Oriente province of the island.

The film utilizes neither voice-over narration nor intertitles (in fact, for several minutes we have no idea what the film may be about), but its interviews, images, and diegetic and nondiegetic music are clearly organized into five, interdependent, segments that produce a record and an idea of life in Baracoa. The segments are: 1) an introduction to the people and the land, 2) an exploration and critique of some historical myths about the city, 3) a search for the meaning of the word Baracoa, 4) a portrait of daily life in Baracoa, and, 5) some final, albeit inconclusive, answers to some of the mysteries of the city.

The first segment is a longish sequence of "people in the street" shots and long shots of the city. It functions as an extended establishing shot, but perversely so. The oddly framed (canted angles, low camera positions, halting camera movements) assortment of individuals who walk by in front of the camera, acknowledging its presence with smiles and waves or with frowns, clarifies little about the nature of the film or about the community. Ordinary individuals at work in shops, school kids going home for lunch, bikers pedaling by are seen. Stylistically disturbing, this sequence serves to introduce the film as something other than reportage, to set up its irreverent but not unkind analysis of life in Baracoa.

The second sequence is an exploration of some of Baracoa's history. It begins conventionally with a low-angle shot of the facade of a colonial church followed by a standard, direct-address interview with a priest standing next to a large wooden cross described as a historical relic. Dated by its wood to Columbus's time, bits of this cross were carried off through the years by devout admirers. Followed by yet another official personage, the city historian offering a speech on the meaning of the city seal, these "official" explanations are undermined by a series of images that, crosscut with the interviews, put them into question while continuing to describe important facets of Baracoa's life. The images depict men at work on wood: lumberjacks bringing a large tree trunk to the saw at a lumbermill and a wood carver chiseling a minute wooden figurine of a woman. What the intercut images (and aggressive sounds) question is not so much the validity of the official history being told, but the relevance of historically arcane knowledge to everyday life in Baracoa. Both the historian and the priest remain "official" figures, cooped up in their ivory towers of historical knowledge surrounded by dead relics, while the people themselves inhabit the streets and woods of the town and therefore have a different kind of experience and knowledge.

That theirs is, regardless of its historical accuracy, an important kind of knowledge is the point of the next sequence, a series of "people in the streets" interviews seeking to discover the meaning of the word "Baracoa." Juxtaposed with each popular interpretation (city of waters, high city, etc.) are two sorts of images: first, the city historian in a tight close-up in front of the city seal, emphatically shaking his head and saying "no," and then, a series of images of the city itself that corroborate, experientially, the popular interpretation. For example, after a barber answers the interviewer's question about Baracoa, with the interpretation that it means "city of water," a montage of water images is seen that underlines the important place of water for the history of the city, for centuries accessible only by water, often devastated by tropical storms, and still highly dependent on the sea for its livelihood. In the film streets are inundated by torrential rains, boats docked at sidewalk posts, large wooden boats either beached, being swabbed, or laboriously replanked. The strategy of juxtaposing "witness" interviews with metaphorical imagery highlights the distance between the voice of the interviewees—regardless of their social status and/or academic credentials—and the voice of the text itself, which is asserted without the aids of titles or self-reflexive gestures, via editing and mise-en-scène.

Although no conclusive answer to the interviewer's question is discovered (on the contrary, less and less likely answers are unearthed), the next sequence develops the texture of daily life in Baracoa in a most unexpected fashion. In marked contrast to the somewhat lyrical music of the prior segments, this segment begins with riotous rap music and a long shot of kids "jiving" in the street. Over a medium shot of a young man in a street corner emblazoned with a sign "No Fumar, No Esmoquin" (No Smoking) (sustained for a surprisingly long time), we hear two unidentified women's voices on the soundtrack: "¡Pucha!" "¿Qué?" "¡Llegó el pollo!" (Pucha! What? The chicken arrived!). What follows is a lively edited montage sequence of images of the townspeople gleefully mobbing the poultry shop and carrying away their live chickens in all sorts of improvised containers (shopping bags, a bicycle's handlebars, their bare bands); a group of kids break-dancing in the street (in the best New York City fashion, on a black linoleum surface and observed by an admiring crowd); chocolate bars being poured, molded, and stamped with the name Baracoa in a factory; a housewife preparing tamales; a household breaking coconuts and preparing coconut milk; large fish being pulled from a boat; a man in a simple boat negotiating some rapids. These metaphoric juxtapositions again highlight the contradictions of Baracoan life, but this time, in the present rather than in historical terms: the pervasive influence of United States culture (Baracoa is still *not* far from the Guantanamo base); the inevitable difficulties of daily life in a small town; the arbitrariness of the food rationing system; the contradiction of live chickens surviving alongside the urban rap phenomenon; the molding effect of the media versus the significance of chocolate production for the city; the survival of anarchic elements next to the inevitable modernization of daily life; and so forth. Both presenting and criticizing—discursively creating—the Baracoan popular in all its modalities, this sequence ironically ends with a nondiegetic voice-over, another unidentified woman's voice screaming: "¡Rosita, hay jamonada!" (Rosita, there is baloney!).

Following this ironic, albeit not unkind, critique, the next sequence concludes by reaffirming the popular as the source of Baracoa's strength and personality. After the city historian finally discloses the official version of the meaning of the word Baracoa (ostensibly derived from an Arawakan word meaning presence of the sea), a townsperson—a welldressed, middle-aged white man—is presented with this information and calmly refuses to accept it as the only truth: "Yo no creo que eso se ajuste a la realidad. Hay que profundizar más esas cuestiones" (I am not sure this fits with reality. I think we have to dig deeper into these issues). And the final word on the issue is ultimately presented by a Black man, who, after arguing that Baracoa is simply "un baúl lleno de buena gente . . . y hospitalidad" (a mountain coffer full of good people . . . and hospitality), introduces himself as Cayamba, "el cantante con la voz más fea del mundo" (the singer with the world's ugliest voice). The film ends with Cayamba's singing about Baracoa serving as voice-over to a series of increasingly more distanced images of the city. Although from a simple description it might seem that the film ends with an unproblematic reassertion of the value of a simplistic notion of the popular literalized as Cayamba's real voice, he is far from a typical representative of a folkloric popular type. Besides being a remarkably poor singer, his lyrics as well as his general demeanor—and his identification as "el trovador guerrillero" (the guerrilla troubadour)—complicate rather than solve the social contradictions already explored by the text.

Kid Chocolate; Uno, dos, eso es; El viaje más largo; and *Un día fui* (and others such as Enrique Colina's *Jau* [1987] and Mayra Vilasis's *Con luz propia* [With Its Own Light, 1988]) are shorts that demonstrate the continued creativity of the Cuban documentary. This creativity has changed much since the high-modernist 1960s and the static 1970s. Much closer to a kind of dialectical postmodern consciousness, it is no longer bound to either indict the past and/or glorify the present, nor to a knee-jerk reflexivity of the means of production (making visible the filmmakers, cameras, mikes, etc.). Instead its reflexivity involves a structural concern over how meaning is created through discourse, of how a cinematic text positions itself in relation to the kind of knowledge that it is producing. Rather than present themselves as the ultimate authority, these texts simultaneously question and believe in themselves and other discourses, up to a certain point. The knowledge produced is no longer something that precedes the text and that is simply being rescued. Instead, it is through the process of turning the complex sociohistorical forces at work in a given situation/person/context into a film—into a discourse—that cultural identity begins to have a voice.

These films were all produced in the late 1980s, in a period of Cuban politics marked by attempts to rectify the mistakes of the past, to eliminate corruption and trickery, and to decentralize some aspects of the national economy. They have been concerned with promoting a healthy, albeit often cynical self-critique as have other ICAIC productions of the period like the fiction short *La Entrevista* (The Interview, 1987) and the fiction feature film *Plaff* (1988) (both directed by a young ICAIC filmmaker, Juan Carlos Tabío). Since then, however, the political climate of Cuba has changed markedly. For one thing, Castro has emphatically refused to follow Gorbachev's perestroika lead and has chosen to maintain a political hardline evidenced in his speeches, policy decisions, and, most recently, the banning of several Soviet publications that glorified glasnost. The 1989 court marshals and executions of high-ranking Cuban military personnel for corruption and drug smuggling have also raised doubts about the stability of the system itself: for such corruption to exist at high levels, there must have been hundreds of others also involved. When compounded by the recent dissolution of almost all Eastern European socialist regimes, the United States' invasion of Panama, and the electoral defeat of the Sandinistas in Nicaragua, these events increase the precariousness of Cuba's international position and make the contradictions of Cuban social life increasingly problematic.

It is still too soon to tell how these political crises will affect cinematic production in the 1990s. But the climate of uncertainty that they have produced was already anticipated and discursively prefigured in these documentary shorts that, refusing to presume to know it all, have gone further in their dialectical questioning, even while continuing to believe.

16

The Battle of Chile

Documentary, Political Process, and Representation (1990)

This essay (along with "At the Limits . . .")—both about the aesthetically innovative and politically militant New Latin American Cinema of the 1960s–1970s—and both published in Julianne Burton's edited volume The Social Documentary in Latin America *(1990), demonstrates López's talent as an astute, yet contrarian analyst of the NLAC. In addition to offering a compelling rereading of the canonical* Batalla de Chile *(1975–1979), the essay contextualizes the film as response to the rise of the Unidad Popular government under Salvador Allende (1970–1973). López also highlights the methods of production employed by Patricio Guzmán and his collaborators (known as El Equipo Tercer Año) and the evolution of their work starting from their first documentary* El primer año *(1971).*

> We maintain that imperfect cinema must above all show the process which generates the problems. It is thus the opposite of a cinema principally dedicated to celebrating results. . . . To analyze a problem is to show the problem (not the process) permeated with judgments which the analysis itself generates a priori. . . . To show the process of a problem . . . is to submit it to judgment without pronouncing the verdict. . . . The subjective element is the selection of the problem, conditioned as it is by the interest of the audience—which is the subject. The objective element is showing the process—which is the object.
>
> —Julio García Espinosa, "For an Imperfect Cinema"

> The first impulse is to film everything that is taking place in order to later find a structure at the moviola. . . . But "everything that takes place" is not really everything that is taking place. . . . What Chile represented, after all, was a sort of twentieth-century Paris Commune.
>
> —Patricio Guzmán in Zuzana Pick,
> "Interview with Patricio Guzmán"

In December 1972 Chile was in a state of chaos. As Salvador Allende's Popular Unity coalition government (called Unidad Popular, or UP) struggled to overcome the many obstacles in the way of its "peaceful road to socialism," a small group of filmmakers headed by Patricio Guzmán decided to undertake an ambitious project: to produce on film a testimonial/documentary record—complex, analytic, dialectical—of this national crisis and its outcome. They eventually produced *The Battle of Chile: The Struggle of a People without Arms* (*La batalla de Chile: La lucha de un pueblo sin armas*)—a three-part, four-and-a-half-hour analysis of Chilean sociopolitical life at its most complex moment, between February and September 1973. It has been recognized as one of the best examples of politically engaged and socially conscious documentary filmmaking in Latin America. If at one end of the spectrum comprising the New Latin American Cinema documentaries we locate *The Hour of the Furnaces* (1968), the montage-based, self-reflexive analytical work by the Grupo Cine Liberación, we must place the apparent immediacy and testimonial power of *Battle* at the other end. However, this testimonial power—acclaimed by critics and audiences alike—is more complexly elaborated than is apparent on the film's dense, informational surface. And it is precisely this textual and political density (which Guzmán himself has described as making the film heavy as a brick) that must be analyzed in relationship to the representational and political options of the Chilean sociopolitical conjuncture.

Popular Unity and the
Practices and Languages of Cinematic Representation

That Popular Unity did not pay sufficient attention to the importance of cultural/ideological production and reproduction in its plans for a democratic and legal transition to socialism is by now, more than fifteen years later, a well-documented, indisputable fact. What was missing from the UP agenda was an understanding of the crucial need for continued direct ideological struggle alongside the overt political warfare. The UP's defeat was largely caused by its inability to exert the hegemonic ideological power necessary to maintain and develop the political majority acquired in 1970.[1] As Armand Mattelart and many others have argued, the official UP policy toward culture—"first access to culture, and *then* rupture with the existing culture"—ignored the crucial role of ideology in society by separating "the delivery of the pre-existing culture . . . from its reception by the dominated classes" (Chanan 1976, 78). Of course, this is not to imply that the UP did not take any measures to influence or control cultural production in Chile. However, its pluralistic and legalistic position prevented it from taking the kind of radical measures needed to counter effectively the ideological strength of antagonistic forces (Mattelart 1980; Smirnow 1979).

The specific problems the UP faced with the cinema have also been well documented and analyzed (Chanan 1976; Bolzoni 1974; Vega, 1977). Chile Films, the official state film agency, was under UP control and supervision, but this was actually a handicap, because the political structure of the coalition (an uneasy mix of Socialists, Communists, and fractions of the Radical and Christian Democratic parties) was reproduced within the administration of Chile Films. Popular Unity had no clear policy for the cinema, and each party represented by the coalition tried to follow its own objectives and not those of the ensemble. Although the daily direction of Chile Films had been assigned to the Committee of Popular Unity Filmmakers, a group headed by Miguel Littín that had earlier proclaimed its allegiance to the UP, Chile Films' resources were far from adequate for the task of building a new national cinema. By 1970 the facilities of Chile Films were thirty years old and in disrepair, and the agency did not even have enough funds to arrange for the installation of equipment purchased in 1969 by the previous regime. Funds for purchasing raw film stock were severely limited, causing even further restrictions on production (Pick 1974). Furthermore, because of a "democratic guarantees" provision that prevented the UP from removing any civil servants from their jobs, incumbent bureaucrats could not be replaced by younger cineastes and technicians, and the institution was saddled with very high payroll expenses. Finally, the potential effectiveness of Chile films was further curtailed because the organization also had little control over film distribution (especially after US distributors stopped exporting their films to Chile in 1971) and did not begin to alter the existing structure of commercial theatrical exhibition (through nationalization) until 1973.

Although institutional and industrial conditions were less than favorable for the development of a strong national cinema, it is important to consider other, less direct and instrumental factors when analyzing Chilean cinema under the UP. How was the process of cinematic representation itself altered under the Popular Unity regime? How did the political and social changes made during this time affect the textual operations of its cinema? Did cinematic representation experience the same—or similar—cataclysmic changes as Chilean society in this period? These kinds of questions—in effect, addressing a sociology of cinematic representation—have rarely been addressed to the cinema produced during the Popular Unity years.

It is always difficult to assess or theorize about the relationship of texts or groups of texts (filmic, literary, or whatever) to specific sociohistorical moments and struggles. As we understand cultural production in general, it is an autonomous, self-referential, and determining process, but one that nevertheless participates in the complexity of any social moment—sometimes prefiguring, sometimes following, but always participating in that sociopolitical instance.

At the risk of oversimplification, we might say that the UP years (whose impetus can be traced as far back as the 1930s) were structurally characterized by ever growing sociopolitical contradictions and polarizations. In spite of their complexity, these contradictions became increasingly more transparent in the 1970–1973 period.[2] As Chilean society was divided into antagonistic blocks that would ultimately exhaust their ability to negotiate with one another, cultural production displayed similar structural characteristics manifested in contradictory bipolar tendencies that simultaneously depended upon and rejected the assumed transparency of meaning production.[3] In the press of the period, for example, we find the hysterical counterrevolutionary aggressiveness of the right in *El Mercurio* versus the measured, intellectualized address of the left in the publications of the UP-controlled Quimantú press. In literature, the anti-poetry of Nicanor Parra countered the revolutionary rhetorical poetry of Pablo Neruda. And in the cinema, the aggressive cinematic self-reflexivity of a Raúl Ruiz stood in sharp contrast to the transparency of newsreel production sponsored by Chile Films.

Caught in the interstices of these general contradictions, the cinema was also affected by its own specific history and other mediating forces at the national as well as the international level. The history of the development of the Chilean cinema before and during the UP is intimately linked with the rise of postwar and anti-Hollywood movements in Europe and the slow emergence of socially conscious modes of filmmaking throughout Latin America. As an integral part of the New Latin American Cinema that emerged from the struggling efforts of Latin American filmmakers in the early 1960s, the representational work of the Chilean cinema must be considered in light of the representational options offered by this complex context.

Elsewhere I have argued that the most central representational characteristic of the New Latin American Cinema is the specific way in which the documentary and fictional modes of filmmaking were combined and transformed as filmmakers of the sixties and seventies attempted to change the social function of the cinema in Latin America. This rearticulation of the basic representational work of the cinema also took place in Chile, but in a fashion specific to that conjuncture, beginning before the UP victory and continuing after its defeat in the "exile cinemas" produced by Chileans all over the world.[4]

Although much less explicitly than in other Latin American countries, the documentary form was taken up by Chilean filmmakers in the years preceding the UP electoral victory in 1970 as a vehicle for the promotion and popularization of the Unidad Popular alliance. Documentary production began in earnest in Chile under the auspices of university cinema programs[5] and university-sponsored TV stations, but it was the 1967 Viña del Mar festival that served as catalyst for the politicization and autocritique of Chilean documentary filmmakers in the context of the New Latin American Cinema.[6]

After the 1967 Viña festival, filmmakers like Alvaro Ramírez, Douglas Hubner, Carlos Flores, and Guillermo Cahn began to use the cinema as an instrument for the analysis of contemporary Chilean social problems: infant malnutrition in *Desnutrición infantil* (Ramírez, 1969), the disenfranchised in *Hermida de la Victoria* (Hubner, 1969), *Casa o mierda* (House or Shit, Flores and Cahn, 1970) and mining problems in *Miguel Angel Aguilera* (Ramírez, 1970).

Following the style of *La hora de los hornos*, Pedro Chaskel and Hector Ríos wanted to develop a cinema that would awaken passive spectators to the injustices and problems of the Frei regime. They produced a film in early 1970 entitled *Venceremos*, the first documentary specifically affiliated with the UP. Like *La hora*, this film was designed to serve as an instrument in the struggle to bring a particular candidate, in this case

Allende, to power. Other films emerged during the electoral campaign that favored the programs of Unidad Popular—for example, *Brigada Ramona Parra* (1970) by Alvaro Ramírez.

Sponsored by the Centro de Cine Experimental (headed by Sergio Bravo) and by the film department of the Central Única de Trabajadores (CUT, the principal workers' union), most of these films were not distributed in the hostile commercial circuit. Instead, they were shown throughout the countryside, in working-class neighborhoods, and in factories. In addition to Chilean films, others, including *La hora de los hornos*, were also shown through these alternative circuits. The Chilean working class has historically been among the most politicized of the continent, and these films served as the focus of important political debates. Overall, the stated goal of militant documentary filmmakers in Chile before Unidad Popular was to "involve the popular masses in the struggles for power and to help them rediscover Chile, giving them a new vision of the present, past, and future of their nation. This vision will be a critical one that interprets reality according to new values and that is integrated with the construction of socialism in Chile" (Bolzoni 1974, 38).[7]

Although highly politicized and distributed almost exclusively within alternative circuits, these early UP documentaries adhered to the tenets of traditional political documentary filmmaking. They sought to be "objective," denunciatory, and persuasive, while also calling attention to conditions that the cinema had previously not recognized or analyzed, and articulating new solutions.

After the UP's electoral victory and the reorganization of Chile Films under the leadership of Miguel Littín and the cineastes of Unidad Popular, documentary production continued, albeit in a different form. Because Chile Films was not able to assume control of Chilean distribution or exhibition, and the films it sponsored and/or produced were generally not welcomed by the commercial sector, documentary films that sought to expose and analyze contemporary social and political problems facing Chile had a difficult time finding an official outlet. Allende's electoral victory had not marked the end of the struggle for cultural and political autonomy; the documentary was being used to promote that victory and to analyze available political and practical options. Rather than denounce conditions, the documentary began to be used as a means to chronicle and analyze the Chilean political process. Over one hundred documentaries were produced by Chile Films between 1970 and 1973, some of which dealt with the need to preserve Chile's natural resources, the workers' struggle to control the national economy, and the need for social and political reforms.[8] As Zuzana Pick has argued, "Each of these films demonstrates that the Chilean documentary movement began to overcome the [idea of] documentary as memory or witness to reality and aspired to transform it into an analytical historical instrument, while [the newsreels] of Chile Films were conceived as the site for informative material and political commentary" (Pick 1984b, 36).[9]

El Equipo Tercer Año and Patricio Guzmán

Patricio Guzmán is among the most accomplished documentary filmmakers to emerge during the Unidad Popular years. Guzmán neither attempted to use the cinema "as a gun" nor followed the socio-scientific mode of, for example, Colombian filmmakers Marta Rodríguez and Jorge Silva in *Chircales* (Brickmakers). Guzmán (and the small group of filmmakers associated with him) adopted the documentary as the only cinematic form appropriate to the complex, multifaceted social and political condition of Chile during Unidad Popular. Although trained in fiction filmmaking in Spain, upon his return to Chile in 1971 Guzmán decided that what was most important was to "film the events that they [in Chile] were living at that moment. . . . You would be sitting in a cafe, working on a script, and all of a sudden a group of picketing workers with red flags would pass by. . . . How could you not film all that? Why distance oneself from that reality?" (Sempere 1977, 54).

Guzmán and his associates undertook to film the day-to-day events of the first year of Unidad Popular; in 1971 they produced *El primer año*, a feature documentary that tried to summarize what took place in that year. Rather than rely on archival material, Guzmán and his team insisted on filming an amazing record of events, but even according to Guzmán, it is too much of a chronicle, too journalistic and commemorative, to provide an analysis of the events recorded. In fact, Guzmán's search for an appropriate mode of cinematic representation for Chile under the UP parallels the increasingly blatant contradictions of the UP conjuncture.

Although Guzmán next embarked on a fiction film project, a Chile Films–sponsored historical reconstruction of the life and legend of Manuel Rodríguez, a Chilean national hero, he once again abandoned fiction "because what was happening was more important than fiction."[10] While shooting *Manuel Rodríguez*, Guzmán and his production team (which included, among others, cameraman Jorge Müller and producer Federico Elton) took to the streets to film a report of daily political activities. "No matter how interesting the *Manuel Rodríguez* project . . . it was impossible not to film what was going on" (Sempere and Guzmán 1977, 69). The streets of Chile in 1972 were physically paralyzed by a number of crippling strikes organized by anti-Unidad Popular forces, and Guzmán and his team filmed the response of the Chilean working class to this paralysis. *La respuesta de octubre* (The Answer to October, 1972) records how the working class organized itself into industrial belts (*cordones industriales*) by taking over factories that had been abandoned by their owners and managers so as to neutralize the economic chaos produced by the strikes. By Guzmán's own admission, the long series of interviews that make up the film is monotonous. The industrial belt was not an immediately visible phenomenon. "You can't see it. You can only see the facade of the factory and a sign. But it is not a parade. It isn't an inauguration or a speech or a demonstration" (Sempere and Guzmán 1977, 72). Yet through their work in this film, Guzmán and his associates began to understand how to find, visualize, and film the "invisible" events at the core of Chilean life. In fact, as the situation worsened, the roots of the crisis were rendered increasingly visible.

Shelving their fiction projects until the time when the country might be under more secure political control, Guzmán and his associates organized themselves to continue their work of documenting the people's struggle against fascist forces in Chile. Because they could no longer count on the support of Chile Films,[11] they obtained simple equipment (an Eclair and a Nagra) from a friendly independent production outfit and raw stock from France through the generosity of cinema verité filmmaker Chris Marker. Rather than run to the streets and film indiscriminately, Guzmán and his team (now called El Equipo Tercer Año) undertook a long theoretical and methodological debate before filmmaking began. Fully conscious of the volatile state of the nation in 1972 and of impending changes, they nevertheless felt that regardless of the final outcome for Chile (whether a civil war or a coup d'état), their film would serve as a valuable historical record of those events. However, they wanted to avoid the agitational or denunciatory style of documentary they all considered typical of the New Latin American Cinema; they sought to produce what they termed an *analytical* documentary, more like an essay than explicit agitprop, which could serve an essential testimonial and analytical function for Chile and all of Latin America in future years. El Equipo Tercer Año surveyed available models of political documentary and fiction filmmaking and analyzed their methodological options. They concluded that they needed to avoid the simple chronological structure they had used in *El primer año* in order to develop a "nucleus" or dialectical approach that would pinpoint "the key areas at which the Chilean class struggle intersects." Guzmán explained:

> Which are the key points through which the proletariat and the peasantry must pass in the conquest of state power? And which are the key points through which the bourgeoisie and its imperialist allies must pass in order to reappropriate that power? If you locate these fifteen or twenty battlegrounds within the larger conflict and pin them down one by one, you are going to have a dialectical vision of what is going on. This was the approach we finally agreed to use. (Burton 1986b, 55)

The extensive preproduction planning carried out by El Equipo Tercer Año would seem to contradict my assertion that sociopolitical contradictions were becoming increasingly obvious. But in fact, the "work" these filmmakers felt was necessary to filming the Chilean conjuncture in 1973 already prefigures the outcome of the crisis itself at a representational level. The ubiquitous assumed transparency of cinematic language challenged the apparent transparency of the social system, disclosing its own insufficiencies. Only the cataclysmic change wrought by the coup d'état—the reestablishment of the hegemony of the oligarchy—would validate El Equipo Tercer Año's complex representational work.

The filming of this tremendously ambitious project took place semi-clandestinely. For as long as the Unidad Popular government retained control of the state, the filmmakers had access to events and were welcomed by workers. But to be able to document the contemporary situation thoroughly, they also had to infiltrate the right and subject themselves to physical danger by participating in all sorts of potentially violent demonstrations.

El Equipo Tercer Año was "in production" for as long as their film supply lasted. When the successful coup made it unsafe to film in the streets, they used their last reels of film to record the first televised messages of the military junta and the broadcast of the bombing of the presidential palace. Soon afterward, the members of the collective left Chile in a prearranged order and also smuggled all the footage and magnetic sound recordings for the film out of the country.[12] After searching unsuccessfully for financial support to complete the project in France, the collective ended up in Cuba, where Alfredo Guevara of the Cuban Film Institute (ICAIC) offered all of the institute's resources and facilities (including the supervision and advice of Julio García Espinosa) necessary to complete the film.

The final product of this experience, the three-part *Battle of Chile*, stands as the epitome of the New Latin American Cinema documentary: direct, engaged, immediate, spontaneous yet analytical, and completed through pan–Latin American cooperation. In fact, no documentary of the New Latin American Cinema other than *The Hour of the Furnaces* has received more popular attention or wider international distribution.

The Critical Response

Ironically, however, *The Battle of Chile* has never been publicly shown in Pinochet's Chile. The public the film was meant to serve as an analysis of a crucial sociopolitical conjuncture has not been and cannot be its audience. Instead, *Battle* has been inserted into a number of extremely different sociopolitical milieus that have decisively affected its reception.

What is most interesting about a survey of the various critical responses to *Battle* is that regardless of their nationalities or political beliefs, most critics have failed to recognize the uniqueness of the film's representational work and have assessed the film as "pure documentary," dealing in facts, history, testimony, and so forth. For example, North American mass media critics uniformly hailed the film's value as a record and for the most part ignored its substantive analytical work or the complexities of its modes of address. Stanley Kauffmann wrote in the *New Republic*, "There is little critical to be said about this picture. It is merely gripping fact, well represented" (1980, 303–04). According to Pauline Kael, "The film seems to give us only the public actions . . . and none of the inner workings" (1978, 82).[13] And Vincent Canby in the *New York Times* (1978, 1) and the reviewers for *Variety* were in almost complete agreement, simply classifying the film as "reportage" with an explicit Marxist bias (Holl 1976; Cart 1980). European critics, although they protested less about the film's alleged "difficulty," also tended subtly to privilege its status as a documentary record over its analytical work. Even Paul Louis Thirard in *Positif* argued that Guzmán prefers to illustrate instead of explain and that this limits the effectiveness of the film (Sempere and Guzmán 1977, 201-03).[14]

When attempting to assess the film's impact on audiences, most critics have been overwhelmed by the film's informational density (its four and a half hours of relentless data), simultaneously claiming that its analysis is excessively detailed and that it does not provide enough background information. Beyond this point, critics have argued either that the film is cold and distancing, or the exact opposite—that it is absorbing. For example, Cuban critic Azucena Isabel argued in her review that the film is effective precisely because of its "conscious distancing" of all emotional impact without seeking to illustrate a specific thesis, while North American critic Rosalie Schwartz claimed that the film was "frightening in its power to absorb the viewer" (Isabel 1977, 194-96; Schwartz 1977-1999, 261).

The Textual Operations of *The Battle of Chile*

This split critical response becomes less paradoxical when we look closely at the textual operations of the film. The film's impact—this simultaneous absorbing and distancing effect—is to a large degree determined by the fictive strategies that are invoked to represent what we necessarily recognize as important documentary footage of crucial historical events.

The most significant of these strategies is Guzmán's extensive use of sequence shots. Rather than depend on montage (like *The Hour of the Furnaces* and, in fact, most political documentaries) to organize and construct an a posteriori reading of the social and political events of this particular moment in Chilean history, the filmmakers set out to film in long takes whenever possible. They were able to do this because of the theoretical and methodological work that preceded and accompanied the actual filming. El Equipo Tercer Año did not want to film everything that was taking place. On the contrary, they followed an original analysis that identified five crucial problems in the Chilean class struggle and filmed only those events that seemed significant within those areas. Guzmán explained in an interview:

> We decided that these fronts of struggle had to be followed up and examined, and anything happening on another front had to be excluded, even if it was very interesting. Within this outline there was room for variation and improvisation.

> This was what we had decided to do: illustrate with images a
> previously proposed outline, without losing in the filming the
> freshness and spontaneity of life, without locking them into a
> set frame. (Pick 1980b, 30)[15]

Once the outline was established, the filmmakers were able to concentrate on the aesthetics of images to a degree unusual in traditional documentary filmmaking of this kind (*témoignage*). "Once the project was clearly worked out on paper and in our heads, we could liberate our expressive capabilities, freeing the camera to make very long takes" (Guzmán in Burton 1977a, 49).

This explicit aesthetic decision required the complex orchestration of the filming process. Guzmán often served as the peripheral eyes of cameraman Jorge Müller, surveying the action, anticipating what was about to happen, and instructing him "to make certain movements [pans, tilts, manual cranes] that are much more readily identified with fictional than with documentary filmmaking" (Burton 1986b, 57).

In the finished film, these sequence shots so laboriously served to alter the traditional relationship between film, filmmakers, and spectators. In the narrative fiction cinema, the sequence shot increases the image's credibility and its indirect persuasiveness. It is generally considered more "realistic" because of its apparent preservation of the unities of time and space. Its extensive use in the documentary, however, rather than emphasizing a real already ostensibly guaranteed by the documentary form, paradoxically brings the document closer to the realm of fiction. It produces a "fiction effect" that, by resisting the manipulation of editing, unmasks the manipulation or "construction" inherent in the simple act of pointing a camera.[16] In *Battle*, sequence shots provide a wealth of detail and evidence of the directiveness of the filming that belies the careful orchestration of the "raw" materials of the real. This is not a film presenting itself as a record of how things "really were" in Chile in 1973, as many critics have argued. It is a precise, calculated, intentionally political, Marxist dialectical analysis of those events that uses the narrative strategies of fiction as a legitimating device. By revealing the means by which the dramatic action has been structured, the sequence shot functions within this documentary as a kind of estrangement device that separates the spectator from the sheer force of rhetoric and that simultaneously suggests (because of its role in fiction) *and* prevents (because this is a documentary) simple identification.

An important example of this operation takes place early in part 1 ("The Insurrection of the Bourgeoisie") during a series of interviews that establish the mood of the people before the March 1973 elections. The filmmakers enter a right-wing apartment, pretending to be representatives of Channel 13 TV.[17] While the microphone interviews the lady of the house, the camera, after remaining on her face for only a few seconds, takes a tour of the well-appointed apartment. What we see underlines the presumed coherence between what she says and her environment. While the woman expresses her conservative political sentiments—in a tone and diction that denote her class position—the camera shows us her furniture, her porcelain figurines, her carefully coiffed, insouciant adolescent son who lights a cigarette taken from a fancy holder resting on a fine wood table. The second-level information provided by this sequence shot is as essential to the analysis presented by the documentary as similarly placed (and therefore underlined) information would be for the plot development of a fiction film. This presentation of information—the visual indictment of the bourgeoisie—simultaneously positions the spectator as a reader/observer of the "real" and as the observer of a preconstructed, intentional operation, directed as a fiction is directed.

Notwithstanding their fictional effect, there is no doubt that the images that assault us in *Battle* are real and that their testimonial force is great. The authenticity of the images and their ability to report directly on the events that took place in Chile in 1973 is interpreted and reorganized for the spectator not only by the sequence shots and by the smoothly invisible editing of Pedro Chaskel, but also by the voiceover narration that situates our reading of the events portrayed by the film.

This authoritarian voice-over marks the distance between this film and traditional conceptions of "direct cinema." Although the sequence shots and the mobile framing, reframing, focus shifts, and movements within the image could code the film as "direct," the voice-over reinscribes the filmic discourse as an authored discourse. The camera may be a "neutral" observer, but the images it produces are orchestrated and controlled by the essential contextual and explanatory information provided by this metadiscourse. Because of the directness of the images, the voice-over performs a double operation that indirectly supports the distancing effect of the sequence shots. By negating the images' ability to stand on their own, the voice-over provides a second line of interpretation, one that is dialectical rather than objective in the traditional sense. It also establishes a specific kind of spectator and address. While the images often seem to position the spectator as a direct observer-participant in the events filmed, the voice-over distances the spectator from emotional identification and encourages a "knowing" stance. The textual operations of *Battle* position the spectator as a knowing subject—one who knows both the outcome of the struggles the film documents and the film's status as an irreplaceable document of those struggles.

This operation is especially apparent at the beginning of part 1. The sound of jet engines and bomb explosions accompanies the credits. After the credits, the source of those sounds is identified: these are the airplanes and the bombs with which the military destroyed the Moneda presidential palace in the September 1973 coup. In long shot, we see the effects of the bombs on the palace. The voice-over—in the English-language version a woman's voice—interjects, "In March 1973, six months before the bombing of the Moneda Palace, the people of Chile go to the polls. . . . The political forces are divided into two sides," as the image places us in the midst of a street demonstration. We know what the outcome will be—there is no narrative enigma in the traditional sense. In fact, the film is structured as an extensive flashback from the spectator's present state of knowledge—signified by the newsreel-like images of the bombing of the palace that were broadcast over television as soon as the military took power.[18] The events presented by the film are thus constructed as leading to a foreknown closure. The voice-over, while insisting on the present tense, always remarks on the future consequences of the events presented, thereby negating the apparent transparency and completeness of the representation. For example, early in part 1, during the presentation of the parliamentary boycott of the UP's anti–black market policies, the narrator makes this statement:

> Although the right was not able to prove anything, the accusations *would follow* their course. The blackmail would be repeated with other high functionaries of Popular Unity: either the ministers give in to the demands of the right or they *will be expelled*. . . . In every instance, a representative of the left *is going to demonstrate* that the accusations did not have any legal basis. (Emphasis added)

Battle's overall flashback structure—emphasized by the fact that part 3, "Popular Power," is structured as a flashback-within-flashback look at the October 1972 crisis from the people's perspective—engages the spectator as a participant in the process of making and recording this particular history (fig. 16.1). The filmmakers' self-reflexivity in the first five minutes of part 1 further contributes to this mode of address. After the shots of

The Battle of Chile | 337

Figure 16.1. The pageantry of Popular Power in *La Batalla de Chile*, part 3. Fair use.

the bombing of La Moneda, we are thrown into the midst of a demonstration, where the handheld camera bounces from one face to another, from one placard and excited shout to the next. In the background of the chanting and singing, we hear the technical commands of the filmmakers: "Sync . . . clapboard . . . ready? go! . . . over here, 'Flaco'!"[19] We see their bodies, especially Guzmán as interviewer holding the microphone, moving among the demonstrators, approaching different individuals, trying to get out of camera range. After several of the cuts in this first sequence, a new shot begins as the camera focuses on a hand tapping the mike to mark the beginning of a take and then quickly reframes or refocuses to approach the subject of the interview. Their privileged location at the beginning underscores the priority accorded to the process of filming the events that mark the crucial "nodal" points of the Chilean class struggle at this historical moment. Furthermore, they introduce the spectator to the historical process and to the process of recording/writing that history as a witness and spectator-participant.

This sense of "history in the making" is further emphasized in the conclusion of part 1 and the beginning of part 2. El Equipo Tercer Año made use of the dramatic footage obtained the day of the *tancazo* (the aborted coup of June 1973) by an Argentine TV cameraman (Leonardo

Henricksen) who filmed his own death as he was threatened and finally shot by an army officer (fig. 16.2). Part 1 ends abruptly, with the turbulent images recorded by the camera falling from the hands of the dying Henricksen. The narrator explains: "Not only did he film his own death. He also filmed, two months before the final coup, the true face of the fascist Chilean military. The imperialist strategy enters its final phase." And in the background, we hear someone's voice screaming, "Watch out! Watch out! Get out of here!" Part 2 ("The Coup d'État") begins with this same footage and voice-over commentary (but without the background voices) (fig. 16.3). The end of Henricksen's final sequence is joined to a sequence filmed by El Equipo Tercer Año's cameraman who, from the other side of the street, witnessed the event.

The development of *Battle* follows the logic of fictive discourses. Each element of the film, especially in parts 1 and 2, is part of a cause-and-effect chain leading to the eventual denouement of the September coup d'état that ends part 2. As Guzmán himself has acknowledged, the filmmakers "probed reality to find in it a narrative line" (Pick 1980b, 30). The film unfolds by establishing a series of events that demand responses from the right and from the left. From the pre-electoral survey of attitudes on both

Figure 16.2. The price of documentary witness: an Argentine cameraman records his own summary execution at the hands of mutinous Chilean troops in *La Batalla de Chile*.

Figure 16.3. The traitorous military under intimate scrutiny: *La Batalla de Chile*, part 2.

sides, the film takes us through the elections, to the increasingly desperate responses of the right, to the left's responses to the right's increasing sabotage activities, and so forth. Because the collective's goal was to present a dialectical analysis, they emphasized conflict, thus bringing the film closer to the traditional structuration of fictional dramas.[20] Their efforts to show events as they unfolded and to juxtapose one series of events to another generate audience expectations that are fulfilled by the subsequent development of the film. Thus the actions filmed are transformed into dramatic actions in the classic sense.

One of the expectations emphasized by the inexorable logic of the cause-and-effect chain, by the introductory sequence, and by the audience's prior knowledge of Chilean events, is the triumph of the right in the September coup d'état. This knowledge and this expectation, fulfilled at the end of part 2, color the filmmakers' and the spectators' relationship to the sequence portraying the right. The iconography and activities of the right—the arm bands and military insignias—are sinister, echoing Nazi and Ku Klux Klan rallies. Their victory at the end of part 2 is, for the film, a pyrrhic one. Although in effect the coup d'état ends the drama, the film continues and finds another locus for dramatic introspection within the left itself rather than in the very visible and ostensibly straightforward conflict between the left and the right. Ultimately, part 3 demonstrates that the militancy of the Chilean people was not sufficiently tapped by the *vía democrática* of Unidad Popular.

The narrative logic underlying this tripartite structure also clearly marks the film as an a posteriori representation, particularly one inflected by exile, neither within the UP conjuncture nor totally outside it. More than other films begun in Chile and finished elsewhere, *The Battle of Chile* highlights the cataclysmic representational/linguistic/ideological effects of the coup d'état and of exile. For those who remained in Chile after the coup, language and representation became suspect: treacherous, deceiving, veiled. Those outside, caught in the time warps of exile, tended to remain within the assumed linguistic and ideological transparency of the UP conjuncture.[21] *The Battle of Chile* is poised between these two conditions: a document shaped by transparency and immediacy that also questions the systems producing these meanings and inscribes a necessarily questioning spectator within its midst.

17

At the Limits of Documentary

Hypertextual Transformation
and the New Latin American Cinema (1990)

This essay ably demonstrates López's tendency to flip conventional readings or frameworks on their heads through the examination of five films from Cuba *(Memorias del subdesarrollo, De cierta manera),* Chile *(El Chacal del Nahueltoro), and Bolivia (El coraje del pueblo and El enemigo principal) from the late 1960s and early 1970s that all mix together documentary and fiction filmmaking practices. She invokes the theories of Genette, Rose, and Hutcheon to interpret these "serious," political films as examples of how parody, understood as a "transformative critical practice, a form that by challenging antecedent texts . . . can disturb preconceptions and prejudices and give rise to new forms of consciousness."*

When we think of the New Latin American Cinema, certain images and adjectives immediately come to mind: a bearded guerrilla, weapon in hand and ammunition belt across his chest; a crowd of peasants defiantly holding up their weapons in protest; a mass demonstration with banners waving. If asked to describe the New Latin American Cinema, we might enlist one of the suggestive phrases that Latin American filmmakers have coined to describe their own practices: an aesthetics of hunger, a cinema of poverty, the camera as gun, an imperfect cinema, a third cinema, an aesthetics of

---

Editors' note: This essay is an expanded version of "Parody, Underdevelopment, and the New Latin American Cinema," *Quarterly Review of Film and Video* 12, nos. 1–2 (1990).

garbage. Most of these terms and images refer us to documentary practices, for, in fact, although the New Latin American Cinema has activated almost every mode, genre, and style of cinematic production, documentary realism—as transformed by different contextual pressures—has served as a springboard for the movement's transformation and retheorizing of the cinematic apparatus and its social functions. Eschewing the traditional distinctions between documentary and fictional modes of filmmaking in its search to produce a "new" cinema with a renewed social function, the New Latin American Cinema has questioned, juxtaposed, transposed, and, ultimately, transformed each mode so that their various ontological and epistemological claims are mediated by the forces of past and present historical contexts.[1] The New Latin American Cinema is best characterized as a transformative cinema—a countercinematic practice for a continent struggling to defy the incapacitating logic of underdevelopment—and the nature of its transformation can be analyzed as a special kind of intertextual mediation where textual operations spill over into social, political, and historical realms.

In light of recent work by Gérard Genette (1982), Margaret Rose (1979), and Linda Hutcheon (1985), among others, this transformative practice can be analyzed as a form of parodic discourse. Although linking the term "parody" to serious, politically motivated texts might seem surprising, since the term is most commonly associated with imitation as ridicule, early uses of the word, its etymology, and contemporary artistic practices justify its use in this context. The prefix "para" refers to something that is simultaneously "beside and against" and ōidē (song), indicates that parody (parōidia) is literally a beside-against song, contrechant, or musical counterpoint. It is this sense of the word, rather than its identification with humorous mockery that has concerned contemporary theorists. Although there is no general consensus among them on the specificity of parodic forms of discourse, all agree at least, on the importance of dissociating the term "parody" from ridiculing imitation and (to different degrees) on its status as a special kind of intertextual transformation. Genette, for example, argues that parody is a form of hypertextuality, a mode that is distinct from other intertextual relations (such as citation, paratextuality, metatextuality, and architextuality), while Rose equates parody with self-reflexivity, and Hutcheon posits it as a form of imitation or repetition with critical distance that permits the ironic signaling of difference within similarity.

For Genette, the defining characteristic of parody as hypertextuality is the relationship between the texts in question. In hypertextuality, Genette

At the Limits of Documentary | 343

argues, a semantic and/or stylistic transformation of text A (the hypotext) takes place in text B (the hypertext). The terms of that transformation vary, but it is the transformation itself—turning texts into palimpsests—that describes the specific character of hypertextuality.[2] Although Genette's exhaustive classification of hypertextual relations as transformative practices is extremely suggestive, his analysis limits the parodic, as a hypertextual category, to its satiric or playful dimensions and subsumes its other possible functions under other hypertextual forms. Because his is primarily a structural schema, Genette's categories are exclusively limited to textual relations. As Hutcheon points out, they ultimately fail to take into account the hermeneutic or interpretive dimension of parody's transformative work.

In Rose's and Hutcheon's less formalistic analyses, however, parody is also analyzed as a transformative *critical* practice, a form that by challenging antecedent texts, conventions, or prevailing modes of thought, can disturb preconceptions and prejudices and give rise to new forms of consciousness. In *The Order of Things* (as Rose points out), Foucault points to the parodic as exemplified by Cervantes's *Don Quixote* as ushering in the critical and self-reflexive modern episteme. As most theorists of parody from Bakhtin to Foucault have argued, parody is central to the promotion of new discursive formations, to the transformation of the discourse of an age. Parody, like *ostranenie* or aesthetic distancing, "lays bare the device" of a text, discourse, or social order and promotes a renewed relationship to the world. However, the "structural and functional relationship of critical revision" mobilized by parody is, according to Hutcheon, always paradoxical (Hutcheon 1985, 15, 26). The capacity of parody to transgress boundaries—its critical potential—is still dependent on the affirmation of that which is being challenged. In Hutcheon's words, "[The] paradox of legalized though unofficial subversion is characteristic of all parodic discourse insofar as parody posits, as a prerequisite to its very existence, a certain aesthetic institutionalization which entails the acknowledgement of recognizable, stable form and conventions" (1985, 74–75). However, this neither negates nor dismisses the revolutionary potential of parodic work. On the contrary, that potential can ultimately only be activated in history, by taking into account the text's inscription in specific sociohistorical conjunctures. Because of its double-voiced nature—a form of discourse with two or more competing "voices" in counterpoint—"parody involves not just a structural *énoncé* but the entire *énonciation* of discourse," in short, a *context* (Hutcheon 1985, 23). In fact, the potential for renewal in parody is especially visible in particular historical periods, such as the 1960s and

1970s in Latin America, that can be described as markedly heteroglot. In such periods, a great number of competing voices or discursive options are available to underline, as Bakhtin would have said, the primacy of context over text for the negotiations necessary for the production of meaning.

In the fictional films of the New Latin American Cinema, the conventions and styles of the documentary—with their claims to immediacy and presence—are semantically and stylistically called into question, while their transformation provides access to a broad historical context that exceeds the analogical realm of fiction and mediates among text, spectator, and social process. The resulting texts, palimpsests of fiction, realism, and the "real," as a result, insert themselves differently into Latin American society.

The Development of the New Latin American Cinema

The New Latin American Cinema is predicated on the consciousness of the cultural ramifications of underdevelopment and dependency. Neither "dependent" nor struggling to become developed, it rejects the entrapment of conventional developmentalist logic and aggressively asserts its own underdevelopment—its hunger, imperfection, violence, and poverty—as an empowering, transformational device. For this cinema to exist, Latin Americans first had to realize that the answer to underdevelopment was not development according to the logic of the metropolis, but revolution. They also had to realize that revolutions could not be successful without the active participation of cultural/ideological forces. The development and maintenance of national cultures became a survival issue, the first step in the establishment of national and continental autonomy. Thus Latin Americans strove to develop and maintain autonomous national cultures in order to challenge attempts at "developing underdevelopment," asserting cultural nationalism as an integral part of the struggle to establish a different order of things on the continent.

Seizing one of the least likely tools for the development of national culture—a mass medium that is inescapably associated with the developed world—Latin Americans attempted to fashion the cinema into an instrument for national and popular expression and a form of resistance to capitalist/imperialist domination. This entailed challenging the cinematic apparatus at every level: technology, aesthetics, language, and modes of production, distribution, and consumption. It also entailed questioning conventional beliefs about the role of the cinema (or any other art) in the maintenance and transformation of society.

At the Limits of Documentary | 345

Establishing the specificity of the New Latin American Cinema was a complex and prolonged process. It involved more than overcoming a general "anxiety of influence" about predecessors and dependence on foreign models. In fact, those imported cinematic models could not simply be directly applied in Latin America; straightforwardly duplicating simple realist forms was perceived as leading to passivity, while extreme modernist and avant-garde forms seemed to run counter to the filmmakers' social concerns and to appeal only to elite audiences. In addition, the characteristics of the dominant Hollywood cinema—transparency, illusionism, commercialism, gloss—were considered inappropriate and counterproductive of cinematic practices seeking to promote sociopolitical liberation.

Faced with the old questions regarding form versus content and debates about realism and modernism, the New Latin American Cinema looked for solutions in history and historiography.[3] Through both contemporary history as exemplified by documentary reportage and fictional reconstructions or rereadings of the past, the New Latin American Cinema assumed the historical as the basic intertext necessary for its own intervention in the region's sociopolitical struggles. Above all, filmmakers sought to emphasize and transform the social and political effectiveness of the cinema. Although the historical focus of the New Latin American Cinema is self-apparent at the content level, this process also challenged the history of cinematic representation itself: the critical juxtaposition or "repetition with critical distance" of traditional cinematic modes—the documentary and the fictional cinemas and their accompanying conventional demands and effects on spectators—in the context of a search for realist, popular, and socially significant representational strategies.

As critical realists, politically committed filmmakers like Fernando Birri and the students at his Documentary School in Santa Fe, Argentina, the first generation of ICAIC filmmakers in Cuba, and some of the practitioners of Cinema Novo in Brazil recognized Latin America's need for a particular kind of critical consciousness of the social, economic, and political aspects of life in an underdeveloped region. This awareness enhanced cinema as an instrument of demystification and "dealienation." These early films and declarations signaled a naïve belief in the camera's ability to record "truths"—to capture a national reality or essence without any mediation—as if a simple inversion of the dominant colonized culture were sufficient to negate that culture and institute a truly national one.

Gradually, the kind of knowledge the cinema was asked to invoke and produce acquired a different character. "Realism," no longer seen as tied to simple perceptual truth or to a mimetic approximation of the real, was increasingly used to refer to a self-conscious material practice. The cinema's powers of representation—its ability to reproduce the surface of the lived world—were activated not as a record or duplication of that surface, but in order to explain it, to reveal its hidden aspects, to disclose the material matrix that determined it. This process was, furthermore, not an end in itself (as it often is in traditional ethnography, for example) but was articulated as part of a larger process of cultural, social, political, and economic renovation. The cinematic analysis of the real was meant to serve as an enabling mechanism for the transformation of that reality. As a representation or restructuring of the "real" conditions of life in Latin America, it sought to bring to light that which was kept in darkness and silence by the sociopolitical and economic mechanisms of underdevelopment. And this light would also illuminate the process of representation itself, questioning the filmmaker's own position in the filmmaking process, their engagement with their subjects, their position as social actors in the universe being recorded. As part of this process, this cinema also sought to provide spectators with a different consciousness of their worlds, to disturb the apparently natural order of things and to break down rationalizations and preconceived ideas.

The best available cinematic model to fulfill this kind of social function was the poetic and morally committed realism proposed by the Italian neorealists, especially when combined with the didactic social commitment of Griersonian documentary, as in Fernando Birri's work for the Documentary School of Santa Fe. Birri's practice combined an essentially documentary impulse—to record the unrecorded as it "really was"—with fictive strategies, a narrative and poetic recreation of events. In subsequent transformations, although the realistic commitment of the documentary remained central, it was increasingly juxtaposed to and mixed with fictional strategies in order to generate different modes of cinematic address more directly associated with social reality and its transformations.

This transformative process that increasingly confuses the traditional distinctions between documentary and fictional modes of filmmaking (and their respective potential social effectiveness) is a central characteristic of the New Latin American Cinema. Within the universe of a given fiction, a historical/real/documentary text is persistently transformed semantically and/or stylistically. Although the terms of the transformation vary widely, this kind of operation transforms texts into palimpsests and reinscribes their textual operations into different orders of social and textual discourse.

The textual operations that embody these representational and discursive challenges are what I have here chosen to call "parodic." Although

At the Limits of Documentary | 347

in the New Latin American Cinema this semantic, pragmatic, and stylistic confrontation is evident in films that are either primarily documentary or primarily fictional, here I shall focus on how the traditional, conventional, historical force of the documentary has been grafted onto the fictional. I will briefly analyze a number of ostensibly fictional films from different countries, each illustrating an increasingly more complex parodic hybridization of documentary and fictional voices. As each voice grapples for ascendancy, it transforms the other's operations while attempting to generate new modes of consciousness for the spectator. These parodic, contestational works simultaneously offer a critical revision of the principal modes of cinematic representation and establish the possibility for a different relationship among cinematic texts, subjects, and contexts: "a perspective on the present and the past which allows [both filmmakers and audiences] to speak TO a discourse from WITHIN it without being totally recuperated by it" (Hutcheon 1986–1987, 206). Documentary material is most obviously crossed with fiction in the New Latin American Cinema, first of all, to provide a context for fictive discourses. But it is also invoked to complicate the relationship between the fiction and its audience, to alter the significance of a film as well as the protocols required for its reception. The parodic relationship between fiction and documentary—a pervasive mixing and sharing of the codes of each mode—sets up a dialectical relationship between identification and distance: "like Brecht's *Verfremdungseffekt*, parody works to distance and, at the same time, to involve both artist and audience in a participatory hermeneutic activity" (Hutcheon 1986–1987, 206).

Memories of Underdevelopment: History as the Present

In *Memorias del subdesarrollo* (*Memories of Underdevelopment*, 1968), one of the most acclaimed works of the New Latin American Cinema, Tomás Gutiérrez Alea makes extensive use of documentary footage of historical and contemporary events to submerge the *angst* of the film's protagonist in a historical context.[4] The film makes use of archival documentary footage of historical events (like the Bay of Pigs invasion) as well as other forms of documentary material such as TV broadcasts, photographs, clips from fiction films, and filmed speeches by Castro. The documentary strategies of *Memories*, however, exceed the simple insertion of documentary material as proofs of authenticity or "realism." The structure of the film itself is predicated on the juxtaposition of the strategies of fictive discourses and the power of the filmic image as document. The relentless introspection of Sergio, the film's protagonist (a frustrated bourgeois intellectual who can neither leave the revolution nor participate fully within it), is constantly juxtaposed to "objective" versions of the world in which he lives. These documentary insertions into the fictive text do not merely serve to guarantee the objectivity of the film's discourse. Rather, in a parodic movement, they relativize the force of that discourse, of any particular discourse, as an indisputable "truth."

The film achieves this balance by inserting its principal character into the "documentary" mise-en-scène. From the beginning of the film, we are introduced to a world that seems "real" rather than fictional—that is, an environment that clearly exceeds the needs and drives of the plot. The dance hall scene that accompanies the credits is shot in an aggressively direct, handheld style associated with documentary. The scenes at the airport, where Sergio says goodbye to his wife and parents, and his ride back to the city on a bus function like slices of everyday Cuban life at the same time that they introduce the protagonist's distance from that life: the richness and authenticity of what we see is not perceived by Sergio himself. Other scenes function similarly, with Sergio serving as the subjective foil against which the documentary force of the mise-en-scène is deployed: at the swimming pool, along the streets of Havana, the view from his telescope, in the Hemingway house. As Enrique Fernández has argued, Sergio functions both as the protagonist of the drama and as the spectator of the transitions and events of a certain period of Cuban history (Fernández 1980, 52-55). And it is his transition from spectator to pseudo-participant—his failed seduction and transformation of Elena—that serves as the central conflict of the film. This transition is articulated as the distance between the fictiveness of the diegesis—Sergio's self-appointed role as a witness or spectator of the revolution—and its insertion into a historical universe that exceeds the boundaries of Sergio's acerbic and limited vision.

The longest explicitly documentary sequence, an elaborate reconstruction of the trial of the Bay of Pigs invaders, is motivated by Sergio's anger at his friend Pablo's assertion that he will assume a political stance once he gets to Miami. Narrated in voice-over by Sergio himself, this sequence analyzes the motivations of the invaders in the context of the aftermath of the events at Playa Girón. Archival footage of the invasion and the public trials as well as still photographs and newsreel footage from the Batista period are used to expand the historical horizon of the narrative as well as to point out the limits of Sergio's own perceptual horizon.

More complex uses of documentary strategies abound. The roundtable discussion on "Literature and Underdevelopment" that Sergio attends, for example, is a reconstruction of an event that actually took place in 1964. At that discussion, one of the participants is Edmundo Desnoes, the author of the novel *Memories of Underdevelopment*, who pontificates on the racial prejudice against Latin Americans in the United States, while a Black attendant silently fills water glasses in the background. During the discussion, the sequence is "fictionalized" through the filter of Sergio's subjective reaction to the events and individuals present (fig. 17.1). As Desnoes lights a cigar, Sergio's voice-over questions Desnoes's actions and his illusions about himself, despite his relatively important position in Cuba: "Eddie, outside [of Cuba] you would be nothing."

In yet another sequence where the documentary emerges next to and within the narrative, Sergio takes Elena to meet a friend at ICAIC. That friend is Tomás Gutiérrez Alea himself, who is introduced viewing a sequence of repeated clips from films censored by Batista officials. When Sergio asks Gutiérrez Alea what he intends to do with the clips, he answers that they will be part of a film he is working on that will have "a bit of everything." Sergio's doubts over whether or not such a film would be released are obviously unfounded, since the film we are watching is precisely the film Alea refers to.

Figure 17.1. Playing himself in the film he coscripted, writer Edmundo Desnoes (*left*) shares the dais with Argentine novelist David Viñas. *Memorias del subdesarrollo* (Tomás Gutiérrez Alea, 1968). Fair use.

By grafting the documentary onto the fictional, juxtaposing a personal/subjective point of view to a historical vision, *Memories of Underdevelopment* complicates the film's point of view to the point where the "story" and its protagonist/spectator within the film are clearly discernible from another position, that of the spectator *of* the film. We see through Sergio's eyes, but what we see also stands on its own, recorded by a camera that sees on its own and that answers Sergio's individual uncertainties with the certainty of the Cuban people's collective transition to socialism.

The Jackal of Nahueltoro: A Criminal Wild Child

More distant from the fictional than *Memories of Underdevelopment*, Miguel Littín's first feature-length film, *El Chacal de Nahueltoro* (*The Jackal of Nahueltoro*, 1969), is an elaborate reconstruction and analysis of a real crime that scandalized Chile in 1960. José del Carmen Valenzuela, called the Jackal of Nahueltoro, was an illiterate vagrant who murdered a woman and her five daughters. Condemned to death, he was educated and acculturated in prison before finally being executed by a firing squad. The film reconstructs the crime and the public attention that it elicited in order to disclose that both the crime and the criminal are the products of a corrupt society that invokes the bourgeois judicial apparatus against those who have been deliberately and completely marginalized from bourgeois society.

The Jackal exhibits a parodic form that directly challenges the relationship between documentary and fiction filmmaking. In fact, the film parodies the mechanisms of "reporting" or documenting by highlighting the dialectic between the (story)*telling* and *showing* functions of fictional narratives and documentaries in an explicitly dialogical fashion.[5] The ultimate crime exposed by the film is that José's first contact with a social order responsive to his physical and spiritual needs occurs inside prison walls. There he learns to tell a story, to compose a poem, to kick a ball, to fashion a guitar; yet he is executed at precisely that point where he is capable of recognizing his social responsibilities.

The Jackal of Nahueltoro begins with a series of statements that position the film (and the spectator) at the limits of the fictional. Statements of "fact" offer the journalistic and legal record of the case of the Jackal as the raison d'être of the film. They thus serve a function opposite to the disclaimers of the conventional fictional cinema that deny any relationship between the fictional work of a given film and similar characters or events in real life. Positioned as a second-order discourse imposed upon an existing discourse about the Jackal, the film begins its operations under the aura of the real, as a documentary reconstruction of prior efforts to document the tragedy—already, in Genette's terms a "hypertext."

The film's distance from the real Jackal and its position as a *commentary* rather than a *documentary* is reinforced throughout the first half by the relations established between the image and the soundtracks. The soundtrack is used as "the record," as the arbiter of different "truths." It is used to give voice to four different kinds of texts, four different interpretations of the Jackal's story: a female voice-over (actually the voice of Shenda Román, the actress who plays Rosa, the Chacal's victim) reading, in a cold and mechanical fashion, the legal record of the case; a news announcer who sensationalizes the search for José and, later, his petition for a pardon; the interviews conducted by a radio reporter in the second half of the film; and the voice of José himself, mostly serving as a voice-over narrator, but also in several brief synchronous conversations (fig. 17.2). None of these voices are colloquial or spontaneous; they are either guarded (the interviews), cold and formal (the legal record), sensationalized (the announcer), or distant (José's voiceover). Even in the conversations between José and the priest or between José and the reporter, language does not serve its usual communicative purposes, for José's halting entreaties ultimately receive no response. Words and sentences function as explicit representations rather than "slices of life" and do not participate in the film's own "representing" work. Spoken or read language thus serves as a record or testimony for the film rather than as a communication device for the characters or as a dramatic device for the film's fictional work.

That fictional work takes place primarily on the image track. The images accompanying the different voices that narrate the texts of the case embody the opposite characteristics of the spoken word. These images, often subjective point-of-view shots, are always impassioned, yet they are also challenged by the authenticity of the direct-cinema documentary style that is used to record them: wild handheld camera movements, awkward transitions, and an oscillating point-of-view structure.

In the first half of the film, conflict is generated by the juxtaposition of the "stories" told in voice-over and the present/past dichotomy of the visual track. The images of the film begin at a "present," the capture and interrogation of José, from which we are led by the soundtrack to José's past. The difference between José's voice-over text and the visualization of

Figure 17.2. The still uncomprehending criminal cornered by the "long arm" of the press and the police. *El Chacal de Nahueltoro* (Miguel Littín, 1969). Fair use.

his tale is parodied by his presentation as a prisoner under interrogation at the same place where the crimes were committed (in Nahueltoro, where a furious crowd screams for his blood in the background). These contrasts clearly serve to relativize the power of all of the discourses offered to the spectator: we are shown and we are told many things from several different perspectives. The scenes of José as a prisoner are brutally direct but reflect the point of view of an invisible participant in the spectacle of his arrest, capture, and interrogation. When he is being questioned by the judge, in contrast, the camera is placed directly between them and functions like a witness by dramatically panning back and forth between the two.

The images of José's arrest and interrogation and the flashback explorations of his life are excruciatingly direct and physical. In José's world, as a child and as an adult, words have little effect against harshness and misery. The elegant words of the rich landowner who refuses to help yet another "little beggar" and the proselytizing of the priest who wants him to take "the body of God" are contrasted to the silence of the officer who does try to offer some material help, as well as against the child's own silence and incomprehension. The boy's future—unending poverty, brutal unrewarded labor, society's scorn—is already present in those early biographical moments. Temporal expansion underscores the most prototypical actions—being picked up for vagrancy as a toddler, hoisting heavy sacks as an adolescent, drinking cheap liquor to the point of unconsciousness as an adult.

Exploiting the potential of the documentary style, the camera probes José's early life and the actions that lead to his crime. It investigates the spaces, refusing to privilege speaking voices and emphasizing the inappropriateness of the conventions of civilization—and the conventions of narration in the fiction cinema—for the lived experiences of someone like José. For example, in the sequence when José meets Rosa (the woman he will murder) the camera tries to remain between them: Rosa and José are always apart, in different off screen spaces. Every time Rosa addresses him, José refuses her gaze. Even his most conventional response to her—chopping wood in exchange for a glass of water—takes place in off screen space, far from the conventions of "civilized" representations.

In the second half, the tone of the film changes to coincide with José's immersion into language and culture under the auspices of the judicial/correctional apparatus. This shift is marked by a freeze-frame of his smiling face after learning, in the prison yard, what to do with a soccer ball. This is the first time we have seen him smile. We subsequently see him cleaned up, getting a haircut, learning how to read, being taught about patriotic moments in the history of Chile, participating in religious ceremonies, weaving baskets (fig. 17.3). Without the hyperactive handheld camera, sequence shots, and shifting past-present perspectives of the first half, this second half increasingly approaches a more conventional fictional representational style. The camera is for the most part static and invisible, simply recording what lies in front of it. José's relations to the individuals he meets in prison are explored through editing. The taming of José exhausts his—and the film's—techniques for resisting cultural and economic aggression, and the film begins to shift its focus. José himself, as portrayed by Nelson Villagra, loses his difference—the marginality that defined him—and becomes simply one more prisoner, in long shots indistinguishable from the others.

This difference is also indicated by a marked shift in the point of view of the film's discourse. The fictional drama abandons the perspective of José to follow the research undertaken by a mustachioed reporter (never identified by name within the diegesis) who records interviews with all those related to the case—the prison chaplain, the judge, the captain of the execution squad—in an effort to construct a vision of the judicial

Figure 17.3. In a paradox expressive of his extreme marginalization, José's only constructive socialization takes places behind bars. *El Chacal de Nahueltoro* (Miguel Littín, 1969). Fair use.

system that could have prevented the execution of José but chooses not to.

The Jackal of Nahueltoro depends upon this grafting of the documentary upon the fictional to unleash its analysis and critique of the Chilean judicial system and of a society that unfairly plays the games of civilization—and enforces its sanctions—against those without the resources to understand or comply with its rules. That it does this successfully does not mean, however, that the film is free from a certain cinematic Manicheanism that privileges the direct—the documentary—against the fictional, associating the former with liberation and the latter with the subjugation and depersonalization of underdevelopment and class society.

One Way or Another: Another Marginalism

Not unlike *The Jackal*, the subject of Sara Gómez's *De cierta manera* (*One Way or Another*, 1974–1977) is also marginalization—specifically, the patterns of cultural resistance to underdevelopment among the underclass. However, the context of this film is radically different. Within the Cuban Revolution, marginalization has ceased to be primarily an economic phenomenon, and *One Way or Another* challenges not only the material conditions of marginalization but also the subtler social mores and attitudes that sustain it. Specifically, the film focuses on how the legacy of marginalization is manifest in contemporary sexual relationships in Cuba.

Unlike *The Jackal*, *One Way or Another* is not interested in eliding the distance between documentary and fictive discourses. In fact, the entire film—especially its genesis—is grounded more in the documentary than in the fictional mode. This is not to say, however, that *One Way or Another* is not a fiction film. The subtitle, *About Real and Fictional People*, unites the fictional and the documentary. But the use of documentary and fictive discourses in the film underlines the differences between both "voices," while clearly demonstrating their conventionality as forms of representation.

In *One Way or Another*, a traditional expository documentary mode—complete with authoritarian voice-over—is set "beside and against" a realist fictional narrative. The narrative is a fairly standard romance. Mario, born in the Havana slum of Las Yaguas and still learning how to adjust to the changes brought about by the revolution, meets and falls in love with Yolanda, a young teacher from a bourgeois family assigned to work in a school in the new community of Miraflores, one of the five new neighborhoods built for the former residents of the Las Yaguas slum (fig. 17.4). Their relationship is fraught with the difficulties that arise from the

Figure 17.4. Mario (Mario Balmaseda) and Yolanda (Yolanda Cuellar) seldom see eye to eye in *De cierta manera* (Sara Gómez, 1974–1977). Fair use.

contradictions between standards of sexual relationships and behavior (like machismo) that are the legacy of marginalization and the material changes brought about by the revolution. Whereas the fictive discourse explores the domestic or interpersonal effects of these changes, the documentary is primarily used to provide a record of changes in the public/social sphere.

The purely documentary segments often rudely interrupt the progression of the classical narrative. Although the voice-over is generally sympathetic, its official and academic tone stands in sharp contrast to the colloquialism and vivacity of the characters' dialogue and their often troubled emotions. After the precredit (a highly charged workers' meeting) and credit sequences, a documentary segment offers concrete information about the elimination of slum areas and their reconstruction into model communities, while the voice-over discusses how defensive cultural patterns born of marginality persist even after the material conditions of marginalization have been attenuated This factual segment solidly positions the narrative romance (which will begin in the next sequence) in the context of a specific social contradiction rather than in a fictive imaginary one, thus disrupting the traditional pleasure that narrative affords us.

Similarly, while Mario and Yolanda exchange life stories early in their relationship, their conversation is interrupted by a minidocumentary—complete with titles and voice-over narration—on the Abacuá secret society.[6] Initiated by Mario's declaration that he once wanted to join the Abacuá, this marked documentary interruption of the diegesis again distances us from the fiction and prevents our simple identification with its characters even though the narrative thread is later resumed (Kaplan 1983, 189–94; Kuhn 1982, 162–67). In total, the film has five explicit documentary narrative interruptions of this kind that serve essentially as distancing devices and as tools for contextualizing markers of social contradiction.

The documentary potential of the cinematic image is also clearly invoked as a parodic intertext for the space where narrative actions are developed. Unlike the standard fiction film, where locations are subordinated to narrative drives, in *One Way or Another* the narrative space becomes a social space where the fictional drives are challenged by social forces. Mario's factory (fig. 17.5), Yolanda's school, the streets, homes, and other settings for the action of the film are used to develop the fictional romance, but they also exert very specific pressures on the fictional structures. As Michael Chanan points out in his perceptive analysis, each "real" location inhabited by "real" people corresponds to a specific aspect of each of the two principal characters' social existence and determines

At the Limits of Documentary | 357

Figure 17.5. Unscripted contention: factory workers debate the ethics of Mario's actions in the conclusion of *De cierta manera* (Sara Gómez, 1974–1977). Fair use.

specific forms of behavior. These physical/social spaces, almost "characters" in their own right, impinge forcefully on the development of the fictional romance (Chanan 1985, 284–93).

Documentary discourses are also used in a less explicit fashion to provide evidence and to support specific narrative dilemmas. In these segments, the documentary and the fictional become almost indistinguishable because the characters of the narrative are given roles in the documentary (or vice versa). This fictional/documentary mixed mode is most often used in relation to Yolanda, while the "full" documentary treatment is invoked primarily in relation to Mario.[7] Thus Yolanda's problems at her school—adjusting to the conditions and needs of less privileged families—are presented through images that are not clearly identified as either documentary or fictional. When she discusses her exasperation with a coworker, for example, we also are shown images of the dire family environment of one of her students. But the status of these images is never clearly identified. Are they documentary or fictional? Later, after we meet the subject of these images, the mother of the delinquent Lázaro, we realize that they are actually both documentary—insofar as the character is real and not played by an actress—as well as an important part of the diegesis of the film. Yolanda is also privileged as the only "character" who leaves the diegesis to address us directly. The first instance of Yolanda's direct address occurs during the first (postcredits) documentary sequence, before we know who she is. Later in the film, after an unpleasant double date, Yolanda is again presented in direct aural and visual address expressing her concerns about the future of her female students.

Although this identification of Yolanda with an undifferentiated documentary/fictional mode of discourse might seem to privilege her role as a social actor, in fact, it segregates Yolanda and her voice into a problematic undefined realm. Neither "real" like Lázaro's mother nor "fictionalized" like Mario, Yolanda is unanchored, both in terms of the public sphere represented through the documentary and in terms of the film's fictional operations. Her problems and her specificity as a middle-class woman are not privileged by documentary explorations, while her fictional role as the difficult, "upper-class," professional girlfriend is undercut by her ability to address us directly through the codes of the documentary.

One Way or Another seems partly to assume the same patriarchal stance that it criticizes by approaching only the male characters of the film with a clearly established dialectical opposition between the documentary/real and the narrative/fictive. The pervasive patriarchal bias that the film analyzes also plays a part in the film's own complex hypertextual documentary and fictional operations.

At the Boundaries of Fiction and Documentary: Historical Reconstruction and the Ukamau Group

More than any other individual or collective within the New Latin American Cinema, Jorge Sanjinés and the Ukamau collective of Bolivia have exploited the margin between documentary and fictional discourses as the most productive way to establish a revolutionary popular cinema—in this instance, for the Andean people. Their films challenge the boundaries of the fictional and the documentary and function as "limit" cases in the search for an authentic, popular, and effective Latin American cinematic practice.

In the dialectical evolution of the work of Sanjinés and Ukamau we can trace the increasing hybridization of the fictional, the documentary, and the historical in their efforts to locate, define, and communicate with their films' target audience. The development of the Ukamau collective's

At the Limits of Documentary | 359

work, from their first film *Ukamau* (1966) to *Get Out of Here!* (*Llosky Kaymanta*, 1977), demonstrates not only the theoretical and practical negotiations undertaken by the group, but also the depth and consistency of their efforts to develop a mode of cinematic discourse—a paradoxical synthesis of fiction and document—that would be true to their subjects, that would be poetic, communicative, critical, and, above all, revolutionary.

This process of transformation began during the production of *Ukamau*, a fictional story exploring the conflict between indigenous and creole (Westernized) cultures in Bolivia. The film was originally conceived as a denunciation of the social and economic exploitation of the Indigenous by the (creole) mestizos. But Sanjinés and his group realized that denunciation was not sufficient, and that

> it was naïve to denounce to the people what they suffered daily. Besides, to whom was that denunciation directed? To those that exercised the oppression? If the film was directed to the people, we had to do more than denounce; we had to pressure the dynamic potential of the people, to begin a call to arms, to tempt the people to pick up the stone that Mayta wields in the last scene [of *Ukamau*]. (Sanjinés 1968, 29–30)[8]

This realization led the collective to seek out ways to make their cinema an agent of change without resorting to the explicitly propagandistic techniques of agitprop documentary.

Their next film *Yawar Mallku* (*Blood of the Condor*, 1969), also fiction based on historical fact, was purported to expose the "principal enemy" they had begun to denounce in *Ukamau*—that is, the penetration of foreign capitalism. Of all the New Latin American Cinema films, *Blood of the Condor* had the most concrete and verifiable sociopolitical impact. The film's denunciation of the population control activities of the US "Progress Corps" (a thin disguise for the Peace Corps) gave rise to a popular campaign that eventually resulted in the Bolivian government's expulsion of the Peace Corps (Sanjinés 1979a, 13–33).

But their experiences making *Blood of the Condor* in an indigenous community and the results of their distribution experiments among the Indigenous convinced the Ukamau group that they had to go further in their efforts to make a popular yet analytical Bolivian cinema that did not fall into either the conventions of fictional or documentary filmmaking.[9] Both *Ukamau* and *Blood of the Condor* were structured to follow the traditional dramatic patterns of fictional narratives. In *Blood of the Condor*, for example, a flashback-within-flashback structure depicts the struggle of a citified Indigenous to buy blood for his dying brother from the Altiplano while simultaneously revealing why the brother was wounded in the first place. He was shot by the police and left to die because he had participated in the castration of the local "Progress Corps" representatives who had sterilized his wife and many other village women without their knowledge. The flashbacks provide greater conventional dramatic suspense, but they also render the film's organization almost unintelligible to Andean villagers whose culture does not make use of them. Similarly, the film's use of close-ups and psychological motivation distanced it from the perceptual, narrative, and social traditions of the indigenous population, reducing its local verisimilitude.[10] As Sanjinés has explained,

> It was not enough that the film was spoken in Quechua, that all the actors were peasants, and that it took their side. . . . It was not that they could not understand what was being said, it was rather a formal conflict at the level of the medium itself which did not correspond to the internal rhythms of our people or their profound conception of reality. (1979b, 31)

After these experiences, Ukamau resolved to reject the conventions of fiction filmmaking:

> Since ours was a cinema that wanted to develop parallel to historic evolution, but that also sought to influence the historical process and to extract its constitutive elements, it could no longer be limited to conventional forms and structures. Its very contents demanded a formal correspondence that would break with molds and traditions because it aspired to results far beyond applause and satisfaction. . . . If it was essential to work with reality and the truth, manipulating live history, everyday history, it was for the same reason indispensable to find forms which would not detract or ideologically betray the contents, as had occurred with *Blood of the Condor*, which used fictional forms to portray historical facts and was unable to document its own truth because of its formal limitations. (1979a, 7)

Their search for a different cinematic language led the Ukamau collective to develop a form of filmmaking as self-conscious historiography, as the inscription of a history in the present. The method of historical reconstruction they developed in films like *Los caminos de la muerte* (The Roads of Death, never completed) and *El coraje del pueblo* (The Courage of the People, 1971) focuses on past events as remembered and witnessed by those who actually lived them.[11] These historical witnesses themselves become protagonists of and active contributors to the films, thus eliminating professional actors, approximating a more collective popular participation, and giving the film "an irrefutable documentary touch" (Sanjinés 1979a, 7).

In *El coraje del pueblo* that documentary "touch" is vividly apparent as a process of self-conscious history-in-the-making. It serves as a constant reminder that we are watching a historical reconstruction that is also an instance of a writing/filming of history itself. The film never completely eschews the fictional; rather, it reinscribes the fictional in terms of the historical and changes the terms of its operation accordingly. Intermingling fictional and documentary modes, *El coraje del pueblo* redistributes the tyrannical weight of respective conventions and attempts a dialogical reappropriation of a specific moment in the history of the Bolivian class struggle.

El coraje del pueblo is a reconstruction of the massacre of miners that took place at the Siglo XX (Twentieth Century) mine on June 24, 1967, the night of the feast of Saint John. Claiming that the miners were directly supporting the guerrilla activities of Che Guevara in the south, the government sent its troops, with orders to kill on sight, into the mining towns while the celebrations were in full swing. Before dawn, hundreds of men, women, and children lay dead in the streets of Siglo XX. Rather than produce a fictional recreation of this event (in the style of *Blood of the Condor*), Ukamau obtained the active cooperation of miners and families who had survived the attack and of soldiers who had participated to reconstruct the events of that night as they were remembered.

Thus *El coraje* functions both as a historical reconstruction of a crucial event in the history of the Bolivian class struggle and as a documentary of one community's collective remembering and recreation of that event. In Sanjinés's assessment, the film is an example of horizontal rather than vertical cinematic practice, of filmmaking with the practical and creative collaboration of the people, rather than a cinema for the people coming, a priori, from outside. In a paradoxical sense, the filmmakers became a part of this collective phenomenon of the Siglo XX community as its instrument of expression, "allowing the community to talk about itself" through them (1979b, 31).

El coraje del pueblo combines documentary and fictional modes in its search for a collective voice. The careful orchestration and sequencing of the material belies a creative intentionality that tries to efface itself in favor of the collectivity. However, the film's double voice constantly calls attention to both "speaking" and "viewing" subject positions within the text. From its very beginning, the film's status as a document and as a recreation is clarified not only through titles that explain its relationship to history, but also through an epic preamble to the events of Saint John's Night that eventually locates the narrative retelling in the present and marks the story itself as past and as an integral part of an even longer historical process.

The film begins with a long prelude in which we see "the people"—identified by a title as the citizens of the town of Catavi in 1942—marching, banners waving, across barren hills and then massacred in cold blood by a troop of soldiers. This sequence is carefully edited, making much use of dynamic graphic principles reminiscent of Eisenstein's montage of attractions. The long cross-cutting between the people walking down a hill and across a plain while the soldiers on a hilltop wait for them to get within firing range builds suspense to an emotional crescendo that finally climaxes, after the shooting is over, in slow panoramic shots of both the despair of the survivors and that of the soldiers—largely of the same poor, indigenous stock as their victims—who had to obey orders. The faces and expressions of the real enemy—heads of government and others allied with the forces of imperialism in Bolivia—are exposed in the next sequence. After an explanatory title that describes what happened at Catavi (four hundred dead, over one thousand wounded), a series of titles and photographs identify those responsible: mine owners, Bolivia's president and prime minister, and the head of the army. The Catavi sequence is followed by a classic documentary montage of still images and titles that trace the history of governmental brutality against the Bolivian miners by detailing other massacres (Potosí in 1947, Siglo XX in 1949, Villa Victoria in 1950, Sora-Sora in 1964, the general military occupation of the mining zones in 1965, the Llallagua massacre in 1965) and by identifying those responsible for the multitude of dead and wounded.

Having outlined a history of brutality against miners up to 1965, the film abruptly changes register. The throbbing percussion music of the montage-documentary-history sequence stops and we are given a long shot of a silent man who sits immobile in a wheelchair by a poor *rancho*, a dog barking somewhere in the distance. This is the present time of the filming, of the act of inscription of *this* history, and the only place where the omniscient voice of an unidentified narrator can exercise its authority. As the camera slowly tracks in, breaking down the distance between the cold facts of history and the physical presence of the historical actor captured by its lens, the voice-over identifies him as Saturnino Condori, a crippled survivor of "the last massacre, the massacre of the night of Saint John, June 24, 1967." On a close-up of Saturnino in direct address, the voice-over takes us inside Siglo XX itself, identifying it as the *escenario* (the setting, the stage) of the worst labor massacre of Bolivia's history. Siglo XX is thus identified both as a historical site and as the site of the fiction (that is, the mise-en-scène of the reconstruction itself). The voice-over continues, first briefly summarizing the importance of mining for the Bolivian economy and of the conditions of life of the Bolivian miner, then identifying several individuals, whom we see briefly on the screen in medium or long shots, as the survivors of the Saint John's Night massacre. Over an extreme long shot of the town, the voice-over assumes its greatest distance: "This is the chronicle of the days before the massacre. We have chosen these men and women for their human value and courage. They weren't heroes, but we believe that their experiences will permit a greater understanding of the people they represent who were mercilessly fired upon."

The narrator then cedes the narration to five historical witnesses who identify themselves (or are named through a title) and address us directly from the same present as the narrator in order to tell us about themselves. The accompanying images detail the individuals' activities in the political actions that led to the massacre: a hunger strike by the women of Siglo XX; the workers' protest against the terrorism of the police and the company guards, and the subsequent beatings and torture inflicted upon their leader; the slowly growing affiliation between the miners and the guerrilla movement led by Che Guevara, the military conscription of miners, the role of university students in setting up an alliance with the guerrillas and the miners.

After displacing an individual focus through these multiple narrators, the film decenters its narration even further by abandoning the perspective of any one individual and attempting to assume the stance of the community itself. The events of Saint John's Night, beginning with the daylight festivities that extended long after dark with traditional bonfires, music, drinking, and dancing, are reconstructed from an omniscient perspective. But because there is no omniscient narrator to direct the discourse, the images serve to collectivize the endeavor, to force the spectator to construct the story as it is being reconstructed from the perspective of the individuals and events featured in various shots. In the darkness, mysterious shapes begin to move. Eventually, as the images become clearer, we see that it is the army, stealthily approaching and preparing to attack. The suspense created by this slow movement, echoing that produced in the first sequence of the encounter between the people of Catavi and the army, is paradoxical. The audience knows that there will be an attack—we have been told so several times by the voice-over narrators. Nevertheless, waiting for the attack becomes suspenseful because of the ambiguity of the images themselves. After a long day of festivities and much drinking, the town is dark and sleepy, and the images, as if from the residents' perspective, are unclear, confusing, dislocated. When the attack begins, events become more and more confused as men and women are dragged from their beds to face firing squads and as isolated pockets of resistance (the emergency siren, the miners' radio station, some armed struggle) emerge throughout the town, only to be quickly vanquished by the ever-growing number of soldiers.

Finally, it is dawn; the massacre is over and all that is left are the dead, the transport by ambulance of the wounded, the crying of the mourners, and the rounding up of prisoners. Four miners who managed to elude the soldiers make their way to a hill and, in a final act of defiance, throw a stick of dynamite into a group of soldiers and prisoners. An air patrol shoots one of them, but the other three manage to escape with their lives. Over shots of the miners' cemetery, the omniscient voice returns the reconstruction to the present by reading a list of some of the names of the dead and by reminding us of the fate of the many orphans and survivors who were "relocated" by the government in an effort to erase the history of the massacre. The film itself, a collective negation of that official erasure and a reinscription of the massacre in a historical context, reminds the spectator of the names of those who ordered the massacre by a quick reiterative montage and ends with a triumphant image of "the people" marching down a hill and across a mesa. Those same images led the people into the range of the army's rifles in the first sequence of the film, but now, the film, by its own articulation, proclaims a critical difference and ends in a dramatic freeze-frame of the people, together, in long shot against the plain.

Although Ukamau's next film, *El enemigo principal* (The Principal Enemy, 1974), incorporates another level of mediation in its historical recreation and representation through the physical presence of an indigenous narrator (*amauta*), *El coraje del pueblo* remains their most successful attempt to *transform* the conventions and effects of the cinema through the formal contrast and synthesis of "opposite" modes of cinematic representation.[12]

Conclusion

The rewriting of people's history through historical fictions, as we have seen in the development of the collective practices of Ukamau and in the work of other filmmakers, has been a central concern of the New Latin American Cinema. Besides adopting and transforming documentary filmmaking strategies, the filmmakers of the New Latin American Cinema have also sought to transform the forms and strategies of fictional filmmaking itself in their efforts to use history and historical fictions to expose and materialize the often-repressed stories of the continent's struggle for liberation. Their search for a popular yet materialist cinematic discourse has led to the extension of the options available for historical narrative in film. By accepting the historical—self-consciously identified as what has been or could be documented—as determining the basic conventions beside and against which to deploy the fictional, the New Latin American Cinema has attempted to establish its own specificity as a transformative practice. Taking on the most central representational given of the cinema—its relationship to the "real" as encoded by documentary and fictional modes—the New Latin American Cinema uses parody to activate viewers and to challenge, transform, and renew with critical distance the social function of the cinema in Latin America. In fact, one may even argue that the New Latin American Cinema is essentially parodic, a cinema that consciously sets itself beside and against the dominant cinema, in counterpoint: a *counter* cinema of underdevelopment.

18

A Poetics of the Trace (2014)

This essay examines the turn toward "subjective" documentaries in Latin American filmmaking in the 2000s, by analyzing three cases: Santiago (Brazil, João Moreira Salles, 2007), Jogo de Cena *(Brazil, Eduardo Coutinho, 2007), and* Alamar *(Mexico, Pedro González Rubio, 2009) that exhibit a "complicated poetics of the trace through their exploration of the dialectics among image, history, performance, and time and how this practice shifts the ground of documentary."*

Emblazoned across the top of his personal website, Chilean documentary filmmaker Patricio Guzmán welcomes visitors with the statement: "Un país sin cine documental es como una familia sin álbum de fotografías" (A country without documentaries is like a family without a photo album), which succinctly articulates the work of the documentary in contemporary Latin America. Without questioning the documentary mission, Guzmán also asserts its affective charge: like a photo album, the documentary is a medium of history but also, in a more complicated fashion, a medium of memory, emotion, and affect. Like the photo album, the documentary holds (or pretends to hold on to) an indexical charge—the photographic trace that Bazin, Barthes, Sontag, and so many others have eloquently written about—while emotionally working on very different and much more complex levels. The documentary—photo album—is also a palimpsest through which the personal and public interface, the traces of which serve to haunt our identities and politics in the present.

In 1990, Julianne Burton and the other contributors to the collection *The Social Documentary in Latin America* persuasively argued that the documentary in Latin America was essentially a practice aligned with the political and sociocultural struggles of the continent, that is to say, a practice firmly planted in and aligned with the public sphere. Jean-Claude Bernardet (1985) astutely dubbed this documentary work sociological, highlighting a focus on collective issues even when individuals and/or communities were at the forefront. By the late 1960s and 1970s, as the cinema was theorized as an instrument for Latin American *concientización* (consciousness-raising) and transformation, documentary "realism" became intertwined with increasingly more complex fictional representational strategies in the effort to generate a different mode of cinematic address more directly associated with social change and ongoing revolutionary processes.[1] In this context, filmmakers like Fernando Solanas, Patricio Guzmán, and Santiago Álvarez remained committed to a political agenda—and the production of specific meanings/messages—while engaging that agenda through increasingly more complex personal documentary poetics.

Through the late 1970s and 1980s (and in the context of failed revolutions and military dictatorships), the Latin American documentary began to lose its attachment to explanatory/demonstrative models and to develop other discursive modalities increasingly more reflexive and subjective. In this respect, Eduardo Coutinho's *Cabra Marcado para Morrer* (Twenty Years After, 1984) is a "hinge" film not only for Brazilian documentary cinema but also for documentary filmmaking in the continent. Returning to the site and subjects of a "sociological" documentary project he had been forced to shelve for twenty years because of the military dictatorship, Coutinho deconstructed the traditional model of the social documentary of the 1960s and opened up important new directions. When the widow of the slain peasant leader appears on camera to retake her real name (Elizabeth Teixeira) among her friends and family, we witness her transformation and reinvention through the excavation of the fragments of her life in clandestinity and her interactions with the filmmaker and crew. This, in a nutshell, will become the nexus of the affectivity articulated by the Latin American documentary of the twenty-first century.[2]

As we look at contemporary documentary production throughout the continent, it is abundantly clear that there remain areas and sites where the documentary continues to be taken up in a direct relationship with specific sociopolitical struggles (the *cine piquetero* and Fernando Solanas's ongoing oeuvre in Argentina, for example). As Michael Chanan argues in *The Politics of Documentary*, it would seem that documentary "has politics in its genes" (2008, 16). Yet, scanning the documentary work of

A Poetics of the Trace | 369

Latin American filmmakers over the past two decades suggests that in addition to its political inflections, the documentary has begun to adopt and to intensify an appeal to the subjective as a fertile realm of exploration and social intervention. Beyond self-reflexivity, the directorial self appears in contemporary documentaries throughout the region in a complicated relationship to the subject(s), as an integral part of what we may call the affective realm of the documentary that exceeds and reasserts the indexical status of nonfiction footage.

In this chapter I outline this shift to the personal, local, and domestic in Latin American documentary practice, with a specific focus on issues of subjectivity, affect, emotion, and indeterminacy. Looking at *Santiago* (Brazil, 2007) by João Moreira Salles, *Jogo de Cena* (Playing, Brazil, 2007) by Eduardo Coutinho, and *Alamar* (Mexico, 2009) by Pedro González-Rubio, this chapter analyzes how these films produce a complicated poetics of the trace through their exploration of the dialectics among image, history, performance, and time and how this practice shifts the ground of documentary spectatorship from "knowledge" or "consciousness" to emotion and affect. In this analysis, the term "trace" stands in for the testimonial function and historical value of the film image as an archive of memory rather than for the materiality of the image imprint.[3] It does not refer to the truth status of the source material per se but to the representation and production of symbolic and affective experiences. Thus I will outline how these films use different discursive modalities—ranging from the subjective (a use of the first person in which the film "speaks, from the point of view of a filmmaker who acknowledges his subjectivity) to "conversations" and self-erasure—to question the very possibility of any "documentary" certainty outside of the affective. I will also unravel how this affective realm is textually set in motion, emphasizing the by now well-known distinction between affect and emotion articulated by Brian Massumi (1996): affect is prior to emotions, an embodied intensity, while emotions are subjective contents, qualified intensities. Documentary affect is, after all, less about how texts are read by spectators than about the multiple relationalities and lines of connectivity established among them.

Santiago: Othering the Self and Exposing the Process

The premise of *Santiago* is deceptively simple. Not unlike what happened with *Cabra Marcado para Morrer*, filmmaker João Moreira Salles returns to an unfinished documentary project about thirteen years later. Yet the reasons for the shelving of the original project and the outcome of the return could not be more different or more indicative of the profound transformation of the documentary in Brazil since 1984.

In 1992 João Moreira Salles had already directed two documentaries (*America* in 1989 had been particularly well received)[4] and ran a production house, VideoFilmes, with his brother, filmmaker Walter Salles. Because of the precipitous decline of support for film production in the early years of the Collor presidency, he was also working in advertising.[5] Using leftover film stock from a commercial shoot, he gathered a small crew and decided to make a documentary about Santiago Badariotti Merlo, an Argentine who had been his family's butler for over thirty years at their mansion in the chic Gávea neighborhood and who was now retired and living in a small apartment in Leblon. The five-day shoot generated about nine hours of material that Moreira Salles later abandoned in the editing process:

> I tried to edit it but I couldn't do it. The film was to be all about Santiago as an exotic character . . . a character that already existed before being filmed, I mean, he existed in my head more than anything. I just wasn't prepared to take in whatever Santiago had to tell me. I had preconceived ideas. (2011)

Thirteen, fourteen years later the material called out to him again and the final film produces a complex commentary on the original footage and the filmmaker's intentions and how the ethics of documentary filmmaking have changed, but also, more importantly, on the work of memory, the radical instability of the documentary, and the importance of affect for contemporary practice.

Santiago begins with three hauntingly beautiful images that echo each other: the camera approaches a framed photograph on a table of the outside of a house, then a photo of a room with an empty bed, and finally a third photo of a chair in an otherwise empty veranda. During this third shot, the voice-over narration that will guide, comment, and question throughout the rest of the film begins: "Thirteen years ago, when I filmed these images, I thought the film would begin like this . . ." Immediately establishing the multiple temporal and historical displacements that the film will have to navigate, this voice-over introduces the "I" and situates memory, or rather, the remembered and forgotten, as the central axis of the film, with the added layering of the fact that the voice we hear is not the filmmaker's but that of his older brother Fernando. The 1992 project, the unfinished documentary about the family butler, will now become multiple narratives: there is still the story of the character Santiago, but there's also a sharing of family histories, an essay on how (not) to make documentaries and a heartfelt homage to the person Santiago, who passed away a few years after the filming. And the film also gains the telling subtitle, "Uma reflexão sobre o material bruto" (A reflection about the raw material). The film operates at three levels: what would have been the documentary that Moreira Salles never finished in 1992 (evidenced by its script, editing storyboards, and one short edited sequence), the character of Santiago, and the footage that never would have been included in the 1992 film, the excess that would have been edited out and that now reveals the most.

The photographs of the empty house, immediately revisited as filmed sequences with graceful and measured camera movements, also begin the film with an important void, an emptiness and attendant melancholia that the filmmaker will struggle to fill. The Gávea mansion is, in Pierre Nora's terms, a *lieux de mémoire*, a site of memory, but an imperfect one, pointing to emptiness rather than a plenitude of symbolic meaning for the "I" of the film. The house remains, but it has lost its history (and its place in History). *Santiago* is an effort to decipher the traces of that lost world (the filmmaker's childhood, the haute bourgeoisie of the Brazilian developmentalist boom of the 1950s, the splendor of Rio de Janeiro as Brazil's capital) and the character Santiago, with his prodigious memory that seems to frighten the filmmaker ("Não te espanta?" [Doesn't it frighten you?], he asks Santiago several times over), and who is the key to that process.

The former butler of the Moreira Salles family is indeed a character. Santiago can discourse with great erudition about the arts in several languages and has translated his passion for the nobility and aristocracy into the lifelong task of documenting it: thirty thousand pages of transcriptions held together with red ribbons imported from Paris. The film presents him in his home—a tiny apartment replete with bric-a-brac and papers—where he is tightly, obsessively framed and constrained by the film and the filmmaker. Whether photographed in the back of his kitchen, his body partially blocked by a typewriter and a doorknob in the foreground; in his bedroom, next to his carefully wrapped typescripts and the edge of an alarm clock in the foreground of the image; or, most remarkably, sitting on the edge of his tub with the doorway and sink in the foreground, Santiago is visually and verbally imprisoned. The filmmaker yells out commands from off screen, prods him to speak, to repeat, to go faster, to not look at the camera, relentlessly and almost cruelly. Never filmed in close-up, he is distant and distanced; blocked by objects, his body always cut off at the knees (fig. 18.1). The static framing—especially when compared to the camera movements in the shots of the house—stresses the length of the moment, the sense of time itself passing, and underlines Santiago's awkwardness

As Moreira Salles comments toward the end of the film, Santiago's discomfort, he realizes, was due to the fact that "he wasn't only a character and I wasn't only a documentary filmmaker. During the five days of filming I never stopped being the son of the owner of the house and he never stopped being the butler." With a singular self-awareness, Moreira Salles discloses, comments upon, and lets us see his own distance from Santiago and how he imposed his own vision and failed to capture perhaps what was most important.

Yet, despite these constraints, in those off moments that would have ended up on the cutting room floor of the original film, we see the edges of a certain subaltern picaresque that evidences Santiago's own agency and self-recognition. As Moreira Salles comments, citing Werner Herzog, what is most interesting of a take is "what occurs gratuitously before and after the action." For example, when asked to talk about the fabulous parties that were held at the Gávea house, Santiago manages to slip in a veiled critique. Describing a party for two hundred with twenty-five waiters, he adds: "and I had to deal with all that." Throughout the film Santiago obediently repeats scenes over and over, but he never lets the camera forget that he is performing. Whenever he finishes a scene, he makes faces at the camera, waves his hands around, and even exclaims in exasperation, "C'est tout!" These are all moments in which Santiago's performativity punctures

Figure 18.1. The static, distant framing in *Santiago* (2007). Fair use.

the deep melancholia of the "I" that comments upon the image, almost making us smile. At the end of the film (which coincides with the end of the filming), he even goes so far as to throw his cane to the ground in a decidedly diva-like fashion. Furthermore, there is one crucial scene in which we can glimpse and revel in the exuberance of Santiago. Filmed in one take and, at Santiago's insistence, focusing only on his hands, the almost five-minute-long sequence of Santiago "exercising" his hands, as if they were ballerinas, is not only of singular visual beauty but paradoxically tells us more about the spirit of Santiago than any close-up of his face could ever convey (fig. 18.2). The ballet of Santiago's hands is an affect machine emblematic of the overall work of the film, simultaneously adrift from meaning-making and sensuously evocative, painfully beautiful, and profoundly sad. It is not only what the hands "do" but what the camera, the film, does with them: with no camera movement, as in most images of Santiago, and no editing, this sequence shot generates a different relationship between temporality and affect and a climactic emotional *durée*.

Beyond the filmmaker's somewhat confessional self-reflexivity, the film also highlights Santiago's thirty-thousand-page accounting of the world's nobility (which in 1992 had not been of any interest whatsoever to the filmmaker), as if looking for evidence that the original footage failed to capture some essential trait or information. Filming fragments of pages, random phrases, the most "sonorous" names of the catalog, Moreira Salles excavates Santiago's collection, remembering Santiago's favorites, finding fragments of poetry and random annotations. Like Santiago, who explains the catalog as his effort to keep these people alive by speaking about them and speaking to them—"The past passes. Things go past. Things are lost"—Moreira Salles struggles to keep Santiago and, through him and his things, his own memories, alive. Like Santiago's hands, the manuscript's pages captured in close-ups acquire an enchanting life of their own: typed words on their way to becoming affective relations.

Figure 18.2. Santiago exercising his hands (*Santiago*, 2007). Fair use.

Toward the end of the film, Moreira Salles introduces a moving segment of audio material. After he turns off the camera, Santiago continues speaking: "Listen, Joãozinho, Joãozinho, there is a short sonnet, very charming . . . I am part of a group of cursed beings . . ." and is interrupted by Moreira Salles who says, "No, that's not needed. We are not going in that direction." Moreira Salles comments that the one time that Santiago tried to tell him something personal, he didn't turn the camera on. Yet, the missed opportunity is even greater, for clearly what Santiago wanted to bring to the fore was his own sexuality, which will remain, like the empty house and the irrecoverable plenitude of the past, a void, visible in the traces and excess of his performances for a camera that, in 1992, did not see.

The self-critique and assessment of a mature documentary filmmaker surveying an earlier project that he now recognizes as flawed lends *Santiago* a melancholic air. Yet that melancholy runs deeper and encompasses the recognition that perhaps Santiago, the person maybe "embalmed" by the film, is the register through which Moreira Salles can trace and begin to unravel the threads of his own life. That the dynasty of the Moreira Salles family is not mentioned as part of the grand catalog hoarded by Santiago is perhaps Santiago's ultimate trump card.

Jogo de Cena: A Manual for Emotion

Few documentary filmmakers have managed to develop a body of work that embodies a consistent ethic, aesthetic, and methodology and that simultaneously establishes a personal realignment of the traditions of the genre. Eduardo Coutinho is one of them. At eighty-plus years of age, Coutinho has become one of the best-known documentary filmmakers in Brazil and, perhaps, in Latin America. His own biography, traversing from militancy as a student, TV-Globo journalism in the 1970s, and absolute insecurity as an independent documentarian in the difficult late 1980s and 1990s to international recognition as a master of the documentary is perhaps worthy of its own documentary treatment.

Already in *Cabra Marcado para Morrer*, his first feature film, Coutinho began to establish the parameters that would define his documentary practice: the ability to reveal the political dimensions of personal lives, a unique way of making evident the universal characteristics of particular stories, and the sensibility to see, predict, and hear the exceptional in the apparently banal. *Cabra* also perfected the filmmaker as character—not only is Coutinho visible onscreen but his presence is as necessary for the historical salvage operation of the film as that of the other participants. In his subsequent documentaries, Coutinho would develop and explore the limits of what he calls his *dispositivo*—the framework of (self-imposed) constraints and devices that delimit his documentary practice in any one project. In *Santa Marta: Duas Semanas no Morro* (1987), for example, he explored the possibilities of a spatially defined *dispositivo* (the favela Santa Marta above Botafogo), began using video (which allowed him to film for two hours without interruptions), and limited the filming to two weeks. He also incorporated into the filmmaking team individuals with prior research experience of the people/location. In *Boca do Lixo* (Scavengers, 1993), again there is a spatial delimitation—a garbage dump in the suburbs of Rio—that defines the film's subjects: the people who live "working" the trash for food and goods to sell. Then he introduces a respect for chronology—the images of the film appear in the order in which they were shot—and an investment in his "characters" or *personagens*: among the many people he filmed, five become characters with whom he has extensive conversations.[6] With *Santo Forte* in 1999, Coutinho began to focus on what Consuelo Lins has dubbed "the art of filming words,"[7] films in which his subjects, in conversation, become characters and relay their stories. *Edifício Master* (Master, a Building in Copacabana, 2002) takes this minimalist aesthetic even further: Coutinho finds his "characters" in the delimited space of an apartment building in the famous neighborhood in Rio de Janeiro. Finally, in *Jogo de Cena*, he unveils the artifice of the conversation as the central axis of the documentary and, thus, of his own practice.

Jogo de Cena begins with the image of a newspaper ad announcing a casting call for women who "have stories to tell" and want to participate in a documentary film (fig. 18.3). Already, that the ad calls for "casting" a documentary is, of course, surprising, but the image itself is also disturbing because of its lack of context. Although we would like to believe that this is indeed a photograph of the ad that was used to cast the film, it is unsettling, abstracted from the reality of a real newspaper/magazine page. Why is there nothing to the right and left of the ad? What are the fragments of ads below and above it and why are they floating? It looks like a legitimate ad, but is it? The image simply suggests an ad, convincing the casual viewer of its veracity, yet it is already a palimpsest of the indeterminacy that will be the guiding thread of the film.

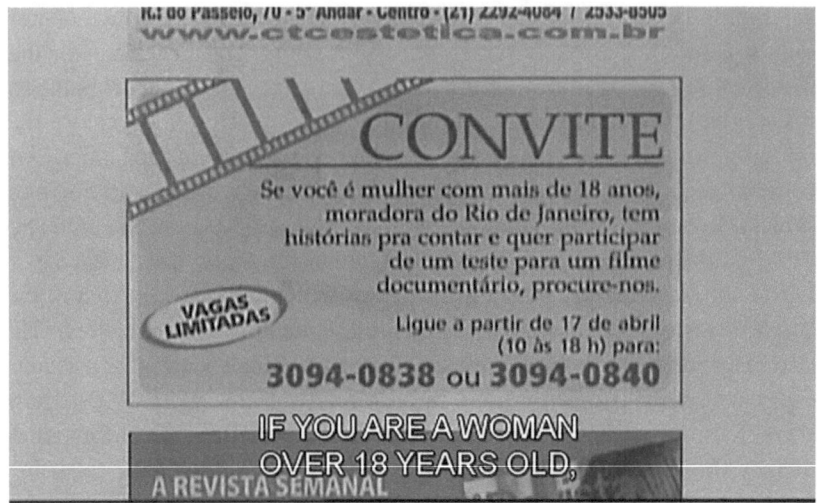

Figure 18.3. Ad announcing a casting call for women who "have stories to tell" (*Jogo de Cena*, 2007). Fair use.

After the ad, the camera follows a woman walking up a narrow set of stairs and entering a stage, where we barely see some technicians, a cameraman, Coutinho seated so that his face is right next to the camera lens (its extension?), and an empty chair, where he tells the woman to sit. The next shot establishes the visual *dispositivo* for the rest of the film: a woman sitting on a chair on a stage telling her story, behind her the red seats of an empty theater. This "theater situation" is disconcerting, since it reverses our expectations about the staging of the proscenium and audiences: the stage, a public space, has been privatized and inverted and will serve as the site for intimate conversations with the filmmaker. Without any kind of identifying information—eventually we learn that her name is Jeckie—the woman begins to speak of her dream of becoming an actress and how she got into the theater group Nós do Morro. Coutinho asks her: "Que te marcou lá?" (What was important for you there?), and she responds: "Eu aprendi a interpretar" (I learned to interpret). And, although her behavior seems oddly artificial, as if she were orating, almost shouting, from a stage, when at Coutinho's behest she performs a bit from *Medea*, the piece she says she is staging, we can believe that indeed she has learned to interpret. Thus the promise of the ad seems fulfilled: the film will feature real women telling their stories.

Gisele is the next woman to occupy the hot seat in front of Coutinho, framed a bit tighter this time, who begins to recount a story of profound loss and redemption: she loses a son at birth but her religious beliefs help her overcome the pain. A few minutes into her testimony, however, when Gisele says, "Eu saí fora do foco do casamento" (I lost the focus on my marriage), a dramatic and memorable cut abruptly shows us the well-known actress Andréa Beltrão, disconcertingly repeating the same line. For the next ten minutes the film will alternate between Gisele and Beltrão, telling the same story.

This is the *jogo*, the game of the film: "real" women tell their stories, reenacted by professional actresses who also comment upon their experiences doing so (fig. 18.4). But there are other games, for, as we soon

Figure 18.4. Reenactment in *Jogo de Cena* (2007). Fair use.

discover, this simple shock of displaced authenticity is not what Coutinho is after. Coutinho's games take place across multiple levels of displaced representations: real women talk about their lives then become models that challenge the representational skills of recognizable actresses (in addition to Beltrão, Fernanda Torres and Marília Pêra) who also comment on camera about the process and thus also speak for themselves. But sometimes, as when we first see Marília Pêra, we do not know whose words she is reenacting. And in the case of the vibrant and animated Nilza, who tells the story of how she conceived her daughter—"uma trepadinha de galo na Praça da Sé em uma guarita de ônibus" (a quickie in the Sé Square in a bus shelter)—we discover we do not even know whose body we've watched. At the end of her story she is framed in a very tight close-up and pointedly shifts her gaze, ostensibly from Coutinho to another space to his right. When she addresses the camera directly, her statement pulls the rug on all spectatorial certainty: "Issa foi o que ela disse" (That's what she said). Only after the credits will the spectator really know that the body that told Nilza's story was that of Débora Almeida, a professional though not very well-known actress (fig. 18.5).

In *Jogo de Cena*, Coutinho takes on the challenge of stealing his characters' words. To the degree that these words and stories are dislocated, repeated, confronted, and commented upon, they lose their truth value, their sociolinguistic fixity. Yet there remains a "factual" dimension—the truth of the falsification—for the spectator ends up witnessing the production of multiple subjectivities through the stories, whether previously "learned"—staged—by the actresses or produced by the women themselves. Thus, the film's reflexivity paradoxically reinforces the dialectic between belief and doubt that underlies all cinematic spectatorship. But rather than any one truth, we are left with multiple expressions of not quite truths that are experienced and felt, a documentary of affectivities. When we already know what's going to be said—such as when we hear the story of Claudilea Cerqueira for the second time—we look and listen for other embodied intensities manifested in the voices, gestures, and facial expressivity of the characters narrating. And we also invest in the stories themselves because they exceed all truth claims: tales of loss, separation, and suffering, of lives turned upside down by tragic events and rebuilt at great cost. As if channeling Douglas Sirk through the documentary, Coutinho invests in the melodramatic imaginary by provoking his characters to tell their stories as punctuated by the pathos and excess emotionality of popular fiction: he documents the emergence of *personagens* through the relationality of affect rather than through the truth values of their testimonies.

A Poetics of the Trace | 379

Figure 18.5. Nilza's surprising revelation in *Jogo de Cena* (2007). Fair use.

Alamar: To the Sea

At the 2009 Toronto International Film Festival, *Alamar*'s international premiere, filmmaker Pedro González-Rubio was asked whether he considered his film a documentary or a fiction. His response was stunning: "It is a film" (Nayman n.d.). Indeed, *Alamar* is a film that resists categorizations and articulates a different cinematic sensibility that actively ignores the distinction between fiction and nonfiction. It is not simply a film that blurs the boundaries but one that poetically refuses to acknowledge them. Not unlike Lisandro Alonso's *La Libertad* (Argentina, 2001) or Oscar Ruíz Navia's *El vuelco del cangrejo* (Colombia, 2009), *Alamar* participates in what critic Robert Koehler has dubbed the global "cinema of in-betweenness," a "zone of cinema . . . in between hardened fact and invented fiction" (n.d.). But, unlike these films, *Alamar* pivots around a remarkably coherent core of affectivity. Beyond the self-reflexivity of *Santiago* or the joyous and melodramatic playfulness of *Jogo de Cena*, *Alamar* simply does not engage in a modernist epistemological debate. Its images, irrespective of their provenance on the spectrum of truth-falsity, simply are. And the film's genius lies in that simplicity.

The provenance of the film is important to understanding its impact. González-Rubio was born in Belgium and traveled the world as a child/adolescent with his parents. He trained in filmmaking in Mexico and London and moved to the Playa del Carmen area in the state of Quintana Roo to get away from Mexico City and a frustrated experience in a mainstream film production. After making his first documentary in the region, *Toro negro* (2005), he visited the Banco Chinchorro preserve (off the southeast coast of the Yucatán Peninsula) and, enchanted by its majestic beauty, decided he had to film there. Originally he wanted to film a story about the last days of a man who returns to Chinchorro before dying. However, after meeting Jorge Machado (the protagonist of *Alamar*), González-Rubio knew that he had found his protagonist even though Jorge looked too healthy to be dying. When he learned about the impending visit from Italy of Machado's young son Natán, he "found the thread of the film . . . Rather than the last days [of someone's life], it would be the first, an initiation trip as well as a farewell. The last days of a father-son relationship" (García 2010). González-Rubio spent about a month with Jorge, traveled to Italy to meet Natán and his mother Roberta Palombini, and then documented the boy's first trip to Banco Chinchorro. They returned to that location one other time, in total spending about one and a half months together living in a palafitte (stilt house) and working in the sea. The film documents the relationship between father, son, and a paternal grandfather figure (played by a local fisherman who is not related to Jorge or Natán) and how they live and work in and with the sea.

The foundation of the film is an observational/ethnographic position. Not unlike traditional ethnographic films, González-Rubio focuses on an ethnographic other Jorge, a sort of noble savage of the sea—and, maintaining a position that is both empathetic and distant, constructs an engaging vision of this otherness, here with an ecological inflection, since the film is not only a register of the Machado men but also serves as preserve. Yet, there are two pivotal differences that perturb the epistemic certainty of the observational mode: the framing story of the family's history that begins and ends the film in Rome and a staging strategy that discloses a disconcerting ability to plan for the unexpected.

The film begins with a brief prologue on "civilization" before the properly documentable scenes begin. The first image of the film is a small black-and-white close-up of Jorge, filmed in a moving car, which is visually and aurally marked as home video footage. "Natán crece, crece, crece" (Natán grows, grows, grows), he says while an off camera, female voice says, in Italian, "Sto registrando" (I am recording). While remaining focused on Jorge, the film captures a perplexing exchange in Italian and Spanish between Jorge and the female voice: the female voice prods Jorge to conjugate the verb *andare* (to go) properly. "Sono andato" (I went), says Jorge, while the female voice demands that he complete the phrase: "'going to' answers which question?" The response she wants—where he is going—she never gets, while we see through the car window a brief image of the instantly recognizable Roman Coliseum. Their voices continue in voice-over as the film shows us a series of photographs and snippets of home videos that briefly encapsulate the relationship between Jorge and Roberta: she's Italian, they met and fell in love at the beach ("a magical time," says Jorge), Roberta got pregnant, Natán was born, they grew apart ("I was unhappy with your reality," says Roberta), they split up. Having summarily presented the history of this family, the film moves to a "present" in which Roberta in Rome is getting Natán ready to go on a trip with Jorge: she wakes him, helps him to shower and packs his bag. When she says goodbye and kisses him, Natán looks off screen right as a dark-skinned male hand enters the frame and reaches out to him.

Having efficiently established the story of separation and heartbreak in civilization with domestic raw materials—home video, photographs—commonly used in first-person documentaries, the film picks up Jorge and Natán as they make their way, in silence, to Banco Chinchorro (eliding the flight from Rome or any image of "civilization" in Mexico), by bus, foot, big motorboat and, finally, with the *abuelo*, on a smaller boat. Here begins the film's story proper, the observable and documentable, a story of father-son love that is also an exploration of nature, of the light and the sea. However, the certainty that the prologue is constructed with found "real" images of this family makes it difficult to read what follows only as an observational exercise. It doesn't impede such a reading, it simply makes it epistemologically uncertain. And the uncertainty is exacerbated by how the journey is presented. The first image we see after the prologue, for example, is a shot of Jorge and Natán boarding a bus, but the camera is already on the bus when they get on, having anticipated their arrival. Similarly, the camera is already on the smaller boat when Jorge and Natán board it from the motorboat. Is this staged or real? How can the camera anticipate so well the characters' movements?

Already in this first sequence of the journey, González-Rubio establishes a singular nondocumentary-like strategy vis-à-vis his documentable subjects that is intimate yet observational, staged yet natural. Thus, for example, except for one instance, the characters steadfastly refuse to acknowledge the presence of the camera and/or the filmmaker. No matter how tight the space—a small boat, the tiny one-room house on stilts—it is as if the camera were invisible. That the spectator knows these spaces are small and confined adds to the indeterminacy of the images. The camera is there, as is the filmmaker; for the characters to not notice it is impossible. González-Rubio has explained the film's remarkable intimacy with its characters as a product of his small crew (himself on camera and a sound person) and his daily lived relationship with them: "the border between our own daily activities and the characters' activities was very blurry. It was very organic" (Tully 2010). Furthermore, without negating an observational stance, his ability to stage and produce strikingly beautiful images in the process of "observing"—for example the breathtaking beauty of Jorge's large, darker-skinned arm across little Natán's seasick body—is delightful as well as unsettling. Similarly, the camera setups are, in general, so measured and elegant that they belie an almost impossible degree of planning for events that are completely unexpected. For example, when Blanquita, the white egret that temporarily stays with them and serves as the film's central metaphor for the inevitability of the end of Natán and Jorge's journey, arrives at the palafitte, González-Rubio manages to be impossibly close, perfectly positioned to capture remarkable images (fig. 18.6).

Alamar has been described as an epic coming-of-age tale, a love story of male bonding, and a celebration of the luminosity of nature. Indeed, it is all these things, but it is also a documentary about the affective mapping of a journey that takes father and son through a magical environment. Mapped onto the poetic paradise of Banco Chinchorro, the growing bond between father and son is felt rather than explained, perceived as it reverberates through the physical work of fishing or diving for lobsters, of cleaning the fish and making meals—and through the beauty of the environment.

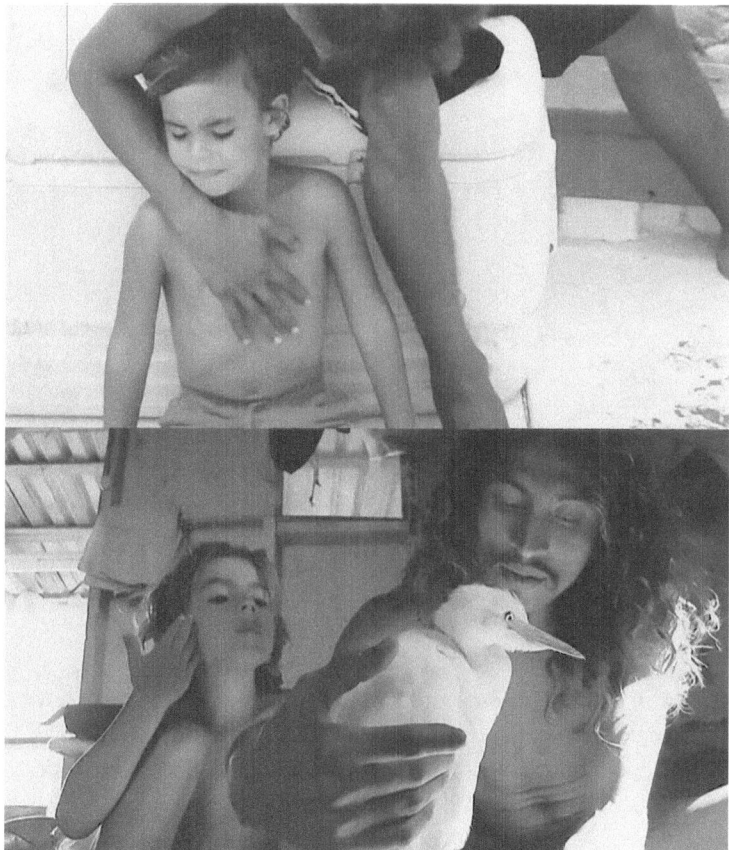

Figure 18.6. Planning for unexpected events: framing in *Alamar* (2009). Fair use.

Tellingly, the documentable film culminates with another magical moment. During breakfast on the morning of what we presume is his last day in Banco Chinchorro, Natán sets out to document, via drawings, all that he has seen and experienced: the stingrays, the two barracudas, Blanquita the egret and . . . the camera (fig. 18.7). Natán's documentary of the affective journey of a five-year-old and his father is, like the film, destined for preservation, an archive. With Jorge's help, he places his drawings in a large glass bottle with a flower petal and, after careful stoppering, casts it out to sea. A message in a bottle or site of memory has been launched, a perfect metaphor for the work of the film itself.

384 | Ana M. López

Figure 18.7. Natán acknowledges the camera (*Alamar*, 2009). Fair use.

Conclusion

Through the analysis of *Santiago, Jogo de Cena*, and *Alamar*, I have tried to argue that beyond a general and generalizable subjective turn in Latin American documentary, filmmakers have begun to forge new trajectories through which to shift the force fields of the documentary. Rather than seek recourse to a regime of social truths or purely personal exploration, these works attempt to explore the interstices of how documentaries—and documentarians—make different kinds of "meaning" by exploring the affective potential of the medium. Instead of the waning of affect presaged by Fredric Jameson in postmodernity (1991), I find in these films an intensification of the affective: their work cannot be understood without an accounting of their affective dimensions. This displacement of the centrality of meaning from documentary practice I have called a poetics of the trace, using trace as a shortcut to something other than signification, as a *punctum* of sensorial memory and experience rather than history. Certainly, in *Santiago*, Moreira Salles unravels the high modernist documentary he failed to make thirteen years earlier through a complex network of aural and visual interventions that engage the spectator at the level of sensation rather than knowledge. We have knowledge of the failed first film and of the author's melancholia, but the film's affective charge exceeds this armature and approximates us to and through Santiago in an entirely different and affective way. In *Jogo de Cena*, everything looks passably "real" yet possibly nothing is. The radical indeterminacy of the performances—and therefore of the images—leads the spectator to two different registers. On the one hand, the visible and audible physical experiences of the performers: how tears erupt and/or are produced, the audible grain and tone of the women's voices, how they shift in their chairs, tilt their heads, breathe. On the other, the stories themselves become a locus of attention: their extraordinary pathos engages us, even as we acknowledge their indeterminacy; we feel through the emotional authenticity of the stories rather than for the characters whose authenticity we have every reason to doubt. Together these registers serve the film to map a thick contemporary structure of feeling rather than a record of the production of a series of subjectivities. Finally, *Alamar* pushes the documentary impulse to its furthest frontier. Here, the documentable is framed by almost clichéd documents of memory and filmed as an enactment. Once again, it is the deployment of sensorial appeals—produced in the physical acts of work, an evolving filial relationship and in relation to a particular landscape and nature—that engages and focuses the spectator. All three films move us in unpredictable ways, functioning in that in-between realm of the affective, and pushing the documentary simultaneously closer to the fictional but also, potentially, closer to its roots.

Part 3

Intersections

Race, Ethnicity, and Gender

Editors' Introduction

This part brings together various essays that showcase López's ongoing interest in how film and television engage with issues of race, ethnicity, and gender. While these concerns are present in essays included in previous parts (such as "From Hollywood and Back" [1998], "Crossing Nations and Genres" [2000], "Tears and Desire" [1994], and "Of Rhythms and Borders" [1997]), the essays featured here focus specifically on the politics of representation and the role of Afro-Cuban, Afro-Brazilian, and Latinx directors and actors in shaping those dynamics. As a group, the essays demonstrate López's interventions into discussions in US-based film studies in the late 1980s about the concept of "Black cinema" and the role and function of stereotypes.[1] Her essays also coincide with analogous critical studies being published in Latin America, such as João Carlos Rodrigues's *O Negro Brasileiro e o Cinema*, originally published in 1988. In addition, her work in this period responds to contemporaneous critical and theoretical shifts—the rise of postcolonial theory, debates about multiculturalism, and efforts to analyze the relationship between film, colonialism, and racism on the part of film studies scholars (Stam 1982–1983; Stam and Spence 1983; Shohat and Stam 1994). Finally, we also must place her work on race and ethnicity in relation to the 1992 quincentennial or five-hundred-year anniversary of the "encounter" between Europeans and indigenous groups in the "Americas"—an event that became a springboard for *Mediating Two Worlds: Cinematic Encounters in the Americas* (1993), one of López's coedited volumes in which two of her essays appeared in revised form ("Tears and Desire" and "Are All Latins from Manhattan?"). Like that volume, we characterize this part as an effort to "throw into relief the [various] sites where vision and knowledge [about race and ethnicity] are produced" (López and Alvarado 1993, xx). Thematically, the essays cover two areas:

the representation of Afro-descendants by Brazilian and Cuban filmmakers of different races/ethnicities and the representation of Latin Americans in US-based film and television. Many essays also grapple with the issue of self-representation and the agency of Afro–Latin American and Latinx directors and actors in countering dominant depictions of "others."

Evident in these essays is López's effort to decenter discussions of race, ethnicity, and audiovisual media as they have been traditionally viewed in relation to Hollywood and to locate them within more specific geocultural contexts, histories, and national ideologies. In "Are All Latins . . ." and "I (Also) Love Ricky" (2012), López's historicizing method provides a means to understand the differential professional trajectories of performers of Latin American descent working in the US film and television industries in the 1930s–1950s. At the same time, such essays help "to problematize traditional notions about Hollywood" and US television (Blasini 2021). Other essays on Brazilian and Cuban filmmaking ("Not Only a Question of Color" [1992] and "African Roots" [1988]) can be seen as an effort at sociohistorical and cultural translation directed at US- and European-based film studies—first and foremost, by arguing for the benefits of contextualized discussions of race and racialization processes. In a broader sense, the essays implicitly undermine the privileging of Hollywood and European industries as touchstones, as well as the underlying tendency to see those well-capitalized cinemas as "more advanced" in aesthetic, ideological, and/or industrial terms. López does this by, for example, recognizing how Brazilian and Cuban historical films from the 1930s–1950s showcased nineteenth-century "enslaved resistance" in a way that would not have been conceivable in contemporaneous Hollywood (López 1992d, 490–91).

Her essays on Latinx actors and directors also challenge the "master [critical] narratives" in vogue in the late 1980s and early 1990s that characterized Hollywood's history of representing "ethnic or racial others" as a long trajectory of absence, marginalization, misrepresentation, and stereotyping—only interrupted occasionally by "a golden, or near-golden, moment when Hollywood . . . sees the light and becomes temporarily more sensitive to an ethnic or minority group," sometimes through the emergence of directors from underrepresented races, ethnicities, and genders (López 1991a, 556). López identifies the ways the US film and television industries' ethnographic impulse to explain and define non-Anglo "others" in particular ways in given historical periods influenced the career trajectory of female stars like Dolores Del Rio and Lupe Vélez, while at the same time pointing to "slippages" that subtly undermined stereotypes. This could be through excessive on-screen performances, as in the spectacular case of Carmen Miranda who outshone duller Anglo protagonists and made the (monolingual Anglo) audience laugh *with* her (rather than at her) through her canny deployment of English. Or, as López notes in "I (Also) Love Ricky," it could be through the exasperated use of Spanish by Desi Arnaz/Ricky Ricardo—a comic trademark of *I Love Lucy* that functioned differently for English- and Spanish-dominant audience members.

These two star studies exemplify the productivity of López's intersectional approach—recognizing how gender impacted the racialized positioning of the performers (and vice versa). In terms of Arnaz, she shows how his talents (as musician and comedian) didn't conform to Hollywood's expectations of Latinx masculinity and, perhaps, prevented his success in film where other, more "typical" Latino actors (like Ricardo Montalbán) thrived. Arnaz's career—like that of Miranda and others—depended on his ability to navigate and negotiate an existing star system with prescribed professional pathways for Latino and Latina actors.

As a group, the essays in this part point toward the historical evolution of the terminology used to refer to peoples of Latin American descent living in the US—both by Hollywood and by scholars. In 1993, "Are All Latins from Manhattan?" took the term "Latin" from an Al Jolson song featured in a 1935 movie (see the epigraph to the chapter), but used the term reflexively to interrogate Hollywood's homogenization of Mediterranean sensuality into the "Latin Lover" type (Rudolph Valentino) and the extension of that type to Mexican actors of European descent in the late silent era (Ramón Novarro, Gilbert Roland, Del Rio). A few years later, in 1996, López and coeditor Chon Noriega addressed terminological issues more directly in *The Ethnic Eye: Latino Media Arts*, one of the earliest volumes to argue for the utility of conceptualizing the work of Chicano/Mexican American, Puerto Rican, Nuyorican, Cuban American audiovisual producers as a (widely varying) group. In their introduction, López and Noriega note the limitations of the term "Latino." Among other things, artists "have rarely ever made 'Latino' works" and often explicitly reject any effort at essentializing across or within ethnic categories (xx). Nonetheless, the editors defend their tactical use of the term as a means to recognize certain "share[d] historical and socio-economic affinities [among those artists included in the volume] that coalesce as a political strategy articulated in the U.S. public sphere."[2] López's own essay for the volume ("Greater Cuba") balances similar imperatives in her discussion of "Cuban/American audiovisual production" by identifying both similarities and differences within that category. She underscores how different generations of filmmakers (from Cuban-born exiles to US-born Cuban Americans) dialogue in varying degrees with shared cultural traditions "from the island" while also addressing their films and videos to differential audiences.

19

Not Only a Question of Color

Afro-Latino/a Images in
Latin American Cinema Today (1992)

In "Not Only a Question of Color . . ." originally published in Tonantzin, *López argues that US (binary) models of racialization cannot be applied to Latin America given the region's more complex cultural, ethnic, and racial past. She also insists on the differences between Latin American countries and, hence, between their different political and ideological discourses on race—most notably, through an in-depth comparison of Brazilian and Cuban cinemas. Finally, the essay examines how the filmic depiction of Afro-descendants in those two countries changed from the 1930s to the 1980s.*

If our knowledge of Latin Americans were based only on Hollywood films, it would be possible to think of the peoples of Latin America as a homogeneous, somewhat "off" colored—not white, yet not quite Black— bunch of energetic dancers (from Carmen Miranda's sambas in the 1940s to lambada in *The Forbidden Dance*), passionate lovers (from Desi Arnaz in *Holiday in Havana* to Raul Julia in *Kiss of the Spider Woman*), and sadistic dictators and military men (from *Pancho Villa* to *Missing* and *Moon over Parador*). That Latin Americans dance, make love, and have often been (subjected to) sadistic dictators is, of course, an irrevocable historical fact. But the cultural, ethnic, and racial history of Latin America is much more complex and heterogeneous than US media would lead us to believe. Rather than a homogeneous "off-white" continent, and despite a common history scarred by colonialism and imperialism, Latin American nations are strikingly diverse and heterogeneous: from the Altiplanos of Bolivia and Peru with majority Quechua and Aymara populations, to the European immigrant majorities of Argentina and Uruguay, and the Afro-Latin majorities of nations that formerly enslaved people[1] like Brazil, Cuba, and other Caribbean islands. Above all, Latin American nations are racially mixed, the result of the so-called "encounter" between worlds being alternatively celebrated or decried this year. Rather than a handy homogeneous "other," then, Latin America presents us with complex identity problems (relationships of self/otherness, of difference and similarity, of center and margin) that are nowhere more evident than in the representations of ethnic and racial differences in its films.

Racial heterogeneity is most pronounced in the cinemas of those nations like Brazil and Cuba that at one time enslaved large numbers of African men, women, and children. When watching either Brazilian or Cuban films, US spectators are often struck by the obvious abundance of "color" on the screen: Black people of every imaginable shade seem to be everywhere, even in films like *Memories of Underdevelopment* (Tomás Gutiérrez Alea, Cuba, 1968) and *Mujer transparente* (various, Cuba, 1990) or *Land in Anguish* (Glauber Rocha, Brazil, 1967), and *Pixote* (Héctor Babenco, Brazil, 1980) that are not explicitly concerned with "Black" issues, history, or culture. In fact, in both of these cinemas, the "nation" represented is hardly ever racially "pure" because in both nations racial identity is not simply an issue of color (black or white) but a complex mixture of color, culture, and social position. Being Black is not just a matter of ascendancy (or the opposite of white), but a negotiable category even within individual families, dependent on the degree of skin color, facial features, and hair quality. In both Cuba and Brazil there are many intermediate shades of black and whiteness, from *café con leche* (coffee and milk) and *mulato*[2] (biracial) to *preto retintos* (dark Black people) and *brancos de Bahia* (whites from Bahia), and racial classifications (and the inherent racism that underlies them) are more fluid and unstable, and thus perhaps more difficult to pin down than in the US. Rather than the US's rabid segregationism, historically, Brazil and Cuba adopted a more paternalistic model that allowed for the possibility of the "whitening" (i.e., improvement) of Black people via a subtly encouraged miscegenation.

But rather than search through these cinemas' histories for "good" or "bad" images of Afro-Latins, it is more productive to discuss how the representation of racial difference is deeply embedded in the specific histories of each of these nations and how each nation's racial ideologies emerge in their cinemas. For despite their shared histories of slavery, abolition, *mestizaje*, and the pervasive presence of Afro-American traditions, each nation's cinema has developed within different social contexts.

Reflecting and reacting to the turmoil that marked the last three decades of the nation's political (various coups d'état and military governments) and economic (inflation, recession, and hyperinflation) history, the Brazilian cinema has gone through various ups and downs since the glory days of the Cinema Novo of the 1960s. The once all-powerful state agency for the cinema, Embrafilme, no longer exists (it was disbanded in 1990), but for more than twenty years it served as the principal funding and distribution gatekeeper, thus in fact, defining the nature of the Brazilian cinema and its filmmakers: primarily ex–Cinema Novo directors, primarily male, primarily white. Despite large numbers of successful and popular Black actors and actresses—from the comedian Grande Otelo to the actress Zezé Motta (*Xica*, Carlos Diegues, 1976)—there have only been a handful of Black directors—Haroldo Costa, Antonio Pitanga, and Zozimo Balbul—and few have managed to make more than one film. Nevertheless, the Brazilian cinema offers perhaps the richest panoply of racial representations of all Latin American cinemas. Although race was not a central concern of the Cinema Novo directors, they were obsessed with the national and with the authentic, and their searches for "Brazilianness" inevitably led them to consider the African heritage and presence in Brazil.

In Cuba, the social context for the cinema could not be more different. When Cuba became a socialist nation in 1959, the revolution imposed social equality among all people, arguing from a materialist perspective that once the economic base of Cuban society was transformed, the discriminations arising from dependent capitalism would disappear. Thus official ideology argued that racism (or sexism), as a superstructural phenomenon, did not need to be addressed directly—via quotas or preferential systems—because the restructuring of the economic base would eventually make it obsolete. In practice, however, this has proven difficult to accomplish. For example, ICAIC, the Cuban Film Institute, remains to this day a primarily white, primarily male organization. Yet this is not as severe an indictment as it may at first appear, but merely a reflection of how difficult it is to overcome centuries of discrimination: ICAIC was set up by white men, many of whom are still active and prolific filmmakers, and the apprenticeship system that helped the institute to develop in the 1960s (and perennially limited resources) has made it painfully slow for younger "others" (Black people, women) to gain access to feature film production. To date, Sergio Giral, a filmmaker who came up in the ranks in the 1960s making documentaries, is ICAIC's premier feature film Black filmmaker. Albeit for different reasons than in Brazil, the Cuban cinema also offers a rich panoply of racial representations. Although rarely addressing racial concerns in a contemporary context because official ideology claims it doesn't exist, the Cuban cinema has specialized in the representation of Afro-Cuban history as part of a general operation of cultural *rescate* (reclamation). (The late Sara Gómez's *One Way or Another* [1974–1977] and its investigation of the presence of Afro-Cuban secret societies like the *machista* Abakuá in contemporary Cuba is one rare exception to this general rule.)

Both the Brazilian and Cuban cinemas have paid much attention to the history of slavery and it is fruitful to compare some films to highlight the representational similarities and differences between them. Unlike the Hollywood cinema, which consistently idealized the antebellum South as an idyllic place with beautiful plantations, benevolent aristocrats, and mostly happy enslaved people (think of *The Birth of a Nation* [1913] and *Gone with the Wind* [1939], for example), neither the Brazilian nor the Cuban cinemas ever allowed themselves such representational excess. For one thing, slavery in both nations was more widespread, occurring throughout the entire national territory, and no area could be segmented off and mythified as territory where people were enslaved. Furthermore, the relatively late dates of abolition (1888 for Brazil, 1887 for Cuba) and the high proportion of Black/biracial citizens (descendants of former enslaved people) in both countries made such a romanticization of slavery impossible. In fact, both national cinemas have emphasized the moment of abolition and enslaved resistance to a degree unthinkable in the classic Hollywood cinema. However, this does not imply that all cinematic representations of slavery in Brazil and Cuba are unproblematic. *Siboney* (Juan Orol, Cuba, 1939), for example, melodramatically focuses on the antislavery sentiments of the young Spanish aristocratic hero rather than on the enslaved Siboney (played by white actress Maria Antonieta Pons), of the title, who serves as little more than the foil against which we measure the hero's good sentiments and properly patriotic actions. Similarly, although *Sinhá Moça* (Tom Payne, Brazil, 1953)—a costume drama centered on a pro-abolitionist young aristocratic woman and her struggles against slavery—goes to great lengths to show slavery as repugnant and to highlight instances of Black rebellion, the film also privileges its white protagonists (Anselmo Duarte and Elaine Lage) and posits abolition as the great moral panacea without questioning the other forces that motivated it.

In contrast, while adapting the traditional melodramatic discourse of the Cuban abolitionist novel *Francisco: el ingenio o las delicias del campo* (1844), *The Other Francisco* (Sergio Giral, Cuba, 1974) questions every element of that discourse: characterizations and their psychological, sociological, and historical accuracy, visual and aural strategies, and political and economic motivations. The novel's progressive status as the first Cuban novel, as a work censored by the Spanish colonial government for challenging colonial institutions, and as the first abolitionist work of historical fiction (it preceded Harriet Beecher Stowe's *Uncle Tom's Cabin* by a decade) is put into question by an ideological analysis of its representational strategies in terms of what it says, how it says it, and what it does not say. The film thus performs an audiovisual ideological "reading" of the novel that serves a double function: it presents a different history of slavery in Cuba—ending with an insurrection of enslaved people rather than with enslaved Francisco's suicide that concluded the novel—and it exemplifies a critical interpretative/viewing practice.

The history of successful Black insurrections—already highlighted in the alternative story of the enslaved Francisco that ends *The Other Francisco*—has been of great significance for both the Brazilian and Cuban cinemas (while, in contrast, such moments in the US's own history of slavery have rarely been the focus of US media representations). In Brazil, for example, two films by Carlos Diegues, *Ganga Zumba* (1963) and *Quilombo* (1984), pay homage to the seventeenth-century republic of fugitive enslaved people Palmares, a community that lasted almost a century and counted as many as twenty thousand inhabitants. Assuming a Black point of view, *Ganga Zumba* tells the story of an enslaved person who discovers he is the grandson of the king of Palmares. Underlying its depiction of slavery's cruelty and dehumanization, the film does not simply portray the enslaved as victims and instead shows them as active agents, even of some of the most grisly but—in the film's analysis—necessary acts of insurrectional violence. Made almost twenty years later, *Quilombo* is less Fanonian and far more celebratory (fig. 19.1). Here, Diegues attempts to recount, in the style of a musical epic, the entire story of Palmares, linking the moments of insurrection and violent struggle with contemporary elements of Afro-Brazilian culture such as the *orixás* or deities of the Afro-inspired rites of *candomblé*, Gilberto Gil's Afro-samba-rock soundtrack, and the symbolic historical reconstructions typical of the Rio carnival samba schools.

Figure 19.1. Ganga Zumba tries to convince Zumbi in *Quilombo* (Carlos Diegues, 1984).

Quilombo's celebration of Afro-Brazilian history and culture was shared by a number of other films of the 1970s and '80s, indicating a marked shift from the mistrust of Black culture evidenced in some earlier Cinema Novo films. While in the 1960s, Afro-Brazilian culture was often posited as alienating and marginalizing—for example, the treatment of religion in Glauber Rocha's *Barravento*—by the late 1970s, films like Nelson Pereira dos Santos's *Tent of Miracles* (1976) celebrated Black culture, religion, and the *mestizaje* intrinsic to Brazil as an important element of national identity.

The importance of Afro-Latin culture for national identity is also highlighted in Cuban films of this same period, especially in *Patakín* (1983), Manuel Octavio Gómez's musical allegory that narrativizes the Santería/Yoruba conflict between good and evil represented by the deities Shango and Ogun. Transposing these Yoruba mythology characters to a stylized modern Havana, the film pits the sexy and sly *mulato*[3] Shango against the earnest and hardworking white Ogun in a comic battle of wits, songs, and dance surrounding their pursuit of the mysterious mulata Caridad. Adapting the style of the Hollywood musical of the 1960s, *Patakín* is like a socialist *West Side Story*, but one in which racial tensions are not the motivation for the principal narrative conflict.

Unlike in the US, where we now have a "Black cinema" that often uncomfortably straddles the frontiers between alternative and mainstream practices and Black and white audiences, the contemporary Brazilian and Cuban cinemas continue to present racial heterogeneity as a social given. Nevertheless, it is true that sometimes both cinemas have tended to elide the racial tensions that undoubtedly exist: in Brazil, via an excessive celebration and carnivalization of race (for example, the sexual prowess of the heroine of *Xica*); in Cuba, via appeals to the official elimination of institutionalized racism (for example, when questioned by his *gusana* [a defector from socialist Cuba] mother about his new wife's racial heritage, the white protagonist of Jesús Díaz's *Lejanía* [Cuba, 1985] responds, "Mother, we don't think like that anymore. Who cares?"). But it is also true that in both cinemas, as in both societies, racial identity and representation are always much more than simply a matter of color.

20

African Roots

Images of Black People in Cuban Cinema (1988)

In "African Roots,"[1] originally published in Black Film Review *as a follow-up to the interview that she and Nicholas Peter Humy conducted with Cuban director Sergio Giral (included as the next chapter in this volume), López argues that debates about the existence of "Black cinema" (that had been utilized to discuss independent filmmaking practices in the US and Great Britain in the 1970s and 1980s) are not transferable to the Cuban case because of its unique history of race relations. After providing a brief history of the representation of Afro-Cubans from the silent period to the present, this essay provides a robust discussion of Cuban filmmaking since the revolution. López comments on the work of Black directors like Giral and Sara Gómez as well as that of others such as Bernabé Hernández, Octavio Cortázar, Luis Felipe Bernaza, Manuel Octavio Gómez, and Tomás Gutiérrez Alea.*

> That I am Black and a film director does not differentiate me in the least from other directors.
>
> —Sergio Giral in López and Humy,
> "Sergio Giral on Filmmaking in Cuba"

This quote from Sergio Giral, the Cuban Film Institute's (ICAIC) only Black feature film director, vividly illustrates the difficulties of approaching the question of a Black cinema in Cuba today. One might assume that Cuba would be one of the most fertile grounds for the development of a clearly defined "Black" cinematic culture, given the legacies of three centuries of slavery under Spanish colonial rule. Thirty percent of the population is Black, there has been extensive miscegenation and syncretism, and there is a marked African character in all forms of cultural expression. But such assumptions are made unjustified by several factors: Cuba's unique position in the Caribbean and its historical evolution as a Spanish colony, US protectorate, and socialist nation.

Racial relations in Cuba were always markedly different than in the US, where the idea of a "Black" cinema distinct from its white counterpart has had the most currency. Largely because of slavery and its abolition, social barriers between Black and white people in Cuba were not as strong as in the US. In fact, the struggle for independence from Spain and the rise of Cuban nationalism seemed to indicate Cuban society was beginning to move away from polarizations along lines of race and color. However, the intensive penetration of US capital, political power, and social conduct between 1899 and 1959 (crucial years for the development of the cinema) decisively sharpened color distinctions in Cuban life. With the importation of American-style racism, whites became more color-conscious to be acceptable to North Americans. Segregation in jobs, economic opportunities, housing, and public facilities grew steadily.[2]

This trend was reversed by the complete social restructuring after the 1959 revolution. Imposing equality of status among all people, the revolution set out to remove all official barriers to Black people. Rather than address the problem of racial inequality via the establishment of quotas and preferential systems, the Cubans tackled the economic system directly. Assuming the material conditions ultimately determine cultural development, they argued that the transformation of the material base of Cuban society would inevitably lead to the cultural transformation of Black people and other groups, like women, discriminated against.

This trajectory is essential to an understanding of Cuban cinema, especially from the perspective of the Black presence in it. When ICAIC was formed in 1959, not only was there not a Black cinema in Cuba, there was hardly a Cuban cinema at all.

As was the case throughout Latin America, the cinema "arrived" early in Cuba. It was imported by European and US film pioneers who traveled "south" to obtain images of exotic foreign lands for their home audiences and widen the market for their own products. Cuban entrepreneurs soon followed, creatively working with substandard equipment and little capital.

Their early films provide us with our first, albeit paradoxical, link between the Afro-Cuban heritage and the cinema. One of the first Cuban films was *Caña y azúcar* (Sugar and Sugar Cane, Manuel Martínez Illas, 1906), a documentary financed with $25,000 from the Manati Sugar Company. Designed to promote the sugar industry, *Caña y azúcar* also inadvertently focused on the motivation for the importation of African people to the US for their enslavement.[3] There was little relationship otherwise between the efforts of Cuban filmmakers and the Afro-Cuban heritage. None of the Cuban film pioneers, or, later, those who attempted to set up production houses modeled on the Hollywood studio system, were Black. Although few films from the silent period survive, contemporary accounts suggest that even when these films seemed to deal with Afro-Cuban themes, they rarely avoided the condescending attitude one would expect from a foreigner or a folklorist.[4] In fact, these films were often made explicitly "as if by a foreigner" to promote the tourist potential of the exotic "Cubanness" of the African heritage (Chanan 1985; Agramonte 1966).

The establishment of ICAIC decisively changed the direction of Cuban cinema.[5] It became Cuban, a cinema that addressed the needs, characteristics, and cultural heritage of the nation. This cinema was devoted to the continued growth and stimulation of the changes required by the revolutionary process. The historical evolution and successes and failures of ICAIC in the intervening twenty-seven years have been well documented and hardly need repeating. Surmounting unbelievable technical, practical, and political odds and using very limited budgets, ICAIC has sustained production of an average of forty feature and short-subject films a year. The ICAIC has nurtured the talent and creativity of its directors to produce films that have gained considerable international renown, and has trained its own filmmakers through an apprenticeship system. It has involved the entire population of Cuba with cinema through innovative distribution and exhibition strategies. ICAIC has actively fostered, through coproductions and collaborative exchanges, the development of the New Latin American Cinema.

Given all these achievements, what has ICAIC done in the area of racial relations? Has ICAIC produced a "Black" Cuban cinema? A cinema dealing with Afro-Cuban themes? Produced by and for Afro-Cubans? The answers are not easy. ICAIC, like all other Cuban institutions, does not recognize race as a differentiating factor. Given that the material base of Cuban society has been fundamentally changed, the social superstructural phenomenon of racism will eventually disappear and is not to be addressed as a special interest, they claim. Filmmakers, as Sergio Giral states earlier, are filmmakers above all else, regardless of their color, gender, or age.

Despite these ideals, Black participation in and access to the cinematic apparatus has been low. After twenty years, Giral remains the only Black feature filmmaker. Yet this is not as serious an indictment as it may appear. Part of ICAIC's strength has been its apprenticeship system. Younger filmmakers are introduced into the system slowly, first gaining experience as documentary filmmakers and gradually assuming responsibility before being permitted to "graduate" into fiction feature filmmaking. That this evolutionary process takes many years to complete should not be surprising given ICAIC's limited resources and the fact that the "fathers" of ICAIC, the men who set up the institute in the 1960s, are still active and prolific filmmakers. The late Sara Gómez, a Black female filmmaker, "came up through the ranks" in this fashion. After producing a number of excellent documentaries in the late 1960s and early '70s, she made her first feature film, *De cierta manera* (*One Way or Another*, 1974–1977). Unfortunately, she died before finishing editing it (fig. 20.1).

Figure 20.1. *De cierta manera* (*One Way or Another*, Sara Gómez, 1974–1977). Fair use.

Part of the second generation of ICAIC fiction filmmakers, Gómez was a contemporary of Giral's. The two trained together and were both under the artistic guidance of Tomás Gutiérrez Alea, one of ICAIC's most prolific and consistent directors. Currently, another Black filmmaker, Rigoberto López, is making documentary shorts and, ostensibly, is "in training" for fiction film production.

The rarity of direct participation by Black people in the Cuban cinema is not, however, an accurate indicator of that cinema's investment in Afro-Cuban themes. Even before Giral and Gómez began making documentaries, there was a marked "Black presence" in the Cuban cinema. Especially in documentary filmmaking, Afro-Cuban traditions, beliefs, rituals, and music have been thoroughly explored. Among the most notable works are a number of documentaries made in the 1960s that explore the religious syncretism typical of Cuban society. (For example, Bernabé Hernández's 1963 shorts, *Abakuá* and *Cultura aborígen*.) In 1968, Octavio Cortázar directed *Acerca de un personaje que unos llaman San Lázaro y otros llaman Babalú* (About a Certain Character That Some Call St. Lazarus and Others Babalú), a twenty-minute documentary using the traditional rituals performed annually on St. Lazarus's Saint Day to explore the relationship between St. Lazarus and the African god Babalú (with whom he is identified in Santería, the folk-based African religion).

A number of documentaries exploring the Afro-Cuban roots of Cuban music and rhythms were also produced in the '60s and '70s. Most notable among these are Sara Gómez's *Y tenemos sabor* (And We've Got Taste, 1968), Luis Felipe Bernaza's *De donde son los cantantes?* (Where Are the Singers From?, 1976), and Octavio Cortázar's *Hablando del punto cubano* (Speaking of Typical Cuban Music, 1972).

In addition to those documentaries dealing explicitly with Afro-Cuban themes, in practical terms, Black people of all shades are very visible in the Cuban cinema. Starting with ICAIC's first productions in the 1960s, the faces in the revolutionary Cuban cinema have reflected the full color spectrum of the Cuban population. It is almost impossible to think of an ICAIC film in which Black people do not appear. Especially in those films reinscribing and celebrating Cuba's history, the historical *cine rescate* of the late 1960s, we see that great care was taken to properly represent the Cuban population in all its racial complexity. In films that address the Cuban War of Independence, like *La primera carga al machete* (The First Charge of the Machete, 1969) by Manuel Octavio Gómez or *La odisea del*

General José (The Odyssey of General José, 1968), we have vivid portrayals of the crucial roles played by Black and biracial people in that struggle.

Even in a film like *Lucía* (Humberto Solás, 1968) Cuba's racial mixture is essential to the film's structure. It is impossible to conceive of the 1895 section of this film without the marked contrast between Raquel Revueltas's lily-white, alienated Lucía and the mestiza, half-crazed Fernandina (Idalia Anreus), who functions as her revolutionary and utterly Cuban alter ego.

In all the ICAIC films, whether fictional or documentary, we see a Cuba that is not racially pure, but an unavoidable mixture of races. It is precisely this point that *Memorias del subdesarrollo* subtly addresses in the scene where Sergio, the protagonist, attends a lecture on "Literature and Underdevelopment." Edmundo Desnoes, the author of the novel *Memorias del subdesarrollo* argues that Latin Americans in the US have the same status as Black people, while the camera emphasizes what the participants don't acknowledge: a white-jacketed Black waiter silently filling water glasses in the background.

The fictional films of the ICAIC have also specifically addressed the problems and history of Black Cubans and Afro-Cuban themes. Gutiérrez Alea's *Cumbite* (1964), for example, is about a Haitian immigrant who, after living fifteen years in Cuba, returns to his village in Haiti. *La última cena* (*The Last Supper*, 1976), also directed by Alea, is set in a sugar plantation in the eighteenth century, shortly after the Haitian uprising of enslaved people, and is based on a documented rebellion of enslaved people. The pious plantation owner decides to reenact the Last Supper Easter week, casting himself as Jesus Christ and twelve of his enslaved workers as the apostles. The enslaved workers, from different regions and exhibiting varying degrees of submission to their brutal existence, are suddenly confronted with a world in which their master washes their feet one night but orders them to work the next day (Good Friday). No longer willing or able to accept their paradoxical and painful status, they rebel and escape; ultimately all but one pay for their freedom with their heads.

Although Alea has consistently addressed Afro-Cuban issues, even in films not explicitly about Afro-Cubans, Giral's fictional oeuvre has been the most notable fictional one addressing the Afro-Cuban heritage. His first three fiction films make up what is usually referred to as ICAIC's "slavery trilogy."

The first film, *El otro Francisco* (*The Other Francisco*, 1974), adapts to the screen the traditional melodramatic discourse of the Cuban abolitionist novel *Francisco: el ingenio o las delicias del campo* (1839). The film questions every element of that discourse: characterizations and their psychological, sociological, and historical accuracy, visual and aural strategies, and political and economic motivations. The book had a progressive status as the first Cuban novel, as a work censored by the Spanish colonial government for challenging colonial institutions, and as the first abolitionist work of historical fiction. Giral's ideological analysis challenges the novel in terms of what it says, how it says it, and what it does not say. The film performs an audiovisual ideological "reading" of the novel, presenting a different history of slavery in Cuba and exemplifying a critical interpretative/viewing practice. The other two films of the trilogy, *El Rancheador* (The Bounty Hunter, 1976) and *Maluala* (1979), explore aspects of the history of slavery. The former focuses on the problematic historical role of the bounty hunters who chased the runaway enslaved people. The latter centers on the strong settlements, or *palenques*, established by runaways in the mountains of eastern Cuba. As Michael Chanan has argued, "The three films of the trilogy taken together show a development of consciousness from singular to collective, from individual resistance to collective struggle, from suicide to battle" (Chanan 1985, 271) and constitute a magnificent tribute and analysis of the history of Cuba's African heritage.

In the last decade, although beset by some internal difficulties, ICAIC has continued to address the Cuban population in its racial complexity. Perhaps the most interesting contemporary Cuban film dealing with a specific Afro-Cuban theme is Manuel Octavio Gómez's *Patakín* (1983), a musical allegory illustrating the classic Santería/Yoruba conflict between the forces of good and evil, represented by the feud between the deities Shango and Ogun. The film transposes these characters from Yoruba mythology to modern-day Havana. It pits the sexy and sly *mulato*[6] Shango against the earnest, hardworking white Ogun in a comic battle of wits, songs, and dance surrounding their pursuit of the mysterious biracial Caridad. Taking on the typical style of the Hollywood musical of the 1960s, with song and dance numbers integrated into the narrative, *Patakín* is like a socialist *West Side Story*, but one in which racial tensions do not fuel the principal narrative conflict.

Another recent film, Giral's latest work, *Plácido* (1986), takes on the history of a biracial Cuban of historical importance, Gabriel de la Concepción Valdés, a poet who assumed the pen name of "Plácido." Now recognized as the most important biracial poet of nineteenth-century Latin America, Plácido was executed during the "Conspiracy of the Ladder" of 1884. Already terrified because the Black population had grown to constitute more than 60 percent of the Cuban population, the colonial order and the creole bourgeoisie's fears of Black uprisings were fueled by rumors of a Black conspiracy. A large number of Black and biracial people were imprisoned, tortured, and executed (with a cruelty rarely seen in Cuba) by the Spanish colonial forces. Plácido's role in this conspiracy has never been clarified, yet he was among the first biracial people to be executed. Whether he was truly involved with the revolutionaries or was manipulated by the colonial order to serve as a scapegoat is not known. As Giral explains in his film, "[Plácido's story] has allowed me to . . . analyze the position of the artist at this particular historical moment, his commitment, his contradictions . . . (and to underline) the importance of commitment because ultimately, whether you are committed or not, you will pay. As we say, 'los justos por los pecadores' (the innocent always pays for the sins of the sinners)" (López and Humy 1986-1987, 4-7).

As was true twenty years ago, Black and biracial people are visible in almost every film produced by ICAIC today. Especially in films dealing with the prerevolutionary period, we often find the inherent racism of prior Cuban sociopolitical life and of life in the United States analyzed in important subplots. For example, Jesús Díaz's *Polvo rojo* (Red Dust, 1982) deals with the efforts of workers to operate a large metal refinery just expropriated from its US owners. Because North American technical support has been withdrawn and the few Cuban engineers who worked there have chosen to leave for the United States, the workers must master the complicated equipment themselves. Within this epic story, an important subplot focuses on the plight of the only Cuban engineer who chooses to stay behind. A biracial man who could "pass" for white in Cuba and who had acquired an education, social status, and a spoiled white bourgeois wife and daughter, he stays behind not only because of his positive feelings toward the revolution, but also because of his resentment toward those who scorned him racially and his certainty that, if he were to go to the United States, there he would always be denigrated and socially disadvantaged because of the color of his skin.

The difference between this prerevolutionary problem and the complexities of revolutionary Cuban society are also highlighted briefly In Jesús Díaz's latest film, *Lejanía* (1985), even though the dramatic conflict of this film is centered around a very specific and limited problem. In the early 1960s, a family leaves a military-age son in Cuba and seeks exile in the United States. The film begins with the son grown, married, and estranged from his family but facing an impending visit from his mother and cousin. It focuses on the difficult emotions surrounding this unexpected visit from the past.

However, an exchange between the mother and son perfectly illustrates the difference in racial attitudes. She says of his wife, "She's not quite white, is she?" to which he responds, "Mother, we don't think like that anymore. Who cares?"

Although we find that racial problems as such are only addressed historically in contemporary Cuban films because the material base for racism no longer exists in contemporary Cuban society, the racial complexity and subtleties of the Cuban population continue to be represented and vividly portrayed. We can only hope that, with time, yet a new generation of ICAIC filmmakers will emerge composed equally of men and women, Black, biracial, and white people, so that the always crucial mechanisms of control and decision-making of the Cuban cinema will be shared in a way truly representative of the Cuban population.

21
Sergio Giral on Filmmaking in Cuba (1986–1987)

WITH NICHOLAS PETER HUMY

Originally published in Black Film Review *this interview with one of the two most prominent Afro-Cuban filmmakers describes Giral's personal and professional trajectory in the US and Cuba, his work at ICAIC (the state film institute), and his films. As López and Humy ask Giral about "the representation of Black people and Black issues" in Cuban cinema and his own position as a filmmaker within ICAIC, the piece demonstrates López's efforts to provide English-language audiences with more informed perspectives about the Cuban industry while at the same time dialoguing with contemporaneous debates in US film studies about ethnicity, race, and film.*

Born in Havana in 1937, Sergio Giral lived for a few years in the United States before returning to Cuba in time to witness the triumph of the revolution in 1959. After making a number of documentaries for the Cuban Film Institute (the ICAIC, or Instituto Cubano de Arte e Industria Cinematográficos) in the 1960s, Giral produced his first feature film, *El otro Francisco* (The Other Francisco) in 1974. This was followed by two other feature films that, like *Francisco*, explored the history of slavery in Cuba: *El Rancheador* (The Bounty Hunter in 1976) and *Maluala* (1979). These three films are known as his "slavery" trilogy. In this interview, Giral discusses his two most recent films—*Techo de vidrio* (The Glass Ceiling, 1982) and *Plácido* (1986)—as well as his experiences at the ICAIC.

411

Giral was interviewed at his Havana home by Ana M. López and Nicholas Peter Humy last August. The interview was later translated by López and edited by Humy.

BFR. You have been with the ICAIC almost from the very beginning, haven't you?

GIRAL. Yes, since 1961. I returned to Cuba from the US in 1959. I did the opposite of what a lot of other Cubans were doing then. I came to Cuba and I found this incredible phenomenon of the revolution. At that time I was barely surviving in the US. I was twenty-two years old and I had no answers. When I returned to Cuba, little by little the revolution began to give me answers, with many contradictions, but with contradictions that were sufficiently rich for me to dedicate myself to them. Time passed, and suddenly I realized that I was staying.

When I arrived in Cuba, I tried to be useful and began to study agricultural engineering at the university. At that time we had a tremendous need to develop our agricultural system. But that profession had nothing to do with my real interests. So I decided I was better off trying to help out in areas that were at least within the realm of my real abilities and possibilities. That's how I became part of the ICAIC—I looked for a way to be useful. There was this new institute and I figured out ways to become affiliated with it.

At that time in Cuba, there were few people skilled in the cinema. The few cinema technicians we had, had either already left or were packing their bags. This was around the time when the US companies left the country and took their employees with them by guaranteeing them jobs in the US. The fledgling industry we had—a micro-industry of publicity and advertising shorts—disappeared. The Cuban cinema emerged from the residue of small efforts and isolated resources left to us.

My apprenticeship, like that of the great majority of ICAIC filmmakers, was autodidactic; it happened while we worked. We began making documentaries right away in order to learn how to make films. And we watched a lot of films. I am part of what is known as the second generation of Cuban filmmakers, a generation that first has been spectators. I grew up in New York—my parents moved to the US in 1953—but I always loved the movies and used to spend every weekend in those Times Square theaters that back then showed great movies all day long for only thirty-five cents or so.

BFR. You are of the second generation of ICAIC filmmakers. How did the third generation emerge?

GIRAL. Once our industry became more developed, it had other needs. So now, for example, one of the prerequisites for entry into the ICAIC, at any level, is to be a graduate of the university in some field that seems somehow related. Before, when I came on board, this wasn't the case. There weren't too many of us with university degrees then. This makes a great difference. We went around the entire operation, doing all kinds of different jobs until we found the ones that we liked and that we were most suited for. Now the young kids come in directly as analysts or as assistant directors, and they stay in those positions for a long time learning and training before they begin to work on their first solo documentary films.

BFR. What is it like to work for the ICAIC today?

GIRAL. Our situation as filmmakers is super-privileged. Of course, we do not profit materially from our work; we do not get rich. But I do *my* work—which is *my* central interest, passion, and obsession—under the best possible conditions.

First of all, I do not have to worry about money. We are paid a monthly salary for our work. For example, we get a year and a half with salary to write a script, to write whatever *you* want wherever *you* want. This is a year and a half of financial and social security. Now, I have a year and a half to produce a script, but if I finish it sooner, say in six months, and I go into the preproduction phase with the script, then I also begin to collect a salary from production budgets. This is a great stimulus; it encourages us to work faster. But it is also a great luxury.

Another thing is that we have tremendous artistic freedom. From the outside, people always miss the point here. The issue of artistic freedom is somehow always wielded against us when people start talking about freedom of expression (which should always be placed in quotation marks in any part of the world anyway). But I will tell you that here I have complete artistic freedom of expression.

BFR. Cuba is culturally very different and very interesting because it is precisely in between most other Latin American nations. It has a unique situation. It doesn't have, for example, the large indigenous population of the Andean countries nor does it have the bourgeois superstructures of, say, Argentina.

GIRAL. Yes, it's a middle ground. And in addition, there's something else very interesting that has an impact on the cinema. Here the filmmaker—and, of course, this also depends on his or her relative experience—is not obligated by material needs and circumstances to always make films for the mass public. You can express yourself, if you so desire, in the most hermetic or most personal way, and if that is your way of expressing yourself, then it is valid and acceptable. Or you can make more popular films, say comedies, if you so desire. You are not always trying to reach the same public, the same subcultural group.

BFR. But I imagine that in the planning of the ICAIC, that has to be mediated. A more popular film here and a more difficult film there, no?

GIRAL. Yes, it is all a matter of equilibrium, of course. We now make some twelve feature-length films a year and approximately forty documentaries, so there's actually a lot of room in the system.

BFR. The most recent films of yours that we know in the US are the films of the slavery trilogy: *The Other Francisco*, *The Bounty Hunter*, and *Maluala*. What about your new films?

GIRAL. My last film is *Plácido*. It was inspired by the life of a poet of the last century named Gabriel de la Concepción Plácido, a poet from Matanzas who had a very interesting history. The most important thing about his life is that he was executed by the Spanish during the war because he was accused of being a conspirator and a traitor. The thing is that no one knows for sure whether he was truly involved with the revolutionaries or whether he was manipulated by the colonial order and made to serve as a scapegoat. This has never been historically clarified. And what his case has allowed me to do is to analyze the position of the artist at this particular historical moment, his compromise, his contradictions. What I seek to do in this film is to underline, to prove, the importance of commitment, of always being committed because ultimately, whether you are committed or not, you will pay. As we say, "los justos por los pecadores" [the innocents always pay for the sins of the sinners]. And that's sad, no?

BFR. In 1982 you made a film that we had not heard about, *Techo de vidrio* [Glass Ceiling].

GIRAL. Yes. Unfortunately, I think it is a failed film. I tried to make a film about contemporary topics, in a more or less critical tone, but I wasn't pleased with the results. It is very difficult for us to broach and elaborate on contemporary topics. Our reality changes so much and so quickly. After all, this is a revolution that is never finished, that never rests.

First of all, I don't like the picture aesthetically. I am very interested in creativity, in the possibility of creating an aesthetic universe in my films. The developed cinemas—the US cinema, for example—have reached that magical stage where they are able to deal with actual problems and with contemporary life within an aesthetic system of its own, which we all accept as appropriate and which we all like. But our approach to contemporary life, to our contemporary cultural realities, has not pleased me so far. Neither mine nor that of other *compañero* filmmakers who have made films on contemporary topics. We are not aesthetically settled yet; we still have not found the aesthetic key for the representation of our contemporary reality.

Glass Ceiling deals with the need to make demands on individuals not only at the level of individual consciousness, but also in terms of social responsibility and in terms of the need to respect social (rather than private) property that belongs to everyone. I actually think that I will take on this topic again, that I will make the film over some day when I find the aesthetic answers that I am looking for. And I will find them.

BFR. What is the difference between the producer, the director, and the screenwriter here in the ICAIC? In the US, as you know, the producer is primarily in charge of finding funds.

GIRAL. The difference is that the producer doesn't have to look for the funds, although he is responsible for them. He is the administrator of all the resources. He answers to the company, represents *its* interests. But here, something else interesting happens. And that is that the director has complete authority during the production process. That is, I can spend my resources in any way I choose. If I have three thousand dollars to do three scenes and I instead choose to invest them all in one, then the producer does not have the authority to stop me.

BFR. Have you completely given up on documentary filmmaking? Are you totally devoted to fiction films?

GIRAL. I had almost forgotten to mention this. I am planning to make a documentary of still photographs, a short film based on the photographs of a friend of mine who has taken some beautiful shots of old Chicago blues men. I love his pictures and am thinking of doing a documentary using only the stills.

Besides this project, I am basically doing only fiction films now. I want to develop an idea—another contemporary problem—for a film on how romantic relationships all over the world, and also here in Cuba, are affected by material, economic concerns and needs. For example, the problem of the professional woman who has to go to the provinces and leave her husband behind in the city. That was inconceivable before, but now it happens all the time, and it changes the nature of romantic relationships. Another topic that interests me is more amusing. A film that would take place in the 1950s, in a cabaret, in the world of the *espectáculo* of the 1950s, but in relation to the mafioso types who controlled that entire world of drugs and prostitution: in other words, the Mafia in the context of Cuba in the 1950s.

BFR. Have you seen *The Cotton Club*?

GIRAL. Yes, and I didn't like it. The film is very beautiful, but it doesn't have any narrative strength. Coppola's films fascinate me though—for example, *The Conversation* and *Rumble Fish*—although this last one is very strange.

BFR. How would you describe the representation of Black people and Black issues in the Cuban cinema and your own position as a Black filmmaker in the ICAIC?

GIRAL. It is very difficult for me to see things from the perspective that is implied in statements such as "Black issues" or "the position of Black people" in the Cuban cinema because our social reality is one that does not make such a phenomenon possible. Such issues do not come up because the problems underlying those issues do not exist here. That I am Black and a film director does not differentiate me in the least from other directors.

Perhaps what I may be able to address more directly are the topics that I have addressed in my films, because here there is direct relationship between my personal experiences as a Black man and a filmmaker and the films that I have made. First of all, I have to indicate that this relationship has been made possible because of the nature of our social life in Cuba. It is the nature of our reality that has permitted me to elaborate, investigate, approach, recreate, and transform my personal experiences and concerns as a Black man into a cinematographic experience. What I have tackled are phenomena that before the revolution were taboo not only for me but also for large segments of the general population.

BFR. In the US, Black filmmakers who have tried to produce a Black cinema have encountered the problem of audiences. The Black audience is used to the Hollywood product; filmmakers want to begin to educate the audience to relate to cinema in different terms. Given that a somewhat parallel situation existed in Cuba at the time of the revolution, could you tell us some of the things that were done to educate this audience?

GIRAL. This is the problem of cultural colonialism. I know the problems of Black filmmakers in the US—I have met many of them and they have also traveled here. And their problems are very, very difficult. The biggest stumbling block is that they are not in power; they don't have power. We have to start from that. It would be an injustice to apply the same principles that we followed here twenty-five years ago because our situation was completely different.

In any case, there are some things that can be said. What did we do? First of all, I must underline that we never rejected any method, approach, or influence a priori. That would have been a terrible mistake. One of the greatest strengths of the Cuban cinema has been its ability to take the best of everything—that is, the best of that culture that colonized us—because we cannot negate it. But we must remain aware that the cinematographic tradition that formed us had, at the same time, another function, and that's where things must change. What function are you going to give your new form of expression? What are you going to be telling the spectator? What are your objectives? You can use the tradition that has subjugated you to new ends.

BFR: Here are you talking about the kind of work you did in *The Other Francisco*, where you took a classic Cuban novel, the classic anti-slavery novel, and turned it upside down?

GIRAL. Yes, you have to take 'their" stories and make them 'yours' . . .

BFR. But I'm not sure you have answered our question. You mention the function of the film—the cinema is designed, is principally used, to entertain according to those 'manipulative' molds. Didn't you have a lot of work to do to develop an audience that would expect and accept something other than that form of entertainment, the Hollywood pleasure machine? Do you have any advice for American independents on how they can go about developing their audience?

GIRAL. Giving advice to American independents is very difficult, and I feel somewhat presumptuous about doing so. Our situations, our realities are so different. In the beginning, we had a great need to create a national film industry. After the American companies left, we had theaters but nothing to show in them. So we had to bring in films from wherever we could get them.

What could I tell these Black filmmakers? I have seen a kind of Black filmmaking that was popular in the 1970s, what was called the Black capitalist movement, that was a kind of Black telephone film.

BFR. You are referring to the "white telephone" films produced in Italy in the '30s?

GIRAL. Yes, many of these films of the '70s remind me of them, and I was astounded because their splendorous vision of Black people was just terrible. I have a friend in New York who used to work for a magazine that shared in this same kind of vision, which has nothing to do with racism, with real social problems, or with the ghetto, but which of course did have a lot to do with the auto-marginalization of the Black self, with self-racism. This is all false, a paralysis.

What I am trying to say is that what is needed is to make a cinema of social approximation, of analysis, and to develop specific aspects of Black society, of the sociology of Black people, of the problems of Black people.

I saw *Purple Rain* and I thought it was an interesting film. I don't know whether the director was Black or white, though I assumed he was white. But it actually does not matter. Sometimes the film seemed very attractive to me, seemed to offer an interesting analysis of the problems of the Black family. But finally the film falls apart because it traces the origins of its hero's problems to that family and limits those problems to the individual, instead of locating them in social reality.

In a Black family in the US, you might have a family situation where the mother is an alcoholic and the father is a bum, but where are you going to locate the origin of problems? In the individual psyche? In the individual's lack of moral fiber? That's ridiculous. You have to look outside the family in order to investigate the nexus of social relations that gives rise to these problems. Otherwise you are lost. These are not psychosexual problems; they are social problems, economic problems, problems of the system—and not only of the political system—but of specific economic systems. Racism, remember, is also an economic system.

22

Are All Latins from Manhattan?
Hollywood, Ethnography, and Cultural Colonialism (1991)

This essay counters the critical tendency during the 1970s–1980s of discussing the representation of people of color in Hollywood cinema in terms of "images" or stereotypes. Drawing on theorists like James Clifford, Edward Said, and Homi K. Bhabha, López suggests that Hollywood "served as an ethnographer of American culture." Seemingly explaining and describing "others," the films ultimately created them in response to given political and historical needs. She first discusses the Good Neighbor Policy as the larger geopolitical context influencing Hollywood's interest in Latin America in the 1930s–1940s, and then examines the trajectories of three female crossover stars (Dolores Del Rio, Lupe Vélez, and Carmen Miranda) who worked in Hollywood before and during that period. She finds that Del Rio and Vélez's careers came to a standstill by the 1940s because they did not fit Hollywood's wartime needs for a particular type of "nonthreatening" ethnic "other." In contrast, Carmen Miranda's career blossomed because she was different enough but still relatable (a strange, but good neighbor)—even though her excessive on-screen performances managed to subtly undermine Hollywood's authority as a reliable ethnographer. This foundational essay subsequently became a model for complex analyses of "Latinos in Hollywood" (Beltrán 2005).

Editors' note: A revised, somewhat shorter edition of this essay was included in *Mediating Two Worlds: Cinematic Encounters in the Americas*, ed. John King, Ana M. López, and Manuel Alvarado (London: British Film Institute, 1993).

> She's a Latin from Manhattan
> I can tell by her mañana
> She's a Latin from Manhattan
> And not Havana.
>
> —Al Jolson in *Go into Your Dance* (1935)

The commonplace of ethnic studies of the Hollywood cinema is to begin with the obvious: the classic Hollywood cinema was never kind to ethnic or minority groups. The standard claim is that, be they Native American, Black, Hispanic, or Jewish, Hollywood represented ethnics and minorities as stereotypes that circulated easily and repeatedly from film to film. More significantly, minorities and ethnics were most noticeable by their absence in classic Hollywood films. Rarely protagonists, ethnics merely provided local color, comic relief, or easily recognizable villains and dramatic foils. When coupled with the pervasiveness of stereotypes, this marginalization or negation completes the usual "pattern" of Hollywood's ethnic representation and its standard assessment as damaging, insulting, and negative.

But Hollywood's relationship to each ethnic and minority group is far more nuanced than this simple narrative at first seems to allow. And, in fact, each of these relationships is unique; each has its own complex history with a specificity derived from Hollywood's position as a socio-culturally bound ethnographer.

What does it mean to say that Hollywood has served as an ethnographer of American culture? First, it means to conceive of ethnography not as a scientific methodology that through detailed description and analysis unearths holistic truths about "other" cultures (Heider 1976, 5–12), but as a historically determined practice of cultural interpretation and representation from the standpoint of participant observation (Clifford 1988). And it also means to think of Hollywood not as a simple reproducer of fixed and homogeneous cultures or ideologies, but as a producer of some of the multiple discourses that intervene in, affirm, and contest the socio-ideological struggles of a given moment. To think of a classic Hollywood film as ethnographic discourse is to affirm its status as an authored, yet collaborative, enterprise, akin in practice to the way contemporary ethnographers have redefined their discipline. James Clifford, for example, has analyzed the discursive nature of ethnography "not as the experience and interpretation of a circumscribed 'other' reality, but rather as a constructive negotiation involving . . . conscious politically significant subjects" (Clifford 1988, 41).

When ethnographers posit their work as "the mutual, dialogical production of a discourse" about culture that "in its ideal form would result in a polyphonic text," we also approach a description of the operations of an ideal, albeit not of Hollywood's cinema (Tyler 1986, 126). The difference lies in the deployment of power relations, what Edward Said (1979) calls the "effect of domination," or the ethnographic, cinematic, and colonial process of designing an identity for the other and, for the observer, a standpoint from which to see without being seen. Obviously, neither ethnography nor the cinema have achieved that ideal state of perfect polyphony or perspectival relativity where the observer-observed dichotomy can be transcended and no participant has "the final word in the form of a framing story or encompassing synthesis." Power relations always interfere. However, both ethnographic and cinematic texts, as discourses, carry the traces of this dialogic-polyphonic process and of the power relations that structure it.

Thinking of Hollywood as ethnographer—as coproducer in power of cultural texts—allows us to reformulate its relationship to ethnicity. Hollywood does not represent ethnics and minorities; it creates them and provides its audience with an experience of them. It evokes them, as the postmodern ethnographer Stephen Tyler might say. Rather than an investigation of mimetic relationships, then, what a critical reading of Hollywood's ethnographic discourse (a meta-ethnography) requires is the analysis of the historical-political construction of self-other relations—the articulation of forms of difference, sexual and ethnic—as an inscription of, among other factors, Hollywood's power as ethnographer, as creator, and translator of otherness.

One characteristic of standard "Hollywood's image of ____" studies is that, no matter how bleakly the overall mimetic accuracy of Hollywood's representations of a particular group is evaluated, the analyst always manages to pinpoint a golden, or near-golden, moment when Hollywood, for complex conjunctural reasons, sees the light and becomes temporarily more sensitive to an ethnic or minority group. In the history of Hollywood's treatment of the American Indian, for example, that moment arrives in the 1960s and 1970s. For other ethnic and minority groups—Jews and Latin Americans, for example—usually there is a significant improvement noticed in the post–World War II period of "social consciousness."[1] What interests me are not the historical specifics of each of these moments, but the fact that such moments of the "discovery" and inscription of ethnic otherness play a critical role in the structure of texts about Hollywood and ethnicity, serving as the linchpin of teleological historical arguments decrying Hollywood's stereotypical, unrealistic, and biased representations of ethnics.

My project is to question precisely this historical-narrative *topos* in the history of Hollywood's representation of Latin Americans. I will focus upon what is perceived as the "golden moment" or "break" in that history—the Good Neighbor Policy years (roughly 1939-1947)—in order to analyze the moment's historical coherence and its function for Hollywood as an ethnographic institution, that is as creator, integrator, and translator of otherness. What happens when Hollywood self-consciously and intentionally assumes the role of cultural ethnographer?

My emphasis is on three stars whose ethnic otherness was articulated according to parameters that shifted as Hollywood's ethnographic imperative became clear: Dolores Del Rio, Lupe Vélez, and Carmen Miranda. That these three figures are Latin American and female is much more than a simple coincidence, for the Latin American woman poses a double threat—sexual and racial—to Hollywood's ethnographic and colonial authority.

The Good Neighbor Policy: Hollywood Zeroes In On Latin America

After decades of portraying Latin Americans lackadaisically and sporadically as lazy peasants and wily señoritas who inhabited an undifferentiated backward land, Hollywood films between 1939 and 1947, featuring Latin American stars, music, locations, and stories flooded US and international markets. By February 1943, for example, thirty films with Latin American themes or locales had been released and twenty-five more were in the works. By April 1945, eighty-four films dealing with Latin American themes had been produced (Rowland 1947, 74, 68). These films seemed to evidence a newfound sensibility, most notably, a sudden respect for national and geographical boundaries. At the simplest level, for example, it seemed that Hollywood was exercising some care to differentiate between the cultural and geographic characteristics of different Latin American countries by incorporating general location shots, specific citations of iconographic sites (for example, Rio de Janeiro's Corcovado Mountain), and some explanations of the cultural characteristics of the inhabitants.

Why did Hollywood suddenly become interested in Latin America? In economic terms, Latin America was the only foreign market available for exploitation during World War II. Before the war, the industry had derived a large percentage of its gross revenues from foreign markets, and upon the closing of the European and Japanese markets, it set out, in Bosley Crowther's words, on "a campaign to woo Latin America" with films of "Pan-American" interest (1949, 21).

Pan-Americanism was also, however, an important key word for the Roosevelt administration, the Rockefeller Foundation, and the newly created (1940) State Department Office of the Coordinator of Inter-American Affairs (OCIAA) headed by Nelson Rockefeller. Concerns about our Southern neighbors' dubious political allegiances and the safety of US investments in Latin America led to the resurrection of the long-dormant Good Neighbor Policy and to the official promotion of hemispheric unity, cooperation, and nonaggression (in part, to erase the memories of the not-so-distant military interventions in Cuba and Nicaragua). Charged with the responsibility of coordinating all efforts to promote inter-American understanding, the OCIAA set up a Motion Picture Section and appointed John Hay Whitney, vice president and director of the film library of the Museum of Modern Art (MoMA) in New York, as its director.[2]

The OCIAA sponsored the production of newsreels and documentaries for Latin American distribution that showed "the truth about the American way," contracted with Walt Disney in 1941 to produce a series of twenty-four shorts with Latin American themes that would "carry the message of democracy and friendship below the Rio Grande," sponsored screenings of films that celebrated the "democratic way" in what became known as the South American embassy circuit, and, together with the Hays Office's newly appointed Latin American expert, began to pressure the studios to become more sensitive to Latin issues and portrayals (Woll 1977–1980; de Usabel 1982). This impetus, when coupled with the incentive of Latin America's imminently exploitable 4,240 movie theaters, was sufficient to stimulate Hollywood to take on the project of educating Latin America about the democratic way of life and its North American audience about its Latin American neighbors.

This self-appointed mission, however, needs to be questioned more closely. How does Hollywood position itself *and* North Americans in relation to the Southern "neighbors"? How is its friendliness constituted? How does it differ from Hollywood's prior circulation of so-called stereotypes and its negligent undifferentiation of the continent?

From an industrial perspective, Hollywood's policies in the Good Neighbor period were directed by the assumption that Latin Americans would flock to see themselves created by Hollywood in glorious Technicolor and with an unexpected linguistic fluency. The pre–Good Neighbor films of the 1930s dealing with Latin Americans (primarily dramatic stories) were notorious for linguistic blunders and regional undifferentiation. They also directly promoted the development of proto-industrial filmmaking in Argentina, Mexico, and Brazil that had already begun to compete for the Latin American market. Furthermore, several Latin American nations had regularly begun to ban or censor Hollywood films deemed offensive to the national character, most notoriously, RKO's *Girl of the Rio* (1932), a film banned by a number of Latin American countries because its lecherous and treacherous central character, Sr. Tostado (Mr. "Toast," "Toasted," or "Crazed"), was considered "the most vile Mexican" ever to appear on the screen (Woll 1977–1980, 33). To forestall censorship and protests and to decrease the competitive edge of national productions, Hollywood began to feature more Latin American actors, songs and dances, and to differentiate among different cultures.

Three basic kinds of Good Neighbor Policy films were produced. First, there were a number of standard, classic Hollywood genre films, with North American protagonists, set in Latin America and with some location shooting, for example, Irving Rapper's *Now Voyager* (1942), with extensive footage shot in Rio de Janeiro; Edward Dmytryk's *Cornered* (1945), shot totally on location in Buenos Aires; and Alfred Hitchcock's *Notorious* (1946), with second-unit location shots of Rio de Janeiro. Then there were B-productions set and often shot in Latin America and that featured mediocre US actors and Latin entertainers in either musicals or pseudo-musical formats, for example, *Mexicana* (1945) starring Tito Guízar, Mexico's version of Frank Sinatra, and the sixteen-year-old Cuban torch singer Estelita; Gregory Ratoff's *Carnival in Costa Rica* (1947) starring Dick Haymes, Vera Ellen, and Cesar Romero; and Edgar G. Ulmer's remake of *Grand Hotel, Club Havana* (1945), starring the starlet Isabelita, Tom Neil, and Margaret Lindsay. Finally, the most successful and most self-consciously "good-neighborly" films were the mid- to big-budget musical comedies set either in Latin America or in the US but featuring, in addition to recognizable US stars, fairly well-known Latin American actors and entertainers.

Almost every studio produced its share of these films between 1939 and 1947, but 20th Century Fox, RKO, and Republic specialized in "good neighborliness" of the musical variety. Fox had Carmen Miranda under contract and produced films that featured her between 1940 and 1946; RKO followed the Rockefeller interest in Latin America by sending Orson Welles on a Good Neighbor tour of Brazil to make a film about Carnival (Stam 1991), and with films such as *Panamericana* (1945); Republic exploited contract players Tito Guízar and Estelita in a number of low-budget musicals such as *The Thrill of Brazil* (1946).

Notwithstanding the number of films produced, and the number of Latin American actors contracted by the studios in this period, it is difficult to describe Hollywood's position with regard to these suddenly welcomed "others" as respectful or reverent.[3] Hollywood (and the United States) needed to posit a complex otherness as the flip side of wartime patriotism and nationalism and in order to assert and protect its colonial-imperialist economic interests. A special kind of other was needed to reinforce the wartime national self, one that—unlike the German or Japanese other—was nonthreatening, potentially but not practically assimilable (that is, nonpolluting to the purity of the race), friendly, fun-loving, and not deemed insulting to Latin American eyes and ears. Ultimately, Hollywood succeeded in all except, perhaps, the last category.

The Transition:
From Indifference to "Difference" across the Bodies of Women

Before the Good Neighbor Policy period, few Latin Americans had achieved star status in Hollywood. In fact, most of the "vile" Latin Americans of the early Hollywood cinema were played by US actors. In the silent period, the Mexican actor Ramón Novarro, one of the few Latin American men to have had a consistent career in Hollywood, succeeded as a sensual yet feminized "Latin Lover" modeled on the Valentino icon (Hansen 1986, 6–32), but the appellation "Latin" always connoted Mediterranean rather than Latin American. Ostensibly less threatening than men, Latin American women fared differently, particularly Dolores Del Rio and Lupe Vélez.

Del Rio's Hollywood career spanned the silent and early sound eras. Although considered exotic, Del Rio appeared in a variety of films, working with directors as diverse as Raoul Walsh, King Vidor, and Orson Welles.[4] After a successful transition to talkies in Edwin Carewe's *Evangeline* (1929), her place in the Hollywood system was unquestionable and further legitimized by her marriage to the respected MGM art director Cedric Gibbons. Undeniably Latin American, Del Rio was not, however, identified exclusively with Latin roles. Hers was a vague upper-class exoticism articulated within a general category of "foreign/other" tragic sensuality. This sensual other, an object of sexual fascination, transgression, fear, and capitulation not unlike Garbo or Dietrich, did not have a specific national or ethnic provenance, simply an aura of foreignness that accommodated her disruptive potential. Her otherness was located and defined on a sexual rather than an ethnic register, and she portrayed, above all, ethnically vague characters with a weakness for North American "white/blond" men: Indigenous maidens, South Seas princesses, Latin American señoritas, and other aristocratic beauties. Although she often functioned as a repeatable stereotype (in her role in *Girl of the Rio*, for example), her undifferentiated sexuality was not easily tamed by the proto-colonial ethnographic imperatives of Hollywood's Good Neighbor period. In a precursor of the Good Neighbor films like *Flying Down to Rio* (1933), the explicit and irresistible sensuality of her aristocratic Carioca character (all she has to do is look at a man across a crowded night club and he is smitten forever) could be articulated because it would be tamed by marriage to the North American hero. However, in the films of the Good Neighbor cycle, that resolution/ partial appeasement of the ethnically undifferentiated sexual threat of otherness she unleashed was no longer available. Likewise, in another pre–Good Neighbor Policy film in which she portrays a Latin American, Lloyd Bacon's *In Caliente* (1935) (fig. 22.1), Del Rio is not identified as a *Mexican* beauty, but as the *world's* greatest dancer. As Carlos Fuentes has remarked, Del Rio was "a goddess threatening to become woman" (1976, 10),[5] and neither category—goddess or woman—was appropriate to Hollywood's self-appointed mission as goodwill imperialist ethnographer of the Americas. Del Rio's persona and her articulation in Hollywood films, in fact, comprise a perfect cinematic example of what Homi K. Bhabha has described as the phenomenon of the colonial hybrid, a disavowed cultural differentiation necessary for the existence of colonial-imperialist authority, where "what is disavowed [difference] is not repressed but repeated as something different—a mutation, a hybrid" (1986, 172).

Del Rio chose to return to Mexico in 1943 and dedicated herself—with a few "returns" to Hollywood, most notably to appear in John Ford's *The Fugitive* (1947) and *Cheyenne Autumn* (1964)—to the Mexican cinema and stage, where she assumed a legendary fame inconceivable in Hollywood.

Are All Latins from Manhattan? | 427

Figure 22.1. As "the world's greatest dancer," Dolores Del Rio was paired with Leo Carillo in Lloyd Bacon's *In Caliente* (1935), where she personifies the perfect cinematic example of the "colonial hybrid." Personal collection of Ana M. López.

The impossibility of her status for Hollywood in 1939–1947 was, however, literally worked through the body of another Mexican actress, Lupe Vélez.

Like Del Rio's, Vélez's career began in the silent period, where she showed promise working with D. W. Griffith in *Lady of the Pavements* (1929) and other directors. But Vélez's position in Hollywood was defined not by her acting versatility, but by her smoldering ethnic identifiability. Although as striking as Del Rio's, Vélez's beauty and sexual appeal were aggressive, flamboyant, and stridently ethnic (fig. 22.2). Throughout the 1930s, she personified the hot-blooded, thickly accented Latin temptress with insatiable sexual appetites, on-screen—in films such as *Hot Pepper* (1933), *Strictly Dynamite* (1934), and *La Zandunga* (1938)—and with her star persona by engaging in much-publicized simultaneous affairs with Gary Cooper, Ronald Colman, and Ricardo Cortez, and marrying Johnny Weissmuller in 1933.[6] (Impossible to imagine a better match between screen

Figure 22.2. Echoes of Lupe Vélez's smoldering sexuality resonate in this publicity shot. Unlike the bearskin upon which she lies, Vélez epitomized the dangerous and potentially untamable aspects of Latin American female sexuality. Personal collection of Ana M. López.

and star biographies: Tarzan meets the beast of the Tropics.) Vélez was, in other words, outrageous, but her sexual excessiveness, although clearly identified as specifically ethnic, was articulated as potentially subsumable. On and off screen, she, like Del Rio, was mated with and married North American men.

The dangers of such explicit on-screen ethnic miscegenation became apparent in RKO's *Mexican Spitfire* six-film series (1939–1943), simultaneously Vélez's most successful films and an index of the inevitability of her failure. Vélez portrayed a Mexican entertainer, Carmelita, who falls in love and marries—after seducing him away from his legitimate Anglo fiancée—Dennis Lindsay, a nice New England man. Much to the dismay of his proper Puritan family, Dennis chooses to remain with Carmelita against all obstacles, including, as the series progressed, specific references to Carmelita's mixed blood, lack of breeding, and social unacceptability, her refusal to put the entertainment business completely behind her to become a proper wife, her inability to promote his (floundering) advertising career, and her apparent lack of desire for offspring. Although the first couple of installments were very successful, the series was described as increasingly redundant, contrived, and patently "absurd" by the press and was cancelled in 1943. Not only had it begun to lose money for RKO, but it also connoted a kind of Latin American otherness anathema to the Good Neighbor mission. Summarily stated, the questions posed by the series could no longer be tolerated because there were no "good neighborly" answers. The ethnic problematic of the series—intermarriage, miscegenation, and integration—could not be explicitly addressed within the new, friendly climate. Ironically highlighting this fictional and ideological question, Vélez, unmarried and five months pregnant, committed suicide in 1944.

Neither Del Rio nor Vélez could be recreated as Good Neighbor ethnics, for their ethnic and sexual power and danger were not assimilable within Hollywood's new, ostensibly friendly, and temperate regime. Del Rio was not ethnic enough and too much of an actress; Vélez was too "Latin" and untamable. Hollywood's new position was defined by its double-imperative as "ethnographer" of the Americas, that is, by its self-appointed mission as translator of the ethnic and sexual threat of Latin American otherness into peaceful good neighborliness *and* by its desire to use that translation to attempt to make further inroads into the resistant Latin American movie market without damaging its national box office. It, therefore, could not advantageously promote either a mythic, goddess-like actress with considerable institutional clout (Del Rio) or an ethnic volcano (Vélez) that was not even subdued by that most sacred of institutions, marriage to a North American. What Hollywood's Good Neighbor regime demanded was the articulation of a different female star persona that could be readily identifiable as Latin American (with the sexual suggestiveness necessary to fit the prevailing stereotype) but whose sexuality was neither too attractive (to dispel the fear/attraction of miscegenation) nor so powerful as to demand its submission to a conquering North American male.

The Perfect "Good Neighbor": Fetishism, Self, and Others

Hollywood's lust for Latin America as ally and market—and its self-conscious attempt to translate and tame the potentially disturbing radical (sexual and ethnic) otherness that the recognition of difference (or lack) entails—are clearest within the constraints of the musical comedy genre. Incorporated into the genre as exotic entertainers, Latin Americans were simultaneously marginalized and privileged. Although they were denied valid narrative functions, entertainment, rather than narrative coherence or complexity, is the locus of pleasure of the genre. Mapped onto the musical comedy form in both deprivative (the denial of a valid narrative function) and supplemental (the location of an excess pleasure) terms, this Hollywood version of "Latin Americanness" participates in the operations of fetishism and disavowal typical of the stereotype in colonial-imperialist discourses (Bhabha 1983, 18–36). This exercise of colonial-imperialist authority would peak, with a significant twist, in the Carmen Miranda films at 20th Century Fox, a cycle that produced a public figure, Miranda (fig. 22.3), that lays bare, with surreal clarity, the scenario of Hollywood's own colonial fantasy and the problematics of ethnic representation in a colonial-imperialist context.[7]

Figure 22.3. Attired in a hyper-version of the traditional *baianas* of Brazilian carnival, Carmen Miranda was the best known Latin American of the 1940s. Personal collection of Ana M. López.

Are All Latins from Manhattan? | 431

In these films, Carmen Miranda functions, above all, as a fantastic or uncanny fetish. Everything about her is surreal, off-center, displaced onto a different regime: from her extravagant hats, midriff-baring multicolored costumes, and five-inch platform shoes to her linguistic malapropisms, farcical sexuality, and high-pitched voice, she is an other, everyone's other. Although not even Brazilian-born (she was born in Portugal to parents who immigrated to Brazil and named her Maria do Carmo Miranda da Cunha), she became synonymous with cinematic "Latin Americanness," with an essence defined and mobilized by herself and Hollywood throughout the continent. As the emcee announces at the end of her first number in Busby Berkeley's *The Gang's All Here*, "Well, there's your Good Neighbor Policy. Come on honey, let's Good Neighbor it."

Miranda was "discovered" by Hollywood "as is," that is, after her status as a top entertainer in Brazil (with more than three hundred records, five films—including the first Brazilian sound feature—and nine Latin American tours) brought her to the New York stage, where her six-minute performance in *The Streets of Paris* (1939) transformed her into "an overnight sensation" (Konder 1982, 17–21).[8] Her explicit Brazilianness—samba song and dance repertoire, Carnival-type costumes—was transformed into the epitome of *latinidad* by a series of films that "placed" her in locales as varied as Lake Louise in the Canadian Rockies, Havana, or Buenos Aires.

Her validity as "Latin American" was based on a rhetoric of visual excess—of costume, performance, sexuality, and musicality—that carried over into the mode of address of the films themselves. Of course, since they were produced at Fox, a studio that depended on its superior Technicolor process to differentiate its product in the marketplace (Gomery 1986, 76–100), these films are also almost painfully colorful, exploiting the technology to further inscribe Latin Americanness as tropicality. For example, although none of the Fox films were shot on location, all include markedly luscious "travelogue-like" sections justifying the authenticity of their locales. Even more significantly, they also include the visual representation of travel, whether to the country in question or "inland," as further proof of the validity of their ethno-presentation within a regime that privileges the visual as the only possible site of knowledge.

Weekend in Havana is a prototypical example. The film begins by introducing the lure of the exotic in a postcredit, narrative establishment montage sequence that situates travel to Latin America as a desirable sightseeing adventure: snow on the Brooklyn Bridge dissolves to a brochure of leisure cruises to Havana, to a tourist guide to "Cuba: The Holiday

Isle of the Tropics," to a window display promoting "Sail to Romance" cruises featuring life-size cardboard cutouts of Carmen Miranda and a Latin band that come to life and sing the title song (which begins, "How would you like to spend the weekend in Havana . . ."). Immediately after, the romantic plot of the musical is set up: Alice Faye plays a Macy's salesgirl whose much-scrimped-for Caribbean cruise is ruined when her ship runs aground. She refuses to sign the shipping company's release and is appeased only with the promise of "romance" in an all-expenses-paid tour of Havana with shipping company executive John Payne.

The trip from the marooned cruise ship to Havana is again represented by an exuberantly colorful montage of the typical tourist sights of Havana—el Morro Castle, the Malecón, the Hotel Nacional, Sloppy Joe's Bar—with a voice-over medley of "Weekend in Havana" and typical Cuban songs. Finally, once ensconced in the most luxurious hotel in the city, Faye is taken to see the sights by Payne. They travel by taxi to a sugar plantation, where Payne's lecture from a tourist book, although it bores Faye to yawns, does serve as a voice-over narration for the visual presentation of "Cubans at work": "Hundreds of thousands of Cubans are involved with the production of this important commodity . . ." These three sequences serve both important narrative and legitimizing functions, testifying to the authenticity of the film's ethnographic and documentary work and eliding the fact that the featured native entertainer, Rosita Rivas (Miranda), is neither Cuban nor speaks Spanish.

More complexly, all the Fox films depend upon Miranda's performative excess to validate their authority as "good neighborly" ethnographic discourses. The films' simple plots—often remakes of prior musical successes and most commonly involving some kind of mistaken identity or similar snafu—further highlight the importance of the Miranda-identified visual and musical regime rather than the legitimizing narrative order. The beginning of *The Gang's All Here*, for example, clearly underlines this operation by presenting a narrativized representation of travel, commerce, and ethnic identity. After the credits, a half-lit floating head singing Ary Baroso's "Brasil" in Portuguese suddenly shifts (in a classic Busby Berkeley syntactical move) to the hull of a ship emblazoned with the name SS *Brazil*, docking in New York and unloading typical Brazilian products: sugar, coffee, bananas, strawberries, and Carmen Miranda. Wearing a hat featuring her native fruits, Miranda finishes the song, triumphantly strides into New York, switches to an English tune, and is handed the keys to the city by the mayor as the camera tracks back to reveal the stage of a nightclub, an Anglo audience to whom she is introduced *as* the Good Neighbor Policy and whom she instructs to dance the "Uncle Sam-ba."

The Fox films' most amazing characteristic is Miranda's immutability and the substitutability of the narratives. Miranda travels and is inserted into different landscapes, but she remains the same from film to film, purely Latin American. Whether the action of the film is set in Buenos Aires, Havana, the Canadian Rockies, Manhattan, or a Connecticut mansion, the on-screen Miranda character—most often named Carmen or Rosita—is remarkably coherent: above all, and against all odds, an entertainer and the most entertaining element in all the films.[9] While the North American characters work out the inevitable romance plot of the musical comedy, Miranda—always a thorn to the budding romance—puts on a show and dallies outrageously with the leading men. Normally not permanently mated with a North American protagonist (with the notable exception of *That Night in Rio*, where she gets to keep Don Ameche, but only because his identical double gets the white girl played by Alice Faye), Miranda, nevertheless, gets to have her fun along the way and always entices and almost seduces with aggressive kisses and embraces at least one, but most often several, of the North American men.

Miranda's sexuality is so aggressive, however, that it is diffused, spent in gesture, innuendo, and salacious commentary. Unlike Vélez, who can seduce and marry a nice WASP man, Miranda remains either contentedly single, attached to a Latin American Lothario (for example, the womanizing manager-cum-gigolo played by Cesar Romero in *Weekend in Havana*), or in the permanent never-never land of prolonged and unconsummated engagements to unlikely North American types. For example, in *Copacabana* she has been engaged for ten years to Groucho Marx and, at the end of the film, they still have separate hotel rooms and no shared marriage vows.

Miranda, not unlike other on-screen female performers (Dietrich in the Von Sternberg films, for example), functions narratively and discursively as a sexual fetish, freezing the narrative and the pleasures of the voyeuristic gaze and provoking a regime of spectacle and specularity. She acknowledges and openly participates in her fetishization, staring back at the camera, implicating the audience in her sexual display. But she is also an ethnic fetish. The look she returns is also that of the ethnographer and its colonial spectator stand-in. Her Latin Americanness is displaced in all its visual splendor for simultaneous colonial appropriation and denial.

Although Miranda is visually fetishized within filmic systems that locate her metaphorically as the emblem of knowledge of Latin

Americanness, Miranda's voice, rife with cultural impurities and disturbing syncretisms, slips through the webs of Hollywood's colonial and ethnographic authority over the constitution and definition of otherness. It is in fact within the aural register, constantly set against the legitimacy of the visual, that Hollywood's ethnographic good neighborliness breaks down in the Fox-Miranda films. In addition to the psychosexual impact of her voice, Miranda's excessive manipulation of accents—the obviously shifting registers of tone and pitch between her spoken and sung English and between her English and Portuguese—inflates the fetish, cracking its surface while simultaneously aggrandizing it. Most obvious in the films where she sings consecutive numbers in each language (*Weekend in Havana* and *The Gang's All Here* are two examples), the tonal differences between her sung and spoken Portuguese and her English indicate that her excessive accent and her linguistic malapropisms are no more than a pretense, a nod to the requirements of a conception of foreignness and otherness necessary to maintain the validity of the text in question as well as her persona as an ethnographic good neighborly gesture. That the press and studio machinery constantly remarked upon her accent and problems with English further highlight their ambiguous status (Woll 1983, 114–15). At once a sign of her otherness as well as of the artificiality of all otherness, her accent ultimately became an efficient marketing device, exploited in advertisements and publicity campaigns: "I tell everyone I know to DREENK Piel's."[10]

Throughout the Good Neighbor films, Miranda remains a fetish, but a surreal one, a fetish that self-consciously underlines the difficult balance between knowledge and belief that sustains it and that lets us hear the edges of an unclassifiable otherness, product of an almost indescribable bricolage, that rejects the totalizing search for truth of the good neighborly Hollywood ethnographer while simultaneously submitting to its designs.

"Are All Latins from Manhattan?"

Miranda's Hollywood career was cut short both by the demise of Hollywood's good neighborliness in the postwar era as well as by her untimely death in 1955.[11] However, Hollywood's circulation and use of her persona as the emblem of the Good Neighbor clearly demonstrates the fissures of Hollywood's work as Latin American ethnographer in this period. With Miranda's acquiescence and active participation, Hollywood ensconced her as the essence of Latin American otherness in terms that, on the surface, were both nonderogatory and simultaneously nonthreatening. First, as a female emblem, her position was always already that of a less-threatening other. In this context, the potential threat of her sexuality—that which was troubling in Vélez, for example—was dissipated by its sheer visual and narrative excess. Furthermore, her legitimizing ethnicity, exacerbated by an aura of the carnivalesque and the absurd, could be narratively relegated to the stage, to the illusory (and tamable) world of performance, theater, and movies. This is perhaps most conclusively illustrated by the frequency with which her persona is used as the emblem of Latin American otherness and exoticism in Hollywood films of the period: in *House across the Bay* (Archie Mayo, 1940) Joan Bennett appears in a Miranda-inspired *baiana* costume; in *Babes on Broadway* (Busby Berkeley, 1941) Mickey Rooney does a number while dressed like her. In *This Our Life* (John Huston, 1942) Bette Davis plays a Miranda record and hums along to "Chica Chica Boom Chic," and in *Mildred Pierce* (Michael Curtiz, 1945) Jo Ann Marlow does a fully costumed Miranda imitation.

At the same time, however, Miranda's textual persona escapes the narrow parameters of the Good Neighbor. As a willing participant in the production of these self-conscious ethnographic texts, Miranda literally asserted her own voice in the textual operations that defined her as *the* other. Transforming, mixing, ridiculing, and redefining her own difference against the expected standards, Miranda's speaking voice, songs, and accents create an other text that is in counterpoint to the principal textual operations. She does not burst the illusory bubble of the Good Neighbor, but by inflating it beyond recognition, she highlights its status as a discursive construct-as-myth.

When we recognize that Hollywood's relationship to ethnic and minority groups is primarily ethnographic—that is, one that involves the coproduction in power of cultural texts—rather than merely mimetic, it becomes possible to understand the supposed break in Hollywood's misrepresentation of Latin Americans during the Good Neighbor Policy years textually as well as in instrumental and ideological terms. It is particularly important to recognize that Hollywood (and, by extension, television) fulfills this ethnographic function, because we are in an era that, not unlike the Good Neighbor years, is praised for its "Hispanization." While the media crows about the 1987–1988 successes of *La Bamba* and *Salsa: The Motion Picture* and a special issue of *Time* proclaims "Magnifico! Hispanic Culture Breaks Out of the Barrio,"[12] it might prove enlightening to look at this particular translation, presentation, and assimilation of Latin American otherness as yet another ethnographic textual creation that must be analyzed as a political coproduction of representations of difference and not as a mimetic narrative challenge.

23

Greater Cuba (1996)

"Greater Cuba" analyzes the work of three generations of US-based filmmakers of Cuban descent, comparing those born and professionalized in Cuba (e.g., Orlando Jiménez-Leal), to those born in Cuba and trained in the US (e.g., León Ichaso), to those who left as small children or who were born in the United States (e.g., Tony Labat). López argues that far from being homogeneous, the Cuban filmmaking community, like the Cuban exile community, is made up of numerous groups. The essay offers a rethinking of the category of "Cuban film," which had been limited to work made on the island after the 1959 revolution, by broadening the category to include filmmakers of Cuban descent working in other locations. "Greater Cuba" influenced the approaches of other scholars—most notably, Juan Antonio García Borrero's notion of "cine sumergido" and his rethinking Cuban film history to include audiovisual production before the revolution and outside of ICAIC (the state film institute) (2001, 2002).

>   I carry this marginality immune to all returns,
>   too much of an habanera to be a new yorker
>   too much a new yorker to be
>   —even to go back to being—
>   anything else.[1]
>
>   —Lourdes Casal, "Para Ana Velford"

Editors' note: This essay is a revision and expansion of "The 'Other' Island: Exiled Cuban Cinema," published in *Jump Cut* (June 1993).

Exile has become a fashionable position from which to "speak." Empowered by postmodern practices that proclaim the decenteredness of contemporary capitalist life and by postcolonial theories of discourse that privilege the hybridity and ambivalence of exile (both inside and outside, belonging yet foreign) as a significant site from which to challenge the oppressive hegemony of the "center" or the "national," the exilic experience—along with borders, margins, and peripheries—has become a central metaphor of contemporary multicultural artistic and critical practices.

Defining what such a position means for cinematic practices is, however, a difficult task.[2] Certainly, in the case of the very rich "Chilean exile cinema," we could argue that the sociohistorical experience of political exile gave rise to a painfully postcolonial, often postmodern, "national" cinema: self-reflexive, nostalgic, produced outside the borders of the nation-state (often even outside the continent itself).[3] But speaking of other less clear-cut "exiled" cinemas in today's increasingly heterogeneous worlds filled with wandering artists and international coproductions is more complicated. And the task becomes even more complex when we seek to find such a cinema within the United States, even in Hollywood itself. Simply being a foreigner—the "outsider" looking in—is not enough. If we take the Chilean exile cinema as a possible model, the principal prerequisite for an exile cinema would seem to be a politically motivated diaspora; in other words, a "forced" political exile without the possibility of return.

In the Chilean case, the tragedy of the diaspora had a special immediacy and political poignancy. Almost universally, cultural circles could respond negatively to Pinochet's regime of terror and sympathetically to the Chilean exiles and to their efforts to position themselves politically and culturally outside their nation. But the last thirty years or so have also witnessed the slow development of an exile cinema/video practice that has been neither as sympathetically received nor as homogeneously articulated. This "other" island, the films and videos of exiled Cubans, has often grated harshly against the sentiments of those for whom *the* island represented our only utopian hope in the Americas.

Certainly one cannot compare the 1973 Chilean debacle with the 1959 Cuban Revolution; if anything, the politics of these events were diametrically opposed and thus gave rise to very different exile populations. Nevertheless, the Cuban exile community is a significant one that cannot be dismissed. Despite Cuba's long history of exile (already marked by wars and displacements when it became "independent" in 1902, political and economic instabilities created mass exoduses in 1925–1933 and 1952–1958), no exodus has been as massive or prolonged as the one provoked by the 1959 revolution. By some (conservative) estimates, as much as 10 percent of the island's present population (ten and a half million, according to the 1987 census) lives in exile (Marshall 1987, 248).[4] This significant part of the "nation" is deeply woven into the history of a "Cuba" that exceeds national boundaries. At the margins of the nation as such, this community functions both as mirror (sharing traditions, codes, symbols, discursive strategies) and as supplement. Furthermore, although a cursory (gringo) look might see the Cuban exile community as homogeneously allied with the far political right because of its continued opposition to the revolution, it is important to note not only its heterogeneity and its historical variances,[5] but also, more specifically, that the exiled filmmakers are not all necessarily typical of the more hysterical and anti-intellectual Miami/New York exile groups that still think of invasions and infiltration, hold fundraisers, elect presidents and mayors in exile, and draw up elaborate postsocialism capitalist reconstruction plans for the island.

Of course, that the majority of Cuban exiles overwhelmingly sought refuge in the United States also had a determining influence on their politics (a reciprocal relationship) and their cinematic/video output.[6] On the one hand, the politics of the Cuban exiles, especially their anti-Castroism, challenged the pro–Cuban Revolution feelings of most people involved in independent/alternative practices; on the other, as yet another exile/Hispanic minority group, they have had few opportunities to "make it" in the entertainment mainstream defined and controlled by Hollywood. Although buttressed by official US policies and actions against Cuba since 1961, Cuban exile film—and video—makers have, paradoxically, had a difficult time articulating their arguments and being heard. Within artistic circles, their exile has, in general, not been a privileged position from which to speak. Their efforts to assemble a national identity within/out of exile—to reconstruct a national history—have often been seen as the marks of a strident ethnocentrism already compromised by their challenges to the island's utopia rather than as anguished cries of exilic loss, liminality, and deterritorialization coupled with the paradoxical need to build, to reterritorialize, themselves anew.

The exile of Cuban filmmakers must be traced back to Cuba itself and to specific events in the island that provoked it. Immediately after the 1959 revolution, the few established producers/filmmakers left Cuba for the United States, among them Manolo Alonso, the "czar" of Cuban film. After nationalization, his film "empire" (studios, etc.) provided the newly formed ICAIC (Instituto Cubano de Arte e Industria Cinematográficos) with a basic infrastructure. Nevertheless, the establishment of ICAIC and the revolutionary government's commitment to the cinema attracted and pleased almost all of the cinephiles, technicians, and amateur filmmakers that had been active in the various (political and apolitical) cine club movements of the 1950s. However, a survey of the first five years of *Cine Cubano* (1960–1965) reveals that of the ten Cuban award-winning feature filmmakers mentioned, five subsequently chose exile: Eduardo Manet, Fausto Canel, Alberto Roldán, Roberto Fandiño, and Francisco Villaverde. Many others involved with ICAIC also chose exile: among them, cinematographers like Ramón Suárez, who photographed Tomás Gutiérrez Alea's films between *Las doce sillas* (The Twelve Chairs, 1962) and *Memorias del subdesarrollo* (Memories of Underdevelopment, 1968); actors like Eduardo Moure, who was the male lead in the first episode of *Lucía* (1968) and in *Historias de la Revolución* (1961); authors/scriptwriters like Edmundo Desnoes (*Memorias del subdesarrollo*), Antonio Benítez-Rojo (*Los sobrevivientes* [The Survivors, 1978]; *Una mujer, un hombre, una ciudad* [A Woman, a Man, a City, 1978]), and René Jordán (*Cuba 58*, 1962); and graphic designers like Antonio Reboiro, who was responsible for many of ICAIC's striking early film posters.[7] What prompted them to leave?

In print, several of the exiled filmmakers have traced their disaffection with the revolution to an event that provoked a national intellectual crisis: the P.M. affair.[8] In 1960, working independently of ICAIC, a group affiliated with the cultural magazine *Lunes de Revolución* (a supplement of the newspaper *Revolución* edited by Carlos Franqui) produced a short film for the magazine's weekly television program. A "free cinema"–style exploration of nightlife in the bars and cafés around the Havana waterfront, the film was called *P.M.* or *Post Meridian* and was directed by Sabá Cabrera Infante (the brother of novelist Guillermo) and Orlando Jiménez-Leal, a young cameraman who had worked for the newsreel production company Cineperiódico. Neither was affiliated with ICAIC. The film aired on television and received a favorable review from Néstor Almendros, who was then a critic in the influential mass-circulation weekly *Bohemia*. Almendros believed the film to be a "jewel of the experimental cinema" that "probed deeply into the reality of an aspect of popular life" (1992, 172). However, when the filmmakers applied to ICAIC for a theatrical exhibition license for the film, it was denied. ICAIC's decision was difficult for many to understand. Those associated with the film and/or with *Lunes* cried "censorship," while ICAIC maintained that the film was irresponsible to the revolution and that they had the right and authority to delay/prohibit its distribution. As Michael Chanan points out, this modest film about the somewhat seedy nighttime activities of marginal Havana types was perhaps only "mildly offensive" (1985, 101), but the historical moment—only six weeks after the Bay of Pigs invasion and Castro's official declaration of the socialist character of the revolution—was tense and emotionally charged. The debate over *P.M.* reached such heights that Castro himself intervened in a famous speech known as "Words to the Intellectuals" that closed a series of meetings among intellectuals held at the National Library. His words were prophetic and have been often quoted: "Within the Revolution, everything; against it, nothing" (Castro 1977, 17).

Despite many claims that the *P.M.* affair was the decisive event that motivated filmmakers to seek exile, most did not leave Cuba until the late 1960s. The debate over *P.M.* revealed that there were various political positions among cultural workers and caused a restructuring of the noncinematic arts scene centered on the closing of *Lunes*, a change in the direction of Casa de las Américas, and the creation of UNEAC (Unión Nacional de Escritores y Artistas de Cuba [National Union of Writers and Artists of Cuba]) in 1961. However, because the cultural agenda suggested by Castro's "Words to the Intellectuals" was not in itself restrictive, it led to a period marked by a certain creative anarchy and a testing of the limits of what was possible under the definition "revolutionary." The tensions that surfaced in this period among artists (primarily writers) and between cultural circles and the revolutionary intelligentsia would not come to a head until 1968–1971, when the polemic case of the writer Heberto Padilla caused an international furor that culminated in a formal "tightening up" of the definition of revolutionary art and culture.[9]

In any case, although Orlando Jiménez-Leal, Sabá Cabrera Infante, and Néstor Almendros (who lost his job in *Bohemia* after the *P.M.* affair) left in 1962–1963, few of those working in ICAIC left Cuba before 1965. The bulk of departures of ICAIC personnel, in fact, occurred in the period 1965–1968.[10] Thus, these departures—although perhaps traceable in spirit to the P.M. affair—were more closely linked to the series of events that began in 1965 with the formation of the Central Committee of the Communist Party and the internment in forced labor camps (called UMAPs: Unidades Militares de Ayuda a la Producción [Military Units to Aid Production]) of homosexuals and other "undesirables" and "deviants" (in 1965–1967). Personally threatening some and morally threatening others, for many within the artistic communities this was "lo que le puso la tapa al porno" (the last straw). (It is interesting to note that no active ICAIC creative personnel left the island during the last massive exodus, the Mariel boat lift of 1980. However, among the "Marielitos" were various former ICAIC workers, most notably Raúl Molina, a documentary director between 1961 and 1966 who was fired from ICAIC because of "ideological conflicts" and worked in "anonymous" nonskilled jobs—farm laborer, gas station attendant—until his departure.)[11]

Despite their scattered departures over more than a decade, many of the exiled Cuban filmmakers, together with others (too young when they left and considered "exiles" as a result of circumstances)[12] who became filmmakers while in exile, have sustained a specific "Cuban" identity: they identify themselves as Cubans, have most often worked with Cuban issues/themes, and, for the most part, maintain an anti-Castro political line. In different ways, their films and videos, especially those of the first and second generations of filmmakers, articulate and attempt to contain the traumas of exile by repeating and denouncing the actual experience (the history of departures) and by symbolically reconstructing the "lost" home (with)in a new imagined community. In fact, their films often participate in what may be called a "Cuban" political culture or political imaginary that exceeds the geographical boundaries of the island nation and that have been a constant feature of Cuban political life at least since the 1890s. Finally, the third generation of exiles, already less liminal and more assimilated, most often bypasses the explicit political discourses typical of the first and second generations, and is more interested in exploring that historically determining, but, in most cases, largely unknown, "Cuban" part of their self-definition as "Cuban Americans."

The First Generation

Of course, not all the exiled filmmakers have continued to make films. Francisco Villaverde, for example, who was part of the Rebel Army's Culture Unit in 1959 and worked at ICAIC between 1960 and 1963 as assistant and director of documentaries, was exiled in 1965, worked for the Associated Press news service in New York, and, since the mid-1970s, has been a literary critic for the *Miami Herald*. None of the authors/scriptwriters have continued to write for the cinema and have found "homes" in academia (Desnoes, Benítez-Rojo) or in journalism (René Jordán is the film critic for the *Miami Herald*).

Manolo Alonso, the "czar" of prerevolutionary Cuban film, settled in the New York–Miami axis and specializes in the production of stage and television musical shows. He and Spanish-language TV magnate René Anselmo were also involved in the establishment of Spanish-language TV channels 41 (New York) and 23 (Miami), and the network Univisión (Rosell 1992). Alonso also seems to have directed the first postrevolutionary Cuban exile film in 1963: *La Cuba de ayer* (Yesterday's Cuba), a two-hour film—primarily footage from prerevolutionary Cuba but also some testimonies and performances by recent exiles—that paints a nostalgic portrait of prerevolutionary life. In 1987 he completed a made-for-Spanish-TV movie, *El milagro del éxodo* (The Miracle of the Exodus), which documents the achievements of Cuban exiles in the United States.

Many others have combined work in advertising or publishing with forays into filmmaking. Orlando Jiménez-Leal, probably one of the best known of the exile filmmakers, worked successfully in Spanish-language advertising in New York, was cinematographer for the Puerto Rican production *La criada malcriada* (The Disobedient Servant, 1965), and eventually set up his own production company, Guede Films, in the late 1970s. Guede Films produced *El Super* (1979), which was directed by Jiménez-Leal and his young brother-in-law León Ichaso and became the first Cuban exile fictional feature to be broadly distributed and exhibited in the United States and to win international awards.[13] (The "first" exile narrative feature shot in the United States was, according to all accounts, Camilo Vila's *Los gusanos* [The Worms, 1977, a rarely seen low-budget feature shot in the Dominican Republic.)[14] Subsequently, Jiménez-Leal went on to direct *The Other Cuba* (1983), a feature-length documentary financed by Italian television (RAI) and, in collaboration with Néstor Almendros, the well-known, highly polemical documentary *Improper Conduct* (1984), produced by French television (Antenne 2) and the Films du Losange (D'Lugo 1996). (Because of generational differences and his split with Jiménez-Leal after *El Super*, I have classified Ichaso as a "second-generation" director and discuss his films later on.) In 1988, Néstor Almendros teamed up with another younger exile, Jorge Ulla, to produce *Nobody Listened*, a documentary denunciation of the treatment of prisoners in Cuban prisons. Most recently, two young Miami Dade Community College professors—Alex Anton and Jorge Cardona, both twenty-seven—filmed *Rompiendo el silencio* (Breaking the Silence, 1994), a documentary about contemporary protest movements in Cuba that features interviews with Cuban dissidents in the island filmed by French journalist Bertrand de la Grange.[15]

It is this "political generation" that most clearly evidences the peculiarity of Cuban exile film, at once closely linked to the island's cultural and political history, but the most different—especially in style—from the island's (ICAIC's) cinema. These films articulate a contradictory, tragic discourse that mythologizes prerevolutionary Cuba in order to radically differentiate it from the revolutionary "present" of the island and link it to these filmmakers' exile. "First-generation" discourse is dependent upon explicit antirevolutionary politics and the documentary form and is, in fact, independent of the age of the exile and of the longevity of his/her diaspora: it is a position available to and used by Cuban exile filmmakers of all ages who still identify themselves primarily as Cuban *political* exiles.

In *The Other Cuba*, for example, Jiménez-Leal devotes over half of the film to a painstaking retelling of the events that led to the triumph of the revolution in 1959 and its early "glory years" (in fact, often using what looks like ICAIC footage) in order to set up its "betrayal" of the exiled ex-followers that he interviews extensively. Attempting to write an "other" history to contribute to the new community's social imaginary (challenging what for many exiles is the US left's blindness to what really happened and also rehabilitating the political allegiances of now-exiled individuals like Carlos Franqui—author of *Family Portrait with Fidel*—who was once an ardent revolutionary and is thus rejected by the Miami exile community), Jiménez-Leal must filmically relive the experiences, positing the authenticity of the struggle against Batista in order provide a link between the island's history and the exiles' "Cuba."[16] Thus, by displacing nationalism from the nation itself, the film creates a space within which the fetishization of the lost "home" (and *patria*) can serve to lessen the trauma of exilic liminality and as a springboard toward a form of assimilation. In doing so, however, the film—and other exile productions—participates in what Nelson Valdés has identified as one of the central characteristics of the "Cuban" political imaginary, the invocation of the theme of betrayal. Valdés argues that in Cuba—before, after, and in exile from the revolution—"political differences . . . turn into charges of betrayal" (1992, 217). In other words, in "Cuban" political discourse, "betrayal" does not simply connote a move away from a given political program, but a breach of personal trust. For the exiles as well as for those on the island (as demonstrated by the late 1980s Ochoa case, where high-ranking officers were accused of drug trafficking), politics requires unconditional personal loyalty, and any wavering or political difference constitutes betrayal. Thus the interviewees' insistent accusations that Castro betrayed his own ideals, his friends, his confidants, and finally the nation itself echo only too familiarly in Cuban ears.

Preceding the markedly different denunciation documentaries, Jiménez-Leal and Ichaso's independent feature *El Super* (based on a play by Iván Acosta) is solidly a film of exile longing and displacement. *El Super* tells the story of Roberto, a former apolitical bus driver who left Cuba in 1968 out of a generalized frustration with the system and ended up becoming the superintendent of a building in New York's Washington Heights. After a decade in New York, Roberto and his wife Aurelia are still struggling with assimilation: they cannot stand the winters, barely speak English, associate primarily with other Latinos, and are deeply disturbed by their teenage daughter's (Elizabeth Peña) increasingly visible Americanness. Roberto, in fact, is in the midst of a deep psychological crisis typical of the exilic condition: longing for a Cuba that never really was and unable to accommodate himself to the harsh realities of his adopted land. The film's solution to his angst—a move to Miami motivated by a job offer and dreams of sun-drenched palm trees and the sounds of Spanish—ends the story on a somewhat hollow triumphant note, for Roberto can never have what he longs for most: not to have left Cuba.

Unlike the denunciation documentaries that followed it, *El Super* displaces the explicitly political to address the experience of exile accommodation at a personal level. Thus, while we may consider the denunciation documentaries as part of the liminal phase of exile, this film that chronologically preceded them is, paradoxically, a film of assimilation that consciously celebrates an already existing new imaginary community.

The Second Generation

Besides these better-known Cuban exile directors, a "new" generation—born in Cuba but trained in the United States—has also emerged. Although there are marked slippages between the first and second generations, this group seems to cohere in in-between spaces: between the United States and Cuba, between the exiles and the North Americans. They are always attempting to "cross over," albeit in different directions. In his witty *Life on the Hyphen: The Cuban-American Way*, Gustavo Pérez Firmat dubs this generation of Cubans in the United States the "one-and-a halfers," for they are *both* first and second generation: they live on the hyphen, may never feel entirely at ease in either US or Cuban culture, but can avail "themselves of the resources—linguistic, artistic, commercial—that both cultures have to offer" (1994, 4–5). As Pérez Firmat goes on to argue, this is the group that has been responsible for the production of intercultural Cuban-American culture: in music, Gloria Estefan and Willie Chirino; in literature, Oscar Hijuelos, José Kozer, Cristina García, and others. In cinema/video, this hyphenated generation is more difficult to identify. Each individual seems to stand at a different point on the ethnic bicultural scale, varying from one-and-an-eighth all the way to one-and-seven-eighths or even perhaps two. I locate León Ichaso, Ramón Menéndez, Jorge Ulla, Miñuca Villaverde, Iván Acosta, and Orestes Matacena in this group. Although their individual trajectories as filmmakers are quite varied, their partial assimilation has meant that they have often felt free to leave behind the explicit denunciations of the first generation in order to focus more and more on the nature of life as exiles; in other words, to wrest exilic nostalgia away from the tragic discourse of dispossession and to recuperate it as ethnic identity—Cuban-American, but also Latino.

Certainly, León Ichaso emblematizes the "crossover" phenomenon. After leaving Jiménez-Leal and teaming up with producer Manuel Arce (and his production company Max Mambru Films), Ichaso tried to build on the success of *El Super* to reach Hollywood. However, when their project to film a Cuban-American screwball comedy entitled *A Short Vacation* was shelved by Universal in 1982 (after spending two years in development, curiously, at the same time that *Scarface* was being planned by the studio), they independently produced their own allegory of failed crossovers, *Crossover Dreams*, in 1985 (fig. 23.1). Starring the Panamanian singer-actor-politician and Harvard-educated lawyer Rubén Blades, the film tells the wry tale of a *salsero*'s struggle to "make it" in the New York City mainstream music scene. Like the tale it tells, *Crossover Dreams* is itself a crossover experience. It isn't simply Cuban-American, but rather a Latino film, deeply marked by the American ethnic experience and the values and narrative strategies of classic Hollywood cinema. Narratively, it tells a story about Latinos in the same terms that similar stories have been told about other ethnic groups' efforts to "make it" in the American mainstream. Visually, however, it offers us a complex map of the rich multicultural and multiethnic space of New York City's Loisaida.

Ichaso's most recent film, *Sugar Hill* (1993), continues this trajectory. The "Cubanness" is even more distant in this film about Harlem life, but what remains is an exquisite attention to place as it participates in the

Figure 23.1. Final scene from León Ichaso and Manuel Arce's *Crossover Dreams*. Fair use.

production of social life in those areas of New York City that are normally invisible. In this incarnation, Ichaso has become, in the words of the *New York Times* reviewer, "a New Yorker at heart" (Gonzalez 1994).

In Ichaso's (and Ramón Menéndez's) films, the Cuban-American experience has been replaced by a more generalized focus that simultaneously reflects the realities of an assimilation that in many cases is already more than thirty years old as well as the commercial imperatives of "entertainment" films that aspire to mass audiences.

Jorge Ulla, another who was exiled quite young, has chosen a markedly different path. In 1978, he directed his first feature film, *Guaguasí*, in the Dominican Republic (not completed or released until 1982). Lushly photographed by Ramón Suárez (who won prizes for *Memories of Underdevelopment*), *Guaguasí* is a fictional tale about the effects of revolutionary policies on a "simple" man who stayed behind, a *guajiro* or peasant who joined the guerrillas accidentally and, after the revolution, became a harsh executioner of his own friends, a betrayer. The film has rarely been seen in the United States, although it was one of the three Latin American films (representing the Dominican Republic) selected in the prenominations for the best foreign film Academy Award category. In 1980, Ulla directed *In Their Own Words* (with Lawrence Ott Jr.), a thirty-minute documentary about the Mariel exodus sponsored by the US Information Agency. Filmed as the exiles were arriving at Key West, the film uses their testimonies to attempt to explain this sudden massive exodus and highlights the experience of leaving and the feelings of these new exiles. Perhaps because of the experience of working on *In Their Own Words*, and despite the fact that he claims a preference for fiction filmmaking, Ulla went on to make documentaries with Orlando Jiménez-Leal (*The Other Cuba*) and Néstor Almendros (*Nobody Listened*), thus joining forces with the "first generation" of exile directors and their passionate politics.

Unlike Ichaso and Ulla, Miñuca Villaverde works in a very personal and poetic style and is one of the most suggestive filmmakers of this group. After working as an experimental filmmaker in New York (under the auspices of the Women's Interart Center) and directing the award-winning shorts *A Girl in Love* and *Poor Cinderella, Still Ironing Her Husband's Shirt*, she moved to Miami with her ex-filmmaker husband Francisco and directed the documentaries *To My Father* (1974) and *Tent City* (1984). *To My Father* is a record of a Cuban-American family's interactions at a time of crisis: waiting for the death of the family patriarch, the filmmaker's own father. *Tent City*, however, assumes a more provocative public stance. Documenting the experiences of those Mariel boat lift exiles who were hard to relocate and had to live in army tents under an expressway in downtown Miami for several months, the film chronicles Villaverde's own fascination with their marginality and dogged persistence to assert their own identities. Since *Tent City*, Villaverde seems to have given up filmmaking and is now a staff writer for the Spanish-language cultural supplement of the *Miami Herald*.

Although more difficult to place than Villaverde and Ulla, Acosta and Matacena have also produced work dealing primarily with exilic assimilation. For example, after writing the play that was adapted for *El Super*, Acosta went on to make *Amigos* (Friends, 1985), a low-budget feature produced by Camilo Viva about the painful assimilation of Mariel exiles into the Miami community: Ramón, who has been in jail for eighteen years, arrives through Mariel and is welcomed by his childhood friend Pablo, but he must learn to deal with the prejudice of the Miami exile community and even the unspoken resentment of his own friend. Although conventionally shot and sometimes haltingly narrated, the film does capture the contradictions of the history of the "waves" of Cuban exile with humor and sensitivity. If *El Super* was the film of exilic assimilation of the 1970s, *Amigos* fulfills the same role in the 1980s, taking us from Key West, through the various Cuban enclaves of Miami, all the way north to Union City, New Jersey.

The Third Generation

Yet a third group of Cuban exiles—what might be called the "Cuban American" (no hyphen) or "third" generation—has been making its presence felt in alternative and independent film and video circles. The individuals in this group are younger, less interested in commercial crossovers, more assimilated, yet still insistently—alternatingly—"Cuban." For example, Enrique Oliver's *Photo Album* (1984) offers a campy yet acute look at the transculturation of exile with tidbits such as a history of the evolution of the Cuban virgin in exile and the exorcism of an overly Americanized teenager by a Santería priest. Multimedia artist Tony Labat has produced a number of tapes dealing with exile and transculturation. Among them, his *ñ* (1982) is a fascinating and very experimental analysis of that letter's inscription of difference while *Kikiriki* (1983) explicitly addresses Labat's own return to Cuba and generates a meditation on machismo, violence, and masculinity. Dinorah de Jesús Rodríguez's *Ochún/Oricha—El Balance—Guerreros: A Trilogy* (1990) explores the African presence in "Cuban" culture. Rafael Elortequi, a University of Miami film school graduate, has done a number of experimental films. Raul Ferrera-Balanquet, a University of Iowa film school graduate and multimedia artist, has produced a series of tapes—among them *Mérida Proscrita* (1990), *We Are Hablando* (1991), *No Me Olvides* (1992), and *Olufina Abuela Balanquet* (1994)—that offer poignant analyses of the difficulties and marginalization of gay Latino life in a North-South context (Negrón-Muntaner 1996; Ortiz 1996). Ela Troyano's filmic range spans from the Warholesque New York downtown avant-garde scene to *How to Kill Her* (1990) (in collaboration with Cuban American playwright Ana María Simo) and *Carmelita Tropicana* (1993), perhaps the most trenchant example of this generation's "Cuban American Way" (Negrón-Muntaner 1996; Muñoz 1996).

Ana María García's work speaks from a different place and with a different voice. She grew up in Puerto Rico, and that island's own complex status coupled with her own long-term commitment to contemporary

Cuba has led her to a documentary practice that is independent, political, and fraught with difficulties. Her first film, *La Operación* (1977–1981), is a denunciation of the planned sterilization of women in Puerto Rico that fits solidly within the parameters of the New Latin American Cinema. Her most recent *Cocolos y Roqueros* (1993) is an incisive analysis of contemporary Puerto Rican identity through music.

Also coming from a different "place" is Andy García's *Cachao* (1992). After his career as a Hollywood actor was well established, García fulfilled his longtime dream of rescuing the brilliant Cuban bass player Israel López "Cachao" from the oblivion of exile by producing a large concert in Miami. This extraordinary show serves as the backbone for this sometimes touching, sometimes cloying documentary, which tracks Cachao and his group through the rehearsals for the show, traces his musical career, and includes interviews with other Cuban exile luminaries like Guillermo Cabrera Infante. Although García rearticulates a Cuban musical past for a Cuban present that does not seem to require the island at all, he cannot bypass the first-generation discourses that demand denunciation and repudiation of the island's present. García has simultaneously argued that with this film he is not searching for roots ("because I never lost them") but that he is also "reliving the Cuba that he never lived" through its music, "which crosses boundaries . . . but has always been the link" to his Cuban heritage (García 1994; Abella 1993).

Nevertheless, this last generation—the Cuban Americans—is perhaps the most distant from the exile experience as such. Overall, their work is not linked to the usual anti-Castro political Cuban-exile agenda. However, their general concern with biculturalism (and the related loss, marginality, and difference) is still couched in the terms of an explicit exilic positionality—a Cubanness slipping into Latinoness—that is unavoidable; and which, full circle, returns them to the mainstream of the contemporary art scene.

Although this generation is also the most distant from the island itself—some left as tiny children, others were born in the United States[17]— its work is, paradoxically, the most closely linked to the island's cinema. In Cuba, an aggressive group of young "amateur" filmmakers, loosely associated with the youth cultural organization Hermanos Sainz (and, in many cases, students at the Instituto Superior de Arte in Havana or the Escuela Internacional de Cine y Televisión in San Antonio de los Baños) and working independently of ICAIC, has begun to express similar cinematic concerns and experimental multimedia approaches. Films and video work such as *Un pedazo de mí* (A Part of Me, Jorge Luis Sánchez, 1989),

Empezar de cero (Starting at Zero, Ibis Gómez García, 1991), *Oscuros rinocerontes enjaulados (Muy a la moda)* (Dark Caged Rhinoceros [Very Much in Fashion], Juan Carlos Cremata, 1991), and *Emma, la mujer marcada* (Emma, the Marked Woman, Camilo Hernández, 1991) tackle topics that the national cinema has shied away from (respectively, marginality in contemporary Cuba, the excessive presence of Martí busts throughout Havana, Cuban irreverence, and notions of cultural identity) in a highly experimental and iconoclastic fashion (Ríos 1991). For both sets of filmmakers, the expressly political—the revolution—is not a direct concern, but a decentered subtext that is subsumed within other categories of life and experience. Perhaps because of their youth, because of their comparatively similar exposure to different varieties of film and video work, or because of a generalized postmodernist climate that has reached into the island itself, the work of the third generation of Cuban American filmmakers and of the new generations emerging in Cuba share a common ground.

In the long and complex history of Cuba and its diaspora, its film and video productions seem to have, partially, effected a graceful reencounter. There is now, it seems, a small "Cuba" that exceeds all national boundaries.

Postscript: The Special Period

When I wrote the first version of this essay a few years ago, that "graceful reencounter" seemed utopian, but not impossible. The Torricelli Act, despite tightening all restrictions on US trade with Cuba, paradoxically liberated cultural exchanges and made the idea of a "Cuban" cinematic practice that exceeded national boundaries seem feasible. In fact, within the island itself, ICAIC's own cinema had begun to make gestures toward a rapprochement with the exile thematic and had undergone a kind of transnationalization that seemed to bypass the previously requisite repudiation of exiles. Whereas in its first thirty years ICAIC had only produced two feature films dealing explicitly with the diaspora and its consequences—*55 Hermanos* (55 Brothers) and *Lejanía* (Parting of the Ways), both directed by Jesús Díaz—two others were released in the early 1990s: *Mujer transparente* (Transparent Woman, 1990), a compilation film with one episode dealing with the trauma of return, and *Vidas paralelas* (Parallel Lives, Pastor Vega, 1992), a fictionalized comparison of life in Union City, New Jersey, and in Havana. In video (coproduced by ICRT [Cuban Radio-Television Institute] and Channel 4 [United Kingdom]),

Estela Bravo produced *Miami-Havana*, a documentary about the emotional traumas of exile focused on a group of Marielitos who were imprisoned in the United States and subsequently returned to the island. Even Cuba's premier director, Tomás Gutiérrez Alea, received a Guggenheim fellowship to work on a script for a sequel to *Memories of Underdevelopment* in collaboration with longtime New Hampshire resident Edmundo Desnoes. Furthermore, his *Strawberry and Chocolate* (1994), an analysis of internal exile produced by official homophobia, became the best-received and most widely seen Cuban film in the United States and was even nominated for an Academy Award.

But the effects of the crisis engendered by the collapse of the Soviet Union (and the withdrawal of all financial subsidies to the island), and the Cuban government's often contradictory, faltering moves toward change, have rippled through the ranks of filmmakers and have produced a different "generation" of exiles that problematizes all chronological sequences. For example, Sergio Giral, a longtime ICAIC director of important films such as *El otro Francisco* (The Other Francisco, 1976) and, most recently, *María Antonia* (1990), now lives in Miami and is on the lecture circuit. Mario Rodríguez Joya, a brilliant photographer and the cinematographer of a good percentage of ICAIC's most successful films, recently moved to Los Angeles. Juan Carlos Cremata (director of *Oscuros rinocerontes enjaulados*) is in Mexico. Creative personnel from other media institutes have also left the island permanently: José Luis Llánez, the director of award-winning ICRT productions, is in Miami, along with Jorge Antonio Crespo and visual artist Nicolás Guillén Landrían (director of *Coffea arábiga*, 1971, which many argue is the best documentary ever produced by ICAIC).

Most recently, two film production students from the ISA (Instituto Superior de Arte)—Carlos Zequeira and Luis Vladimir Ceballos—arrived in Miami with potentially incendiary footage featuring interviews with Cuban *roqueros* (heavy metal fans) who nihilistically (politically?) contaminated themselves with the Human Immunodeficiency Virus and are currently interned in the "La Conchita" *sidatorio* (AIDS asylum). Although not even a documentary as such, the footage generated a minor journalistic storm, including coverage in the *Miami Herald* and a feature in the *New York Times Magazine*. Early in 1995, Tomás Gutiérrez Alea also made headlines when he became a Spanish citizen, although he declared his intention to continue living in Cuba and argued that the rationale for the citizenship change was to facilitate coproduction deals.

Although none of these filmmakers have yet to secure financing for film production in the United States—either for new projects or to complete existing ones—their presence here will undoubtedly produce a new "wave" of exile productions that will speak with yet another voice and will project yet another set of experiences and contradictions of exile, within exile, and for nationness.

That these and other images have been and continue to be extraordinarily powerful weapons in the struggles for definition of the "Cuban" nation was amply demonstrated in the debacle that followed the much-touted "Diálogo" conference held in Havana in April 1994. Officially entitled "La Nación y la Emigración" (the nation and immigration), the three-day conference was sponsored by the Cuban government to discuss Cuba's relation to its diaspora and featured a plane full of invited exiles from the United States and other countries. Although the conversations and debates held during the conference may or may have not proved useful in opening up relations between the United States and Cuba, their significance was superseded by a twelve-minute video. Shot surreptitiously during a closing reception hosted by Fidel for the delegates, the tape was mysteriously (with or without official permission) sold to the international press two days later, before the delegates had returned to Miami. It featured a number of Cuban Americans paying their compliments to Fidel and vying for his attention. The "star" of the video was Miami-based attorney Magda Montiel, who had hoped to win a Florida congressional seat on the Democratic ticket. When her turn came to greet Fidel, she shook his hand, kissed and hugged him, and emotionally said, "Thank you for what you have done for my people. You have been a great teacher to me." Aired insistently on every Spanish-language news broadcast for two or three days, this video clip dashed not only Montiel's political career, but all hopes for a Cuba-US dialogue. For the Miami media and the Miami community, the conference immediately became a "love fest" between Fidel and the treacherous exiles who had betrayed their "real" identity as Cubans. And, once again, the theme of betrayal asserted itself against all odds—and against all conference participants and future dealings between Cuba and the exile community.

Some months later, in the summer of 1994, the yet unresolved *balsero* crisis unleashed yet another set of complications for Cuban-US relations, which further compromised the exile position. No longer smoothly generational and symmetrical (if it ever was), the panorama of Cuban exile has recently become a marked palimpsest of accommodation, assimilation, and transnationality; of comfort, work, and misery. And new work in film and video will undoubtedly reflect upon, engage with, and help generate new sites for the utterly unstable yet sometimes utterly privileged position of "Greater Cuba."

24

I (Also) Love Ricky

The Oft-Forgotten Cuban-in-the-Text (2012)

This essay examines the well-known US TV sitcom I Love Lucy *(1951–1957). Whereas López's earlier star studies analyzed female performers (1991, 1998), this essay examines the series' male star (Cuban-born Desi Arnaz) and the reasons behind the show's immense success. López argues that* I Love Lucy's *unique ability to focus on an interethnic/racial marriage between a Latinx man and an Anglo woman (a rarity for US movies and television at the time) depended on the publicized parallels established between Lucille Ball and Arnaz's on-screen and off screen lives, as well as the aura and allure of Cuba for the early 1950s US public. While recognizing how comic moments often depended on racist presumptions of Ricky/Desi's inferiority (e.g., his accented English; his use of Spanish when exasperated by Lucy), the essay also suggested that the showcasing of Cuban Spanish (and Cuban music) functioned as a point of pride for Latinx audiences, and as a sign that socio-economic success might not depend on assimilation.*

Lucille Ball and the television series *I Love Lucy* have been successfully recuperated for feminism via the valorization of the surprising performative impact of her physical comedy against the narrative containment that subjugated her to the power of the patriarchy by the end of each episode.

Editors' note: Originally published in Spanish as "Yo también amo a Ricky: el cubano que muchas veces se olvida" (2012), this essay was translated by Laura Podalsky and Ana M. López. The translation includes minor changes and the inclusion of additional illustrations.

There has been no such reconsideration of Desi Arnaz. Her costar, husband, and producer has been too easily dismissed as a patriarchal figure whose supposed ethnic inferiority allowed Lucy to manipulate, trick, and outperform him. For example, in one of the most interesting analyses of the TV series, Patricia Mellencamp deals summarily with the character of Ricky in a single paragraph that concludes as follows:

> Although he is "tall, dark, and handsome," not the usual slapstick type, his representation as the Latin lover/bandleader/crooner and slapstick foil for Lucy's pies in the face suggests that Lucy's resistance to patriarchy might be more palatable because it is mediated by a racism which views Ricky as inferior. (1986, 90)

If one of her goals is to "rethink Freud's construction of the radical underpinnings and 'liberating' function of jokes, the comic, and humor [as] yet another 'foreign' policy of potential containment for U.S. women" (1986, 82), Mellencamp only establishes the most obvious ties to the actual foreign character of Ricky and fails to follow through on the implications of her otherwise astute observation. We can find something similar in another article on Lucille Ball's star image published in *Cinema Journal* in 1990. In it, Alexander Doty examines the ethnicity of Ricky as the inevitable result of that of Desi Arnaz. He argues that for Ricky to be taken as a credible spouse for Lucy in the conservative and racist 1950s, "the character of Arnaz had to be a version of himself"—that is, an entertainer rather than a banker (1990, 4). Neither Mellencamp nor Doty deepen their analyses to account more specifically for the impact of Ricky and his ethnicity on the show (given his humor, popularity, and fans). However, their articles do open up interesting pathways to begin that work—first, by analyzing the interdependent cross-coding of ethnic and gendered representations and notions of resistance and resistant readings; and, second, by broadening the analysis of the star text in order to account specifically for ethnic relations and conflicts. In my view, *I Love Lucy* can continue to be seen as a proto-feminist parable of containment, but it also serves as an ethnic chronicle that lays bare the tensions and conflicts of interethnic relationships.

I Love Lucy could never escape from the ethnic issues embedded within it. This was not a text that simply "featured" an ethnic character to showcase local color. Rather, one of its main protagonists was Cuban (and the husband of the lead actress). It was masterminded and produced by a Cuban who, in fact, "gave voice" to the show itself: the "I" in *I Love*

I (Also) Love Ricky | 457

Lucy, after all, could only have referred to Ricky Ricardo/Desi Arnaz. What was a Cuban doing in the most successful program on network television in the 1950s and how did he get there? How should we understand his presence in a program that ultimately codified the conventions, structures, and styles of the sitcom; that was probably the most popular comedy ever broadcast; and that was the first sitcom to be seen by ten million households in the US?

The life of Desiderio Arnaz y Acha is well chronicled in his autobiography: *A Book* (1987). He was born into a prestigious upper-class family that left for the US when his father, a right-wing senator, fell out of political favor in 1933 after a revolution that overthrew the dictator Gerardo Machado. The family left the island to save their lives after a crowd set fire to their house.[1] In Miami, broke and alone, the two Arnazes—Desi was seventeen years old when he joined his father there in 1934—hustled to survive. The young Desi left behind his dreams to go to Notre Dame and law school and began to work in local clubs in 1936 because the job paid better than anything else he could find and it was a way of exploiting skills he had previously considered only useful to flirt with young women. Soon, he had made it big in the world of entertainment and in 1939 appeared on Broadway in the Rodgers and Hart show *Too Many Girls*. According to his own rather breathless recounting of this period, by then he had already taught the whole Atlantic coast to dance the conga. A year later, he repeated his success in Hollywood in the film version of *Too Many Girls* (George Abbott, 1940). By then, the year of his lightning-fast marriage to Lucille Ball, *Variety* had described him "as the hottest ticket on vaudeville and cabaret since Carmen Miranda hit these shores" (cited in Harris 1991, 85).

The comparison with Carmen Miranda was not coincidental. The success of both Miranda and Arnaz was emblematic of the Good Neighbor Policy's efforts to establish a "friendlier" relationship with Latin American countries (Arnaz even participated as a goodwill ambassador in a 1941 tour of Mexico by Hollywood celebrities that kicked off that policy) and to take advantage of the renewed cultural interest in the exoticism of Latin America.[2] But [there were also differences between the professional trajectories of the two]. After a short run on Broadway, Miranda rocketed to fame in Hollywood (where she was featured as the embodiment of the Good Neighbor Policy itself in *The Gang's All Here*). While Arnaz's Hollywood future had seemed promising after his appearance in *Bataan* (Tay Garnett, 1943) after a short interruption serving in the army during the war, his film career quickly fizzled. There didn't seem to be much interest in his type—that is, a Latino who could do comedy, sing, and dance—

and the interest that did exist seemed focused on Mexican newcomer Ricardo Montalbán. While it was possible for Carmen Miranda to take advantage of Hollywood's interest in promoting a fetishized version of the Latin American woman (López 1991a), Arnaz wasn't able to reproduce her screen success (perhaps because of the competition from Montalbán) and, instead, remained primarily a band leader and nightclub entertainer.[3]

Consequently, even though he wasn't a movie star, when Arnaz and Ball began to actively pursue the possibility of working together on television (to save both their ailing marriage and careers), Arnaz did have an identifiable successful public persona as a Latino musical entertainer. Doty is no doubt correct that the character of Ricky Ricardo was tied to Arnaz himself, to his well-known career and extraordinarily well-publicized marriage to Ball. In this context, the genesis of the character of Ricky is quite revealing. The inspiration behind *I Love Lucy* was the Ball radio program *My Favorite Husband*, in which she played the ditzy wife of a boring WASP bank president. The radio program was itself based on a novel, Isabel Scott Rorick's *Mr. and Mrs. Cugat*. Although the novel did not explicitly refer to the popular bandleader Xavier Cugat, the Cuban connections would have been difficult to miss at the time, especially since it was well known that Cugat had given Arnaz an important opportunity at the beginning of his career. It is interesting that Ball had tried, unsuccessfully, to convince the show's producers to cast Arnaz for the role of the husband. On the pilot for *I Love Lucy* (first titled *The Lucille Ball–Desi Arnaz Show*), the characters were Larry López, a struggling Latinx go-getter rather than a successful band leader and his wife, Lucy López, a housewife with dreams of show-business stardom. The much tighter link subsequently forged between the Ricardos on *I Love Lucy* and the star images of Arnaz and Ball suggests a clear strategy aimed at legitimizing a potentially unacceptable ethnicity via recourse to the hypostatized and well known "real" lives of the two stars. Thus the miscegenation of the main couple and Ricky's ascendant career in show business became acceptable because they could be read in relation to the existing relationship of Ball and Arnaz, despite the fact that the producers at CBS initially had opposed this tie as "unbelievable."

That said, the rags-to-riches Arnaz story does not sufficiently account for the sudden appearance and enduring popularity of a show on national television featuring a successful Latino (more or less) happily married to an Anglo woman. The show's ethnicity also relates to the specificity of the medium itself and the more general sociocultural and political climate in the early 1950s. Once legitimized by their preestablished star personas, Ricky's ethnicity and his marriage to Lucy could be exploited as a means to further distinguish television from Hollywood (in films, Latinxs never—or hardly ever—ended up with Anglo women). It's also important to note that even if classic television had the tendency to produce personalities rather than "stars" (indeed, becoming a star at that time meant moving from TV to film), in this case, the conflation of their off screen lives and their TV characters was so flawless that it catapulted them immediately to stardom. (For example, the fetishization of the ties between the "real" and the televisual would never have been as picture-perfect as the well-known episode of *I Love Lucy* linking the on-air birth of Little Ricky to the off screen birth of Desi Arnaz Jr.).

More significantly, however, to be Cuban in the early 1950s had an alluring, almost exotic connotation rather than today's typical Latino aura of dangerous marginality, or, in the case of old-time Cuban exiles, political conservatism. Before 1959, Cuba was associated with sunny beaches, sex, and gambling, not with the revolution or with political exiles. This island of easy pleasures, a stone's throw from US shores, was best known on the mainland for impassioned/passionate music: Pérez Prado's mambos, Arnaz's congas, the rhumba, and later, the cha-cha-cha. During the years of *I Love Lucy*'s peak popularity (1950–1957), being Cuban in the US meant, essentially, having a sense of rhythm. And nobody had a better sense of rhythm than the "Rey de Babalú": it was so strong that it flowed genetically into Little Ricky who could play the drums as well as his dad by age three.

A simple commutation test (of the type proposed by John O. Thompson [1978] to analyze performance styles) is useful for identifying the ethnic effect of Ricky on *I Love Lucy*. Ricky could never have been a white Anglo-Saxon—a "Richard," for example. Many of the comedic premises of the show disappear unless Lucy's husband is an "ethnic type" with an accent. At the same time, as he had to be a successful entertainer at the point of crossover stardom, he couldn't be any sort of ethnic. In fact, he had to be Latin American: a Frenchman à la Maurice Chevalier would have been too sophisticated; a Jewish artist would have been too earthy (traumas of the *Jazz Singer* type would not be allowed!). Could Ricky have been played by Ricardo Montalbán? The Mexican actor, albeit handsome and visibly and audibly "Latinx," would have been too stiff and dignified to roll with Lucy's punches, and wouldn't have been credible as a nightclub entertainer. The only contemporary substitute for Arnaz might have been Cesar Romero. As the prototypical "tall, dark, and good-looking" Latino, Romero played musically inclined gigolos and lovers throughout the 1940s, often in Fox's Good Neighbor musical comedies. He had the handsome huskiness and expressive face of Arnaz, albeit without the latter's musical abilities. Is it merely a coincidence that Romero was a first-generation Cuban American?

If, as the commutation test seems to suggest, Cubanness was an essential factor of the Ricky character in *I Love Lucy*, then how does that Cubanness function on a textual level? Above all, it was the only ethnic characteristic that was clearly recognizable—not in relation to other ethnic attributes, but rather to their absence in the figure of Lucy. The former Miss McGillicuddy is, after all, a white Anglo-Saxon Protestant bearing the iconic red (hair), white (skin), and blue (eyes) features that distinguish "America." She is the norm against which Ricky is defined as *other* when she calls him "an attractive Cuban," a "Cuban hunk," or "a gorgeous Cuban." Ricky is insistently recognized as Cuban. Note that in almost every episode (and most particularly in the ones right before the fateful, assimilationist move to Connecticut) Ricky is identified as Cuban or does something that identifies him as such—like speaking in Spanish. And [as he is always Cuban], Lucy reflexively/automatically assumes the identity of being Anglo-Saxon, an identity that is as important to her role as that of woman, wife, and actress.

What functions does Ricky's ethnicity serve in the show? In *I Love Lucy*, as in the majority of Hollywood classical films, the cross-coding of gender and sexuality with the ethnic tended to obscure ethnicity. More specifically, Ricky's Cubanness is made textually explicit in three different ways: narratively, musically, and linguistically. His Cubanness has a narrative function in almost every episode and serves as the thematic center of entire episodes (for example, when Lucy meets Ricky's mother) or sets up specific gags (for instance, when Lucy recreates her idea of Cuba—palm trees, sarapes, sombreros, bananas, a donkey, and a chicken coop—and dresses like Carmen Miranda so that Ricky feels "at home").

The program's use of music is particularly illustrative. In almost every episode, Ricky sings musical numbers, typically in his nightclub whose very name (initially the Tropicana and later Club Babalú) resonates with Cubanness. The cabaret space itself is encoded as Cuban—or at the very least as Latinx. First and foremost, it is a place where Spanish—whether spoken or sung—fits right in and can be used for communication. Ricky's musicians are also apparently Cuban and the audience is thrilled when he sings in Spanish. Although his musical repertoire goes beyond the Cuban musical canon, the island's songs are always well represented. Moreover, Ricky and his band always play Cuban instruments—most notably, the conga drums as represented in those iconic photos identifying him almost entirely with that instrument (figs. 24.1a–c).

Figures 24.1a–c. Desi Arnaz and the conga drums. Personal collection of Ana M. López.

Linguistically, Cubanness erupts into *I Love Lucy* when Ricky mispronounces words in English and bursts into Spanish in almost every episode. And what role do those untranslated outbursts of Spanish serve? Undoubtedly, they are a source of much mirth for Anglo-Saxon audiences; the lively reaction of the studio audience underscores that quite clearly. Usually pointing to Ricky's exasperation with Lucy (or vice versa), these monologues use the linguistic difference to encode the social and gender differences between the two characters. Consider, in the episode "Never Do Business with Friends" (season 2, episode 32), the early scene with the washing machine. After Lucy exasperates Ricky complaining about her broken washing machine and stringing laundry to dry all across the kitchen, Ricky storms off screen behind the hanging laundry, looking for the door and muttering, in Spanish, "Ay Dios mío, esta mujer está completamente loca," at which points Lucy turns sideways from her laundry and smirks with obvious satisfaction (fig. 24.2).

Ethnic difference, measured in terms of Ricky's linguistic incompetence, allows Lucy to affirm a certain superiority over her husband: her Americanness. At the same time, the linguistic difference also serves as a sign of Ricky's ongoing lack of assimilation. Despite his professional success, he continues to be an *other* who doesn't speak English well (enough), and who has to revert to Spanish when his emotions overcome him or when he invokes popular forms of wisdom that he, notwithstanding, knows perfectly well how to translate. Thus, Fred Mertz also can poke fun at Ricky's accent, as in the Lucy and Bob Hope episode, season 6, episode 1 (the episode with Lucy and Bob Hope), or use "Cuban" as an epithet when

Figure 24.2. A scene from "Never Do Business with Friends" from the TV show *I Love Lucy*. Fair use.

he gets upset (the episode with the washing machine described earlier). Authorized by Lucy's racist humor, Fred's expressions—even without the cover of gender—appear similarly harmless and simply "funny."

That said, if we pull back from this critical focus on the mainstream audience in order to interpret the series from an ethnic perspective, we can see that the outbreaks of Spanish in *I Love Lucy* might have had a different effect. Rather than serving as a marginalizing marker of otherness (of the inability to assimilate), Ricky's use of Spanish also can be seen as a sign of cultural pride: even as a successful artist and even though he doesn't need to, he continues to use the mother tongue. His Spanish, unmistakably Cuban and grammatically correct, would be a welcomed reminder of cultural specificity—a singularity that is always on the verge of disappearing in the context of immigrant experiences. For Spanish-speaking viewers, Ricky's monologues were not a stream of incomprehensible sounds (as they were for monolingual English audience members); his words were a form of direct communication: they are understood. Moreover, his eruptions in Spanish were often far racier than what was allowed on English-language television in the 1950s (for example, "Mira que jode la mujer esta"/Look how this woman is screwing up) and established a rather risqué connection with audiences who could understand them.

In addition, from an ethnic perspective, even the main narrative conceit of the program itself looks different. It could be said, for example, that the Latinx public—especially Cuban viewers—might have seen Lucy, but really tuned in to watch Ricky. Despite the actress's interpretative prominence, Ricky's power—as husband, as the Law—is narratively and legally authorized. It is Ricky who puts limits on Lucy's craziness, extricates her from problems, and protects her as if she were a little girl. And, in so doing, he affirms for an ethnic audience not only the obvious patriarchal imperative but also an almost inconceivable ethnic superiority. Lucy's clownishness always puts such power on trial; she invariably tries to be cleverer, to pull one over on him, to deceive him or do something better than he does. But in the end Ricky always proves to be in control and to be right. In spite of the ongoing questioning that comes into play tangentially in relation to gender roles (in which the Mertzes, especially Fred, participate), the Latino does win at the end, albeit somewhat paradoxically.

Perhaps the most decisive proof of the enduring importance of *I Love Lucy* for Latinx audiences and the possible Latinx readings of the program

464 | Ana M. López

is Oscar Hijuelos's Pulitzer Prize–winning novel *The Mambo Kings Play Songs of Love* (1989) that invokes Ricky Ricardo, *I Love Lucy*, and Desi Arnaz himself (Desi Arnaz Jr. plays Ricky Ricardo in the film version of the novel) as *the* central cultural icons of New York's Latinx community in the first half of the 1950s. The novel's recreation of a "real" episode of *I Love Lucy*—in which the Castillo brothers appear on the program as Ricky's Cuban cousins—restructures the program's ethnic and gender relationships in a revealing way. The episode makes use of the Cubanness of the Castillo brothers and their relationship with Ricky (defined through their shared ethnicity and musicality) to displace Lucy's interpretative gamesmanship—making it impossible for her to undermine what has been understood as Ricky's ethnic power. Framed by an iconic television screen from the 1950s in the film version of the novel (1992, Arne Glimcher), the clips of the program are a hit with the "real" Latinx community gathered in the living room to watch the show together (fig. 24.3).

This audience, like the one in the studio, laughs at the jokes but takes particular delight when the Castillo brothers repeatedly say, "No hablamos

Figure 24.3. A recreation of a "real" episode of *I Love Lucy* in the film version of Oscar Hijuelos's novel *The Mambo Kings Play Songs of Love*. Fair use.

inglés" (We don't speak English). For the purposes of my argument, what is even more significant is how *The Mambo Kings* . . . places *I Love Lucy* at the dramatic climax of the novel's nostalgic and historically imperfect/fuzzy narration of the origins of the construction of Cuban American identity. In so doing, the novel affirms and confirms the power of televised images and stories in the construction of the history of our ethnic past.

Part 4

Final Thoughts, Metacritical Reflections

25

López on López

Liminal Words (2012)

This short essay served as the opening to López's Hollywood, Nuestra América y los Latinos *(2012), the first Spanish-language volume to translate and compile many of her essays. The collection foregrounded her scholarship on early cinema as well as popular cinema and television from later periods. Directed at a Spanish-language audience, "Liminal Words" provides a synthetic overview of the rise of English-language Latin Americanist film studies and its relationship to Latin American–based studies.*

Hollywood, Nuestra América y los Latinos includes ten essays that deal with a constellation of issues related to Latin American–Latinx cinema, mass media, and their histories. With the exception of "I (Also) Love Ricky" all of the essays have appeared before in English-language journals, books, and small-circulation periodicals; a few have been translated into other languages. So why pull them together here [in Spanish] and why now?

In this second decade of the twenty-first century, we are surrounded by discourses outlining how new technologies and interconnected economic systems have profoundly altered mass media practices and have transnationalized or globalized what once may have been national. Indeed, it's impossible to deny that the intensification of globalization and its discontents over the last two decades or so have profoundly altered how the

---

Editors' note: This essay was translated by Laura Podalsky and Ana M. López, and includes minor changes.

cinema and mass media have been produced, positioned, and experienced. That said, the essays included in this volume argue that Latin American cinema has *always* already been, to one degree or another, a transnational phenomenon. I contend that it is imperative to examine the art, practice, and experience of Latin American film historically and continentally, not only to understand its totality—in other words, its past, present, and future—but also to trace the aggregation and disaggregation of the national in the cinema and mass media across the region and beyond. To talk about "the national" is, of course, to invoke the cinema's place in the creation of all those imaginary communities to which we pledge love and allegiance.

This overarching argument about the transnational nature of Latin American cinema in the past as well as the present has a great deal to do with the particular genesis of this scholarship and the history of Latin American film studies in the US. Thirty years ago [in the early 1980s], English-language studies of Latin American cinema were almost entirely identified with the New Latin American Cinema. The emerging "new" cinemas of Brazil, Cuba, and Argentina—linked to evolving social movements and to the renewal of the pan–Latin American dreams of Martí and Bolívar ("Nuestra America"/Our America)—had captured the imagination of US-based and other scholars. As I wrote in a 1991 review essay (1991d), unlike other national cinemas that were introduced into English-language studies via translations of "canonical master histories" written by nationals (e.g., the German cinema, as studied through the works of Siegfried Kracauer and Lotte Eisner), the various cinemas of Latin America were first introduced to English-language film studies in the 1970s ahistorically, through articles about contemporaneous films and events that offered, above all, political readings and assessments. In general, this initial phase of English-language studies of Latin American cinemas was plagued by challenges that continued to haunt researchers throughout the 1980s: the difficulty of accessing the films themselves, the lack of historical data, and unverifiable secondary sources. Above all, [these early studies] displayed a blissful disregard of the critical and historical labor written in Spanish and Portuguese and published in Latin America itself.

But in the 1980s a new generation of scholars—most of whom had been trained in the field of film studies as practiced in US universities—placed Latin America on the map of that discipline. They produced essays that were still passionate and committed, and continued to focus primarily on the New Latin American Cinema. Many of us writing about the New Latin American Cinema back then also participated in its development, decried the setbacks produced by the region's authoritarian regimes, identified new critical paradigms—for example, the notion of exile cinemas—and heralded various "returns" of national cinemas under emerging democracies. We also struggled to insert the movement into the theoretical debates of the period. With historical hindsight, it is now clear that some of our work back then may have identified too closely with the NLAC: critical distance and acuity are difficult to achieve when immersed in a constantly changing vortex of political, social, and aesthetic forces. Yet by the end of the decade and in the 1990s and beyond, it became clear that a [marked] shift had taken place in English-language studies of Latin American cinema. In line with a general turn with the discipline of film studies, we took up the challenges of historicizing Latin American cinema [studies].

What does it mean to "do" film history? Thirty or forty years ago [in the 1970s–1980s], this meant producing a chronicle of dates, names, inventions, directors, and films loosely to some social determinants. Of course, not all of the names and films could be included in any one account and the presumption was that what was included was aesthetically valuable, worthy of mention, or, at least, significant for some later development. These canonical film histories set the stage for what was valued and, therefore, for what was studied and discussed. By default, these early chronicles were also exclusionary. This was not necessarily malicious, but rather the simple result of being bound by the perspective of the individual historian and his (de facto) universe of knowledge and expectations.

In the 1980s, the work of film historians was also sharply distinct from that of film critics. While the former were almost exclusively concerned with contextual issues (the production and reception of films), the latter were primarily preoccupied with the texts [themselves] and with the close reading of film style and structure. One tradition was anchored in the field of history and relied upon its positivist heritage, eventually evolving to privilege exhaustive archival research, corroboration, and sound historiographical practices. For their part, film critics were more closely aligned with the practices of literary studies and the close analysis of texts. To put it in simple terms, film historians might have accused film scholars of dealing with dense and impenetrable theoretical systems in which individual films existed in a social and historical vacuum, while for other film studies scholars, the work of film historians appeared to be theoretically naïve, positivist, and reductive of the semantic and linguistic complexity of the films themselves.

In the study of Latin American cinema, the divide was even more sharply etched, this time not across disciplinary lines but across the Rio Grande. Again, to put it in the simplest terms, the "real" film history was the domain of Latin American–based experts who, especially in Mexico,[1] were in the process of developing some of the most outstanding bodies of historical research, whereas US and European scholars specialized in textual exegesis. There were, at this time, many acrimonious debates, some more productive than others, most mired in the "First" versus the "Third" World debates of the era ([for example, how] First World intellectuals were "colonizing" the cultural practices of the Third World, etc.). But beyond those debates, the reality was that most English-language Latin American film scholarship analyzed texts and most Latin American–based scholars eschewed formal textual analysis in favor of sociohistorical investigations.

Throughout the 1990s, however, the field gracefully abandoned the "text-context" dualism to move toward a productive contextualization of film that uses a wide variety of sources as evidence and attends to the historical, social, and cultural contexts without forsaking textual analysis. The essays included in *Hollywood, Nuestra América y los Latinos* are emblematic of this shift in the field of Latin American film studies, as they question and analyze the uneven and complex creation (and, indeed, existence) of national cinemas in the continent, even as they engage with issues that are perhaps only available to those speaking and writing from a specific scholarly position. In my case, I speak as a scholar of Latin American cinema who works and lives outside of Latin America, and as someone without the recourse of a Latin American nationality as a guarantor of authenticity. I think that this "marginality immune to all returns," as noted by my exiled compatriot Lourdes Casal (1981, 61), is less a handicap than a productive point of departure. It is precisely the fact of not *being in* or really *being from* that has allowed me to identify and analyze connections, tendencies, processes, decentered modernities, and continental pathways that may have been impossible to appreciate by someone situated within the nation and the national. It's not that it's a better or worse viewpoint; it's simply an other.

I don't have time in this essay to thank all of my colleagues, friends, and students (in the US and other places) who have influenced and contributed to my work throughout the years. I must mention, however, several key moments and individuals that shifted my world and my perspectives. One of these was my first return Cuba to do research in the Cinemateca. I will always be grateful to Pastor Vega, who listened to my plea for sponsorship, and to Teresa Toledo and Mayuya Douglas who guided me through this and many other phases of discovery. *Maestro* Julio García Espinosa never failed to be a source of inspiration, and Ambrosio Fornet, a fountain of wisdom. To my indispensable Lola Calviño, Norberto Codina, and Juan Antonio García Borrero, I owe decades of support and friendship. Finally, if it weren't for the talent of my translator María Teresa Ortega, the judgment of my editor Alfredo Prieto, and the confidence of Olga Marta Pérez, director of Ediciones UNIÓN, *Hollywood, Nuestra América y los Latinos* would not have been possible. I am thankful to all of them for the opportunity to make this modest contribution to the bibliography and debate of Latin American cinema in Cuba.

I hope that this perspective on Latin American cinema, and on the Latino in Hollywood cinema, might be useful for the future of our cinemas as well as our way of approaching and understanding them.

—Ana M. López

New Orleans, October 2011

"Siete Veces Ana"

An Afterword

NILO COURET

I first read Ana's work as an undergraduate student at Columbia University in a Latin American film survey taught by Richard Peña. Hers was an "other" history of Latin American cinema that made room for the margins in order to challenge the categories normally used to construct film historical discourses: "If we cannot pin the movement down to a nation, to a hard-and-fast periodization, to the artistry of individual auteurs, or to a general dominant aesthetic, then we have to begin by investigating other alternatives for structuring [film] history" (López 1991c, 310). Even in Ana's earliest work lay an invitation to historicize otherwise, to understand the messiness of the archive, the ambivalence of the apparatus, and the limitations of the national.

I first realized I was following in her footsteps during a graduate seminar at the University of Iowa on Latin American cinema taught by Kathleen Newman. Ana had also completed her PhD at the University of Iowa, and Kathleen shared some ephemera from the Iowa Conferences on Latin American Film that Ana had organized in 1985 and 1986. Ana also programmed a screening series that made room for films from the entire region and inspired my own program of Latin American comedies screening at Iowa in 2010. The hand-stapled program for the 1986 conference featured her work-in-progress on parody in New Latin American Cinema. In the later published piece, which gets overshadowed by her more well-known articles, she argues for reading Latin American cinema parodically, where the "para-" refers to something that is simultaneously beside and against. In Ana's earliest work also lay an invitation to read otherwise, to understand the shortcomings of the symptomatic because the region's cinema was neither simply derivative (beside) nor simply opposed (against) to American and European cinemas.

I first taught Ana in an upper-level undergraduate class on global melodrama. I paired her classic "Tears and Desires" (1994b) with *María Candelaria*. I had designed the class with Ana's essay in mind because it calls on us to study the melodramatic mode outside the American context by attending to the social function of the mode in its cultural and historical specificity. In the case of melodrama, the genre's social function pertains to gender as it intersects with the nation: from the self-abnegating mother to the streetwalking prostitute. Although the melodrama and its female protagonist often allegorize the nation, Ana seemed to prefer the characters that meet tragic ends and challenge the facile resolution of the story (and by extension the nation). Ana makes room for such marginal figures because their tears register material and ideological constraints and their desires challenge the moral order. Ana teaches us that excess and affects matter because they invite us to imagine how the world should be.

I first met Ana at the International Congress on Hispanic Cinemas: In Transition in Madrid in 2012 on a panel organized by Laura Podalsky. In a conference featuring mostly panels on the Spanish transition to democracy, ours was a session on the transition to sound. The standing-room-only crowd came to hear from the illustrious members of the panel, but only me—a no-name ABD—and Ana were able to make the trip. The audience was there for Ana, and yet Ana made room for me. I nervously raced through my paper before Ana's presentation on the radiophonic imaginary in Latin America. Hers was a far-reaching discussion of radio aesthetics in early sound cinema that would go on to shape the paper I had presented on Luis Sandrini, which became one of my first published pieces, my job talk, and a major chapter in my first book.

Ana first approached me two years later at the Society for Cinema and Media Studies after I had finished my graduate study and was a junior professor at the University of Michigan. She sat next to me in the audience at a midday panel. Before the session began she said, "I downloaded your dissertation." Ana paused, and in that breath, I braced for the worst. Perhaps she felt my work too pedantic? too ahistorical? too formalist? too speculative? She congratulated me and quickly added, "When is it going to be a book?" Later in that conference, she made room for me at the bar and generously heard my ideas for the book and other work in progress. She offered much advice, quickly remarking that I tended to like the beginnings of things and that I needed to have the resolve to see my projects to the end: "Finish the book!" I asked Ana how she came upon my dissertation and she explained that she uses different library resources to stay apprised of new research, especially recent dissertations and scholarship published in Latin America.

I invited Ana to read the manuscript for the book three years later before submitting it for peer review. I wanted the book to take the lessons of "Early Cinema and Modernity" into the transition and industrial eras of Latin American film. Ana's foundational essay argued that cinema was a way of "playing with and at modernity," and I wanted to propose that studio film comedy was such an exercise in play (López 2000b, 49). Although Ana enjoyed the book, she asked me: "Who is your audience?" When I told her it was she, she remarked that I needed to write a book that was not for an audience of one and to make room for others in my scholarship.

I asked Ana to be a part of a panel at Visible Evidence in Buenos Aires, inviting an ABD candidate to our panel in the hopes of paying forward the opportunity I'd had in Madrid. Ana presented on travelogues in early cinema and mentioned how she finds herself drawn to impossible projects, ones with no official archive, no extant texts or objects of study, or no received theoretical framework. In this way, her more recent projects try to make room for future scholarship: How might pornography make us reassess histories of early cinema? How did radio shape the movie musical? How do Cuban online music videos challenge the models of monetization on YouTube? She is animated by such projects because to answer why they are impossible is to understand the conditions of possibility of Latin American culture.

I return to Ana's work at the start of every project. I read Ana because she invites me to ask: What can cinema do? For her, cinema is a "global, intertextual experience" (2000b, 49). Hers is an approach that looks to cinema not only for its narratives but for the relations it makes possible. Cinema makes room for play between texts, between histories, between regions, between genres, between identities, between media, and between people. Perhaps it isn't cinema but rather Ana who enables such relations to take place. My career has been made possible by the room she made for me.

Notes

Introduction: At the Interface and Beyond

1. Her groundbreaking role in US-based film studies is acknowledged through her inclusion in the SCMS Fieldnotes interviews with pioneers of film and media studies (Venegas 2017; SCMS Fieldnotes).

2. Ana López, *Hollywood, Nuestra América y los Latinos* (Havana: Ediciones Unión, 2012) compiled (and translated) a more limited selection of her essays, focusing primarily on essays on early cinema and on popular cinema and television from later periods.

3. The current volume includes English-language translations of "Palabras liminares" and "Yo también amo a Ricky" from *Hollywood, Nuestra América y los Latinos*, as well as "Historia nacional, historia transnacional" from *Horizontes del segundo siglo: investigación y pedagogía del cine mexicano, latinoamericano y chicano* (1998b).

4. See, for example, Burton's 1986 *Cinema and Social Change in Latin America: Conversations with Filmmakers*. Burton would include two of López's essays on the New Latin American Cinema (1990a and 1990b) in her 1990 edited volume *The Social Documentary in Latin America*.

5. Allen had already left Iowa, and Doane and Rosen had just finished up their degrees before López entered the program. Rodowick, Petro, and Jenkins (who completed an MA at Iowa) were there with her at the same time.

6. Around the same time, German scholar Peter Schumann's *Historia del cine latinoamericano* (1987) published a comprehensive (and somewhat teleological) history of filmmaking in Latin American countries that characterized the NLAC as the apex of filmmaking in the region. US and British scholars such as Julianne Burton, Michael Chanan, Randal Johnson, Robert Stam, and Chilean-Canadian scholar Zuzana Pick made extremely important contributions to translating the filmmakers' manifestos and disseminating interviews (Burton 1986a; Chanan 1983), identifying and analyzing key aspects of the NLAC (Burton 1990), providing

overviews of national cases (Chanan 1976, 2004 [1985]; Johnson 1984; Johnson and Stam 1995 [1982]), and exploring the institutional and aesthetic foundations across the NLAC (Pick 1993).

And this is to say nothing of the innumerable contributions of Latin American critics and scholars. These Portuguese-, Spanish-, and French-language accounts are too numerous to summarize here but include new magazines like *Cine Cubano* and primary-source volumes such as *Hojas del cine: testimonios y documentos del nuevo cine latinoamericano*, vols. 1–3 (1988), along with monographs like Pick (1980a), Hennebelle and Gumucio Dagrón (1981), Paranaguá (1985), Valjalo and Pick (1984), and Xavier (1983).

7. In this effort, López's work complemented Paulo Antonio Paranaguá's call to recognize not only Hollywood but also European influences on Latin American filmmaking. See "Triángulo" (Paranaguá 2003).

8. Chon Noriega also was one of the cofounders of the National Association of Latino Independent Producers (NALIP). For more information on Noriega's trajectory, see his SCMS Fieldnotes interview with Stephen Charbonneau (2021).

9. For more information on the caucus, see Charles Ramirez Berg's account in his SCMS Fieldnotes interview with Mary Beltrán (2016).

Editors' Introduction to Part 1

1. Within this rising interest in transnational approaches to Latin American cinemas, some scholars made the case for the continued relevance of the nation as the "principle site for both the production and reception of movies" (King 2004, 304, as cited in Tierney 2018, 6). It's important to note that the original edition of King's excellent *Magical Reels* was published in 1990 before the emergence of transnational approaches to cinemas. Since that time, Joanna Page (2009), Sarah Barrow (2018) and other scholars have reaffirmed the saliency of the national as an analytical category for accounts of film in Latin America. See also Poblete (2017) and Shaw et al. (2017).

2. For the aforementioned reasons, the transnational turn can be distinguished from comparative approaches that have long been part of Latin American film studies (Hennebelle and Gumucio Dagrón 1981; Paranaguá 1985; Burton 1986a; Schumann 1987; see also Lusnich 2011 for an overview of such studies) and continue into the present with more recent volumes that compare, for example, Argentine and Brazilian cinemas or Brazilian and Mexican cinemas (Rêgo and Rocha 2011; Andermann and Fernández Bravo 2013; Gordon 2009). That said, some of López's own essays might be characterized as comparativist (2000b and 2000c).

3. The numerous accounts of Soviet director Sergei Eisenstein and Spanish filmmaker Luis Buñuel's influence on Mexican filmmaking in the 1930s–1950s

exemplify this tendency of tracing aesthetic "advancements" to forces outside the region.

1. A Cinema for the Continent (1994)

1. Editors' note: As noted in the introduction to this part, López would not invoke the term "transnational" explicitly until a few years later in "Historia nacional, historia transnacional" (1998b).
2. In comparison, Argentina (the next largest film producer) released only between thirty and sixty films per year in this same period.
3. For example, *Santa* (Saint, Antonio Moreno, 1931), *La mujer del puerto* (The Woman of the Port, Arcady Boytler and Rafael Sevilla, 1933), *Dos monjes* (Two Monks, Juan Bustillo Oro, 1934), *Redes* (Nets, Fred Zinnemann, 1934), *El compadre Mendoza* (Godfather Mendoza, Fernando de Fuentes, 1933), and *¡Vámonos con Pancho Villa!* (Let's Go with Pancho Villa!, Fernando de Fuentes, 1935). These films explored familiar genre territory—melodrama, social consciousness, and revolution/action films—but with a subtlety and freshness that astounds the contemporary viewer. Thus, for example, although Andrea Palma's tragic sex worker of *La mujer del puerto* reminds us of Von Sternberg's work with Marlene Dietrich, the film also introduces a different kind of female persona into the universe of Mexican cinema: not simply a sex worker with a heart of gold like the protagonist of *Santa*, Andrea Palma's character embodies a tragic sexuality that transcends the stereotype. Similarly, Fernando de Fuentes's films about revolutionary themes/heroes go beyond the expected: both films refuse to idealize the revolution and the revolutionary process and present us with genuinely tragic heroes caught in the wheels of social movements that spin out of their control into corruption, anarchy, and stagnation.
4. Editors' note: Unless otherwise indicated, all translations from this and other foreign-language sources are by López.
5. Even Argentina imports Mexican films in 1940–1941(de Usabel 1982, 172).
6. The exception is, of course, *Doña Bárbara*, an adaptation of a novel by the Venezuelan writer Rómulo Gallegos. It is interesting to note that even before *Doña Bárbara*, the Venezuelan market had already proven to be one of the most profitable for the Mexican industry. Two years earlier, *Simón Bolívar* had already broken all box office records in Caracas (de Usabel 1982, 182).
7. As early as 1933, for example, the Cuban singer/actress Rita Montaner had already appeared in the Mexican film *La noche del pecado* (The Night of Sin, Miguel Contreras Torres) with her "Conjunto Tropical."
8. As of 1947, for example, few of Havana's theaters showed only US films, since the city (population seven hundred thousand) seemed to prefer the

few available national productions and Mexican films above all others (de Usabel 1982, 220).

9. With, obviously, some exceptions, most notably Manuel Barbachano Ponce's coproduction with Cuba of *Cuba baila* (Cuba Dances, 1960) directed by Julio García Espinosa.

10. As witnessed, for example, in the use of a gigantic classic Mexican film poster in Ela Troyano's ode to *latinidad*, *Carmelita Tropicana* (1993).

2. National History, Transnational History (1998)

1. Editors' note: López offers a more detailed analysis of *La balandra Isabel llegó esta tarde* in "Crossing Nations and Genres: Traveling Filmmakers," chapter 8 in this volume.

2. Editors' note: *The Cuban Image* was republished in an updated version, *Cuban Cinema* (2004), which included several new chapters.

4. Early Cinema and Modernity in Latin America (2000)

1. Unless otherwise noted, all translations from foreign-language sources are my own.

2. Whereas I use "modernity" to refer to both the idea of the modern as well as a particular disposition toward lived experience that encompasses various ideological and discursive paradigms, "modernization" refers more specifically to the processes of change that result from the introduction of certain technologies into the various spheres of private and social life.

3. This term was coined by Arjun Appadurai in reference to the introduction of cricket to India: "The indigenization [of a cultural practice imported by the colonizers] is often a product of collective and spectacular experiments with modernity, and not necessarily of the surface affinities of a new cultural form with existing patterns in the [new nation's] cultural repertoire" (1995, 24).

4. With three exceptions: the general comparative study by Paranaguá (1985), which begins with the silent period; Paranaguá's subsequent essays on silent cinema (1997a and 1997b); and his rather cursory and inadequately documented survey in Ann Marie Stock (1997) Although the groundbreaking volume, edited by Guy Hennebelle and Alfonso Gumucio Dagrón (1981), was the first to attempt to present comparable histories of filmmaking throughout the continent, its format—a national cinema per chapter—and the uneven quality of the research/contributions dilute its comparative usefulness.

5. By 1911, more than eleven thousand miles of track had been laid. Mexico was so thoroughly blanketed by railways that fewer than two thousand miles of track have been added since the Díaz regime.

6. See De los Reyes's discussion of how the practice of kissing in Mexico changed after the circulation of explicit cinematic kisses and the innovation of darkened public spaces—movie theaters—in which they could be exchanged is especially relevant here (1995a, 267–89).

7. Raúl Rodríguez comments on the clearly political intentions of *Simulacro de un incendio*: the firefighters were aligned with the Spanish colonial government and fought against the liberating army, the film featured a Spanish actress, and, in its initial screening, was featured with three other shorts about the Spanish military.

8. The "sonorization" was accomplished according to the system developed by Gaumont and Pathé in France. First, the soundtrack was recorded on a disk; later, while playing the record on a gramophone, they filmed the actors or actresses pretending to sing or recite. During projection, the film would be synchronized to the gramophone, whose sound was amplified by speakers near the screen. The equipment to reproduce sound was actually manufactured in Buenos Aires by Eugenio Py.

9. In his 1910 inaugural speech, Nilo Peçanha declared that his would be a government of "peace and love."

10. As early as 1897, for example, the major Mexico City daily *El Mundo* featured a column signed by "Lumière" that presented what can only be described as "fragments" or cinematic views of everyday urban life. An exemplary article from November 28, 1897, is reprinted in de los Reyes (1972, 237–38).

11. All accounts of the new medium describe its *technology* in excruciating detail over and above its effects, giving precise technical information about how the illusion of movement was produced. See, for example, the description of the Cinématographe that appeared in the Buenos Aires newspaper *La Prensa* on April 3, 1896 (Caneto et al. 1996, 23), and the one published in the Mexican daily *El Mundo* on August 23, 1896 (de los Reyes 1972, 217–22).

12. What Porfirio Díaz's closest advisers—the Mexican power elite—called themselves in reference to their conviction that Mexico would be transformed (i.e., modernized) through science and technology.

13. Soon after the sinking of the USS *Maine* in Havana harbor on February 15, 1998, US Edison and Biograph cameramen began to produce views and shorts of the events unfolding in Cuba. Throughout 1898, and especially after the US entered the war, they extended the cinema's capacity as a visual newspaper (often in collaboration with the Hearst organization) and, for the first time, used the medium to elicit patriotic sentiments in US audiences, revealing the medium's ideological and propagandistic force. The difficulties of filming in real battles also led to many "reconstructions" of famous events, most notoriously Albert E. Smith and J. Stuart Blackton's reconstruction of the Battle of Santiago Bay in New York, using a tub of water, paper cut-out ships, and cigar smoke. Many credit the enthusiasm generated by these films with the revitalization of the lagging motion picture business in the US; the ongoing production of a few firms set the commercial foundation for the US industry.

14. The term was coined by Roberto Schwarz (1992) to explain the juxtaposition of modernizing ideologies such as liberalism within traditional social structures such as the enslaving Brazilian monarchy. Misplaced or out-of-place "ideas" lead to significant discursive dislocations, which critically reveal the fissures of allegedly universal concepts.

15. This is an astounding example of the speed of cinematic diffusion, not only of technology but also of modes of commercialization and spectatorship. According to Charles Musser's research, American Biograph began its overseas expansion in 1897, establishing a London office in March. It was one of the characteristics of the Biograph operators to provide locally shot scenes to theater operators in order to enhance the programs' popularity (1990, 157, 172).

16. According to Tom Gunning's periodization, after the waning of the "cinema of attractions" dominance (circa 1905), early narrative forms developed that enabled filmmakers to experiment with the specific cinematic narrative language that would become standardized as the "classic Hollywood narrative style" around 1915–1917. This "transitional" period of more than a decade was volatile and ambivalent; D. W. Griffith's narrative ambitions of the period were far from the norm (1998, 262–66).

17. The modernist effort to reconceptualize origins, which typically attributes to indigenous traditions the significance of a primitive past (Chow 1995).

18. The Mexican Revolution was extraordinarily long and complex. It began in 1910, when Francisco Madero, a wealthy Chihuahuan and opponent of Porfirio Díaz, issued his "Plan of San Luis Potosí" manifesto calling for revolts against the tyrant. The government was unable to defeat the small bands of revolutionaries attacking government installations and, after Díaz resigned in May 1911, Madero headed a provisional regime. In 1913, Díaz supporters in Mexico City staged a coup leading to an artillery duel with the forces of General Victoriano Huerta, whom Madero had ordered to put down the rebellion. Known as the Decena Trágica, the "tragic ten," the fighting lasted for ten days during which hundreds of bystanders were slaughtered. The result was that Huerta toppled Madero and ostensibly arranged for his assassination. This bloody assumption of power had wide repercussions: Emiliano Zapata in Morelos and Francisco "Pancho" Villa in Chihuahua rallied to Venustiano Carranza's call for a drive to unseat the usurper; their coalition became known as the "Constitucionalistas." Zapata's movement included the more radical elements and Carranza's the bourgeois, reform-minded groups, while Villa's group was populist, rural, and without a well-defined political position.

Years of bloody civil wars and complex political maneuverings involving the various factions and the US and other world powers followed, including the occupation of Veracruz by US troops in April 1914. In July of that year, Huerta escaped and the constitutionalist armies of Obregón and Carranza arrived in Mexico City, where a struggle for power ensued among the victors. After the Aguascalientes convention, General Eulalio Gutiérrez was named provisional president, but Carranza set up a parallel government in Veracruz, which US forces had just evacuated. The following years—1915 and 1916—were possibly the worst years of the struggle, with all the factions fighting each other, derailing trains, issuing currencies, and creating absolute chaos, including Villa's attack on the US town of Columbus, New Mexico, which provoked a punitive expedition led by US General John J. Pershing.

Finally, in February 1917, war with the US was averted and a new constitution promulgated; its labor, land tenure, and social welfare provisions and anticlericalism were the most radical in the world at that time. Venustiano Carranza was elected president in March of the same year. The struggle was not yet over, however, and revolts against Carranza's government soon broke out. Zapata in Morelos had remained insurgent (he was finally assassinated in 1919); Pancho Villa took up arms again. Finally, in 1920, Alvaro Obregón released the Aguas Prietas Plan, calling for an uprising. It was backed by Pancho Villa and most of the army. A few weeks later, Carranza was assassinated while trying to flee to Veracruz with a good part of the treasury. Obregón was subsequently elected president and the Revolution was officially over, leaving behind more than a million dead.

19. Francisco Serrador, an early entrepreneur, expanded his business and, by the mid-1910s, had created what is often referred to as an "exhibition trust." He created the company Companhia Cinematográfica Brasileira in 1911 with a broad base of investors to focus on distribution and exhibition. It proceeded to acquire and/or build theaters throughout Brazil, especially in Rio de Janeiro. The company also became the exclusive agent of the principal European producers and featured imports prominently (Araújo 1976, 369–70, 396; Araújo 1981, 210–25).

20. Fox arrived in 1915, Paramount's Companhia de Películas de Luxo da América do Sul in 1916, Universal in 1921, MGM in 1926, Warner Bros. in 1927, and First National and Columbia in 1929 (Johnson 1997, 34–36).

6. From Hollywood and Back: Dolores Del Rio, a Trans(national) Star (1998)

1. With one notable exception, Christine Gledhill's *Stardom: Industry of Desire* (1991), which recognizes this problem and includes an essay on three Indian female stars and an essay of Dorothy Dandridge, Lena Horne, and questions of race.

2. One exception is the work of Paulo Antonio Paranaguá (1985, 1996).

3. It is a curious coincidence that Gunther Lessing, her attorney for these proceedings, was the same lawyer that some years earlier had negotiated the contract between Pancho Villa and the Mutual Film Corporation.

4. For First National: *Joanna* (Carewe, 1925), *High Steppers* (Carewe, 1926), and *Pals First* (Carewe, 1926). For Fox: *What Price Glory?* (Raoul Walsh, 1926), *Loves of Carmen* (Raoul Walsh, 1927), *The Gateway of the Moon* (Raoul Walsh,

1927), *The Red Dancer of Moscow* (Raoul Walsh, 1928), and *No Other Woman* (Leon Tellegen, 1928). For MGM: *The Trail of '98* (Clarence Brown, 1928). For Universal: *The Whole Town's Talking* (Edward Laemmle, 1926). For United Artists: *Resurrection* (Carewe, 1927), *Ramona* (Carewe, 1928), *Revenge* (Carewe,1928), *Evangeline* (Carewe,1929), and *The Bad One* (George Fitzmaurice, 1930).

5. Editors' note: Unless otherwise noted all translations from foreign-language sources are López's own.

6. Either because he had lost his star or for other reasons, Carewe's career fizzled after he lost Lolita. He remarried his former wife, Mary Aiken, remade *Revenge* with Lupe Vélez in the Del Rio role, and committed suicide in 1940.

7. As Eileen Bowser describes it, "This kind of shot is almost a Raoul Walsh trademark" (1969, 62).

8. Eliding not only their nationalities, but, in light of Gibbons's well-known preference for men and Del Rio's own relationship with Garbo at the time, their sexual preferences as well (Madsen 1995).

9. Of course, although the Production Code was not fully enforced through the Production Code Administration until 1934, it had already been adopted in 1930 (Jacobs 1991).

10. Cecil Beaton was apparently not taken with her at all, and he described her as "difficult" to photograph because "she had fixed ideas on how she should pose" (Vickers 1985, 130, 158). The famous Beaton photograph with Del Rio clad only in a lei was reprinted illustrating Carlos Monsiváis's article "Dolores del Río: Las responsibilidades del rostro" (1983), 52; translated in Monsiváis (1997a).

11. Aurelio de los Reyes credits her eye/eyebrow expressivity to Emilio Fernández's influence (1996, 105–07).

12. A significant prologue added to the film at the insistence of Joseph Breen, the head of the Production Code Administration, disclaims any identification with Mexico and links the story to contemporary cold war issues, describing it as a "timeless and topical story" that is "still being played in many parts of the world."

13. Mesa-Bains's *An Ofrenda for Dolores del Rio* (1984) was reconstructed in 1990 for the CARA (Chicano Art: Resistance and Affirmation) show at the Wright Gallery at UCLA (Griswold del Castillo, McKenna, and Yarbro-Bejarano 1991, 63).

14. For an interesting analysis of the Mesa-Bains altars, see Jennifer A. González (1993, 82–91).

7. The São Paulo Connection: The Companhia Cinematográfica Vera Cruz and *O Cangaceiro* (1998)

1. Editors' note: Unless otherwise indicated, all translations from foreign-language sources are López's own.

Notes to Chapter 7 | 487

2. This last argument is proffered by Gini Brentani, originally hired as secretary to (and who later became Mrs.) Jacques Deheinzelin, who argues that "que nos vivemos numa sociedade de classes e evidente. Mas qualquer um dos brasileiros da Vera Cruz podia tranquilamente almoçar com o mulatto . . . e depois jantar na casa de Ciccilo no mesmo dia sem se sentir deslocado, enguanto que os ingleses jamais fariam isso" (it is obvious that we live in a classicist society. However, any of the Brazilians at Vera Cruz could easily have lunch with a mulatto . . . and then dine at Ciccilo's house [Francisco Antonio Paulo Matarazzo Sobrinho, the Brazilian industrialist mentioned at the beginning of this essay] that very evening without ever feeling out of place, whereas the English would never do that [translation by the editors]) (Galvão 1981, 114).

3. Pereira de Almeida, originally an actor, was a central figure of the Teatro Brasileiro de Comedia, an important playwright, and one of the original cofounders of Vera Cruz.

4. Pereira de Almeida had already recognized the value of television when he stole Amácio Mazzaropi from TV-Tupi and the early program Radio Alegre. Legend has it that he and Tom Payne were having a drink at Nick's Bar, near the Vera Cruz studios, in 1951, when they saw Mazzaropi on TV and decided to invite him to Vera Cruz.

5. In the 1960s, Vera Cruz participated in a number of coproductions, using its studios and technical facilities (for example, *Noite vazia*, Walter Hugo Khoury, 1964), but most frequently it rented its facilities to TV producers, especially TV Excelsior, which filmed telenovelas there. Brothers Walter Hugo and William Khoury purchased the Vera Cruz studios and archives though not the land, which belonged to the Bank of the State of São Paulo, in the 1960s, in a very complicated deal the details of which have not yet been clearly elucidated. See Pereira de Almeida's interview (Galvão 1981, 166–78).

6. The announcement of the Centro Experimental Alberto Cavalcanti the same year of the centenary of Cavalcanti's birth was, ironically, the only public recognition of the date in Brazil. As Amir Labaki argued in the *Folha de São Paulo* (1997): "Reafirma-se Cavalcanti, assim, como un desconhecido no próprio pais. Não há justificativa exceto preconceito, descaso, e covardia" (This simply reaffirms that Cavalcanti is an unknown in his own country. There is no justification for this, except prejudice, neglect and cowardice [translation by the editors]).

7. "Guilhenne de Almeida comeca a dirigir novo filme," *Folha de São Paulo* (Ilustrada), March 7, 1997.

8. Editors' note: In line with current usage, we have altered some of the original text to acknowledge slavery as a violent process inflicted on people as part of the colonialist endeavor, and not an identity.

9. Prints (and videotapes) with different endings are still circulating. In one version, Galdino's death is not shown. In others, according to Lima Barreto produced by demand of Columbia Pictures for US distribution, the official posse

finally catches up to the *cangaceiros* right after Teodoro dies and kills Galdino. Brazilian sources identify the version in which Teodoro's and Galdino's deaths are juxtaposed as the definitive one, although in the published script of the film Galdino dies at the hands of the posse.

10. In 1953, a primarily French jury (fifteen out of nineteen jurors) headed by Jean Cocteau awarded the Grand Prize to Clouzot's *Le Salaire de la peur* and eight special international prizes. At this time Cannes juries were able to create and dispense as many awards beyond the Grand Prize as they wished, which led Alex Viany to characterize the award harshly as a consolation prize (1987, 10).

11. In their Latin music–inspired album *Pirata* (1989), which also includes other paeans to Latin American cowboy figures in songs titled "Tex," "Santiago," and "Amigo."

12. And as much of a productive hybrid as later films praised for their generic mixing such as *Macunaima* (Joaquim Pedro de Andrade, 1969) or even those whose hybridity is rarely discussed (for example, *Os Cafajestes* [Ruy Guerra, 1962], a rewriting of French New Wave style and melodrama).

13. A Lebanese immigrant, Benjamin Abrahão was an entrepreneur and adventurer who arrived in Brazil in the 1910s and ended up working as a sort of marketing adviser for Padre Cícero in Juazeiro do Norte in Ceará in the 1930s. He called himself a journalist and claimed to have studied in France. Apparently introduced to Lampião when he went to Padre Cícero to receive his decoration as a captain of the armed forces, Abrahão convinced Lampião to pose for a photograph. Some years later, in 1936, Abrahão got the backing of a newly established production company (Ademar Albuquerque's Aba-filmes) and went into the *sertão* with a 35-mm camera to film what he hoped would become a very successful and profitable documentary of the *cangaceiros* in action. Although a complete amateur, Abrahão was rather resourceful, resorting to handholding the camera in order to better follow the *cangaceiros*' actions, and his footage is fascinating. Lampião was cooperative, careful to present himself, surrounded by creature comforts, as the "king" of the *cangaço*. Unfortunately for Abrahão and Aba-filmes, the film's romanticized presentation of Lampião did not please the Getúlio Vargas government—after all, federal forces had been trying to capture Lampião for years!—and the film was banned in Brazil's first act of official federal censorship. Abrahão's footage has been preserved by a private collector in Bahia and was incorporated into the 1997 film *Baile Perfumado* (Paulo Caldas, Lírio Fereira).

14. The phenomenon of *cangaceiros* began around 1880, when the Northeast suffered one of the most severe droughts in its history, and armed groups robbed warehouses and estates and distributed goods to the thousands of migrants who wandered around the region (called the *Retirantes*). Thus, it began as social banditry, in the style of Robin Hood. With the abolition of slavery in 1888 and the proclamation of the Republic in 1899, conditions in the Northeast declined even further and the *cangaço* grew, maintaining its Robin Hood–esque attitude and

adding to it a spirit of social justice and revenge. The *cangaceiros* were mystical and violent and believed that the only way to avoid starvation and/or slavery to the *latifundio* system was armed struggle. Their principal enemy was injustice, specifically that of the *Coronéis*, the feudal landowners of the Northeast, and that of the government, which regularly organized posses to attempt to control them. The most famous of all *cangaceiros* was Virgulino Lampião, who formed a group in 1916, at age nineteen, after his parents were murdered by order of a local Pernambuco *Coronel*. His group grew in size and power, using guerrilla tactics to combat and demoralize government forces for over two decades. The federal government even tried to co-opt him, offering him arms, uniforms, money, and the title "Captain 1" to fight against the Prestes Column (another rebel movement commanded by Luis Carlos Prestes, who would become Brazil's most famous communist leader). Lampião took the money, arms, and title, and used them to fight the government *macacos* even more fiercely. In 1929 he met María Bonita in the interior of Bahia, a young and very beautiful woman who went on to become his constant companion in love and battle: their relationship is the source of the greatest romantic myth of Brazilian culture. When Getúlio Vargas came to power in 1930, his economic industrialization plan prioritized the elimination of the *latifundios* and the *cangaceiros*. Lampião reacted splendidly and fought the government troops spectacularly, beginning to attract attention as the "King" of the *cangaço*. Finally, in 1938, he, María Bonita, and a small troop were ambushed and machine-gunned in Gruta de Anjicos, Bahia. Eleven *cangaceiros*, including Lampião and María Bonita, were beheaded and their heads were sent to Salvador, where they were exhibited in a museum until the 1980s. With Lampião's death, the other *cangaceiro* groups were quickly defeated. A year later, the last two *cangaceiros*, "Corisco and his wife Dadá," were finally defeated.

15. "Mulher, mulher rendeira; mulher mulher rendá; Tu me ensina a fazer renda; eu te ensino a namorar" [Lacemaker, lacemaker; woman of lace; You teach me how to make lace; I'll teach you how to make love].

16. This is an explicitly cinematic effect and production. In Lima Barreto's script there is little musicality and the *cangaceiros* express themselves in the camp through rhymes and spontaneous poetry reminiscent of *literatura de cordel* (Barreto 1984, 74–82).

17. Born Héctor Julio Pande Bernabé in Argentina, the painter Carybé is another interesting example of a putative "foreigner" who participated in the film. For decades considered one of the most respected visual chroniclers of Bahia (and the illustrator of many Jorge Amado books), Carybé began his lifelong project when he arrived in Bahia with the desire to draw and interview Lampião. He arrived too late and had to resign himself to drawing his decapitated head, already housed in a museum. In the 1950s he managed to get a job with the Ministry of Education to draw Bahian scenes and never again left. His designs

for the film established its visual look and are yet another important instance of the hybridizations at work in the text.

18. It is interesting to note that both Carlos Coimbra and Aurélio Teixeira, the principal *nordestern* directors, were direct heirs of the Vera Cruz tradition. Coimbra entered the cinema through an internship with editor Oswald Haffenrichter, while Teixeira participated in a number of São Paulo productions with ex–Vera Cruz personnel (i.e., Tom Payne's *Arará vermelha*, 1956; Anselmo Duarte's *Absolutamente certo*, 1957).

19. After then-president Fernando Collor de Mello closed Embrafilme in 1990, Brazilian production went into a deep crisis that lasted until the mid-1990s when, fueled by new federal tax incentives for investments in culture (the Audiovisual and Rouanet laws) and a series of state and municipal production initiatives (in, for example, Rio, São Paulo, and Ceará), production increased dramatically.

20. Mirinow arrived in Brazil in 1940 to work for Vera Cruz and remained working at the Teatro Brasileiro de Comedia until 1960. Subsequently he moved to New York, where he worked for CBS (doing makeup for the Beatles before their appearance on *The Ed Sullivan Show* and in films such as *The Godfather*) ("Maquiador . . . ," 1997).

8. Crossing Nations and Genres: Traveling Filmmakers (2000)

1. Thus, for example, although it is impossible to consider the phenomenon of post-Pinochet Chilean exile without taking into account pancontinental collaborations, the pan–Latin American influences upon the seemingly far more insular Cuban ICAIC (Instituto Cubano de Arte e Industria Cinematográficos) cinema or the Brazilian Cinema Novo movement have yet to be investigated.

2. One exception to this rule is Paulo Antonio Paranaguá's *Cinema na América Latina: Longe de Deus e perto de Hollywood*. Albeit brief, this is to my knowledge the only comparative, continental historical study of Latin American cinema to date.

3. For the most detailed account of the Hollywood "Hispanic" cinema, see Juan B. Heinink and Robert G. Dickson (1990), Emilio García Riera's *México visto por el cine extranjero*, 6 vols. (1987–1990) and his *Historia documental del cine mexicano*, vol. 1 (1993a).

4. The history of the creation of the Lumiton studios is an interesting one. Four friends (César José Guerico, Enrique Telémanco Susini, Luis Romero Carranza, and Miguel Mugica) who owned a radio company received a large cash payment from ITT (International Telegraph and Telephone) to give up the business. With the funds, they decided to go into movie production. They bought a camera in the United States, bought a lot in the Buenos Aires neighborhood of Munro, and built a studio from the ground up. At its peak, the studio had more

than four hundred employees. See interview with Lumiton set designer Richard Canord in Homero Alsina Thevenet (1978, 189–209).

5. Four-week shooting schedules were the norm for a feature film. During production, it was common for employees to sleep on the studio grounds. The top talent had the use of a special "chalet" on the property that had been acquired with the original lot and retained for this purpose (Ortiz 1982, 206–07).

6. Editors' note: Unless otherwise specified, all translations from Spanish and Portuguese sources are by López.

7. In terms of the imaginary geography of the film, La Guaira is clearly figured as a more remote outpost than Isla Margarita and is a place where wild forces and desires take root and where social mores and customs are wildly dislocated. However, geographically, La Guaira is in fact more central to the nation, as it is the port for the capital city of Caracas. Ostensibly La Guaira should have been a modernizing force even in the late 1940s rather than, as in the film, an almost anachronistic site for the occult, the forbidden, and the foreign. It is interesting co speculate how geographical consciousness might have affected the Venezuelan viewer in 1949.

8. The scene when Segundo awakens in Esperanza's less-than-bourgeois abode may well be one of the most effective and elegantly constructed in the film, conveying its complex message economically via pointed glances, reframings, rack focus, and excellent editing.

9. De Córdova was, himself, a traveler. He appeared in a number of Hollywood films in 1939–1947, including *For Whom the Bell Tolls* (Frank Turtle, 1943) and *Frenchman's Creek* (Mitchell Leisen, 1944). Di Núbila claims that in 1947, de Córdova's star had begun to wane: "His star was in complete decadence. . . . Despite the success of his Hollywood films, Mexican producers were no longer interested in him" (1959b, 94). But as Emilio García Riera argues, given how extraordinarily busy de Córdova was in 1947, this hardly makes sense: he filmed *La diosa arrodillada* (Roberto Gavaldón) and *Algo flota sobre el agua* (Alfredo B. Crevenna) in Mexico; *New Orleans* (Arthur Lubin) in the United States; a US-Mexico coproduction, *The Adventures of Casanova* (Roberto Gavaldón); and finally, *Dios se lo pague* (Luis César Amadori) in Argentina (1971, 238). Whatever the case may be, this last film, the most popular Latin American film of the decade, transformed him into the most recognizable and bankable male star in the continent. In subsequent years he continued his pancontinental travels, filming regularly in Mexico, Argentina, and even Brazil (in two other films with Christensen).

9. Tears and Desire: Women and Melodrama in the "Old" Mexican Cinema (1994)

1. This period of the Latin American cinema has generated much solid historical/archival research. For Mexico, see especially Emilio García Riera, *His-*

toria documental del cine mexicano, 10 vols. to date, and Moises Viñas (1987). In English, see Carl J. Mora (1982). For a succinct and well-informed comparative historical analysis of this period in English, see John King (1990).

2. Although the Mexican cinema would not take off on an industrial scale until the 1936 international success of the *comedia ranchera* (ranch comedy) *Allá en el Rancho Grande* (*Over on the Big Ranch*, Fernando de Fuentes), melodramatic films were a staple from the 1930s through the 1960s. Aided by US wartime policies (and US resentment of Argentina's neutrality), the Mexican cinema thrived during the war and immediate postwar periods, producing 124 films in 1950, the majority of which were melodramas. I am using the term "melodrama" here loosely, for the Mexican cinema (and other Latin American cinemas, especially Brazil's and its *chanchadas*) proved extraordinarily adept at generic mixing. I use the word "melodramatic" in its broadest sense, as a structuring principle of expectations and conventions against which individual films establish their uniqueness as singular products, while recognizing that the term has a different currency in Latin America than in the United States or Europe.

3. An Aztec legend claimed that Quetzalcoatl, a feathered serpent god, would come from the East to redeem his people on a given day of the Aztec calendar, which, coincidentally, was the same day (April 21, 1519) that Cortéz and his men (fitting the description of Quetzalcoatl) landed in Vera Cruz. Thus Malintzin Tenepal became Cortéz's translator, strategic adviser, and eventually mistress, believing that she was saving her people. This is how recent scholarship has reinterpreted the four-hundred-year-old legacy of female betrayal, the founding moment of the Mexican nation (Alarcón 1983).

4. However, women did not win the right to vote in national elections until 1953.

5. The *género chico*, or *teatro frívolo*, was a vaudeville-like theatrical genre that developed in neighborhood playhouses and tents. While the bourgeois theater staged classical melodramas from Spain and France that outlined the parameters of decent behavior and exalted heightened sensibilities in perfect academic Spanish, the *género chico* thrived with popular characters and satire. Carnivalesque in the Bakhtinian sense, it included in its repertory taboo words and gestures and popular speech while exalting the grotesque and demanding a constant interaction between players and audience (Lamb 1975; Mañón 1932).

6. For an extensive analysis of María Félix's career and star persona, see Paco Ignacio Taibo (1985).

7. Editors' note: We retain the term "prostitute" in this essay to acknowledge how the term has been used to mystify the figure of the sex worker in the texts of Mexican culture with which López engages. But we also use the term "sex worker" in plot summaries of the relevant films to demystify this construction and to acknowledge that sex work is not an identity but a job these female characters do.

8.

The Perverted One
To you, life of my soul, perverted woman whom I love
To you, ungrateful woman
To you, who makes me suffer and makes me cry
I consecrate my life to you, product of evil and innocence.
All of my life is yours, woman
I want you, even if they call you perverted.

9. As Eduardo Galeano summarizes it in *Century of the Wind*, "Lara exalts the Lost Woman, in whose eyes are seen sun-drunk palm trees; he beseeches Love from the Decadent One, in whose pupils boredom spreads like a peacock's tail; he dreams of the sumptuous bed of the silky-skinned Courtesan; with sublime ecstasy he deposits roses at the feet of the Sinful One and covers the Shameful Whore with incense and jewels in exchange for the honey of her mouth" (1988, 110).

10. As Jorge Ayala Blanco indicates, in a few months between 1947 and 1948 alone, precisely coinciding with the Mario Rodríguez Alemán sexenio, over twelve *cabaretera* films were produced (1968, 137).

11. The Lara song "Aventurera" had already been featured in the 1946 María Félix film *La Devoradora* (Fernando de Fuentes). At the time, Lara and Félix were enjoying a much-publicized, albeit short-lived, marriage, and he ostensibly wrote the song explicitly for her.

10. Our Welcomed Guests: Telenovelas in Latin America (1995)

1. From all accounts, it seems that the Latin American radionovela and its successor, the telenovela, were first introduced and successfully marketed in Cuba. Inspired by the success of novela pioneer Felix B. Caignet (whose radionovela *El derecho de nacer* [*The Right to Be Born*, 1948] was heard all over the continent and was subsequently remade in film, telenovela, comic book, and even book form), tycoon Goar Mestre built a Cuban media empire as powerful in its day as Brazil's TV-Globo is today. Early Cuban telenovelas were not that widely exported, but many individuals with expertise in this field, especially writers, went into exile after the 1959 revolution and subsequently played important roles in the development of the telenovela format in other countries. Thus the Cuban writer Delia Fiallo has authored a large number of successful Venezuelan *culebrones* (big snakes, the popular Venezuelan term for long serial narratives, whether on radio or TV) and Gloria Magadan (who was hired by Colgate in the US and loaned

out to its Brazilian subsidiary) was essential to the development of the telenovela in Brazil in the 1960s.

2. In 1950, *Time* magazine, describing the success of Cuban radionovelas like Caignet's *El derecho de nacer* throughout Latin America (and even within the Spanish-speaking US), articulated the difference between the Caignet-style and US soaps: "Caignet knew how to give a new twist to the radio soap opera to please Latin tastes and achieved unprecedented success. He knew how to reproduce the daily climaxes, the racking sobs, the lack of subtlety, and the sonorous disquieting narrator. But he also moved the action from the soap opera's kitchens and living rooms to places as exotic as the coffee fields of Palma Soriano. And while the North American serials tended to steer clear of sexual problems, Caignet threw himself fully into the furies of passion, abortion and illegitimacy" (González 1988, 47–48).

3. The telenovela star system has produced fascinating ancillary markets. Besides stimulating the appearance of famous singers as characters (for example, Nydia Caro, José Luis Rodríguez, Lizette, Iris Chacón, and, most recently, Celia Cruz), telenovela actors (for example, Lucia Méndez and Verónica Castro) have also become singers and entertainers and have spilled out onto other programs and media. Furthermore, telenovelas have generated a large-scale pan–Latin American fan and information industry, with countless magazines (for example, *Telerevista*, *TV y novelas*, *Show*, and, in Brazil, *Amiga*) and TV and radio shows devoted to disseminating information about stars, focusing on their fictional characters as well as their personal lives.

4. The *show de auditorium* or variety program is another unique Latin American TV genre that evolved through the adaptation of US programming. Like the telenovela, the *show de auditorium* originated on radio as an adaptation of the US variety show format and, after undergoing local transformations, was transferred to TV. Generally aired on weekends (when there are no telenovelas), the *shows* are extraordinarily popular. Televisa's *Siempre en Domingo* (Always on Sundays), for example, is beamed live to over a dozen nations and has the world's largest audience for a regularly scheduled program (Holston 1986). TV-Globo's *Fantástico*, another Sunday program, has been on the air since the early 1970s and has an audience share of close to 90 percent (based on the nationally produced IBOPE ratings). Currently, US-based Univisión is producing perhaps the most popular of all *shows de auditorium*, *Sábado Gigante* (Giant Saturday). Hosted by Don Francisco, a Chilean national of German descent (real name, Mario Kreutzberger), *Sábado* is a descendent of a Chilean *show* that has aired regularly for more than thirty years and is cited in the *Guinness Book of Records* as "the world's longest running TV show with a single host without ever showing a repeat." The three-and-a-half-hour show (a combination of game shows, documentaries, audience-participation skits, travelogues, talk shows, and beauty contests) is produced in Miami and exported to eighteen countries. It has made Don Francisco one of the most popular characters of Spanish-language television and a recognizable

figure throughout the continent. Everyone loves Don Francisco. See "Univisión's Don Rules Saturday" (Anon. 1992) and Daisann McLane (1988).

5. To preempt rival networks from challenging its supremacy by airing imported telenovelas, Globo has even resorted to buying, but never programming, the most popular products. This was the case, for example, with Televisa's extraordinarily popular *Simplemente María* (a five-hundred-episode telenovela that surpassed all sales records in the 1970s—over US$20 million—and even engendered a 1980s remake), which was purchased by Globo but never aired.

6. TV-Globo broke into the international market in the early 1980s with the success of *A Escrava Isaura* (1981), a historical telenovela set in the colonial period with a vaguely abolitionist theme. *Isaura* was sold widely throughout Latin America (its Spanish-dubbed version even aired on Univisión in the US), Europe, and Asia. It was named the best television program of the decade in Poland, caused Cuban officials to reschedule meetings to avoid competing with it, and resulted in a triumphant world tour for Lucelia Santos (the lead actress) who was feted like royalty even in China.

7. Following the pattern exploited by Hollywood interests for international trade, telenovela producers sell their product at differential rates, according to the characteristics of the market. Most often, the determining factor is the number of TV sets in the market in question, but other considerations may be taken into account as well. Thus, for example, when TV-Globo sells its telenovelas to Cuban television, it charges an average of US$250 per episode rather than its usual US$5,000–15,000 for "older" products. Furthermore, to facilitate sales to foreign debt-ridden nations, the larger producers have set up a barter system whereby programs are exchanged for advertising time. Since 1985, Televisa has demanded four minutes for each program hour sold to US-based multinationals. Similarly, when TV-Globo sold *A Escrava Isaura* and *Dancin' Days* to China, it accepted advertising time instead of currency (Mattelart and Mattelart 1990, 12).

8. The exception is Colombia, where the Colombian Radio and Television Institute (Inravisión) legislated that, as of July 1, 1987, prime-time telenovelas had to be domestically produced. However, this measure was intended to protect national producers from the popularity of Mexican and Brazilian telenovelas, and not from US serials (Mattelart and Mattelart 1990, 11).

9. Nevertheless, as Robert Allen suggests in his analysis of the term "soap opera" in the US, class denigration usually also lies behind devaluation by gender (1985, 8–9).

10. Martín-Barbero sketches an interesting history of Latin American melodramas that highlights, for example, the relationship between popular serial literature and oral storytelling traditions (such as the reader in Cuban tobacco factories) and the roots of Argentine *radioteatro* (rather than radionovela) in traveling circus spectacles and their "theatrical" troupes (Martín-Barbero and Muñoz

1992, 39–60). For an analysis of the relationship between intellectual elites and radio, see Ana Maria Fadul (1984).

11. Even regional variants sustain this principle. In Brazil telenovelas are simply called novelas (but in Portuguese, the novel is more generally called a *romance*). In Venezuela, the term *culebrones* (big snakes) is often used derogatorily, but its gender connotation would obviously be male rather than female.

12. Doris Sommer (1991) uses the term "foundational fiction" to refer to the relationship between popular nineteenth-century romance novels and nation-building in Latin America.

13. One of the earliest Cuban critiques of melodrama (cinematic, radial, and televisual) was produced by critics/filmmakers Enrique Colina and Daniel Díaz Torres (1971). Reynaldo González's study (1988) of radio serial narratives continues in this tradition. A more subtle analysis of the place and pleasure of melodrama in television serial narratives is found in Julio García Espinosa (1993).

14. The work undertaken to improve serial narrative production has been extensive. A large number of training and informational seminars have been held for production personnel under the auspices of the ICRT. Furthermore, in the context of the 1989 Havana Film Festival, the ICRT organized an important seminar on the telenovela with presentations and debates among researchers and producers from various Latin American countries. The Centro de Investigaciones Sociales of the ICRT has also focused much attention on the telenovela: they have researchers dedicated almost exclusively to serial narrative, have developed an extensive dossier on telenovela research throughout the world, and have undertaken various studies of the peculiarities of the Cuban audience/context. Most recently, in an innovative experiment in conjunction with the Facultad de Cine, Radio y Televisión of the Instituto Superior de Arte, two students produced a thesis that included not only a historical study of the Cuban telenovela, but also the production *and* analysis of perhaps the first contemporary Cuban telenovela to have been a popular success: *Pasión y prejuicio* (Passion and Prejudice), aired in 1993. The students, Anabel Leal and Reinaldo Cruz, were simultaneously actors, assistant directors, and analysts/chroniclers of the production and reception process. They attribute the success of the telenovela not only to its story and protagonists, but also to its production strategy. For the first time in the history of the ICRT, a production was organized on a semi-industrial model: the director and producer were given free rein to hire personnel and to make budgetary decisions. Furthermore, the production team was given a financial incentive (considerable salary bonuses) to complete the project on time and under budget (Bobes 1993, 4–9).

15. Editors' note: In line with current usage, we have altered some of the original text to acknowledge slavery as a violent process inflicted on people as part of the colonialist endeavor, and not an identity.

16. In a country that for decades refused to grant "star" status to domestic film/TV actors and actresses, the attention-loving and quite sophisticated personnel

of the Brazilian telenovelas became instant national symbols. When visiting Cuba, even second- and third-echelon actors and actresses are treated like national treasures. They are officially welcomed like diplomatic dignitaries (and regularly meet with Fidel Castro and high party officials), but they are also popularly received with an adulation that knows almost no bounds. Accompanying a Globo actor in Havana, for example, is a gruesome ordeal: chambermaids won't leave their room; every cook, sous-chef, and dishwasher in every restaurant must make their acquaintance; telephone operators will stay on the line during their calls; they are unable to make public appearances without causing a mob scene. Thus, even years after the airing of *A Escrava Rosaura*, Lucelia Santos is still a national heroine and Maitê Proença—the star of the second-most-watched Brazilian import, *Dona Beija*—is still considered a national sex symbol and, despite her Germanic blonde and blue-eyed physique, a paradigmatic Brazilian beauty. More perversely, Rubens de Falco (the actor who played the villain in *Isaura*) has essentially disappeared from the Brazilian television scene but in Cuba is still feted and treated as a *gran galán*. It is not surprising, then, that like de Falco, many ex-Globo actors and actresses return periodically to Cuba to recharge their faltering star egos.

17. For an interesting in-depth analysis of this period, see Alma Guillermoprieto (1993).

18. Most of its non-telenovela programming—news, variety shows, music specials, talk shows, and sitcoms—is produced in the US, in Telemundo's studios in Hialeah, Florida.

19. The deal was quite advantageous: Azcárraga had sold Univisión to Hallmark for US$600 million and the new partnership reacquired it for US$550 million.

20. As this chapter was being prepared, Telemundo was unable to refinance its US$300 million outstanding debts and went into bankruptcy proceedings in August 1993. Its programming has changed little since then, but it is expected that it will have to curtail some of its more expansive production plans (Anon. 1993, 43).

21. The entire menu of first-run telenovelas available on Univisión in late 1993 evidences a heightened consciousness of a larger "Hispanic" world at Televisa. In addition to *Valentina* and *Dos mujeres, un camino*, the 8:00 p.m. slot is occupied by *Corazón salvaje*, a remake of a classic historical telenovela written in the 1940s by Caridad Bravo Adams, a veteran who learned the craft writing serials for prerevolutionary Cuban radio and TV. The stellar cast includes many well-known figures as well as César Evora, a Cuban actor who has not made a break with Cuba (and who also starred in Cuba's first successful telenovela in 1993). Replacing *Valentina* in the 7:00 p.m. slot and already airing in half-hour episodes at 7:30 since December 1993 is *Mas allá del puente*, a continuation of one of Televisa's most successful serials, *De frente al sol*. Written by the Cuban actor/writer René Muñóz, with extensive location shooting throughout Mexico and the Caribbean, it features an expansive cast, including the special appearance

of the veteran Mexican/US actress Katy Jurado (best known in the US for her role as Chihuahua in *High Noon*).

11. Of Rhythms and Borders (1997)

1. For an interesting discussion centered on Cuban music, see Leonardo Acosta (1989).
2. "If I dragged through this world the shame of having been and the pain of no longer being." With the exception of some short phrases or unless otherwise noted, all translations from foreign-language sources are López's own.
3. As Roberto Guidi has argued, the Valentino version of the tango, "a fantastic combination of rumba, paso doble, cueca and apache dance," became *the* international stereotype of the tango as dance" (cited by Couselo 1976, 129).
4. The list of potential examples is vast and spans all genres, although the Hollywood melodrama seems to have been especially attracted to Latin sounds. For example, in the inappropriately titled *Bolero* (Wesley Ruggles, 1934), Carlos Gardel look-alike George Raft ravishes Carole Lombard on the dance floor to the tango "El choclo"; Jean Arthur and Charles Boyer consummate their love to the tune of "La cumparsita" in *History Is Made at Night* (Prank Borzage, 1937); and Joan Bennett sings "Chula Chihuahua" in *House across the Bay* (Archie Mayo, 1940) while dressed like Carmen Miranda.
5. Thus Desi Arnaz as the Chicano marine Felix Martínez in *Bataan* (Tay Garnett, 1943) is also known as "the Jitterbug Kid."
6. Both Chihuahua and Pearl Chavez are heirs to the erotic mestiza legacy of Jane Russell's Rio in *The Outlaw* (Howard Hughes, 1940). Functioning as another narrative "third term," Rio is also an emblem of the indeterminacy of the Hollywood mestiza.
7. It seems appropriate to note that the association of pure musical performativity with ethnically and racially differentiated rhythms was only encouraged by those musicals where Anglo principal characters engaged in "ethnic" dance. For example, as Rick Altman points out, in the Astaire and Rogers films ethnic rhythms are always used for the specialty numbers that stress the dancing itself rather than the narrative romance (*Flying Down to Rio*, *Swing Time*) and in the "new" dances introduced at the end of their films together until *Top Hat* (1935) (1987, 165).
8. An important exception to this rule is the aristocratic Brazilian character who only dances socially, played by the Mexican actress Dolores Del Rio in *Flying Down to Rio* (Thornton Freeland, 1933).
9. One should also account for the production of musical multilinguals, especially for the Paramount-Joinville series begun in1930 (with *Luces de Buenos Aires*), featuring the great Argentine tango star Carlos Gardel.

10. As Antonio Benítez-Rojo argues: "What happens when there arrives, or there is imposed commercially a 'foreign' signifier, let's say the big band music of the 1940s or the rock music of the past thirty years? Well, among other things, the mambo, the cha-cha-cha, the bossa novas, the bolero, salsa, and reggae happen.... Caribbean music did not become Anglo Saxon, but rather the latter became Caribbean within a play of differences" (1992, 21).

11. Ever mindful of its capitalist prerogatives, Hollywood studios began to invest in Mexican productions as early as 1937–1938, attracting talent and using Mexican locations but also capitalizing on the success of Mexican films throughout Latin America (García Riera 1969a).

12. For example, in *La vendedora de Harrod's* (Defilippia Novoa, 1921), *Buenos Aires tenebroso* (Juan Glize, 1917), *El guapo del arrabal* (Julio Irigoyen, 1923), and in most of José Agustín Ferreyra's silent film productions, especially *El tango de la muerte* (1917), *Mientras Buenos Aires duerme* (1921), and *La costurerita que dio aquel mal paso* (1926).

13. This is the term used by Domingo Di Núbila (1959a, 18).

14. According to Couselo, Latin American distributors often valued Argentine films according to the number of tangos included: the more tangos, the higher the receipts (1976, 1314).

15. Thus, for example, in Miguel Zacarías's *La cuna vacía* (The Empty Cradle, 1937), the Manichean split between the virgin and the whore is inscribed in the musical difference between Ana, who sings pure and spiritual operatic airs, and Elena, who suggestively enjoys her danzón performances.

16. Editors' note: We retain the term "prostitute" in this essay to acknowledge how the term has been used to mystify the figure of the sex worker in the texts of Mexican culture with which López engages. But we also use the term "sex worker" in plot summaries of the relevant films to demystify this construction and to acknowledge that sex work is not an identity but a job these female characters do.

17. As Jorge Ayala Blanco indicates, in a few months between 1947 and 1948, precisely coinciding with the beginning of the Mario Rodríguez Aleman sexenio, over twelve *cabaretera* films were produced (1968, 137).

18. The Lara song "Aventurera" had already been featured in the 1946 María Félix film *La devoradora* (Fernando de Fuentes). At the time, Lara and Félix were enjoying a much publicized, albeit short-lived, marriage.

19. Editors' note: In line with current usage, we have altered some of the original text to acknowledge slavery as a violent process inflicted on people as part of the colonialist endeavor, and not an identity.

20. "I dance the mambo, son, guaracha, or rumba, for all of them have sandunga, just like the African rhythm." For a detailed analysis of this and other Cuban films of the period, see Laura Podalsky (1994).

21. The film was also released with the title ¡*Ay que bonitas piernas!* (Oh What Beautiful Legs!).

22. For a detailed analysis of this fascinating film, see Ayala Blanco (1968) and my "Tears and Desire: Women and Melodrama in the 'Old' Mexican Cinema" (1994b).

23. With the exception of Carlos Diegues's *Escola de Samba, Alegria de Viver* (Samba School, Joy of Life), one of the episodes of the compilation film *Cinco Vezes Favela* (Five Times Favela, 1962). However, despite its title, this film does not position samba as a popular form of cultural capital. It argues, instead, that samba is one of the instruments that blocks class consciousness in the urban favelado and is thus vastly different from Pereira dos Santos's films.

24. For more details and an astute analysis, see Michael Chanan (1985).

25. For the sake of this argument, I am excluding the emphasis upon Andean indigenous music in the films of the region such as *La tierra prometida* (Miguel Littín, 1973, Chile), with music by Inti-Illimani, or the films of Jorge Sanjinés in Bolivia and Peru.

26. For an insightful analysis of this film and Fernando Solanas's *Sur*, see Kathleen Newman, "National Cinema after Globalization: Fernando Solanas' *Sur* and the Exiled Nation" (1993).

27. Editors' note: Throughout this essay we have replaced the term "transvestite" with transgender and later trans woman to acknowledge that we are looking at this film from a different position to the original context of its production. But we also acknowledge that there is a conversation to be had about the film's exploration of gender. In the present moment it makes sense to refer to the film's trans characters, Suzy and Karla, as trans women, but in the film Julia simply refers to them as "unas amigas que tienen un show" (two [girl]friends who have a show) and it also puts an emphasis on Suzy's (Tito Vasconcelos) performance of dual gender identities. Another more local term that was used pejoratively in the 1980s and 1990s, but which, we stress, has subsequently been reclaimed, is *travesti*.

12. Mexico (2012)

1. Had space and time limitations allowed it, I would have liked to explore a third locale where musicality is invoked in the classic Mexican cinema, albeit not as frequently, the *vecindad* or working-class neighborhood. The transformation of the *barrio* into a musical space was facilitated primarily by the extraordinary success of Pedro Infante as the exemplary worker/family man "Pepe el Toro" in three films by Ismael Rodríguez, *We the Poor* (*Nosotros los Pobres*, 1948), *You the Rich* (*Ustedes los ricos*, 1948), and *Pepe el Toro* (1953). Subsequently, it was also exploited very effectively by the great singer/dancer/comedian Tin Tan (German Valdés) in films like *The King of the Neighborhood* (*El rey del barrio*, Gilberto Martínez Solares, 1949) and *El ceniciento* (Gilberto Martínez Solares, 1952).

2. It is interesting to note that President Lázaro Cárdenas had *mariachis* accompany him during his political campaign and invited a band to play at his inauguration (Velázquez and Vaughan 2006, 111).

3. The music of the *jarabe tapatío* was composed in Guadalajara in the nineteenth century. According to Pérez Montfort, the dance began to be identified as "typically Mexican" as early as 1918 to 1919, when the dance company of the Russian ballerina Anna Pavlova staged a very well-received version in Mexico City, sponsored by local producers and artists like Adolfo Best Maugard. In 1924, Minister of Education José Vasconcelos consolidated its Mexicanness by decreeing that the *jarabe* would be taught in all Mexican public schools, de facto determining that the *jarabe* would supersede local dance traditions and embody the unity of the nation (1994, 118–21).

4. Editors' note: We retain the term "prostitute" in this essay to acknowledge how the term has been used to mystify the figure of the sex worker in the texts of Mexican culture with which López engages. But we also use the term "sex worker" in plot summaries of the relevant films to demystify this construction and to acknowledge that sex work is not an identity but a job these female characters do.

5. In fact, the first radionovela produced by XEW in 1932 was *The Three Musketeers* (*Los Tres mosqueteros*), written by Alejandro Galindo (later an important filmmaker) and his brother Marco Aurelio ("Historia de W Rádio Mexico").

6. Although *comedia ranchera* is often translated as "ranch comedy," comedy is only one of the elements of the genre and this translation misleads by eliding musical and dramatic elements.

7. The point of reference is Rick Altman's highly influential 1984 article, "A Semantic/Syntactic Approach to Film Genre."

8. Jorge Ayala Blanco traces the antecedents of the *ranchera* genre to parodies in Spanish theater of the early 1900s, the *sainete* (light comedic moments, futile complications, misunderstandings as narrative motors, the arbitrary resolution of sentimental conflicts, and the clever use of language), the *zarzuela* (or light operetta) theatrical genre (sung interludes directly contributing to the narrative, the expression of communal happiness through song), regional literature, prior efforts to represent *hacienda* life in the silent Mexican cinema, burlesque theater in Mexico City, and Mexican folkloricism (1985, 69–70).

9. *Rancho Grande* was also seen throughout the Spanish-speaking Latin American market and subtitled versions were even released in the US (always the market most resistant to cinematic imports). But even this first moment of nationalist expansion was mediated by Hollywood. International distribution was coordinated by United Artists, who struck a most advantageous agreement with the film's producer (a 40 to 60 percent split of gross revenues). Until United Artists got out of Latin American distribution in the 1950s, *Rancho Grande* was

one of its highest-grossing films, in 1939 surpassed only by *Modern Times* and *The Garden of Allah* (de Usabel 1982, 140–41).

10. It is important to note that this is exactly how contemporary audiences would have perceived this sequence: the adult that appears on-screen is, above all, Jorge Negrete, not just the adult character Chavo.

11. Lucha Reyes was, in fact, the female counterpart to Negrete's super-macho *charro*. According to Yolando Moreno Rivas, cited by Velázquez and Vaughan, she lost her voice during a singing tour in Europe and returned to Mexico singing in a totally unexpected way: "she lavished her voice, coughing, moaning, crying, laughing, cursing—and stopped in the middle of a number to take a drink. Singing of love, abandonment, and torment, she came to personify the temperamental, passionate, strong, and tragic *'mujer mexicana bravía'*" (2006, 112).

12. *Two of a Kind* (*Tal para cual*, Rogelio A. González, 1952) featured Jorge Negrete and Luis Aguilar, *The Sons of María Morales* (*Los hijos de María Morales*, Fernando de Fuentes, 1952) starred Pedro Infante and Antonio Badu, and *The Three Happy Compadres* (*Los tres alegres compadres*, Julián Soler, 1951) went even further by featuring three big stars, Jorge Negrete, Pedro Armendáriz, and Andrés Soler.

13. It is important to note that, while in *Rancho Grande* the "secret" had to do with the girl's shame and the audience is in on the truth, here it is about the man and the audience is kept in the dark.

14. As an indigenous woman who became the interpreter and mistress of Hernán Cortés during the conquest of Mexico, La Malinche is a deeply ambivalent figure, with associations ranging from victimization to treachery.

15. Parts of this section are adapted from López (1994b).

16. During the Cárdenas sexenio, the labor unions and *campesino* organizations were reorganized, urban and industrial workers gained unionization rights and wage increases, and the government finally fulfilled the promises of the revolution by expropriating and redistributing more than five hundred million acres to about eight hundred thousand *campesinos*. Under his leadership, the work of the Secretaría de Educación Pública and its socialist educational program, focused on the empowerment and enfranchisement of rural communities, also acquired renewed vigor (Knight 1994). With a strong nationalist and populist agenda, Cárdenas had widespread popular support that was almost unanimous when he masterminded the expropriation of foreign oil companies in 1938.

17. The musical cast of *Revancha* is a who's who of the musical celebrities of the era: Agustín Lara (playing a blind pianist, his prototypical role), Toña la Negra, Pedro Vargas, and the trio Ángeles del Infierno.

18.

> Sell your love expensively, adventuress.
> Put the price of grief on your past.
> And he who wants the honey from your mouth
> Must pay with diamonds for your sin

Notes to Chapter 14 | 503

Since the infamy of your destiny
Withered your admirable spring.
Make your road less difficult,
Sell your love dearly, adventuress.

13. Before Exploitation: Three Men of the Cinema in Mexico (2009)

1. Since 1926, Mexican regulations required Spanish for all radio broadcasts, 25 percent Mexican music content, and banned religious programming (Hayes 2000).

2. The first radionovela produced by XEW in 1932 was *Los tres mosqueteros* (The Three Musketeers) written by Alejandro Galindo and his brother Marco Aurelio. See "Historia de W Radio Mexico," http://www.wradio.com.mx/historia.asp?id=1 96949, accessed July 1, 2008.

3. The D.F. or Distrito Federal was officially created on December 31, 1928.

4. That privilege has been reserved for the films of Fernando de Fuentes, Arcady Boytler, Alejandro Galindo, and, to a lesser degree, Juan Bustillo Oro, Gabriel Soria, and Miguel Contreras Torres.

5. In an interview with Alejandro Pelayo for the 1982 TV series *Los que hicieron nuestro cine* (The Ones Who Created Our Cinema), Orol claimed that audiences laughed at moments when they were meant to cry. He reedited it and rereleased it in second-run theaters, where it apparently did much better (De la Vega Alfaro 1987, 25).

6. Similar to *Redes* but independent of the state, *Janitzio* (1934, released 1935; dir. Carlos Navarro) also exalted the indigenous (and provided Emilio Fernández with his first starring role).

7. A contemporary critic called it "perhaps the least Mexican of the films made in Mexico" (De la Vega Alfaro 1992, 110).

8. Orchestrated by the newspaper *Excelsior* in Mexico City in an effort to counter the very liberal initiatives promoting sex education and women's rights emanating from the liberal state of Yucatan (Acevedo 1982, 8).

9. Although it is tempting to suggest a link between Bohr and the drug abuse exploitation films making the rounds in the United States around this same time (such as Dwain Esper's *Narcotic*, 1933), there is no evidence that this was the case.

14. (Not) Looking for Origins: Postmodernism, Documentary, and *America* (1993)

1. Editors' note: Unless otherwise stated, all translations are López's own.

2. The year 1989 was a year of drastic changes for Brazilian society. Racked by hyperinflation, which by November had reached a high of 50 percent per month, the nation devoted itself to the preparations for its first presidential election in twenty-five years. Despite the nonintervention of the military establishment, a new constitution, and a democratically elected congress, the country seemed simultaneously to be at a standstill, waiting for a new leader, and to be spinning out of control. The media, especially television, was playing its usual role in capitalist developing societies, serving up its usual fare of entertainment programming, news reporting, and political advertising (two one-hour blocks per day—one in the morning, one during prime time—on radio and television, apportioned free of charge to the more than twenty-five different political parties according to the size of their constituencies).

3. For information about the history of the development of Brazilian television, see Alcir Henrique da Costa, Inimá Ferreira Simões, and Maria Rita Kehl (1986); Fernando Barbosa Lima, Gabriel Priolло, and Arlindo Machado (1985); and Michèle Mattelart and Armand Mattelart (1989).

4. João Moreira Salles, the son of a former ambassador to the United States who is also the owner of one of the largest Brazilian banks, obtained financing for the production from a number of companies (most notably CrediCard and the Companhia Brasileira de Metalurgia e Mineração) under legislation known as the "lei Samey," which gave tax breaks in exchange for corporate cultural financing. (This legislation was abolished in 1990, shortly after the airing of *America*, when newly elected president Fernando Collor de Mello introduced an economic plan that eliminated all state support for cultural activities.)

5. *Pantanal* was Manchete's first serious challenge to Globo's hold on the prime-time audience. Set in the swampy Pantanal region (rather than in an urban center or a bucolic past), the telenovela's slower rhythms, earthiness, ecological sensibilities, *and* explicit nudity and sexuality consistently attracted more viewers than the Globo telenovela it was aired against (*A Rainha da Sucata* [The Queen of Scraps]). With its hegemony seriously challenged, Globo underwent a series of almost hysterical programming changes designed to recapture its audience. However, now accustomed to changing channels (and given the growing popularity of TV sets equipped with remote control units that facilitate channel switching), Brazilian audiences have remained comparatively fickle since then.

6. The term itself has been subject to various ideological appropriations and is marked by a wide variety of interpretations. For useful discussions of the various postmodern positions, see: Jonathan Arac (1986); Stanley Aronowitz and Henry Giroux (1991); Hal Foster (1983); Andreas Huyssen (1986); Andrew Ross (1988).

7. See, for example, Roberto da Matta (1978).

15. Revolution and Dreams: The Cuban Documentary Today (1992)

1. Editors' note: Chanan published a revised and updated version of *The Cuban Image* in 2004 under the new title *Cuban Cinema*. All translations, unless otherwise stated, are López's own.

2. The documents collected in the "Cuba" section of the anthology *Hojas de cine: Testimonios y documentos del nuevo cine latinoamericano* (Fundacion Mexicana de Cineastas 1988) provide ample proof of the scope, range, and depth of the debates of the 1960s and 1970s.

3. The period 1986–1988 was one of great economic crisis. In 1986, Cuba was unable to meet some of its foreign debt payments and, when unable to renegotiate the debt, suspended all payments. Internally, this crisis was reflected throughout 1986–1988 in various policy changes causing much controversy. For example, the cost of urban transport increased by 100 percent (the first increase since 1959), consumer electricity increased by 40 percent, the number of subsidized workers' lunchrooms was drastically reduced, and scarce food products became available in government-run "parallel markets" at prohibitively high prices. Also in 1986, the short-lived but thriving private farmers' markets were prohibited because of profiteering charges. Finally, the public fights against governmental corruption (which culminated in 1989) began in 1987 with the firing of over three hundred government employees.

4. As defined by Bill Nichols (1985) "voice" refers to "that which conveys to us a sense of the text's social point of view, of how it is speaking to us and how it is organizing the material it is presenting to us" (260).

5. In particular, Sara Gómez's *Iré a Santiago* (1964), a gentle portrait of Santiago de Cuba and its people that takes its name from a poem by Lorca.

16. *The Battle of Chile*: Documentary, Political Process, and Representation (1990)

1. For an interesting analysis of the Chilean debacle from a Gramscian perspective, see John Hoffman (1984).

2. As Raúl Zurita has convincingly argued, this is apparent first of all within language itself as the growing sociopolitical dislocation in Chile forced oral expression and conversation to become increasingly transparent and self-evident: "One understands . . . because one is in disagreement and language becomes more transparent as the intermediary space of negotiation narrows" (1985, 301).

3. Interestingly, Stuart Hall finds a similar phenomenon in his analysis of the relationship of the photomagazine *Picture Post* to wartime Great Britain,

a society undergoing a revolutionary transformation and crisis akin to that of Chile under the UP (1972).

4. For an extensive filmography and analysis of the Chilean exile cinema, the "cinema of resistance," see Zuzana Pick (1984a).

5. Among university programs, the most important was that of the Catholic University in Santiago. Other centers of experimental/political cinematic activity were the Cine Club Universitario, the Centro de Cine Experimental, the Cinemateca Universitaria, and the Cine-Club Viña del Mar. The visit of Dutch documentarist Joris Ivens in the early 1960s (when he filmed his *Valparaíso*) was also an important stimulus to the young filmmakers who worked with him and attended his seminars.

6. The 1967 Viña del Mar festival represented a first step in the collaborative process of creating a new, pan–Latin American cinema. The importance of this event was officially recognized at the 1987 International Festival of New Latin American Cinema in Havana, with a complete retrospective of the films shown at Viña two decades earlier.

7. Declarations collected by the editors of *Cine y liberación*. Editors' note: All translations, unless otherwise stated are López's own.

8. Chile Films also produced many newsreels analyzing current events, but these newsreels, like their documentaries, provoked the anger of the established commercial sector and even, in some cases, fights in the theaters (Pick et al. 1981, 206).

9. A subsequent version of Pick's essay appears in chapter 5 of Julianne Burton's *The Social Documentary in Latin American Cinema* (1990).

10. The historical film was itself planned as a kind of documentary of the popular rewriting (and ideologically motivated deformation) of the legend of the nineteenth-century Chilean hero Manuel Rodríguez (see Sempere and Guzmán 1977, 60, 75).

11. Chile Films had been paralyzed by internal problems and the US blockade that made the importation of raw film stock impossible.

12. Cameraman Jorge Müller was not able to leave the country. He was arrested by the military police and like many of Latin America's "disappeared," he is assumed dead, though his fate has never been made public.

13. This is by far the most thorough critical review available in the North American mass press.

14. Sempere and Guzmán (1977) also reprints other reviews, including Luis Marcorelles's glowing assessment of the film for *Le Monde*.

15. The five fronts of struggle identified by El Equipo Tercer Año were the control of production and distribution, the counteroffensive by revolutionary forces, the transformation of the relations of production, the ideological fight in education and information, and the battle plan. These five areas were identified in what was essentially the shooting script, published as "Guión esquema del filme," in *Cine Cubano* 91–92 (1977): 49–51, and reprinted in Patricio Guzmán (1977).

16. "A film using the sequence-shot is still a communicative instrument that signifies on other levels as well as that of direct representation (which in itself is already incomplete and intentional); it is still a work in which the place occupied by the signifiers is the support and root of the place occupied by the signified, by the diegesis" (Bettetini 1973, cited by Williams 1980, 221).

17. Channel 13 was the principal TV station controlled by the right.

18. This sequence of the bombing of La Moneda is one of the few not actually filmed by El Equipo Tercer Año. Another crucial sequence not filmed by them is the ending of part 1, the cameraman's filming of his own death (Sempere and Guzmán 1977, 97).

19. "Flaco" was Jorge Müller's nickname.

20. See Mayra Vilasis (1983) for an analysis of dramaturgy and the documentary.

21. This phenomenon has been well documented. For a journalistic account, see Ariel Dorfman (1981). For an analysis of how this "silencing" and "shrouding" of expression has redefined the nature of art in Pinochet's Chile, see Nelly Richard (1986). See also Hernán Vidal (1985).

17. At the Limits of Documentary: Hypertextual Transformation and the New Latin American Cinema (1990)

1. Although the discursive claims and effects of the fictional cinema have been theorized at great length, the documentary has so far escaped this kind of detailed analysis. The most suggestive work on the documentary as a signifying practice appears in Bill Nichols (1982). Michael Renov (1986) points out this lack and begins an analysis of the metaphysics of the nonfiction film.

2. The other four categories of transtextual relations identified by Genette do not have this transformative character. Citation or simple intertextuality, for example, is characterized by the copresence of two or more texts. Paratextuality refers to the relations between a text and all those ancillary textual fragments that name or place it: titles, subtitles, intertitles, prefaces, advertisements, and so forth. Metatextuality refers to a commentative relation, whatever links a text that speaks of another without necessarily citing it. In Genette's terms, this is "a critical relation *par excellence*" (1982, 10). Finally, architextuality refers to a silent relation between a text and generic and/or taxonomic categories. Genette has dedicated a separate volume to the analysis of this kind of transtextual relation (1979).

3. Given the diversity of the New Latin American Cinema, it is useless to attempt to encase the movement within the structures of traditional aesthetic typologies. Even the most modern and ostensibly politicized of these typologies— for example, Jean-Luc Comolli and Paul Narboni's (1971) hierarchy of progressiveness in the cinema—fail to account for the necessarily contextual effects and

transformations of any one tradition or practice within the New Latin American Cinema. I cite Comolli and Narboni here, because it is their typology of progressive texts that seems to have inspired Teshome Gabriel's similar typology of the Third Cinema (1982). Gabriel proposes a three-step genealogy of the Third Cinema that progresses from (1) dependence on Hollywood and (2) national cinemas that decolonize content without altering form, to (3) guerrilla cinema that radically alters all the structures of the cinematic apparatus. Problematic because of its exclusive emphasis on textual systems (especially in stages 1 and 2), this genealogy also insists on a seriality that is difficult to sustain given the unequal development of film practices in the different nations that participate in the New Latin American Cinema project.

4. That this documentary material is often invisible to North American audiences and critics, who insist on viewing this film as the anguished cry of an intellectual alienated and oppressed by the revolution, is significant in the context of contemporary theoretical arguments regarding the importance of specific reading formations for cinematic reception and meaning production. The contradictory positions of North American critics vis-à-vis this film have been explored by Julianne Burton (1977b), Daniel Díaz Torres (1976), and Tomás Gutiérrez Alea himself (1982).

5. This is a distinction ultimately based on a Platonic conception of art as imitation. For an analysis of the problems of this distinction for theories of filmic narration, see Edward Branigan (1984, 190–96).

6. The Abacuá is a secret religious society based on the practices, legends, rites, languages, and symbols of some of the enslaved Africans imported into Cuba. It developed in the marginal sectors of Havana and Matanzas provinces as an all-male sect that promoted certain religious beliefs and also functioned to protect the interests of its (Black and white) members.

7. Besides the documentary sequence that begins the film proper, the other four sequences are motivated by Mario: a sequence on the 1960s census and literacy campaign that was crucial for his development, the "essay" on the Abacuá sect, a biographical sketch of one of Mario's friends (singer and ex-boxer Guillermo Díaz, "another real person in this film"), and the demolition and rehabilitation of a slum like the one where he grew up.

8. All translations are López's own.

9. For details of their experiences with the community of Kaata while making the film, see Sanjinés (1979a, 15) and Jean-René Huleu, Ignacio Ramonet, and Serge Toubiana (1974). After an incredibly difficult journey carrying equipment to this distant village, Ukamau members sought out the assistance and cooperation of the villagers through their chief rather than from the community itself. They were unsuccessful until many days later when they agreed to participate in a community religious ceremony where they received a favorable prophecy from a reading of coca leaves. From this experience, the Ukamau group learned that

it could not impose its own organizational or social standards upon the deeply communal and collective social organization of the indigenous population.

10. It is interesting to note that these are the same techniques of the traditional cinema that in Robert Kolker's analysis save the film from excessive simplicity. Dismissing the film as "crude" for its refusal to use a more modern and sophisticated cinematic language, Kolker fails to take into account the cultural traditions of the audience to whom the film was directed (1983, 298–300).

11. When *Los caminos de la muerte* was almost 70 percent complete, the original negative was destroyed through a developing error in a German laboratory. Sanjinés and others believe that this was a deliberate act of sabotage. *El coraje del pueblo* was originally produced for Italian television in 1969, during the temporary period of democracy that followed the death of Bolivian president René Barrientos. By the time the film was finished in 1971, however, the political climate had changed and the film could not be exhibited in Bolivia. Its release elsewhere was delayed by RAI, which initially deleted the sequences that identified those responsible for the massacre. In fact, in 1975 Antonio Eguino (the film's director of photography) was arrested by the Bolivian military when his participation in the film was exposed through a confiscated contraband copy of the film.

12. Based on the events in the guerrilla movement narrated in *Perú 1965: Una Experiencia Liberatadora* by Héctor Béjar (a militant member of the ELN [National Liberation Army]), *El enemigo principal* was shot in 1974 (in Peru) by a new Ukamau collective organized after Sanjinés was forced into exile by the 1971 political crisis. Although the film was generally well received, its political analysis of guerrilla interactions with indigenous populations has been questioned as excessively *foco*-oriented. This strategy derives from tactics developed during the Cuban Revolution as theorized by Régis Debray (1967). For a discussion of *foquismo* and the political interpretation of this film, see Alfonso Gumucio Dagrón (1982, 295–300).

18. A Poetics of the Trace (2014)

1. The opposite process—the irruption of the documentary in the fictional—was also an important characteristic of the New Latin American Cinema movement. See López 1990a, 1990b, and 1991d.

2. It is not surprising that *Cabra* is one of the three films chosen by Fredric Jameson in his 1990 *Signatures of the Visible* to discuss what he called a neodocumentary turn, tracing the emergence of a new concept of the real as both encountered and produced by the film.

3. See the discussions in Wahlberg (2008) and Doane (2007).

4. See "(Not) Looking for Origins," chapter 14 in this volume, for López's 1991 essay on this TV series.

5. When he was president, from 1990 to 1992, Fernando Collor de Mello dismantled state funding for film production in Brazil.

6. Coutinho prefers the term "conversation" to the more traditional interview.

7. Paper presented at the conference Fiction/Fact in Brazilian Documentary Film at New York University in 2010 and also developed in her book *O documentário de Eduardo Coutinho: televisão, cinema e video.*

Editors' Introduction to Part 3

1. López published her essays on the representation of Black people in Brazilian and Cuban cinema in important journals like *Black Film Review* (published between 1984 and 1995) and *Tonantzin* founded in the mid-1980s.

2. We recognize that the gender-neutral, nonbinary term "Latinx" is more commonly used since the mid-2010s and may, indeed, be an appropriate way to characterize López's essays in this section given their emphasis on heterogeneity. That said, we also wanted to recognize the historical evolution of audiovisual scholarship in this area and to avoid forcing a later nomenclature onto essays written in prior periods.

19. Not Only a Question of Color: Afro-Latino/a Images in Latin American Cinema Today (1992)

1. Editors' note: In line with current usage, we have altered some of the original text to acknowledge slavery as a violent process inflicted on people as part of the colonialist endeavor, and not an identity.

2. Editors' note: The term *mulato* meaning biracial is commonly used in the Spanish Caribbean and has none of the negative connotations of the term's straight English-language translation. López's use of the Spanish term here indicates its common and uncontested usage in Cuba. We also note however that in the present moment use of the term is currently under discussion in Cuba.

3. Editors' note: We retain López's use of the Spanish term *mulato* (biracial) and direct readers to note 2 for an explanation.

20. African Roots: Images of Black People in Cuban Cinema (1988)

1. Editors' note: We have adjusted the original title ("African Roots: Images of Black People in Cuban Cinema") in order to respond to current practices in the field.

Notes to Chapter 22 | 511

2. The most notable study of Cuban slavery remains Manuel Moreno Fraginals's exhaustive three volumes entitled *El Ingenio* (1964). Also useful are Moreno Fraginals (1974) and Franklin W. Knight (1974).

3. Editors' note: In line with current usage, we have made small changes to the text to acknowledge slavery as a violent process inflicted on people as part of the colonialist endeavor, and not an identity.

4. It is unfortunate that hardly any films from the silent period of Cuban filmmaking have survived the ravages of time and accidental fires, in particular, the work of film pioneer Enrique Díaz Quesada. The titles of most of his films suggest a persistent preoccupation and interest in Afro-Cuban traditions. His 1917 *La hija del policía o el poder de los Ñañigos* (The Policeman's Daughter or the Power of the Ñañigos), for example, dealt with the Ñañigo or Abakuá secret society, which is also one of the subjects investigated in Sara Gómez's 1974 *De cierta manera* (*One Way or Another*).

5. The historical evolution and achievements of the ICAIC have been well documented and surveyed in texts such as Chanan (1985) and Julianne Burton (1981).

6. Editors' note: López's use of the term *mulato* reflects what was, in difference to the term in English, a common and uncontested use in Spanish in Cuba and elsewhere in the Spanish Caribbean. However, the editors would also like to draw attention to the fact that, in the present moment, the term and its usefulness are under discussion in Cuba.

22. Are All Latins from Manhattan? Hollywood, Ethnography, and Cultural Colonialism (1991)

1. For an interesting and useful survey of the literature on the cinematic representation of ethnics and minorities, see Allen L. Woll and Randall M. Miller (1987).

2. For a popular assessment of the power of the cinema as democratic propaganda for the American way of life in South America, see Florence Horn (1941, 59-64). Horn glowingly describes how well a young Brazilian and her housewife "friends" understand and recognize "America" because of their constant exposure to US films. After reading the following sentence, one wonders whether Orson Welles might have also read this piece before setting off on his OCIAA-sponsored Brazilian project in 1942: "He [the Brazilian boy] returns home, almost without exception, to tell his friends that it's all true—and even more so" (60). For self-assessments of the power and efficacy of the Good Neighbor Policy, see Nelson Rockefeller (1944, 15; 1943, 16–17).

3. As does Woll's analysis of this period (1977–1980). In particular, Woll praises the "unheard" of cultural sensitivity of RKO's *Flying Down to Rio* (1933),

a film that featured Dolores Del Rio as a Carioca enchantress and Rio de Janeiro as a city defined by its infinite romantic possibilities and as the South American meeting place of new US communication technologies and capital: airplanes for Southern travel, telegraphs for speedy communication, records and movies for music and romance. See Sergio Augusto (1988, 352–61).

4. Del Rio's Hollywood filmography includes, among other titles, *What Price Glory?* (1926, Walsh); *The Loves of Carmen* (1927, Walsh); *Ramona* (1928, Carewe); *The Red Dance* (1928, Walsh); *The Trail of '98* (1929, Brown); *Evangeline* (1929, Carewe); *The Bird of Paradise* (1932, Vidor); *Flying Down to Rio* (1933, Freeland); *Wonder Bar* (1934, Bacon); *Madame DuBarry* (1934, Dieterle); *In Caliente* (1935, Bacon); *The Lancer Spy* (1937, Ratoff); and *Journey into Fear* (1941, Foster). In *Journey into Fear*, Del Rio worked closely with Orson Welles (the first director of the film), with whom she had previously collaborated in the Mercury Theater production *Father Hidalgo* (1940) and during the production of *Citizen Kane* (1941).

5. López's own translation.

6. For the best summary/analysis of Vélez's career, see Gabriel Ramírez (1986).

7. Between 1940 and her death in 1955, Miranda made fourteen films: ten for 20th Century Fox, one for United Artists, two for MGM, and one for Paramount. The Fox "cycle," between 1940 and 1946, consisted of *Down Argentine Way* (1940, Cummings); *That Night in Rio* (1941, Cummings); *Weekend in Havana* (1941, Lang); *Springtime in the Rockies* (1942, Cummings); *The Gang's All Here* (1943, Berkeley); *Four Jills in a Jeep* (1944, Seiter); *Greenwich Village* (1944, Lang); *Something for the Boys* (1944, Seiler); *Doll Face* (1946, Seiler); and *If I'm Lucky* (1946, Seiler).

8. In a review of *The Streets of Paris*, Harry C. Pringle wrote in 1939 that "[the opening] was a pleasant but not an exciting evening until, at approximately 10 o'clock, six young men appeared on the stage and were followed by a vibrant young woman wearing an exotic dress and a turban hat with bananas, peaches, pears and other fruit stand wares on it. . . . But the magic of her appeal lay in the degree to which she seemed to be having an enormously good time: that, and in the implication that she loved everybody in general and all men in particular" (Barsante, 1985, 12).

9. Among others, see, for example, the *Variety* reviews of her Fox films—especially of *Down Argentine Way* (October 9, 1940), *Springtime in the Rockies* (November 24, 1942), and *That Night in Rio* (March 12, 1941)—which specifically comment upon the weakness of the romance narratives and the strength of her musical comedic performances.

10. Full-page advertisement for Piel's Light Beer in the New York *Daily Mirror*, July 25, 1947: "A lighting flash along Broadway means Carmen Miranda!

That Luscious, well-peppered dish! She glitters like a sequin, with her droll accent and spirited dances. And Carmen goes for Piel's—with all its sparkle and tang! 'I tell everyone I know to DREENK Piel's' she exclaims."

11. Miranda died at the age of forty-four, of a heart attack, on August 5, 1955, after taping a television program with Jimmy Durante. By this time—after a series of less than memorable screen appearances, alcohol and drug abuse, and a nervous breakdown in 1954—Miranda's presence had waned considerably. Although she was still a recognizable star, she had begun to work far more for television than for the cinema.

12. Special issue of *Time*, July 11, 1988.

23. Greater Cuba (1996)

1. Editors' note: Unless otherwise noted, all translations from Spanish-language sources are López's own.

2. Hamid Naficy has begun this project (1991).

3. The literature on the Chilean exile cinema is quite extensive, but for a good summary see Zuzana Pick (1987).

4. Less conservative figures indicate the possibility that as much as 12 percent of the present Cuban population (or 1.2 million) lives abroad (Fuentes-Pérez 1988).

5. For example, the earliest exiles have been quite unforgiving of those who collaborated with Castro and the revolution and whose subsequent change of political opinion has not convinced them. Thus, Carlos Franqui, an ex-Castro ally, is not very welcome in Miami circles (he lives in Italy): when he was introduced to the audience awaiting a screening of *The Other Cuba* (based, partly, on his story) at the Miami Film Festival in 1985, the audience's resounding boos convinced him to remain in his seat rather than go up on the stage and face the crowds (Fernández 1985).

6. Various exiled film workers did *not* come to the United States immediately—most notably, Néstor Almendros, who left Cuba to become a world-famous cinematographer in France and only came to the United States when he began to work for Hollywood producers in the late 1970s. (Almendros died in Paris in 1992.) Humberto López Guerra produced a documentary in Sweden entitled *Castro y Cuba*. Fausto Canel spent ten years in Spain and directed several films— *La espera* (Power Game), *La espuela* (The Spur), and *María la Santa* (Maria, the Saint)—and a TV serial (*El juglar y la Reina* [The Joker and the Queen]) before moving to the United States and directing *Campo minado*, a feature-length documentary about the return of democracy to the Southern Cone. He is presently living in Hollywood and working on the screenplay adaptation of his novel *Ni tiempo para pedir auxilio* (1991).

7. Tracking the journeys of Cuban exiles involved with film and video is a difficult task, which has become even more complicated in the last few years. I have relied on personal knowledge, some accounts published in the Spanish-language press and in the *Miami Herald*, and Maria Eulalia Douglas's *Diccionario de Cineastas Cubanos, 1959-1987* (1989), which identifies past and present ICAIC personnel (including those that had left as of 1987). José Antonio Evora—former *Cine Cubano* editor and current Guggenheim fellow—has also been a most helpful informant.

8. See, for example, Néstor Almendros (1987); and Guillermo Cabrera Infante (1985).

9. Padilla, an award-winning (UNEAC, 1968) yet disaffected poet, was arrested for dissidence in 1971. His subsequent public confession and apology, the ban on his books, and the government's refusal to allow him to travel (until his final departure via Spain in 1980) caused an international scandal that provoked the first split between Cuba and international intellectual circles. For an excellent assessment and compilation of important documents, see Lourdes Casal (1971).

10. In fact, this chronology somewhat contradicts the sociological understanding of the nature of the various "waves" of Cuban exiles. According to sociologists Amaro and Portes, for example, the first wave, 1959-1962, consisted primarily of elites who already had well-established business/connections in the United States. The second wave, 1962-1965, were the middle-class professionals who "escaped" for political and ideological reasons. The exiles of the third wave (1965-1974) increasingly were "those who searched" for better economic opportunities (Amaro and Portes 1972).

11. See Jorge Ulla, Lawrence Ott, and Miñuca Villaverde (1986, 158). Molina, who wrote the preface to this publication of the scripts of Ulla's and Villaverde's films, now lives in New York and works in the Latin American Department of Associated Press.

12. In addition to those that accompanied their parents into exile, the Cuban diaspora also included a number of children and teenagers sent by their parents to the United States (between 1960 and 1963) in response to rumors that the government was about to impose child custody laws that would give the state absolute authority over all children. Over several years, fourteen thousand children were met by the Catholic Charities organization, which set up camps in Miami and later relocated the children to orphanages and foster homes throughout the United States.

13. *El Super* won the grand prize at the Mannheim festival, a festival award at Biarritz, and was selected for a Mostra at the Venice festival in 1979.

14. I have been unable to view this film. However, all accounts indicate that it was produced on a shoestring budget and barely distributed within south Florida. The story was set in the late 1950s and focuses on five prisoners who undergo tests of emotional endurance and political conviction in between sessions

with a sadistic interrogator in a revolutionary guerrilla group. It was based on a 1975 play by Eduardo Corbe, photographed by Ramón Suárez, produced by Camilo Vila and Danilo Bardisa, and starred, among others, Orestes Matacena.

15. *Rompiendo el silencio* aired on Miami Univision affiliate Channel 23 on October 1, 1994. It is also available on video from the producers.

16. I use "Cuba" to refer to the greater nation, beyond the geographical confines of the island, that includes the exiled communities.

17. With the exception of Ferrera-Balanquet, who was over eighteen when he left Cuba during the Mariel exodus.

24. I (Also) Love Ricky: The Oft-Forgotten Cuban-in-the-Text (2012)

1. Strangely enough, in *A Book*, Arnaz characterized the coup of 1952 (that served as a prelude to the Batista dictatorship) as a "communist insurgency," almost as if he were trying to align himself with the perspective and sense of loss of the later generation of exiles who left the island after 1959.

2. In *A Book*, Arnaz explains that he was asked to participate not because of his star status, but because he spoke Spanish and could report directly on Mexico's reaction to the tour to the State Department and the Rockefeller "people."

3. Although Desi Arnaz did make a couple of interesting and moderately successful feature films essentially playing himself—*Cuban Pete* (1946, Jean Yarbrough) and *Holiday in Havana* (1949, Jean Yarbrough)—which possibly served as precursors for his subsequent Ricky Ricardo.

25. López on López: Liminal Words (2012)

1. See, for example, Emilio García Riera's eighteen-volume *Historia documental del cine mexicano* ([1969] 1992–1997); the almost anthropological reconstruction of [Mexico's] silent film patrimony by Aurelio de los Reyes in *Los orígenes del cine mexicano, 1896–1900* (Mexico City: FFCE, 1983b) and *Filmografía del cine mudo mexicano* (Mexico City: Filmoteca UNAM, 1986).

Works Cited

Abella, Alex. 1993. "The New Rhythm of Florida." *Los Angeles Times Magazine*, May 23, 38.
Acevedo, M. 1982. *El 10 de mayo*. Mexico City: Cultura SEP/Martín Casillas.
Acheson, K., and C. Maule. 1994. "Understanding Hollywood's Organization and Continuing Success." *Journal of Cultural Economics* 18, no. 4: 271–300.
Acosta, Leonardo. 1989. "From the Drum to the Synthesizer: Study of a Process." *Latin American Perspectives* 16, no. 2: 29–46.
Adamo, Sam. 1998. "The Sick and the Dead: Epidemic and Contagious Disease in Rio de Janeiro, Brazil." In *Cities of Hope: People, Protests, and Progress in Urbanizing Latin America, 1870–1930*, edited by Ron Pineo and James A. Baer, 218–39. Boulder, CO: Westview Press.
Agramonte, Arturo. 1966. *Cronología del cine cubano*. Havana: Ediciones ICAIC.
Agramonte, A., and L. Castillo. 2003. *Ramón Peón: El hombre de los glóbulos negros*. Havana: Editorial de Ciencias Sociales.
Alarcón, Nancy. 1983. "Chicana's Feminist Literature: A Re-vision through Malintzin, or Malintzin: Putting Flesh Back on the Object." In *This Bridge Called My Back: Writings by Radical Women of Color*, edited by Cherríe Moraga and Gloria Anzaldúa, 182–90. New York: Women of Color Press.
Alfaro Moreno, Rosa María. n.d. "Usos sociales populares de la telenovela en el mundo urbano." Mimeo.
Alfaro Salazar, H., and A. Ochoa Vega. 1997. *Espacios distantes . . . aún vivas: Las salas cinematográficas de la Ciudad de México*. Mexico City: Universidad Autónoma Metropolitana.
Allen, Robert. 1985. *Speaking of Soap Operas*. Chapel Hill: University of North Carolina Press.
Almendros, Néstor. 1987. "A los dictadores les gusta el cine." *Noticias de arte New York*, September, 10–12.
Almendros, Néstor. 1992. "P.M." In *Cinemanía: ensayos sobre el cine*. Barcelona: Seix Barral.

Altman, Rick. 1984. "A Semantic/Syntactic Approach to Film Genre." *Cinema Journal* 23, no. 3: 6–18.
Altman, Rick. 1987. *The American Film Musical*. Bloomington: Indiana University Press.
Altman, Rick. 1989. "Dickens, Griffith, and Film Theory Today." *South Atlantic Quarterly* 88 (Spring): 321–59.
Altman, Rick. 2004. "Cinema Sound at the Crossroads: A Century of Identity Crises." In *Le son en perspectives*, edited by D. Nasta and D. Huvelle, 13–46. Brussels: Peter Lang.
Alvaray, Luisela. 2021. Email correspondence with editors.
Amaro, Nelson, and Alejandro Portes. 1972. "Una sociología del exilio: situación de los grupos cubanos en los Estados Unidos." *Aportes* 23 (January): 6–24.
Andermann, Jens, and A. Fernandez Bravo, eds. 2013. *New Brazilian and Argentine Cinema: Reality Effects*. London: Palgrave Macmillan.
Anderson, Benedict. 1991. *Imagined Communities*, 2nd ed. London: Verso.
Anon. 1986. "Telenovela Is Something Else." *Variety*, March 12, 142.
Anon. 1992. "Univisión's Don Rules Saturday." *Variety*, March 23, 74, 96.
Anon. 1993. "Telemundo Turns to Chapter 11." *Variety*, August 9, 43.
Antola, Livia, and Everett M. Rogers. 1984. "Television Flows in Latin America." *Communication Research* 11, no. 2: 185–203.
Appadurai, Arjun. 1995. "Playing with Modernity: The Decolonization of Indian Cricket." In *Consuming Modernity: Public Culture in a South Asian World*, edited by Carol Breckenridge, 23–48. Minneapolis: University of Minnesota Press.
Appadurai, Arjun, and Carol Breckenridge. 1995. "Public Modernity in India." In *Consuming Modernity: Public Culture in a South Asian World*, edited by Carol Breckenridge, 1–22. Minneapolis: University of Minnesota Press.
Arac, Jonathan, ed. 1986. *Postmodernism and Culture*. Minneapolis: University of Minnesota Press.
Araújo, Vicente de Paulo. 1976. *A Bela Época do Cinema Brasileiro*. São Paulo: Perspectiva/ Secretaria da Cultura, Ciencia e Tecnologia.
Araújo, Vicente de Paulo. 1981. *Salões, Circos e Cinemas de São Paulo*. São Paulo: Perspectiva.
Arnaz, Desi 1987. *A Book*. New York: William Morrow.
Aronowitz, Stanley, and Henry Giroux. 1991. *Postmodern Education: Politics, Culture and Social Criticism*. Minneapolis: University of Minnesota Press.
Augusto, Sergio. 1988. "Hollywood Looks at Brazil: From Carmen Miranda to Moonraker." In *Brazilian Cinema*, edited by Randall Johnson and Robert Stam, 352–61. Austin: University of Texas Press.
Aura, Alejandro. 1990. *La hora íntima de Agustín Lara*. Mexico City: Cal y Arena.
Ayala Blanco, Jorge. 1968. *La aventura del cine mexicano*. Mexico City: Ediciones Era.

Ayala Blanco, Jorge. 1979. *La aventura del cine mexicano*. Mexico City: Ediciones Era, 1979.
Ayala Blanco, Jorge. 1986. *La condición del cine mexicano*. Mexico City: Editorial Posada.
Ayala Blanco, J., and M. I. Amador. 1980. *Cartelera cinematográfica 1930-39*. Mexico City: UNAM.
Baer, Nicholas. 2018. "Historical Turns: On Caligari, Kracauer and New Film History." *Research in Film and History* 1: 1-16.
Barbosa Lima, Fernando, Gabriel Priollo, and Arlindo Machado. 1985. *Televisão e Vídeo*. Rio de Janeiro: Zahar.
Barreto, Lima. 1984. *O Cangaceiro*. Fortaleza: Edicões Universidade Federal do Ceará/CAPES.
Barrow, Sarah. 2018. *Contemporary Peruvian Cinema: History, Identity and Violence on Screen*. London: I. B. Tauris, 2018.
Barsante, Cassio Emmanuel. 1985. *Carmen Miranda*. Rio de Janeiro: Editorial Europa.
Basadre, Jorge. 1968-1970. *Historia de la República del Perú, 1822-1933*. Lima: Editorial Universitaria.
Batson, L. D. 1929. "The Extent of the Development of Radio Over the World." *Annals of the American Academy of Political and Social Science* 142 (March): 21-31.
Baudrillard, Jean. 1986. *America*. Rio de Janeiro: Rocco.
Baudrillard, Jean. 1989. *America*. Translated by Chris Turner. London: Verso.
Beaume, Georges. 1952. "Dolores Del Rio: Reine du Mexique." *Cinémonde* 932 (June 13): 9-11.
Bedoya, Ricardo. 1992. *100 años de cine en el Perú: una historia crítica*. Lima: Universidad de Lima/ Instituto de Cooperación Iberoamerica.
Beltrán, Mary C. 2005. "The New Hollywood Racelessness: Only the Fast, Furious (and Multiracial) Will Survive." *Cinema Journal* 44, no. 2: 50-67.
Beltrán, Mary. 2009. *Latina/o Stars in U.S. Eyes: The Making and Meanings of Film and TV Stardom*. Urbana: University of Illinois Press.
Beltrán, Mary. 2016. SCMS Fieldnotes: Interview with SCMS Latino Caucus Founder Charles Ramírez Berg. https://vimeo.com/148806387.
Benítez-Rojo, Antonio. 1992. *The Repeating Island*. Translated by James E. Maraniss. Durham, NC: Duke University Press.
Benjamin, Walter. 1969. "The Storyteller." In *Illuminations*, 83-109. New York: Schocken.
Berger, Dina. 2006. "A Drink between Friends: Mexican and American Pleasure Seekers in 1940s Mexico." In *Adventures into Mexico*, edited by Nicholas Dagen Bloom, 13-34. Lanham, MD: Rowman & Littlefield.
Bernardet, Jean-Claude. 1985. *Cineastas e Imagens do Povo*. São Paulo: Brasiliense.
Besañez, Miguel. 1981. *La lucha por la hegemonía en México*. Mexico City: Siglo XXI.

Besas, Peter. 1992. "Globo Grabs the TV Jackpot in Brazil." *Variety*, March 23, 82.
Besas, Peter. 1993. "A Novel Rise to the Top." *Variety*, October 11, 1818.
Bettetini, Gianfranco. 1973. *The Language and Technique of the Film*. The Hague: Mouton Publishers.
Bhabha, Homi K. 1983. "The Other Question . . ." *Screen* 24, no. 6: 18–36.
Bhabha, Homi K. 1986. "Signs Taken for Wonders: Questions of Ambivalence and Authority under a Tree Outside Delhi, May 1917." In *Race, Writing, and Difference*, edited by Henry Louis Gates Jr., 163–84. Chicago: University of Chicago Press, 1986.
Bhabha, Homi K. 1990a. "DissemiNation: Time, Narrative, and the Margins of the Modern Nation." In *Nation and Narration*, edited by Homi K. Bhabha, 291–322. New York: Routledge.
Bhabha, Homi K. 1990b. Introduction. In *Nation and Narration*, edited by Homi K. Bhabha, 1–7. New York: Routledge.
Bhabha, Homi K. 1994. *The Location of Culture*. London: Routledge, 1994.
"Bird of Paradise." 1983. In *Variety Film Reviews*, vol. 4, 13. New York: Garland.
Blasini, Gilberto. 2021. Email correspondence with editors.
Bobes, Marilyn. 1993. "La increíble y un poco triste historia de la telenovela cubana." *Revolución y cultura* 3 (May–June): 4–9.
Bodeen, De Witt. 1967. "The Career of Dolores Del Rio." *Films in Review* (May): 266–67.
Bohr, José. 1987. *Desde el balcón de mi vida*. Buenos Aires: Sudamericana.
Bolzoni, Francesco. 1974. *El cine de Allende*. Valencia: Fernando Torres Editor.
Bordwell, David, Janet Staiger, and Kristin Thompson. 1985. *The Classical Hollywood Cinema: Film Style and Mode of Production to 1960*. London: Routledge.
Bordwell, David, and Kristin Thompson. 1994. *Film History: An Introduction*. New York: McGraw-Hill.
Bowser, Eileen. 1969. *Film Notes*. New York: Museum of Modern Art.
Branigan, Edward. 1984. *Point of View in the Cinema*. New York: Mouton.
Brennan, Timothy. 1990. "The National Longing for Form." In *Nation and Narration*, edited by Homi K. Bhabha, 44–70. New York: Routledge.
Brissac Peixoto, Nelson. 1987. *Cenários em Ruínas: A Realidade Imaginária Contemporânea*. São Paulo: Editora Brasiliense.
Brissac Peixoto, Nelson. 1989. *America: Depoimentos* and *America: Imagens*. Rio de Janeiro: VideoFilmes/Companhia das Letras.
Brooks, Peter. 1976. *The Melodramatic Imagination*. New Haven, CT: Yale University Press.
Brunner, José Joaquín. 1993. "Notes on Modernity and Postmodernity." Translated by John Beverly. *Boundary 2* 20, no. 3 (Fall): 34–54.
Burton, Julianne. 1977a. "Politics and the Documentary in People's Chile: An Interview with Patricio Guzman on *The Battle of Chile*." *Socialist Review* 35, no. 7 (September–October): 36–87.

Burton, Julianne. 1977b. "Memories of Underdevelopment in the Land of Over-development." *Cineaste* 8, no. 1: 16–21.
Burton, Julianne. 1981. "Cuba." In *Les Cinemas de L'Amérique Latine*, edited by Guy Hennebelle and Alfonso Gumucio Dagrón, 258–313. Paris: L'Herminier.
Burton, Julianne. 1986a. *Cinema and Social Change in Latin America: Conversations with Filmmakers.* Austin: University of Texas Press.
Burton, Julianne. 1986b. "Politics and the Documentary in People's Chile: An Interview with Patricio Guzmán on *The Battle of Chile*." In *Cinema and Social Change in Latin America: Conversations with Filmmakers*, edited by Julianne Burton, 36–68. Austin: University of Texas Press.
Burton, Julianne. 1990. *The Social Documentary in Latin America*. Pittsburgh: University of Pittsburgh Press.
Bustillo Oro, J. 1984. *Vida cinematográfica.* Mexico City: Cineteca Nacional.
Butler, Judith. 1990a. *Gender Trouble.* New York: Routledge.
Butler, Judith. 1990b. "Lana's 'Imitation': Melodramatic Repetition and the Gender Performative." *Genders* 9 (Fall): 1–18.
Cabrera Infante, Guillermo. 1985. "Cuba's Shadow." *Film Comment* 21, no. 3: 43–45.
Canby, Vincent. 1978. "Guzman Documentary." *New York Times*, January 13, sec. C7, 1.
Caneto, Guillermo, et al. 1996. *Historia de los primeros años del cine en la Argentina, 1895–1910.* Buenos Aires: Fundación Cinemateca Argentina.
Cano, Federico Medina, and Marta Ines Montoya Ferrer. 1989. *Telenovela: el milagro del amor.* Medellín, Colombia: Universidad Pontífica Bolivariana.
Caparelli, Sergio. 1982. *Televisão e Capitalismo no Brazil.* Porto Alegre: L and PM Editores.
Carbone, Giancarlo. 1992. *El cine en el Perú, 1897–1950; testimonios.* Lima: Universidad de Lima.
Carrasco, Jorge V. 2005. *Pedro Infante, estrella del cine.* Mexico City: Giron.
Carson, Diane, Linda Dittmar, and Janice R. Welsch, eds. 1994. *Multiple Voices in Feminist Film Criticism.* Minneapolis: University of Minnesota Press.
Cart. 1980. "La batalla. De Chile-III." *Variety*, May 17.
Casal, Lourdes, ed. 1971. *El caso Padilla: literatura y revolución en Cuba.* Miami: Ediciones Universal.
Casal, Lourdes. 1981. "Para Ana Velford." In *Palabras juntan revolución.* Havana: Casa de las Américas.
Castro, Fidel. 1977. "Palabras a los intelectuales." In *Política cultural de la Revolución Cubana: Documentos*, 5–47. Havana: Editorial de Ciencias Sociales.
Cavalcanti, Alberto. 1952. *Filme e Realidade.* Rio de Janeiro: Livraria Editora.
Cavalcanti de Paiva, Salvyano. 1952. "O Cinema Brasileiro na Mesa de Operacões." *Manchete* 21 (September 13): 14.
Chanan, Michael. 1976. *Chilean Cinema.* London: British Film Institute.

Chanan, Michael. 1983. *Twenty-Five Years of the New Latin American Cinema*. London: Channel Four Books.
Chanan, Michael. 1985. *The Cuban Image: Cinema and Cultural Politics in Cuba*. London and Bloomington: British Film Institute and Indiana University Press.
Chanan, Michael. 2004. *Cuban Cinema*. London: University of Minnesota Press.
Chanan, Michael. 2008. *The Politics of Documentary*. London: British Film Institute.
Charbonneau, Stephen. 2021. SCMS Fieldnotes: Chon A. Noriega, interviewed by Stephen Charbonneau. https://vimeo.com/499886357.
Charney, Leo, and Vanessa R. Schwartz. 1995. Introduction. In *Cinema and the Invention of Modern Life*, 1–14. Berkeley: University of California Press.
Chow, Rey. 1995. *Primitive Passions*. New York: Columbia University Press.
Claxton, R. H. 2007. *From Parsifal to Perón: Early Radio in Argentina, 1920–1944*. Gainesville: University Press of Florida.
Clifford, James. 1988. *The Predicament of Culture: Twentieth-Century Ethnography, Literature, and Art*. Cambridge: Harvard University Press.
Colina, Enrique, and Daniel Díaz Torres. 1971. "Ideología del melodrama en el viejo cine latinoamericano." *Cine Cubano* 73–75: 14–26.
Collier, Simon. 1988. "Carlos Gardel and the Cinema." In *The Garden of Forking Paths: Argentine Cinema*, edited by John King and Nissa Torrents, 15–26. London: National Film Theater/British Film Institute.
Colomina de Rivera, Marta, ed. 1968. *El huésped alienante: estudio sobre audencia y efecto de las radio-telenovelas en Venezuela*. Maracaibo, Venezuela: Universidad del Zulia.
Comolli, Jean-Louis. 1978. "Historical Fictions: A Body Too Much." Translated by Ben Brewster. *Screen* 19, no. 2: 41–54.
Comolli, Jean-Luc, and Paul Narboni. 1971. "Cinema/Ideology/Criticism." *Screen* 12, no. 1: 27–38.
Conde, Maite. 2018. *Foundational Films: Early Cinema and Modernity in Brazil*. Oakland: University of California Press.
Cook, David. 1996. *A History of Narrative Film*, 3rd ed. New York: Norton.
Cook, Pam. 1988. "Women in the Western." In *The BFI Companion to the Western*, edited by Edward Buscombe, 240–43. London: Andre Deutsch/British Film Institute.
Corliss, Richard. 2007. "Learning Pedro Infante." *Time*, April 15.
Cosentino, Olivia. 2021. Email correspondence with editors.
Costa Lima, Luiz. 1986. *Sociedade e Discurso Ficcional*. Rio de Janeiro: Editora Guanabara.
Couret, Nilo. 2018. *Mock Classicism: Latin American Film Comedy, 1930–1960*. Oakland: University of California Press.
Couselo, Jorge Miguel. 1976. *El tango en el cine*. Vol. 8 of *La historia del tango*. Buenos Aires: Corregidor.

Crafton, Donald. 2004. "Mindshare: Telephone and Radio Compete for the Talkies." In *Allegories of Communication: Intermedial Concerns from Cinema to the Digital*, edited by J. Fullerton and J. Olsson, 141–56. Rome: John Libbey.
Crofts, Stephen. 1993. "Reconceptualizing National Cinema." *Quarterly Review of Film and Video* 14: 49–67.
Crowther, Bosley. 1949. "*That Night in Rio.*" *New York Times*, March 10, 21.
Crowther, Bosley. 1954. "*Cangaceiro.*" *New York Times Film Reviews*, September 4, 19.
Cuarterolo, Andrea. 2013. *De la foto al fotograma: relaciones entre cine y fotografía en la Argentina (1840–1933)*. Montevideo: Centro de la Fotografía Ediciones.
da Costa, Alcir Henrique, Inimá Ferreira Simões, and Maria Rita Kehl. 1986. *Um País no Ar: Historia da TV Brasileira em 3 Canais*. São Paulo: Brasiliense.
Da Matta, Roberto. 1978. *Carnavais, Malandros e Herois*. Rio de Janeiro: Zahar.
Danan, Martine. 1995. "Marketing the Hollywood Blockbuster in France." *Journal of Popular Film and Video* 23, no. 3: 131–40.
Dávalos Orozco, Federico. 1996. *Albores del cine mexicano*. Mexico City: Clio.
Debray, Régis. 1967. *The Revolution in the Revolution*. New York: Monthly Review.
De Certeau, Michel. 1984. *The Practice of Everyday Life*. Berkeley: University of California Press.
de la Mora, Sergio. 2006. *Cinemachismo: Masculinities and Sexuality in Mexican Film*. Austin: University of Texas Press.
De la Vega Alfaro, Eduardo. 1987. *Juan Orol*. Guadalajara: Centro de Investigaciones y Enseñanzas Cinematográficas.
De la Vega Alfaro, Eduardo. 1992. *Pioneros del cine sonoro Vol. 3 Juan Orol*. Guadalajara: Centro de Investigaciones y Enseñanzas Cinematográficas.
De la Vega Alfaro, Eduardo. 1995. "Origins, Development and Crisis of the Sound Cinema (1929–64)." In *Mexican Cinema*, edited by Paulo Antonio Paranaguá, 79–93. London: British Film Institute.
De la Vega Alfaro, Eduardo, and Patricia Torres San Martín. 1997. *Adela Sequeyro*. Guadalajara: Universidad de Guadalajara/Universidad Veracruzana.
de la Vega, Alicia. 1979. *Re-visión del cine chileno*. Santiago, Chile: Editorial Aconagua.
de los Reyes, Aurelio. 1972. *Los orígenes del cine en México*. Mexico City: UNAM.
de los Reyes, Aurelio. 1983a. *Cine y sociedad en México, 1896–1930: Vivir de sueños*. Mexico City: UNAM.
de los Reyes, Aurelio. 1983b. *Los orígenes del cine mexicano*. Mexico City: Fondo de Cultural Economica.
de los Reyes, Aurelio. 1985. *Con Villa en México: testimonios de los camarógrafos norteamericanos en la Revolución*. Mexico City: UNAM.
de los Reyes, Aurelio. 1986. *Filmografía del cine mudo mexicano, 1896–1920*. Mexico City: UNAM.
de los Reyes, Aurelio. 1987. *Medio siglo de cine mexicano (1886–1947)*. Mexico City: Trillas.

de los Reyes, Aurelio. 1988. "Nacimiento de un mito: Dolores del Río." In *Historia, leyendas y mitos de México: Su expresión en el arte*, 311–30. Mexico City: Universidad Autónoma de México.

de los Reyes, Aurelio. 1995a. "Los besos y el cine." In *El arte y la vida cotidiana: XVI coloquio internacional de Historia del Arte*, edited by Elena Estrada de Garlero, 267–89. Mexico City: UNAM.

de los Reyes, Aurelio. 1995b. "The Silent Cinema." In *Mexican Cinema*, edited by Paulo Antonio Paranaguá, 63–77. London: British Film Institute.

de los Reyes, Aurelio. 1996. *Dolores Del Rio*. Mexico City: Servicios Codumex.

De Luca, Tiago. 2014. *Realism of the Senses in World Cinema: The Experience of Physical Reality*. London: I. B. Tauris.

de Orellana, Margarita. 2004. *Filming Pancho Villa: How Hollywood Shaped the Mexican Revolution*. London: Verso

de Orellana, Margarita. 1991. *La mirada circular: El cine norteamericano de la Revolución Mexicana*. Mexico City: Joaquín Mortiz.

Dennison, Stephanie, and Song Hwee Lim, eds. 2006. *Remapping World Cinema: Identity, Culture and Politics in Film*. London: Wallflower Press.

Desmond, Jane. 1997. "Embodying Difference: Issues in Dance and Cultural Studies." In *Everynight Life: Culture and Dance in Latin/o America*, edited by Celeste Fraser Delgado and José Esteban Muñoz, 33–64. Durham, NC: Duke University Press.

de Usabel Gaizca, S. 1982. *The High Noon of American Films in Latin America*. Ann Arbor, Michigan: UMI Research Press.

Dever, Susan. 2003. *Celluloid Nationalism and Other Melodramas: From Post-Revolutionary Mexico to fin de siglo Mexamérica*. Albany: State University of New York Press.

Díaz López, Marina. 1996. "*Allá en el Rancho Grande*: la configuración de un género nacional en cl cine mexicano." *Secuencias* 5: 9–30.

Díaz Torres, Daniel. 1976. "Cine cubano en EE.UU." *Cine Cubano* 86–87 (1976): 65–71.

Di Núbila, Domingo. 1959a. *Historia del cine argentino*, vol. 1. Buenos Aires: Cruz de Malta.

Di Núbila, Domingo 1959b. *Historia del cine argentino*, vol. 2. Buenos Aires, Argentina: Editorial Cruz de Malca.

Di Núbila, Domingo. 1998. *La época de oro: historia del cine argentino*, vol. 1. Buenos Aires: Ediciones del Jilguero.

D'Lugo, Marvin. 1996. "From Exile to Ethnicity: Néstor Almendros and Orlando Jiménez Leal's *Improper Conduct* (1984)." In *The Ethnic Eye: Latino Media Arts*, edited by Chon Noriega and Ana M. López, 171–82. Minneapolis: University of Minnesota Press.

D'Lugo, Marvin. 2003. "Authorship, Globalization and the New Identity of Latin American Cinema: From the Mexican Ranchera to Argentine 'Exile.'"

In *Rethinking Third Cinema*, edited by Wimal Dissanayake and Anthony Guneratne, 103–25. London: Routledge.
D'Lugo, Marvin. 2010. "Aural Identity, Genealogies of Sound Technologies, and Hispanic Transnationality on Screen." In *World Cinemas, Transnational Perspectives*, edited by Nataša Ďurovičová and Kathleen Newman, 160–84. New Brunswick, NJ: Routledge.
Doane, Mary Ann. 1987. *The Desire to Desire: The Woman's Film of the 1940s*. Bloomington: Indiana University Press.
Doane, Mary Ann. 2007. "Indexicality: Trace and Sign: Introduction." *Differences: A Journal of Feminist Cultural Studies* 18, no. 1: 1–6.
Dorfman, Ariel. 1981. "The House That Neruda Built." *Village Voice*, December 13, 59–68.
Doty, Alexander. 1990. "The Cabinet of Lucy Ricardo: Lucille Ball's Star Image." *Cinema Journal* 4 (Summer): 3–22.
Douglas, Maria Eulalia. 1989. *Diccionario de cineastas cubanos, 1959–1987*. Havana: Cinemateca de Cuba/Universidad de los Andes, 1989.
Douglas, Maria Eulalia. 1996. *La tienda negra: el cine en Cuba (1897–1990)*. Havana: La Cinemateca de Cuba, 1996.
Douglas, Susan J. 2004. *Listening In: Radio and the American Imagination*. Minneapolis: University of Minnesota Press, 2004.
Ďurovičová, Nataša. 1992. "Translating America: The Hollywood Multilinguals, 1929–1933." In *Sound Theory, Sound Practice*, edited by Rick Altman, 138–53. New York: Routledge.
Ďurovičová, Nataša, and Kathleen Newman. 2010. *World Cinema: Transnational Perspectives*. New York: Routledge.
Dyer, Richard. 1981. "Entertainment and Utopia." In *Genre: The Musical, A Reader*, edited by Rick Altman, 175–89. London: Routledge & Kegan Paul/British Film Institute.
Ellner, Rebecca. 1997. "Tropicalizing Latin Americanness: Hollywood, Ethnicity, and the Colonial Discourse." MA thesis, Tulane University.
Elsaesser, Thomas. 1991. "Tales of Sound and Fury: Observations on the Family Melodrama." In *Imitations of Life: A Reader on Film and Television Melodrama*, edited by Marcia Landy, 68–92. Detroit: Wayne State University Press.
Elsaesser, Thomas. 2004. "The New Film History as Media Archaeology." *Cinémas: revue d'études cinematographiques/Cinémas: Journal of Film Studies* 14, nos. 2–3: 75–117.
España, Claudio. 1999. "El modelo institucional: formas de representación en la edad de oro." In *Cine argentino: industria y clasicismo, vol. 1 (1933–1956)*, edited by Claudio España, 22–159. Buenos Aires: Fondo Nacional de las Artes.
Espinoza, Belkis, and Jorge Luis Llópiz. 1989. *Cine cubano: 30 años en revolución*. Havana: Centro de Promoción y Estudio del Cine "Saul Yelín."

Ezra, Elizabeth, and Terry Rowden. 2006. *Transnational Cinema: The Film Reader.* London: Routledge, 2006.
Fadul, Ana Maria. 1984. "Literatura, Rádio e Sociedade." In *Literatura em Tempo de Cultura de Massa*, edited by Lígia Averbuck and Regina Ziberman. São Paulo: Nobel.
Falicov, Tamara. 2021. Email correspondence with editors.
Fein, Seth. 1994. "Hollywood, U.S.-Mexican Relations and the Devolution of the 'Golden Age' of Mexican Cinema." *Film-Historia* 4, no. 2: 103–35.
Fein, Seth. 1998a. "Cold-War Hollywood in Postwar Mexico: Anticommunism and Transnational Feature-Film Production." In *Visible Nations*, edited by Chon Noriega, 82–111. Minneapolis: University of Minnesota Press.
Fein, Seth 1998b. "Transnationalization and Cultural Collaboration: Mexican Film Propaganda during World War II." *Popular Cinemas/Popular Cultures: Studies in Latin American Popular Culture* 17: 105–28.
Fernandes, Ismael. 1987. *Memoria da Telenovela Brasileira.* São Paulo: Brasiliense.
Fernández, Adela. 1986. *El Indio Fernández: vida y mito.* Mexico City: Panorama.
Fernández, Enrique. 1980. "Witnesses Always Everywhere: The Rhetorical Strategies of *Memories of Underdevelopment.*" *Wide Angle* 4, no. 2: 52–55.
Fernández, Enrique. 1985. "Miami's Autores." *Film Comment* 21, no. 3 (May–June): 46–48.
Feuer, Jane. 1993. *The Hollywood Musical*, 2nd ed. Bloomington: Indiana University Press.
Flinn, Caryl. 1992. *Strains of Utopia: Gender, Nostalgia, and Hollywood Film Music.* Princeton: Princeton University Press.
Foster, Hal, ed. 1983. *The Anti-aesthetic: Essays on Postmodern Culture.* Port Townsend, WA: Bay Press.
Franco, Jean. 1986. "The Incorporation of Women: A Comparison of North American and Mexican Popular Narrative." In *Studies in Entertainment: Critical Approaches to Mass Culture*, edited by Tania Modleski, 119–38. Bloomington: Indiana University Press.
Franco, Jean. 1989. *Plotting Women: Gender and Representation in Mexico.* New York: Columbia University Press.
French, William E. 1991. "In the Path of Progress: Railroads and Moral Reform in Porfirian Mexico." In *Railroad Imperialism*, edited by Clarence B. Davis and Kenneth E. Wilbrun, 85–102. New York: Greenwood.
Fuentes, Carlos. 1976. "El Rostro de la Escondida." In *Dolores del Río*, edited by Luis Gasca. San Sebastián, Spain: 24th Festival Internacional de Cine.
Fuentes, Carlos. 1982. *Orquídeas a la luz de la luna.* Barcelona: Seix Barral.
Fuentes-Pérez, Ileana. 1988. "By Choice or by Circumstance: The Inevitable Exile of Artists." In *Outside Cuba/Fuera de Cuba*, 19–28. New Brunswick, NJ, and Miami: Office of Hispanic Arts, Rutgers University, and the Research Institute for Cuban Studies, University of Miami.

Gabriel, Teshome. 1982. *Third Cinema in the Third World.* Ann Arbor, MI: UMI Research Press.
Gabus Mendes, O. 1929. "De São Paulo." *Cinearte* 183 (August 29): 20–21.
Galeano, Eduardo. 1988. *Century of the Wind.* New York: Pantheon.
Galvão, Maria Rita. 1980. *30 Anos do Cinema Paulista (1950–1980).* São Paulo: Fundação Cinemateca Brasileira.
Galvão, Maria Rita. 1981. *Burguesia e Cinema: o Caso Vera Cruz.* Rio de Janeiro: Civilização/Embrafilme.
Galvão, Maria Rita. 1987. "Le Muet." In *Le cinéma brésilien*, edited by Paulo Paranaguá, 51–64. Paris: Centre Georges Pompidou.
Galvão, Maria Rita, and Carlos Roberto de Souza. 1987. "Le parlant et les tentatives industrielles: années trente, quarante, cinquante." In *Le cinéma brésilien*, edited by Paulo Antonio Paranaguá, 67–89. Paris: Centre Pompidou.
Galvão, Maria Rita, and Jean-Claude Bernardet. 1983. *O Nacional e o Popular na Cultura Brasileira.* São Paulo: Brasiliense/EMBRAFILME.
García, Alfredo. 2010. "Entrevista a Pedro González Rubio. Director de *Alamar*. Mejor película de 12 Bafici." *Tierra en Trance* 10. http://tierraentrance.miradas.net/2010/10/entrevistas/entrevista-a-pedro-González-rubio-director-de-alamar-mejor-pelicula-de-12-bafici.html. Accessed September 1, 2013.
García, Rocío. 1994. "Andy García debuta como director." *Aquí New Orleans* (January): 16.
García Borrero, Juan Antonio. 2001. *Guía crítica del cine cubano de ficción.* Havana: Arte y literatura.
García Borrero, Juan Antonio. 2002. *Rehenes de la sombra: ensayos sobre el cine cubano que no se ve.* Huesca: Festival de Cine de Huesca, Filmoteca de Andalucía, Casa de América.
García Canclini, Néstor. 1997. "Will There Be a Latin American Cinema in the Year 2000? Visual Culture in a Postnational Era." In *Framing Latin American Cinema: Contemporary Critical Approaches*, edited by Ann Marie Stock, 246–58. London: University of Minnesota Press.
García Espinosa, Julio. 1983. "For an Imperfect Cinema." In *Twenty-Five Years of the New Latin American Cinema*, edited by Michael Chanan, 28–33. London: British Film Institute.
García Espinosa, Julio. 1993. "La *telenovela*, ou le 'ragot' élevé à la catégorie de l'art dramatique." *Cinémas d'Amérique Latine* 1: 52–55.
García Márquez, Gabriel. 1982. *Obra periodística.* Vol. 2, *Entre cachacos 1*, edited by Jacques Gilard. Barcelona: Brugera.
García Riera, Emilio. 1969. *Historia documental del cine mexicano*, vol. 1. Mexico City: Ediciones Era.
García Riera, Emilio. 1970. *Historia documental del cine mexicano*, vol. 2. Mexico City: Ediciones Era.

García Riera, Emilio. 1971. *Historia documental del cine mexicano*, vol. 3. Mexico City: Ediciones Era.
García Riera, Emilio. 1972. *Historia documental del cine mexicano*, vol. 4. Mexico City: Ediciones Era.
García Riera, Emilio 1974. *Historia documental del cine mexicano*, vol. 6. Mexico City: Ediciones Era.
García Riera, Emilio. 1987a. *México visto por el cine extranjero*, vol. 1. Guadalajara: Ediciones Era/Universidad de Guadalajara.
García Riera, Emilio. 1987b. *México visto por el cine extranjero*, vol. 3. Guadalajara: Ediciones Era/Universidad de Guadalajara.
García Riera, Emilio. 1993a. *Historia documental del cine mexicano*, vol. 1. Guadalajara: Universidad de Guadalajara.
García Riera, Emilio. 1993b. *Historia documental del cine mexicano*, vol. 2. Guadalajara: Universidad de Guadalajara.
García Riera, Emilio. 1993c. *Historia documental del cine mexicano*, vol. 3. Guadalajara: Universidad de Guadalajara.
García Riera, Emilio. 1993d. *Historia documental del cine mexicano*, vol. 4. Guadalajara: Universidad de Guadalajara.
García Riera, Emilio. 1993e. *Historia documental del cine mexicano*, vol. 5. Guadalajara: Universidad de Guadalajara.
García Riera, Emilio. 1993f. *Historia documental del cine mexicano*, vol. 6. Guadalajara: Universidad de Guadalajara.
Gatti, J. 2000. "Lusofonia no Cinema Brasileiro: Notas sobre a Presença de Línguas no Cinema." In *Estudos de cinema: SOCINE II e III*, 86–97. São Paulo: Annablume.
Gazetas, Aristides. 2000. *An Introduction to World Cinema*. Jefferson, NC: McFarland.
Genette, Gérard. 1979. *Introduction á l'architexte*. Paris: Editions de Seuil.
Genette, Gérard. 1982. *Palimpsestes: La littérature au second degré*. Paris: Editions du Seuil.
Gledhill, Christine. 1987. "The Melodramatic Field: An Investigation." In *Home Is Where the Heart Is: Studies in Melodrama and the Woman's Film*, edited by Christine Gledhill, 5–39. London: British Film Institute.
Gledhill, Christine. 1991. *Stardom: Industry of Desire*. New York: Routledge, 1991.
Gledhill, Christine. 1992. "Speculations on the Relationship between Soap Opera and Melodrama." *Quarterly Review of Film and Video* 14, nos. 1–2: 103–24.
Godoy Quezada, Mario. 1966. *Historia del cine chileno, 1902–1966*. Santiago de Chile: Anon.
Gomery, Douglas. 1986. *The Hollywood Studio System*. New York: St. Martin's Press.
Gómez Rial, S. 1999. "Compañía Argentina de Films Río de la Plata: los románticos del micrófono." In *Cine argentino: industria y clasicismo, vol. 1 (1933–1956)*, edited by Claudio España, 250–63. Buenos Aires: Fondo Nacional de las Artes.

Gonzalez, David. 1994. "Harlem Was on Their Mind." *New York Times*, February 20, H11.
González, Jennifer A. 1993. "Rhetoric of the Object: Material Memory and the Artwork of Amalia Mesa-Bains." *Visual Anthropology Review* 9, no. 1 (Spring): 82–91.
González, Reynaldo. 1988. *Llorar es un placer*. Havana: Editorial Letras Cubanas.
González Ordosgoicci, Enrique Ali. 1991. *Diez ensayos de cultura venezolana*. Caracas, Venezuela: Fondo Editorial Tropykos.
Gordon, Richard A. 2009. *Cannibalizing the Colony: Cinematic Adaptations of Colonial Literatures in Mexico and Brazil*. West Lafayette, IN: Purdue University Press.
Griswold del Castillo, Richard, Teresa McKenna, and Yvonne Yarbro-Bejarano, eds. 1991. *Chicano Art: Resistance and Affirmation, 1965–1985*. Los Angeles: Wright Art Gallery, UCLA.
Guback, Thomas. 1969. *The International Film Industry: Western Europe and America since 1945*. Bloomington: Indiana University Press.
Guevara, Alfredo. 1988. "Reflexión nostálgica sobre el futuro." In *El nuevo cine latinoamericano en el mundo de hoy*, 7–8. Mexico City: Universidad Nacional Autónoma de Mexico.
Guillermoprieto, Alma. 1993. "Obsessed in Rio." *New Yorker*, August 16, 44–55.
Gumucio Dagrón, Alfonso. 1982. *Historia del cine en Bolivia*. La Paz: Editorial Los Amigos del Libro.
Gunning, Tom. 1990. "The Cinema of Attractions: Early Film, Its Spectator, and the Avant-Garde." In *Early Cinema: Space, Frame, Narrative*, edited by Thomas Elsaesser and Alan Barker, 56–62. London: British Film Institute, 1990.
Gunning, Tom. 1998. "Early American Film." In *The Oxford Guide to Film Studies*, edited by John Hill and Pamela Church Gibson, 255–71. New York: Oxford University Press.
Gutiérrez Alea, Tomás. 1982. "Memorias de *Memorias*." In *Dialéctica del espectador*, 59–72. Havana: Cuadernos de la Revista Unión.
Guzmán, Patricio. 1977. "Guión esquema del filme." In *La Batalla de Chile: la lucha de un pueblo sin armas*. Pamplona: I. Peralta Ediciones/Editorial Ayuso.
Hall, Stuart. 1972. "The Social Eye of *Picture Post*." *Working Papers in Cultural Studies* 2 (Spring): 71–120.
Hansen, Miriam. 1986. "Pleasure, Ambivalence, Identification: Valentino and Female Spectatorship." *Cinema Journal* 25 (Summer): 6–32.
Hansen, Miriam. 1997. "Early Cinema, Late Cinema: Transformations of the Public Sphere." In *Viewing Positions: Ways of Seeing Films*, edited by Linda Williams, 134–54. New Brunswick, NJ: Rutgers University Press.
Hardy, Phil. 1988. "Music." In *The BFI Companion to the Western*, edited by Edward Buscombe, 193–95. London: Andre Deutsch/British Film Institute.

Harris, Warren G. 1991. *Lucy and Desi*. New York: Simon & Schuster.
Hayes, Joy Elizabeth. 2000. *Radio Nation: Communication, Culture, and Nationalism in Mexico, 1920–1950*. Tucson: University of Arizona Press.
Heider, Karl G. 1976. *Ethnographic Film*. Austin: University of Texas Press.
Heinink, Juan B., and Robert G. Dickson. 1990. *Cita en Hollywood: antología de las películas norteamericanas habladas en castellano*. Bilbao, Spain: Ediciones Mensajero.
Hennebelle, Guy, and Alfonso Gumucio Dagrón. 1981. *Les Cinémas d'Amérique Latine d'Aujourd'hui*. Paris: l'Herminier.
Hershfield, Joanne. 2000. *The Invention of Dolores del Rio*. Minneapolis: University of Minnesota Press.
Higbee, Will, and Song Hwee Lim. 2010. "Concepts of Transnational Cinema: Towards a Critical Transnationalism in Film Studies." *Transnational Cinemas* 1, no. 1 (2010): 7–21.
Higson, Andrew. 1989. "The Concept of a National Cinema." *Screen* 30, no. 4 (1989): 36–46.
Higson, Andrew. 2000. "The Limiting Imagination of a National Cinema." In *Cinema and Nation*, edited by Mette Hjort and Scott MacKenzie, 63–74. London: Routledge.
Hijuelos, Oscar. 1989. *The Mambo Kings Play Songs of Love*. New York: Farrar, Straus & Giroux.
Hill, John. 1986. *Sex, Class and Realism: British Cinema, 1956–1963*. London: British Film Institute.
Hill, John, and Pamela Church Gibson, eds. 1998. *The Oxford Guide to Film Studies*. New York: Oxford University Press.
Hintz, Eugenio. 1988. *Historia y filmografía del cine uruguayo*. Montevideo: Ediciones de la Plaza.
"Historia de W Radio Mexico." http://www.wradio.com.mx/historia.asp?id=196949. Accessed July 1, 2008.
Hjort, Mette. 2010. "On the Plurality of Cinematic Transnationalism." In *World Cinemas, Transnational Perspectives*, edited by Nataša Ďurovičová and Kathleen Newman, 12–33. New York: Routledge.
Hoffman, John. 1984. *The Gramscian Challenge*. Oxford: Basil Blackwell.
Hojas de cine: testimonios y documentos del nuevo cine latinoamericano. 1988. Mexico City: Fundación Mexicana de Cineastas.
Holl. 1976. "*La batalla de Chile-II: el golpe de estado.*" *Variety*, July 14.
Holston, Mark. 1986. "Tuning In to Televisa." *Americas* (March–April): 24–29.
Horn, Florence. 1941. "*Formidavel, Fabulosissimo.*" *Harper's*, no. 184 (December): 59–64.
Huleu, Jean-René, Ignacio Ramonet, and Serge Toubiana. 1974. "Entretien avec Jorge Sanjinés." *Cahiers du Cinema* 253: 6–21.

Hutcheon, Linda. 1985. *A Theory of Parody: The Teachings of Twentieth-Century Art Forms*. New York: Methuen.
Hutcheon, Linda. 1986–1987. "The Politics of Postmodernism: Parody and History." *Cultural Critique* 5: 179–207.
Huyssen, Andreas. 1986. *After the Great Divide*. Bloomington: Indiana University Press.
Infante, José Pedro. 2007. *Pedro Infante: el dolor inmortal*. Mexico City: Grupo Nelson, 2007.
Isabel, Azucena. 1977. "El golpe de estado." In *Chile: el cine contra el fascismo*, edited by Pedro Sempere and Patricio Guzmán, 194–96. Valencia: Fernando Torres, Editor.
Jacobs, Lea. 1991. *The Wages of Sin*. Madison: University of Wisconsin Press.
Jameson, Fredric. 1984. "Postmodernism, or the Cultural Logic of Late Capitalism." *New Left Review* 146 (July–August): 53–92.
Jameson, Fredric. 1990. *Signatures of the Visible*. New York: Routledge.
Jameson, Fredric. 1991. *Postmodernism or the Cultural Logic of Late Capitalism*. London: Verso.
Jarvinen, Lisa. 2012. *The Rise of Spanish-Language Filmmaking: Out from Hollywood's Shadow, 1929–39*. New Brunswick, NJ: Rutgers University Press.
Jencks, Charles. 1986. *What Is Postmodernism?* New York: Academy Editions.
Johnson, Randal. 1984. *Cinema Novo x 5: Masters of Contemporary Brazilian Film*. Austin: University of Texas Press.
Johnson, Randal. 1997. *The Film Industry in Brazil: Culture and the State*. Pittsburgh: University of Pittsburgh Press.
Johnson, Randal, and Stam, Robert, eds. 1995 [1982]. *Brazilian Cinema: Expanded Edition*. New York: Columbia University Press.
Johnson, Timothy W. 1982. "What Price Glory?" In *Magill's Survey of Cinema: Silent Films*, vol. 3, 1210. Englewood Cliffs, NJ: Salem Press.
Kael, Pauline. 1978. "*The Battle of Chile*." *New Yorker*, January 23, 82.
Kandell, Jonathan. 1988. *La Capital: The Biography of Mexico City*. New York: Random House.
Kaplan, E. Ann. 1983. *Women and Film: Both Sides of the Camera*. New York: Methuen, 1983.
Kaplan, E. Ann. 1987. "Mothering, Feminism, and Representation: The Maternal in Melodrama and the Woman's Film, 1910–40." In *Home Is Where the Heart Is: Studies in Melodrama and the Woman's Film*, edited by Christine Gledhill, 123–29. London: British Film Institute.
Kauffmann, Stanley. 1980. "*The Battle of Chile*." In *Before My Eyes: Film Criticism and Comment*, 303. New York: Harper and Row.
Koehler, Robert. n.d. "Agrarian Utopias/Dystopias: The New Nonfiction." *Cinema Scope* 40. http://cinema-scope.com/features/features-agrarian-utopiasdystopias-the-new-nonfiction/. Accessed August 30, 2013.

Kolker, Robert. 1983. *The Altering Eye*. New York: Oxford University Press.
Konder, Rodolfo. 1982. "The Carmen Miranda Museum: The Brazilian Bombshell Is Still Box Office in Rio." *Americas* 34, no. 5 (1982): 17–21.
King, John. 1990. *Magical Reels: A History of Cinema in Latin America*. London: Verso.
King, John. 2000a [1990]. *Magical Reels: A History of Cinema in Latin America*. New Edition. London: Verso
King, John, ed. 2000b. *An Argentine Passion: The Life and Work of Maria Luisa Bemberg*. London: Verso, 2000.
King, John. 2004. "Cinema in Latin America." In *Cambridge Companion to Latin American Modern Culture*, edited by John King, 282–313. Cambridge: Cambridge University Press.
King, John, Ana M. López, and Manuel Alvarado. 1993. *Mediating Two Worlds: Cinematic Encounters in the Americas*. London: British Film Institute.
Kirby, Lynne. 1997. *Parallel Tracks: The Railroad and Silent Cinema*. Durham, NC: Duke University Press, 1997.
Knight, Alan. 1994. "The Cardenismo: Juggernaut or Jalopy?" *Journal of Latin American Studies* 26: 73–107.
Knight, Franklin W. 1974. *The African Dimensions in Latin American Societies*. New York: Macmillan.
Kuhn, Annette. 1982. *Women's Pictures: Feminism and Cinema*. London: Routledge & Kegan Paul.
Labaki Amir. 1997. "Quem Tem Medo de Cavalcanti?" *Folha de São Paulo*, February 2.
Lamb, Ruth S. 1975. *Mexican Theater of the Twentieth Century*. Claremont, CA: Ocelot Press.
Landy, Marcia, ed. 1991. Introduction. In *Imitations of Life: A Reader on Film and Television Melodrama*, 13–30. Detroit: Wayne State University Press.
Lang, Robert. 1989. *American Film Melodrama: Griffith, Vidor, Minnelli*. Princeton, NJ: Princeton University Press.
Leal, Norberto Willis. 1982. *O Nordeste no Cinema*. Salvador: Universidade Federal da Paraiba/Universidade Federal da Bahia.
Lefere, R., and N. Lie. 2016. *Transnational perspectivas sobre la transnacionalidad del cine hispano*. Leiden: Brill.
Levental, Larry. 1993. "Want a Bigger Slice? You Bake a Bigger Pie." *Variety*, January 18, 62.
Lins, Consuelo. 2004. *O Documentário de Eduardo Coutinho: Televisão, Cinema e Video*. Rio de Janeiro: Jorge Zahar.
López, Ana M. 1985a. "A Short History of Latin American Film Histories." *UFVA Journal* 37, no. 1: 55–69.
López, Ana M. 1985b. "The Melodrama in Latin America: Telenovelas, Film, and the Currency of a Popular Form." *Wide Angle* 7, no. 3: 4–13.

López, Ana M. 1986. "Towards a 'Third' and 'Imperfect' Cinema: A Theoretical and Historical Study of Filmmaking in Latin America." Director: J. Dudley Andrew. PhD thesis communication studies, University of Iowa, 1986.
López, Ana M. 1987. "Unleashing the Margins: Argentine Cinema, 1956–1976." In *The Garden of Forking Paths: Argentine Cinema*, ed. John King and Nissa Torrents, 49–80. London: British Film Institute/National Film Theater.
López, Ana M. 1988a. "African Roots: Images of Blacks in Cuban Cinema." *Black Film Review* 4, no. 3: 5–9.
López, Ana M. 1988b. "An 'Other' History: The New Latin American Cinema." *Radical History Review* 41 (Spring): 93–116.
López, Ana M. 1990a. "At the Limits of Documentary: Hypertextual Transformation and the New Latin American Cinema." In *The Social Documentary in Latin America*, edited by Julianne Burton, 403–32. Pittsburgh: University of Pittsburgh Press.
López, Ana M. 1990b. "*Battle of Chile*: Documentary, Political Process, and Representation." In *The Social Documentary in Latin America*, edited by Julianne Burton, 267–97. Pittsburgh: University of Pittsburgh Press.
López, Ana M. 1990c. "Parody, Underdevelopment, and the New Latin American Cinema." *Quarterly Review of Film and Video* 12, nos. 1–2: 63–71.
López, Ana M. 1991a. "Are All Latins from Manhattan? Hollywood, Ethnography, and Cultural Colonialism." In *Unspeakable Images: Ethnicity and the American Cinema*, edited by Lester D. Friedman, 404–24. Urbana: University of Illinois Press.
López, Ana M. 1991b. "Celluloid Tears: Melodrama in the Classic Mexican Cinema." *Iris* 13 (Summer): 29–52.
López, Ana M. 1991c. "An 'Other' History: The New Latin American Cinema." In *Resisting Images: Essays on Cinema and History*, edited by R. Sklar and C. Musser, 308–30. Philadelphia, PA: Temple University Press.
López, Ana M. 1991d. "Setting Up the Stage: A Decade of Latin American Film Scholarship." *Quarterly Review of Film and Video* 13: 239–60.
López, Ana M. 1992a. "The Melodrama in Latin America: Telenovelas, Film, and the Currency of a Popular Form." In *Imitations of Life: A Reader on Film and Television Melodrama*, edited by Marcia Landy, 596–606. Detroit: Wayne State University Press.
López, Ana M. 1992b. "Revolution and Dreams: The Cuban Documentary Today." *Studies in Latin American Popular Culture* 11: 45–57.
López, Ana M. 1992c. "(Not) Looking for Origins: Postmodernism, Documentary and America." In *Theorizing Documentary*, edited by Michael Renov, 151–63. London: Routledge.
López, Ana M. 1992d. "Not Only a Question of Color: Afro-Latino/a Images in Latin American Cinema." *Tonantzin* 9, no. 1: 20.

López, Ana M. 1993. "The 'Other' Island: Exiled Cuban Cinema." *Jump Cut* 38: 7–15.
López, Ana M. 1994a. "A Cinema for the Continent." In *The Mexican Cinema Project*, edited by Chon Noriega and Steven Ricci, 7–12. Los Angeles: UCLA Film and Television Archive.
López, Ana M. 1994b. "Tears and Desire: Women and Melodrama in the 'Old' Mexican Cinema." In *Multiple Voices in Feminist Film Criticism*, edited by Diane Carson, Linda Dittmar, and Janice R. Welsch, 254–70. Minneapolis: University of Minnesota Press.
López, Ana M., trans. 1995a. *Cuba: La isla posible*. Barcelona: Centre de Cultura Contemporània de Barcelona / Ediciones Destino.
López, Ana M. 1995b. "Our Welcomed Guests: *Telenovelas* in Latin America." In *To Be Continued . . . Soap Operas around the World*, edited by Robert Allen, 256–75. London: Routledge.
López, Ana M. 1996. "Greater Cuba." In *The Ethnic Eye: Latino Media Arts*, edited by Chon Noriega and Ana M. López, 38–58. Minneapolis: University of Minnesota Press.
López, Ana M. 1997. "Of Rhythms and Borders." In *Everynight Life: Culture and Dance in Latin/o America*, edited by Jose Muñoz and Celeste Fraser Delgado, 310–44. Durham, NC: Duke University Press.
López, Ana M. 1998a. "From Hollywood and Back: Dolores Del Rio, a (Trans) National Star." *Studies in Latin American Popular Culture* 17: 5–33.
López, Ana M. 1998b. "Historia nacional, historia transnacional." In *Horizontes del segundo siglo: Investigación y pedagogía del cine mexicano, latinoamericano y chicano*, edited by Patricia Torres San Martín, Julianne Burton, and Angel Miquel, 75–81. Guadalajara: Universidad de Guadalajara/IMCINE.
López, Ana M. 1998c."The São Paulo Connection: The Companhia Cinematográfica Vera Cruz and *O Cangaceiro*." *Nuevo Texto Crítico* 11, no. 1: 127–54.
López, Ana M. 1999. "*O Cangaceiro*: estilos híbridos para un espacio nacional cinematográfico." *Archivos de la Filmoteca* 31 (1999): 172–83.
López, Ana M. 2000a. "Crossing Nations and Genres: Travelling Filmmakers in Latin America." In *Visible Nations*, edited by Chon Noriega, 33–50. Minneapolis: University of Minnesota Press.
López, Ana M. 2000b. "Early Cinema and Modernity in Latin America." *Cinema Journal* 40, no. 1 (Fall): 48–78.
López, Ana M. 2000c. "Facing Up to Hollywood." In *Reinventing Film Studies*, edited by Christine Gledhill and Linda Williams, 419–37. London: Edward Arnold.
López, Ana M. 2006. "The State of Things: New Directions in Latin American Film History." *Americas* 63, no. 2: 197–203.
López, Ana M. 2009. "Before Exploitation: Three Men of Cinema in Mexico." In *Latsploitation: Exploitation Cinema and Latin America*, edited by Victoria Ruétalo and Dolores Tierney, 13–33. London: Routledge.

López, Ana M. 2010. "La investigación cinematográfica en América Latina." *Observatorio del Cine Latinoamericano*.
López, Ana M. 2011. "Geographical Imaginaries." *Studies in Hispanic Cinemas* 7, no. 1: 3-8.
López, Ana M. 2012a. "Mexico." In *The International Film Musical*, edited by Corey Creekmur and Linda Mokdad, 121-40. Edinburgh: University of Edinburgh Press.
López, Ana M. 2012b. "Palabras Liminales." In *Hollywood, Nuestra América y los Latinos*, 5-10. Havana: Ediciones Unión.
López, Ana M. 2014a. "Calling for Intermediality: Latin American Mediascapes." *Cinema Journal* 54, no. 1: 135-41.
López, Ana M. 2014b. "A Poetics of the Trace." In *New Documentaries in Latin America*, edited by Vinicius Navarro and Juan Carlos Rodríguez, 25-43. London: Palgrave Macmillan.
López, Ana M. 2017. "Film and Radio Intermedialities in Early Latin American Sound Cinema." In *The Routledge Companion to Latin American Cinema*, edited by Marvin D'Lugo, Ana M. López, and Laura Podalsky, 316-28. London: Routledge.
López, Ana M., and Nicholas Peter Humy. 1986-1987. "Sergio Giral on Filmmaking in Cuba." *Black Film Review* 3, no. 1: 4-7.
López Guerra, Humberto. 1991. *Ni tiempo para pedir auxilio*. Miami: Ediciones Universal.
López Navarro, Julio. 1994. *Películas chilenas*. Santiago, Chile: Editorial La Neria.
Lusnich, Ana Laura. 2011. "Pasado y presente en los estudios comparados del cine latinoamericano." *Comunicación y Medios* 24: 25-42.
Lusnich, Ana Laura. 2014. "Del comparativismo al transnacionalismo: Bases para un estudio del cine argentino y mexicano del período clásico-industrial." *Toma Uno* 3: 99-109.
Lusnich, Ana Laura, Alicia Aisemberg, and Andrea Cuarterolo, eds. 2017. *Pantallas transnacionales: el cine argentino y mexicano del período clásico*. Mexico City: Cineteca Nacional México.
Machado, R. 1987. "A Produção Paulista de 1914 a 1922." In *História do Cinema Brasileiro*, edited by Fernão Ramos, 99-127. São Paulo: Art Editora.
MacLaird, Misha. 2013. *Aesthetics and Politics in the Mexican Film Industry*. London: Palgrave Macmillan.
Madsen, Alex. 1995. *The Sewing Circle: Female Stars Who Loved Other Women*. New York: Carol.
Mañón, Manuel. 1932. *Historia del teatro popular de México*. Mexico City: Editorial Cultura.
"Maquiador Participa das Duas Producões." 1997. *O Estado de São Paulo*, October 24.
Maranghello, César. 2005. *Breve historia del cine argentino*. Barcelona: Laerte, S.A. Ediciones.

Marshall, Peter. 1987. *Cuba Libre*. Boston: Faber and Faber.
Martín-Barbero, Jesús. 1987. *De las medias a las mediaciones: comunicación, cultura y hegemonía*. Barcelona: Ediciones Gili.
Martín-Barbero, Jesús. 1992. "Transformaciones del género: de la telenovela en Colombia a la telenovela colombiana." In *Televisión y melodrama*, edited by Martín-Barbero and Muñoz, 61–106. Bogotá: Tercer Mundo Editores.
Martín-Barbero, Jesús, and Sonia Muñoz, eds. 1992. *Televisión y melodrama*. Bogotá: Tercer Mundo Editores.
Martínez Gandía, Rafael. 1930. *Dolores del Río: la triunfadora*. Madrid: Compañía Iberoamericana de Publicaciones, S.A.
Massumi, Brian. 1996. "The Autonomy of Affect." In *Deleuze: A Critical Reader*, edited by Paul Patton, 217–39. Oxford: Blackwell.
Matallana, Andrea. 2006. *Locos por la radio: Una historia social de la radiofonía en la Argentina, 1923–1947*. Buenos Aires: Prometeo.
Mattelart, Armand. 1979. *Multinational Corporations and the Control of Culture: The Ideological Apparatuses of Imperialism*. Atlantic Heights, NJ: Humanities Press.
Mattelart, Armand. 1980. *Mass Media, Ideologies and the Revolutionary Movement*. Atlantic Highlands, NJ: Humanities Press.
Mattelart, Armand. 1983. *Transnationals and the Third World: The Struggle for Culture*. South Hadley, MA: Bergin & Garvey.
Mattelart, Michèle, and Armand Mattelart. 1989. *O Carnaval das Imagens: A Ficção na TV*. Translated by Suzana Calazans. São Paulo: Brasiliense.
Mattelart, Michèle, and Armand Mattelart. 1990. *The Carnival of Images*. Translated by David Buxton. New York: Bergin & Garvey.
McLane, Daisann. 1988. "Couch Batata." *Village Voice*, April 26, 49.
Medin, Tzvi. 1990. *El sexenio alemanista*. Mexico City: Grijalbo.
Mellencamp, Patricia. 1986. "Situation Comedy, Feminism, and Freud: Discourses of Gracie and Lucy." In *Studies in Entertainment: Critical Approaches to Mass Culture*, edited by Tania Modleski, 80–95. Bloomington: Indiana University Press.
Mendes Catani, Afránio. 1987. "Amácio Mazzaropi: 30 Anos de Presença no Cinema Brasileiro." In *Historia do Cinema Brasileiro*, edited by Fernão Ramos, 191–298. São Paulo: Art Editora.
Mendible, Myra, ed. 2007. *From Bananas to Buttocks: The Latina Body in Popular Film and Culture*. Austin: University of Texas Press
Miller, Toby. 1998a. "Hollywood and the World." In *The Oxford Guide to Film Studies*, edited by John Hill and Pamela Church Gibson, 371–81. London: Oxford University Press.
Miller, Toby. 1998b. *Technologies of Truth: Cultural Citizenship and the Media*. Minneapolis: University of Minnesota Press.
Miquel, Angel. 2005. *Disolvencias: literatura, cine y radio en México (1900–1950)*. Mexico City: Fondo de Cultura Económica, 2005.

Modleski, Tania. 1982. *Loving with a Vengeance: Mass Produced Fantasies for Women*. London: Methuen.
Molina Guzmán, Isabel. 2014. *Dangerous Curves: Latina Bodies in the Media*. New York: New York University Press.
Monsiváis, Carlos. 1976. "El cine nacional." In *Historia general de México*, vol. 4, 434–59. Mexico City: El Colegio de México, 1976.
Monsiváis, Carlos. 1981. "Crónica de sociales: María Félix en dos tiempos." In *Escenas de pudor y liviandad*, 161–68. Mexico City: Grijalbo.
Monsiváis, Carlos. 1982a [1977]. *Amor perdido*. Mexico City: Era.
Monsiváis, Carlos. 1982b. "Reir llorando (notas sobre la cultura popular urbana)." In *Política cultural del estado mexicano*, edited by Moisés Ladrón de Guevara, 14–91. Mexico City: Ed. GEFE/SEP.
Monsiváis, Carlos. 1983. "Dolores del Río: Las responsabilidades del rostro." *México en el arte* 1: 53–65.
Monsiváis, Carlos. 1986. "Quien fue Pedro Infante." *Revista Encuentro* (April): 1–16.
Monsiváis, Carlos. 1990. "Sociedad y cultura." In *Entre la guerra y la estabilidad política: El México de los 40*, edited by Rafael Loyola, 259–80. Mexico City: Grijalbo.
Monsiváis, Carlos. 1994. *A través del espejo: el cine mexicano y su público*. México: Ediciones el Milagro.
Monsiváis, Carlos. 1995. "Mythologies." In *Mexican Cinema*, translated by Ana M. López, edited by Paulo Antonio Paranaguá, 117–27. London: British Film Institute.
Monsiváis, Carlos. 1997a. "Dolores Del Rio: The Face as Institution." In *Mexican Postcards*, translated by John Kraniauskas, 71–87. London: Verso.
Monsiváis, Carlos. 1997b. *Mexican Postcards*. Translated by John Kraniauskas. London: Verso.
Monteiro, José Carlos. 1996. *Cinema Brasileiro: Historia Visual*. Rio de Janeiro: FUNARTE.
Mora, Carl J. 1982. *Mexican Cinema: Reflections of a Society, 1896–1980*. Berkeley: University of California Press.
Mora, Carl J. 1985. "Feminine Images in Mexican Cinema: The Family Melodrama; Sara Garcia, 'The Mother of Mexico'; and the Prostitute." *Studies in Latin American Popular Culture* 4: 228–35.
Moraga, Cherríe. 1986. "From a Long Line of Vendidas: Chicanas and Feminism." In *Feminist Studies/Critical Studies*, edited by Teresa de Lauretis, 173–90. Bloomington: Indiana University Press.
Morais da Costa, Fernando. 2008. *O Som no Cinema Brasileiro*. Rio de Janeiro: Editora Viveiros de Castro.
Moreira Salles, João. 2011. "João Moreira Salles talks about *Santiago*, Part V." https://my.scottishdocinstitute.com/joao_moreira_salles_talks_about_santiago_part_v. Accessed June 10, 2013.

Moreno Fraginals, Manuel. 1964. *El Ingenio*. Havana: UNESCO.
Moreno Fraginals, Manuel, ed. 1974. *Africa in Latin America*. New York: Holmes and Meir.
Mosk. 1953. "O Cangaceiro." In *Variety Film Reviews*, vol. 8. New York: Garland.
Mota Martinez, Fernando, and Maria Esther Núñez Herrera. 1998. *Locutores en acción: vida y hazañas de quienes hicieron la radio mexicana*. Mexico City: Asociación Nacional de Locutores.
Moura, Roberto. 1987. "A Bela Época (Primórdios–1912)." In *História do Cinema Brasileiro*, edited by Fernão Ramos, 13–20. São Paulo: Art Editora.
Mulvey, Laura. 1986. "Melodrama In and Out of the Home." In *High Theory/Low Culture*, edited by Colin McCabe, 80–100. New York: St. Martin's Press.
Muñoz, José Esteban. 1996. "Flaming Latinas: Ela Troyano's *Carmelita Tropicana: Your Kunst Is Your Waffen* (1993)." In *The Ethnic Eye: Latino Media Arts*, edited by Chon Noriega and Ana M. López, 129–42. Minneapolis: University of Minnesota Press.
Musser, Charles. 1990. *The Emergence of Cinema: The American Screen to 1907*. Berkeley: University of California Press.
Naficy, Hamid. 1991. "Exile Discourse and Televisual Fetishization." *Quarterly Review of Film and Video* 13, nos. 1–3: 85–116.
Nagib, Lúcia. 2011. *World Cinema and the Ethics of Realism*. New York: Continuum.
Nagib, Lúcia, Chris Perriam, and Rajinder Dudrah, eds. 2012. *Theorizing World Cinema*. London: I.B. Tauris, 2012.
Navitski, Rielle. 2017. *Public Spectacles of Violence: Sensational Cinema and Journalism in Early Twentieth-Century Mexico and Brazil*. Durham, NC: Duke University Press.
Navitski, Rielle. 2021. Email correspondence with editors.
Nayman, Adam. N.d. "Surfing on the Wave of Reality: Pedro González-Rubio's *Alamar*." *CinemaScope* 42. https://cinema-scope.com/cinema-scope-magazine/interviews-surfing-on-the-wave-of-reality-pedro-gonzalez-rubios-alamar/. Accessed July 1, 2013.
Negrón-Muntaner, Frances. 1996. "Drama Queens: Latino Gay and Lesbian Independent Film/Video." In *The Ethnic Eye: Latino Media Arts*, edited by Chon Noriega and Ana M. López, 59–78. Minneapolis: University of Minnesota Press.
Nesbet, A. 2003. *Savage Junctures: Sergei Eisenstein and the Shape of Thinking*. London: I. B. Tauris.
Neto, Fernando Paulino. 1997. "Vera Cruz Prepara Volta em Setembro." *Folha de São Paulo*, August 12.
Newman, Kathleen. 1993. "National Cinema after Globalization: Fernando Solanas' *Sur* and the Exiled Nation." In *Mediating Two Worlds: Cinematic Encounters in the Americas*, edited by John King, Ana López, and Manuel Alvarado, 242–57. London: British Film Institute.

Nichols, Bill. 1982. *Ideology and the Image*. Bloomington: Indiana University Press.
Nichols, Bill. 1985. "The Voice of Documentary." In *Movies and Methods II*, edited by Bill Nichols, 258–73. Berkeley: University of California Press.
Nichols, Bill. 1988. "The Voice of Documentary." In *New Challenges for Documentary*, edited by Alan Rosenthal, 48–63. Los Angeles: University of California Press.
Nieto, Jorge, and Diego Rojas. 1992. *Tiempos del Olympia*. Bogotá: Fundación Patrimonio Fílmico Colombiano.
Nora, Pierre. 1989. "Between Memory and History: Les Lieux de Memoire." *Representations* 26 (1989): 7–24.
Nordenstreng, Kaarle, and Tapio Varis. 1974. *Television Traffic: A One-Way Street?* Paris: UNESCO.
Noriega, Chon. 1993. "Internal Others: Hollywood Narratives 'about' Mexican Americans." In *Mediating Two Worlds: Cinematic Encounters in the Americas*, edited by John King, Ana López, and Manuel Alvarado, 52–66. London: British Film Institute.
Noriega, Chon, and Ana M. López, eds. 1996. *The Ethnic Eye: Latino Media Arts* Minneapolis: University of Minnesota Press.
Noronha, Jurandyr. 1997. *Pioneros do Cinema Brasileiro*. CD-ROM.
Novo, Salvador. 1946. *Nueva grandeza mexicana*. Mexico City: Hermes.
Novo, Salvador. 1951. *Este y otros viajes*. Mexico City: Stylo.
Nowell-Smith, Geoffrey. 1987. "Minnelli and Melodrama." In *Home Is Where the Heart Is: Studies in Melodrama and the Women's Film*, edited by Christine Gledhill, 70–74. London: British Film Institute.
Nowell-Smith, Geoffrey, ed. 1996. *The Oxford History of World Cinema*. Oxford: Oxford University Press.
Ochoa Gautier, Ana María. 2006. "El sonido y el largo siglo XX." *Revista Número* 51. www.revistanumero.com/51/sonido.htm. Accessed December 1, 2016.
O'Neil, Brian. 1998. "Yankee Invasion of Mexico or Mexican Invasion of Hollywood? Hollywood's Renewed Spanish-Language Production of 1938–39." *Studies in Latin American Popular Culture* 17: 79–104.
Oroz, Silvia. 1991. *Melodrama: O Cinema de Lágrimas da América Latina*. Rio de Janeiro: Rio Funda Editora.
Ortiz, Christopher. 1996. "The Forbidden Kiss: Raúl Ferrera-Balanquet and Enrique Novelo-Cascante's *Mérida Proscrita* (1990)." In *The Ethnic Eye: Latino Media Arts*, edited by Chon Noriega and Ana M. López, 244–59. Minneapolis: University of Minnesota Press.
Ortiz, Mecha. 1982. *Mecha Ortiz*. Buenos Aires: Editorial Moreno.
Ortiz, Renato, Silvia Helena Simoes, and Jose Mario Ortiz Ramos. 1989. *Telenovela: Historia e Produção*. São Paulo: Brasiliense.
Page, Joanna. 2009. *Crisis and Capitalism in Contemporary Argentine Cinema*. Durham, NC: Duke University Press.

Paranaguá, Paulo Antonio. 1985. *Cinema na América Latina: Longe de Deus e perto de Hollywood*. Porto Alegre: L&PM.
Paranaguá, Paulo Antonio. 1987. "Tableau Synoptique: culture et societé au Brésil." In *Le cinéma brésilien*, edited by Paulo Antonio Paranaguá. Paris: Centre Georges Pompidou.
Paranaguá, Paulo Antonio. 1990. "Cinéma, culture et societé à Cuba: tableaux synoptique." In *Le cinéma cubain*, edited by Paulo Antonio Paranaguá, 13–48. Paris: Centre Georges Pompidou.
Paranaguá, Paulo Antonio. 1992. "Dix raisons pour aimer ou détester le cinéma mexicain et pour exclure toute indifférence." In *Le cinéma mexicain*, 9–23. Paris: Editions du Centre Pompidou.
Paranaguá, Paulo Antonio, ed. 1995a. *Mexican Cinema*. Translated by Ana López. London: British Film Institute.
Paranaguá, P. A. 1995b. "Ten Reasons to Love or Hate the Mexican Cinema." In *Mexican Cinema*, edited by P. A. Paranaguá, 1–13. London: British Film Institute.
Paranaguá, Paulo Antonio. 1996. *Vera Cruz: retrospectiva*. Festival Internacional de Biarritz.
Paranaguá, Paulo Antonio. 1997a. "América busca su imagen" [CHK]. In *Historia general del cine*, vol. 4. *América (1915-1928)*, edited by Jenaro Talens and Santos Zunzunegui, 129–57. Madrid: Cátedra.
Paranaguá, Paulo Antonio. 1997b. "El cine silente latinoamericano: primeras imágenes de un centenario." *La Gran Ilusión* 6: 32–39.
Paranaguá, Paulo Antonio. 2003. "Triángulo." In *Tradición y modernidad en el cine de América Latina*, 89–96. Madrid: Fondo de Cultura Económica.
Parker, David S. 1998. "Civilizing the City of Kings: Hygiene and Housing in Lima, Peru." In *Cities of Hope: People, Protests and Progress in Urbanizing Latin America, 1870-1930*, edited by Ron F. Pineo, 153–78. London: Routledge.
Parrish, James Robert. 1978. *The Hollywood Beauties*. New York: Arlington House.
Paterson, Richard, ed. 1982. *Brazilian Television in Context*. London: British Film Institute.
Paz, Octavio. 1961. *The Labyrinth of Solitude: Life and Thought in Mexico*. New York: Grove Press.
Pedelty, Mark. 1999. "The Bolero: The Birth, Life, and Decline of Mexican Modernity." *Latin American Music Review/Revista de Música Latinoamericana* 20, no. 1: 30–58.
Peña Ovalle, Priscilla. 2011. *Dance and the Hollywood Latina: Race, Sex, and Stardom*. New Brunswick, NJ: Rutgers University Press.
Pérez Firmat, Gustavo. 1994. *Life on the Hyphen: The Cuban-American Way*. Austin: University of Texas Press.
Pérez Montfort, Ricardo. 1994. *Estampas de nacionalismo popular mexicano: ensayos sobre cutura popular y nacionalismo*. Mexico City: Ciesas.

Pérez Turrent, Tomás. 1995. "The Studios." In *Mexican Cinema*, edited by Paulo Antonio Paranaguá and translated by Ana M. López, 133–44. London: British Film Institute.
Petro, Patrice. 1989. *Joyless Streets: Women and Melodramatic Representation in Weimar Germany*. Princeton, NJ: Princeton University Press.
Pick, Zuzana. 1974. "Le cinéma chilien sous le signe de l'Union Populaire: 1970–1973." *Positif* 155: 35–41.
Pick, Zuzana. 1980a. "Le 'Nouveau cinéma' d'Amérique latine: développement culturel, économique et sociopolitique depuis 1960." PhD thesis.
Pick, Zuzana. 1980b. "Interview with Patricio Guzmán." *Cinetracts* 3, no. 1: 29–34.
Pick, Zuzana. 1984a. "Cronología del cine chileno en el exilio 1973/1983." *Literatura chilena: creación y crítica* 27: 15–21.
Pick, Zuzana. 1984b. "La imagen cinematográfica y la representación de la realidad." *Literatura chilena: creación y crítica* 27: 34–40.
Pick, Zuzana. 1987. "Chilean Cinema in Exile, 1973–1986." *Framework* 34: 40–57.
Pick, Zuzana M. 1993. *The New Latin American Cinema: A Continental Project*. Austin: University of Texas Press.
Pick, Zuzana, Juan Verdejo, and Gaston Ancelovici. 1981. "Chili." In *Les Cinémas de l'Amérique latine*, edited by Guy Hennebelle and Alfonso Gumucio Dagrón, 189–227. Paris: l'Herminier.
Piedra, José. 1990. "Through Blues." In *Do the Americas Have a Common Literature?*, edited by Gustavo Pérez Firmat, 107–29. Durham, NC: Duke University Press.
Piedra, José. 1991. "Poetics for the Hip." *New Literary History* 22: 633–675.
Pilcher, Jeffrey M. 2001. *Cantinflas and the Chaos of Mexican Modernity*. Wilmington, DE: Scholarly Resources.
Poblete, Juan. 2017. "National Cinema." In *The Routledge Companion to Latin American Cinema*, edited by Marvin D'Lugo, Ana. M. López, and Laura Podalsky, 17–30. London: Routledge.
Podalsky, Laura. 1994. "Negotiating Differences: National Cinemas and Co-productions in Pre-revolutionary Cuba." *Velvet Light Trap* 34: 59–70.
Polan, Dana. 1988. "Postmodernism and Cultural Analysis Today." In *Postmodernism and Its Discontents: Theories, Practices*, edited by E. Ann Kaplan, 45–58. New York: Verso.
Pollak-Eltz, Angelina. 1972. *Vestigios africanos en la cultura del pueblo venezolano*. Caracas, Venezuela: Universidad Católica Andrés Bello.
Poniatowska, Elena. 1993. "Dolores Del Rio." In *Todo México*, vol. 2, 7–39. Mexico City: Editorial Diana.
Poppe, Nicolas. 2021. *Alton's Paradox: Foreign Film Workers and the Emergence of Industrial Cinema in Latin America*. Albany: State University of New York Press.
Pratt, Mary Louise. 1991. "Arts of the Contact Zone." *Profession*, 33–40.

Pratt, Mary Louise. 1992. *Imperial Eyes: Travel Writing and Transculturation.* New York: Routledge.
Pumarejo, Tomás López. 1987. *Aproximación a la telenovela* Madrid: Ediciones Catedra.
Quijano, Aníbal. 1993. "Modernity, Identity, and Utopia in Latin America." Translated by John Beverly. *Boundary 2* 20, no. 3 (Fall 1993): 140–55.
Quiroz Velasco, Teresa. 1987. "La telenovela en el Perú." *Diálogos de la comunicación* 18: 74–84.
Rama, Angel. 1996. *The Lettered City.* Translated by John Charles Chasteen. Durham, NC: Duke University Press, 1996.
Ramírez, Gabriel. 1986. *Lupe Vélez: la mexicana que escupía fuego.* Mexico City: Cineteca Nacional.
Ramírez Berg, Charles. 1992. *Cinema of Solitude: A Critical Study of Mexican Film, 1967–1983.* Austin: University of Texas Press.
Ramos, Fernão, ed. 1987. *Historia do Cinema Brasileiro.* São Paulo: Art Editora.
Ramsaye, Terry. 1926. *A Million and One Nights.* New York: Simon & Schuster.
Rêgo, Cacilda, and Carolina Rocha, eds. 2011. *New Trends in Argentine and Brazilian Cinema.* Bristol: Intellect.
Renov, Michael. 1986. "Re-thinking Documentary: Toward a Taxonomy of Mediation." *Wide Angle* 8, nos. 3/4: 71–77.
Reyes de la Maza, Luis. 1973. *El cine sonoro en México.* Mexico City: UNAM.
Richard, Alfred Charles, Jr. 1992. *The Hispanic Image on the Silver Screen: An Interpretative Filmography from Silents into Sound, 1895–1935.* New York: Greenwood.
Richard, Nelly. 1986. *Margins and Institutions: Art in Chile since 1973*, a special issue of *Art and Text* 21.
Ríos, Alejandro. 1991. "Otro cine cubano de hoy." *Cine Cubano* 133 (November–December): 53–57.
Rocha, Glauber. 1963. *Revisão Crítica do Cinema Brasileiro.* Rio de Janeiro: Civilizacão Brasileira.
Rockefeller, Nelson. 1943. "Will We Remain Good Neighbors after the War? Are We Killing Our Own Markets by Promoting Industrialization in Latin America?" *Saturday Evening Post*, November 6, 16–17.
Rockefeller, Nelson. 1944. "Fruits of the Good Neighbor Policy." *New York Times Magazine*, May 14, 15.
Rodríguez, Raúl. 1993. *El cine silente en Cuba.* Havana: Letras Cubanas.
Rogers, Everett, and Livia Antola. 1985. "*Telenovelas*: A Latin American Success Story." *Journal of Communication* 35: 24–35.
Romero, José Luis, and Luis Alberto Romero. 1983. *Buenos Aires: Historia de cuatro siglos.* Buenos Aires: Editora Abril.
Rose, Margaret A. 1979. *Parody/Meta-Fiction: An Analysis of Parody as a Critical Mirror to the Writing and Reception of Fiction.* London: Croom Helm.

Rosell, Rosendo. 1992. "¿Por qué no acordarnos hoy de . . . Manolo Alonso?" In *Vida y milagros de la farándula cubana*, vol. 2, 226–28. Miami: Ediciones Universal.
Ross, Andrew, ed. 1988. *Universal Abandon? The Politics of Postmodernism*. Minneapolis: University of Minnesota Press, 1988.
Rowland, Donald W. 1947. *History of the Office of the Coordinator of Inter-American Affairs*. Washington: Government Printing Office.
Ruétalo, Victoria, and Dolores Tierney. 2009. *Latsploitation, Exploitation Cinemas, and Latin America*. London: Routledge.
Sadlier, Darlene, ed. 2009. *Latin American Melodrama: Passion, Pathos, and Entertainment*. Urbana: University of Illinois Press.
Sadoul, Georges. 1953. "A Cannes, ou *Le Salaire de la peur* reste favori, le cinéma japonais marque des points." *Les Lettres Françaises* (April 30–May 7).
Said, Edward. 1979. *Orientalism*. New York: Random House.
Salles Gomes, Paulo Emilio. 1982. "O Gosto da Realidade." In *Crítica de Cinema no Suplemento Literario*, vol. 2. Rio de Janeiro: Paz e Terra/Embrafilme.
Salles Gomes, Paulo Emilio. 1986. "Mauro e Dois Outros Grandes." In *Paulo Emilio: Um Intelectual na Linha da Frente*, edited by Décio de Almeida Prado. São Paulo: Brasiliense/Embrafilme.
Salles Gomes, Paulo Emilio. 1995. "Cinema: A Trajectory within Underdevelopment." In *Brazilian Cinema*, edited by Randal Johnson and Robert Stam, 244–55. New York: Columbia University Press, 1995.
Sánchez Prado, Ignacio. 2014. *Screening Neoliberalism: Transforming Mexican Cinema 1988–2012*. Nashville, TN: University of Nashville Press.
Sanjinés, Jorge. 1968. "Sobre *Ukumau*." *Cine Cubano* 48: 28–33.
Sanjinés, Jorge. 1979a. "Cine revolucionario: la experiencia boliviana." In *Teoría y practica de un cine junto al pueblo*, edited by Grupo Ukamau, 13–33. Mexico City: Siglo Veintiuno.
Sanjinés, Jorge. 1979b. "We Invent a New Language through Popular Culture." Translated by John King. *Framework* 20: 31–33.
Sargent, Charles S. 1994. "Argentina." In *Latin American Urbanization: Historical Profiles of Major Cities*, edited by Gerald Michael Greenberg, 1–38. Westport, CT: Greenwood Press.
Schaefer, Eric. 1999. *Bold! Daring! Shocking! True! A History of Exploitation Films, 1919–1959*. Durham, NC: Duke University Press.
Schatz, Thomas. 1988. *The Genius of the System: Hollywood Filmmaking in the Studio Era*. New York: Pantheon.
Schement, Jorge Reina, and Everett M. Rogers. 1984. "Media Flows in Latin America." *Communication Research* 11, no. 2: 305–20.
Schiller, Herbert. 1976. *Communication and Cultural Domination*. White Plains, NY: International Arts and Sciences.
Schivelbusch, Wolfgang. 1971. *The Railroad Journey: Trains and Travel in the Nineteenth Century*. Translated by Anselm Hollo. New York: Urizen Books.

Schnitman, Jorge A. 1984. *Film Industries in Latin America: Dependency and Development*. Norwood, NJ: Ablex.
Schumann, Peter B. 1987. *Historia del cine latinoamericano*. Buenos Aires: Legasa.
Schwarz, Roberto. 1992. *Misplaced Ideas: Essays on Brazilian Culture*. Translated by John Gledson. London: Verso.
Schwartz, Rosalie. 1977–1979. "Battle of Chile." *PCCLAS Proceedings* 6: 260–62.
SCMS (Society of Cinema and Media Studies) Field Notes. https://www.cmstudies.org/page/fieldnotes.
Senna, Orlando. 1997. "*Cangaço:* Os Guerreiros da Terra do Sol." *Cinemas d'Amérique Latine* 5: 17–34.
Sempere, Pedro. 1977. "Cine contra el fascismo: conversación con Patricio Guzmán." In *Chile: el cine contra el fascismo*, edited by Pedro Sempere and Patricio Guzmán. Valencia: Fernando Torres, Editor.
Sempere, Pedro, and Patricio Guzmán. 1977. *Chile: el cine contra el fascismo*. Valencia: Fernando Torres, Editor.
Serna, Enrique. 1993. *Jorge el bueno: La vida de Jorge Negrete*, 3 vols. Mexico City: Clio.
Serna, Laura Isabel. 2014. *Making Cinelandia: American Films and Mexican Culture before the Golden Age*. Durham, NC: Duke University Press.
Serna, Laura Isabel. 2021. Email correspondence with the editors.
Shaw, Lisa, Luis Duno-Gottberg, Joanna Page, and Ignacio M. Sánchez Prado. 2017. "National Cinemas (Re)ignited: Film and the State." In *The Routledge Companion to Latin American Cinema*, edited by Marvin D'Lugo, Ana. M. López, and Laura Podalsky, 44–61. London: Routledge.
Shipman, David. 1970. "Dolores del Rio." In *The Great Movie Stars: The Golden Years*, 154–56. New York: Crown.
Shohat, Ella. 1989. *Israeli Cinema: East/West and the Politics of Representation*. Austin: University of Texas Press.
Shohat, Ella, and Robert Stam. 1994. *Unthinking Eurocentrism: Multiculturalism and the Media*. London: Routledge.
Sinclair, John. 1990. "Spanish-Language Television in the United States: Televisa Surrenders Its Domain." *Studies in Latin American Popular Culture* 9: 39–63.
Sklar, Robert. 1993. *Film: An International History of the Medium*. New York: Prentice-Hall.
Smirnow, Gabriel. 1979. *The Revolution Disarmed*. New York: Monthly Review.
Smith, Paul Julian. 2017. *Queer Mexico: Cinema and Television since 2000*. Detroit: Wayne State University Press.
Smith, Paul Julian. 2018. *Spanish and Latin American Television Drama: Genre and Format Translation*. London: School of Advanced Study University of London/Institute of Modern Languages Research.
Smith, Paul Julian. 2019. *Multiplatform Media in Mexico: Growth and Change since 2010*. Cham, Switzerland: Palgrave Macmillan, 2019.

Solanas, Fernando, and Octavio Getino. 1976. "Towards a Third Cinema." In *Movies and Methods*, edited by Bill Nichols, 44–64. Berkeley: University of California Press.
Solar, Steve, ed. 1991. *Literatura latinoamericana en cine*. New York: Motion Picture Export Association of America.
Sommer, Doris. 1991. *Foundational Fictions: The National Romances of Latin America*. Berkeley: University of California Press.
Sontag, Susan. 1966. "Death of Tragedy." In *Against Interpretation*, 132–39. New York: Dell.
Stam, Robert. 1982–1983. "Slow Fade to Afro: The Black Presence in Brazilian Cinema." *Film Quarterly* 36, no. 2: 16–32.
Stam, Robert. 1989. *Subversive Pleasures: Bakhtin, Cultural Criticism, and Film*. Baltimore, MD: Johns Hopkins University Press.
Stam, Robert. 1991. "Bakhtin, Polyphony and Ethnic/Racial Representation." In *Unspeakable Images: Ethnicity and the American Cinema*, edited by Lester D. Friedman, 251–76. Urbana: University of Illinois Press.
Stam, Robert, and Louise Spence. 1983. "Colonialism, Racism, and Representation." *Screen* 24, no. 2: 2–20.
Stephanson, Anders. 1987. "Regarding Postmodernism: A Conversation with Fredric Jameson." *Social Text* 17 (Fall): 29–54.
Sterne, Jonathan. 2003. *The Audible Past: Cultural Origins of Sound Reproduction*. Durham, NC: Duke University Press.
Stock, Ann Marie, ed. 1997. *Framing Latin American Cinema: Contemporary Critical Perspectives*. Minneapolis: University of Minnesota Press.
Stock, Ann Marie. 1999. "Authentically Mexican? *Mi Querido Tom Mix* and *Cronos* Reframe Critical Questions." In *Mexico's Cinema: A Century of Film and Filmmakers*, edited by Joanne Hershfield and David R. Maciel, 267–86. Wilmington, DE: Scholarly Resources.
Straubhaar, Joseph D. 1984. "Brazilian Television: The Decline of American Influence." *Communication Research* 11, no. 2: 221–40.
Syder, Andrew, and Dolores Tierney. 2005. "Mexploitation/Exploitation: Or How a Mexican Wrestler Almost Found Himself in a Sword and Sandals Epic." In *Horror International*, edited by Steven Schneider and Tony Williams, 33–55. Detroit: Wayne State University Press.
Taibo, Paco Ignacio, I. 1984. *Siempre Dolores*. Barcelona: Planeta.
Taibo, Paco Ignacio. 1985. *María Félix: 47 pasos por el cine*. Mexico City: Joaquin Mortiz/Planeta.
Tello, Max. R. 1986. "Carmín: juventud divino tesoro." In *Libra Bianco: América Latina*, edited by Ivano Cipriani. Turin: Teleconfronto.
Thevenet, Homero Alsina, ed. 1978. *Reportaje al cine argentino: los pioneros del sonoro*. Buenos Aires: Editorial Abril.
Thévenot, Jean. 1953. "Festival de Cannes." *Les Lettres Françaises* (April 23–30): 10.

Thompson, John O. 1978. "Screen Acting and the Commutation Test." *Screen* 19, no. 2: 55–69.
Thompson, K. 1985. *Exporting Entertainment: America in the World Film Market, 1907-1934*. London: British Film Institute.
Tierney, Dolores. 1997. "Silver Sling-Backs and Mexican Melodrama: *Salón México* and *Danzón*." *Screen* 38, no. 4: 360–71.
Tierney, Dolores. 2003. "José Mojica Marins and the Cultural Politics of Marginality in Third World Cinema." *Journal of Latin American Cultural Studies* 13, no. 1: 63–78.
Tierney, Dolores. 2007. *Emilio Fernández: Pictures in the Margins*. London: Routledge.
Tierney, Dolores. 2018. *New Transnationalisms in Contemporary Latin American Cinemas*. Edinburgh: Edinburgh University Press.
Tomlinson, John. 1991. *Cultural Imperialism: A Critical Introduction*. London: Frances Pinter.
Trejo Delarbre, Raul, ed. 1985. *Televisa, el quinto poder*. Mexico City: Editorial Claves Latinoamericanas.
Tully, Michael. 2010. "A Conversation with Pedro González-Rubio." *Hammer to Nail*. https://www.hammertonail.com/interviews/a-conversation-with-pedro-gonzalez-rubio-alamar/. Accessed July 1, 2013.
Turim, Maureen. 1987. "French Melodrama: Theory of a Specific History." *Theater Journal* 39, no. 3 (October): 307–27.
Turnstall, Jeremy. 1977. *The Media Are American: Anglo-American Media in the World*. London: Constable.
Tyler, Stephen A. 1986. "Post-Modern Ethnography: From Document of the Occult to Occult Document." In *Writing Culture: The Poetics and Politics of Ethnography*, edited by James Clifford and George Marcus, 122–40. Berkeley: University of California Press.
Ulla, Jorge, Lawrence Ott, and Miñuca Villaverde. 1986. *Dos filmes del Mariel: el éxodo cubano de 1980*. Madrid: Editorial Playor.
Valdés, Nelson. 1992. "Cuban Political Culture: Between Betrayal and Death." In *Cuba in Transition*, edited by Sandor Halebsky and John M. Kirk, 207–28. Boulder, CO: Westview Press.
Valdés Rodríguez, José Manuel. 1966. "*O Cangaceiro*." In *Cine en la Universidad de la Habana*. Havana: Empresa de Publicaciones Mined.
Valjalo, David, and Zuzana M. Pick. 1984. *10 años de cine chileno 1973/1983*. Los Angeles, CA/Santiago de Chile: Ediciones de la Frontera.
Vasconcelos, José. 1925. *La raza cósmica: misión de la raza iberoamericana*. Barcelona: Agencia Mundial de Librería.
Vasudevan, Ravi. 1989. "The Melodramatic Mode and the Commercial Hindi Cinema: Notes on Film History, Narrative and Performance in the 1950s." *Screen* 30 (Summer): 29–50.

Vaughan, Mary Kay. 1997. *Cultural Politics in Revolution: Teachers, Peasants, and Schools in Mexico, 1930-1940*. Tucson: University of Arizona Press.
Vaughan, Mary Kay, and Stephen E. Lewis. 2006. Introduction. In *The Eagle and the Virgin: Nation and Cultural Revolution in Mexico, 1920-40*, edited by Mary Kay Vaughan and Stephen E. Lewis, 1-20. Durham, NC: Duke University Press.
Vázquez Millares, Angel, ed. 1970. *Danzón*. Havana: Coordinación Provincial de la Habana.
Vega, Alicia, ed. 1977. *Re-visión del cine chileno* Santiago, Chile: Editorial Aconcagua-CENECA.
Velázquez, Mario, and Mary Kay Vaughan. 2006. "*Mestizaje* and Musical Nationalism in Mexico." In *The Eagle and the Virgin: Nation and Cultural Revolution in Mexico, 1920-1940*, edited by Mary Kay Vaughan and Stephen E. Lewis, 94-118. Durham, NC: Duke University Press.
Venegas, Cristina. 2017. SCMS Fieldnotes: Ana Lopez Interviewed by Cristina Venegas. https://vimeo.com/215947929.
Venegas, Cristina. 2021. Email communication with the editors.
Viany, Alex. 1987. *Introdução ao Cinema Brasileiro*. Rio de Janeiro: Alhambra/Embrafilme.
Vickers, Hugo. 1985. *Cecil Beaton*. London: Weidenfeld & Nicolson.
Vidal, Hernán, ed. 1985. *Fascismo y experiencia literaria: reflexiones para un recanonización*. Minneapolis: Society for the Study of Contemporary Hispanic and Lusophone Revolutionary Literatures.
Vieira, João Luiz. 1987. "A Chanchada e o Cinema Carioca (1930-1955)." In *História do Cinema Brasileiro*, edited by Fernão Ramos, 129-88. São Paulo: Art Editora.
Vieira, João Luiz. 2003. "Apresentação: Encontro com o Cinema Brasileiro." *Centro Cultural Banco de Brasil* (May): 18-23.
Vieira, João Luiz, and Robert Stam. 1985. "Parody and Marginality: The Case of Brazilian Cinema." *Framework* 28: 20-49.
Vieira, João Luiz, and Robert Stam. 1990. "Parody and Marginality: The Case of Brazilian Cinema." In *The Media Reader*, edited by Manuel Alvarado and John O. Thompson, 82-104. London: British Film Institute.
Vilasis, Mayra. 1983. "Comunicación y dramaturgia en el cine documental." *Cine Cubano* 105: 61-66.
Viñas, Moises, ed. 1987. *Historia del cine mexicano*. Mexico City: UNAM/UNESCO.
Vincendeau, Ginnette. 1989. "Melodramatic Realism: On Some French Women's Films in the 1930s." *Screen* 30 (Summer): 51-65.
Vink, Nico. 1988. *The Telenovela and Emancipation: A Study on TV and Social Change in Brazil*. Amsterdam: Royal Tropical Institute.
Wahlberg, Malin. 2008. *Documentary Time: Film and Phenomenology*. Minneapolis: University of Minnesota Press.

Walter, Richard J. 1996. "Buenos Aires." In *Encyclopedia of Latin American History and Culture*, vol. 1, edited by Barbara Tenenbaum et al., 480–83. New York: Scribner's.
Wasko, Janet. 1994. *Hollywood in the Information Age: Beyond the Silver Screen*. Austin: University of Texas Press.
Williams, Alan. 1992. "Historical and Theoretical Issues in the Coming of Recorded Sound to the Cinema." In *Sound Theory, Sound Practice*, edited by Rick Altman, 126–37. New York: Routledge.
Williams, Christopher. 1980. *Realism and the Cinema: A Reader*. London: Routledge & Kegan Paul.
Winston, Brian. 1988. "Direct Cinema: The Third Decade." In *New Challenges for Documentary*, edited by Alan Rosenthal, 517–29. Los Angeles: University of California Press.
Woll, Allen L. 1980 [1977]. *The Latin Image in American Film*. Los Angeles, CA: UCLA Latin American Series.
Woll, Allen L. 1978. *The Films of Dolores del Rio*. New York: Gordon Press.
Woll, Allen L. 1983. *The Hollywood Musical Goes to War*. Chicago: Nelson Hall.
Woll, Allen L., and Randall M. Miller, eds. 1987. *Ethnic and Racial Images in American Film and Television: Historical Essays and Bibliography*. New York: Garland.
Xavier, Ismail. 1982. "Allegories of Underdevelopment: From the 'Aesthetics of Hunger' to the 'Aesthetics of Garbage.'" PhD dissertation, New York University.
Xavier, Ismail. 1983. *Sertão/Mar: Glauber Rocha e a Estética da Fome*. São Paulo: Brasiliense/Embrafilme.
Xavier, Ismail. 1993. *Alegorias do Subdesenvolvimento: Cinema Novo, Tropicalismo, Cinema Marginal*. São Paulo: Editora Brasiliense.
Yaeger, Gertrude. 1990. "*Angel Malo* [Bad Angel], A Chilean Telenovela." *Studies in Latin American Popular Culture* 9: 249–65.
Zurita, Raúl. 1985. "Chile: literatura, lenguaje y sociedad (1973–1983)." In *Fascismo y experiencia literaria: reflexiones para una recanonización*, edited by Hernan Vidal, 299–331. Minneapolis: Institute for the Study of Ideologies and Literature.

Index

20th Century Fox (Fox), 113, 425, 430, 431, 432, 433, 434, 459, 485n20, 485n4, 512n7, 512n9
See also Good Neighbor films

Abacuá (Abakuá), 356, 396, 508n6-7, 511n4
Acosta, Iván, 445, 446, 448
African heritage, 395, 403, 407
Afro-Brazilian, 223, 389, 397-398
See also *Quilombo* (1984)
Afro-Cuban, 172, 177, 235, 241, 389, 396, 401-410, 411, 511n4
See also *De cierta manera/One Way or Another* (1974-1977)
Afro-Latin/o/a, 393-399
See also Latin/s/x/os/as
Afro-Venezuelan, 171, 175, 177, 178
Alamar (2009), 367, 369, 379-385
Allá en el Rancho Grande (*Rancho Grande* 1936), 19-22, 47-49, 100, 104, 156, 232, 255-259, 260, 292-293, 492n2, 501-2n9, 502n13
Allende, Salvador, 42, 323, 324, 328
Almendros, Néstor, 35, 440, 441, 443, 448, 513n6, 514n8
Alonso, Manolo, 234, 439, 443
Altman, Rick, 4, 92, 188, 227, 229, 245, 251, 498n7, 501n7

Alvaray, Luisela, xiii, 3, 184
America (1989), 185, 295-308, 370
Amaro, Blanquita, 234, 235, 252
Anderson, Benedict, 211, 222, 296
Arau, Alfonso, 27, 34, 37, 57
Argentina Sono Films, 167, 169, 230-231
Armendáriz, Pedro, 33, 41, 126, 130, 131, 502n12
Arnaz, Desi (Ricky Ricardo), 228, 230, 391, 393, 455-465, 498n5, 515n1-3
See also *I Love Lucy*
Atlântida, 49, 135, 232
Ayala Blanco, Jorge, 26, 49, 104, 199, 260, 261, 266, 493n10, 499n17, 500n22, 501n8
Aventurera (1950), 199-200, 201, 233, 236, 267-268, 493n11, 499n18
¡Ay Jalisco .... no te rajes! (1941), 259-260
Azcárraga Vidaurreta, Emilio, 130, 216, 253, 273
Azcárraga Milmo, Emilio, 216, 217, 497n19

balandra Isabel llegó esta tarde, La (1949), 33, 139, 163, 170-179
Barbachano Ponce, Manuel, 35, 241, 310, 482n9

549

Barreto, Lima, 50, 136, 138, 141, 150–153, 158–159, 161, 487n9, 489n16
Batalla de Chile, La (*The Battle of Chile*, 1975–1979), 53, 185, 323–340
Bay of Pigs (Playa Girón), 347, 348, 441
Beltrán, Mary, 109, 419, 480n9
Benítez-Rojo, Antonio, 240, 440, 442, 499n10
Bernardet, Jean-Claude, 140, 141, 142, 368
Bernaza, Luis Felipe 311, 401, 405
Best Maugard, Adolfo, 92, 110, 112, 501n3
Bhabha, Homi K., 5, 7, 9, 14, 222–223, 296, 419, 426, 430
biracial, 394, 396, 406–409, 510n2
 See also *mulato/a*
Black Film Review, 401, 411, 510n1
Blasini, Gilberto, xiii, 3, 5, 390
Blood of the Condor (1969)
 See *Yawar Mallku* (1969)
Bohr, José, 33, 47, 59, 139, 185, 271–293, 503n9
bolero, see Music
Boytler, Arcady, 47, 139, 263, 276, 503n4
Buñuel, Luis, 24, 32, 139, 165, 198, 480–481n3
Burton (Carvajal) Julianne, 3, 4, 323, 331, 334, 367, 479n4, 479n6, 480n2, 506n9, 508n4, 511n5
Bustillo Oro, Juan, 46, 91, 104, 106, 195, 503n4
 See also *Cuando los hijos se van*

cabaretera, 28, 185, 189–190, 197, 198–201, 232–233, 236, 251, 252, 263–269, 281, 291, 493n10, 499n17
 See also Ninón Sevilla, Maria Antonieta Pons
Cabra Marcado para Morrer (1984), 303, 368, 369, 374–375, 509n2
Cangaceiro, O (1953), 50, 51, 135, 138, 140, 144, 147–161
Cantinflas, 18, 27, 148
Carewe, Edwin, 112–115, 425, 486n6
Carmelita Tropicana (1993) 8, 449, 482n10
Casal, Lourdes, 437, 472, 514n9
Castro, Fidel, 52, 53, 320, 347, 441, 445, 450, 497n16, 513n5, 513n6
Cavalcanti, Alberto, 32, 50, 136, 140, 142, 144, 158, 165, 487n6
Chacal de Nahueltoro, El (1969) 53, 185, 341, 350–355
Chanan, Michael, 34, 42, 311, 325, 356–357, 368, 403, 407, 441, 479n6, 482n2, 500n24, 505n1, 511n5
cha-cha-cha, see Music
chanchada, 7, 50, 51, 136–137, 141, 145, 153, 191, 231–232, 234, 238, 492n2
Channel 13, 212, 217, 335, 507n17
Chile Films, 33, 139, 168–169, 325–326, 328–330, 506n8, 506n11
Christensen, Carlos Hugo, 14, 29, 32–33, 139, 163, 166–179, 491n9
Cine Cubano, 26, 54, 440, 480n6, 506n15, 514n7
Cinédia, 49, 135, 231
Cinema Novo, 30, 32, 33, 51, 52, 54, 166, 236–238, 345, 395, 398, 490n1
 in relation to Vera Cruz, 135, 137, 142, 144, 160, 165
Classical cinema, see Golden Age
Clifford, James, 7, 419, 420, 421

Colina, Enrique (and Daniel Díaz
    Torres), 26, 54, 183, 496n13
    See also cultural colonization
colonialism, 191, 389, 393
colonization, 22, 49, 189
    See also cultural colonization
Columbia Pictures, 51, 143, 148,
    485n20, 487n9
comedia ranchera, 20–23, 28, 48–49,
    156, 171–172, 177, 232, 235,
    236, 251, 252, 255–264, 268–269,
    292–293, 492n2, 501n6, 501n8
    See also Allá en el Rancho Grande
    (1936)
coproductions, 9, 13, 24–25, 31, 33,
    35, 56–58, 139, 143, 164–165,
    241, 242, 243, 403, 435–436, 438,
    452, 482n9, 487n5, 491n9
coraje del pueblo, El (1971), 341,
    361–365, 509n11
Cortázar, Octavio 67, 401, 405
Cosentino, Olivia, xiii, 3, 91
Couret, Nilo, 3, 10, 61, 186, 475–
    477
Coutinho, Eduardo, 303, 367, 368,
    369, 374–379, 510n6
coup d'état, 53, 170, 330, 331, 336,
    337, 338, 339, 340, 438, 484n18,
    515n1
Crofts, Stephen, 9, 17, 44
Cuando los hijos se van (1941), 91,
    104–106, 195–196
Cuban cinema, 30, 34–35, 52–54,
    71–72, 98, 212, 233–234, 237,
    240–243, 293, 393–399, 401–409,
    411–414, 415–417
    and coproductions, 24–25, 33,
    56–57, 139, 482n9
    documentaries, 309–321, 403,
    404–406, 413, 416, 440–441,
    442, 443–444, 448, 449–451, 452,
    513n6
    in "Greater Cuba," 391–392,
    437–454
    See also ICAIC
Cuba baila (1960), 237, 239–241,
    482n9
Cuban Revolution (1959) 212, 236,
    309–321, 354, 395, 401, 402, 411,
    437, 438, 439, 451, 493n1, 509n12
cultural colonialism, 417, 419–436, 472
cultural colonization (media
    imperialism), 10, 26, 38, 184,
    236, 344
    as emblematized by melodrama and
    telenovelas, 54, 203–205
    as theorized by dependency theory,
    5, 6, 38, 51–55, 58, 62, 203–205
    See also New Latin American
    Cinema (NLAC)
cultural studies, 1, 4, 61, 183–184, 188

Danzón (1991), 7, 27, 225, 243–249
danzón, 7, 222–223, 244–249,
    264–265, 499n15
De cierta manera (One Way or
    Another 1974–1977), 185, 341,
    354–358, 396, 404, 511n4
De Córdova, Arturo, 33, 41, 139, 171,
    173–174, 176, 178–179, 491n9
de Fuentes, Fernando, 47, 287, 292,
    481n3, 503n4
    See also Allá en el Rancho Grande,
    Doña Bárbara
Del Rio, Dolores, 8, 33, 34, 41, 59,
    109–134, 139, 197–198, 275, 390,
    391, 419, 422, 425–428, 429,
    486n6, 486n8, 486n10, 498n8,
    511–512n3-4
de la Mora, Sergio, 186, 263
de los Reyes, Aurelio, 7, 47, 65, 67,
    73, 75, 77, 78, 81, 85, 86, 87,
    98, 115, 122, 124, 132, 274, 275,
    483n10–11, 486n11, 515n1

dependency theory, *see* cultural colonization
Desnoes, Edmundo, 349, 406, 440, 442, 452
Díaz, Jesús, 311, 399, 408, 451
See also *Lejanía* (1985)
Díaz, Porfirio, 47, 69, 75, 77, 78, 83, 482n5, 483n12, 484n18
Porfirian, 76, 78, 194, 200–201, 258
Porfiriato, 47, 73
Disney, Walt, 110, 233, 423
documentary, 1, 5–6, 50, 136, 153, 158, 183, 185, 295–308, 309–321, 323–340, 341–365, 367–385, 488n13
impulse in early cinema, 66, 69–76, 83–88
impulse in films from the 1940s–50s, 151, 172, 173, 177–178
impulse in NLAC, 341–365, 507n1, 508n4, 508n7, 509n1
See also Cuban cinema-documentary
día fui, Un (1987), 309, 314, 317–320
Di Núbila, Domingo, 7, 80, 93, 167, 179, 491n9, 499n13
Documentary School (Santa Fe), 345, 346
Doña Bárbara (1943), 23, 170, 196, 481n6
Dos tipos de cuidado (1952), 261–263, 269
Douglas, María Eulalia (Mayuya), 309, 473, 514n7
Ďurovičová, Nataša, 13, 15, 37, 44

early cinema, xvii, 1, 9–10, 61–90, 469, 477, 479n2
Eisenstein, Sergei, 32, 45–46, 47, 139, 150, 152–153, 165, 275–276, 287, 362, 480n3
Elsaesser, Thomas, 4, 92, 184
Embrafilme, 54, 143, 161, 395, 490n19

enemigo principal, El (1974), 341, 365, 509n12
Equipo Tercer Año, El, 323, 329–333, 337, 338, 506n15, 507n18
ethnic, 117, 121, 132, 227–228, 229, 242, 243, 390, 391, 393, 394, 419–436, 446, 455–465
ethnicity (ethnic identity), 188, 224, 226, 227, 230, 249, 389–392, 411, 419–436, 446, 455–465
See also *mestizaje*
exploitation films, 27, 183, 185–186, 271–293, 503n9
Evangeline (1929) 114, 117, 425, 486n4, 512n4
exile (and cinema/television), 1, 33, 179, 217, 243, 299, 471, 500n26, 509n12
and Chile, 30, 327, 340, 438, 490n1, 506n4, 513n3
and Cuba, 8, 392, 408–409, 437–454, 459, 472, 483n1, 513–515 (*see also* Desi Arnaz)

Falicov, Tamara, xiii, 3
Fein, Seth, 31, 59, 111, 129
Félix, María, 18, 28, 84, 196–197, 200, 492n6, 493n11, 499n18
Fernández, Emilio, 14, 31, 125–126, 128, 130, 150–151, 152–153, 165, 265, 276, 486n11, 503n6
See also *María Candelaria, Flor silvestre*
Ferreyra, José Agustín, 94, 103, 231, 232, 499n12
Figueroa, Gabriel, 20, 48, 126, 130, 152, 258, 265
Flor silvestre (1943), 23, 126, 127
Flying Down to Rio (1933), 120, 121–124, 228, 426, 498n7–8, 511–512n3, 512n4
folletín (serial literature), 103, 184, 206, 209, 495n10

Index | 553

foundational (fictions) (Doris Sommer), 81–82, 170, 171–172, 178, 222, 496n12
Fugitive, The (1947), 130–131, 426
Franqui, Carlos, 440, 444, 513n5

Galvão, Maria Rita, 50, 75, 137, 139–140, 141, 142, 144, 159, 487n2, 487n5
Gang's All Here, The (1943), 22, 431–432, 434, 457, 512n7
García Espinosa, Julio, 2, 52, 237, 239–240, 241, 237, 323, 332, 473, 482n9, 496n13
García Riera, Emilio, 7, 21, 23, 24, 43, 49, 115, 120, 127, 128, 225, 227, 229, 260, 261, 264, 265, 266, 280, 490n3, 491n9, 491n1, 499n11, 515n1
García, Sara, 105–106, 194–196, 200, 282, 293
Gardel, Carlos, 100, 230, 498n4, 498n9
Genette, Gérard, 341, 342, 343, 351, 507n2
género chico (*teatro frívolo*) (popular theatre), 193, 256, 492n5
Girl of the Rio (1932), 119, 424, 426
Giral, Sergio, 35, 396–397, 401, 403–408, 411–418, 452
See also *Maluala, El otro Francisco*
Gledhill, Christine, 1, 37, 129, 184, 187, 188, 209, 485n1
globalization (in filmmaking), 34, 35, 38–39, 55–58
Globo (TV-), 143, 204, 207–208, 211, 213, 214, 295, 299–300, 374, 493n1, 494n4, 495n5-7, 496–497n16, 504n5
Golden Age
as national/transnational, 17–28, 29–35, 164–165, 178–179
of Mexican cinema, 27, 30, 45–49, 59, 111, 126, 130, 164, 184, 187–201, 247, 251–269

Gómez, Manuel Octavio 398, 401, 405, 407
Gómez, Sara, 314, 354, 396, 401, 404, 405, 505n5, 511n4
González-Rubio, Pedro, 369, 379–382
Good Neighbor Policy/films (1939–1947), 22–23, 42, 121, 228, 230, 419, 422–426, 429–435, 457, 459, 511n2
See also Carmen Miranda, Desi Arnaz, 20th Century Fox
Grupo Cine Liberación, 52–53, 324
Grupo Ukamau (Ukamau collective), 185, 358–365, 508–509n9, 509n12
Guevara, Alfredo, 312, 314, 332
See also ICAIC
Guízar, Tito, 20, 100, 256–259, 424–425
Gumucio Dagrón, Alfonso, 479–480n6, 480n2, 480n6, 482n4, 509n12
Gutiérrez Alea, Tomás, 34, 35, 53, 58, 185, 241, 310, 312, 347–350, 401, 405, 406, 440, 452, 508n4
See also *Memorias del subdesarollo* (1968)
Guzmán, Patricio, 35, 53, 185, 323–340, 367, 368

Hennebelle, Guy, 479–480n6, 480n2, 480n6, 482n4
"Hispanic" cinema/films (Hollywood), 31, 33, 44, 45, 46, 49, 93, 165, 282, 490n3
Hollywood, 6, 7, 8, 9, 14–15, 18, 19, 21, 22, 23, 24, 26, 27, 31, 32, 33, 34, 37–59, 245–246, 420–436
and Dolores Del Rio, 109–127
and "Latin" and Latin American music, 225–230, 242–243, 498n1
historical control over international film markets, 39–44

Hollywood *(continued)*
  involvement in the Mexican
  industry during WWII, 129
  See also Good Neighbor Policy,
  "Hispanic" cinema/films
Humy, Nicholas Peter, 401, 411–418
hora de los hornos, La (The Hour of the Furnaces, 1968), 53, 324, 327–328, 332, 333
Hutcheon, Linda, 6, 341, 342, 343, 347

ICAIC (Instituto Cubano de Arte e Industria Cinematográficos), 30, 34, 35, 54, 67, 139, 241–242, 309–314, 320, 332, 345, 349, 395–396, 401–409, 411–416, 437, 440–442, 444, 450–452, 490n1, 511n5
Ichaso, León, 242, 437, 443, 445–446, 447, 448
ICRT (Instituto Cubano de Radio y Televisión), 213, 452, 496n14
Ídolos de la radio (1934), 91, 100–102
I Love Lucy, 230, 391, 455–465
imperfect cinema, 52, 323, 341
In Caliente (1935), 120, 426, 427, 512n4
indigenous, 26, 38, 44, 54, 55, 66, 67, 76, 81, 86, 126, 128, 130, 132, 155, 164, 198, 206, 265, 359, 360, 362, 365, 389, 413, 484n17, 500n25, 502n14, 503n6, 508–509n9, 509n12
Infante, Pedro, 189, 255, 261, 500n1, 502n12
Instituto Superior de Arte (ISA), 450, 452, 496n14
intermedial(ity), 10, 92–107
Ivens, Joris, 35, 310, 506n5

Jackal of Nahueltoro, The, see *Chacal de Nahueltoro, El*

Jameson, Frederic, 300, 302, 303, 307, 384, 509n2
Jiménez Leal, Orlando 437, 440–441, 443, 444, 445, 448
  See also El Super (1979), *The Other Cuba* (1983)
Jogo de Cena (2007), 367, 369, 374–379, 380, 384, 385
Johnson, Randal, 39, 50, 137, 141, 479–480n6, 480n6, 485n20

Kid Chocolate (1987), 309, 312–314
King, John, 6, 13, 52, 92, 184, 187, 480n1, 491–492n1

Lamarque, Libertad, 23, 33, 100, 139, 168, 189, 197–199, 200, 231, 235, 252
Lampião (Virgulino Ferreira), 147, 153, 161, 488n13, 488–489n14, 489n17
Lara, Agustín, 45, 200–201, 232–233, 254–255, 267, 493n9, 493n11, 499n18, 502n17
Latin/s/x/os/as, 1, 3, 7–9, 27, 34, 109–135, 217, 221–222, 225, 228–229, 242, 389–394, 419–436, 437–454, 455–465, 510n2
  See also Afro-Latin/o/a
Latinidad, 112, 222, 228, 229, 235, 431, 482n10, 482n10
Lejanía (1985) 311, 399, 408, 451
Littín, Miguel, 35, 53, 185, 325, 328, 350, 352, 354, 500n25
Llorona, La (1934), 185, 271, 272, 276–281
Lucía (1968), 53, 406, 440
Lumiton, 32, 167–169, 231, 490–491n4
  See also Carlos Hugo Christensen
Luponini (El Terror de Chicago) (1935), 47, 287, 289–292

Index | 555

Madre querida (1934), 91, 103–104, 185, 194, 271, 287–289, 292
MacLaird, Misha, 3, 186
Maluala (1979), 407, 411, 414
Malinche, La (Malintzin), 191, 200, 263, 277, 280, 492n3, 502n14
See also *La Llorona*
mambo, see Music
Mambo Kings, The (1992), 219, 242, 464, 465
María Candelaria (1943), 23, 126, 127–128, 131, 265, 476
Mariel (boat lift/exodus), 442, 448, 515n17
Marker, Chris, 35, 310, 330
Martín-Barbero, Jesús, 2, 62, 184, 203, 205, 210, 211–212, 495n10
Matacena, Oreste, 446, 448, 514–515n14
Mattelart, Armand, 62, 325, 504n3
Mazzaropi, Amácio, 143, 145, 147, 160, 487n4
melodrama, 1, 6–7, 10, 19, 23, 28, 33, 46, 47, 103, 144–145, 172, 176, 178, 183–184, 185, 186, 187–201, 245–248, 378, 476, 492n2, 495n10–16
and Vera Cruz productions, 144–145
as conservative (*see* Colina, Enrique), 54, 213
as women's (woman's) film, 7, 188, 195, 197
family melodrama, 104, 190, 193–196, see also *Cuando los hijos se van*, *Madre querida*
maternal melodrama, 49, 195, 268, 287–289, see also *Madre querida*
and music, 232, 245, 246, 251, 252, 255, 256, 498n4
radionovelas, 103–104, 184, 195, 206, 255, 274, 281, 287, 289, 493–494n1–2, 501n5

See also *cabaretera*, radio-radionovelas, telenovela
Memorias del subdesarrollo (*Memories of Underdevelopment*, 1968), 53, 185, 341, 347–365, 394, 406, 440, 447, 452
memory, 132, 144, 157, 176, 226–227, 258, 304, 315, 316, 329, 367, 369–371, 383, 384, 385
See also *Santiago* (2007), *Alamar* (2009)
Mesa-Bains, Amalia, 110, 132, 133, 134, 486n13–14
mestiza/o/os, 254, 273, 359, 406, 498n6
mestizaje, 177, 229, 254, 395, 398
See also racial mixture/ing
Mexican cinema, 17–28, 29, 32, 33, 34, 45–49, 59, 74, 77, 87, 111–112, 126–130, 139, 151, 165, 166, 184, 187–201, 232, 235–236, 240, 245, 251–269, 271–293, 426
Mexican (film) industry, 6, 18–19, 47, 236, 275, 481n6
Mexican Revolution, 83, 190, 192–193, 253, 256, 259, 265, 286, 484–485n18
the films of (1911–1916), 82–85
mexicanidad, 254, 256–257
Miranda, Carmen, 8, 121, 124, 228, 231, 235, 236, 391, 393, 419, 422, 425, 430–435, 457–458, 460, 498n4, 512n7, 512–513n10, 513n11
See also *The Gang's All Here* (1943), *Weekend in Havana* (1941)
Modernity (being modern), 61–90, 96–97, 107, 136, 147, 161, 200–201, 252–253, 264, 272, 273, 282, 295–296, 308, 472, 482n2–3
and new aural economies, 96–98, 107
cinema as sign of, 272–273, 477

modernization, 10, 63, 65–66, 68, 80, 89, 91, 107, 129, 130, 147, 190, 193, 195, 203–205, 209, 482n2, 491n7
Monsiváis, Carlos, 2, 90, 124, 126, 188, 192–193, 196, 201, 232, 258, 261, 262, 486n10
Montalbán, Ricardo, 228, 391, 458, 459
Montaner, Rita, 234, 235, 252, 481n7
Moreira Salles, João, 367, 295–308, 369–374, 384, 504n4
　See also *Santiago* (2007)
Moreno, Antonio, 32, 45, 94, 139, 165, 189, 263, 481n3
movie theaters, 48
　in Latin America (1940), 166, 423
　in Peru, 66
　in Mexico City during the revolution, 83
　in Mexico, fitted for sound (1930), 98
　in Mexico (1930), 275
mujer del puerto, La (1933), 47, 139, 263, 281, 284, 481n3
Mulata (1953), 25, 201, 268
mulato/a, 316, 394, 398, 407, 510n2, 511n6
Music, 221–269, 221–250, 460, 498–503
　and Latinidad/Latinness, 222, 235
　and national identity/nationness, 222–224, 230–236, 238–241, 249–250, 251–269
　bolero, 7, 232–233, 235, 245, 247, 254–255, 264, 267, 499n10, see also Agustín Lara
　bossa nova, 229
　cha-cha-cha, 222, 229, 235 252, 459
　mambo, 229, 234, 235, 242, 252, 267 459, 499n10, 499n20
　mariachi, 222, 254, 257

　ranchera, 20, 48, 99, 222, 232, 254, 255, 256–257, 274
　rumba, 189, 224, 234, 235, 242, 248, 252, 267, 498n3, 499n20
　salsa, 7, 219, 222, 229, 499n10
　son, 7, 235, 252
　See also danzón, Agustín Lara, rumbera, samba, tango
musicals(s), the, xvii, 6–7, 101, 120–121, 145, 157, 183–185, 227–228, 232, 242, 245–246, 292, 424–425, 430, 432–433, 498n7, 499n15, 502n17
　and the Golden Age, 251–269
　and the new cinemas of the 1950s–60s/80s, 236–242

national cinema(s), 98, 111–112, 117, 144, 164, 191–192, 234, 253, 470–471, 472, 482n4
　and co-productions, 56–57
　and globalization, 35, 57, 89
　debates about, studies of, 9, 13–14, 17, 29–31, 32, 35
　in Argentina, 52, 167–168
　in Brazil, 32, 52, 191
　in Chile, 168–169
　in Cuba, 34, 52, 56–57
　in Mexico, 19, 23, 126–130, 139, 271–274, 277–278, 287, 293
　in presence of/opposition to Hollywood, 38, 42–44, 45–49, 52, 56, 191
　in Venezuela, 166–178
　See also Golden Age, Vera Cruz
national culture, 31, 44, 46, 141, 170, 253, 274
　and the New Latin American cinema, 344
national identity, 8, 9, 80, 170, 189, 191–193, 254, 305–306, 308, 398, 439, 465, 470

Index | 557

in *America* (1993), 295–296, 298, 304–309
See also music
nationalism(ist/istic)/nationness, 18–19, 21, 25, 33, 46–48, 59, 64, 76–79, 81, 82, 86, 111–112, 126, 135, 139, 140–141, 153, 177, 190, 194, 211, 222, 223, 246, 250, 254, 264, 273, 277, 286, 344, 395, 402, 403, 425, 431, 453, 460–464, 501n3, 501n9, 502n16
Americanness, 445, 462
and Cuba, 402, 437–454
and early cinema, 79–82, 86–89
and early sound cinema, 99,
and music, 99, 222, 233, 237
and silent cinema, 87–89, 93, 100, 253
Brazilianess, 141, 147, 305, 395, 431
Cubanness, 35, 219, 241, 403, 446, 450, 460–464
Mexicanness, 33, 118, 127, 129, 132, 134, 236, 277
Navitski, Rielle, xiii, 3, 10, 61, 91
Negrete, Jorge, 18, 28, 198, 255, 259–261, 293, 502n10-12
New Latin American Cinema (NLAC), 5–6, 8, 9, 26, 30, 37, 38, 52–55, 111, 225, 236, 242, 323–340, 341–365, 368, 403, 450, 470–471, 479–480n6, 507–508n3, 509n1
as pancontinental, 163, 164, 178
See also Cinema Novo, Imperfect Cinema, Grupo Ukamau, El Equipo Tecer Año, Third Cinema, Grupo Cine Liberación
Newman, Kathleen, 475, 500n26, 500n26
Nichols, Bill, 304, 505n4, 507n1
Noriega, Chon, 3, 8, 17, 59, 221, 229, 391, 480n8

Office of the Coordinator of Inter-American Affairs (OCIAA), 42, 121, 129, 423, 511n2
One Way or Another (1974–1977), see *De cierta manera*
Orol, Juan, 24, 25, 33, 35, 46, 59, 91, 103–104, 139, 185, 194, 266, 271–293, 396, 503n5
Other Cuba, The (1983), 443, 444–445, 448, 513n5
otro Francisco, El (*The Other Francisco* 1974), 397, 406–407, 411, 414, 452

Palma, Andrea, 199, 268, 481n3
Paranaguá, Paulo Antonio, 2, 21, 31, 48, 62, 65, 92, 136, 151, 230, 231, 480n6-7, 480n2, 482n4, 485n2, 490n2
Patakín (1983), 242, 398, 407
Paz, Octavio, 191, 297, 304, 307
Peón, Ramón, 185, 233–234, 271–293
Pereira dos Santos, Nelson, 53, 236–239, 398, 500n23
Phillips, Alex, 32, 126, 139, 165, 276, 281, 285, 286
Piedra, José, 224, 248, 267
Pick, Zuzana, 324, 325, 329, 334, 338, 479–480n6, 506n4, 506n8-9, 513n3
Plácido (1986), 407–408, 411, 414–415
Pons, María Antonieta, 24, 33, 198, 234, 235, 252, 266, 396
postcolonial, theory, film analysis (-ism), 5, 7, 9, 13, 58, 184, 186, 303, 389, 438
See also Homi K. Bhabha, Edward Said
prostitute, figure of (as mythified in Mexican culture), 200–201, 233, 255, 263, 476, 492n7, 499n16, 501n4
See also sex worker

¿Quién mató a Eva? (1934), 47, 284–285, 289
Quilombo (1984), 242, 397–398

RKO, 22, 130, 227, 424, 425, 428, 429, 511n3
race/racial/racialization, 1, 8, 124, 178, 212, 223, 349, 389–391, 393–399, 401–409, 411–418, 419–436
  racial identity, 394, 399
  racial mixture/ing (racially mixed), 24–25, 394, 406, see also *mulato, mestizaje*
  racism 126, 389, 394, 395, 399, 402, 403, 408, 409, 418, 456
  See also biracial
radio (intermedialities with film), 1, 9–10, 91–107, 144, 158, 167, 189, 195, 221–222, 238, 243, 253, 272–273, 287–289, 292, 293, 351, 364, 477, 490n4, 496n10, 497n21
radio (in development of popular music forms), 45, 254–255, 274
radio (intermedialities with television), 143, 203–220, 458, 487n4, 494n3-4 (see also *I Love Lucy*)
radio and popular music (importance in development of star system), 189, 230–231, 254–255, 258, 259
radionovelas, 46, 99, 101–102, 103, 105, 184, 206, 255, 274, 281, 287, 289, 493n1, 494n2, 495n10, 501n5, 503n2
  See also Jorge Negrete, Tito Guízar, Pedro Infante
radionovela, see melodrama
radiophonic imaginary, 9–10, 91–107, 231, 288, 476
rancheras, see *comedia ranchera*, music-ranchera

Redes (1934), 32, 46, 165, 286–287, 481n3, 503n6
Rio, 40 Graus (1955), 236–237
Rio, Zona Norte (1957), 237–239
Rockefeller, Nelson (The Rockefeller Foundation), 121, 423, 425, 511n2, 515n2
  See also Office of the Coordinator of Inter-American Affairs (OCIAA)
Rocha, Glauber, 53, 137, 142, 152–153, 159, 160, 242, 394, 398
Rose, Margaret, 341, 342, 343
Ruétalo, Victoria, 3, 186, 276
rumba, see music
rumbera, 35, 197, 198, 201, 235–236, 240, 267–268
  See also María Antonieta Pons, music-rumba, Ninón Sevilla

Sagrario (1933), 272, 280–281
Said, Edward, 5, 7, 419, 421
Salles Gomes, Paulo Emilio, 141, 144, 158–159
Salles, João Moreira
  See Moreira Salles, João
Salón México (1948), 265–266, 267
salsa, see music
samba, 99, 145, 222–223, 229, 231, 235–236, 237–239, 252, 267, 393, 397, 431, 500n23
Sánchez Prado, Ignacio, xiii, xvii, 186
sangre manda, La (1934), 185, 271–272, 281–286
Sanjinés, Jorge, 53, 185, 358–362, 500n25, 508n9, 509n11, 509n12
  See also *Blood of the Condor*, Grupo Ukamau
Santa (1931), 32, 45, 94, 139, 165, 189, 232, 259, 263, 281, 481n3
santería, 175, 176, 177, 219, 398, 405, 407, 449
  See also Yoruba

Santiago (2007), 367, 369–374, 380, 384–385
Serna, Laura Isabel, xiii, 14, 61
Serrador, Francisco, 74, 75, 82, 485n19
sex worker, 45, 167, 267, 268, 481n3, 497n7, 499n16, 501n4
Sevilla, Ninón, 24, 33, 139, 189, 197, 198–200, 201, 235, 236, 252, 266–268
silent film/period/era, 19, 30, 61–90, 92–94, 96–97, 103, 107, 109, 112–114, 116–117, 118, 129, 150, 158, 165, 225, 230–231, 253, 263, 273, 275, 277, 391, 401, 403, 425, 427, 482n4, 499n12, 501n8, 511n4, 515n1
See also early cinema
Sinhá Moça (1953), 140, 144–145, 396–397
slavery, 145, 395–397, 402, 406–407, 411, 414, 487n8, 488–489n14, 496n15, 499n19, 510n1, 511n2–3
See also Sergio Giral, *El otro Francisco* (1974), *Maluala* (1979)
Solanas, Fernando, 7, 53, 243, 368, 500n26
See also Grupo Cine Liberación
Solás, Humberto, 53, 312, 406
Spanish Civil War, 30, 31, 139, 164, 166
Stam, Robert, 7, 39, 50, 62, 137, 192, 305, 389, 425, 479–480n6
stardom (transnational), 31, 33, 109–134, 275
See also Desi Arnaz, Arturo de Córdova, Dolores Del Rio, Libertad Lamarque, Carmen Miranda, Lupe Vélez
star system(s), 6, 22, 49, 111, 129, 178, 189, 206–207, 217, 262, 391, 494n3, 496–497n16
Latin American, 95, 178, 189, 206
Mexican, 22, 49, 129, 262

US Latino crossover, 217, 391, 419, 446, 459
See also telenovelas
stereotypes, 21, 49, 110, 198, 240, 241, 389, 390, 419, 420, 424, 426, 429–430, 481n3, 498n3
Suárez, Ramón, 440, 447, 514–515n14
Super, El (1979), 443, 445, 446, 448, 449, 514n13

TV-Tupi, 143, 211, 487n4
tango, 99–103, 167, 189, 198, 221–222, 223, 224, 225, 228, 230–231, 232, 235, 243, 252, 498n3–4, 499n12, 499n14
tango films/melodramas, 232, 243
See also Carlos Gardel, Libertad Lamarque
teatro frívolo (*género chico*) (popular theatre), 193, 256, 492n5
Telemundo, 207–208, 216–217, 497n18, 497n20
telenovelas, 1, 6, 34, 161, 184, 203–220, 299, 493–497
and national identity, 211–220
and star system, 206–207, 209, 217, 494n3
as a melodramatic mode of expression, 206, 208–210, 215
Brazilian, 210, 211, 213–215, 299–300, 487n5, 493–494n1, 495n8, 504n5
Colombian, 210, 211–212
Cuban, 212–214, 493n1
Mexican, 210, 214, 216–218
US Spanish language, 216–220
Venezuelan, 207, 210, 215, 216, 493n1
Televisa, 204, 207, 214, 216–218, 494n4, 495n5, 495n7, 497n21
Tico-tico no fubá (1952), 145, 146, 158, 159
Tierney, Dolores, 6, 29, 186, 265–266, 276, 480n1

Tin Tan (Germán Valdés), 23, 235, 500n1
Third Cinema, 53, 341, 507–508n3
Toledo, Teresa, 309, 473
Tovar, Lupita, 32, 165, 275
Troyano, Ela, 8, 449, 482n10
  See also *Carmelita Tropicana* (1993)
transnational cinema (as the product of global forces), 17, 29–35, 37, 55–59, 64, 296, 308, 469–470, 480n1–2, 481n1
  New Latin American Cinema as, 30–31, 163–164
  transnational turn in film scholarship, 9–10, 13–15, 29–30
  transnationality of Cuban cinema, 34–35
  transnationality of Golden Age Mexican Cinema, 9, 14, 129–132, 267
  transnationality of Hollywood, 40–41, 117–118, *see also* "Hispanic" cinema/film
  transnationality/transnationalization of *telenovelas*, 184, 203, 205, 212–214, 216–220
traveler/traveling film personnel, 14, 31–35, 109–134, 163–179, 275–276, 293
  See also stardom (transnational)
traveling filmmakers, *see* transnational cinema
TV-Globo, *see* Globo

Ukamau Group, *see* Grupo Ukamau
Ulla, Jorge, 443, 446, 447–448, 514n11
  See also *The Other Cuba* (1983)
Unidad Popular (UP, Popular Unity), 42, 323–331, 336, 340

United Artists, 21, 48, 113, 114, 118, 486n4, 501n9, 512n7
Univisión, 27, 208, 216–217, 219, 443, 494n4, 495n6, 497n19, 497–498n21, 515n15

Vega, Pastor, 451, 472–473
Vélez, Lupe, 8, 227, 275, 390, 419, 422, 425, 427–429, 433, 435, 486n6, 512n6
Venegas, Cristina, xiii, 3, 4, 479n1
Vera Cruz, Companhia Cinematográfica, 32, 37, 38, 49–51, 135–161, 165, 487n2–5, 490n18, 490n20
  See also Alberto Cavalcanti
viaje más largo, El (1987), 309, 314–317, 320
Viany, Alex, 140, 141–142, 151–152, 488n10
Villaverde, Miñuca, 446, 448, 514n11
Viña del Mar Film Festival, 312, 327, 506n5–6
Vieira, João Luiz, 7, 93, 100, 234

Weekend in Havana (1941), 228, 431–433, 434, 512n7
Welles, Orson, 110, 125, 425, 511n2, 512n4
Woll, Allen, 42, 115, 118, 119, 121, 228, 423, 424, 434, 511n1, 511–512n3

Xavier, Ismael, 154, 305, 480n6
XEW, 103, 105, 253–254, 255, 273–274, 501n5, 503n2

Yawar Mallku (*Blood of the Condor*, 1969), 53, 185, 359–361
Yoruba, *see* santería

www.ingramcontent.com/pod-product-compliance
Lightning Source LLC
Chambersburg PA
CBHW051842300426
44117CB00006B/237